Bharat's

FOREIGN DIRECT INVESTMENTS in INDIA

Bharat

COMMITTED TO QUALITY AND EXCELLENCE

INVITATIONS TO AUTHORS

We invite Judges, Lawyers, law Teachers and other legal experts to write books for us. We firmly believe that authors form strong pillars of our organisation. We offer very attractive terms to handsomely compensate them for the time and money spent and for the efforts contributed by them.

We also invite all those, who have manuscripts ready and are looking for favourable opportunities for publishing them, to please get in touch with us.

We appreciate and value quality in content and the presentation of the text of the books we produce. On our part, we assure them of quality production.

FREE DOWNLOAD from www.bharatlaws.com*

Instead of providing a Free CD, as a step forward towards innovation and in tune with changing technologies, we are instead facilitating a free download of PowerPoint presentation of FEMA from our website **www.bharatlaws.com.**

Steps to FREE DOWNLOAD of data from www.bharatlaws.com:

- Purchase a copy of *Bharat's* Foreign Direct Investments in India, 3rd edn.. You can obtain the Serial No. by scratching the scratch card on the front cover of the Book. Ensure that the Serial No. placed on the front cover is not already scratched/visible.
- *Books with pre-scratched serial Nos. will be automatically treated as sold and are not returnable in any case.*
- Visit **www.bharatlaws.com**
- Choose Foreign Direct Investments in India, 3rd edn. from Downloads on Home Page.
- Fill the proforma and download the file on your Desktop (this may take a few minutes depending on the size of the file and speed of your internet). *It is a one-time download data only.* In case of any subsequent problem, please contact Ravi Puliani at Mobile: 0-9810267553
- Install the software through the fdii03.exe file and you can view and read the PowerPoint presentation.
- *The download of data is possible only once with the serial number.*

* The free download data of present edition will be available on the website only upto 30 days from the release of next edition *i.e.* 4th edn.

Bharat's

FOREIGN DIRECT INVESTMENTS in INDIA

with New FDI Policy, dated 10-4-2012

Web-download of PowerPoint Presentation on FEMA

By

CA. KAMAL GARG

BHARAT LAW HOUSE PVT. LTD.
New Delhi
2012

First Edition 2010
Third Edition 2012

By the same author

- Statutory Audit under Companies Act
- CARO
- Guide to Bank Audit
- Guide to Tax Audit
- Foreign Direct Investments in India
- IFRS Concepts & Application
- Company Balance Sheet & Profit and Loss Account
- Handbook on Internal Auditing
- Auditor's Practice Manual
- Accounting Standards and IFRS
- Compounding of Offences under Company Law & FEMA
- Handbook on Valuation
- Consolidated Financial Statements
- Interim Financial Reporting under AS, Ind-AS & IFRS
- Understanding Goods & Service Tax
- Professional Approach to Advanced Auditing
- Systematic Approach to Auditing & Assurance
- Mercantile Laws (for CPT)

PRICE ₹ 750

ISBN: 978-81-7733-801-0

Printed in India

WITH THE BLESSINGS OF "MATA VAISHNO DEVI"

Published by D.C. Puliani for Bharat Law House Pvt. Ltd.
T-1/95, Mangolpuri Industrial Area, Phase-I, New Delhi-110 083.
Printed at Shanti Enterprises, New Delhi
(Phones 2791 0001-03)

Bharat?

Bharat is a 'trade-name' for a group of concerns, popularly known as Bharat Law House and Bharat Law House Pvt. Ltd.

Bharat is one of the most reputed publishers of law books with an experience of over five decades. We possess a very diverse range of publications covering not only the area of taxation — direct and indirect — but also company law, capital market, finance, industrial law, foreign exchange, commercial, civil and criminal laws.

Bharat's new and most ambitious venture of publishing the Budget Publications has received an unprecedented success. They establish new heights of accuracy, authenticity and excellence. The students publications for CA, CS, CWA, CFA, MBA, graduate and post-graduate studies have carved out a niche for themselves. As such, we adequately serve the needs of students and the professionals.

Bharat works hard to make things easy for you. We want our passion for excellence to translate in your satisfaction. Ours is a professionally qualified team-work with strong in-house capabilities. Our strength lies in the patronage of legal luminaries in every field. We strive for accuracy, authenticity and sincerity. No wonder our publications adorn the bookshelves of the discerning, judicious and the learned readers.

Bharat invites you to be a member of its family; share your thoughts and expertise with the readers and 'live forever'.

Dedicated
to my
PARENTS

PREFACE TO THE THIRD EDITION

It gives me immense pleasure to present before the readers the third edition of the book "Foreign Direct Investments in India". The present book is incorporated with the Consolidated FDI policy issued by the Department of Industrial Policy and Promotion, Ministry of Commerce and Industry, Government of India, *vide* its Circular D/o IPP F. No. 5(2)/2012, dated 10-4-2012, which is effective from April 10th, 2012. This book will serve as a ready referencer for the Corporates, Chartered Accountants and other professionals involved, directly or indirectly, in the matters pertaining to FDI.

This book is equipped with the following features:

1. Analysis of various definitions through illustrations;
2. Sectoral Investment Cap for FDI;
3. Guidelines for Foreign Investment in Downstream Entities;
4. Issue of Shares under FDI;
5. GDR/ADR/FCCB/FCEB;
6. External Commercial Borrowing (ECB);
7. Issue of Securities of Indian Entity;
8. Transfer of shares and convertible debentures of an Indian Company;
9. Acquisition and transfer of Immovable Property in India;
10. Establishment of Branch Office/Liaison Office in India;
11. Current Account Transactions with illustrations;
12. Remittance and Reporting Requirements;
13. CCI Guidelines;
14. Consolidated FDI Policy.

I would like to acknowledge my mentor Mr. Sanjay Kumar Goyanka, Chartered Accountant; my brother Mr. Vimal Garg; my friends CA Amit Kumar Goyal; CA Stuti Gupta and Mrs. Meera Kishore for their constant encouragement and motivation. I would also like to acknowledge my professional colleagues Mr. Sunil Keswani, M. Com, PGDBM; Mr. Ravish Bhateja, MBA; Mr. L. Muralidharan, CA, CWA; Mr. P. Subbaraman, MBA, MFT; Mr. Vijay K. Bhalla, CA; Mr. Mahavir Aggarwal, CA and my teacher Dr. K. Venkata Subramanian for sharing their inputs for this book.

I am grateful to the Puliani brothers of M/s Bharat Law House Pvt. Ltd. for bringing out this publication in its present content and form.

The readers may send their queries and suggestions at my e-mail id cakamalgarg@gmail.com.

24th April, 2012 KAMAL GARG
New Delhi

CONTENTS AT A GLANCE

ABOUT THE AUTHOR

Mr. Kamal Garg is a fellow member of the Institute of Chartered Accountants of India. He is first class graduate from Deen Dayal Upadhyaya College, University of Delhi. His areas of interest include accounting and auditing. He has contributed articles for Students' Newsletter of ICAI and other professional journals. He has participated at Seminars as a speaker and is an eminent faculty on auditing. He has addressed innumerable workshops on Accounting Standards and IFRS across India including almost all the metros. He is also a guest speaker at Pristene's Knowledge Group (PKG), Mumbai. He has to his credit the following books for the professionals and students which are widely acclaimed:

- Statutory Audit under Companies Act
- CARO
- Guide to Bank Audit
- Guide to Tax Audit
- Foreign Direct Investments in India
- IFRS Concepts & Application
- Company Balance Sheet & Profit and Loss Account
- Handbook on Internal Auditing
- Auditor's Practice Manual
- Accounting Standards and IFRS
- Compounding of Offences under Company Law & FEMA
- Handbook on Valuation
- Consolidated Financial Statements
- Interim Financial Reporting under AS, Ind-AS & IFRS
- Understanding Goods & Service Tax
- Professional Approach to Advanced Auditing
- Systematic Approach to Auditing & Assurance
- Mercantile Laws (for CPT)

For IFRS Corporate Training
& Consultancy, contact
cakamalgarg@gmail.com or 0-9811054015.

DETAILED CONTENTS

Chapter 4

ORIGIN, TYPE, ELIGIBILITY, CONDITIONS AND ISSUE/TRANSFER OF INVESTMENT

Chapter 5

CALCULATION, ENTRY ROUTE, CAPS, ENTRY CONDITIONS, ETC. OF INVESTMENT

Chapter 6

POLICY ON ROUTE, CAPS AND ENTRY CONDITIONS

Chapter 7

REMITTANCE, REPORTING AND VIOLATION

Chapter 8

CURRENT ACCOUNT TRANSACTIONS

Chapter 9

Chapter 10

Chapter 11

Appendix 1

THE FOREIGN EXCHANGE MANAGEMENT ACT, 1999

CHAPTER I

Preliminary

CHAPTER II

Regulation and Management of Foreign Exchange

Appendix 2

CONSOLIDATED FDI POLICY

Chapter 1
INTRODUCTION

SYNOPSIS

Foreign Direct Investment (FDI) plays an important role in the long-term economic development of a country not only as a source of capital but also for enhancing competitiveness of the domestic economy through transfer of technology, strengthening infrastructure, raising productivity and generating new employment opportunities. FDI also has an important role in enhancing exports. In India, FDI is considered as one of the developmental tool. The policy of the Government of India is to strive to maximize the developmental impact and spin-offs of FDI. While the Government encourages, and indeed, welcomes FDI in all the sectors where it is permitted, the Government is especially looking for large FDI inflows in the development of infrastructure, technological upgradation of Indian industry through 'greenfield' investments in manufacturing, and in projects having the potential for creating employment opportunities on a large scale. With its highly-skilled and cost-effective manpower, it offers immense opportunities not only for Business Process Outsourcing, but increasingly for the higher end of the value chain in Knowledge Process Outsourcing and Engineering Process Outsourcing. In order to further improve the investment climate, a major rationalization of the FDI policy and associated procedures was recently undertaken by my Ministry.

India, the largest democracy and 4th largest economy (in terms of purchase power parity) in the world. India is also the tenth most industrialized country in the world. With its consistent growth performance and abundant high-skilled manpower, India provides enormous opportunities for investment, both domestic and foreign. Since the beginning of economic reforms in 1991, major reform initiatives have been taken in the fields of investment, trade, financial sector, exchange control simplification of procedures, enactment of competition and amendments in the intellectual property rights laws, etc. India provides a liberal, attractive, and investor friendly investment climate.

Foreign direct investment (FDI) plays a multidimensional role in the overall development of the host economies. It may generate benefits through bringing in non-debt-creating foreign capital resources, technological upgrading, skill enhancement, new employment, spill-overs and allocative efficiency effects. While FDI is expected to create positive outcomes, it may also generate negative effects on the host economy. The costs to the host economy can arise from the market power of large firms and their associated ability to generate high profits. Much of the existing empirical evidence suggests that the positive effects offset negatives, thus providing net economic benefits for the host economies.

FDI-enabled firms in manufacturing sectors provide employment to about 15.6 lakh persons accounting for about 4 to 5 per cent of the total employment in the organised sector. Small cities provide employment to about 7.9 lakh workers. Sectors providing a relatively high share of employment in small cities include transport equipment; growing and processing of crops; construction parts; textiles; and non-metallic mineral products. The study (by NCAER) concludes that the FDI in manufacturing sectors has significant reach in small cities, thus generating linkages with suburban and rural regions of India. The major FDI-receiving sectors have strong backward and/or forward linkages with the economy. The sectors with strong backward and forward linkages include construction; fuels; chemicals; and metallurgical industries. The sectors with strong backward linkages include electrical equipment; drugs and pharmaceuticals; food processing; and textiles, among others. Service sectors, telecommunications, and consultancy services have strong forward linkages (NCAER Study, August 2009).

1. Capital Formation *vis-à-vis* FDI Policy

Capital formation is an important determinant of economic growth. While domestic investments add to the capital stock in an economy, FDI plays a complementary role in overall capital formation and in filling the gap between domestic savings and investment. At the macro-level, FDI is a non-debt-creating source of additional external finances. At the micro- level, FDI is expected to boost output, technology, skill levels, employment and linkages with other sectors and regions of the host economy. While the quantity of FDI is important, equally important is the quality of FDI. The major factors that might provide growth impetus to the host economy include the extent of localisation of the output of the foreign firm's plant, its export orientation, the vintage of technology used, the research and development (R&D) best suited for the host economy, employment generation, inclusion of the poor and rural population in the resulting benefits, and productivity enhancement. Many developing countries, including India, have started receiving significant amounts of FDI in the past two decades. A large quantum of such FDI originates from high-income countries including the United States and the EU, while south-south FDI flows have also been increasing.

Prior to 1991, the FDI policy framework in India was highly regulated. The government aimed at exercising control over foreign exchange transactions. All dealings in foreign exchange were regulated under the Foreign Exchange Regulation Act (FERA), 1973, the violation of which was a criminal offence. Through this Act, the government tried to conserve foreign exchange resources for the economic development of the nation. Consequently the investment process was plagued with many hurdles including unethical practices that became part of bureaucratic procedures. Under the deregulated regime, FERA was consolidated and amended to introduce the Foreign Exchange Management Act (FEMA), 1999. The new Act was less stringent and aimed at improving the capital account management of foreign exchange in India. The Act sought to facilitate external trade and payments and to promote orderly development and maintenance of the foreign exchange market in India. It resulted in improved access to foreign exchange.

FDI policy is reviewed on continued basis and changes in sectoral policy/ sectoral equity cap are notified through Press Notes by the Secretariat for Industrial Assistance (SIA), Department of Industrial Policy & Promotion (DIPP). All Press Notes are available at DIPP website (www.dipp.gov.in). FDI Policy is also notified by Reserve Bank of India (RBI) under Foreign Exchange Management Act (FEMA) 1999.

2. FDI-related Institutions

There are three primary institutions in India that handle FDI-related issues: the Foreign Investment Promotion Board (FIPB), the Secretariat for Industrial Assistance (SIA), and Foreign Investment Implementation Authority (FIIA).

3. Foreign Investment Promotion Board (FIPB)

The Foreign Investment Promotion Board (FIPB), Department of Economic Affairs (DEA), Ministry of Finance is the nodal single-window agency for all matters relating to FDI as well as promoting investment in the country. It is chaired by the Secretary, Industry (Department of Industrial Promotion and Policy). Its objective is to promote FDI in India:

(*i*) by undertaking investment promotion activities in India and abroad;

(*ii*) by facilitating investment in the country by international companies, non-resident Indians and other foreign investors;

(*iii*) through purposeful negotiations/discussions with potential investors;

(*iv*) through early clearance of proposals submitted to it; and

(*v*) by reviewing policies and putting in place appropriate institutional arrangements, transparent rules and procedures and guidelines for investment promotion and approvals.

4. Secretariat for Industrial Assistance (SIA)

The Secretariat for Industrial Assistance (SIA) has been set up by the Government of India in the Department of Industrial Policy and Promotion, Ministry of Commerce & Industry to provide a single-window service for entrepreneurial assistance, investor facilitation, receiving and processing all applications which require government approval, conveying government decisions on applications filed, assisting entrepreneurs and investors in setting up projects (including liaison with other organisations and state governments) and monitoring the implementation of projects. It also notifies all government policy decisions relating to investment and technology, and collects and publishes monthly production data for select industry groups. The SIA website provides chat time during fixed hours when all questions are answered. During other times, investors are encouraged to write e-mails and the Secretariat assures a reply within 24 hours.

5. Foreign Investment Implementation Authority (FIIA)

The Government of India has set up the Foreign Investment Implementation Authority (FIIA) to facilitate quick translation of Foreign Direct Investment (FDI) approvals into implementation, and to provide a pro-active one-stop after-care service to foreign investors by helping them obtain necessary approvals, sort out operational problems and meet with various government agencies to find solutions to their problems. The proforma for making a reference to the Foreign Investment Implementation Authority (FIIA) can be downloaded from the website. The Secretariat for Industrial Assistance (SIA) in the Department of Industrial Policy & Promotion (DIPP) functions as the Secretariat of the FIIA.

6. Foreign Investment Policy

Foreign investment is permitted in virtually every sector, except those of strategic concern such as defence (opened up recently to a limited extent) and rail transport. Foreign companies are permitted to set up 100 per cent subsidiaries in India. No prior approval from the exchange control authorities (RBI) is required, except for certain specified activities.

According to the current policy, FDI can come into India in two ways:

Automatic route: FDI in sectors/activities *to the extent permitted* under the automatic route does not require any prior approval either by the government or the Reserve Bank of India (RBI). The investors are only required to notify the concerned regional office of the RBI within 30 days of receipt of inward remittances and file the required documents with that office within 30 days of issue of shares to foreign investors.

Prior Government Approval route: In the limited category of sectors requiring prior government approval, the proposals are considered in a time-bound and transparent manner by the Foreign Investment Promotion Board (FIPB) under the Department of Economic Affairs, Ministry of Finance. Approvals of composite proposals involving foreign investment/ foreign technical collaboration are also granted on the recommendations of the FIPB.

7. Legal Framework

Foreign Direct Investments under Automatic Approval and Government Approval are regulated by the Foreign Exchange Management Act, 1999 (FEMA *vide* Reserve Bank's Notification FEMA. 20/2000-RB, dated May 3, 2000 as amended from time to time). If a foreigner or foreign company or a person resident outside India wants to invest in India either in the manufacturing sector or service sector, including the housing sector, insurance, banking, telecommunications, etc., the foreigner, foreign company or a person resident outside India has to pay due attention to the conditions, regulations and procedures which are stipulated by various applicable Rules and Regulations.

8. Consolidated FDI Policy [w.e.f. April 1st, 2010 as amended w.e.f. April 10th, 2012]

The Department of Industrial Policy and Promotion, Ministry of Commerce and Industry, Government of India, has issued a consolidated FDI policy (hereinafter the "policy") *vide* its Circular D/o IPP F. No. 5(14)/2009-FC, dated 31-3-2010, which shall be effective from April 1st, 2010 (now reviewed and revised vide its Circular D/o IPP F. No. 5(2)/2012-FC, dated 10-4-2012). The policy attached to this circular is divided into six Chapters and nine Annexures. The structure of these Chapters and Annexures is given below:

1.	Chapter 1	Intent and Objective
2.	Chapter 2	Definitions
3.	Chapter 3	General Conditions on FDI
4.	Chapter 4	Calculation of Foreign Investment
5.	Chapter 5	Foreign Investment Promotion Board (FIPB)
6.	Chapter 6	Sector Specific Conditions on FDI
7.	Chapter 7	Remittance, Reporting and Violation

ANNEXURES

1.	Annex 1	Form FC-GPR
2.	Annex 2	Terms and conditions for Transfer of Shares/Convertible Debentures, by way of Sale, from a Person Resident in India to a Person Resident Outside India and from a Person Resident Outside India to a Person Resident in India
3.	Annex 3	Documents to be submitted by a person resident in India for transfer of shares to a person resident outside India by way of gift
4.	Annex 4	Definition of "relative" as given in section 6 of Companies Act, 1956
5.	Annex 5	Report by the Indian company receiving amount of consideration for issue of shares/Convertible debentures under the FDI Scheme

6. Annex 6 Know Your Customer (KYC) Form in respect of the non-resident investor
7. Annex 7 Annual Return on Foreign Liabilities and Assets
8. Annex 8 Form FC-TRS
9. Annex 9 Form DR
10. Annex 10 Form DR - Quarterly

As per para 1.1.3 to para 1.1.4, this circular consolidates into one document all the prior policies/regulations on FDI which are contained in FEMA, 1999, RBI Regulations under FEMA, 1999 and Press Notes/Press Releases/ Clarifications issued by DIPP and reflects the current 'policy framework' on FDI. It is clarified that this is a consolidation/compilation and comprehensive listing of most matters on FDI and is not intended to make changes in the extant regulations. This Consolidation deals comprehensively with all aspects of FDI Policy which are covered under the various Press Notes/Press Releases/ Clarifications issued by DIPP. It has been decided that from now onwards a consolidated circular would be issued after one year to update the FDI policy. This consolidated circular will, therefore, be superseded by a circular to be issued on 29-3-2013 (DIPP Press Release 10-4-2012). All earlier Press Notes/Press Releases/Clarifications on FDI issued by DIPP which were in force and effective as on March 31, 2012 stand rescinded as on March 31, 2011. The present circular consolidates and subsumes all such/these Press Notes/Press Releases/ Clarifications as on March 31, 2012.

Chapter 2
INTENT AND OBJECTIVE

'Investment' is usually understood as financial contribution to the equity capital of an enterprise or purchase of shares in the enterprise. 'Foreign investment' is investment in an enterprise by a Non-Resident irrespective of whether this involves new equity capital or re-investment of earnings. Foreign investment is of two kinds — (*i*) Foreign Direct Investment (FDI) and (*ii*) Foreign Portfolio Investment (para 1.1.1).

International Monetary Fund (IMF) and Organization for Economic Cooperation and Development(OECD) define FDI similarly as a category of cross border investment made by a resident in one economy (the direct investor) with the objective of establishing a 'lasting interest' in an enterprise (the direct investment enterprise) that is resident in an economy other than that of the direct investor. The motivation of the direct investor is a strategic long term relationship with the direct investment enterprise to ensure the significant degree of influence by the direct investor in the management of the direct investment enterprise. Direct investment allows the direct investor to gain access to the direct investment enterprise which it might otherwise be unable to do. The objectives of direct investment are different from those of portfolio investment whereby investors do not generally expect to influence the management of the enterprise. In the Indian context, FDI is defined in Para 2.1.11 of this Circular (see next Chapter). It is the policy of the Government of India to attract and promote productive FDI from nonresidents in activities which significantly contribute to industrialization and socio-economic development. FDI supplements the domestic capital and technology.

1. The Legal basis

Foreign Direct Investment by non-resident in resident entities through transfer or issue of security to person resident outside India is a 'Capital account transaction' and Government of India and Reserve Bank of India regulate this under the FEMA, 1999 and its various regulations. Keeping in view the current requirements, the Government from time to time comes up with new regulations and amendments/changes in the existing ones through order/allied rules, Press Notes, etc. The Department of Industrial Policy and Promotion (DIPP), Ministry of Commerce & Industry, Government of India makes policy pronouncements on FDI through Press Notes/ Press Releases which are notified by the Reserve Bank of India as amendment to Notification No. FEMA 20/2000-RB, dated May 3, 2000. These notifications take effect from the date of issue of Press Notes/Press Releases. The procedural instructions are issued by the Reserve Bank of India *vide* AP DIR (Series) Circulars. The regulatory framework over a period of time thus consists of Acts, Regulations, Press Notes, Press Releases, Clarifications, etc.

Accordingly, the circular of consolidated FDI policy consolidates into one document all the prior policies/regulations on FDI which are contained in FEMA, 1999, RBI Regulations under FEMA, 1999 and Press Notes/Press Releases/ Clarifications issued by DIPP and reflects the current 'policy framework' on FDI. *It is clarified that this is a consolidation/compilation and comprehensive listing of most matters on FDI and is not intended to make changes in the extant regulations.* This Consolidation deals comprehensively with all aspects of FDI Policy which are covered under the various Press Notes/Press Releases/ Clarifications issued by DIPP. It should be noted that w.e.f. April 1st, 2010 onwards a consolidated circular would be issued every six months to update the FDI policy. This consolidated circular will, therefore, be superseded by a circular to be issued on September 30, 2010.

It should be reiterated here that all earlier Press Notes/Press Releases/ Clarifications on FDI issued by DIPP which were in force and effective as on March 31, 2012 stand rescinded as on March 31, 2012. The present circular consolidates and subsumes all such/these Press Notes/Press Releases/ Clarifications as on March 31, 2012. Notwithstanding the rescission of earlier Press Notes/Press Releases/Clarifications, anything done or any action taken or purported to have been done or taken under the rescinded Press Notes/Press Releases/Clarifications prior to March 31, 2012 shall, in so far as it is not inconsistent with those Press Notes/Press Releases/Clarifications, be deemed to have been done or taken under the corresponding provisions of this circular and shall be valid and effective. It is the *intent and objective* of the Government to promote foreign direct investment through a policy framework which is transparent, predictable, simple and clear and reduces regulatory burden. The system of periodic consolidation and updation is introduced as an investor friendly measure. While this circular consolidates FDI Policy Framework, the legal edifice is built on notifications issued by RBI under FEMA. Therefore, any changes notified by RBI from time to time would have to be complied with and where there is a need/scope of interpretation, the relevant FEMA notification will prevail.

> *Intent is an anticipated outcome that is intended or that guides one's planned actions. "Intent and motive should not be confused. Motive is what prompts a person to act, or fail to act. Intent refers only to the state of mind with which the act is done or omitted." Objective is the mission, purpose, or standard that can be reasonably achieved within the expected timeframe and with the available resources.*

Chapter 3
ANALYSIS OF IMPORTANT DEFINITIONS

SYNOPSIS

Chapter 2 of the consolidated FDI policy, effective from April 1st 2010, contains forty definitions on various aspects. These definitions are discussed as below.

1. AD Category-I Bank

As per para 2.1.1 'AD Category-I Bank' means a bank (Scheduled Commercial, State or Urban Cooperative) which are authorized under Section 10(1) of FEMA to undertake all current and capital account transactions according to the directions issued by the RBI from time to time.

Section 10(1) of FEMA stipulates that, the Reserve Bank may, on an application made to it in this behalf, authorize any person to be known as authorized person to deal in foreign exchange or in foreign securities, as an authorized dealer, money changer or off-shore banking unit or in any other manner as it deems fit.

2. Authorised Bank

'Authorized Bank' means a bank including a co-operative bank (other than an authorized dealer) authorized by the Reserve Bank to maintain an account of a person resident outside India (para 2.1.2)

3. Authorised Dealer

'Authorized Dealer' means a person authorized as an authorized dealer under subsection (1) of section 10 of FEMA.

4. Authorised Person

'Authorized Person' means an authorized dealer, money changer, offshore banking unit or any other person for the time being authorized under Sub-section (*a*) of Section 10(1) of FEMA to deal in foreign exchange or foreign securities.

Categories of 'Authorised Persons are as follows [RBI circular No. 25/AP (FL) No. 2, dated 6-3-2006:

Category	Entities	Permitted Activities
Authorised Dealer – Category I	Commercial Banks, State Coop Banks, Urban Coop Banks	All current and capital account transactions as per RBI directions issued from time to time
Authorised Dealer – Category II	Upgraded FFMCs, Coop Banks, Regional Rural Banks (RRBs), others	Specified non-trade related current account transactions (discussed below) and all activities permitted to FFMC
Authorised Dealer – Category III	Select Financial and other Institutions	Transactions incidental to the foreign exchange

Category	Entities	Permitted Activities
Full Fledged Money Changers (FFMC)	Department of Post, Urban Coop Banks, Other FFMC	Purchase of foreign exchange and sale for private and business visits abroad.

5. Person

'Person' *includes*:

(*i*) an individual;

(*ii*) a Hindu undivided family;

(*iii*) a company;

(*iv*) a firm;

(*v*) an association of persons or a body of individuals whether incorporated or not;

(*vi*) every artificial juridical person, not falling within any of the preceding subclauses; and

(*vii*) any agency, office, or branch owned or controlled by such person.

It should be noted here that the definition of person as given above as per para 2.1.27, is inclusive definition and this definition is worded exactly as given under section 2(u) of FEMA.

6. Person of Indian Origin (PIO)

'Person of Indian Origin' (PIO) means a citizen of any country other than Bangladesh or Pakistan, if:

(*i*) he at any time held Indian Passport;

(*ii*) he or either of his parents or any of his grandparents was a citizen of India by virtue of the Constitution of India or the Citizenship Act, 1955 (57 of 1955); or

(*iii*) the person is a spouse of an Indian citizen or a person referred to in subclause (*i*) or (*ii*).

It should be noted here that this definition under para 2.1.28 is not given under Foreign Exchange Management Act. But this definition is given under Regulation 2(*xii*) of Foreign Exchange Management (Deposit) Regulations, 2000.

7. Person Resident in India

'Person resident in India' *means*—

(*i*) a person residing in India for more than one hundred and eighty-two days during the course of the preceding financial year but *does not include*—

(A) A person who has gone out of India or who stays outside India, in either case—

(*a*) for or on taking up employment outside India, or

(*b*) for carrying on outside India a business or vocation outside India, or

(*c*) for any other purpose, in such circumstances as would indicate his intention to stay outside India for an uncertain period;

(B) A person who has come to or stays in India, in either case, otherwise than—

(*a*) for or on taking up employment in India; or

(*b*) for carrying on in India a business or vocation in India, or

(*c*) for any other purpose, in such circumstances as would indicate his intention to stay in India for an uncertain period;

(*ii*) any person or body corporate registered or incorporated in India,

(*iii*) an office, branch or agency in India owned or controlled by a person resident outside India,

(*iv*) an office, branch or agency outside India owned or controlled by a person resident in India.

It should be noted here that the definition of person as given above as per para 2.1.29, is exhaustive definition as the word 'means' has been used and this definition is worded exactly as given under section 2(*v*) of FEMA.

8. Person Resident Outside India

'Person resident outside India' means a person who is not a Person resident in India [para 2.1.30]. This definition is again worded exactly as that give under section 2(*w*) of FEMA.

It should be noted that if a person goes outside India in such circumstances that his period of outside India is not certain, then it cannot be said that he has intention to stay outside India for an uncertain period. Further, the words residing in India for more than one hundred eighty two days implies that compulsive stay in India will not be considered. The word 'reside' implies some kind of permanency. Therefore, in case where an airhostess employed by an airline outside India is accommodated at a 'base' in India during the layover, her staying in India cannot be regarded as period of residence in India. It would be worthwhile to mention here that the citizenship is not relevant for determining the residential status of a person under FEMA. Further, the period of stay has to be considered in respect of *preceding* financial year and not for the current year.

Case Study: Mr. Ram had resided in India during the Financial Year 2006-2007 for less than 183 days. He again came to India on 1st May, 2007 for higher studies and business and stayed upto 15th July, 2008. State under the Foreign Exchange Management Act, 1999 (read with Consolidated FDI Policy).

(*i*) If Mr. Ram can be considered 'person Resident in India' during the Financial year 2007-2008; and

(*ii*) Is citizenship relevant for determining such a status?

Recommendation: No. Mr. Ram cannot be considered 'Person resident in India' during the financial year 2007-2008 notwithstanding the purpose or duration of his stay in India during 2007-2008. An individual has to be present in India for more than 182 days in the *preceding* financial year. Mr. Ram does not satisfy this condition for the financial year 2007-2008. Further, citizenship is not relevant for determining the residential status.

Case Study:

(*i*) How will you determine whether particular business units like a factory or office is a 'person resident in India' under Foreign Exchange Management Act, 1999?

(*ii*) 'Printex Computer' is a Singapore based company having several business units all over the world. It has a unit for manufacturing computer printers with its Headquarters in Pune. It has a Branch in Dubai which is controlled by the Headquarters in Pune. What would be the residential status under FEMA, 1999 of printer units in Pune and that of Dubai branch?

Recommendation:

(*i*) Section 2 of FEMA, 1999 defines the term "person resident in India". According to Section 2(*iii*), all business units in India will be "resident in India" even though these units are owned or controlled by a person resident outside India. Similarly all business units outside India will be 'resident in India' provided the business units are either owned or controlled by a person resident in India [Section 2(*v*)(*iv*)]. It is necessary to determine the residential status of the person who owns or controls the business unit.

(*ii*) Printex Computer being a Singapore based company would be person resident outside India [(Section 2(*w*)] Section 2(*u*) defines 'person' under clause (*viii*) thereof, as person would include any agency, office or branch owned or controlled by such person. The term such person appears to refer to a person who is included in clause (*i*) to (*vi*). Accordingly Printex unit in Pune, being a branch of a company would be a 'person'. Section 2(*v*) defines a person resident in India. Under clause (*iii*) thereof person resident in India would include an office, branch or agency in India owned or controlled by a person resident outside India. Printex unit in Pune is owned or controlled by a person resident outside India, and hence it, would be a 'person resident in India.' However, Dubai Branch though not owned is controlled by Print unit in Pune which is a person resident in India. Hence prima facie, it may be possible to hold a view that the Dubai Branch is a person resident in India.

Case Study: Examine whether the following branches can be considered as a 'Person resident in India' under Foreign Exchange Management Act, 1999:

(*i*) ABC Limited, a company incorporated in India established a branch at London on 1st January, 2008.

(*ii*) M/s XYZ, a foreign company, established a branch at New Delhi on 1st January, 2008. The branch at New Delhi controls a branch at Colombo.

Recommendation:

(*i*) Any person or body corporate registered or incorporated body in India is a resident in India [section 2(*v*)(*ii*)]. 'Person' includes a company [section 2(*u*)]. An office, branches or agency outside India owned or controlled by a person resident in India is a person resident in India. [Section 2(*v*)(*iv*)].

In view of the above provisions in FEMA, 1999 London branch established by ABC Ltd, a company incorporated in India, is a 'person resident in India' under the Act from the date of establishment i.e. 1st January, 2003.

(*ii*) According to Section 2(*v*)(*iii*) of FEMA, 1999 an office, branch or agency in India owned or controlled by a person resident outside India is a person resident in India'. Only a body corporate registered or incorporated in India is a 'person resident in India'. According to section 2(*w*), 'person resident outside India' means a person who is not resident in India. Hence M/s XYZ, foreign company is a 'resident outside India. But the branch at New Delhi owned by M/s XYZ is a 'resident in India' within the meaning of section 2(*v*)(*iii*) from the date of establishment i.e. 1st January, 2003. The branch at Colombo controlled by the branch at New Delhi referred to in the question is a person 'resident in India' within the meaning of section 2(*v*)(*iii*) read with section 2(*v*)(*iv*).

Case Study: Mr. Sekhar resided for a period of 150 days in India during the Financial year 2003-2004 and thereafter went abroad. He came back to India on 1st April, 2004 as an employee of a business organization. What would be his residential status during the financial year 2004-2005?

Recommendation: According to the provisions of section 2(*v*) of the Foreign Exchange Management Act, 1999, a person in order to qualify for the purpose of being treated as a "Person Resident in India" in any financial year, must reside in India for a period of more than 182 days during the preceding financial year. In the given case, Mr. Sekhar has resided in India for a period of only 150 days, *i.e.*, less than 182 days, during the financial year 2003-2004. Hence he cannot be considered as a "Person Resident in India" during the financial year 2004-2005 irrespective of the purpose or duration of his stay.

Case Study:

(*i*) MKP Limited, an Indian company having its Registered Office at Mumbai, India established a branch at New York U.S.A. on 1st April, 2009.

(*ii*) WIP Ltd., a company incorporated and registered in London established a branch at Chandigarh in India on 1st April, 2009.

(*iii*) WIP Ltd.'s Singapore branch which is controlled by its Chandigarh branch.

Recommendation:

(*i*) As per provisions of section 2(*v*)(*ii*) of the Foreign Exchange Management Act, 1999 (FEMA) any person or body corporate registered or incorporated in India is a "Person resident in India". As per section 2(*v*) of the said Act the term "person" includes a company. Section 2(*v*)(*iv*) of the said Act states that an office, branch or agency outside India owned or controlled by a person resident in India is a "Person resident in India".

In the light of the above provisions of FEMA, the residential status of the New York branch of MKP Ltd is that of a "Person resident in India" from the date of its establishment since it is owned by a person, i.e., a company, resident in India.

(*ii*) As per provisions of section 2(*v*)(*iii*) of the Foreign Exchange Management Act, 1999 (FEMA) an office, branch or agency in India owned or controlled by a person resident outside India is a "Person resident in India". Section 2(*w*) of the said Act states that a person who is not resident in India is a "Person resident outside India".

On application of the above provisions of FEMA, it can be concluded that WIP Ltd. is a "Person resident outside India" and since it owns a branch in Chandigarh, India, the residential status of the said Chandigarh branch is that of a "Person resident in India" from the date of its establishment.

(*iii*) As per provisions of section 2(*v*)(*iv*) of the Foreign Exchange Management Act, 1999 (FEMA) an office, branch or agency outside India owned or controlled by a person resident in India is a "Person resident in India". Here, the Singapore branch of WIP Ltd. is controlled by its Chandigarh branch which is a "Person resident in India". Therefore, the residential status of the Singapore branch of WIP Ltd. shall be that of a "Person resident in India".

Case Study: Mr. Sekhar resided in India for a period of 150 days in India during the financial year 2006-07 and thereafter went abroad. He came back to India on 1st April, 2007 as an employee of a business organization. What would be his residential status during the financial year 2009-2010.

Recommendation: In accordance with the provisions of Section 2(*v*) of the Foreign Exchange Management Act, 1999, as contained in section 2(*v*) a person in order to qualify for the purpose of being treated as a "Person Resident in India" in any financial year, must reside in India for a period of more than 182 days during the preceding financial year. In the given case, Mr. Sekhar has resided in India for a period of only 150 days, *i.e.*, less than 182 days, during the financial year 2009-2010. Hence he cannot be considered as a "Person Resident in India" during the financial year 2009-2010 irrespective of the purpose or duration of his stay.

9. Resident Entity

'Resident Entity' *means* 'Person resident in India' *excluding* an individual [para 2.1.34].

10. Resident Indian Citizen

'Resident Indian Citizen' shall be interpreted in line with the definition of 'person resident in India' as per FEMA, 1999, *read in conjunction with* the Indian Citizenship Act, 1955 [para 2.1.35].

The above definition makes it clear that for a person to be called as Resident Indian Citizen has to satisfy both the following limbs:

(*a*) he should be Indian citizen under the Indian Citizenship Act, 1955; *and*

(*b*) he should be person resident in India as per [section 2(*v*) of] FEMA, 1999

SYNOPSIS OF THE CITIZENSHIP ACT, 1955 (*www.mha.nic.in*)

Introduction:

The Constitution of India provides for a single citizenship for the entire country. The provisions relating to citizenship at the commencement of the Constitution are contained in Articles 5 to 11 in Part II of the Constitution of India. The Citizenship Act enacted by the Parliament in 1955 provides for acquisition and determination of citizenship.

Modes of acquiring Indian citizenship:

***By Birth* (*section 3*):** A person born in India on or after 26th January 1950 but before 1st July 1987 is a citizen of India by birth irrespective of the nationality of his parents. A person born in India on or after 1st July, 1987, is considered as a citizen of India only if either of his parents is a citizen of India at the time of his birth. Further, those born in India on or after 7th January 2004 are considered citizens of India only if both of their parents are citizens of India or one of whose parents is a citizen of India and the other is not an illegal migrant at the time of their birth.

***By Descent* (*section 4*):** A person born outside India on or after 26th January, 1950 but before 10th December, 1992 is a citizen of India by descent, if his father was a citizen of India at the time of his birth. A person born outside India on or after 10th December, 1992, is considered as a citizen of India if either of his parents is a citizen of India at the time of his birth. From 07th January, 2004, a person born outside India shall not be a citizen of India by virtue of this Section, unless his birth is registered at an Indian consulate within one year of the date of birth or with the permission of the Central Government, after the expiry of the said period. An application, for registration of the birth of a minor child, to an Indian consulate under Section 4(1) shall be made in Form I and shall be accompanied by an undertaking in writing from the parents of such minor child that he or she does not hold the passport of another country.

By Registration **(*section 5*):** Citizenship of India by registration can be acquired by—

(*a*) persons of Indian origin, who or either of whose parents was born in undivided India and who are ordinarily resident in India for seven years;

(*b*) persons of India origin who are ordinarily residents in any country or place outside undivided India;

(*c*) persons who are or have been married to a citizen of India and who are ordinarily resident in India for five years;

(*d*) minor children both whose parents are Indian citizens;

(*e*) a citizen of Singapore and Canada who is resident in India for five years and eight years respectively.

By Naturalisation **(*section 6*):** Citizenship of India by naturalisation can be acquired by a foreigner who is ordinarily resident in India for twelve years (continuously for the twelve months preceding the date of application and for eleven years in the aggregate in the fourteen years preceding the twelve months).

11. Company Controlled by Resident Indian Citizens, etc.

As per para 2.1.7, a company is considered as "controlled" by resident Indian citizens if the resident Indian citizens *and* Indian companies, which are owned and controlled by resident Indian citizens, have the power to appoint a majority of its directors in that company.

It should be noted here that the word *'and'* is used in this definition. By applying rule of logical construction, it should be interpreted that the word 'and' should be construed as 'and/or'. Further, it should also be worthwhile to note here that this definition uses two control limbs, namely:

(*i*) Control by Resident Indian Citizens;

(*ii*) Control by Indian Companies, which are *owned and controlled* by Resident Indian Citizens.

Resident Indian Citizen has been defined in para 2.1.35 of the Consolidated Policy as noted above. Further, as per para 2.1.19, ***"Indian Company"*** means a company incorporated in India under the Companies Act, 1956. Thus, it should be construed that if a company is incorporated in India (thus being an Indian Company) but is "either owned or controlled" (*i.e.* not owned and controlled) by resident Indian citizens, and such an Indian Company 'controls' any company, then the latter shall not be considered as "company controlled by resident Indian citizens, etc. It would be pertinent to mention here that for the purpose of 'owning and controlling', what constitutes owning and controlling is not spelled out by para 2.1.7. Further, it seems to be explicitly sufficient from the given definition that for the purpose of a company to be called as being controlled by resident Indian citizens, etc. the only criteria that need to be there is it's (i.e. the Indian Company) power to appoint a majority of its directors. The shareholding criteria is not given in this para but is covered in para 2.1.26 (see point 15) under which a company may be taken as a company 'owned' (as contrasted to 'control' used in this para) by resident Indian citizens. Hence, the following repercussions follow in respect of an Indian Company:

(*a*) firstly, it should be owned and controlled by resident Indian citizens; and

(*b*) secondly, it should have the power to appoint majority of its directors.

If both the above conditions are satisfied then a company would be known as a company controlled by resident Indian citizens, etc.

Since the words, "owned" and "controlled" are not defined in this policy much will depend upon the facts and circumstances of each case. However, a derivation could be that ownership means holding of more than 50% of the capital in a company. This also seems to the intention as followed from para 2.1.26 (see point 15). In respect of 'control', a bit of guidance can be taken from Accounting Standard (AS) 18 on Related Parties of Companies (Accounting Standards) Rules, 2006. Para 10 of AS 18 states that, Control refers to:

(*a*) ownership, directly or indirectly, of more than one half of the voting power of an enterprise, or

(*b*) control of the composition of the board of directors in the case of a company or of the composition of the corresponding governing body in case of any other enterprise, or

(*c*) a substantial interest in voting power and the power to direct, by statute or agreement, the financial and/or operating policies of the enterprise.

Para 11 of AS 18 further states that, an enterprise is considered to control the composition of the Board of Directors of the company, if it has the power, without the consent or concurrence of any other person, to appoint or remove all or a majority of directors of that company. An enterprise is deemed to have the power to appoint a director if any of the following conditions is satisfied:

(*a*) a person cannot be appointed as director without the exercise in his favour by that enterprise of such a power as aforesaid; or

(*b*) a person's appointment as director follows necessarily from his appointment to a position held by him in that enterprise; or

(*c*) the director is nominated by that enterprise; in case that enterprise is a company, the director is nominated by that company/subsidiary thereof.

12. Company Controlled by Non Resident Entities

As per para 2.1.8, an entity is considered as 'controlled' by 'non resident entities', if non-residents have the power to appoint a majority of its directors. A question may arise here as to whether only non resident entities are covered here to be taken as controlling a company or it includes even a non resident individual. The situation becomes quite explorable considering the definitions of non resident entity and non resident Indian given in point 13 and point 14 below read with the definition of resident entity give in point 9 above. As may be noted in point 9, the definition excludes individual. Someone may as a matter of corollary opine that non resident entity does not include individual. This opinion may further be strengthened on account of the fact that para 2.1.25 (see point 14) has defined non resident Indian separately as it means an individual resident outside India who is a citizen of India or is an individual of Indian origin. But in author's opinion, because of the usage of broad words "person resident outside India" in para 2.1.24 (see point 13), the intention of policy makers seems to be to consider even non resident individuals for the purpose of determining whether the companies are controlled by non resident entities (and/or individuals).

13. Non Resident Entity

'Non resident entity' means a 'person resident outside India' as defined under FEMA [para 2.1.24].

14. Non Resident Indian

'Non Resident Indian' (NRI) means an individual resident outside India who is a citizen of India or is an individual of Indian origin [para 2.1.25].

15. Company Owned by Resident Indian Citizens

A company is considered as 'owned' by resident Indian citizens if more than 50% of the *capital* in it is *beneficially owned* by resident Indian citizens and/or Indian companies, which are ultimately owned and controlled by resident Indian citizens [para 2.1.26]. In addition to the discussion under point 11, this para (as well as para 2.1.27 as given in point 16) uses the word 'capital' but without making any distinction between equity capital and preference capital. The question arises as to whether preference capital should be considered for the purpose of ownership criteria or not, the reason being, as per section 85 (as reproduced below) of the Companies Act, 1956,

(1) "Preference share capital" means, with reference to any company limited by shares, whether formed before or after the commencement of this Act,

that part of the share capital of the company which fulfils both the following requirements, namely:—

(*a*) that as respects dividends, it carries or will carry a preferential right to be paid a fixed amount or an amount calculated at a fixed rate, which may be either free of or subject to income-tax; and

(*b*) that as respect capital, it carries or will carry, on a winding up or repayment of capital, a preferential right to be repaid the amount of the capital paid-up or deemed to have been paid up, whether or not there is a preferential right to the payment of either or both of the following amounts namely:—

(*i*) any money remaining unpaid, in respect of the amounts specified in clause (*a*), up to the date of the winding up or repayment of capital; and

(*ii*) any fixed premium or premium on any fixed scale, specified in the memorandum or articles of the company.

Explanation: Capital shall be deemed to be preference capital, notwithstanding that it is entitled to either or both of the following rights, namely:—

(*i*) that, as respects dividends, in addition to the preferential right to the amount specified in clause (*a*), it has a right to participate, whether fully or to a limited extent, with capital not entitled to the preferential right aforesaid;

(*ii*) that, as respects capital, in addition to the preferential right to the repayment, on a winding up, of the amounts specified in clause (*b*), it has a right to participate, whether fully or to a limited extent, with capital not entitled to that preferential right in any surplus which may remain after the entire capital has been repaid.

(2) "Equity share capital" means, with reference to any such company, all share capital which is not preference share capital.

(3) The expressions "preference share" and "equity share" shall be construed accordingly.

Para 2.1.5 of this policy states that 'Capital' means equity shares; fully, compulsorily & mandatorily convertible preference shares; fully, compulsorily & mandatorily convertible debentures. Any other type of instruments like warrants, partly paid shares etc. are not considered as capital and cannot be issued to person resident outside India. However, additionally, para 3.2.1 and 3.2.2 of this policy has made it clear that Indian companies can issue equity shares, fully, compulsorily and mandatorily convertible debentures and fully, compulsorily and mandatorily convertible preference shares subject to pricing guidelines/valuation norms prescribed under FEMA Regulations. The pricing of the capital instruments should be decided/determined upfront at the time of issue of the instruments. Accordingly, other types of Preference shares/Debentures *i.e.* non-convertible, optionally convertible or partially convertible for issue of which funds have been received on or after May 1, 2007 are considered as debt.

This definition (as well as that given in point 16) also does not define as to what constitutes "beneficial ownership". As per Black Law Dictionary (2nd Pocket ed. 2001 pg. 508), beneficial owner is a legal term where specific property rights ("use and title") in equity belong to a person even though legal title of the property belongs to another person. This often relates where the legal title owner has implied trustee duties to the beneficial owner."

16. Entity Owned by Non Resident Entities

An entity is considered as 'owned' by 'non resident entities', if more than 50% of the capital in it is beneficially owned by non-residents [para 2.1.27].

17. FDI

As per para 2.1.11, 'FDI' means investment by non-resident entity/person resident outside India in the capital of the Indian company under Schedule 1 of FEM (Transfer or Issue of Security by a Person Resident Outside India) Regulations 2000 [details given in later chapter].

18. Investing Company

'Investing Company' means an Indian Company holding only investments in another Indian company, directly or indirectly, other than for trading of such holdings/securities (para 2.1.20).

As per AS 13, Investments are assets held by an enterprise for earning income by way of dividends, interest, and rentals, for capital appreciation, or for other benefits to the investing enterprise. Assets held as stock-in-trade are not 'investments'. Further, as per section 2(*za*) of FEMA, "security" means shares, stocks, bonds and debentures, Government securities as defined in the Public Debt Act, 1944 (18 of 1944), savings certificates to which the Government Savings Certificates Act, 1959 (46 of 1959) applies, deposit receipts in respect of deposits of securities and units of the Unit Trust of India established under sub-section (1) of section 3 of the Unit Trust of India Act, 1963 (52 of 1963) or of any mutual fund and includes certificates of title to securities, but does not include bills of exchange or promissory notes other than Government promissory notes or any other instruments which may be notified by the Reserve Bank as security for the purposes of this Act.

19. Investment on Repatriable Basis

As per para 2.1.21, 'Investment on repatriable basis' means investment, the sale proceeds of which, net of taxes, are eligible to be repatriated out of India and the expression 'investment on non-repatriable basis' shall be construed accordingly.

It should be noted here that as per section 2(*y*) of FEMA, "repatriate to India" means bringing into India the realised foreign exchange and—

(*i*) the selling of such foreign exchange to an authorised person in India in exchange for rupees; or

(*ii*) the holding of realised amount in an account with an authorised person in India to the extent notified by the Reserve Bank,

and includes use of the realised amount for discharge of a debt or liability denominated in foreign exchange and the expression "repatriation" shall be construed accordingly.

20. Joint Venture

As per para 2.1.22, 'Joint Venture' (JV) means an Indian entity incorporated in accordance with the laws and regulations in India in whose capital a *foreign entity* makes an investment para [2.1.23]. Although, the expression foreign entity has not been expressly defined in this policy but it may be safely taken to include company controlled by non resident entities, non resident entities, entity owned by non resident entities, as discussed above in the preceding paragraphs. Under AS 27, a joint venture is a contractual arrangement whereby two or more parties undertake an economic activity, which is subject to joint control.

21. Foreign Institutional Investor

'Foreign Institutional Investor' (FII) means an entity established or incorporated outside India which proposes to make investment in India and which is registered as a FII in accordance with the SEBI (FII) Regulations 1995 (para 2.1.14).

22. Foreign Venture Capital Investor

As per para 2.1.15, 'Foreign Venture Capital Investor' (FVCI) means an investor incorporated and established outside India, which is registered under the Securities and Exchange Board of India (Foreign Venture Capital Investor) Regulations, 2000 [SEBI (FVCI) Regulations] and proposes to make investment in accordance with these Regulations.

23. Government Route

As per para 2.1.16, 'Government route' means that investment in the capital of resident entities by nonresident entities can be made only with the prior approval from FIPB, Ministry of Finance or SIA, DIPP as the case may be.

24. Indian Venture Capital Undertaking

'Indian Venture Capital Undertaking' (IVCU) means an Indian company:—

(*i*) whose shares are not listed in a recognised stock exchange in India;

(*ii*) which is engaged in the business of providing services, production or manufacture of articles or things, but does not include such activities or sectors which are specified in the negative list by the SEBI, with approval of Central Government, by notification in the Official Gazette in this behalf (para 2.1.19).

25. SEZ

'SEZ' means a Special Economic Zone as defined in Special Economic Zone Act, 2005 (para 2.1.37).

26. Transferable Development Rights

As per para 2.1.39, 'Transferable Development Rights' (TDR) means certificates issued in respect of category of land acquired for public purposes either by the Central or State Government in consideration of surrender of land by the owner without monetary compensation, which are transferable in part or whole.

27. Venture Capital Fund

As per para 2.1.40, 'Venture Capital Fund' (VCF) means a Fund established in the form of a Trust, a company including a body corporate and registered under Securities and Exchange Board of India (Venture Capital Fund) Regulations, 1996, which

(*i*) has a dedicated pool of capital;

(*ii*) raised in the manner specified under the Regulations; and

(*iii*) invests in accordance with the Regulations.

28. Depository Receipt

Under para 2.1.8 of this policy, 'Depository Receipt' (DR) means a negotiable security issued outside India by a Depository bank, on behalf of an Indian company, which represent the local Rupee denominated equity shares of the company held as deposit by a Custodian bank in India. DRs are traded on Stock Exchanges in the US, Singapore, Luxembourg, etc. DRs listed and traded in the US markets are known as American Depository Receipts (ADRs) and those listed and traded anywhere/elsewhere are known as Global Depository Receipts (GDRs).

29. Erstwhile Overseas Corporate Body (OCB)

As per para 2.1.9, 'Erstwhile Overseas Corporate Body' (OCB) means a company, partnership firm, society and other corporate body owned directly or indirectly to the extent of at least sixty percent by non-resident Indian and includes overseas trust in which not less than sixty percent beneficial interest is held by non-resident Indian directly or indirectly but irrevocably and which was in existence on the date of commencement of the Foreign Exchange Management (Withdrawal of General Permission to Overseas Corporate Bodies (OCBs)) Regulations, 2003 the Regulations and immediately prior to such commencement was eligible to undertake transactions pursuant to the general permission granted under the Regulations.

30. FCCB

As per para 2.1.10, 'Foreign Currency Convertible Bonds'(FCCB) means a bond issued by an Indian company expressed in foreign currency, the principal and interest of which is payable in foreign currency. FCCBs are issued in accordance with the Foreign Currency Convertible Bonds and ordinary shares (through depository receipt mechanism) Scheme 1993 and subscribed by a non-resident entity in foreign currency and convertible into ordinary shares of the issuing company in any manner, either in whole, or in part.

31. Capital Account Transaction

'Capital account transaction' means a transaction which alters the assets or liabilities, including contingent liabilities, outside India of persons resident in India or assets or liabilities in India of persons resident outside India, and includes transactions referred to in sub-section (3) of section 6 of FEMA (para 2.1.6). This definition is worded exactly as it stands in section 2(*e*) of FEMA (details given in later chapter).

Section 6(3) of FEMA stipulates that, without prejudice to the generality of the provisions of sub-section (2), the Reserve Bank may, by regulations prohibit, restrict or regulate the following,—

(*a*) transfer or issue of any foreign security by a person resident in India;

(*b*) transfer or issue of any security by a person resident outside India;

(*c*) transfer or issue of any security or foreign security by any branch, office or agency in India of a person resident outside India;

(*d*) any borrowing or lending in foreign exchange in whatever form or by whatever name called;

(*e*) any borrowing or lending in rupees in whatever form or by whatever name called between a person resident in India and a person resident outside India;

(*f*) deposits between persons resident in India and persons resident outside India;

(*g*) export, import or holding of currency or currency notes;

(*h*) transfer of immovable property outside India, other than a lease not exceeding five years, by a person resident in India;

(*i*) acquisition or transfer of immovable property in India, other than a lease not exceeding five years, by a person resident outside India;

(*j*) giving of a guarantee or surety in respect of any debt, obligation or other liability incurred,—

  (*i*) by a person resident in India and owed to a person resident outside India; or

  (*ii*) by a person resident outside India.

It would be worthwhile to mention here that current account transaction has not been defined by this policy. However, as per section 2(*j*) of FEMA, "current account transaction" means a transaction other than a capital account transaction and without prejudice to the generality of the foregoing such transaction includes,—

(*i*) payments due in connection with foreign trade, other current business, services, and short-term banking and credit facilities in the ordinary course of business,

(*ii*) payments due as interest on loans and as net income from investments,

(*iii*) remittances for living expenses of parents, spouse and children residing abroad, and

(*iv*) expenses in connection with foreign travel, education and medical care of parents, spouse and children.

Appendix

Issue of Foreign Currency Convertible Bonds and Ordinary Shares (Through Depository Receipt Mechanism) Scheme, 1993[1]

Central Government hereby notifies the following scheme, for facilitating issue of Foreign Currency Convertible Bonds and Ordinary Shares Through Global Depository Mechanism by Indian Companies, namely:—

1. Short title and commencement.—(1) This scheme may be called the Issue of Foreign Currency Convertible Bonds and Ordinary Shares (Through Depository Receipt Mechanism) Scheme, 1993.

(2) It shall be deemed to have come into force with effect from the first day of April, 1992.

2. Definitions.—In this scheme, unless the context otherwise requires,—

(*a*) "Domestic Custodian Bank" means a banking company which acts as a custodian for the ordinary shares or foreign currency convertible bonds of an Indian company which are issued by it against global depository receipts or certificates;

(*b*) "foreign currency convertible bonds" means bonds issued in accordance with this scheme and subscribed by a non-resident in foreign currency and convertible into ordinary shares of the issuing company in any manner, either in whole, or in part, on the basis of any equity related warrants attached to debt instruments;

(*c*) "Global Depository Receipts" means any instrument in the form of a depository receipt or certificate (by whatever name it is called) created by the Overseas Depository Bank outside India and issued to non-resident investors against the issue of ordinary shares or Foreign Currency Convertible Bonds of issuing company;

(*d*) "issuing company" means an Indian company permitted to issue Foreign Currency Convertible Bonds or ordinary shares of that company against Global Depository Receipts;

(*e*) "Overseas Depository Bank" means a bank authorised by the issuing company to issue Global Depository Receipts against issue of Foreign Currency Convertible Bonds or ordinary shares of the issuing company;

(*f*) the words and expressions not defined in the Scheme, but defined in the Income-tax Act, 1961 (43 of 1961), or the Companies Act, 1956 (1 of

1 GSR No. 700(E), dated 12-11-1993.

1956), or the Securities and Exchange Board of India Act, 1992 (15 of 1992), or the Rules and Regulations framed under these Acts, shall have the meaning respectively assigned to them, as the case may be, in the Income-tax Act or the Companies Act, or the Securities and Exchange Board of India Act.

[1][(*g*) "a software company" means a company engaged in manufacture or production of software where not less than 80 per cent of the company's turnover is from software activities;

(*h*) "information technology software and information technology services" means the companies which deal with such activities as defined in recommendation No. 19(*a*) and (*b*) of the Notification dated 25th July, 1998 issued by the Planning Commission.]

3. Eligibility for issue of convertible bonds or ordinary shares of issuing company.—(1) An issuing company desirous of raising foreign funds by issuing foreign currency convertible bonds or ordinary shares for equity issues through Global Depository Receipt is required to obtain prior permission of the Department of Economic Affairs, Ministry of Finance, Government of India.

[2][(*i*) An Indian Company may sponsor an issue of ADRs/GDRs with an overseas depository against shares held by its shareholders at a price to be determined by the Lead Manager, in respect of:—

(*a*) Divestment by shareholders of their holdings of Indian companies listed in India.

(*b*) Divestment by shareholders of their holdings of Indian companies not listed in India but which are listed overseas.

(*ii*) Such a facility would be available *pari passu* to all categories of shareholders of the company whose shares are being sold in the ADR/GDR market overseas.

(*iii*) An approved intermediary under the scheme, would be an Investment Banker registered with the Securities and Exchange Commission in the USA, or under Financial Services Authority in U.K., or the appropriate regulatory authority in Germany, France, Singapore or in Japan.

(*iv*) Such issues would need to conform to the Foreign Direct Investment Policy and other mandatory statutory requirements and detailed guidelines issued in this regard. The provisions of paragraph (4B) of Schedule I to Foreign Exchange Management (Transfer or Issue of Security by a Person Resident

---

1 Inserted by Foreign Currency Convertible Bonds and Ordinary Shares (Through Depository Receipt Mechanism) Amendment Scheme, 1999, w.e.f. 23-6-1998 in respect of "Indian Software Companies" and w.e.f. 16-9-1998 in respect of "Information technology software and information technology services".

2 Inserted by Issue of Foreign Currency Convertible Bonds and Ordinary Shares (Through Depository Receipt Mechanism) (Amendment) Scheme-II, 2002, dated 29-7-2002, w.e.f. 29-7-2002.

Outside India) Regulations, 2000 as notified by Reserve Bank of India *vide* Notification No. FEMA 41/2001-RB, dated March 2, 2001, would also need to be adhered to.]

[1][(1)(A) An Indian company, which is not eligible to raise funds from the Indian capital market including a company which has been restrained from accessing the securities market by the Securities and Exchange Board of India (SEBI) will not be eligible to issue (*i*) Foreign Currency Convertible Bonds and (*ii*) Ordinary Shares through Global Depository Receipts under the Foreign Currency Convertible Bonds and Ordinary Shares (Through Depository Receipt Mechanism) Scheme, 1993.

(1)(B) Unlisted Indian Companies issuing Global Depository Receipts/ Foreign Currency Convertible Bonds shall be required to simultaneously list in the Indian Stock Exchange(s).]

[2][3(1)(Ba) The unlisted companies issuing Global Depository Receipts/ Foreign Currency Convertible Bonds that have taken verifiable "effective steps," before 31st August, 2005 would be exempted from the requirement of prior or simultaneous listing provided these companies complete their issues latest by 31st December, 2005.

Explanation.—"Effective steps", for the above purpose, will mean the following:—

(*a*) That the company has completed due diligence and filed offering circular in the overseas exchange(s); or

(*b*) That approval of overseas exchange(s) has been obtained; or

(*c*) That the payment of listing fees is made; or

(*d*) Approval of the Reserve Bank of India under Foreign Exchange Management Act, 1999, where applicable, for meeting issue related expenses has been obtained.

It is clarified that private placements of issues, where no offering circular was placed before the overseas exchange(s), would not qualify for "effective steps".]

[3][(1)(C) Erstwhile Overseas Corporate Bodies (OCBs) who are not eligible to invest in India through the portfolio route and entities prohibited to buy, sell or deal in securities by SEBI will not be eligible to subscribe to (*i*) Foreign Currency Convertible Bonds and (*ii*) Ordinary Shares through Global Depository Receipts under the Foreign Currency Convertible Bonds and Ordinary Shares (Through Depository Receipt Mechanism) Scheme, 1993.]

---

1 Inserted by Foreign Currency Convertible Bonds and Ordinary Shares (Through Depository Receipt Mechanism) (Amendment) Scheme, 2005, w.e.f. 31-8-2005.

2 Inserted by Foreign Currency Convertible Bonds and Ordinary Shares (Through Depository Receipt Mechanism) (Second Amendment) Scheme, 2005, w.e.f. 14-9-2005.

3 Inserted by Foreign Currency Convertible Bonds and Ordinary Shares (Through Depository Receipt Mechanism) (Amendment) Scheme, 2005, w.e.f. 31-8-2005.

(2) An issuing company seeking permission under sub-paragraph (1) shall have a consistent track record of good performance (financial or otherwise) for a minimum period of three years, on the basis of which an approval for finalising the issue structure would be issued to the company by the Department of Economic Affairs, Ministry of Finance.

(3) On the completion of finalisation of issue structure in consultation with the Lead Manager to the issue, the issuing company shall obtain the final approval for proceeding ahead with the issue from the Department of Economic Affairs.

Explanation.—For the purposes of sub-paragraphs (2) and (3) "issue structure" means any of the requirements which are provided in the paragraphs 5 and 6 of this scheme.

(4) The foreign currency convertible bond shall be denominated in any freely convertible foreign currency and the ordinary shares of an issuing company shall be denominated in Indian rupees.

(5) When an issuing company issues ordinary shares or bonds under this scheme, that company shall deliver the ordinary shares or bonds to a Domestic Custodian Bank who will, in terms of agreement, instruct the Overseas Depository Bank to issue Global Depository Receipt or certificate to non-resident investors against the shares or bonds held by the Domestic Custodian Bank.

(6) A Global Depository Receipt may be issued in the negotiable form and may be listed on any international stock exchanges for trading outside India.

(7) The provisions of any law relating to issue of capital by an Indian company shall apply in relation to the issue of Foreign Currency Convertible Bonds or the ordinary shares of an issuing company and the issuing company shall obtain the necessary permission or exemption from the appropriate authority under the relevant law relating to issue of capital.

[1][**3A.** Indian companies engaged in information technology software and information technology services are eligible to offer to their non-resident/ resident permanent employees (including Indian and overseas working directors) global depository receipts against the issue of ordinary shares under the scheme subject to the operational guidelines/conditions issued from time to time by the Government.]

[2][**3B.** Indian companies engaged in information technology software and information technology services as defined in recommendation No. 19(*a*) and (*b*) of the Notification dated 25-7-1998 issued by the Planning Commission, are

---

1 Inserted by Foreign Currency Convertible Bonds and Ordinary Shares (Through Depository Receipt Mechanism) Amendment Scheme, 1999, w.e.f. 23-6-1998 in respect of "Indian Software Companies" and w.e.f. 16-9-1998 in respect of "Information technology software and information technology services".

2 Inserted by Foreign Currency Convertible Bonds and Ordinary Shares (Through Depository Receipt Mechanism) Amendment Scheme, 2000, w.e.f. 16-6-2000.

eligible to offer also to the non-residents/residents permanent employees (including Indian and overseas working directors) of their subsidiary companies, incorporated in India or abroad and engaged in information technology software and information technology services, global depository receipts against the issue of ordinary shares under the scheme subject to the eligibility conditions and operational guidelines/conditionalities announced from time to time by the Government.]

[1][**3C.** Indian Companies registered in India and engaged in the following sectors/areas, where 80% of turnover is from these sectors/areas of the operation/business of the company in the three previous financial years, are eligible to offer Global Depository Receipts against the issue of ordinary shares under the Scheme to their non-resident/resident permanent employees (including Indian and overseas working directors) and also of their subsidiary companies, incorporated in India or abroad, subject to the eligibility conditions and operational guidelines/conditionalities announced from time to time by the Government:—

(*i*) Information Technology (as defined in the recommendation No. 19(*a*) and (*b*) of Gazette Notification, dated 25-7-1999 issued by the Planning Commission) and Entertainment Software.

(*ii*) Pharmaceuticals.

(*iii*) Biotechnology.

(*iv*) Any other activities within the knowledge based sector as notified by the Government from time to time.

These norms would also be available for multi-product diversified companies which do not conform to the criteria of 80% turn over as mentioned above but having an average annual export earnings of ₹ 100 Crores from the sectors mentioned above in the three previous financial years.]

4. Limits of foreign investment in the issuing company.—The ordinary shares and Foreign Currency Convertible Bonds issued against the Global Depository Receipts shall be treated as direct foreign investment in the issuing company. The aggregate of the foreign investment made either directly or indirectly (through Global Depository Receipts Mechanism) shall not exceed 51% of the issued and subscribed capital of the issuing company:

Provided that the investments made through Offshore Funds or by Foreign Institutional Investors will not form part of the limit laid down in this paragraph.

5. Issue structure of the Global Depository Receipts.—(1) A Global Depository Receipt may be issued for one or more underlying shares or bonds held with the Domestic Custodian Bank.

---

1 Inserted by Issue of Foreign Currency Convertible Bonds and Ordinary Shares (Through Depository Receipt Mechanism) (Amendment) Scheme, 2001, w.e.f. 15-9-2000.

(2) The Foreign Currency Convertible Bonds and Global Depository Receipts may be denominated in any freely convertible foreign currency.

(3) The ordinary shares underlying the Global Depository Receipts and the Shares issued upon conversion of the Foreign Currency Convertible Bonds will be denominated only in Indian currency.

(4) The following issues will be decided by the issuing company with the Lead Manager to the issue, namely:—

(*a*) public or private placement;

(*b*) number of Global Depository Receipts to be issued;

[1][(*ca*) *Listed Companies.*—The pricing should not be less than the higher of the following two averages:

(*i*) The average of the weekly high and low of the closing prices of the related shares quoted on the stock exchange during the six months preceding the relevant date;

(*ii*) The average of the weekly high and low of the closing prices of the related shares quoted on a stock exchange during the two weeks preceding the relevant date.

The 'relevant date' means the date thirty days prior to the date on which the meeting of the general body of shareholders is held, in terms of section 81(1A) of the Companies Act, 1956, to consider the proposed issue.]

[2][(*ca*)(*i*) *Listed companies.*—The companies issuing Global Depository Receipts that have taken verifiable "effective steps", before 31st August, 2005 would be exempt from the requirement of the pricing guidelines at para 5(4)(*ca*) provided these companies complete their issues latest by 31st December, 2005.

Explanation.—"Effective steps", for the above purpose, will mean the following:

(*a*) That the company has completed due diligence and filed offering circular in the overseas exchange(s); or

(*b*) That approval of overseas exchange(s) has been obtained; or

(*c*) That the payment of listing fees is made; or

(*d*) Approval of the Reserve Bank of India under Foreign Exchange Management Act, 1999, where applicable, for meeting issue related expenses has been obtained.

---

1 Substituted by Foreign Currency Convertible Bonds and Ordinary Shares (Through Depository Receipt Mechanism) (Amendment) Scheme, 2005, w.e.f. 31-8-2005.

2 Inserted by Foreign Currency Convertible Bonds and Ordinary Shares (Through Depository Receipt Mechanism) (Second Amendment) Scheme, 2005, w.e.f. 14-9-2005.

It is clarified that private placements of issues, where no offering circular was placed before the overseas exchange(s), would not qualify for "effective steps".]

[1][(*cb*) *Unlisted Companies*.—The pricing should be in accordance with Reserve Bank of India Regulations notified under Foreign Exchange Management Act, 1999;]

[2][(*cc*) The companies going in for an offering in the domestic market and a simultaneous or immediate following on offering (within 30 days of domestic issue) through ADR/GDR issues wherein GDRs/ADRs are priced at or above. The domestic price, would be exempt from the requirement given at (*ca*)(*i*) and (*ii*) above. Companies going for such simultaneous or immediate follow on offering in the ADR/GDR market will have to take SEBI's approval for such issue, which will specify the percentage to be offered in the domestic and ADR/GDR markets;]

(*d*) the rate of interest payable on Foreign Currency Convertible Bonds; and

(*e*) the conversion price, coupon, and the pricing of the conversion options of the Foreign Currency Convertible Bonds.

[3][(*i*) *Listed Companies*.—The conversion price of the Foreign Currency Convertible Bonds should be in accordance with para 5(4)(*ca*) *ibid*.]

[4][(*a*) *Listed companies*.—The companies issuing Foreign Currency Convertible Bonds that have taken verifiable "effective steps", before 31st August, 2005 would be exempt from the requirement of the pricing guidelines at para 5(4)(*e*)(*i*) provided these companies complete their issues latest by 31st December, 2005.

Explanation.—"Effective steps", for the above purpose, will mean the following:

(*a*) That the company has completed due diligence and filed offering circular in the overseas exchange(s); or

(*b*) That approval of overseas exchange(s) has been obtained; or

(*c*) That the payment of listing fees is made; or

(*d*) Approval of the Reserve Bank of India under Foreign Exchange Management Act, 1999, where applicable, for meeting issue related expenses has been obtained.

---

1 Substituted by Foreign Currency Convertible Bonds and Ordinary Shares (Through Depository Receipt Mechanism) (Amendment) Scheme, 2005, w.e.f. 31-8-2005.

2 Inserted by the Issue of Foreign Currency Covertible Bonds and Ordinary Shares (Through Depository Receipt Mechanism) (Amendment) Scheme, 2005, w.e.f. 17-11-2005.

3 Inserted by Foreign Currency Convertible Bonds and Ordinary Shares (Through Depository Receipt Mechanism) (Amendment) Scheme, 2005, w.e.f. 31-8-2005.

4 Inserted by Foreign Currency Convertible Bonds and Ordinary Shares (Through Depository Receipt Mechanism) (Second Amendment) Scheme, 2005, w.e.f. 14-9-2005.

It is clarified that private placements of issues, where no offering circular was placed before the overseas exchange(s), would not qualify for "effective steps".]

[1][(*ii*) *Unlisted Companies.*—The conversion price of the Foreign Currency Convertible Bonds should be in accordance with Reserve Bank of India Regulations notified under Foreign Exchange Management Act, 1999.]

(5) There would be no lock-in-period for the Global Depository Receipts issued under this scheme.

6. Listing of the Global Depository Receipts.—The Global Depository Receipts issued under this scheme may be listed on any of the Overseas Stock Exchanges, or Over the Counter Exchanges or through Book Entry Transfer Systems prevalent abroad and such receipts may be purchased, possessed and freely transferable by a person who is a non-resident within the meaning of section 2(*q*) of the Foreign Exchange Regulation Act, 1973 (46 of 1973) subject to the provisions of that Act.

7. Transfer and redemption.—(1) A non-resident holder of Global Depository Receipts may transfer those receipts, or may ask the Overseas Depository Bank to redeem those receipts. In the case of redemption, Overseas Depository Bank shall request the Domestic Custodian Bank to get the corresponding underlying shares released in favour of the non-resident investor, for being sold directly on behalf of the non-resident, or being transferred in the books of account of the issuing company in the name of the non-resident.

[2][(1)(*a*) The Global Depository Receipts redeemed and underlying shares sold in terms of para 7(1) of the Scheme may be reissued to the extent of such redemption and sale made in the domestic market. Such reissuance will be in terms of Foreign Exchange Management (Transfer or Issue of Security by a Person Resident Outside India) Regulations, 2000, as amended from time to time and the guidelines issued in this regard.]

(2) In case of redemption of the Global Depository Receipts into underlying shares, a request for the same will be transmitted by the Overseas Depository Bank to the Domestic Custodian Bank in India, with a copy of the same being sent to the issuing company for information and record.

(3) On redemption, the cost of acquisition of the shares underlying the Global Depository Receipts shall be reckoned as the cost on the date on which the Overseas Depository Bank advises the Domestic Custodian Bank for redemption. The price of the ordinary shares of the issuing company prevailing in the Bombay Stock Exchange or the National Stock Exchange on the date of the

---

1 Inserted by Foreign Currency Convertible Bonds and Ordinary Shares (Through Depository Receipt Mechanism) (Amendment) Scheme, 2005, w.e.f. 31-8-2005.

2 Inserted by Issue of Foreign Currency Covertible Bonds and Ordinary Shares (Through Depository Receipt Mechanism) (Amendment) Scheme, 2002, w.r.e.f. 2-3-2001.

advice of redemption shall be taken as the cost of acquisition of the underlying ordinary shares.

(4) For the purposes of conversions of Foreign Currency Convertible Bonds, the cost of acquisition in the hands of the non-resident investors would be the conversion price determined on the basis of the price of the shares at the Bombay Stock Exchange, or the National Stock Exchange, on the date of conversion of Foreign Currency Convertible Bonds into shares.

8. Taxation on Foreign Currency Convertible Bonds.—(1) Interest payments on the bonds, until the conversion option is exercised, shall be subject to deduction of tax at source at the rate of ten per cent.

(2) Tax on dividend on the converted portion of the bond shall be subject to deduction of tax at source at the rate of ten per cent.

(3) Conversion of Foreign Currency Convertible Bonds into shares shall not give rise to any capital gains liable to income-tax in India.

(4) Transfers of Foreign Currency Convertible Bonds made outside India by a non-resident investor to another non-resident investor shall not give rise to any capital gains liable to tax in India.

9. Taxation on shares issued under Global Depository Receipt Mechanism.—(1) Under the provisions of the Income-tax Act, income by way of dividend on shares will be taxed at the rate of 10 per cent. The issuing company shall transfer the dividend payments net after deducting tax at source to the Overseas Depository Bank.

(2) On receipt of these payments of dividend after taxation, the Overseas Depository Bank shall distribute them to the non-resident investors proportionate to their holdings of Global Depository Receipts evidencing the relevant shares. The holders of the depository receipts may take credit of the tax deducted at source on the basis of the certification by the Overseas Depository Bank, if permitted by the country of their residence.

(3) All transactions of trading of the Global Depository Receipts outside India, among non-resident investors, will be free from any liability to income-tax in India on capital gains therefrom.

(4) If any capital gains arise on the transfer of the aforesaid shares in India to the non-resident investor, he will be liable to income-tax under the provisions of the Income-tax Act. If the aforesaid shares are held by the non-resident investor for a period of more than twelve months from the date of advice of their redemption by the Overseas Depository Bank, the capital gains arising on the sale thereof will be treated as long-term capital gains and will be subject to income-tax at the rate of 10 per cent under the provisions of section 115AC of the Income-tax Act. If such shares are held for a period of less than twelve months from the date of redemption advice, the capital gains arising on the sale thereof will be treated as short-term capital gains and will be subject to tax at the

normal rates of income-tax applicable to non-residents under the provisions of the Income-tax Act.

(5) After redemption of the depository receipts into underlying shares, during the period, if any, during which these shares are held by the redeeming non-resident foreign investor who has paid for these shares in foreign exchange at the time of purchase of the Global Depository Receipt, the rate of taxation of income by way of dividends on these shares would continue to be at the rate of 10 per cent, in accordance with section 115AC(1) of the Income-tax Act. The long-term capital gains on the sale of these redeemed underlying shares held by non-resident investors in the domestic market shall also be charged to tax at the rate of 10 per cent, in accordance with the provisions of section 115AC(1).

(6) When the redeemed shares are sold on the Indian Stock Exchanges against payment in rupees, these shares shall go out of the purview of section 115AC of the Income-tax Act and income therefrom shall not be eligible for the concessional tax treatment provided thereunder. After the transfer of shares where consideration is in terms of rupees payment, the normal tax rates would apply to the income arising or accruing on these shares.

(7) Deduction of tax at source on the amount of capital gains accruing on transfer of the shares would be made in accordance with sections 195 and 196C of the Income-tax Act.

10. Application of avoidance of double taxation agreement in case of Global Depository Receipts.—(1) During the period of fiduciary ownership of shares in the hands of the Overseas Depository Bank, the provisions of Avoidance of Double Taxation Agreement entered into by the Government of India with the country of residence of the Overseas Depository Bank will be applicable in the matter of taxation of income from dividends from underlying shares and interest on Foreign Currency Convertible Bonds.

(2) During the period, if any, when the redeemed underlying shares are held by the non-resident investor on transfer from fiduciary ownership of the Overseas Depository Bank, before they are sold to resident purchasers, the Avoidance of Double Taxation Agreement entered into by the Government of India with the country of residence of the non-resident investor will be applicable in the matter of taxation of income from the dividends from the said underlying shares, or interest on Foreign Currency Convertible Bonds, or any capital gain arising out of transfer of underlying shares.

11. Gift-tax and wealth-tax.—The holding of the depository receipts in the hands of non-resident investors and the holding of the underlying shares by the Overseas Depository Bank in a fiduciary capacity and the transfer of the Global Depository Receipts between non-resident investors and the Overseas Depository Bank shall be exempt from wealth-tax under the Wealth-tax Act, 1957 (27 of 1957), and from gift-tax under the Gift-tax Act, 1958 (18 of 1958).

Additional information to be filed by companies applying for permission to float global issues

1. Name of the Company & Address for Communication.
2. Existing Business.
3. Profile on Proposed Expansion/Diversification Project with breakup requirements of Rupee and F.E. Components.
4. Existing Resources

Equity	Year ending in March			Debt	Year ending in March		
	1993	1992	1991		1993	1992	1991
(*i*) Authorised Capital				(*i*) Secured Loans			
(*ii*) Issued & paid up capital				(*a*) Banks & FIs.			
(*iii*) Reserves & Surplus				(*b*) Debentures			
(*a*) General Reserve				(*c*) Other loans			
(*b*) Development Rebate Reserve				(*ii*) Unsecured Loans Deposits & Loans Deferred Liabilities			
(*c*) Investment Allowance Reserve				(*iii*) Current Liabilities Over Drafts from Banks and other short-term Borrowings.			
(*d*) Capital Reserve							
(*e*) Other Reserves							

5. Fixed Assets

   I. (*i*) Gross Block
   (*ii*) Additions and Accretions during the year
   (*iii*) Depreciation
   (*iv*) Net Block

   II. Work in Progress

6.	Year ending in March		
	1993	1992	1991
(*i*) Sales & Other income			
(*ii*) Operating Expenses			
(*iii*) Interest on Loans			
(*iv*) Profit before Depreciation			
(*v*) Depreciation			
(*vi*) Profit before Tax			
(*vii*) Provision for Taxation			
(*viii*) Profit before Appropriations			
(*ix*) Dividend and other appropriations			
(*x*) Profit Transferred to General Reserves			

7. Capacity and Utilisation

Products	Year	Units	Installed Capacity P.A.	Production during the year	Capacity Utilisation percentage

	Year ending in March		
	1993	1992	1991
8. Financial Results and Management Ratios			
(*i*) Net Worth			
(*ii*) Capital employed			
(*iii*) Capital-turnover ratio			
(*iv*) Equity-Debt Ratio (Long term)			
(*v*) Profitability			
(*a*) Profit margin $\frac{\text{Net Profit}}{\text{Income}} \times 100 = \%$ age			
(*b*) Return on equity $\frac{\text{Net Profit}}{\text{Equity}} \times 100$			
(*c*) Return on Net Worth $\frac{\text{Net Profit}}{\text{Net Worth}} \times 100$			
(*d*) Return on Total Investment $\frac{\text{Net Profit}}{\text{Total Investment}} \times 100$			
(*e*) Return on total capital employed $\frac{\text{Net Profit}}{\text{Resources}} \times 100$			
(*iv*) Liquidity Ratio Current ratio $= \frac{\text{Current Assets}}{\text{Current Liabilities}}$			
(*vii*) Revenue per worker for the year $= \frac{\text{Income}}{\text{Total Employment}}$			
9. Statutory Liabilities (Disputed and otherwise) & Defaults			
10. Defaults in respect of interest/instal-ments to Loans from Banks/Financial Institutions			
11. Exports & Imports			
(*a*) F.O.B. value Exports			
(*b*) Exported to (Countries)			
(*c*) Imports			
(*i*) Capital Equipment			
(*ii*) Materials, Components, Consumables			
(*d*) Other Foreign Currency Expenditure			
(*e*) Foreign debt liabilities			

12. Salient features of the prospective corporate plans and diversification proposals with special reference to foreign exchange requirements.

Format of Approval for Finalising the Issue Structure

Government of India
Ministry of Finance, Department of Economic Affairs
(Investment Division), New Delhi

To Dated the ....

M/s. ....

....

Subject: Your Application for a GDR/ADR/IDR issue for an amount of ....

Dear Sir,

I am directed to refer to your Letter No. .... dated .... on the subject mentioned above and to convey Government of India's approval 'in principle' to the mobilisation of foreign currency resources equivalent to .... through issue of GDR/ADR/IDRs to cover the Foreign Currency needs for your .... projects and other related corporate needs.

2. The approval is subject to the understanding that the foreign currency resources raised through the proposed issue should be mandatorily remitted to India immediately after the issue.

3. This approval is valid for a period of six months from the date of issue of this letter.

4. You are now requested to finalise the detailed parameters of the proposed GDR/ADR/IDRs offering for consideration and final approval by the Government of India.

Yours faithfully,

( )

Director (Foreign Investments)

Indicative items of final approval for Foreign Currency Convertible Bonds Issues

Issuer
Lead Manager
Co. Lead Manager(s)
Principal Amount
Currency
Issue price (& premium, if any)
Coupon (& payment dates)
Conversion Premium
Maturity
Listing of Bonds
Optional Redemption by Issuer (Call)
Optional Redemption by Investor (Put)
Form and Denomination
Status
Cross Default Provisions
Negative Pledge Provisions
Taxation
Commissions
Reimbursible Expenses
Governing Laws

Indicative items in the final approval for Euro-Equity Issues through GDR Mechanism

Issuer
Lead Manager
Co. Lead Manager(s)
Overseas Depository Institution
Indian Custodian
Issue Structure and Denomination (No. of underlying shares represented by the GDRs).
Issue Amount (Principal amount)
Greenshoe Option (Additional amount in % terms which may be retained, if offered)
Warrants attached, if any
Currency of issue
G.D.R. Listing
Underlying Shares Listing
Standstill period (No further equity shares, or interests in equity shares, for a specified time period from the date of issue)
Trading provision
Settlement provisions
Selling Commission
Underwriting Commission and Management Fees
Legal Expenses, Printing Expenses, Depository Fees, and other out of pocket expenses.
Taxation
Governing Laws.

Chapter 4

ORIGIN, TYPE, ELIGIBILITY, CONDITIONS AND ISSUE/ TRANSFER OF INVESTMENT

SYNOPSIS

1. Origin of Investment in India

A non-resident entity (other than a citizen of Pakistan or an entity incorporated in Pakistan) can invest in India, subject to the FDI Policy. A citizen of Bangladesh or an entity incorporated in Bangladesh can invest in India under the FDI Policy, only under the Government route.

NRIs resident in Nepal and Bhutan as well as citizens of Nepal and Bhutan are permitted to invest in the capital of Indian companies on repatriation basis, subject to the condition that the amount of consideration for such investment shall be paid only by way of inward remittance in free foreign exchange through normal banking channels.

Overseas Corporate Bodies (OCBs) have been derecognized as a class of Investors in India with effect from September 16, 2003. Erstwhile OCBs which are incorporated outside India and are not under the adverse notice of RBI can make fresh investments under FDI Policy as incorporated non-resident entities, with the prior approval of Government of India if the investment is through Government route; and with the prior approval of RBI if the investment is through Automatic route.

A FII may invest in the capital of an Indian company either under the FDI Scheme/Policy or the Portfolio Investment Scheme. 10% individual limit and 24% aggregate limit for FII investment would still be applicable even when FIIs invest under the FDI scheme/policy. The Indian company which has issued shares to FIIs under the FDI Policy for which the payment has been received directly into company's account should report these figures separately under item No. 5 of Form FC-GPR (Post-issue pattern of shareholding) so that the details could be suitably reconciled for statistical/monitoring purposes. A daily statement in respect of all transactions (except derivative trade) have to be submitted by the custodian bank in floppy/soft copy in the prescribed format directly to RBI to monitor the overall ceiling/sectoral cap/statutory ceiling. No person other than registered FII/NRI as per Schedules II and III of Foreign Exchange Management (Transfer or Issue of Security by a Person Resident Outside India) Regulations of FEMA 1999, can invest/trade in capital of Indian Companies in the Indian Stock Exchanges directly i.e. through brokers like a Person Resident in India.

The Reserve Bank of India has prescribed following guidelines in respect of portfolio investment scheme via AP (DIR Series) Circular No. 53, dated December 17, 2003:

1. A SEBI registered FII/approved sub-account is permitted to open a Foreign Currency denominated Account and/or a Special Non-Resident Rupee Account and to transfer sums from the foreign currency account to the rupee account for making genuine investments

in the securities in terms of the SEBI (FIIs) Regulations, 1995. The sums may be transferred from foreign currency account to rupee account at the prevailing market rate and the Authorised Dealer may transfer repatriable proceeds (after payment of tax) from the rupee account to the foreign currency account.

2. The Special Non-Resident Rupee Account may be credited with the proceeds of sale of shares/debentures, dated Government securities, Treasury Bills etc., dividend, income received by way of interest, forward contracts booked etc., by compensation received towards sale/renouncements of right offerings of shares and income earned on securities lent under SEBI's Securities Lending Scheme, 1997 after deduction of appropriate tax, if any subject to the condition that the Authorized Dealer should obtain confirmation from the investee company/FII concerned that tax at source, wherever necessary, has been deducted from the gross amount of dividend/interest payable/ approved income to the share/debenture/Government securities holder at the applicable rate, in accordance with the Income Tax Act.

3. The Special Non-Resident Rupee Account may be debited for purchase of shares/debentures, dated Government securities, Treasury Bills etc., and for payment of fees to applicant FIIs' local Chartered Accountant/Tax Consultant where such fees constitute an integral part of their investment process.

4. The SEBI registered FII/sub-account is/are permitted to purchase shares/convertible debentures of an Indian company through offer/ private arrangement subject to the applicable ceiling and the Indian company is permitted to issue such shares provided that: (*i*) in the case of public offer, the price of shares to be issued is not less than the price at which shares are issued to residents; and (*ii*) in the case of issue by private placement, the price is not less than the price arrived at in terms of SEBI guidelines or guidelines issued by the erstwhile Controller of Capital Issues, as applicable. Purchases can also be made of PCDs/FCDs/Right Renunciations/Warrants/Units of Domestic Mutual Fund Schemes.

5. FII shall not engage in short selling and shall take delivery of securities purchased and give delivery of securities sold. There shall be no squaring off of transactions during the no-delivery period of a security.

6. The SEBI registered FII shall restrict allocation of its total investment between equities and debt in the Indian capital market in the ratio of 70:30. The FII may form a 100% debt fund and get such fund registered with SEBI.

7. The purchase of equity shares by a single SEBI registered FII/sub-account in each company shall not exceed 10% (ten percent) of the

paid-up equity capital of the company. The purchase of equity shares by each foreign corporate and foreign individual shall not exceed 5% of the paid-up equity capital of the company within the overall aggregate limit of 24% or the sectoral cap/statutory ceiling, as applicable. These limits shall include acquisition of shares in primary/ secondary market.

8. SEBI registered FII may trade in all exchange traded derivative contracts on the stock exchanges in India subject to the position limits as prescribed by SEBI from time to time. The SEBI registered FII/sub-account may open a separate sub-account of their Special Non-Resident Rupee Account through which all receipts and payments pertaining to trading/investment in exchange traded derivative contracts including initial margin and mark to market settlement, transaction charges, brokerage etc., will be made. Further transfer between the Special Non-Resident Rupee Account and the sub account maintained for the purpose of trading in exchange traded derivative contracts can be freely effected. However, repatriation of the rupee amount will be effected only through their Special Non-Resident Rupee Account subject to payment of relevant taxes. The Authorised Dealer may keep proper records of the sub account and submit them to Reserve Bank as and when required.

9. SEBI registered FIIs/sub-accounts may keep with the Trading Member/Clearing Member amount sufficient to cover the margins prescribed by the Exchange/Clearing House and such amounts as may be considered necessary to meet the immediate needs.

10. A daily statement in respect of all transactions (except derivative trade) should be submitted in floppy/soft copy in the prescribed format directly to the Chief General Manager, Exchange Control Department, Reserve Bank of India, Foreign Investment Division, Central Office, Central Office Building, Mumbai-400 001 to monitor the overall ceiling/sectoral cap/statutory ceiling. When the total holdings of FIIs reach within 2% of the applicable limit, Reserve Bank will issue a notice to all designated branches of Authorised Dealers stating that any further purchases of shares of the said company require prior approval of Reserve Bank. No purchases shall be made once the prescribed overall ceiling/sectoral cap/statutory limit is reached.

A Foreign Venture Capital Investor (FVCI) may contribute upto 100% of the capital of a Venture Capital Fund/Indian Venture Capital Undertaking and may also set up a domestic asset management company to manage the fund. All such investments are allowed under the automatic route subject to SEBI & RBI regulations and FDI Policy. However FVCIs are also allowed to invest as non-resident entities in other companies subject to FDI Policy.

2. Types of Instruments

Indian companies can issue equity shares, fully, compulsorily and mandatorily convertible debentures and fully, compulsorily and mandatorily convertible preference shares subject to pricing guidelines/valuation norms prescribed under FEMA Regulations. The pricing of the capital instruments should be decided/determined upfront at the time of issue of the instruments. Other types of Preference shares/Debentures i.e. non-convertible, optionally convertible or partially convertible for issue of which funds have been received on or after May 1, 2007 are considered as debt. Accordingly all norms applicable for ECBs (see chapter 10 for details) relating to eligible borrowers, recognized lenders, amount and maturity, end-use stipulations, etc. shall apply. Since these instruments would be denominated in rupees, the rupee interest rate will be based on the swap equivalent of London Interbank Offered Rate (LIBOR) plus the spread as permissible for ECBs of corresponding maturity

The inward remittance received by the Indian company via issuance of DRs and FCCBs are treated as FDI and counted towards FDI.

(*a*) *Issue of shares by Indian Companies under FCCB/ADR/GDR*

Indian companies can raise foreign currency resources abroad through the issue of FCCB/DR (ADRs/GDRs), in accordance with the Scheme for issue of Foreign Currency Convertible Bonds and Ordinary Shares (Through Depository Receipt Mechanism) Scheme, 1993 (See Appendix) and guidelines issued by the Government of India there under from time to time.

A company can issue ADRs/GDRs if it is eligible to issue shares to person(s) resident outside India under the FDI Policy. However, an Indian listed company, which is not eligible to raise funds from the Indian Capital Market including a company which has been restrained from accessing the securities market by the Securities and Exchange Board of India (SEBI) will not be eligible to issue ADRs/GDRs.

Unlisted companies, which have not yet accessed the ADR/GDR route for raising capital in the international market, would require prior or simultaneous listing in the domestic market, while seeking to issue such overseas instruments. Unlisted companies, which have already issued ADRs/GDRs in the international market, have to list in the domestic market on making profit or within three years of such issue of ADRs/GDRs, whichever is earlier. ADRs/GDRs are issued on the basis of the ratio worked out by the Indian company in consultation with the Lead Manager to the issue. The proceeds so raised have to be kept abroad till actually required in India. Pending repatriation or utilization of the proceeds, the Indian company can invest the funds in:—

(*a*) Deposits, Certificate of Deposits or other instruments offered by banks rated by Standard and Poor, Fitch, IBCA, Moody's, etc. with rating not below the rating stipulated by Reserve Bank from time to time for the purpose;

(*b*) Deposits with branches of Indian Authorized Dealers outside India; and

(*c*) Treasury bills and other monetary instruments with a maturity or unexpired maturity of one year or less.

(*d*) There are no end-use restrictions except for a ban on deployment/ investment of such funds in real estate or the stock market. There is no monetary limit up to which an Indian company can raise ADRs/GDRs.

(*e*) The ADR/GDR proceeds can be utilized for first stage acquisition of shares in the disinvestment process of Public Sector Undertakings/ Enterprises and also in the mandatory second stage offer to the public in view of their strategic importance.

Voting rights on shares issued under the Scheme shall be as per the provisions of Companies Act, 1956 and in a manner in which restrictions on voting rights imposed on ADR/GDR issues shall be consistent with the Company Law provisions. Voting rights in the case of banking companies will continue to be in terms of the provisions of the Banking Regulation Act, 1949 and the instructions issued by the Reserve Bank from time to time, as applicable to all shareholders exercising voting rights.

Erstwhile OCBs who are not eligible to invest in India and entities prohibited from buying, selling or dealing in securities by SEBI will not be eligible to subscribe to ADRs/GDRs issued by Indian companies. The pricing of ADR/GDR issues should be made at a price determined under the provisions of the Scheme of issue of Foreign Currency Convertible Bonds and Ordinary Shares (through Depository Receipt Mechanism) Scheme, 1993 and guidelines issued by the Government of India and directions issued by the Reserve Bank, from time to time.

The pricing of sponsored ADRs/GDRs would be determined under the provisions of the Scheme of issue of Foreign Currency Convertible Bonds and Ordinary Shares (Through Depository Receipt Mechanism) Scheme, 1993 and guidelines issued by the Government of India and directions issued by the Reserve Bank, from time to time.

(*b*) *Two-way Fungibility Scheme*

A limited two-way Fungibility scheme has been put in place by the Government of India for ADRs/GDRs. Under this Scheme, a stock broker in India, registered with SEBI, can purchase shares of an Indian company from the market for conversion into ADRs/GDRs based on instructions received from overseas investors. Re-issuance of ADRs/GDRs would be permitted to the extent of ADRs/GDRs which have been redeemed into underlying shares and sold in the Indian market.

(c) *Sponsored ADR/GDR issue*

An Indian company can also sponsor an issue of ADR/GDR. Under this mechanism, the company offers its resident shareholders a choice to submit their shares back to the company so that on the basis of such shares, ADRs/GDRs can be issued abroad. The proceeds of the ADR/GDR issue are remitted back to India and distributed among the resident investors who had offered their Rupee denominated shares for conversion. These proceeds can be kept in Resident Foreign Currency (Domestic) accounts in India by the resident shareholders who have tendered such shares for conversion into ADRs/GDRs.

3. Eligibility of FDI in Resident Entities

(*a*) *FDI in an Indian Company*

Indian companies including those which are micro and small enterprises can issue capital against FDI. This policy has not defined as to when an enterprise may be referred to as micro and small enterprise. For this purpose, reference may be made to section 7 of the Micro, Small and Medium Enterprises Development Act, 2006 (MSMED Act), the Central Government may, for the purposes of this Act, by notification classify any class or classes of enterprises, whether proprietorship, Hindu undivided family, association of persons, co-operative society, partnership firm, company or undertaking, by whatever name called:

(A) In the case of the enterprises engaged in the manufacture or production of goods as:

- (*i*) a *micro enterprise*, where the investment in plant and machinery does not exceed twenty five lakh rupees;
- (*ii*) a *small enterprise*, where the investment in plant and machinery is more than twenty five lakh rupees but does not exceed five crore rupees; or
- (*iii*) a *medium enterprise*, where the investment in plant and machinery is more than five crore rupees but does not exceed ten crore rupees;

(B) In the case of the enterprises engaged in providing or rendering of services as:

- (*i*) a *micro enterprise*, where the investment in equipment does not exceed ten lakh rupees;
- (*ii*) a *small enterprise*, where the investment in equipment is more than ten lakh rupees but does not exceed two crore rupees; or
- (*iii*) a *medium enterprise*, where the investment in equipment is more than two crore rupees but does not exceed five crore rupees

For the removal of doubt, it is hereby clarified that in calculating the investment in plant and machinery, the cost of pollution control, research and development, industrial safety devices and such other items as may be specified, by notification, shall be excluded.

(*b*) *FDI in Partnership Firm/Proprietary Concern*

A Non-Resident Indian (NRI) or a Person of Indian Origin (PIO) resident outside India can invest by way of contribution to the capital of a firm or a proprietary concern in India on *non-repatriation basis* provided:

(*a*) Amount is invested by inward remittance or out of NRE/FCNR (B)/NRO account maintained with Authorized Dealers/Authorized banks;

(*b*) The firm or proprietary concern is not engaged in any agricultural/ plantation or real estate business or print media sector;

(*c*) Amount invested shall not be eligible for repatriation outside India.

Investments with repatriation benefits: NRIs/PIO may seek prior permission of Reserve Bank for investment in sole proprietorship concerns/partnership firms with repatriation benefits. The application will be decided in consultation with the Government of India.

Investment by non-residents other than NRIs/PIO: A person resident outside India other than NRIs/PIO may make an application and seek prior approval of Reserve Bank for making investment by way of contribution to the capital of a firm or a proprietorship concern or any association of persons in India. The application will be decided in consultation with the Government of India.

Restrictions: An NRI or PIO is not allowed to invest in a firm or proprietorship concern engaged in any agricultural/plantation activity or real estate business (i.e. dealing in land and immovable property with a view to earning profit or earning income there from) or engaged in Print Media.

(*c*) *FDI in Trusts*

FDI in Trusts other than VCF is not permitted.

(*d*) *FDI in other Entities*

FDI in resident entities other than those mentioned above is not permitted.

(*e*) *FDI in Limited Liability Partnerships (LLPs)*

FDI in LLPs is permitted, subject to the following conditions:

(*a*) FDI will be allowed, through the Government approval route, only in LLPs operating in sectors/activities where 100% FDI is allowed, through the automatic route and there are no FDI-linked performance conditions (such as 'Non Banking Finance Companies' or 'Development of Townships, Housing, Built-up infrastructure and Construction-development projects' etc.).

(*b*) LLPs with FDI will not be allowed to operate in agricultural/plantation activity, print media or real estate business.

(*c*) An Indian company, having FDI, will be permitted to make downstream investment in an LLP only if both-the company, as well as the LLP- are operating in sectors where 100% FDI is allowed, through the automatic route and there are no FDI-linked performance conditions.

(*d*) LLPs with FDI will not be eligible to make any downstream investments.

(*e*) Foreign Capital participation in LLPs will be allowed only by way of cash consideration, received by inward remittance, through normal banking channels or by debit to NRE/FCNR account of the person concerned, maintained with an authorized dealer/authorized bank.

(*f*) Investment in LLPs by Foreign Institutional Investors (FIIs) and Foreign Venture Capital Investors (FVCIs) will not be permitted. LLPs will also not be permitted to avail External Commercial Borrowings (ECBs).

(*g*) In case the LLP with FDI has a body corporate that is a designated partner or nominates an individual to act as a designated partner in accordance with the provisions of Section 7 of the LLP Act, 2008, such a body corporate should only be a company registered in India under the Companies Act, 1956 and not any other body, such as an LLP or a trust.

(*h*) For such LLPs, the designated partner "resident in India", as defined under the *'Explanation' to Section 7(1) of the LLP Act, 2008*, would also have to satisfy the definition of "person resident in India", as prescribed under Section 2(*v*)(*i*) of the Foreign Exchange Management Act, 1999.

(*i*) The designated partners will be responsible for compliance with all the above conditions and also liable for all penalties imposed on the LLP for their contravention, if any.

(*j*) Conversion of a company with FDI, into an LLP, will be allowed only if the above stipulations are met and with the prior approval of FIPB/Government.

4. Conditions on Issue/Transfer of Shares

(a) Issue of Capital Instruments

The capital instruments should be issued within 180 days from the date of receipt of the inward remittance or by debit to the NRE/FCNR (B) account of the non-resident investor. In case, the capital instruments are not issued within 180 days from the date of receipt of the inward remittance or date of debit to the NRE/FCNR (B) account, the amount of consideration so received should be refunded immediately to the non-resident investor by outward remittance through normal banking channels or by credit to the NRE/FCNR (B) account, as the case may be. Non-compliance with the above provision would be reckoned as a contravention under FEMA and would attract penal provisions. In exceptional cases, refund of the amount of consideration outstanding beyond a period of 180 days from the date of receipt may be considered by the RBI, on the merits of the case.

(b) Issue price of shares

Issue price of shares to persons resident outside India under the FDI Policy, shall be on the basis of SEBI guidelines in case of listed companies. In case of unlisted companies, valuation of shares has to be done by a Chartered Accountant in accordance with the guidelines issued by the erstwhile Controller of Capital Issues (CCI).

(c) Foreign Currency Account

Indian companies which are eligible to issue shares to person(s) resident outside India under the FDI Policy may be allowed to retain the share subscription amount in a Foreign Currency Account, with the prior approval of RBI.

(d) Transfer of shares and convertible debentures

Subject to FDI sectoral policy, foreign investors can also invest in Indian companies by purchasing/acquiring existing shares from Indian shareholders or from other non-resident shareholders. General permission has been granted to non-residents/NRIs for acquisition of shares by way of transfer subject to the following:

(*a*) A person resident outside India (other than NRI and erstwhile OCB) may transfer by way of sale or gift, the shares or convertible debentures to any person resident outside India (including NRIs);

(*b*) NRIs may transfer by way of sale or gift the shares or convertible debentures held by them to another NRI.

(*c*) *In both the above cases, the 'Existing Venture/tie-up condition' as defined in this policy (see Chapter 5 for details) would apply.*

(*d*) A person resident outside India can transfer any security to a person resident in India by way of gift;

(*e*) A person resident outside India can sell the shares and convertible debentures of an Indian company on a recognized Stock Exchange in India through a stock broker registered with stock exchange or a merchant banker registered with SEBI;

(*f*) A person resident in India can transfer by way of sale, shares/convertible debentures (including transfer of subscriber's shares), of an Indian company in sectors other than financial services sectors (i.e. Banks, NBFC, Insurance, ARCs, CICs, infrastructure companies in the securities market viz. Stock Exchanges, Clearing Corporations, and Depositories, Commodity Exchanges, etc.) under private arrangement to a person resident outside India, subject to the guidelines given in Annex-2 (discussed later) of this policy.

(*g*) General permission is also available for transfer of shares/convertible debentures, by way of sale under private arrangement by a person resident outside India to a person resident in India, subject to the guidelines given in Annex-2 (discussed later) of this policy.

(*h*) The above General Permission also covers transfer by a resident to a non-resident of shares/convertible debentures of an Indian company, engaged in an activity earlier covered under the Government Route but now falling under Automatic Route, as well as transfer of shares by a non-resident to an Indian company under buyback and/or capital reduction scheme of the company. However, this General Permission is not available in case of transfer of shares/debentures, from a Resident to a Non-Resident/Non-Resident Indian, of an entity engaged in any activity in the financial services sector (*i.e.* Banks, NBFCs, ARCs, CICs, Insurance, infrastructure companies in the securities market such as Stock Exchanges, Clearing Corporations, and Depositories, Commodity Exchanges, etc.);

(*i*) The Form FC-TRS should be submitted to the AD Category-I Bank, within 60 days from the date of receipt of the amount of consideration. The onus of submission of the Form FC-TRS within the given timeframe would be on the transferor/transferee, resident in India;

(*j*) The sale consideration in respect of equity instruments purchased by a person resident outside India, remitted into India through normal banking channels, shall be subjected to a Know Your Customer (KYC) check by the remittance receiving AD Category I bank at the time of receipt of funds. In case, the remittance receiving AD Category I bank is different from the AD Category I bank handling the transfer transaction, the KYC check should be carried out by the remittance receiving bank and the KYC report be submitted by the customer to the AD Category I bank carrying out the transaction along with the Form FCTRS

(e) Escrow

AD Category I banks have been given general permission to open Escrow account and Special account of non-resident corporate for open offers/exit offers and delisting of shares. The relevant SEBI (SAST) Regulations or any other applicable SEBI Regulations/provisions of the Companies Act, 1956 will be applicable.

(f) Prior permission of RBI in certain cases for transfer of capital instruments

The following instances of transfer of capital instruments from resident to non-residents by way of sale require prior approval of RBI:

(*a*) Transfer of capital instruments of an Indian company engaged in financial services sector (*i.e.* Banks, NBFCs, Asset Reconstruction Companies, CICs, Insurance companies, infrastructure companies in the securities market such as Stock Exchanges, Clearing Corporations, and Depositories, Commodity Exchanges, etc.);

(*b*) Transactions which attract the provisions of SEBI (Substantial Acquisition of Shares & Takeovers) Regulations, 1997;

(*c*) The activity of the Indian company whose capital instruments are being transferred falls outside the automatic route and the approval of the FIPB has been obtained for the said transfer;

(*d*) The transfer is to take place at a price which falls outside the pricing guidelines specified by the Reserve Bank from time to time;

(*e*) Transfer of capital instruments where the non-resident acquirer proposes deferment of payment of the amount of consideration, prior approval of the Reserve Bank would be required. Further, in case approval is granted for a transaction, the same should be reported in Form FC-TRS, to an AD Category I bank for necessary due diligence, within 60 days from the date of receipt of the full and final amount of consideration. The link office of the AD Category-I Bank will consolidate such Form FC-TRS details and report the same to the Central Office of RBI.

The transfer of capital instruments of companies engaged in sectors falling under the Government Route from residents to non-residents by way of sale or otherwise requires Government approval followed by permission from RBI.

A person resident in India, who intends to transfer any capital instrument, by way of gift to a person resident outside India, has to obtain prior approval from

Reserve Bank. While forwarding applications to Reserve Bank for approval for transfer of capital instruments by way of gift, the documents mentioned in **Annex-3** of this policy (see table below) should be enclosed. Reserve Bank considers the following factors while processing such applications:

(*a*) The proposed transferee (donee) is eligible to hold such capital instruments under Schedules 1, 4 and 5 of Notification No. FEMA 20/2000-RB, dated May 3, 2000, as amended from time to time;

(*b*) The gift does not exceed 5 per cent of the paid-up capital of the Indian company/each series of debentures/each mutual fund scheme;

(*c*) The applicable sectoral cap limit in the Indian company is not breached;

(*d*) The transferor (donor) and the proposed transferee (donee) are close relatives as defined in Section 6 of the Companies Act, 1956, as amended from time to time. The current list is reproduced in **Annex-4** of this policy (see table below);

(*e*) The value of capital instruments to be transferred together with any capital instruments already transferred by the transferor, as gift, to any person residing outside India does not exceed the rupee equivalent of USD 25,000 *during the calendar year;*

(*f*) Such other conditions as stipulated by Reserve Bank in public interest from time to time.

(A) Documents to be submitted by a person resident in India for Transfer of shares to a person resident outside India by way of Gift (Annex 3)

(*i*) Name and address of the transferor (donor) and the transferee (donee);

(*ii*) Relationship between the transferor and the transferee;

(*iii*) Reasons for making the gift;

(*iv*) In case of Government dated securities and treasury bills and bonds, a certificate issued by a Chartered Accountant on the market value of such security;

(*v*) In case of units of domestic mutual funds and units of Money Market Mutual Funds, a certificate from the issuer on the Net Asset Value of such security;

(*vi*) In case of shares and debentures, a certificate from a Chartered Accountant on the value of such securities according to the guidelines issued by the Securities & Exchange Board of India or the erstwhile CCI for listed companies and unlisted companies, respectively;

(*vii*) Certificate from the concerned Indian company certifying that the proposed transfer of shares/convertible debentures by way of gift from resident to the nonresident shall not breach the applicable sectoral cap/FDI limit in the company and that the proposed number of shares/convertible debentures to be held by the nonresident transferee shall not exceed 5 per cent of the paid up capital of the company;

(*viii*) An undertaking from the resident transferor that the value of security to be transferred together with any security already transferred by the transferor, as gift, to any person residing outside India does not exceed the rupee equivalent of USD 25,000 *during a calendar year.*

(B) Definition of "Relative" as given in Section 6 of Companies Act, 1956 (Annex 4):

A person shall be deemed to be a relative of another, if, and only if:

(*a*) they are members of a Hindu undivided family ; or

(*b*) they are husband and wife ; or

(*c*) the one is related to the other in the manner indicated in Schedule IA (as under)

1. Father.
2. Mother (including step-mother).
3. Son (including stepson).
4. Son's wife.
5. Daughter (including step-daughter).
6. Father's father.
7. Father's mother.
8. Mother's mother.
9. Mother's father.
10. Son's son.
11. Son's son's wife.
12. Son's daughter.
13. Son's daughter's husband.
14. Daughter's husband.
15. Daughter's son.
16. Daughter's son's wife.
17. Daughter's daughter.
18. Daughter's daughter's husband.
19. Brother (including step-brother).
20. Brother's wife.
21. Sister (including step-sister).
22. Sister's husband.

(g) Conversion of ECB/Lumpsum Fee/Royalty into Equity

Indian companies have been granted general permission for conversion of External Commercial Borrowings (ECB) (excluding those deemed as ECB) in convertible foreign currency into shares/preference shares, subject to the following conditions and reporting requirements:

(*a*) The activity of the company is covered under the Automatic Route for FDI or the company has obtained Government approval for foreign equity in the company;

(*b*) The foreign equity after conversion of ECB into equity is within the sectoral cap, if any;

(*c*) Pricing of shares is as per SEBI regulations or erstwhile CCI guidelines in the case of listed or unlisted companies respectively;

(*d*) Compliance with the requirements prescribed under any other statute and regulation in force; and

(*e*) The conversion facility is available for ECBs availed under the Automatic or Government Route and is applicable to ECBs, due for payment or not, as well as secured/unsecured loans availed from non-resident collaborators;

(*f*) General permission is also available for issue of shares/preference shares against lump sum technical know-how fee, royalty, under automatic route or SIA/FIPB route, subject to pricing guidelines of SEBI/CCI and compliance with applicable tax laws.

5. Issue of Instruments

(a) Issue of Rights/Bonus Shares

FEMA provisions allow Indian companies to freely issue Rights/Bonus shares to existing non-resident shareholders, subject to adherence to sectoral cap, if any. However, such issue of bonus/rights shares has to be in accordance with other laws/statutes like the Companies Act, 1956, SEBI (Issue of Capital and Disclosure Requirements) Regulations, 2009 (in case of listed companies), etc. The price of shares offered on rights basis by the Indian company to non-resident shareholders shall not be lower than the price at which such shares are offered to resident shareholders.

(b) Prior permission of RBI for Rights issue to erstwhile OCBs

OCBs have been derecognised as a class of investors from September 16, 2003. Therefore companies desiring to issue rights share to such erstwhile OCBs will have to take specific prior permission from RBI. As such, entitlement of rights share is not automatically available to erstwhile OCBs. However bonus shares can be issued to erstwhile OCBs without the approval of RBI.

(c) Additional allocation of rights share by residents to non-residents

Existing nonresident shareholders are allowed to apply for issue of additional shares/fully, compulsorily and mandatorily convertible debentures/fully, compulsorily and mandatorily convertible preference shares over and above their rights share entitlements. The investee company can allot the additional rights share out of unsubscribed portion, subject to the condition that the overall issue of shares to non-residents in the total paid-up capital of the company does not exceed the sectoral cap.

(d) Acquisition of shares under Scheme of Merger/Demerger/Amalgamation

Mergers/demergers/amalgamations of companies in India are usually governed by an order issued by a competent Court on the basis of the Scheme submitted by the companies undergoing merger/demerger/amalgamation. Once the scheme of merger or demerger or amalgamation of two or more Indian companies has been approved by a Court in India, the transferee company or new company is allowed to issue shares to the shareholders of the transferor company resident outside India, subject to the conditions that:

(*i*) the percentage of shareholding of persons resident outside India in the transferee or new company does not exceed the sectoral cap, and

(*ii*) the transferor company or the transferee or the new company is not engaged in activities which are prohibited under the FDI policy.

(*e*) *Issue of shares under Employees Stock Option Scheme* (*ESOPs*)

Listed Indian companies are allowed to issue shares under the Employees Stock Option Scheme (ESOPs), to its employees or employees of its joint venture or wholly owned subsidiary abroad who are resident outside India, other than to the citizens of Pakistan. ESOPs can be issued to citizens of Bangladesh with the prior approval of FIPB. Shares under ESOPs can be issued directly or through a Trust subject to the condition that:

(*a*) The scheme has been drawn in terms of relevant regulations issued by the SEBI, and

(*b*) The face value of the shares to be allotted under the scheme to the non-resident employees does not exceed 5 per cent of the paid-up capital of the issuing company.

Unlisted companies have to follow the provisions of the Companies Act, 1956. The Indian company can issue ESOPs to employees who are resident outside India, other than to the citizens of Pakistan. ESOPs can be issued to the citizens of Bangladesh with the prior approval of the FIPB.

The issuing company is required to report the details of such issues to the Regional Office concerned of the Reserve Bank, within 30 days from the date of issue of shares.

Terms and Conditions for Transfer of Shares/Convertible Debentures, by Way of Sale, From A Person Resident in India to A Person Resident Outside India and From A Person Resident Outside India to A Person Resident in India (Annex 2).

In order to address the concerns relating to pricing, documentation, payment/receipt and remittance in respect of the shares/convertible debentures of an Indian company, *other than a company engaged in financial service sector*, transferred by way of sale, the parties involved in the transaction shall comply with the guidelines set out below.

(*f*) *Parties involved in the transaction*

Parties involved in the transaction are:

(*a*) seller (resident/non-resident),

(*b*) buyer (resident/non-resident),

(*c*) duly authorized agent/s of the seller and/or buyer,

(*d*) Authorised Dealer bank (AD) branch, and

(*e*) Indian company, for recording the transfer of ownership in its books.

(*g*) *Pricing Guidelines*

The under noted pricing guidelines are applicable to the following types of transactions:

(*i*) Transfer of shares, by way of sale under private arrangement by a person resident in India to a person resident outside India;

(*ii*) Transfer of shares, by way of sale under private arrangement by a person resident outside India to a person resident in India.

(*h*) *Transfer by Resident to Non-resident*

In case of transfer by Resident to Non-resident (*i.e.* to incorporated non-resident entity other than erstwhile OCB, foreign national, NRI, FII), the price of shares transferred by way of sale by resident to a non-resident *shall not be less than:*

(*a*) the ruling market price, in case the shares are *listed* on stock exchange,

(*b*) fair valuation of shares done by a Chartered Accountant as per the guidelines issued by the erstwhile Controller of Capital Issues, in case of *unlisted* shares.

The price per share arrived at should be certified by a Chartered Accountant.

(*i*) *Transfer by Non-resident to Resident*

In case of transfer by Non-resident (*i.e.* by incorporated non-resident entity, erstwhile OCB, foreign national, NRI, FII) to Resident, the sale of shares by a non-resident to resident shall be in accordance with Regulation 10B(2) of Notification No. FEMA 20/2000-RB, dated May 3, 2000 which is as below:

(*a*) Where the shares of an Indian company are traded on stock exchange:

(*i*) the sale is at the prevailing market price on stock exchange and is effected through a merchant banker registered with Securities and Exchange Board of India or through a stock broker registered with the stock exchange;

(*ii*) if the transfer is other than that referred to in clause (*i*), the price shall be arrived at by taking the average quotations (average of daily high and low) for one week preceding the date of application with 5 per cent variation. Where, however, the shares are being sold by the foreign collaborator or the foreign promoter of the Indian company to the existing promoters in India with the objective of passing management control in favour of the resident promoters the proposal for sale will be considered at a price which may be higher by up to a ceiling of 25 per cent over the price arrived at as above,

(*b*) Where the shares of an Indian company are not listed on stock exchange or are *thinly traded*:

(*i*) if the consideration payable for the transfer does not exceed ₹ 20 lakh per seller per company, at a price mutually agreed to between the seller and the buyer, based on any valuation methodology currently in vogue, on submission of a certificate from the statutory auditors of the Indian company whose shares are proposed to be transferred, regarding the valuation of the shares; and

(*ii*) if the amount of consideration payable for the transfer exceeds ₹ 20 lakh per seller per company, at a price arrived at, at the *seller's option*, in any of the following manner, namely:

(A) a price based on earning per share (EPS linked to the Price Earning (P/E) multiple), or a price based on the Net Asset Value (NAV) linked to book value multiple, whichever is higher;

or

(B) the prevailing market price in small lots as may be laid down by the Reserve Bank so that the entire shareholding is sold in not less than five trading days through screen based trading system;

or

(C) where the *shares are not listed* on any stock exchange, at a price which is lower of the two independent valuations of share, one by statutory auditors of the company and the other by a Chartered Accountant or by a Merchant Banker in Category 1 registered with Securities and Exchange Board of India.

Explanation:

(*i*) *Thinly Traded Share:* A share is considered as thinly traded if the annualized trading turnover in that share, on main stock exchanges in India, during the six calendar months preceding the month in which application is made, is less than 2 percent (by number of shares) of the listed stock.

(*ii*) For the purpose of arriving at Net Asset Value per share, the miscellaneous expenses carried forward, accumulated losses, total outside liabilities, revaluation reserves and capital reserves (except subsidy received in cash) shall be reduced from value of the total assets and the net figure so arrived at shall be divided by the number of equity shares issued and paid up. *Alternatively*, intangible assets shall be reduced from the equity capital and reserves (excluding revaluation reserves) and the figure so arrived at shall be divided by the number of equity shares issued and paid up. The NAV so calculated shall be used in conjunction with the average BV multiple of Bombay Stock Exchange National Index during the calendar month immediately preceding the month in which application is made and BV multiple shall be discounted by 40 per cent.

(*iii*) For computing the price based on Earning Per Share, the earning per share as per the latest balance sheet of the company shall be used in conjunction with the average Price Earnings Multiple of Bombay Stock Exchange National Index for the calendar month preceding the month in which application is made and Price Earning shall be discounted by 40 per cent.

***(j)* Responsibilities/Obligations of the parties**

All the parties involved in the transaction would have the responsibility to ensure that the relevant regulations under FEMA are complied with and consequent on transfer of shares, the relevant individual limit/sectoral caps/ foreign equity participation ceilings as fixed by Government are not breached. Settlement of transactions will be subject to payment of applicable taxes, if any.

(k) Method of payment and remittance/credit of sale proceeds

The sale consideration in respect of the shares purchased by a person resident outside India shall be remitted to India through normal banking channels. In case the buyer is a Foreign Institutional Investor (FII), payment should be made by debit to its Special Non-Resident Rupee Account. In case the buyer is a NRI, the payment may be made by way of debit to his NRE/FCNR (B) accounts. However, if the shares are acquired on non-repatriation basis by NRI, the consideration shall be remitted to India through normal banking channel or paid out of funds held in NRE/FCNR (B)/NRO accounts.

The sale proceeds of shares (net of taxes) sold by a person resident outside India may be remitted outside India. In case of FII, the sale proceeds may be credited to its special Non-Resident Rupee Account. In case of NRI, if the shares sold were held on repatriation basis, the sale proceeds (net of taxes) may be credited to his NRE/FCNR(B) accounts and if the shares sold were held on non repatriation basis, the sale proceeds may be credited to his NRO account subject to payment of taxes.

The sale proceeds of shares (net of taxes) sold by an OCB may be remitted outside India directly if the shares were held on repatriation basis and if the shares sold were held on non-repatriation basis, the sale proceeds may be credited to its NRO (Current) Account subject to payment of taxes, except in the case of OCBs whose accounts have been blocked by Reserve Bank.

(l) Documentation

Besides obtaining a declaration in Form FC-TRS (in quadruplicate), the AD branch should arrange to obtain and keep on record the following documents:

For sale of shares by a person resident in India:

(*i*) Consent Letter duly signed by the seller and buyer or their duly appointed agent indicating the details of transfer i.e. number of shares to be transferred, the name of the investee company whose shares are being transferred and the price at which shares are being transferred. In case there is no formal Sale Agreement, letters exchanged to this effect may be kept on record;

(*ii*) Where Consent Letter has been signed by their duly appointed agent, the Power of Attorney Document executed by the seller/buyer authorizing the agent to purchase/sell shares;

(*iii*) The shareholding pattern of the investee company after the acquisition of shares by a person resident outside India showing equity participation of residents and nonresidents category-wise (*i.e.* NRIs/OCBs/foreign nationals/incorporated non-resident entities/FIIs) and its percentage of paid up capital obtained by the seller/buyer or their duly appointed agent from the company, where the sectoral cap/limits have been prescribed;

(*iv*) Certificate indicating fair value of shares from a Chartered Accountant;

(*v*) Copy of Broker's note if sale is made on Stock Exchange;

(*vi*) Undertaking from the buyer to the effect that he is eligible to acquire shares/convertible debentures under FDI policy and the existing sectoral limits and Pricing Guidelines have been complied with;

(*vii*) Undertaking from the FII/sub account to the effect that the individual FII/Sub account ceiling as prescribed by SEBI has not been breached.

For sale of shares by a person resident outside India:

(*i*) Consent Letter duly signed by the seller and buyer or their duly appointed agent indicating the details of transfer i.e. number of shares to be transferred, the name of the investee company whose shares are being transferred and the price at which shares are being transferred;

(*ii*) Where the Consent Letter has been signed by their duly appointed agent the Power of Attorney Document authorizing the agent to purchase/sell shares by the seller/buyer. In case there is no formal Sale Agreement, letters exchanged to this effect may be kept on record;

(*iii*) If the sellers are NRIs/OCBs, the copies of RBI approvals evidencing the shares held by them on repatriation/non-repatriation basis. The sale proceeds shall be credited NRE/NRO account, as applicable;

(*iv*) Certificate indicating fair value of shares from a Chartered Accountant;

(*v*) No Objection/Tax Clearance Certificate from Income Tax authority/ Chartered Accountant;

(*vi*) Undertaking from the buyer to the effect that the Pricing Guidelines have been adhered to.

(m) Reporting requirements

Reporting of transfer of shares between residents and non-residents and vice versa is to be done in Form FC-TRS. The Form FC-TRS should be submitted to the AD Category I bank, within 60 days from the date of receipt of the amount of consideration. The onus of submission of the Form FC-TRS within the given timeframe would be on the transferor/transferee, resident in India. The AD Category I bank, would forward the same to its link office. The link office would consolidate the Forms and submit a monthly report to the Reserve Bank (To the Chief General Manager-in-Charge, Reserve Bank of India, Foreign Exchange Department, Foreign Investment Division, Central Office, Mumbai). For the purpose the Authorized Dealers may designate branches to specifically handle such transactions. These branches could be staffed with adequately trained staff for this purpose to ensure that the transactions are put through smoothly. The ADs may also designate a nodal office to coordinate the work at these branches and also ensure the reporting of these transactions to the Reserve Bank.

When the transfer is on private arrangement basis, on settlement of the transactions, the transferee/his duly appointed agent should approach the investee company to record the transfer in their books along with the certificate in the Form FC-TRS from the AD branch that the remittances have been received by the transferor/payment has been made by the transferee. On receipt of the certificate from the AD, the company may record the transfer in its books.

The actual inflows and outflows on account of such transfer of shares shall be reported by the AD branch in the R-returns in the normal course. In addition the AD branch should submit two copies of the Form FC-TRS received from their constituents/customers together with the statement of inflows/outflows on account of remittances received/made in connection with transfer of shares, by way of sale, to IBD/FED/or the nodal office designated for the purpose by the bank in the enclosed proforma (which is to be prepared in MS-Excel format). The IBD/FED or the nodal office of the bank will in turn submit a consolidated monthly statement in respect of all the transactions reported by their branches together with copies of the FC-TRS Forms received from their branches to Foreign Exchange Department, Reserve Bank, Foreign Investment Division, Central Office, Mumbai in soft copy (in MS-Excel) by e-mail to fdidata@rbi.org.in.

Shares purchased/sold by FIIs under private arrangement will be by debit/credit to their Special Non Resident Rupee Account. Therefore, the transaction should **also** be reported in Form LEC (FII) by the designated bank of the FII concerned. Shares/convertible debentures of Indian companies purchased under Portfolio Investment Scheme by NRIs, OCBs cannot be transferred, by way of sale under private arrangement.

On receipt of statements from the AD, the Reserve Bank may call for such additional details or give such directions as required from the transferor/transferee or their agents, if need be.

General Clarifications *vide* Circular 1 of 2011 as on March 31, 2011:

(*a*) **Pricing of Convertible instruments (*Paragraph 3.2.1 of Circular 1 of 2011*):** Instead of specifying the price of convertible instruments upfront, companies will now have the option of prescribing a conversion formula, subject to the FEMA/SEBI guidelines on pricing. This would help the recipient companies in obtaining a better valuation based upon their performance.

(*b*) **Inclusion of fresh items for issue of shares against non-cash considerations (*Paragraph 3.4.6 of Circular 1 of 2011*):** The existing policy provides for conversion of only ECB/lump-sum fee/Royalty into equity. A discussion paper on the possibility and need for inclusion of additional items into equity had been released by DIPP in September, 2010. After stakeholder consultations, Government has now decided to permit issue of equity, under the Government route, in the following cases, subject to specific conditions:

  (*a*) import of capital goods/machinery/equipment (including second-hand machinery)

  (*b*) pre-operative/pre-incorporation expenses (including payments of rent etc.)

This measure, which liberalises conditions for conversion of non-cash items into equity, is expected to significantly ease the conduct of business.

(*c*) **Removal of the condition of prior approval in case of existing joint ventures/technical collaborations in the 'same field" (*Paragraph 4.2.2 of Circular 2 of 2010*):** A discussion paper had been released by DIPP last year on the need for review of this condition. There is a felt need to attract fresh investment and technology inflows into the country, as also to reduce the levels of State intervention in the commercial sphere. Keeping in view the above, Government has decided to abolish this condition. It is expected that this measure will promote the competitiveness of India as an investment destination and be instrumental in attracting higher levels of FDI and technology inflows into the country.

6. CCI Guidelines

Guidelines for valuation of equity shares of companies and the business and net assets of branches (*Ministry of Finance, Department of Economic Affairs F. No. 11(21) CCI (11)/90, dated 13-7-1990):* Ministry of Finance, Department of Economic Affairs has issued the following guidelines for valuation:

Part I

General

1. These are operating guidelines for valuation of equity shares of companies. Briefly, they will be referred to as "Valuation Guidelines".
2. These are purely administrative instructions for internal official use and are, therefore, not to be quoted, cited or published as the official guidelines of the government.
3. They will be effective from the date of their issue and will be applicable to all pending and future cases arising for consideration in the Department of Economic Affairs, Ministry of Finance.
4. Specially, these guidelines will be applicable to the valuation of:
   (*a*) Equity shares of companies, private and public limited;
   (*b*) Indian business/net assets of the sterling tea companies; and
   (*c*) Indian business/net assets of the branches of foreign companies.

Part II

Principles and method of valuation

6. The objective of the valuation process is to make a reasonable judgment of the value of the equity share of a company or of the business and net assets of a branch in cases arising for valuation under the Foreign Exchange Regulation Act, 1973 and the Capital Issues (Control) Act, 1947.

The best reasonable judgment of the value will be referred to as the "Fair Value" (FV) and it will be arrived at on the basis of the following in the manner described in the subsequent paragraphs:

(1) Net Asset Value (NAV).

(2) Profit Earning Capacity Value (PECV).

(3) Market Value (MV), in the case of listed shares.

6.1 Net Asset value (NAV).—The Net Asset Value, *as at the latest audited balance sheet date*, will be calculated starting from the total assets of the company or of the branch and deducting therefrom all debts, dues, borrowings and liabilities including current and likely contingent liabilities and preference capital, if any.

In other words, it should represent the true "net worth" of the business after providing for all outside present and potential liabilities. In the case of companies, the Net Asset Value as calculated from the assets side of the balance sheet in the above manner will be cross checked with equity share capital plus free reserves and surplus, less the likely contingent liabilities.

6.2 In calculating the Net Asset Value, the following points shall particularly be kept in view:

(*i*) *Proposed bonus issue or fresh equity:* If a new bonus issue or a fresh issue of equity capital is proposed, it shall be taken into account. The face value of the fresh issue of equity capital will be added to the existing net worth as at the latest balance sheet date and the resulting "net worth" will be divided by the enlarged equity capital base, including the fresh issue as well as new bonus issue.

(*ii*) *Intangible assets:* Intangible assets like goodwill, patents, trademarks, copyright, etc. will not be taken into account in calculating the assets.

(*iii*) *Revaluation:* Revaluation of fixed assets, if any, will ordinarily not be taken into account. But if the revaluation had taken place long ago, say nearly 15 years ago, it may not be reasonable to deduct it from the total assets.

(*iv*) *Reserves:* Any reserve which has not been created out of genuine profits or out of cash will not be taken into account, e.g. amalgamation reserve or reserve created by changing the method of depreciation or reserve created by revaluation of fixed assets, etc.

(*v*) *Provision for Gratuity:* Provision for gratuity based on actuarial valuation, but net of taxes, as well as provision for any other terminal benefits due to the employees will be provided for and deducted as liabilities.

(*vi*) *Other Liabilities:* Liabilities like arrears of preference dividend, unclaimed dividends, dividends not provided for separately but proposed to be paid out of reserves, miscellaneous expenditure to the extent not written off, debt balance on profit and loss account, arrears of depreciation, etc. will be provided for and deducted from the total assets, so also, adequate provision will be made for bad and doubtful debts.

(*vii*) *Contingent Liabilities:* In the case of contingent liabilities, a judgment must be made of the liabilities that are likely to impair the net worth of the company and it should be provided for on the liabilities side. In order to do so, the clarifications necessary may be obtained from the company and their auditors.

(*viii*) *Provision for Depreciation:* In the matter of provision for depreciation, the following approach will be adopted:

(*a*) If the company has consistently been following the straightline method of depreciation, the depreciation as provided for in the accounts may be accepted in calculating the Net Asset Value and it is not necessary to reckon depreciation according to the written down value method as claimed by the company for income-tax purposes.

(*b*) If, however, within the preceding 5 years, the company has *switched over* from written down value method to straightline method, then the provision for depreciation will be reckoned according to the written down value method as if the company has not made the *switch over*. For this purpose, the company should be asked to furnish the necessary information especially the depreciation claimed for income-tax purposes. Where, however, a company follows right from the beginning the straightline method for depreciation of new fixed assets, although it might be following the written down value method of valuation for the older assets, the depreciation as provided for in the accounts of the company will be accepted both for the old and new assets because this cannot be regarded as a *switch over* in the method of depreciation. The criterion for determining whether there has been a *switch over* or not is thus whether there has been a change in the method of depreciation in respect of the same fixed assets within the preceding five years.

(*c*) In the case of valuation of branches, the provision for depreciation will always be reckoned according to the written down value method. If the accounts are based on the straightline method, then the company must be asked to furnish the depreciation provision according to the written down value method.

6.3 The calculation of the Net Assets Value will be recorded, with the necessary details, in the proforma shown in Annexure 1.

7.1 Profit Earning Capacity Value (PECV).—The Profit Earning Capacity Value will be calculated by capitalising the average of the after tax profits at the following rates:

(*i*) 15% in the case of manufacturing companies.

(*ii*) 20% in the case of trading companies.

(*iii*) 171/2% in the case of 'intermediate' companies that is to say, companies whose turnover from trading activity is more than 40% but less than 60% of their total turnover.

7.2 While ordinarily, the capitalisation rate for a manufacturing company will be 15%, there may be exceptional cases where the capitalisation rate may have to be liberalised in order to ensure fair and equitable valuation. Such cases, where discretion may need to be exercised, are illustrated below:

(*i*) Where, in the case of a listed share, the average of the Net Asset Value and the Profit Earning Capacity Value based on 15% capitalisation rate is less than the average market price by a substantial margin, say by over 20%. In such cases, the company would usually have the following characteristics, *viz.* a track record of high and consistent dividend payments and bonus issues, established position as market leader in its field, a good reputation for the quality and integrity of its management etc., and these would be reflected in the market price of the share.

(*ii*) Where a company has a high profitability rate as revealed by the percentage of the after tax profits to the equity capital of the company.

(*iii*) Where a company has diversified its activities and is a multi unit company, as a result of which it would be in a position to sustain its overall profits even if anyone part of its operations runs into difficulties.

In such cases, the capitalisation rate of 15% could be liberalised suitably upto maximum of 12% with a view to arriving at a fair and equitable valuation. Needless to emphasise, this discretion should be exercised with great care and caution after taking into account all relevant factors.

7.3 The crux of estimating the Profit Earning Capacity Value lies in the assessment of the future maintainable earnings of the business. While the past trends in profits and profitability would serve as a guide, it should not be overlooked that the valuation is for the future and that it is the future maintainable stream of earnings that is of greater significance in the process of valuation. All relevant factors that have a bearing on the future maintainable earnings of the business must, therefore, be given due consideration.

7.4 The provision for taxation, the method of computation of the average profits and the treatment of the profitability of the fresh issue of capital, if any, are of particular importance in the calculation of the future maintainable earnings. These are dealt with in the following paragraphs:

7.5 Provision for taxation.—For computation of profits after tax, provision for taxation will be assumed on the following basis:

(*a*) *Widely held public limited companies.*—Provision for taxation will be assumed at the current statutory rate under the Income-tax Act. If, however, "the actual tax liability" as shown in the audited accounts of the company is more than the current statutory rate, then the actuals will be assumed subject to a maximum statutory limit of income-tax plus surtax on companies under the Income-tax Act. The expression "actual tax liability" will mean the average of the tax liability (in percentage points) for the preceding three years or the actual tax liability in the latest accounting year, whichever is higher.

(*b*) *Tea companies.*—Provision for taxation will be assumed at 70% in consideration of the fact that on 40% of their profits, they have to pay central income-tax, while on the remaining 60% of the profits, they have to pay the state agricultural income-tax, and that in addition, they may have to pay surtax also.

(*c*) *Branches*.—For branches converting themselves into public or private limited companies, provision for taxation will be assumed at 70% although as branches, they may be paying tax at the rate of 73.5%.

(*d*) *Private limited companies and closely held public companies*.—In the case of private limited companies, which propose to continue as private limited companies, provision for taxation will be the actual liability shown in the accounts of the company, subject to a minimum of the current statutory rate. If, however, the private limited company is being converted into a public limited company, the actuals will be restricted to a maximum of 70%. This position will hold good for closely held public limited companies also (i.e. public limited companies not listed nor proposed to be listed on the stock exchange).

7.6 Method of computation of average profits.—Keeping in view that the objective is to arrive at a true and realistic estimate of the future maintainable earnings of the business, the following approach will be adopted in computing the average profits:

(1) It should broadly be checked that the profits shown in the audited accounts of the company are "true" profits and that there has been no attempt at "window dressing" of the accounts to inflate the profits. In particular, it is important to exclude non-recurring miscellaneous income of an abnormal nature or magnitude, writing back of provision etc.

(2) Ordinarily, the averaging of profits will be done for the latest three years for which audited accounts are available. But in appropriate cases, *e.g.* where the capital base of the company and/or the fresh issue is of a sizeable order or where the profits show erratic variation or where the premium involved is substantial or where the industry concerned is subject to cyclical trends, e.g. "tea industry", it would be advisable to take into account the profits of the latest five years in order to arrive at a fair and realistic, estimate of the future maintainable earnings.

(3) If the year to year variation in the profits of the last three years can be considered to be normal (a thumb rule for determining which could be that the annual variation does not exceed about 20% and the maximum does not vary by more than 50% from the minimum) the average may be calculated on the basis of a simple arithmetical average. But if the profits are rising consistently from year to year at a steady ratio and there are reasons to believe that the rising trend will be maintained, the average may be calculated on a weighted basis giving a weightage of 3 for the latest year, 2 for the middle year and 1 for the farthest year. In such cases, it will be pertinent to look into the accounts of the preceding two years also to check that the rising trend in profits is stable. Conversely, if the profits are declining consistently from year to year, it would be advisable to assume the profits of only the latest year because any average—simple or weighted—will give a higher figure than the profits of the latest year, and it will not be rational to assume a higher profit in a

situation of consistently declining profits. Here also, it would be advisable to look into the accounts of the last five years to take a judgment on the trend in profits.

(4) If a business has sustained losses in all the three years or even in the latest two years, the profit earning capacity value will have to be regarded as 'nil', because it would not then be realistic to assume that the business would earn profits in the near future. But if the business has sustained a loss in only one of the three years (the latest year could also be the odd year of loss) and there are reasons to believe that the loss in that year was a freak loss and does not represent the true earning potential of the business, it would be open to exclude the freak year and work out an average based on the working results of the remaining four of the latest five years. If, however, that average turns out to be more than the profits of the latest year, then it would be advisable to assume, as a measure of abundant caution, the profits of the latest year.

It will be evident from the above that in the assessment of the future maintainable earnings, the exercise of discretion and judgment cannot altogether be avoided and that all facts and circumstances must be given the consideration before a view is taken.

7.7 Treatment of the profitability of the fresh issue of capital.—In deciding upon the profitability of the additional capital being raised, the following factors must be looked into:

(*a*) The purpose for which the capital is being raised; whether it is to finance a definite new or expansion project for which the company holds a letter of intent or an industrial licence.

(*b*) Whether the expansion or the new project is "on the ground" and tangible progress has been made in implementing the project.

(*c*) The forecast of future profits and profitability of the project.

7.8 Where the fresh issue of capital is for the purpose of financing and expansion or new project and there are reasons to believe that the project would maintain the profitability of the business, it could be assumed that the fresh capital would contribute to the profits upto maximum of 50% of the existing rate of profitability; in other words the maximum will be calculated as under:

$$\frac{1/2 \times \text{Fresh capital}}{\text{Existing Net Worth}} \times \text{Existing profits after tax}$$

This will be added to the existing profits after tax and the total will be divided by the enlarged capital base to arrive at the future maintainable earnings per share.

But where the fresh capital is sought to be raised not for financing a concrete new or expansion project, but for general reasons like modernisation and replacement of assets, dilution of foreign equity or for getting the shares listed on the stock exchange, it would not be advisable to assume that the fresh capital will contribute to the profitability of the business in any tangible manner in the near future. In such cases, while the fresh issue of capital will be taken into account, no additional profits will be assured.

7.9 The calculation of profit earning capacity value will be recorded with the necessary details in the proforma shown in Annexure II.

8.1 Market value.—The question of market value acting as a guiding factor for valuation will obviously arise only in those cases where the shares being valued are listed on the stock exchange. In such cases, the market value will be taken cognisance of in the following manner:

(1) The average market price will be determined taking into account the stock market quotations in the preceding three years (after making appropriate adjustments for bonus issues and dividend payments) as under:

(*a*) The high and low of the preceding two years; and

(*b*) The high and low of each month in the preceding 12 months.

(2) The average market price will be kept in the background as a relevant factor while setting the fair value (FV) unless there are reasons to believe that the market price is vitiated by speculative transactions or manipulative practices.

(3) The reasonableness of the fair value will be checked against the average market price on the following lines:

(*a*) if the average of the net asset value and the profit earning capacity value on 15% capitalisation rate is less than the average market price by about 20% only, then the average will be regarded the fair value (FV).

(*b*) if, however, the average of the net asset value and the profit earning capacity value is less than the average market price by a substantial margin, say by over 20%, then the profit earning capacity value may be reworked by liberalising suitably the capitalisation rate of 15% in the following manner:

- If the average market price is more than 20% to 50% of the fair value, the capitalisation rate will be 12%;
- If the average market price is more than 50% to 75% of the fair value, the capitalisation rate will be 10%;
- If the average market price is more than 75% and above of the fair value, the capitalisation rate will be 8%.

The fair value will be determined on the basis of the average of the net asset value and the reworked profit earning capacity value. Thus, while the market value will not be a direct "input", in valuation, it will be recognised and made use of in the aforesaid manner while determining the fair value of a listed share.

8.2 The details of the market price and the calculation of the average market price will be recorded in the proforma shown in Annexure III.

9.1 Fair value (FV).—As indicated in para 5 above, the final valuation based on best reasonable judgment will be called the fair value (FV).

9.2 In the case of companies, the average of the net asset value and the profit earning capacity value based on the 15% capitalisation rate will be the starting point for determining the fair value. The following principles will be kept in view in arriving at the fair value:

(1) In the case of a listed share, if the average of the net asset value and the profit earning capacity value on 15% capitalisation rate is less than the average market price by about 2% only, then the average will be regarded as the fair value.

(2) If, however, the average of the net asset value and the profit earning capacity value is less than the average market price by a substantial margin, *i.e.* by over 20%, then the profit earning capacity value may be reworked by liberalising suitably the capitalisation rate of 15% upto a maximum of 8%. The fair value will be determined on the basis of the net asset value and the reworked profit earning capacity value.

(3) As a matter of prudence, it may be desirable to deduct at least one year's dividend per share from the average of the net asset and profit earning capacity values to arrive at the fair value. A cushion of this order may be required as a safeguard against future uncertainties.

(4) Where the profit earning capacity value is 'nil' or negligible, the fair value should be limited to half of the net asset value. If, however, the net assets comprise mostly of liquid assets like cash and bank balances or easily realisable bank debts, the fair value may be fixed upto two-thirds of the net asset value or upto the actual cash and bank balances, if the latter is even higher. The rationale to the proposition is that if the business chooses to liquidate itself, it is likely to realise at least this value.

(5) If the share is neither listed nor proposed to be listed, the average of NAV and PECV should be discounted by at least 1:15% to take account of the restricted mobility of the share.

9.3 In the case of sterling tea companies and branches, the fair value will be determined on the basis of the principles outlined in paras 10 and 11 below.

10.1 Valuation of sterling tea companies.—The "financial" valuation (as distinguished from the "physical" valuation done by the tea board) of the Indian business of sterling tea companies in the context of their Indianisation under FERA, will be done on the basis of the following principles:

(*a*) The net asset value (NAV) will be calculated in the usual manner after deducting all contingent liabilities as well as the "UK assets and liabilities". In particular, the profits remittable to the parent company upto the date of valuation shall be deducted, as they are to be regarded as debts due to the parent company. Any revaluation of fixed assets will also be deducted from the total assets as explained in para 6.2(*iii*) above, unless the revaluation has taken place long ago. It should, however, be kept in view that the exclusion of revaluation does not lead to untenable results or to erratic valuation as between companies with similar assets.

(*b*) Care should be taken to ensure that all income tax liabilities are deducted from the assets before arriving at the NAV. For this purpose, the income-tax department should be consulted to ascertain the income-tax dues receivable from the sterling companies.

(*c*) The profit earning capacity value (PECV) will be calculated by taking the average of the pre-tax profits of the five years from 1972-76 deducting 70% for tax provision and capitalising the after-tax profits to arrive at by 15%.

(*d*) if the net asset value (NAV) is less than the profit earning capacity value (PECV), then the NAV will be taken as the fair value of the Indian business. But if the NAV is more than the PECV then the average of the two will be taken as the fair value. This is to ensure that the NAV is backed by adequate profit potential and that the valuation does not in any event exceed the NAV.

10.2 The final valuation will be determined on the basis of the tea board's report and the comments of the Ministry of Commerce thereon, after taking into consideration all relevant factors.

11. Valuation of branches.—The valuation of branches of foreign companies in the context of their Indianisation under FERA will be done on the basis of the following principles:

(1) Each case will be considered on its own merits because the method of Indianisation may differ from case to case depending on its circumstances.

(2) If the Indian company proposes to take over only the business of the foreign branch together with specified assets and liabilities with the foreign branch, it need not be objected to, unless there are reasons to justify a contrary view.

(3) As far as possible the income-tax liability of the branch may be left to be discharged by the branch itself and the Indian company may not be saddled with this liability. This may require the branch being left with sufficient assets, e.g., the remittances to be made on account of past profits and head office liabilities, cash and bank balances out of the current assets, etc.

(4) Where the foreign branch is allowed to continue with a portion of the assets and liabilities, it is only for the purpose of its "winding-up" after recovering the assets and discharging the liabilities. But it will not be permitted to carry on any manufacturing, trading or commercial activity. If at the time of its winding-up, the assets exceed the liabilities, the surplus will be repatriated by it with the approval of the Reserve Bank.

(5) As regards valuation it may be done on the basis of the book value of the fixed assets plus the current assets less the current and contingent liabilities being actually taken over by the Indian company subject to the condition that it is backed by profit earning potential. For this purpose, the profit earning capacity value (PECV) will be calculated on the basis of the average pre-tax profits of the last three years, tax provisions at 70% and capitalisation at 15%. If the PECV is less than the net asset value mentioned above, then the valuation will be done on the basis of the average of the two values. In other words, the valuation should not in any event exceed the net assets value of the assets being taken over by the Indian company, and should not involve any payment directly or indirectly for intangible assets like goodwill, etc.

(6) As a general proposition it would be better to exclude the unremitted profits and head office liabilities due to the parent company as if they are debts due to it, rather than to include them in the consideration payable by the Indian company.

Each case will, however, have to be considered on its own merits because there could be cases where a suitable capital base for the Indian company and foreign share in that capital base upto the level permitted by FERA would be dependent on the unremitted profits and head office liabilities forming a part of the total consideration.

12. Valuation on the basis of "willing buyer—willing seller" concept.— While, as a general rule, the concept of "willing buyer—willing seller" is not acceptable for various reasons, the price agreed to between the parties can be accepted in the following two categories of cases:

I. Small value cases.—If the total consideration involved does not exceed ₹ 5 lakhs and the shares being transferred do not constitute more than 10% of the total equity shareholding of the company, the transaction may be approved if the price agreed to between the parties does not exceed—

(*i*) the ruling market price, if it is a listed share,

(*ii*) the price as certified by the auditors of the company if it is not a listed share.

To guard against the possibility of splitting the shares into small value transactions, only one such transaction in the same shares should ordinarily be allowed in a period of one year.

II. Cases where the fair value is close to the price agreed to between the parties.—If the fair value as determined according to these guidelines is less than the price agreed to between the parties by a very small margin only, say by about 10% only, it would be preferable not to disturb the price that the parties to the transaction have negotiated and settled amongst themselves.

General

13. It is important to stress the fact that however elaborate and detailed the guidelines may be, the process of valuation cannot possibly be reduced to uniform and inflexible arithmetical exercise. In the ultimate analysis, valuation will have to be tempered by the exercise of judicious discretion and judgment taking into account all relevant factors. There will always be several factors, e.g., quality and integrity of the management, present and prospective competition, yield on comparable securities and market sentiment, etc. which are not evident from the face of the balance sheets but which will strongly influence the worth of a share. Similarly, the accounts might be "window dressed" with a view to presenting a brighter picture of the company's working results. The guidelines are intended to provide the basic framework for valuation and to minimise the element of subjective consideration. While they should be applied fairly and consistently in all cases, they should not be regarded as eliminating the exercise of discretion and judgment needed to arrive at a fair and equitable valuation.

14. It would be useful to compare the basis of the valuation according to these guidelines with that of the company's auditors. On the one hand, this will help reduce errors in calculation as well as a better understanding of the facts of the case, and on the other, this will enable us to explain the basis of our valuation to the company concerned.

Annexure I

Name of the company ______________________________

According to the audited balance sheet as at ______________________

Net Asset Value (NAV)

₹ lakhs	₹ lakhs
Total assets: ______________	Shareholders funds__________
Deduct all liabilities	(1) Equity capital __________
1. Preference capital ______________	(2) Free Reserves __________
2. Secured and unsecured borrowings _____	Total ______________
3. Current liabilities ______________	Deduct contingent liabilities
4. Contingent liabilities ______________	1.
5.	2.
6.	3.
7.	4.
	5.

Net worth:

Add: (1) Fresh capital issue (Face value)

Total Net Worth

Number of shares, including fresh and bonus issues

Net asset value (NAV) per share

Net asset value (NAV) according to the company's auditors

Annexure II

Profit Earning Capacity Value (PECV)

Year profit before tax	Profits after tax	Dividend declared
1.		
2.		
3.		
4.		
5.		
__________	__________	__________

Average profits before tax (On the basis of simple or weighted average as the case may be)	: __________
Deduct	: __________
Provision for taxation at ________	: __________
Average profits after tax	: __________
Deduct: Preference dividend	: __________
Net profit after tax	: __________
Add: Contribution to profits by fresh issue, if any	: __________
Total profits after tax	: __________
Number of equity shares, including fresh and bonus issue	: __________
Earnings per share (EPS)	: __________
Profit earning capacity value (PECV) at 15% capitalisation rate (*i.e.* by multiplying EPS by 6.66)	: __________
PECV according to the company's auditors	: __________

Annexure III

Average Market Price

	High	Low	Remarks
1. Year			
2. Year			
3. Latest year			
4. Month-wise			
1.			
2.			
3.			
(for preceding 12 months)			

Average market price on the above basis:

Appendix

Foreign Exchange Management (Transfer or Issue of Security by a Person Resident Outside India) Regulations, 2000

Notification No. GSR 406(E) [FEMA 20/2000-RB], dated 3-5-2000[1]

1 Published in the Gazette of India, Extraordinary No. 255, dated 8-5-2000, Part II, section 3(*i*).

In exercise of the powers conferred by clause (*b*) of sub-section (3) of section 6 and section 47 of the Foreign Exchange Management Act, 1999 (42 of 1999), the Reserve Bank makes the following regulations to prohibit, restrict or regulate, transfer or issue security by a person resident outside India, namely:—

1. Short title and commencement.—(1) These Regulations may be called the Foreign Exchange Management (Transfer or Issue of Security by a Person Resident Outside India) Regulations, 2000.

(2) They shall come into effect on the 1st day of June, 2000.

2. Definitions.—In these regulations, unless the context requires otherwise,—

(*i*) "Act" means the Foreign Exchange Management Act, 1999 (42 of 1999);

[1][(*ia*) "Asset reconstruction company" (ARC) means a company registered with the Reserve Bank of India under section 3 of the Securitisation and Reconstruction of Financial Assets and Enforcement of Security Interest Act, 2002 (SARFAESI Act);]

[2][(*ii*) "Capital" means equity shares, preference shares and convertible debentures;]

[3][(*iia*) "entity incorporated outside India" means an entity incorporated/ registered under the relevant statutes, laws of the host country;]

[4][(*iib*) "preference shares" means compulsorily and mandatorily convertible preference shares;]

[5][(*iic*) "debenture" means compulsorily and mandatorily convertible debenture;]

(*iii*) "registered Foreign Institutional Investor (FII)" means the foreign institutional investor registered with SEBI;

---

1 Inserted by Foreign Exchange Management (Transfer or Issue of Security by a Person Resident Outside India) (Second Amendment) Regulations, 2006, w.r.e.f. 8-11-2005 [FEMA 149/2006-RB].

2 Substituted by Foreign Exchange Management (Transfer or Issue of Security by a Person Resident Outside India) (Second Amendment) Regulations, 2008 [Notification No. FEMA 179/2008-RB, dated 22-8-2008] w.e.f. 1.5.2007 for the following:

'(*ii*) "Capital" means equity shares, preference shares, convertible preference shares and convertible debentures.'

3 Inserted by the Foreign Exchange Management (Transfer or Issue of Security by a Person Resident Outside India) (Third Amendment) Regulations, 2003, w.e.f. 23-10-2003 [FEMA 100/2003-RB].

4 Inserted by Foreign Exchange Management (Transfer or Issue of Security by a Person Resident Outside India) (Second Amendment) Regulations, 2008 [Notification No. FEMA 179/2008-RB, dated 22-8-2008] w.e.f. 1.5.2007.

5 Inserted by Foreign Exchange Management (Transfer or Issue of Security by a Person Resident Outside India) (Second Amendment) Regulations, 2008 [Notification No. FEMA 179/2008-RB, dated 22-8-2008] w.e.f. 8.6.2007.

[1][(*iiia*) "Foreign venture capital investor" means an investor incorporated and established outside India which proposes to make investment in venture capital fund(s) or venture capital undertakings(s) in India and is registered with SEBI under the SEBI (Foreign Venture Capital Investors) Regulations, 2000;]

[2][(*iiib*) "Foreign Central Bank" means an institution/organization/body corporate established in a country outside India and entrusted with the responsibility of carrying out central bank functions under the law for the time being in force in that country;]

(*iv*) "Government approval" means approval from the Secretariat for Industrial Assistance (SIA), Department of Industrial Policy and Promotion, Government of India or as the case may be, Foreign Investment Promotion Board (FIPB) of the Government of India;

(*v*) "Indian company" means a company incorporated in India;

[3][(*va*) "Indian venture capital undertaking" means a company incorporated in India whose shares are not listed on a recognized stock exchange in India and which is not engaged in an activity under the negative list specified by SEBI;]

(*vi*) "Investment on repatriation basis" means an investment the sale proceeds of which are, net of taxes, eligible to be repatriated out of India, and the expression "Investment on non-repatriation basis", shall be construed accordingly;

(*vii*) "Joint Venture (JV)" and "Wholly Owned Subsidiary" shall have the meanings respectively assigned to them in the Foreign Exchange Management (Transfer and Issue of Foreign Security) Regulations, 2000;

[4][(*viia*) NRI shall have the same meaning assigned to him under the Foreign Exchange Management (Deposit) Regulations, 2000;]

(*viii*) [5][* * *] "Overseas Corporate Body (OCB)", shall have the meanings

---

1 Inserted by the Foreign Exchange Management (Transfer or Issue of Security by a Person Resident Outside India) (Amendment) Regulations, 2000, w.e.f. 26-12-2000.

2 Inserted *vide* Foreign Exchange Management (Transfer or Issue of Security by a Person Resident Outside India) (Amendment) Regulations, 2007 [Notification No. FEMA 166/2007-RB, dated 17-10-2007]

3 Inserted by the Foreign Exchange Management (Transfer or Issue of Security by a Person Resident Outside India) (Amendment) Regulations, 2000, w.e.f. 26-12-2000.

4 Substituted by the Foreign Exchange Management (Transfer or Issue of Security by a Person Resident Outside India) (Fourth Amendment) Regulations, 2004, w.e.f. 30-8-2004 [FEMA 122/2004-RB] for the following:

"(*viia*) 'non-resident Indian ('NRI') shall have the meaning assigned to it in clause (*iv*) of regulation 2 of the Foreign Exchange Management (Investment in Firm or Proprietary Concern in India) Regulations, 2000;"

Earlier it was inserted by the Foreign Exchange Management (Transfer or Issue of Security by a Person Resident Outside India) (Second Amendment) Regulations, 2003, w.e.f. 18-6-2003.

5 The words "Non-resident Indian (NRI)" omitted by the Foreign Exchange Management (Transfer or Issue of Security by a Person Resident Outside India) (Second Amendment) Regulations, 2003, w.e.f. 18-6-2003.

respectively assigned to them in the Foreign Exchange Management (Deposit) Regulations, 2000;

(*ix*) "SEBI" means the Securities and Exchange Board of India established under the Securities and Exchange Board of India Act, 1992 (15 of 1992);

(*x*) "Secretariat for Industrial Assistance" means Secretariat for Industrial Assistance in the Department of Industrial Policy and Promotion, Ministry of Commerce and Industry, Government of India;

(*xi*) "Transferable Development Rights (TDR)" shall have the same meaning as assigned to it in the regulations made under sub-section (2) of section 6 of the Act;

[1][(*xia*) "Venture capital fund" means a fund established in the form of a trust, a company including a body corporate and registered under the Securities and Exchange Board of India (Venture Capital Fund) Regulations, 1996, which has a dedicated pool of capital raised in a manner specified under the said Regulations and which invests in venture capital undertakings in accordance with the said Regulations;]

(*xii*) the words and expressions used but not defined in these regulations shall have the same meanings respectively assigned to them in the Act.

3. Restriction on issue or transfer of security by a person resident outside India.—Save as otherwise provided in the Act, or rules or regulations made thereunder, no person resident outside India shall issue or transfer any security:

Provided that a security issued prior to, and held on, the date of commencement of these regulations, shall be deemed to have been issued under these regulations and shall accordingly be governed by these regulations:

Provided further that the Reserve Bank may, on an application made to it and for sufficient reasons, permit a person resident outside India to issue or transfer any security, subject to such conditions as may be considered necessary.

4. Restriction on an Indian entity to issue security to a person resident outside India or to record a transfer of security from or to such a person in its books.—Save as otherwise provided in the Act or rules or regulations made thereunder, an Indian entity shall not issue any security to a person resident outside India or shall not record in its books any transfer of security from or to such person:

Provided that the Reserve Bank may, on an application made to it and for sufficient reasons, permit an entity to issue any security to a person resident outside India or to record in its books transfer of security from or to such person, subject to such conditions as may be considered necessary.

---

1 Inserted by the Foreign Exchange Management (Transfer or Issue of Security by a Person Resident Outside India) (Amendment) Regulations, 2000, w.e.f. 26-12-2000.

5. Permission for purchase of shares by certain persons resident outside India[1].—[2][(1)(*i*)] A person resident outside India (other than a citizen of Bangladesh or Pakistan [3][* * *]) [4][or an entity incorporated outside India] (other than an entity in Bangladesh or Pakistan), may purchase shares or convertible debentures of an Indian company under Foreign Direct Investment Scheme, subject to the terms and conditions specified in Schedule 1.

[5][(*ii*) Notwithstanding anything contained in sub-regulation (*i*) above, a person who is a citizen of Bangladesh or an entity incorporated in Bangladesh may, with the prior approval of the Foreign Investment Promotion Board of the Government of India, purchase shares and convertible debentures of an Indian company under Foreign Direct Investment Scheme, subject to the terms and conditions specified in Schedule 1.]

(2) A registered Foreign Institutional Investor (FII) may purchase shares or convertible debentures of an Indian company under the Portfolio Investment Scheme, subject to the terms and conditions specified in Schedule 2:

[6][* * *]

[7][Provided further that foreign institutional investors shall not invest in the paid up equity capital of asset reconstruction companies].

[8][(3) (*i*) A Non-resident Indian (NRI) may purchase shares or convertible

---

1 Refer AP (DIR Series) Circular No. 73, dated 8-6-2007 (also Press Note, dated 30-4-2007) for revised guidelines in respect of foreign investments in preference shares and AP (DIR Series) Circular No. 74, dated 8-6-2007 for revised guidelines in respect of foreign investments in debentures.

2 Sub-regulation (1) re-numbered as (1)(*i*) *vide* Foreign Exchange Management (Transfer or Issue of Security by a Person Resident Outside India) (Second Amendment) Regulations, 2007 [Notification No. FEMA 167/2007-RB, dated 23-10-2007].

3 The words "or Sri Lanka" omitted by the Foreign Exchange Management (Transfer or Issue of Security by a Person Resident outside India) (Fourth Amendment) Regulations, 2004, w.e.f. 30-8-2004 [FEMA 122/2004-RB].

4 Substituted for "or an entity outside India, whether incorporated or not" by the Foreign Exchange Management (Transfer or Issue of Security by a Person Resident outside India) (Third Amendment) Regulations, 2003, w.e.f. 23-10-2003 [FEMA 100/2003-RB].

5 Inserted *vide* Foreign Exchange Management (Transfer or Issue of Security by a Person Resident Outside India) (Second Amendment) Regulations, 2007 [Notification No. FEMA 167/2007-RB, dated 23-10-2007].

6 Omitted by the Foreign Exchange Management (Transfer or Issue of Security by a Person Resident Outside India) (Fifth Amendment) Regulations, 2005, w.e.f. 22-7-2005. [FEMA 138/2005-RB]. Prior to omission it read as under:

"Provided that the FII shall not purchase shares or convertible debentures of an Indian company which is engaged in the print media sector."

Earlier, it was inserted by the Foreign Exchange Management (Transfer or Issue of Security by a Person Resident Outside India) (Amendment) Regulations, 2001, w.e.f. 16-2-2001.

7 Inserted by Foreign Exchange Management (Transfer or Issue of Security by a Person Resident Outside India) (Second Amendment) Regulations, 2006, w. r.e.f. 8-11-2005 [FEMA 149/2006-RB].

8 Substituted by Foreign Exchange Management (Transfer or Issue of Security by a Person Resident Outside India) (Amendment) Regulations, 2002, w.e.f. 29-11-2002 [corrected by Notification No. GSR 551(E), dated 31-8-2004] for the following:"(3) A non-resident → →

debentures of an Indian Company on a Stock Exchange under Portfolio Investment Scheme, subject to the terms and conditions specified in Schedule 3 [1][* * *].

(*ii*) A non-resident Indian [2][* * *] may purchase shares or convertible debentures of an Indian company on non-repatriation basis other than under Portfolio Investment Scheme subject to the terms and conditions specified in Schedule 4 [3][* * *].

[4][(4) A non-resident Indian or a registered Foreign Institutional Investor or a Foreign Central Bank may purchase securities, other than shares or convertible debentures of an Indian company, subject to the terms and conditions specified in Schedule 5.]

[5][(5) A foreign venture capital investor registered with SEBI may make investment in a venture capital fund or an Indian venture capital undertaking, in the manner and subject to the terms and conditions specified in Schedule 6.]

→ → Indian or an overseas corporate body may purchase shares or convertible debentures of an Indian company—

(*i*) on a stock exchange under the Portfolio Investment Scheme, subject to the terms and conditions specified in Schedule 3; or/and

(*ii*) on non-repatriation basis other than under Portfolio Investment Scheme, subject to the terms and conditions specified in Schedule 4:

[1][Provided that the NRI/OCB shall not purchase shares or convertible debentures of an Indian company which is engaged in the print media sector.]"

1 Inserted by the Foreign Exchange Management (Transfer or Issue of Security by a Person Resident Outside India) (Amendment) Regulations, 2001, w.e.f. 16-2-2001.

1 Omitted by the Foreign Exchange Management (Transfer or Issue of Security by a Person Resident Outside India) (Fifth Amendment) Regulations, 2005, w.e.f. 22-7-2005. [FEMA 138/2005-RB]. Prior to omission it read as under:

"provided that the NRI shall not purchase shares or convertible debentures of an Indian Company which is engaged in Print Media sector."

2 The words "or an Overseas Corporate Body" omitted by Foreign Exchange Management [Withdrawal of General Permission to Overseas Corporate Bodies (OCBs)] Regulations, 2003, w.e.f. 23-10-2003.

3 Omitted by the Foreign Exchange Management (Transfer or Issue of Security by a Person Resident Outside India) (Fifth Amendment) Regulations, 2005, w.e.f. 22-7-2005. [FEMA 138/2005-RB]. Prior to omission it read as under:

"provided that the NRI [* * *] shall not purchase shares or convertible debentures of an Indian Company which is engaged in Print Media sector."

Earlier, the words "or OCB" omitted by Foreign Exchange Management [Withdrawal of General Permission to Overseas Corporate Bodies (OCBs)] Regulations, 2003, w.e.f. 23-10-2003.

4 Substituted vide Foreign Exchange Management (Transfer or Issue of Security by a Person Resident Outside India) (Amendment) Regulations, 2007 [Notification No. FEMA 166/2007-RB, dated 17-10-2007]. Prior to substitution, sub-regulation (4) read as under:

"(4) A non-resident Indian @[* * *] or a registered Foreign Institutional Investor may purchase securities, other than shares or convertible debentures of an Indian company, subject to the terms and conditions specified in Schedule 5."

@ The words "or an overseas corporate body" omitted by Foreign Exchange Management [Withdrawal of General Permission to Overseas Corporate Bodies (OCBs)] Regulations, 2003, w.e.f. 23-10-2003.

5 Inserted by the Foreign Exchange Management (Transfer or Issue of Security by a Person Resident Outside India) (Amendment) Regulations, 2001, w.e.f. 16-2-2001.

[1][* * *]

[2][(6) A registered Foreign Institutional Investor (FII) having valid approval under the Foreign Exchange Regulation Act, 1973 or under the Foreign Exchange Management Act, 1999 may trade in all exchange traded derivative contracts approved by RBI/SEBI subject to the limits and margin requirement prescribed by RBI/SEBI as well as the stipulations regarding collateral securities as directed by the Reserve Bank from time to time.]

[3][(7) A Non-Resident Indian (NRI) may invest in exchange traded derivative contracts approved by SEBI from time to time out of INR funds held in India on non-repatriable basis subject to the limits prescribed by SEBI. Such investments will not be eligible for repatriation benefits.]

6. Acquisition of right shares.—(1) A person resident outside India may purchase equity or preference shares or convertible debentures offered on right basis by an Indian company which satisfies the conditions specified in sub-regulation (2).

(2) An Indian company which satisfies the following conditions, may offer to a person resident outside India, equity or preference shares or convertible debentures on right basis, namely:—

(*i*) the offer on right basis does not result in increase in the percentage of foreign equity already approved, or permissible under the Foreign Direct Investment Scheme in terms of these regulations;

[4][(*ii*) the existing non-resident shareholders may apply for issue of additional shares, and the investee company may allot the same subject to the condition that the overall issue of shares to non-residents in the total paid-up capital does not exceed the sectoral cap;]

---

1 Omitted by the Foreign Exchange Management (Transfer or Issue of Security by a Person Resident Outside India) (Fifth Amendment) Regulations, 2005, w.e.f. 22-7-2005. [FEMA 138/2005-RB]. Prior to omission it read as under:

"Provided that the foreign venture capital investor shall not purchase shares or convertible debentures of an Indian company which is engaged in the print media sector."

2 Substituted by Foreign Exchange Management (Transfer or Issue of Security by a Person Resident Outside India) (Second Amendment) Regulations, 2008 [Notification No. FEMA 179/2008-RB, dated 22-8-2008] w.e.f. 31.12.2007 for the following:

*"(6) A registered Foreign Institutional Investor (FII) having valid approval under FERA 1973 or under FEMA, 1999 may trade in all exchange traded derivative contracts approved by SEBI from time to time subject to the limits as prescribed by SEBI."

* Earlier this sub-regulation was inserted by the Foreign Exchange Management (Transfer or Issue of Security by a Person Resident Outside India) (Amendment) Regulations, 2003, w.e.f. 17-1-2003 [FEMA 85/2003-RB].

3 Inserted by the Foreign Exchange Management (Transfer or Issue of Security by a Person Resident Outside India) (Amendment) Regulations, 2003, w.e.f. 17-1-2003 [FEMA 85/2003-RB].

4 Inserted by the Foreign Exchange Management (Transfer or Issue of Security by a Person Resident Outside India) (Amendment) Regulations, 2003, w.r.e.f. 12-11-2002 [FEMA 76/2002-RB]. [Corrected by Notification No. 555(E), dated 31-8-2004].

[1][(*iii*)] the existing shares or debentures against which shares or debentures are issued by the company on right basis were acquired and are held by the person resident outside India in accordance with these regulations;

[2][(*iv*) The offer on right basis to the persons resident outside India shall be:

(*a*) in the case of shares of a company listed on a recognized stock exchange in India, at a price as determined by the company;

(*b*) in the case of shares of a company not listed on a recognized stock exchange in India, at a price which is not less than the price at which the offer on right basis is made to resident shareholders.]

(3) The right shares or debentures purchased by the person resident outside India shall be subject to same conditions including restrictions in regard to repatriability as are applicable to the original shares against which right shares or debentures are issued:

Provided that the amount of consideration for purchase of right shares or debentures is paid by way of inward remittance in foreign exchange through normal banking channels or by debit to NRE/FCNR account, when the shares or debentures are issued on repatriation basis:

Provided further that in respect of the shares or debentures issued on non-repatriation basis, the amount of consideration may also be paid by debit to NRO/NRSR/NRNR account.

[3][**6A. Acquisition of bonus shares.**—An Indian company may issue bonus shares to its non-resident shareholders, subject to the following conditions:—

(*a*) the shares against which bonus shares are issued by the company (hereinafter referred to as 'the original shares') were acquired or held by the non-resident shareholder in accordance with the Rules/Regulations applicable to such acquisition;

(*b*) the bonus shares acquired by the non-resident shareholder shall be subject to the same condi-tions including restrictions in regard to repatriability as are applicable to the original shares.]

---

1 Renumbered by the Foreign Exchange Management (Transfer or Issue of Security by a Person Resident Outside India) (Amend-ment) Regulations, 2003, w.r.e.f. 12-11-2002 [FEMA 76/2002-RB]. [Corrected by Notification No. 555(E), dated 31-8-2004].

2 Substituted by the FEM (Transfer or Issue of Security by a Person Resident Outside India) (Amendment) Regulations, 2010 [Notification No. FEMA 205/2010-RB, dated 7-4-2010. Earlier, clause (iv) read as under:

*"(*iv*) the offer on right basis to the persons resident outside India is at a price which is not lower than that at which the offer is made to resident shareholders."

* Renumbered by the Foreign Exchange Management (Transfer or Issue of Security by a Person Resident Outside India) (Second Amendment) Regulations, 2003, w.r.e.f. 12-11-2002 [FEMA 76/2002-RB]. [Corrected by Notification No. 555(E), dated 31-8-2004].

3 Inserted by the Foreign Exchange Management (Transfer or Issue of Security by a Person Resident Outside India) (Second Amendment) Regulations, 2003, w.e.f. 18-6-2003.

[1][**6B. Report to RBI.**—A company issuing rights shares or bonus shares in terms of these Regulations shall report to the Reserve Bank in Form FC-GPR as stipulated in Paragraph 9(1)(B) of Schedule 1 to these Regulations.]

7. Issue and acquisition of shares after merger or de-merger or amalgamation of Indian companies.—Where a Scheme of merger or amalgamation of two or more Indian companies or a reconstruction by way of de-merger or otherwise of an Indian company, has been approved by a Court in India, the transferee company or, as the case may be, the new company may issue shares to the shareholders of the transferor company resident outside India, subject to the following conditions, namely:—

(*a*) the percentage of shareholding of persons resident outside India in the transferee or new company does not exceed the percentage specified in the approval granted by the Central Government or the Reserve Bank, or specified in these regulations:

Provided that where the percentage is likely to exceed the percentage specified in the approval or the regulations, the transferor company or the transferee or new company may, after obtaining an approval from the Central Government, apply to the Reserve Bank for its approval under these regulations;

(*b*) the transferor company or the transferee or new company shall not engage in agriculture, plantation or real estate business or trading in TDRs; and

(*c*) the transferee or the new company files a report within 30 days with the Reserve Bank giving full details of the shares held by persons resident outside India in the transferor and the transferee or the new company, before and after the merger/amalgamation/reconstruction, and also furnishes a confirmation that all the terms and conditions stipulated in the scheme approved by the Court have been complied with.

8. Issue of shares under Employees Stock Options Scheme to persons resident outside India.—(1) An Indian company may issue shares under the Employee's Stock Options Scheme, by whatever name called, to its employees or employees of its joint venture or wholly owned subsidiary abroad who are resident outside India, directly or through a Trust:

Provided that—

(*a*) the scheme has been drawn in terms of regulations issued under the Securities Exchange Board of India Act, 1992; and

---

1 Substituted by Foreign Exchange Management (Transfer or Issue of Security by a Person Resident Outside India) (Second Amendment) Regulations, 2008 [Notification No. FEMA 179/2008-RB, dated 22-8-2008] w.e.f. 22.8.2008 for the following:

**6B. Report to RBI.*—A company issuing right shares or bonus shares in terms of regulation 6 or regulation 6A, as the case may be, shall, within thirty days from the date of issue, report the transaction in Form FC-GPR to the Regional Office of the Reserve Bank of India under whose jurisdiction the registered office of the company is situated.

* Earlier this Regulation was inserted by the Foreign Exchange Management (Transfer or Issue of Security by a Person Resident Outside India) (Second Amendment) Regulations, 2003, w.e.f. 18-6-2003.

(*b*) face value of the shares to be allotted under the scheme to the non-resident employees does not exceed 5% of the paid-up capital of the issuing company.

(2) The Trust and the issuing company shall ensure that value of shares held by persons resident outside India under the scheme does not exceed the limit specified in clause (*b*) of sub-regulation (1).

(3) The issuing company shall furnish to the Reserve Bank, within thirty days from the date of issue of shares under the scheme, a report giving the following particulars/documents,—

(*i*) names of persons to whom shares are issued under the scheme and number of shares issued to each of them;

(*ii*) a certificate from the Company Secretary of the issuing company that the value of shares issued under the scheme does not exceed 5% of the paid up capital of the issuing company and that the shares are issued in compliance with the regulations issued by the SEBI in this behalf.

9. Transfer of shares and convertible debentures of an Indian company by a person resident outside India.—(1) Subject to the provisions of sub-regulation (2), a person resident outside India holding the shares or debentures of an Indian company in accordance with these regulations, may transfer the shares or debentures so held by him, in compliance with the conditions specified in the relevant Schedule of these regulations.

[1][(2) (*i*) A person resident outside India, not being a non-resident Indian or an overseas corporate body, may transfer by way of sale or gift the shares or convertible debentures held by him or it to any person resident outside India;[1]

(*ii*) A non-resident Indian [2][* * *] may transfer by way of sale or gift the shares or convertible debentures held by him or it to another non-resident Indian [3][* * *] only:

---

1 Substituted by the Foreign Exchange Management (Transfer or Issue of Security by a Person Resident Outside India) (Second Amendment) Regulations, 2003, w.e.f. 18-6-2003 for the following:

"(2) (*i*) A person resident outside India, not being a non-resident Indian or an overseas corporate body, may transfer by way of sale, the shares or convertible debentures held by him to any person resident outside India:

Provided that the person to whom the shares are being transferred has obtained prior permission of Central Government to acquire the shares if he has previous venture or tie up in India through investment in shares or debentures or a technical collaboration or a trade mark agreement or investment by whatever name called in the same field or allied field in which the Indian company whose shares are being transferred is engaged.

(*ii*) A non-resident Indian or an overseas corporate body may transfer by way of sale, the shares or convertible debentures held by him or it to another non-resident Indian or an overseas corporate body only.

(*iii*) A person resident outside India may transfer any security held by him, to a person resident in India by way of gift."

2 The words "or an overseas corporate body" omitted by Foreign Exchange Management [Withdrawal of General Permission to Overseas Corporate Bodies (OCBs)] Regulations, 2003, w.e.f. 23-10-2003.

3 The words "or overseas corporate body", ibid.

Provided that the person to whom the shares are being transferred, in terms of clauses (*i*) and (*ii*), has obtained prior permission of Central Government to acquire the shares if he has previous venture or tie up in India through investment in shares or debentures or a technical collaboration or a trade mark agreement or investment by whatever name called in the same field or allied field in which the Indian company whose shares are being transferred is engaged:

Provided further that the restriction in clauses (*i*) and (*ii*) shall not apply to the transfer of shares to international financial institutions such as Asian Development Bank ('ADB'), International Finance Corporation ('IFC'), Commonwealth Development Corporation ('CDC'), Deutsche Entwicklungs Gescelscchaft ('DEG') and transfer of shares of an Indian company engaged in information technology sector.

(*iii*) A person resident outside India holding the shares or convertible debentures of an Indian company in accordance with these Regulations,—

(*a*) may transfer the same to a person resident in India by way of gift;

(*b*) may sell the same on a recognised Stock Exchange in India through a registered broker.]

10. Prior permission of Reserve Bank in certain cases for transfer of security.—A. Transfer by way of gift or sale by a person resident in India.

A person resident in India who proposes to transfer to a person resident outside India [1][not being erstwhile OCBs]:—

[2][(*a*) (*i*) any security, by way of gift, shall make an application to the Reserve Bank for its approval.

(*ii*) The Reserve Bank may grant such approval on being satisfied of the following conditions:

(*a*) The donee is eligible to hold such a security under Schedules 1, 4 and 5 of these Regulations.

(*b*) The gift does not exceed 5% of the paid up capital of the Indian company/each series of debentures/each mutual fund scheme.

(*c*) The applicable sectoral cap/foreign direct investment limit in the Indian company is not breached.

(*d*) The donor and the donee are relatives as defined in section 6 of the Companies Act, 1956.

---

1 Inserted by Foreign Exchange Management (Transfer or Issue of Security by a Person Resident Outside India) (Second Amendment) Regulations, 2005, [Notification No. FEMA-131/2005-RB] w.r.e.f. 4-10-2004.

2 Substituted by Foreign Exchange Management (Transfer or Issue of Security by a Person Resident Outside India) (Fourth Amendment) Regulations, 2005, [Notification No. FEMA-137/2005-RB] w.e.f. 22-7-2005 for the following:

"(*a*) any security, by way of gift, shall make an application to the Reserve Bank furnishing the following information, namely:—

(*i*) Name and address of the transferor and the proposed transferee;

(*ii*) Relationship between the transferor and the proposed transferee;

(*iii*) Reasons for making the gift;"

(*e*) The value of security to be transferred by the donor together with any security transferred to any person residing outside India as gift in the calendar year does not exceed the rupee equivalent of USD 25,000.

(*f*) Such other conditions as considered necessary in public interest by the Reserve Bank.

(*iii*) The application for approval referred to in sub-clause (*i*) shall contain the following information/documents:

(*a*) Name and address of the donor and the donee.

(*b*) Relationship between the donor and the donee.

(*c*) Reasons for making the gift.

(*d*) In case of Government dated securities and treasury bills and bonds, a certificate issued by a Chartered Accountant on the market value of such securities.

(*e*) In case of units of domestic mutual funds and units of Money Market Mutual Funds, a certificate from the issuer on the Net Asset Value of such security.

(*f*) In case of shares and debentures, a certificate from a Chartered Account on the value of such securities according to the guidelines issued by the Securities and Exchange Board of India or the erstwhile CCI with regard to listed companies and unlisted companies respectively.

(*g*) Certificate from the concerned Indian company certifying that the proposed transfer of shares/convertible debentures, by way of gift, from resident to the non-resident shall not breach the applicable sectoral cap/FDI limit in the company and that the proposed number of shares/convertible debentures to be held by the non-resident transferee shall not exceed 5% of the paid up capital of the company.]

[1][(*b*) any share/convertible debenture of an Indian Company whose activities fall under Annexure B to Schedule 1, other than item Nos. 1, 2 and 3 and subject to the Sectoral Limits specified therein, shall transfer such shares/ debentures[2] without prior approval of Government and RBI if the same is by way of sale subject to the following:

---

1 Substituted by Foreign Exchange Management (Transfer or Issue of Security by a Person Resident Outside India) (Second Amendment) Regulations, 2005, w.r.e.f. 4-10-2004. Prior to substitution clause (*b*) read as under:

"(*b*) any share/convertible debenture of an Indian company, by way of sale, shall obtain the Government approval for the transfer and thereafter apply to the Reserve Bank for its approval, which may be granted subject to such conditions as are considered necessary by Reserve Bank, including the price at which such sale may be made."

2 In terms of AP (DIR Series) Circular No. 62, dated 24.5.2007, AD Category-I banks are permitted to open Escrow account and Special account on behalf of non-resident corporates, without prior approval of the Reserve Bank, for acquisition/transfer of shares/convertible debentures through open offers/delisting/exit offers.

(*i*) that the Indian Company whose shares or convertible debentures are proposed to be transferred is not engaged in rendering any financial service;

(*ii*) that the transfer does not fall within the purview of the provisions of SEBI (Substantial Acquisition of Shares and Takeovers) Regulations, 1997; and

(*iii*) that the concerned parties adhere to pricing guidelines, documentation and reporting requirements for such transfers as may be specified by Reserve Bank, from time to time;

[1][(*c*) any security by way of sale, shall make an application to the Reserve Bank for its approval if,—

(*i*) the activity of the Indian company, whose securities are being transferred, falls outside the Automatic Route, and the approval of the FIPB has been obtained for the said transfer;

(*ii*) the activity of the Indian company whose securities are being transferred, falls under the financial services sector;

(*iii*) the transfer falls within the purview of the provisions of SEBI (Substantial Acquisition of Shares and Takeover) Regulations, 1997; and

(*iv*) the transfer is to take place at a price which falls outside the pricing guidelines specified by Reserve Bank, from time to time.]

Explanation.—For the purpose of this Regulation, "financial services" shall mean service rendered by banking and non-banking companies regulated by the Reserve Bank, insurance, companies regulated by Insurance Regulatory and Development Authority (IRDA) and other companies regulated by any other financial regulator as the case may be.]

B. Transfer by way of sale not convered by regulation 9 by a person resident outside India—

(1) [2][* * *]

[3][(2) A person resident outside India, may transfer share or convertible

---

1 Inserted by Foreign Exchange Management (Transfer or Issue of Security by a Person Resident Outside India) (Second Amendment) Regulations, 2008 [Notification No. FEMA 179/2008-RB, dated 22-8-2008] w.e.f. 10.2.2006.

2 Clause (1) omitted by Foreign Exchange Management (Transfer or Issue of Security by a Person Resident Outside India) (Second Amendment) Regulations, 2005, [Notification No. FEMA-131/2005-RB] w.r.e.f. 4-10-2004. Prior to omission clause (1) read as under:

"(1) Transfer by way of sale not covered by regulation 9 by a person resident outside India of the shares/convertible debentures held by him to a person resident in India, shall require prior permission of the Reserve Bank, for which application in Form TS 1 may be made to the Reserve Bank."

3 Substituted by Foreign Exchange Management (Transfer or Issue of Security by a Person Resident Outside India) (Second Amendment) Regulations, 2005, w.r.e.f. 4-10-2004. Prior to omission clause (2) read as under:

"(2) While considering the grant of permission, the Reserve Bank shall take into account the following factors, namely:—

(*a*) where the shares of an Indian company are traded on stock exchange,— →→

→→ (*i*) the sale is at the prevailing market price on stock exchange and is effected through a merchant banker registered with Securities and Exchange Board of India or through a stock broker registered with the stock exchange;

(*ii*) if the transfer is other than that referred to in clause (*i*), the Reserve Bank will satisfy itself that the shares are proposed to be sold at a price arrived at by taking the average quotations (average of daily high and low) for one week preceding the date of application with 5 per cent variation. Where, however, the shares are being sold by the foreign collaborator or the foreign promoter of the Indian company to the existing promoters in India with the objective of passing management control in favour of the resident promoters the proposal for sale will be considered at a price which may be higher by upto a ceiling of 25 per cent over the price arrived at as above,

(*b*) where the shares of an Indian company are not listed on stock exchange or are thinly traded,—

(*i*) if the consideration payable for the transfer does not exceed ₹20 lakh per seller per company, at a price mutually agreed to between the seller and the buyer, based on any valuation methodology currently in vogue, on submission of a certificate from the statutory auditors of the Indian company whose shares are proposed to be transferred, regarding the valuation of the shares, and

(*ii*) if the amount of consideration payable for the transfer exceeds ₹20 lakhs per seller per company, at a price arrived at, at the seller's option, in any of the following manner, namely:—

(A) a price based on earning per share (EPS linked to the Price Earning (P/E) multiple, or a price based on the Net Asset Value (NAV) linked to book value multiple, whichever is higher, or

(B) the prevailing market price in small lots as may be laid down by the Reserve Bank so that the entire shareholding is sold in not less than five trading days through screen based trading system;

(*c*) where the shares are not listed on any stock exchange, at a price which is lower of the two independent valuations of share, one by statutory auditors of the company and the other by a Chartered Accountant or by a Merchant Banker in Category 1 registered with Securities and Exchange Board of India.

Explanation:—

(*i*) A share is considered as thinly traded if the annualised trading turnover in that share, on main stock exchanges in India, during the six calendar months preceding the month in which application is made, is less than 2 per cent (by number of shares) of the listed stock.

(*ii*) For the purpose of arriving at Net Asset Value per share, the miscellaneous expenses carried forward, accumulated losses, total outside liabilities, revaluation reserves and capital reserves (except subsidy received in cash) shall be reduced from value of the total assets and the net figure so arrived at shall be divided by the number of equity shares issued and paid up. Alternatively, intangible assets shall be reduced from the equity capital and reserves (excluding revaluation reserves) and the figure so arrived at shall be divided by the number of equity shares issued and paid up. The NAV so calculated shall be used in conjunction with the average BV multiple of Bombay Stock Exchange National Index during the calendar month immediately preceding the month in which application is made and BV multiple shall be discounted by 40 per cent.

(*iii*) For computing the price based on Earning Per Share, the earning per share as per the latest balance sheet of the company shall be used in conjunction with the average Price Earning Multiple of Bombay Stock Exchange National Index for the calendar month preceding the month in which application is made and Price Earning shall be discounted by 40 per cent."

debenture of an Indian Company, without the prior permission of the Reserve Bank, by way of sale, to a person resident in India subject to the adherence to pricing guidelines, documentation and reporting requirements for such transfers as may be specified by Reserve Bank from time to time.]

11. Remittance of sale proceeds.—(1) No remittance of sale proceeds of an Indian security held by a person resident outside India shall be made otherwise than in accordance with these regulations and the conditions specified in the relevant Schedule.

(2) An authorised dealer may allow the remittance of sale proceeds of a security (net of applicable taxes) to the seller of shares resident outside India:

Provided—

(*a*) the security was held by the seller on repatriation basis;

(*b*) either the security has been sold on a recognised stock exchange in India through a stock broker at the ruling market price as determined on the floor of the exchange, or the Reserve Bank's approval has been obtained in other cases for sale of the security and remittance of the sale proceeds thereof; and

(*c*) a no objection/tax clearance certificate from the Income-tax authority has been produced.

[1][**12. Pledge of shares of company incorporated in India**

(*i*) Any person being a promoter of a company registered in India (borrowing company), which has raised external commercial borrowing, may pledge the shares of the borrowing company or that of its associate resident companies for the purpose of securing the external commercial borrowing (ECB) raised by the borrowing company:

Provided that no person shall pledge any such share unless no-objection has been obtained from a bank which is an authorised dealer.

(*ii*) A bank which is an authorised dealer may grant 'no objection' for pledge of shares under clause (*i*) after satisfying itself of the following:

(*a*) the underlying ECB is strictly in compliance with the extant ECB guidelines,

(*b*) the loan agreement has been signed by both the lender and the borrower,

(*c*) there exists a security clause in the Loan Agreement requiring the borrower to create charge on financial securities, and

(*d*) the borrower has obtained Loan Registration Number (LRN) from the Reserve Bank: [2][(Amendment) Rules, 2009.]

---

1 Inserted by Foreign Exchange Management (Transfer or Issue of Security by a Person Resident Outside India) (Amendment) Regulations, 2009, w.r.e.f. 11-7-2008 [FEMA 202/2009-RB, dated 10-11-2009].

2 This seems to be a superfluous entry and needs to be deleted.

Provided that the 'no objection' may be granted by a bank which is an authorised dealer subject to the following conditions, namely:—

(*a*) the period of such pledge shall be co-terminus with the maturity of the underlying external commercial borrowing;

(*b*) in case of invocation of pledge, transfer shall be in accordance with the extant FDI policy and directions issued by the Reserve Bank;

(*c*) the Statutory Auditor has certified that the borrowing company will utilize/has utilised the proceeds of the external commercial borrowing for the permitted end-use/s only.]

Schedule 1

[*See* regulation 5(1)]

Foreign Direct Investment Scheme[1]

1. Purchase by a person resident outside India of equity/preference/ convertible preference shares and convertible debentures issued by an Indian company.—[2][(1) A person resident outside India referred to in clauses (*i*) and (*ii*) of sub-regulation (1) of Regulation 5, may purchase shares or convertible debentures issued by an Indian company up to the extent and subject to the terms and conditions set out in this Schedule.]

[3][(2) If the person purchasing the shares under this Scheme proposes to be a collaborator or proposes to acquire the entire shareholding of a new Indian company, he should obtain prior permission of Central Government if he has, as on January 12, 2005, an existing joint venture or technology transfer/trademark agreement in the same field as that of such Indian company.]

[4][Provided that no prior permission of Central Government shall be required

---

1 Refer also AP (DIR Series) Circular No. 73, dated 8-6-2007 (also Press Note, dated 30-4-2007 of Ministry of Finance) for revised guidelines in respect of foreign investments in preference shares and AP (DIR Series) Circular No. 74, dated 8-6-2007 for revised guidelines in respect of foreign investments in debentures.

2 Substituted vide Foreign Exchange Management (Transfer or Issue of Security by a Person Resident Outside India) (Second Amendment) Regulations, 2007 [Notification No. FEMA 167/2007-RB, dated 23-10-2007]. Prior to substitution, para 1(1) read as under:

"(1) A person resident outside India referred to in sub-regulation (1) of regulation 5, may purchase shares or convertible debentures issued by an Indian company up to the extent and subject to the terms and conditions set out in this Schedule."

3 Substituted by Foreign Exchange Management (Transfer or Issue of Security by a Person Resident Outside India) (Second Amendment) Regulations, 2008 [Notification No. FEMA 179/2008-RB, dated 22-8-2008] w.e.f. 12.1.2005 for the following:

"(2) If the person purchasing the shares under this Scheme proposes to be collaborator or proposes to acquire the entire shareholding of a new Indian company, he should obtain a prior permission of Central Government if he has a previous venture or tie-up in India through investment in shares or debentures or a technical collaboration or a trade mark agreement or investment by whatever name called in the same field or allied field in which the Indian company issuing the shares is engaged."

4 Inserted by Foreign Exchange Management (Transfer or Issue of Security by a Person Resident Outside India) (Second Amendment) Regulations, 2008 [Notification No. FEMA 179/2008-RB, dated 22-8-2008] w.e.f. 12.1.2005. →→

for investments to be made by Venture Capital Funds registered with SEBI; investments by multinational financial institutions; or where in the existing joint-venture investment by either of the parties is less than 3 per cent; or where the existing joint venture/collaboration is defunct or sick or for transfer of shares of an Indian company engaged in Information Technology sector or in the mining sector, if the existing joint venture or technology transfer/trade mark agreement of the person to whom the shares are to be transferred are also in the Information Technology sector or in the mining sector for same area/mineral.]

2. Automatic route of Reserve Bank for issue of shares by an Indian company.—[1][(1) An Indian company, not engaged in any activity/sector mentioned in Annexure A to this Schedule, may issue shares or convertible debentures to a person resident outside India, subject to the limits prescribed in Annexure B to this Schedule, in accordance with the Entry Routes specified therein and the provisions of Foreign Direct Investment Policy, as notified by the Ministry of Commerce & Industry, Government of India, from time to time:

Provided that the shares or convertible debentures are not being issued by the Indian company with a view to acquire existing shares of any Indian company.

Explanation.—A company which proposes to embark on expansion programme to undertake activities or manufacture items included in Annexure B to this Schedule may issue shares or debentures out of fresh capital proposed to be issued by it for the purpose of financing expansion programme, up to the

---

→ → *Note*: The substituted para is retrospectively effective from 12-1-2005 keeping in tune with the fact that Press Note No. 1 (2005 Series) was issued by DIPP, Ministry of Commerce on this date.

1 Substituted by Foreign Exchange Management (Transfer or Issue of Security by a Person Resident Outside India) (Second Amendment) Regulations, 2008 [Notification No. FEMA 179/2008-RB, dated 22-8-2008] w.e.f. 10.2.2006 for the following:

"(1) An Indian company which is not engaged in any activity, or in manufacturing of item included in Annexure 'A' to this Schedule, may issue shares or convertible debentures to a person resident outside India, referred to in paragraph 1 upto the extent specified in Annexure B, subject to compliance with the provisions of the Industrial Policy and Procedures as notified by Secretariat for Industrial Assistance (SIA) in the Ministry of Commerce and Industry, Government of India, from time to time:

Provided that:

(*i*) the activity of the issuer company does not require an industrial licence under the provisions of the Industries (Development and Regulation) Act, 1951 or under the locational policy notified by Government of India under the Industrial Policy of 1991 as amended from time to time;

(*ii*) the shares or convertible debentures are not being issued by the Indian company with a view to acquiring existing shares of any Indian company.

Explanation.—A company which proposes to embark on expansion programme to undertake activities or manufacture items included in Annexure B to this Schedule may issue shares or debentures out of fresh capital proposed to be issued by it for the purpose of financing expansion programme, upto the extent indicated in Annexure B, subject to compliance with the provisions of this paragraph."

Note: The substituted Para is retrospectively effective from 10.2.2006 keeping in tune with the fact that Press Note No. 4 (2006 Series) was issued by DIPP, Ministry of Commerce on this date.

extent indicated in Annexure B, subject to compliance with the provisions of this paragraph.]

[1][(2) *Omitted.*]

[2][(2)] A company which is a small scale industrial unit and which is not engaged in any activity or in manufacture of items included in Annexure A, may issue shares or convertible debentures to a person referred to in paragraph 1, to the extent of 24% of its paid-up capital:

Provided that such a company may issue shares in excess of 24% of its paid up capital if—

(*a*) it has given up its small scale status,

(*b*) it is not engaged or does not propose to engage in manufacture of items reserved for small scale sector, and

(*c*) it complies with the ceilings specified in Annexure B.

[3][(3)] Notwithstanding anything contained in clause (3) an Export Oriented Unit or a Unit in Free Trade Zone or in Export Processing Zone or in a Software Technology Park or in an Electronic Hardware Technology Park may issue shares or convertible debentures to a person resident outside India referred to in paragraph 1 in excess of 24 per cent provided it complies with the ceilings specified in Annexure B.

[4][[5][(4)] An Indian company, otherwise eligible to issue shares under this Schedule may issue equity/preference shares, subject to pricing guidelines as given in paragraph 5 of this Schedule, to a person resident outside India.—

(*i*) being a provider of technology/technical know-how, against Royalty/ Lump sum fees due for payment;

---

1 Omitted by Foreign Exchange Management (Transfer or Issue of Security by a Person Resident Outside India) (Second Amendment) Regulations, 2008 [Notification No. FEMA 179/2008-RB, dated 22-8-2008]. Before omission, sub-paragraph (2) read as under:

"(2) A trading company incorporated in India may issue shares or convertible debentures to the extent of 51 per cent of its capital, to persons resident outside India referred to paragraph 1, subject to the condition that remittance of dividend to the shareholders outside India is made only after the company has secured registration as an Export/Trading/Star Trading/Super Trading House from the Directorate General of Foreign Trade, Ministry of Commerce, Government of India, New Delhi."

2 Renumbered for (3), (4) and (5) by Foreign Exchange Management (Transfer or Issue of Security by a Person Resident Outside India) (Second Amendment) Regulations, 2008 [Notification No. FEMA 179/2008-RB, dated 22-8-2008].

3 Renumbered for (3), (4) and (5) by Foreign Exchange Management (Transfer or Issue of Security by a Person Resident Outside India) (Second Amendment) Regulations, 2008 [Notification No. FEMA 179/2008-RB, dated 22-8-2008].

4 Inserted by the Foreign Exchange Management (Transfer or Issue of Security by a Person Resident Outside India) (Fifth Amendment) Regulations, 2004, w.e.f. 27-11-2004 [FEMA 125/2004-RB].

5 Renumbered for (3), (4) and (5) by Foreign Exchange Management (Transfer or Issue of Security by a Person Resident Outside India) (Second Amendment) Regulations, 2008 [Notification No. FEMA 179/2008-RB, dated 22-8-2008].

(*ii*) against External Commercial Borrowing (ECB) (other than import dues deemed as ECB or Trade credit as per RBI Guidelines):

Provided that the foreign equity in the company after the conversion of Royalty/Lumpsum fee/ECB into equity is within the sectoral cap notified, if any.]

[1][**3. Issue of shares by a company requiring the Government approval.**— An Indian company intending to issue shares to a person resident outside India in accordance with these Regulations shall obtain prior approval of the Foreign Investment Promotion Board of Government of India if the company:

(*a*) is engaged or proposes to engage, in any activity given in Annexure A(A) to this Schedule; or

(*b*) falls under the FIPB route as stipulated under the column "Entry Route" in Annexure B to this Schedule; or

(*c*) proposes to issue shares to a person resident outside India against considerations other than inward remittance i.e., against royalty/ lumpsum fee due for payment; or

(*d*) proposes to issue shares to a person resident outside India, on or after November 28, 2003, against External Commercial Borrowings (ECBs) [excluding those deemed as ECBs] received in convertible foreign currency.]

4. Issue of shares by International offering through ADR and/or GDR.— (1) An Indian company may issue its Rupee denominated shares to a person resident outside India being a depository for the purpose of issuing Global Depository Receipts (GDRs) and/or American Depository Receipts (ADRs):

Provided the Indian company issuing such shares—

(*a*) has an approval from the Ministry of Finance, Government of India to issue such ADRs and/or GDRs or is eligible to issue ADRs/GDRs in terms of the relevant scheme in force or notification issued by the Ministry of Finance,

---

1 Substituted by Foreign Exchange Management (Transfer or Issue of Security by a Person Resident Outside India) (Second Amendment) Regulations, 2008 [Notification No. FEMA 179/2008-RB, dated 22-8-2008] w.r.e.f. 29-11-2003 for the following:

"3. *Issue of shares by a company requiring the Government approval.*—A company which is engaged or proposes to engage in any activity specified in Annexure 'A' or which proposes to issue shares to a person resident outside India beyond the sectoral limits stipulated in Annexure 'B' *[either directly or by conversion of ECB/Royalty/Lump sum fee] or which is otherwise not eligible to issue shares to a person resident outside India, may issue shares to a person resident outside India referred to in paragraph 1, provided it has secured prior approval of Secretariat for Industrial Assistance or, as the case may be of the Foreign Investment Promotion Board of the Government of India and the terms and conditions of such an approval are complied with."

* These words were earlier inserted by Foreign Exchange Management (Transfer or Issue of Security by a Person Resident Outside India) (Fifth Amendment) Regulations, 2004 [Notification No. FEMA 125/2004-RB] w.e.f. 27-11-2004.

Note: The substituted Para is retrospectively effective from 29-11-2003 keeping in tune with the fact that Press Note No. 5 (2003 Series) was issued by DIPP, Ministry of Commerce on this date.

(*b*) is not otherwise ineligible to issue shares to persons resident outside India in terms of these regulations, and

(*c*) the ADRs/GDRs are issued in accordance with the Scheme for issue of Foreign Currency Convertible Bonds and Ordinary Shares (Through Depository Receipt Mechanism) Scheme, 1993 and guidelines issued by the Central Government thereunder from time to time.

(2) The Indian company issuing shares under sub-paragraph (1), shall furnish to the Reserve Bank, full details of such issue in the [1][Form DR], within 30 days from the date of closing of the issue.

(3) The Indian company issuing shares against ADRs/GDRs shall furnish a quarterly return in the [2][Form DR Quarterly] to Reserve Bank within fifteen days of the close of the calendar quarter.

(4) Pending repatriation or utilisation of foreign exchange resources raised in terms of clause (1) the Indian company may invest the foreign currency funds in—

[3][(*a*) deposits with or Certificate of Deposit or other instruments offered by banks who have been rated by Standard and Poor, Fitch, IBCA or Moody's, etc., and such rating not being less than the rating stipulated by Reserve Bank from time to time for the purpose,]

(*b*) deposits with branch outside India of an authorised dealer in India, and

(*c*) treasury bills and other monetary instruments with a maturity or unexpired maturity of the instrument of one year or less.

[4][**4A**. A registered broker in India may purchase shares of an Indian Company on behalf of a person resident outside India, for the purpose of converting the shares so purchased into ADRs/GDRs:

Provided that—

(*i*) the shares are purchased on a recognized stock exchange;

(*ii*) the Indian company has issued ADRs/GDRs;

(*iii*) the shares are purchased with the permission of Custodian of the ADRs/GDRs of the concerned Indian company and are deposited with the Custodian;

---

1 Substituted for the words 'form specified in Annexure C' by Foreign Exchange Management (Transfer or Issue of Security by a Person Resident Outside India) (Second Amendment) Regulations, 2008 [Notification No. FEMA 179/2008-RB, dated 22-8-2008].

2 Substituted for the words 'form specified in Annexure D' by Foreign Exchange Management (Transfer or Issue of Security by a Person Resident Outside India) (Second Amendment) Regulations, 2008 [Notification No. FEMA 179/2008-RB, dated 22-8-2008].

3 Substituted by the Foreign Exchange Management (Transfer or Issue of Security by a Person Resident Outside India) (Third Amendment) Regulations, 2004, w.e.f. 16-6-2004 [FEMA 118/2004-RB] for the following:

"(*a*) deposits with or Certificate of Deposits or other instruments of banks who have been rated not less than A1 + by Standard and Poor or P1 by Moody's for short-term obligations,"

4 Inserted by the Foreign Exchange Management (Transfer or Issue of Security by a Person Resident Outside India) (Amendment) Regulations, 2001, w.e.f. 2-3-2001.

(*iv*) the number of shares so purchased shall not exceed ADRs/GDRs converted into underlying shares and shall be subject to sectoral caps as applicable;

(*v*) the non-resident investor, broker, Custodian and the overseas depository comply with the provisions of the Scheme for Issue of Foreign Currency Convertible Bonds and Ordinary Shares (Through Depository Receipt Mechanism) Scheme, 1993 and guidelines issued thereunder by the Central Government from time to time.]

[1][**4B.** An Indian company may sponsor an issue of ADRs/GDRs with an overseas depository against shares held by its shareholders at a price to be determined under the provisions of the Scheme for Issue of Foreign Currency Convertible Bonds and Ordinary Shares (Through Depository Receipt Mechanism) Scheme, 1993 and guidelines issued by the Government of India and the reporting requirements as directed by Reserve Bank, from time to time.]

[2][**5. Issue price.**—Price of shares issued to persons resident outside India under this Schedule, shall not be less than—

(*a*) the price worked out in accordance with the SEBI guidelines, as applicable, where the shares of the company is listed on any recognised stock exchange in India;

---

1 Substituted by Foreign Exchange Management (Transfer or Issue of Security by a Person Resident Outside India) (Second Amendment) Regulations, 2008 [Notification No. FEMA 179/2008-RB, dated 22-8-2008] for the following:

*"4B. (*i*) An Indian company may sponsor an issue of ADRs/GDRs with an overseas depository against shares held by its shareholders at a price to be determined by the Lead Manager.

(*ii*) The proceeds of the issue shall be repatriated to India within a period of one month.

(*iii*) The sponsoring company shall comply with the provisions of the Scheme for Issue of Foreign Currency Convertible Bonds and Ordinary Shares (Through Depository Receipt Mechanism) Scheme, 1993 and guidelines issued thereunder by the Central Government from time to time.

(*iv*) The sponsoring company shall furnish full details of such issue in a form specified in Annexure C to the Foreign Investment Division, Exchange Control Department, Reserve Bank of India, Central Office, Mumbai within 30 days from the date of closure of the issue."

* Earlier it was inserted by Foreign Exchange Management (Transfer or Issue of Security by a Person Resident Outside India) (Amendment) Regulations, 2001 w.e.f. 2-3-2001.

2 Substituted by the FEM (Transfer or Issue of Security by a Person Resident Outside India) (Amendment) Regulations, 2010 [Notification No. FEMA 205/2010-RB, dated 7-4-2010]. Earlier, paragraph 5 read as under:

"5. *Issue price.*—Price of shares issued to persons resident outside India under this Schedule, shall not be less than—

(*a*) the price worked out in accordance with the SEBI guidelines, 1[as applicable] where the issuing company is listed on any recognised stock exchange in India, and

(*b*) fair valuation of shares done by a chartered accountant as per the guidelines issued by the erstwhile Controller of Capital Issues, in all other cases."

1 Inserted by the Foreign Exchange Management (Transfer or Issue of Security by a Person Resident Outside India) (Second Amendment) Regulations, 2003, w.e.f. 18-6-2003.

(*b*) the fair valuation of shares done by a SEBI registered Category-I Merchant Banker or a Chartered Accountant as per the discounted free cash flow method, where the shares of the company is not listed on any recognised stock exchange in India; and

(*c*) the price as applicable to transfer of shares from resident to non-resident as per the pricing guidelines laid down by the Reserve Bank from time to time, where the issue of shares is on preferential allotment.]

[1][**5A.** *Omitted.*]

[3][**6. Issue price of ADRs/GDRs.**—The pricing of ADRs/GDRs to be issued to a person resident outside India shall be determined under the provisions of[2] the Scheme for Issue of Foreign Currency Convertible Bonds and Ordinary Shares

---

1 Omitted by Foreign Exchange Management (Transfer or Issue of Security by a Person Resident Outside India) (Second Amendment) Regulations, 2008 [Notification No. FEMA 179/2008-RB, dated 22-8-2008]. Before omission, this para read as under:

"[1]5A. *Issue price of ADRs/GDRs.*—Price of ADRs/GDRs to be issued to a person resident outside India may be decided by the Indian company—

(*a*) where the issue is on public offer basis, in consultation with the lead manager to the issue; and

(*b*) in other cases, as provided in paragraph 5 above."

1 Earlier it was inserted by Foreign Exchange Management (Transfer or Issue of Security by a Person Resident Outside India) (Second Amendment) Regulations, 2003 w.e.f. 18-6-2003.

2 Substituted by Foreign Exchange Management (Transfer or Issue of Security by a Person Resident Outside India) (Second Amendment) Regulations, 2008 [Notification No. FEMA 179/2008-RB, dated 22-8-2008]. Before substitution paragraph 6 relating to 'Dividend Balancing' read as under:

"*6. Dividend balancing.*—Where a company is engaged in any of the industries in the consumer goods sector, specified in Annexure E, or in any other activity where the condition of dividend balancing has been stipulated in terms of the provisions of Industrial Policy and Procedures notified by Secretariat for Industrial Assistance, the cumulative outflow of foreign exchange on account of payment of dividend over a period of seven years from the date of commencement of commercial production to investors outside India shall not exceed cumulative amount of export earning of the company during those years:

Provided that—

(*a*) the restriction under this paragraph shall not apply—

(*i*) in respect of shares held in such a company by International Finance Corporation (IFC), the Deustche Entwicklungs Gescelschaft (DEG), the Commonwealth Development Corporation (CDC) and Asian Development Bank (ADB);

(*ii*) to a company that has completed a period of seven years from the date of commencement of commercial production;

†[(*iii*) to obligations arising out of dividends declared/remitted after 14th July, 2000, i.e., the date on which conditions of dividend balancing was withdrawn.]

††[(*b*) * * *]"

† Earlier it was inserted by Foreign Exchange Management (Transfer or Issue of Security by a Person Resident Outside India) (Second Amendment) Regulations, 2003 w.e.f. 18-6-2003.

†† Omitted, *ibid.* Prior to omission, it read as under:

"(*b*) in case of an existing company that has issued fresh equity to persons resident outside India under these regulations, the restriction shall apply to the fresh shares from the date of their issue."

(Through Depository Receipt Mechanism) Scheme, 1993 and guidelines issued by the Government of India from time to time.]

7. Rate of dividend on preference shares.—The rate of dividend on preference shares or convertible preference shares issued under these regulations shall not exceed 300 basis points over the Prime Lending Rate of State Bank of India prevailing as on the date of the Board meeting of the company in which issue of such shares is recommended.

8. Mode of payment for shares issued to persons resident outside India.—A company in India issuing shares or convertible debentures under this Schedule to a person resident outside India shall receive the amount of consideration for such shares—

(*i*) by inward remittance through normal banking channels, or

(*ii*) by debit to NRE/FCNR account of the person concerned maintained with an authorised dealer/authorised bank.

[1][*Explanation*.—Conversion of Royalty/Lumpsum fee due for payment or conversion ECB, as given elsewhere in this Schedule, shall be treated as consideration for issue of shares within the meaning of this paragraph:]

[2][Provided that if the shares or convertible debentures are not issued within 180 days from the date of receipt of the inward remittance or date of debit to **NRE/FCNR(B)** account, the amount of consideration so received shall be refunded to the person concerned by outward remittance through normal banking channels or by credit to his **NRE/FCNR(B)** account, as the case may be:

Provided further that the Reserve Bank may, on an application made to it and for sufficient reasons permit an Indian company to refund the amount of consideration received towards issue of security, if such amount is outstanding beyond a period of 180 days from the date of receipt.]

9. Report by the Indian company.—(1) An Indian company issuing shares or convertible debentures in accordance with these Regulations shall submit to Reserve Bank,—

(A) not later than 30 days from the date of receipt of the amount of consideration, a [3][report in form specified in Annexure C to this Schedule] indicating:—

(*i*) Name and address of the foreign investors,

(*ii*) Date of receipt of funds and their rupee equivalent,

---

1 Inserted by the Foreign Exchange Management (Transfer or Issue of Security by a Person Resident Outside India) (Fifth Amendment) Regulations, 2004, w.e.f. 27-11-2004 [FEMA 125/2004-RB].

2 Provisos inserted vide Foreign Exchange Management (Transfer or Issue of Security by a Person Resident Outside India) (Third Amendment) Regulations, 2007 [Notification No. FEMA 170/2007-RB, dated 13-11-2007].

3 Substituted for the word 'report' by Foreign Exchange Management (Transfer or Issue of Security by a Person Resident Outside India) (Second Amendment) Regulations, 2008 [Notification No. FEMA 179/2008-RB, dated 22-8-2008].

(*iii*) Name and address of the authorised dealer through whom the funds have been received, and

(*iv*) Details of the Government approval, if any.

(B) not later than 30 days from the date of issue of shares, a report in Form FC-GPR together with,—

(*i*) a certificate from the Company Secretary of the company accepting investment from persons resident outside India certifying that—

(*a*) all the requirements of the Companies Act, 1956 have been complied with;

(*b*) terms and conditions of the Government approval, if any, have been complied with;

(*c*) the company is eligible to issue shares under these regulations; and

(*d*) the company has all original certificates issued by authorised dealers in India evidencing receipt of amount of consideration [1][in accordance with paragraph 8];

(*ii*) a certificate from Statutory Auditors or Chartered Accountant indicating the manner of arriving at the price of the shares issued to the persons resident outside India:

[2][Provided that, in addition to above, the company shall report the conversion of ECB into equity, in ECB-2 Return of the respective month in case of full conversion of ECB. In case of partial conversion of ECB, the converted portion shall be reported in Form FC-GPR to the concerned Regional Office of the Reserve Bank and non-converted portion in Form ECB-2.]

[3][(C) the amount of consideration received by Indian company as advance against equity shall be reported to the Regional Office of the Reserve Bank under whose jurisdiction the Registered Office of the Company operates in the form specified in "Annexure C" within 30 days of receipt thereof.]

10. Permission for retaining share subscription money received from persons resident outside India in a foreign currency account.—Reserve Bank may, on an application made to it and on being satisfied that it is necessary so to do, permit an Indian company issuing shares to persons resident outside India under this Schedule, to retain the subscription amount in a foreign currency account, subject to such terms and conditions as it may stipulate.

---

1 Substituted for the words 'in accordance with paragraph 9' by Foreign Exchange Management (Transfer or Issue of Security by a Person Resident Outside India) (Second Amendment) Regulations, 2008 [Notification No. FEMA 179/2008-RB, dated 22-8-2008].

2 Inserted by the Foreign Exchange Management (Transfer or Issue of Security by a Person Resident Outside India) (Fifth Amendment) Regulations, 2004, w.e.f. 27-11-2004 [FEMA 125/2004-RB].

3 Inserted by Foreign Exchange Management (Transfer or Issue of Security by a Person Resident Outside India) (Second Amendment) Regulations, 2008 [Notification No. FEMA 179/2008-RB, dated 22-8-2008].

[1][ANNEXURE A

(*See* paragraph 2 of Schedule 1)

(A) All Activities/Sectors would require prior approval of the Government of India for FDI in the following circumstances:—

(*i*) where provisions of Press Note 1 (2005 Series) issued by the Government of India are attracted;

(*ii*) where more than 24 per cent foreign equity is proposed to be inducted for manufacture of items reserved for the Small Scale sector.

(B) Sectors prohibited for FDI

(*i*) Retail Trading (except single brand product retailing);

(*ii*) Atomic Energy;

(*iii*) Lottery Business;

(*iv*) Gambling and Betting;

(*v*) Business of chit fund;

(*vi*) Nidhi Company;

(*vii*) Trading in Transferable Development Rights (TDRs);

(*viii*) Activities/sector not opened to private sector investment.]

[2][Annexure B

(*See* paragraph 2 of Schedule 1)

Sector-specific policy for Foreign Investment

In the following sectors/activities, FDI up to the limit indicated below is allowed subject to other conditions as indicated. In Sectors/Activities not listed below, FDI is permitted up to 100 per cent on the automatic route subject to sectoral rules/regulations applicable.

Sr. No.	*Sector/Activity*	*FDI Cap/ Equity*	*Entry Route*	*Other conditions*
	Agriculture			
1.	Floriculture, Horticulture, Development of Seeds, Animal Husbandry, Pisciculture, Aquaculture, Cultivation of	100%	Automatic	—

---

1 Annexure A substituted by Foreign Exchange Management (Transfer or Issue of Security by a Person Resident Outside India) (Second Amendment) Regulations, 2008 [Notification No. FEMA 179/2008-RB, dated 22-8-2008].

Note: Earlier Annexure A was substituted by Foreign Exchange Management (Transfer or Issue of Security by a Person Resident Outside India) (Second Amendment) Regulations, 2003 w.e.f. 18-6-2003.

2 Annexure B substituted by Foreign Exchange Management (Transfer or Issue of Security by a Person Resident Outside India) (Second Amendment) Regulations, 2008 [Notification No. FEMA 179/2008-RB, dated 22-8-2008].

Note: Earlier Annexure B was substituted by Foreign Exchange Management (Transfer or Issue of Security by a Person Resident Outside India) (Second Amendment) Regulations, 2003 w.e.f. 18-6-2003.

Sr. No.	*Sector/Activity*	*FDI Cap/ Equity*	*Entry Route*	*Other conditions*
	Vegetables & Mushrooms under controlled conditions and services related to agro and allied sectors. NB: Besides the above, FDI is not allowed in any other agricultural sector/activity			
2.	Tea Sector, including tea plantation NB: Besides the above, FDI is not allowed in any other plantation sector/activity	100%	FIPB	Subject to divestment of 26% equity in favour of Indian partner/Indian public within 5 years and prior approval of State Government concerned in case of any change in future land use.
	Industry			
	Mining			
3.	Mining covering exploration and mining of diamonds & precious stones; gold, silver and minerals.	100%	Automatic	Subject to Mines & Minerals (Development & Regulation) Act, 1957 (www.mines.nic.in) Press Note 18 (1998) and Press Note 1 (2005) are not applicable for setting up 100% owned subsidiaries insofar as the mining sector is concerned, subject to a declaration from the applicant that he has no existing joint venture for the same area and/or the particular mineral.
4.	Coal & Lignite mining for captive consumption by power projects, and iron & steel, cement production and other eligible activities permitted under the Coal Mines (Nationalisation) Act, 1973.	100%	Automatic	Subject to provisions of Coal Mines (Nationalization) Act, 1973. (www.coal.nic.in)
5.	Mining and mineral separation of titanium bearing minerals and ores, its value addition and integrated activities. NB: FDI will not be allowed in mining of "prescribed substances" listed in Government of India Notification No. S.O. 61(E), dated 18-1-2006 issued by the Department of Atomic Energy.	100%	FIPB	Subject to sectoral Regulations and the Mines and Minerals (Development & Regulation) Act, 1957 and the following conditions— (*i*) value addition facilities are set up within India along

Sr. No.	*Sector/Activity*	*FDI Cap/ Equity*	*Entry Route*	*Other conditions*
				with transfer of technology; (*ii*) disposal of tailings during the mineral separation shall be carried out in accordance with Regulations framed by the Atomic Energy Regulatory Board such as Atomic Energy (Radiation Protection) Rules, 2004 and the Atomic Energy (Safe Disposal of Radioactive Wastes) Rules, 1987.
	Manufacturing			
6.	Alcohol-Distillation & Brewing	100%	Automatic	Subject to license by appropriate authority.
7.	Cigars & Cigarettes-Manufacture	100%	FIPB	Subject to industrial license under the Industries (Development & Regulation) Act, 1951.
8.	Coffee & Rubber processing & warehousing	100%	Automatic	—
9.	Defence production	26%	FIPB	Subject to licensing under Industries (Development & Regulation) Act, 1951 and "guidelines on FDI in production of arms & ammunition.
10.	Hazardous chemicals, viz., hydrocyanic acid and its derivatives; phosgene and its derivatives; and isocyanates and diisocyan-tes of hydrocarbon.	100%	Automatic	Subject to industrial license under the Industries (Development & Regulation) Act, 1951 and other sectoral Regulations.
11.	Industrial explosives - Manufacture.	100%	Automatic	Subject to industrial license under the Industries (Development & Regulation) Act, 1951 and Regulations under Explosives Act, 1898
	Power			
12.	Power including generation (except Atomic energy); transmission, distribution and Power trading.	100%	Automatic	Subject to provisions of the Electricity Act, 2003 (www.powermin.nic.in)

Sr. No.	*Sector/Activity*	*FDI Cap/ Equity*	*Entry Route*	*Other conditions*
	Services			
	Civil Aviation Sector			
13.	Airports —			
	(*a*) Greenfield projects	100%	Automatic	Subject to sectoral Regulations notified by Ministry of Civil Aviation (www.civilaviation.nic.in)
	(*b*) Existing projects	100%	FIPB beyond 74%	Subject to sectoral Regulations notified by Ministry of Civil Aviation (www.civilaviation.nic.in)
14.	Air Transport Services including Domestic Scheduled Passenger Airlines; Non-Schedules Airlines; Chartered Airlines; Cargo Airlines; Helicopter and Seaplane Services.			
	(*a*) Scheduled Air Transport Services/Domestic Scheduled Passenger Airline.	49% - FDI; 100% - for NRIs investment	Automatic	Subject to no direct or indirect participation by foreign airlines and sectoral Regulations. (www.civilaviation.nic.in)
	(*b*) Non-Scheduled Air Transport Service/Non-Scheduled airlines, Chartered airlines, and Cargo airlines.	74% - FDI 100% - for NRIs investment	Automatic	Subject to no direct or indirect participation by foreign airlines in Non-Scheduled and Chartered airlines. Foreign airlines are allowed to participate in the equity of companies operating Cargo airlines. Also subject to sectoral Regulations. (www.civilaviation.nic.in)
	(*c*) Helicopter Services/ Seaplane services requiring DGCA approval.	100%	Automatic	Foreign airlines are allowed to participate in the equity of companies operating Helicopter and seaplane services. Also subject to sectoral Regulations. (www.civilaviation.nic.in)
15.	Other services under Civil Aviation Sector.			
	(*a*) Ground Handling Services	74% - FDI 100% - for NRIs investment	Automatic	Subject to sectoral Regulation and security clearance.
	(*b*) Maintenance and Repair organizations; flying training institutes; and	100%	Automatic	—

Sr. No.	*Sector/Activity*	*FDI Cap/ Equity*	*Entry Route*	*Other conditions*
	technical training institutions.			
16.	Asset Reconstruction Companies.	49% (only FDI)	FIPB	Where any individual investment exceeds 10% of the equity, provisions of section 3(3)(*f*) of Securitization and Reconstruction of Financial Assets and Enforcement of Security Interest Act, 2002 should be complied with. (www.finmin.nic.in)
17.	Banking - Private sector.	74% (FDI+ FII) Within this limit, FII investment not to exceed 49%	Automatic	Subject to guidelines for setting up branches/ subsidiaries of foreign banks issued by RBI. (www.rbi.org.in)
18.	Broadcasting.			
	(*a*) FM Radio	FDI+FII investment up to 20%	FIPB	Subject to guidelines notified by Ministry of Information & Broadcasting. (www.mib.nic.in)
	(*b*) Cable network	49% (FDI+ FII)	FIPB	Subject to Cable Television Net-work Rules (1994), notified by Ministry of Information & Broadcasting. (www.mib.nic.in)
	(*c*) Direct-To-Home	49% (FDI+FII). Within this limit, FDI component not to exceed 20%	FIPB	Subject to guidelines issued by Ministry of Information & Broadcasting. (www.mib.nic.in)
	(*d*) Setting up hardware facilities such as up-linking, HUB, etc.	49% (FDI+ FII)	FIPB	Subject to Up-linking Policy notified by Ministry of Information & Broadcasting. (www.mib.nic.in)
	(*e*) Up-linking a News & Current Affairs TV Channel	26% (FDI+ FII)	FIPB	Subject to guidelines issued by Ministry of Information & Broadcasting. (www.mib.nic.in)

Sr. No.	*Sector/Activity*	*FDI Cap/ Equity*	*Entry Route*	*Other conditions*
	(*f*) Up-linking a Non-news & Current Affairs TV Channel	100%	FIPB	Subject to guidelines issued by Ministry of Information & Broadcasting. (www.mib.nic.in)
19.	Commodity Exchanges	49% (FDI+FII) FDI - 26% FII - 23%	FIPB	FII purchases shall be restricted to secondary market. Subject to regulations specified by concerned Regulators.
20.	Construction Development projects, including housing, commercial premises, resorts, educational institutions, recreational facilities, city and regional level infrastructure, townships. NB: FDI is not allowed in Real Estate Business.	100%	Automatic	Subject to conditions notified vide Press Note 2 (2005 Series) including : (*a*) Minimum capitalization of US $ 10 million for wholly owned subsidiaries and US$ 5 million for joint venture. The funds would have to be brought within six months of commencement of business of the Company. (*b*) Minimum area to be developed under each project-10 hectares in case of development of serviced housing plots; and built-up area of 50,000 sq. mts. in case of construction development project; and any of the above in case of a combination project. [Note 1: For investment by NRIs, the conditions mentioned in Press Note 2 (2005) are not applicable. Note 2: For investment in SEZs, Hotels & Hospitals, conditions mentioned in Press Note 2 (2005) are not applicable]
21.	Courier services for carrying packages, parcels and other items which do not come within the ambit of the Indian Post Office Act, 1898.	100%	FIPB	Subject to existing laws and exclusion of activity relating to distribution of letters, which is exclusively reserved for the State. (www.indiapost.gov.in)

Sr. No.	*Sector/Activity*	*FDI Cap/ Equity*	*Entry Route*	*Other conditions*
22.	Infrastructure companies in securities markets namely, Stock Exchanges, Depositories and Clearing Corporations	49% (FDI+FII) FDI - 26% FII - 23%	FIPB	FII purchases shall be restricted to secondary market. Subject to regulations specified by concerned Regulators.
23.	Credit Information Companies	49% (FDI+FII) Within this limit, FII investment not to exceed 24%	FIPB	Foreign Investment in CIC will be subject to Credit Information Companies (Regulation) Act, 2005. Subject to regulations specified by concerned Regulators.
24.	Industrial Parks both setting up and in established Industrial Parks	100%	Automatic	Conditions in Press Note 2 (2005) applicable for construction development projects would not apply provided the Industrial Parks meet with the undermentioned conditions— (*i*) it would comprise of a minimum of 10 units and no single unit shall occupy more than 50% of the allocable area; and (*ii*) the minimum percentage of the area to be allocated for industrial activity shall not be less than 66% of the total allocable area.
25.	Insurance	26%	Automatic	Subject to licensing by the Insurance Regulatory & Development Authority. (www.irda.nic.in)
26.	Investing companies in infrastructure/services sector (except telecom sector)	100%	FIPB	Where there is a prescribed cap for foreign investment, only the direct investment will be considered for the prescribed cap and foreign investment in an investing company will not be set off against this

Sr. No.	*Sector/Activity*	*FDI Cap/ Equity*	*Entry Route*	*Other conditions*
				cap provided the foreign direct investment in such investing company does not exceed 49% and the management of the investing company is with the Indian owners.
27.	Non-Banking Finance Companies — (*i*) Merchant banking (*ii*) Underwriting (*iii*) Portfolio Management Services (*iv*) Investment Advisory Services (*v*) Financial Consultancy (*vi*) Stock Broking (*vii*) Asset Management (*viii*) Venture Capital (*ix*) Custodial Services (*x*) Factoring (*xi*) Credit Rating Agencies (*xii*) Leasing & Finance (*xiii*) Housing Finance (*xiv*) Forex Broking (*xv*) Credit card Business (*xvi*) Money changing business (*xvii*) Micro credit (*xviii*) Rural credit	100%	Automatic	Subject to: (*a*) Minimum capitalization norms for fund based NBFCs - US$ 0.5 million to be brought upfront for FDI up to 51%; US$ 5 million to be brought upfront for FDI above 51% and up to 75%; and US$ 50 million out of which US$ 7.5 million to be brought upfront and the balance in 24 months, for FDI beyond 75% and up to 100%. (*b*) Minimum capitalization norms for non-fund based NBFC activities - US$ 0.5 million. (*c*) Foreign investors can set up 100% operating subsidiaries without the condition to disinvest a minimum of 25% of its equity to Indian entities subject to bringing in US$ 50 million without any restriction on number of operating subsidiaries without bringing additional capital. (*d*) Joint venture operating NBFCs that have 75% or less than 75%

Sr. No.	*Sector/Activity*	*FDI Cap/ Equity*	*Entry Route*	*Other conditions*
				foreign investment will also be allowed to set up subsidiaries for undertaking other NBFC activities subject to the subsidiaries also complying with the applicable minimum capital inflow. (*e*) Compliance with the guidelines of the RBI.
28.	Petroleum & Natural Gas sector			
	(*a*) Refining	49% in case of PSUs.	FIPB (in case of PSUs)	Subject to Sectoral policy and no divestment or dilution of domes- tic equity in the existing PSUs.
		100% in case of Private companies	Automatic (in case of private companies)	(www.petroleum.nic.in)
	(*b*) Other than Refining and including market study and formulation; investment/ financing; setting up infrastructure for marketing in Petroleum & Natural Gas sector.	100%	Automatic	Subject to sectoral Regulations issued by Ministry of Petroleum & Natural Gas. (www.petroleum.nic.in)
29.	Print Media —			
	(*a*) Publishing of newspaper and periodicals dealing with news and current affairs	26%	FIPB	Subject to guidelines notified by Ministry of Information & Broadcasting. (www.mib.nic.in)
	(*b*) Publishing of scientific magazines/specialty journals/periodicals	100%	FIPB	Subject to guidelines issued by Ministry of Information & Broadcasting. (www.mib.nic.in)
30.	Telecommunications			
	(*a*) Basic and cellular, Unified Access Services National/International Long Distance, V-Sat, Public Mobile Radio Trunked Services	74% (Including FDI, FII, NRI, FCCBs, ADRs,	Automatic up to 49%. FIPB beyond 49%.	Subject to guidelines notified in the Press Note 3 (2007 Series) dated April 19, 2007.

Sr. No.	*Sector/Activity*	*FDI Cap/ Equity*	*Entry Route*	*Other conditions*
	(PMRTS), Global Mobile Personal Communications Services (GMPCS) and other value added telecom	GDRs, convertible preference shares, and proportionate foreign equity in Indian promoters/ Investing Company)		
	(*b*) ISP with gateways, radio-paging, end-to-end bandwidth.	74%	Automatic up to 49%. FIPB beyond 49%.	Subject to licensing and security requirements notified by the Department of Telecommunications (www.dotindia.com)
	(*c*) (*a*) ISP without gateway,	100%	Automatic up to 49%.	Subject to the condition that such companies shall divest 26% of their equity in favour of Indian public in 5 years, if these companies are listed in other parts of the world. Also subject to licensing and security requirements, where required. (www.dotindia.com)
	(*b*) infrastructure provider providing dark fibre, right of way, duct space, tower (Category I);		FIPB beyond 49%.	
	(*c*) electronic mail and voice mail.			
	(*d*) Manufacture of telecom equipments	100%	Automatic	Subject to sectoral requirements. (www.dotindia.com)
31.	Trading			
	(*a*) Wholesale/cash & carry trading	100%	Automatic	Subject to guidelines for FDI in trading issued by Department of Industrial Policy & Promotion vide Press Note 3 (2006 Series) dated February 10, 2006.
	(*b*) Trading for Exports	100%	Automatic	
	(*c*) Trading of items sourced from small scale sector	100%	FIPB	

Sr. No.	*Sector/Activity*	*FDI Cap/ Equity*	*Entry Route*	*Other conditions*
	(*d*) Test marketing of such items for which a company has approval for manufacture	100%	FIPB	Subject to the condition that the test marketing approval will be for a period of two years and investment in setting up manufacturing facilities commences simultaneously with test marketing.
	(*e*) Single Brand Product retailing	51%	FIPB	
32.	Satellites -Establishment and operation	74%	FIPB	Subject to sectoral guidelines issued by Department of Space/ ISRO. (www.isro.org)
33.	Special Economic Zones and Free Trade Warehousing Zones covering setting up of these Zones and setting up units in the Zones	100%	Automatic	Subject to Special Economic Zones Act, 2005 and the Foreign Trade Policy. (www.sezindia.nic.in)
34.	Drugs & Pharmaceutical including those involving recombinant DNA technology.	100%	Automatic	—

[1][ANNEXURE C

Report by the Indian company receiving amount of consideration for issue of shares as per Foreign Direct Investment Scheme

[To be filed by the company through its Authorised Dealer Category-I bank not later than 30 days from the date of receipt of the amount of consideration with the Regional Office of the RBI under whose jurisdiction the Registered Office of the company making the declaration is situated, called for in terms of para 9(1)(A) of Schedule I to Notification No. FEMA 20/2000-RB, dated May 3, 2000.]

Permanent Account Number (PAN) of the investee company given by the IT Department | | | | | | | | | | | | | | |

No.	*Particulars*	*(In Block Letters)*
1.	Name of the Indian company	
	Address of the Registered Office	

---

1 Inserted by Foreign Exchange Management (Transfer or Issue of Security by a Person Resident Outside India) (Second Amendment) Regulations, 2008 [Notification No. FEMA 179/2008-RB, dated 22-8-2008].

Note: This format conforms to what is provided by Annexure II and Annexure III to AP (DIR Series) Circular No. 44, dated 30-5-2008.

No.	*Particulars*	*(In Block Letters)*	
	Fax		
	Telephone		
	e-mail		
2.	Details of the foreign investor/ collaborator		
	Name		
	Address		
	Country		
3.	Date of receipt of funds		
4.	Amount	In foreign currency	In Indian Rupees
5.	Whether investment is under Automatic Route or Approval Route	Automatic Route/Approval Route	
	If Approval Route, give details (ref. No. of FIPB approval and date)		
6.	Name of the AD through whom the remittance is received		
7.	Address of the AD		

A copy of the FIRC evidencing the receipt of consideration for issue of shares/convertible debentures as above is enclosed.

(Authorised signatory of the investee company) (Authorised signatory of the AD)

(Stamp) (Stamp)

For use of the Reserve Bank only:

Unique Identification Number for the remittance:

Know Your Customer (KYC) Form in respect of the non-resident investor

Registered Name of the Remitter/Investor	
(Name, if the investor is an Individual)	
Registration Number (Unique Identification Number* in case remitter is an Individual)	
Registered Address (Permanent Address if remitter Individual)	
Name of the Remitter's Bank	
Remitter's Bank Account No.	
Period of banking relationship with the remitter	

*Passport No., Social Security No. or any Unique No. certifying the bona fides of the remitter as prevalent in the remitter's country.

We confirm that all the information furnished above is true and accurate as provided by the overseas remitting bank of the non-resident investor.

(Signature of the Authorised Official of the AD bank receiving the remittance)

Date:

Place:

Stamp:]

[1][**ANNEXURE D**

FC-GPR

PART - A

(To be filed by the company through its Authorised Dealer Category-I bank with the Regional Office of the RBI under whose jurisdiction the Registered Office of the company making the declaration is situated as and when fresh investment in the Company is received, along with the documents mentioned in item No. 4 of the undertaking enclosed in this form)

Permanent Account Number (PAN) of the investee company given by the IT Department | | | | | | | | | | | | | | |

Date of issue of shares | | | | | | | | | | | | | | | | | | |

No.	Particulars	(In Block Letters)
1.	Name	
	Address of the Registered Office	
	State	
	Registration No. given by Registrar of Companies	
	Whether existing company or new company (strike off whichever is not applicable)	Existing company/New company

---

1 Annexure D containing Form FC-GPR substituted for 'FC-GPR' by Foreign Exchange Management (Transfer or Issue of Security by a Person Resident Outside India) (Second Amendment) Regulations, 2008 [Notification No. FEMA 179/2008-RB, dated 22-8-2008].

Note: Earlier Form FC-GPR was substituted by the Foreign Exchange Management (Transfer or Issue of Security by a Person Resident Outside India) (Second Amendment) Regulations, 2003, w.e.f. 18-6-2003 and thereafter it was revised in terms of AP (DIR Series) Circular No. 40, dated 20-4-2007. The present format as per Annexure D conforms to what is provided by Annexure I to AP (DIR Series) Circular No. 44, dated 30-5-2008.

No.	Particulars	(In Block Letters)
	If existing company, give registration number allotted by RBI for FDI, if any	
	Telephone	
	Fax	
	e-mail	
2.	Description of the main business activity NIC Code	
	Location of the project and NIC code for the district where the project is located	
	Percentage of FDI allowed as per FDI policy	
	State whether FDI is allowed under Automatic Route or Approval Route (strike out whichever is not applicable)	Automatic Route/Approval Route
3.	Details of the foreign investor/collaborator*	
	Name Address Country Constitution/Nature of the investing Entity [Specify whether 1. Individual 2. Company 3. FII 4. FVCI 5. Foreign Trust 6. Private Equity Fund 7. Pension/Provident Fund 8. Sovereign Wealth Funds4 9. Partnership/Proprietorship firm 10. Financial Institution 11. NRIs/PIOs 12. others (please specify)] Date of incorporation	

***If there are more than one foreign investor/collaborator, separate Annex may be included for items 3 and 4.**

4.	Particulars of Shares/Convertible Debentures Issued		
	(*a*) Nature and date of issue		
	Nature of issue	*Date of issue*	*Number of shares/convertible debentures*
1.	IPO/FPO		
2.	Preferential allotment/private placement		
3.	Rights		
4.	Bonus		
5.	Conversion of ECB		
6.	Conversion of royalty (including lump sum payments)		
7.	Conversion against import of capital goods by units in SEZ		
8.	ESOPs		
9.	Share Swap		
10.	Others (please specify)		
	Total		

(*b*) Type of security issued

No.	*Nature of security*	*Number*	*Maturity*	*Face value*	*Premium*	*Issue Price per share*	*Amount of inflow**
1.	Equity						
2.	Compulsorily Convertible Debentures						
3.	Compulsorily Convertible Preference shares						
4.	Others (please specify)						
	Total						

(*i*) In case the issue price is greater than the face value please give break up of the premium received.

(*ii*) *In case the issue is against conversion of ECB or royalty or lump sum payment or against import of capital goods by units in SEZ, a Chartered Accountant's Certificate certifying the amount of the outstanding on the date of conversion.

	(*c*) Break up of premium	Amount
	Control Premium	
	Non-competition fee	
	Others@	
	Total	
	@please specify the nature	
	(*d*) Total inflow (in Rupees) on account of issue of shares to non-residents (including premium, if any) vide	
	(*i*) Remittance through AD: (*ii*) Debit to NRE/FCNR A/c with Bank .... (*iii*) Others (please specify) Date of reporting of (*i*) and (*ii*) above to RBI under Para 9(1) A(*i*) of Notification No. FEMA 20/2000-RB, dated May 3, 2000, as amended from time to time.	
	(*e*) Disclosure of fair value of shares issued**	
	We are a listed company and the market value of a share as on date of the issue is*	
	We are an un-listed company and the fair value of a share is*	

**before issue of shares *(Please indicate as applicable)

5.	Post issue pattern of shareholding						
		Equity			*Compulsorily convertible Preference Shares/Debentures*		
	Investor category (*a*) Non-Resident	*No. of shares*	*Amount (Face Value)* ₹	%	*No. of shares*	*Amount (Face Value)* ₹	%
	1. Individuals						
	2. Companies						
	3. FIIs						
	4. FVCIs						
	5. Foreign Trusts						
	6. Private Equity Funds						

	7. Pension/Provident Funds						
	8. Sovereign Wealth Funds						
	9. Partnership/ Proprietorship firms						
	10. Financial Institutions						
	11. NRIs/PIOs						
	12. Others (please specify)						
	Sub-total						
	(*b*) Resident						
	Total						

Declaration to be filed by the authorised representative of the Indian company: (Delete whichever is not applicable and authenticate).

We hereby declare that:

1. We comply with the procedure for issue of shares as laid down under the FDI scheme as indicated in Notification No. FEMA 20/2000-RB, dated 3rd May, 2000 as amended from time to time.

2. The investment is within the sectoral cap/statutory ceiling permissible under the Automatic Route of RBI and we fulfil all the conditions laid down for investments under the Automatic Route namely (strike off whichever is not applicable) —

(*a*) Foreign entity/entities—(other than individuals), to whom we have issued shares have existing joint venture or technology transfer or trademark agreement in India in the same field and Conditions stipulated in Press Note 1 of 2005 Series dated January 12, 2005 have been complied with.

Or

(*b*) Foreign entity/entities—(other than individuals), to whom we have issued shares do not have any existing joint venture or technology transfer or trademark agreement in India in the same field.

(*c*) We are not an SSI unit.

Or

We are a SSI unit and the investment limit of 24 per cent of paid-up capital has been observed/requisite approvals have been obtained.

(*d*) Shares issued on rights basis to non-residents are in conformity with Regulation 6 of the RBI Notification No. FEMA 20/2000-RB, dated 3rd May, 2000, as amended from time to time.

Or

(*e*) Shares issued are bonus shares.

Or

(*f*) Shares have been issued under a scheme of merger and amalgamation of two or more Indian companies or reconstruction by way of de-merger or otherwise of an Indian company, duly approved by a Court in India.

Or

(*g*) Shares are issued under ESOP and the conditions regarding this issue have been satisfied.

3. Shares have been issued in terms of SIA/FIPB approval No. .... dated ....

4. We enclose the following documents in compliance with Paragraph 9(1)(B) of Schedule 1 to Notification No. FEMA 20/2000-RB, dated 3rd May, 2000:

(*i*) A certificate from our Company Secretary certifying that—

(*a*) all the requirements of the Companies Act, 1956 have been complied with;

(*b*) terms and conditions of the Government approval, if any, have been complied with;

(*c*) the company is eligible to issue shares under these Regulations; and

(*d*) the company has all original certificates issued by authorised dealers in India evidencing receipt of amount of consideration in accordance with paragraph 8 of Schedule 1 to Notification No. FEMA 20/2000-RB, dated 3rd May, 2000.

(*ii*) A certificate from Statutory Auditors/Chartered Accountant indicating the manner of arriving at the price of the shares issued to the persons resident outside India.

5. Unique Identification Number given for all the remittances received as consideration for issue of shares/convertible debentures (details as above), by RBI:

R														

(Signature of the Applicant)* : ....

(Name in Block Letters) : ....

(Designation of the signatory) : ....

Place:

Date:

(*To be signed by Managing Director/Director/Secretary of the Company)

Certificate to be filed by the Company Secretary of the Indian Company Accepting the Investment:

(As per Para 9(1)(B)(i) of Schedule 1 to Notification No. FEMA 20/2000-RB, dated 3rd May, 2000)

In respect of the above-mentioned details, we certify the following:

1. All the requirements of the Companies Act, 1956 have been complied with.
2. Terms and conditions of the Government approval, if any, have been complied with.
3. The company is eligible to issue shares under these Regulations.
4. The company has all original certificates issued by AD Category-I banks in India, evidencing receipt of amount of consideration in accordance with paragraph 8 of Schedule 1 to Notification No. FEMA 20/2000-RB, dated May 3, 2000.

(Name & Signature of the Company Secretary) (Seal)

For use of the Reserve Bank only:

Unique Identification Number for the FC-GPR : G															

FC-GPR

PART - B

(*i*) This part of the return to be submitted to the Director, Balance of Payment Statistical Division, Department of Statistics & Information Management, Reserve Bank of India, C8, 3rd Floor, Bandra-Kurla Complex, Bandra (E), Mumbai - 400051; Tel: 2657 1265, 2657 2513, Fax: 26570848; email:surveyfla@rbi.org.in

(*ii*) This is an annual return to be submitted by 31st of July every year by all companies, pertaining to all investments by way of direct/portfolio investments/re-invested earnings/ others in the Indian company made during the previous years (i.e., the information in Part B submitted by July 31, 2007 will pertain to all the investments made in the previous years up to March 31, 2007). The details of the investments to be reported would include all foreign investments made into the company which is outstanding as on the balance sheet date. The details of overseas investments in the company both under Direct/portfolio investment may be separately indicated. Please use end-March Market prices/exchange rates for compiling the relevant information.

Permanent Account Number (PAN) of the investee company given by the IT Department														

No.	Particulars	(In Block Letters)
1.	Name Address State	
	Registration No. given by the Registrar of Companies	
2.	Name of the Contact Person : Tel. Fax :	Designation : E-mail :
3.	Account closing date :	
4.	Details of changes if any, with regard to information furnished earlier (Change in name of company/Change of location, activities, etc.)	
5.	Whether listed company or unlisted company	Listed/unlisted
5.1	If listed, (i) Market value per share as at end-March (ii) Net Asset Value per share as on date of latest Audited Balance Sheet	
5.2	If unlisted, Net Asset Value per share as on date of latest Audited Balance Sheet	
6.	Foreign Direct Investment (FDI)	

Amount in Lakhs of Rupees

		*Foreign Liabilities In India**		*Foreign Assets Outside India†*	
		Outstanding at end-March of Previous Year	*Outstanding at end-March of Current Year*	*Outstanding at end-March of Previous Year*	*Outstanding at end-March of Current Year*
	6.0 Equity Capital				
	6.1 Other Capital‡				

No.	*Particulars*		(*In Block Letters*)		
	6.2 Disinvestment during the year				
	6.3 Retained earnings during the year**				
7.	Portfolio and Other Investment				
	[Please furnish here the outstanding investments other than those mentioned under FDI above]				
	7.0 Equity Securities				
	7.1 Debt Securities				
	7.1-1 Bonds and Notes				
	7.1-2 Money Market Instruments				
	7.2 Disinvestment during the year				
8.	Financial Derivatives (notional value)				
9.	Other Investment				
	9.1 Trade Credit				
	9.1-1 Short-Term				
	9.1-2 Long-Term				
	9.2 Loans*	Please see the note below			
	9.3 Others				
	9.3-1 Short-Term				
	9.3-2 Long-Term				

<table>
<tr><td rowspan="2">10</td><td colspan="7">Shareholding pattern as at end-March</td></tr>
<tr><td rowspan="2">Investor category Nature of investing entity</td><td colspan="3">Equity</td><td colspan="3">Compulsorily convertible Preference Shares/Debentures</td></tr>
<tr><td></td><td>No. of shares</td><td>Amount (Face Value) ₹</td><td>%</td><td>No. of shares</td><td>Amount (Face Value) ₹</td><td>%</td></tr>
<tr><td></td><td>(a) Non-Resident</td><td></td><td></td><td></td><td></td><td></td><td></td></tr>
<tr><td></td><td>1. Individuals</td><td></td><td></td><td></td><td></td><td></td><td></td></tr>
<tr><td></td><td>2. Companies</td><td></td><td></td><td></td><td></td><td></td><td></td></tr>
<tr><td></td><td>3. FIIs</td><td></td><td></td><td></td><td></td><td></td><td></td></tr>
<tr><td></td><td>4. FVCIs</td><td></td><td></td><td></td><td></td><td></td><td></td></tr>
<tr><td></td><td>5. Foreign Trusts</td><td></td><td></td><td></td><td></td><td></td><td></td></tr>
<tr><td></td><td>6. Private Equity Funds</td><td></td><td></td><td></td><td></td><td></td><td></td></tr>
<tr><td></td><td>7. Pension/Provident Funds</td><td></td><td></td><td></td><td></td><td></td><td></td></tr>
<tr><td></td><td>8. Sovereign Wealth Funds</td><td></td><td></td><td></td><td></td><td></td><td></td></tr>
<tr><td></td><td>9. Partnership/Proprietor-ship firms</td><td></td><td></td><td></td><td></td><td></td><td></td></tr>
<tr><td></td><td>10. Financial Institutions</td><td></td><td></td><td></td><td></td><td></td><td></td></tr>
<tr><td></td><td>11. NRIs/PIOs</td><td></td><td></td><td></td><td></td><td></td><td></td></tr>
<tr><td></td><td>12. Others (please specify)</td><td></td><td></td><td></td><td></td><td></td><td></td></tr>
<tr><td></td><td>Sub-Total</td><td></td><td></td><td></td><td></td><td></td><td></td></tr>
<tr><td></td><td>(b) Resident</td><td></td><td></td><td></td><td></td><td></td><td></td></tr>
<tr><td></td><td>Total</td><td></td><td></td><td></td><td></td><td></td><td></td></tr>
<tr><td>11.</td><td>Persons employed during the financial year ending March 31®</td><td colspan="3"></td><td colspan="3"></td></tr>
<tr><td></td><td>Directly</td><td colspan="3"></td><td colspan="3"></td></tr>
<tr><td></td><td>Indirectly</td><td colspan="3"></td><td colspan="3"></td></tr>
<tr><td></td><td>Total</td><td colspan="3"></td><td colspan="3"></td></tr>
</table>

Signature of the authorised Official : ....

Name (in block letters) : ....

Designation : ....

Place : Date:

[1][Annexure E]

(*Omitted*)

[2][FORM DR

[Refer to paragraph 4(2) of Schedule I]

Return to be filed by an Indian Company who has arranged issue of GDR/ADR

Instructions:

The form should be completed and submitted to the Reserve Bank of India, Foreign Investment Division, Central Office, Mumbai.

1. Name of the company :
2. Address of registered office :

---

1 Annexure E omitted by Foreign Exchange Management (Transfer or Issue of Security by a Person Resident Outside India) (Second Amendment) Regulations, 2008 [Notification No. FEMA 179/2008-RB, dated 22-8-2008]. Before omission 'Annexure E' read as under:

Annexure E

(*See paragraph 6 of Schedule I*)

List of 22 industries in respect of which dividend balancing is applicable

1. Manufacture of food and food products
2. Manufacture of dairy products
3. Grain mill products
4. Manufacture of bakery products
5. Manufacture and refining of sugar (vacuum pan sugar factories)
6. Production of common salt
7. Manufacture of Hydrogenated oil (Vanaspati)
8. Tea processing
9. Coffee
10. Manufacture of beverages, tobacco and tobacco products
11. Distilling, rectifying and blending of spirits, wine industries, malt liquors and malt, production of country liquors and toddy
12. Soft drinks and carbonated water industry
13. Manufacture of cigar, cigarettes, cheroot and cigarette tobacco
14. Manufacture of wood and wood products, furniture and fixtures
15. Manufacture of leather and fur/leather products
16. Tanning, curing, finishing, embossing and japanning of leather
17. Manufacture of footwear (excluding repair) except vulcanised for moulded rubber or plastic footwear
18. Manufacture of footwear made primarily of vulcanised or moulded products
19. Prophylactics (rubber contraceptive)
20. Motor cars
21. Entertainment electronics (VCRs, Colour TVs, CD Players, Tape Recorders)
22. White goods (Domestic Refrigerators, Domestic Dishwashing Machines, Programmable Domestic Washing Machines, Microwave Ovens, Air conditioners)."

2 Form DR substituted for Annexure C by Foreign Exchange Management (Transfer or Issue of Security by a Person Resident Outside India) (Second Amendment) Regulations, 2008 [Notification No. FEMA 179/2008-RB, dated 22-8-2008]

Note: Earlier Annexure C was substituted by the Foreign Exchange Management (Transfer or Issue of Security by a Person Resident Outside India) (Second Amendment) Regulations, 2003, w.e.f. 18-6-2003.

3. Address for correspondence :
4. Existing business (please give the NIC Code of the activity in which the company is predominantly engaged) :
5. Details of the purposes for which GDRs/ADRs have been raised :

   If funds are deployed for overseas investment, details thereof.
6. Name and address of the depository abroad :
7. Name and address of the lead/manager investment/merchant banker :
8. Name and addresses of the sub-managers to the issue :
9. Name and address of the Indian custodians :
10. Details of FIPB approval (please quote the relevant NIC Code if the GDRs are being issued under the automatic route) :
11. Whether any overall sectoral cap for foreign investment is applicable. If yes, please give details. :
12. Details of the equity capital : Before issue After issue

    (*a*) Authorised capital

    (*b*) Issued and paid-up capital

    (*i*) Held by persons resident in India

    (*ii*) Held by foreign investors other than FIIs/NRIs/PIOs/OCBs (A list of foreign investors holding more than 10 per cent of the paid-up capital and number of shares held by each of them should be furnished)

    (*iii*) Held by NRIs/PIOs/OCBs

    (*iv*) Held by FIIs.

    Total equity held by non-residents

    (*c*) Percentage of equity held by non-residents to total paid-up capital
13. Whether issue was on private placement basis. If yes, please give details of the investors and ADRs/GDRs issued to each of them :
14. Number of GDRs/ADRs issued :
15. Ratio of GDRs/ADRs to underlying shares :

16. Issue related expenses :
   (*a*) Fee paid/payable to merchant bankers/lead manager
      (*i*) Amount (in US $, etc.)
      (*ii*) Amount as percentage to the total issue
   (*b*) Other expenses
17. Whether funds are kept abroad; if yes, name and address of the bank :
18. Details of the listing arrangement
    Name of stock exchange
    Date of commencement of trading
19. The date on which ADRs/GDRs issue was launched :
20. Amount raised (in US $) :
21. Amount repatriated (in US $) :

Certified that all the conditions laid down by Government of India and Reserve Bank of India have been complied with.

Sd/-
Chartered Accountant

Sd/-
Authorised Signatory of the Company]

[1][Form DR-Quarterly]

[Refer to paragraph 4(3) of Schedule I]

Quarterly Return

(To be submitted to the Reserve Bank of India,
Foreign Investment Division, Central Office, Mumbai)

1. Name of company :
2. Address :
3. GDR/ADR issue launched on :
4. Total No. GDRs/ADRs issued :
5. Total amount raised :
6. Total interest earned till end of quarter :
7. Issue Expenses and commissions, etc. :
8. Amount repatriated :

---

1 Form DR-Quarterly substituted for Annexure D by Foreign Exchange Management (Transfer or Issue of Security by a Person Resident Outside India) (Second Amendment) Regulations, 2008 [Notification No. FEMA 179/2008-RB, dated 22-8-2008].

Note: Earlier Annexure D was substituted by the Foreign Exchange Management (Transfer or Issue of Security by a Person Resident Outside India) (Second Amendment) Regulations, 2003, w.e.f. 18-6-2003.

9. Balance kept abroad details :
   (*i*) Banks deposits
   (*ii*) Treasury bills
   (*iii*) Others (please specify)
10. No. of GDRs still outstanding
11. Company's share price at the end of the quarter :
12. GDR price quoted on overseas stock exchange as at the end of the quarter

Certified that funds raised through ADRs/GDRs have not been invested in stock market or real estate.

Sd/-	Sd/-
Chartered Accountant	Authorised Signatory of the Company]

Schedule 2

[*See* regulation 5(2)]

Purchase/sale of shares and/or convertible debentures of an Indian company by a registered Foreign Institutional Investor under Portfolio Investment Scheme

1. Purchase/sale of shares and/or convertible debentures.—[1][(1) A registered Foreign Institutional Investor (FII) may purchase the shares and convertible debentures of an Indian company under Portfolio Investment Scheme.

(2) The purchase of shares/convertible debentures under sub-paragraph (1) shall be made through registered broker on recognized stock exchange in India.]

(3) The amount of consideration for purchase of shares/debentures shall be paid out of inward remittance from abroad through normal banking channels or out of funds held in an account maintained with the designated branch of an authorised dealer in India, in accordance with these regulations.

(4) The total holding by each FII/SEBI approved sub-account of FII shall not exceed 10% (ten per cent) of the total paid-up equity capital or 10% (ten per cent) of the paid-up value of each series of convertible debentures issued by an

---

1 Substituted by the Foreign Exchange Management (Transfer or Issue of Security by a Person Resident Outside India) (First Amendment) Regulations, 2004, w.e.f. 1-1-2004 [FEMA 108/2004-RB] for the following:

"(1) A registered Foreign Institutional Investor (FII) may, through the Securities and Exchange Board of India, apply to the Reserve Bank for permission to purchase the shares and convertible debentures of an Indian company under Portfolio Investment Scheme. The permission may be granted by Reserve Bank subject to such terms and conditions as may be considered necessary.

(2) The registered FII permitted by the Reserve Bank under sub-paragraph (1), shall purchase the shares/convertible debentures of an Indian company through registered brokers on recognised stock exchanges in India."

Indian company and the total holdings of all FIIs/sub-accounts of FIIs put together shall not exceed 24 per cent of paid-up equity capital or paid up value of each series of convertible debentures:

[1][Provided that the limit of 24 per cent referred to in this paragraph may be increased upto the sectoral cap/statutory ceiling, as applicable, by the Indian company concerned by passing a resolution by its Board of Directors followed by passing of a special resolution to that effect by its General Body.]

Explanation.—For arriving at the ceiling on holdings of FIIs, shares/ convertible debentures acquired both through primary as well as secondary market will be included. However, the ceiling will not include investment made by FII through offshore Funds, Global Depository receipts and Euro-Convertible Bonds.

[2][(5) A registered FII is permitted to purchase shares/convertible debentures of an Indian company through offer/private placement, subject to the ceiling specified in sub-paragraph (4) of this paragraph and the Indian company is permitted to issue such shares:

Provided that—

(*i*) in case of public offer, the price of the shares to be issued is not less than the price at which shares are issued to residents, and

(*ii*) in case of issue by private placement, the price is not less than the price arrived in terms of SEBI guidelines or guidelines issued by erstwhile Controller of Capital Issues, as applicable.]

[3][(6) A registered FII may undertake short selling as well as lending and borrowing of securities subject to such conditions as may be stipulated by the Reserve Bank of India and the SEBI from time to time.]

---

1 Substituted by the Foreign Exchange Management (Transfer or Issue of Security by a Person Resident Outside India) (Amendment) Regulations, 2001, [FEMA 45/2001-RB] w.e.f. 20-9-2001 for the following:

"Provided that the limit of 24 per cent referred to in this paragraph may be increased to [1][49 per cent] by the Indian company concerned by passing a resolution by its Board of Directors followed by passing of a special resolution to that effect by its General Body."

1 Inserted by the Foreign Exchange Management (Transfer or Issue of Security by a Person Resident Outside India) (Amendment) Regulations, 2001, w.e.f. 2-3-2001.

2 Substituted by the Foreign Exchange Management (Transfer or Issue of Security by a Person Resident Outside India) (Second Amendment) Regulations, 2003, w.e.f. 18-6-2003 for the following:

"(5) A registered FII may also be permitted to purchase shares/convertible debentures of an Indian company through private placement/arrangement, subject to the ceilings specified in sub-paragraph (4) of this paragraph."

3 Inserted *vide* Foreign Exchange Management (Transfer or Issue of Security by a Person Resident Outside India) (Amendment) Regulations, 2008, w.r.e.f. 31-12-2007 [Notification No. GSR 575(E) [FEMA 175/2008-RB], dated 22-2-2008].

2. Maintenance of account by a registered FII for routing transactions of purchase and sale of shares/convertible debentures.—[1][A registered Foreign Institutional Investor may open a Foreign Currency Account and/or a Special Non-Resident Rupee Account with a designated branch of an authorized dealer for routing the receipt and payment for transaction relating to purchase and sale of shares/convertible debentures under this Scheme, subject to the following conditions:

(*i*) The Account shall be funded by inward remittance through normal banking channels or by credit of sale proceeds (net of taxes) of the shares/convertible debentures sold on stock exchange.

(*ii*) The funds in the account shall be utilized for purchase of shares convertible debentures in accordance with the provisions of paragraph 1 of this Scheme or for remittance outside India.

(*iii*) The funds from Foreign Currency Account of the registered FII may be transferred to Special Non-Resident Rupee account of the same FII and vice versa.]

3. Remittance of sale proceeds of shares/convertible debentures.—The designated branch of an authorised dealer may allow remittance of net sale proceeds (after payment of taxes) or credit the net amount of sale proceeds of shares/convertible debentures to the foreign currency account or a Non-resident Rupee Account of the registered Foreign Institutional Investor concerned.

4. Investment by certain other investors.—[2][A domestic asset management company or portfolio manager, who is registered with SEBI as a foreign

---

1 Substituted by the Foreign Exchange Management (Transfer or Issue of Security by a Person Resident Outside India) (First Amendment) Regulations, 2004, w.e.f. 1-1-2004 [FEMA 108/2004-RB] for the following:

"The Reserve Bank may, on application, permit a registered Foreign Institutional Investor to open a Foreign Currency Account and/or a Non-resident Rupee Account with a designated branch of an authorised dealer for routing the receipt of and payment for transactions relating to purchase and sale of shares/convertible debentures under this Scheme, subject to the following conditions:—

(*i*) The account shall be funded by inward remittance through normal banking channels or by credit of sale proceeds (net of taxes) of the shares/convertible debentures sold on stock exchange.

(*ii*) The funds in the account shall be utilised for purchase of shares/ convertible debentures in accordance with the provisions of paragraph 1 of this Scheme or for remittance outside India.

(*iii*) The funds from Foreign Currency Account of the registered FII may be transferred to Non-resident Rupee Account of the same FII and *vice versa*."

2 Substituted by the Foreign Exchange Management (Transfer or Issue of Security by a Person Resident Outside India) (First Amendment) Regulations, 2004, w.e.f. 1-1-2004 [FEMA 108/2004-RB] for the following:

"(1) Reserve Bank may, subject to such terms and conditions as it may consider necessary permit a domestic asset management company or portfolio manager who is registered with SEBI as a foreign institutional investor for managing the funds of a sub-account, to make investment under the Scheme on behalf of:—

(*i*) a person resident outside India who is a citizen of a foreign state, or →→

institutional investor for managing the fund of a sub-account may make investment under the Scheme on behalf of—

(*i*) a person resident outside India who is a citizen of a foreign state, or

(*ii*) a body corporate registered outside India:

Provided such investment is made out of funds raised or collected or brought from outside through normal banking channel.]

[1][* * *]

[2][(2)] Investments permitted to be made under sub-paragraph (1) shall not exceed 5% (five per cent) of the total paid-up equity capital or 5% (five per cent) of the paid-up value of each series of convertible debentures issued by an Indian company, and shall also not exceed the overall ceiling specified in sub-paragraph (4) of paragraph 1 of this Schedule.

Schedule 3

[*See* regulation 5(3)(*i*)]

Purchase/sale of shares and/or convertible debentures by an NRI [3][* * *] on a Stock Exchange in India on repatriation and/or non-repatriation basis under Portfolio Investment Scheme

1. A Non-resident Indian (NRI) [4][* * *] may purchase/sell shares and/or convertible debentures of an Indian company, through a registered broker on a recognised stock exchange, subject to the following conditions:—

[5][(*i*) NRIs may purchase and sell shares/convertible debentures under the Portfolio Investment Scheme through a branch designated by an

---

→→ (*ii*) a body corporate registered outside India:

Provided such investment is made out of funds raised or collected or brought from outside India through normal banking channel."

1 Omitted by the Foreign Exchange Management (Transfer or Issue of Security by a Person Resident Outside India) (First Amendment) Regulations, 2004, w.e.f. 1-1-2004 [FEMA 108/2004-RB]. Prior to omission it read as under:

"(2) The application to Reserve Bank for permission under sub-paragraph (1) may be made through SEBI."

2 Renumbered for "(3)", *ibid.*

3 The words "/OCB" omitted by Foreign Exchange Management (Transfer or Issue of Security by a person resident outside India) Regulations, 2001, w.e.f. 29-11-2001.

4 The words "or an Overseas Corporate Body (OCB)" omitted by Foreign Exchange Management (Transfer or Issue of Security by a person resident outside India) Regulations, 2002, w.r.e.f. 29-11-2001.

5 Substituted by the Foreign Exchange Management (Transfer or Issue of Security by a Person Resident Outside India) (Second Amendment) Regulations, 2003, w.e.f. 18-6-2003 for the following:

"(*i*) the NRI 1[* * *] designates a branch of an authorised dealer for routing his 2[* * *] transactions relating to purchase and sale of shares/convertible debentures under this Scheme, and routes all such transactions only through the branch so designated;"

1 The words "/OCB" omitted by Foreign Exchange Management (Transfer or Issue of Security by a person resident outside India) Regulations, 2002, w.r.e.f. 29-11-2001.

2 The words "/its" omitted by Foreign Exchange Management (Transfer or Issue of Security by a person resident outside India) Regulations, 2002, w.r.e.f. 29-11-2001.

authorised dealer for the purpose and duly approved by the Reserve Bank of India;]

(*ii*) the paid-up value of shares of an Indian company, purchased by each NRI [1][* * *] both on repatriation and on non-repatriation basis, does not exceed 5 per cent of the paid-up value of shares issued by the company concerned;

(*iii*) the paid-up value of each series of convertible debentures purchased by each NRI [2][* * *] both on repatriation and non-repatriation basis does not exceed 5 per cent of the paid-up value of each series of convertible debentures issued by the company concerned;

(*iv*) the aggregate paid-up value of shares of any company purchased by all NRIs [3][* * *] does not exceed 10 per cent of the paid-up capital of the company and in the case of purchase of convertible debentures the aggregate paid-up value of each series of debentures purchased by all NRIs [4][* * *] does not exceed 10 per cent of the paid-up value of each series of convertible debentures:

Provided that the aggregate ceiling of 10 per cent referred to in this clause may be raised to 24 per cent if a special resolution to that effect is passed by the General Body of the Indian company concerned;

(*v*) the NRI [5][* * *] investor takes delivery of the shares purchased and gives delivery of shares sold;

(*vi*) payment for purchase of shares and/or debentures is made by inward remittance in foreign exchange through normal banking channels or out of funds held in NRE/FCNR account maintained in India if the shares are purchased on repatriation basis and by inward remittance or out of funds held in NRE/FCNR/NRO/NRNR/NRSR account of the NRI [6][* * *] concerned maintained in India where the shares/debentures are purchased on non-repatriation basis;

[7][(*vii*) * * *]

---

1 The words "or OCB" omitted by Foreign Exchange Management (Transfer or Issue of Security by a person resident outside India) Regulations, 2002, w.r.e.f. 29-11-2001.

2 *Ibid.*

3 The words "and OCBs" omitted by Foreign Exchange Management (Transfer or Issue of Security by a person resident outside India) Regulations, 2002, w.r.e.f. 29-11-2001.

4 *Ibid.*

5 The words "or OCB" omitted by Foreign Exchange Management (Transfer or Issue of Security by a person resident outside India) Regulations, 2002, w.r.e.f. 29-11-2001.

6 The words "/OCB" omitted by Foreign Exchange Management (Transfer or Issue of Security by a person resident outside India) Regulations, 2002, w.r.e.f. 29-11-2001.

7 Omitted by Foreign Exchange Management (Transfer or Issue of Security by a person resident outside India) Regulations, 2002, w.r.e.f. 29-11-2001. Prior to omission, it read as under:

"(*vii*) the Overseas Corporate Body (OCB) informs the designated branch of the authorised dealer immediately on the holding/interest of NRIs in the OCB becoming less than 60 per cent."

2. Report to Reserve Bank.—[1][The link office of the designated branch of an authorised dealer referred to in paragraph 1 shall furnish to the Chief General Manager, RBI, ECD, Central Office, Mumbai, a report on daily basis on PIS transactions undertaken by it, such report to be furnished on line or on floppy or in hard copy in a format supplied by Reserve Bank.]

[2][**3. Remittance/credit of sale/maturity proceeds of shares and/or debentures.**—The net sale/maturity proceeds (after payment of taxes) of shares and/or debentures of an Indian company purchased by NRI [3][* * *] under this scheme, may be allowed by the designated branch of an authorised dealer referred to in paragraph 1,—

(*a*) to be credited to NRO account of the NRI [4][* * *] investor where the payment for purchase of shares and/or debentures sold was made out of funds held in NRO account or where the shares and/or debentures were purchased on non-repatriation basis, or

(*b*) at the NRI [5][* * *] investor's option, to be remitted abroad or credited to his/its NRE/FCNR/NRO account of the NRI, where shares and/or debentures were purchased on repatriation basis.]

---

1 Substituted by Foreign Exchange Management (Transfer or Issue of Security by a person resident outside India) (Amendment) Regulations, 2002, w.r.e.f. 29-11-2001 for the following:

"The link office of the designated branch of an authorised dealer referred to in paragraph 1, shall furnish to the Chief General Manager, Reserve Bank of India (ECD), Central Office, Mumbai a report on daily basis giving the following details—

(*a*) Name of the Non-resident Indian, or OCB.

(*b*) Company-wise number of shares and/or debentures and paid-up value thereof, purchased and/or sold by each NRI/OCB."

2 Substituted by the Foreign Exchange Management (Transfer or Issue of Security by a Person Resident Outside India) (Second Amendment) Regulations, 2003, w.e.f. 18-6-2003 for the following:

"3. *Remittance/credit of sale/maturity proceeds of shares and/or debentures.*—The net sale/maturity proceeds (after payment of taxes) of shares and/or debentures of an Indian company purchased by NRI or OCB under this Scheme, may be allowed by the designated branch of an authorised dealer referred to in paragraph 1,—

(*a*) to be credited to NRSR account of the NRI or OCB investor where the payment for purchase of shares and/or debentures sold was made out of funds held in NRSR account, or

(*b*) at the NRI or OCB investor's option, to be credited to his/its NRO or NRSR account, where the shares and/or debentures were purchased on non-repatriation basis, or

(*c*) at the NRI or OCB investor's option, to be remitted abroad or credited to his/its NRE/FCNR/NRO/NRSR account, where shares and/or debentures were purchased on repatriation basis."

3 The words "or OCB" omitted by Foreign Exchange Management [Withdrawal of General Permission to Overseas Corporate Bodies (OCBs)] Regulations, 2003, w.e.f. 23-10-2003.

4 The word "or OCB" omitted by Foreign Exchange Management [Withdrawal of General Permission to Overseas Corporate Bodies (OCBs)] Regulations, 2003, w.e.f. 23-10-2003.

5 The words "or OCB" omitted by Foreign Exchange Management [Withdrawal of General Permission to Overseas Corporate Bodies (OCBs)] Regulations, 2003, w.e.f. 23-10-2003.

Schedule 4

[*See* regulation 5(3)(*ii*)]

Purchase and sale of shares/convertible debentures by a Non-resident Indian (NRI) [1][* * *] on non-repatriation basis

1. Prohibition on purchase of shares/convertible debentures of certain companies.—No purchase of shares or convertible debentures of an Indian company shall be made under this Scheme if the company concerned is a Chit Fund or a Nidhi company or is engaged in agricultural/plantation activities or real estate business or construction of farm houses or dealing in Transfer of Development Rights.

Explanation.—For the purpose of this paragraph, real estate business shall not include development of township, construction of residential/commercial premises, roads, bridges, etc.

2. Permission to purchase and/or sell shares/convertible debentures of an Indian company.—Subject to paragraph 1, a Non-resident Indian [2][* * *] may, without any limit, purchase on non-repatriation basis, shares or convertible debentures of an Indian company issued whether by public issue or private placement or right issue:

[3][Provided that the person to whom the shares are being transferred, shall obtain prior permission of the Central Government to acquire the shares if he has, as on January 12, 2005, an existing joint venture or technology transfer/trademark agreement in the same field as that of the company of which the shares or convertible debentures to be acquired by him.

---

1 The words "or an Overseas Corporate Body (OCB)" omitted by Foreign Exchange Management [Withdrawal of General Permission to Overseas Corporate Bodies (OCBs)] Regulations, 2003, w.e.f. 23-10-2003.

2 The words "or an Overseas Corporate Body" omitted by Foreign Exchange Management [Withdrawal of General Permission to Overseas Corporate Bodies (OCBs)] Regulations, 2003, w.e.f. 23-10-2003.

3 Substituted by Foreign Exchange Management (Transfer or Issue of Security by a Person Resident Outside India) (Second Amendment) Regulations, 2008 [Notification No. FEMA 179/2008-RB, dated 22-8-2008] for the following:

*[Provided that the person to whom the shares are being transferred, has obtained prior permission of Central Government to acquire the shares if he has previous venture or tie up in India through investment in shares or debentures or a technical collaboration or a trade mark agreement or investment by whatever name called in the same field or allied field in which the Indian company whose shares are being transferred is engaged:

Provided further that this restriction shall not apply to the transfer of shares to International Financial Institutions such as Asian Development Bank ('ADB'), International Finance Corporation ('IFC'), Commonwealth Development Corporation ('CDC'), Deutsche Entwicklungs Gescelscchaft ('DEG') and transfer of shares of an Indian company engaged in information technology sector.]

* Earlier these Provisos were inserted by Foreign Exchange Management (Transfer or Issue of Security by a Person Resident Outside India) (Second Amendment) Regulations, 2003, w.e.f. 18-6-2003.

Provided further that no prior permission of Central Government shall be required for:—

(*a*) transfer of shares to multinational financial institutions such as Asian Development Bank (ADB), International Finance Corporation (IFC), Commonwealth Development Corporation (CDC), Deutsche Entwicklungs Gescelscchaft (DEG).

(*b*) transfer of shares of an Indian company engaged in Information Technology sector or in the mining sector, if the existing joint venture or technology transfer/trademark agreement of the person to whom the shares are to be transferred are also in the Information Technology sector or in the mining sector for same area/mineral.

(*c*) investments to be made by Venture Capital Funds registered with SEBI; investments by multinational financial institutions or where in the existing joint-venture investment by either of the parties is less than 3 per cent; or where the existing joint venture/collaboration is defunct or sick.]

3. Method of payment for purchase of shares/convertible debentures.— The amount of consideration for purchase of shares or convertible debentures of an Indian company on non-repatriation basis, shall be paid by way of inward remittance through normal banking channels from abroad or out of funds held in NRE/FCNR/NRO/NRSR/NRNR account maintained with an authorised dealer or as the case may be with an authorised bank in India:

Provided that in the case of an NRI [1][* * *] resident in Nepal and Bhutan, the amount of consideration for purchase of shares or convertible debentures of an Indian company on non-repatriation basis, shall be paid only by way of inward remittance in foreign exchange through normal banking channels.

4. Sale/Maturity proceeds of shares or convertible debentures

(*i*) The sale/maturity proceeds (net of applicable taxes) of shares or convertible debentures purchased under this Scheme shall be credited only to NRSR account where the purchase consideration was paid out of funds held in NRSR account and to NRO or NRSR account at the option of the seller where the purchase consideration was paid out of inward remittance or funds held in NRE/FCNR/NRO/NRNR account.

(*ii*) The amount invested in shares or convertible debentures under this Scheme and the capital appreciation thereon shall not be allowed to be repatriated abroad.

---

1 The word "/OCB" omitted by Foreign Exchange Management [Withdrawal of General Permission to Overseas Corporate Bodies (OCBs)] Regulations, 2003, w.e.f. 23-10-2003.

Schedule 5

[*See* regulation 5(4)]

Purchase and sale of securities other than shares or convertible debentures of an Indian company by a person resident outside India

[1][**1. Permission to Foreign Institutional Investors for purchase of securities.**—A registered Foreign Institutional Investor may purchase on repatriation basis, dated Government securities/treasury bills listed non-convertible debentures/bonds, commercial papers issued by an Indian company and units of domestic mutual funds, Security Receipts issued by Asset Reconstruction Companies and Perpetual Debt instruments eligible for inclusion

---

1 Substituted by Foreign Exchange Management (Transfer or Issue of Security by a Person Resident Outside India) (Second Amendment) Regulations, 2008 [Notification No. FEMA 179/2008-RB, dated 22-8-2008] for the following:

*"1. A registered foreign institutional investor may purchase, on repatriation basis, dated Government securities/treasury bills, non-convertible debentures/bonds issued by an Indian company, units of domestic mutual funds and security receipts issued by asset reconstruction companies either directly from the issuer of such securities or through a registered stock broker on a recognized stock exchange in India:

Provided that—

**[(*i*) The FII shall restrict allocation of its total investment between equity and debt instructions (including dated Government securities and treasury bills in the Indian capital market) in the ratio of 70: 30, and]

(*ii*) If the FII desires to invest up to 100 per cent in dated Government securities including treasury bills, non-convertible debentures/bonds issued by an Indian company, it shall form a 100 per cent debt fund and get such fund registered with the SEBI.

(*iii*) The total holding by a single FII in each tranche of scheme of security receipts shall not exceed 10 per cent of the issue and the total holdings of all FIIs put together shall not exceed 49 per cent of the paid up value of each tranche of scheme of security receipts issued by the asset reconstruction companies."

* Earlier this Paragraph was substituted by Foreign Exchange Management (Transfer or Issue of Security by a Person Resident Outside India) (Second Amendment) Regulations, 2006 w.e.f. 8-11-200 [FEMA 149/2006-RB] for the following:

"*1. Permission to Foreign Institutional Investors for purchase of securities.*—A registered Foreign Institutional Investor may purchase, on repatriation basis, dated Government securities/treasury bills, @[listed non-convertible debentures/bonds, commercial paper] issued by an Indian company and units of domestic mutual funds either directly from the issuer of such securities or through a registered stock broker on a recognised stock exchange in India:

Provided that—

(*i*) the FII shall restrict allocation of its total investment between equity and debt instruments (including dated Government Securities and Treasury Bills in the Indian capital market) in the ratio of 70:30, and

(*ii*) if the FII desires to invest upto 100 per cent in dated Government Securities including Treasury Bills, non-convertible debentures/bonds issued by an Indian company, it shall form a 100% debt fund and get such fund registered with SEBI."

** Earlier this provision was dispensed with vide AP (DIR Series) Circular No. 25, dated 17-10-2008.

@ Italicised words were inserted by Foreign Exchange Management (Transfer or Issue of Security by a Person Resident Outside India) (Amendment) Regulations 2006.

as Tier I capital and Debt capital instruments as upper Tier II capital issued by banks in India to augment their capital (the definitions of Tier I capital and Tier II capital will be the same as clarified by Reserve Bank, Department of Banking Operations and Development and modified from time to time); subject to the limits prescribed by RBI and SEBI from time to time; either directly from the issuer of such securities or through a registered stock broker on a recognised Stock Exchange in India:

Provided that:

[1][(*i*) *Omitted.*

(*ii*) *Omitted.*

(*i*) The total holding by a single FII in each tranche of scheme of Security Receipts shall not exceed 10 per cent of the issue and the total holdings of all FIIs put together shall not exceed 49 per cent of the paid up value of each tranche of scheme of Security Receipts issued by the Asset Reconstruction Companies; and

(*ii*) The investment by all FIIs in Perpetual Debt instruments (Tier I) should not exceed an aggregate ceiling of 49 per cent of each issue, and investment by individual FII should not exceed the limit of 10 per cent of each issue. The investment by FIIs in Debt capital instruments (Tier II) shall be within the limits stipulated by SEBI for FII investment in corporate debt:]

Provided further that FIIs may offer such securities as permitted by the Reserve Bank from time to time as collateral to the recognized Stock Exchanges in India for their transactions in exchange traded derivative contracts as specified in sub-regulation (6).[2]]

2. Permission to Non-resident Indian [3][* * *] for purchase of securities.—[4][1A. A Non-resident Indian may, without limit, purchase on repatriation basis,—

1 Clauses (*i*) and (*ii*) of the first proviso omitted and clauses (*iii*) and (*iv*) renumbered as (*i*) and (*ii*) by Foreign Exchange Management (Transfer or Issue of Security by a Person Resident Outside India) (Amendment) Regulations, 2009, w.r.e.f. 17-10-2008 [FEMA 202/2009-RB, dated 10-11-2009]. Prior to omission clauses (*i*) and (*ii*) read as under:

"(*i*) the FII shall restrict allocation of its total investment between equity and debt instruments (including dated Government Securities and Treasury Bills in the Indian capital market) in the ratio of 70:30;

(*ii*) if the FII desires to invest up to 100 per cent in dated Government Securities including Treasury Bills, listed non-convertible debentures/bonds issued by an Indian company, it shall form a 100 per cent debt fund and get such fund registered with SEBI;"

2 It should be sub-regulation (6) of Regulation 5. The authorities concerned should undertake to get it corrected.

3 The words "and overseas corporate body" omitted by Foreign Exchange Management [Withdrawal of General Permission to Overseas Corporate Bodies (OCBs)] Regulations, 2003, w.e.f. 23-10-2003.

4 Substituted by Foreign Exchange Management (Transfer or Issue of Security by a Person Resident Outside India) (Second Amendment) Regulations, 2008 [Notification No. FEMA 179/2008-RB, dated 22-8-2008] w.e.f. 25-1-2006 for the following: →→

(*i*) Government dated securities (other than bearer securities) or treasury bills or units of domestic mutual funds;

(*ii*) bonds issued by a public sector undertaking (PSU) in India;

(*iii*) shares in Public Sector Enterprises being disinvested by the Government of India, provided the purchase is in accordance with the terms and conditions stipulated in the notice inviting bids.

1B. A Non-resident Indian may purchase on repatriation basis perpetual debt instruments eligible for inclusion as Tier I capital and Debt capital instruments as upper Tier II capital issued by banks in India to augment their capital, as stipulated by Reserve Bank from time to time. The investments by all NRIs in Perpetual Debt instruments (Tier I) should not exceed an aggregate ceiling of 24 per cent of each issue and investments by a single NRI should not exceed 5 per cent of each issue. Investment by NRIs in Debt capital instruments (Tier II) shall be in accordance with the extant policy for investment by NRIs in other debt instruments.]

(2) A Non-resident Indian [1][* * *] may, without limit, purchase on non-repatriation basis, dated Government securities (other than bearer securities), treasury bills, units of domestic mutual funds, units of Money Market Funds in India, or National Plan/Savings Certificates[2].

[3][(3) A Multilateral Development Bank which is specifically permitted by Government of India to float rupee bonds in India may purchase Government dated securities.]

[4][**2A. Permission to Foreign Central Banks for purchase of Government Securities.**—A Foreign Central Bank may purchase and sell dated Government securities/treasury bills in the secondary market — subject to the conditions as may be stipulated by the Reserve Bank from time to time.]

→ → "(1) A Non-resident Indian @[* * *] may, without limit, purchase on repatriation basis,–

(*i*) Government dated securities (other than bearer securities) or treasury bills or units of domestic mutual funds;

(*ii*) bonds issued by a public sector undertaking (PSU) in India;

(*iii*) shares in Public Sector Enterprises being disinvested by the Government of India, provided the purchase is in accordance with the terms and conditions stipulated in the notice inviting bids."

@ The words "or an overseas corporate body", omitted by Foreign Exchange Management [Withdrawal of General Permission to Overseas Corporate Bodies (OCBs)] Regulations, 2003, w.e.f. 23-10-2003.

1 The words "or an overseas corporate body" omitted by Foreign Exchange Management [Withdrawal of General Permission to Overseas Corporate Bodies (OCBs)] Regulations, 2003, w.e.f. 23-10-2003.

2 In terms of Master Circular 13/2010-11, dated 1-7-2010, Government of India has notified that NRIs are not permitted to make investments in Small Savings Schemes including PPF.

3 Inserted by the Foreign Exchange Management (Transfer or Issue of Security by a Person Resident Outside India) (Fourth Amendment) Regulations, 2003, w.e.f. 22-11-2003 [FEMA 106/2003-RB].

4 Inserted vide Foreign Exchange Management (Transfer or Issue of Security by a Person Resident Outside India) (Amendment) Regulations, 2007 [Notification No. FEMA 166/2007-RB, dated 17-10-2007]

3. Method of payment of purchase consideration.—(1) A registered Foreign Institutional Investor who purchases securities under the provisions of this Schedule shall make the payment for purchase of such securities either by inward remittance through normal banking channels or out of funds held in Foreign Currency Account or Non-resident Rupee Account maintained by the Foreign Institutional Investor with a designated branch of an authorised dealer with the approval of Reserve Bank in terms of paragraph 2 of Schedule 2.

(2) A Non-resident Indian [1][* * *] who purchases securities on repatriation basis, under sub-paragraph (1) of paragraph 2 of this Schedule, shall make payment either by inward remittance through normal banking channels or out of funds held in his/its NRE/FCNR account.

(3) A Non-resident Indian [2][* * *] who purchases securities on non-repatriation basis, under sub-paragraph (2) of paragraph 2 of this Schedule, shall make payment either by inward remittance through normal banking channels or out of funds held in his/its NRE/FCNR/NRO/NRSR/NRNR account.

[3][(4) A Multilateral Development Bank which purchases Government dated securities under this Schedule, shall make payment either by inward remittance through normal banking channels or out of funds held in the account opened with the specific approval of RBI.]

4. Permission for sale of securities.—A person resident outside India who has purchased securities in accordance with this Schedule may (*a*) sell such securities through a registered stock broker on a recognised stock exchange, or (*b*) tender units of mutual funds to the issuer for repurchase or for payment of maturity proceeds or (*c*) tender Government securities/treasury bills to the Reserve Bank for payment of maturity proceeds.

5. Remittance/credit of sale/maturity proceeds.—(*i*) In the case of a registered Foreign Institutional Investor who has sold securities in accordance with paragraph 4, the designated branch of an authorised dealer referred to in sub-paragraph (1) of paragraph 3 may allow remittance of net sale/maturity proceeds (after payment of taxes) or credit the net amount of sale/maturity proceeds of such securities to the foreign currency account or Non-resident Rupee Account of the FII investor maintained in accordance with the provisions of paragraph 2 of Schedule 2.

(*ii*) In the case of a Non-resident Indian [4][* * *] who has sold securities in

1 The words "or an overseas corporate body" omitted by Foreign Exchange Management [Withdrawal of General Permission to Overseas Corporate Bodies (OCBs)] Regulations, 2003, w.e.f. 23-10-2003.

2 *Ibid.*

3 Inserted by the Foreign Exchange Management (Transfer or Issue of Security by a Person Resident Outside India) (Fourth Amendment) Regulations, 2003, w.e.f. 22-11-2003 [FEMA 106/2003-RB].

4 The words "or an overseas corporate body" omitted by Foreign Exchange Management [Withdrawal of General Permission to Overseas Corporate Bodies (OCBs)] Regulations, 2003, w.e.f. 23-10-2003.

accordance with paragraph 4, the net sale/maturity proceeds (after payment of taxes) of such securities, may be —

(*a*) credited only to NRSR account of the NRI investor where the payment for purchase of securities sold was made out of funds held in NRSR account, or

(*b*) credited, at the NRI [1][* * *] investor's option, to his/its NRO or NRSR account, where the payment for the purchase of the securities sold was made out of funds held in NRO account, or

(*c*) remitted abroad or at the NRI [2][* * *] investor's option, credited to his/its NRE/FCNR/NRO/ NRSR/NRNR account, where the securities were purchased on repatriation basis in accordance with sub-paragraph (1) of paragraph 2 and the payment for purchase of the securities sold was made by inward remittance through normal banking channels or out of funds held in NRE/FCNR account.

[3][(*iii*) In the case of sale of Government dated securities by a Multilateral Development Bank, the net maturity proceeds (after payment of taxes) may be remitted abroad or credited to fund account opened with the prior permission of the Reserve Bank.]

Form TS 1

Application for transfer of shares of a company registered in India by a non-resident to a person resident in India

Instructions

1. The application should be completed in duplicate and submitted to the concerned Regional Office of Reserve Bank under whose jurisdiction the Head/Registered Office of the company, whose shares are to be transferred, is situated if the transferor is a foreign company/foreign national resident outside India.

2. The application may be signed either by the transferor or the transferee attaching therewith consent in writing of the other party or a copy of the sale/purchase agreement.

Documentation

1. Photocopies of Reserve Bank's approval(s) for acquiring and holding shares by the transferor, if specific approval was granted by Reserve Bank for holding/acquisition of shares, if applicable.

2. In case the shares proposed to be transferred are listed on a Stock Exchange, a certificate from a Chartered Accountant certifying the average

---

1 The words "or OCB" omitted by Foreign Exchange Management [Withdrawal of General Permission to Overseas Corporate Bodies (OCBs)] Regulations, 2003, w.e.f. 23-10-2003.

2 *Ibid.*

3 Inserted by the Foreign Exchange Management (Transfer or Issue of Security by a Person Resident Outside India) (Fourth Amendment) Regulations, 2003, w.e.f. 22-11-2003 [FEMA 106/2003-RB].

quotation (average of daily high and low) for one week preceding the date of application.

3. In case of unlisted/thinly traded shares, valuation of the shares on basis of any valuation methodology in vogue, if the total consideration is upto ₹ 20 lakhs.

4. In case of unlisted thinly traded shares where the total consideration exceeds ₹ 20 lakhs, two valuation certificates for the shares of the company, one from the statutory auditors of the company and the other from an independent Chartered Accountant/SEBI registered Category-I Merchant Banker.

Or

Documentary evidence showing Price Earnings (PE) and Book Value (BV) multiples of Bombay Stock Exchange National Index (BSEN) for the calendar month immediately preceding the date of application and a certificate showing the Earnings per Share (EPS) and Net Asset Value (NAV) of the shares of the company as per the latest audited Balance Sheet.

1. Particulars of the transferor:

A. If the transferor is a corporate body

(*i*) Name and address

(*ii*) Place of incorporation

(*iii*) Total shareholding in the investee company

(*iv*) Particulars of Reserve Bank approval/s for acquiring/holding shares

(*v*) Number and face value of the shares proposed to be sold/ transferred

(B) If the transferor is an individual

(*i*) Full name and address

(*ii*) Number of shares held in the Indian company

(*iii*) Reserve Bank's approval number/s and date(s) (if any) for acquiring/holding the shares

(*iv*) Number and face value of shares proposed to be sold/transferred

2. Particulars of the Indian company whose shares are to be sold/transferred

(*i*) Name and address

(*ii*) Place of incorporation

(*iii*) Total paid-up capital	No. of shares	Amount
(*a*) Equity		

(*b*) Preference

(*c*) Held by

(*i*) **Non-resident**	**Equity**		**Preference**	
	No. of shares	Percentage to total paid-up equity shares	No. of shares	Percentage to total paid-up preference shares
(*a*) Foreign nationals/corporate bodies [other than included in (*b*) below]				
(*b*) NRIs/Overseas corporate bodies predominantly owned by NRIs				
(*ii*) **Residents**:				
(*a*) Indian Promoters				
(*b*) Others				
Total				

3. Particulars of the buyers/transferee:

   (*i*) Name and address

   (*ii*) Place of incorporation

4. Whether the shares are quoted on a recognised Stock Exchange? Yes/No

   (*i*) If the shares are quoted on the Stock Exchange, whether the sale is proposed to be effected on the floor of the Stock Exchange to the general public at the prevailing market price? Yes/No

   (*ii*) If the sale (of the quoted shares) is by way of private arrangement, please furnish the following:

   (*a*) the average of quotations (average of daily high and low) for one week preceding the date of application duly certified by a Chartered Accountant. [item 2 under Documentation]

   (*b*) the proposed sale price

5. If the sale/transfer is of non-listed as well as of listed but not regularly traded shares, the proposed sale price [to be supported by a Chartered Accountants' certificate as indicated in Item 4 under Documentation]
6. Whether the transferor/transferee requires any permission under the Companies Act/MRTP Act. If so, whether such permission has been received from the appropriate authority.
7. Reason for the proposed sale/transfer of shares
8. Any other information which the applicant wishes to furnish in support of this application.

I/We declare that the particulars given above are true and correct to the best of my/our knowledge and belief.

Place: ....

Date: .... (Stamp and signature of the transferor/ transferee as the case may be)

[1][**Schedule 6**

[*See* regulation 5(5)]

Investment in an Indian venture capital undertaking by a registered foreign venture capital investor

1. Investment by foreign venture capital investor.—(1) A registered Foreign Venture Capital Investor (FVCI) may, through the Securities and Exchange Board of India, apply to the Reserve Bank for permission to invest in Indian Venture Capital Undertaking (IVCU) or in a VCF or in a scheme floated by such VCFs. Permission may be granted by the Reserve Bank subject to such terms and conditions as may be considered necessary.

(2) The registered FVCI permitted by the Reserve Bank under sub-paragraph (1), may purchase equity/equity linked instruments/debt/debt instruments, debentures of a IVCU or of a VCF through initial public offer or private placement or in units of schemes/funds set up by a VCF.

(3) The amount of consideration for investment in VCFs/IVCUs shall be paid out of inward remittance from abroad through normal banking channels or out of funds held in an account maintained with the designated branch of an authorised dealer in India in accordance with para 2.

2. Maintenance of account by the registered FVCI for investment in IVCUs/VCFs or schemes/funds set up by the VCFs.—The Reserve Bank may,

---

1 Inserted by the Foreign Exchange Management (Transfer or Issue of Security by a Person Resident Outside India) (Amendment) Regulations, 2000, w.e.f. 26-12-2000.

on application, permit a FVCI which has received 'in principle' registration from SEBI to open a foreign currency account and/or a rupee account with a designated branch of an authorised dealer with the following permissible transactions:—

(*i*) crediting inward remittance received through normal banking channels or the sale proceeds (net of taxes) of investments;

(*ii*) making investment in accordance with the provisions of paragraph 1 above;

(*iii*) transferring funds from the foreign currency account of the FVCI to their own rupee account;

(*iv*) remitting funds from the foreign currency or rupee account subject to payment of applicable taxes;

(*v*) meeting local expenses of the FVCI.

3. Forward cover.—Authorised dealers may offer forward cover to FVCIs to the extent of total inward remittance. In case the FVCI has made any remittance by liquidating some investments, original cost of the investments will be deducted from the eligible cover.

4. Valuation of investments.—The FVCI may acquire by purchase or otherwise or sell shares/convertible debentures/units or any other investment held by it in the IVCUs or VCFs or schemes/funds set up by the VCFs at a price that is mutually acceptable to the buyer and the seller/issuer. The FVCI may also receive the proceeds arising out of the liquidation of VCFs or schemes/funds set up by the VCFs.

5. Adherence to SEBI Guidelines.—FVCIs shall abide by the relevant regulations/guidelines issued by the Securities and Exchange Board.]

Chapter 5
CALCULATION, ENTRY ROUTE, CAPS, ENTRY CONDITIONS, ETC. OF INVESTMENT

SYNOPSIS

1. Calculation of total foreign investment *i.e.* Direct and indirect foreign investment in Indian companies

Investment in Indian companies can be made both by non-resident as well as resident Indian entities. Any non-resident investment in an Indian company is direct foreign investment. Investment by resident Indian entities could again comprise of both resident and non-resident investment. Thus, such an Indian company would have indirect foreign investment if the Indian investing company has foreign investment in it. The indirect investment can also be a *cascading investment i.e.* through multi-layered structure.

For the purpose of computation of indirect Foreign investment, Foreign Investment in Indian company shall include all types of foreign investments *i.e.* FDI; investment by FIIs (holding as on March 31); NRIs; ADRs; GDRs; Foreign Currency Convertible Bonds (FCCB); fully, compulsorily and mandatorily convertible preference shares and fully, compulsorily and mandatorily convertible Debentures regardless of whether the said investments have been made under Schedule 1, 2, 3 and 6 of FEMA (Transfer or Issue of Security by Persons Resident Outside India) Regulations.

2. Guidelines for Calculation of total Foreign Investment *i.e.* Direct and Indirect Foreign Investment in an Indian Company

(a) Counting the Direct Foreign Investment

All investment directly by a non-resident entity into the Indian company would be counted towards foreign investment.

(b) Counting of Indirect Foreign Investment

The foreign investment through the investing Indian company would not be considered for calculation of the indirect foreign investment in case of Indian companies which are 'owned **and** controlled' by resident Indian citizens and/or Indian Companies which are owned and controlled by resident Indian citizens.

For cases where condition given in above para is not satisfied *or* if the investing company is owned **or** controlled by 'non resident entities', the entire investment by the investing company into the subject Indian Company would be considered as indirect foreign investment. However, it is provided that, as an exception, the *indirect foreign investment in only the 100% owned subsidiaries* of operating-cum-investing/investing companies, will be limited to the foreign investment in the operating-cum-investing/investing company. This exception is made since the downstream investment of a 100% owned subsidiary of the holding company is akin to investment made by the holding company and the downstream investment should be a mirror image of the holding company. This exception, however, is strictly for those cases where the entire capital of the downstream subsidiary is owned by the holding company.

Case Study: If the indirect foreign investment is being calculated for Company X which has investment through an investing Company Y having foreign investment, the following would be the method of calculation:

(A) where Company Y has foreign investment less than 50%- Company X would not be taken as having any indirect foreign investment through Company Y.

(B) where Company Y has foreign investment of say 75%; and

(I) invests 26% in Company X, the entire 26% investment by Company Y would be treated as indirect foreign investment in Company X;

(II) invests 80% in Company X, the indirect foreign investment in Company X would be taken as 80%

(III) where Company X is a wholly owned subsidiary of Company Y (*i.e.* Company Y owns 100% shares of Company X), then only 75% would be treated as indirect foreign equity and the balance 25% would be treated as resident held equity. The indirect foreign equity in Company X would be computed in the ratio of 75: 25 in the total investment of Company Y in Company X.

The total foreign investment would be the sum total of direct and indirect foreign investment. The aforementioned methodology of calculation would apply at every stage of investment in Indian Companies and thus to each and every Indian Company.

Introduction of specific provision for downstream investment through internal accruals {*Para 4.6.6(iv)*}**:** It has now been explicitly clarified that downstream investments through internal accruals are permissible, subject to following of guidelines for downstream investments by Indian companies which are "owned and/or controlled by non-resident entities". This clarity was necessary as the FDI policy states that for the purpose of downstream investment, the operating-cum-investing/investing companies would have to bring in requisite funds from abroad and not leverage funds from the domestic market for such investments. While this would not preclude companies from making downstream investments through 'internal accruals', it had been noticed that, in certain cases, some companies had started accessing the Government approval route for downstream investments through internal accruals. (Circular 2 of 2010 as on September 30, 2010).

Guidelines for foreign investment into investing companies /downstream investment by Indian Companies 'owned and/or controlled by non resident entities' as per Para 4.1 (para 4.6.4):

The Policy on downstream investment comprises policy for (*i*) only operating companies (*ii*) operating-cum-investing companies (*iii*) only investing companies as below:

(*i*) *Only operating companies:*

Foreign investment in such companies would have to comply with the relevant sectoral conditions on entry route, conditionalities and caps with regard to the sectors in which such companies are operating.

(*ii*) *Operating-cum-investing companies:*

(a) Foreign investment into such companies would have to comply with the relevant sectoral conditions on entry route, conditionalities and caps with regard to the sectors in which such companies are operating.

(b) Further, the subject Indian companies into which downstream investments are made by such companies would have to comply with the relevant sectoral conditions on entry route, conditionalities and caps in regard of the sector in which the subject Indian companies are operating.

(*iii*) *Investing companies:*

(a) Foreign Investment in Investing Companies will require the prior Government/FIPB approval, regardless of the amount or extent of foreign investment.

(b) The Indian companies into which downstream investments are made by such investing companies would have to comply with the relevant sectoral conditions on entry route, conditionalities and caps in regard of the sector in which the subject Indian companies are operating.

For the purpose of downstream investment, the operating cum investing companies and the investing companies would have to bring in requisite funds from abroad and not leverage funds from domestic market for such investments. This would, however, not preclude downstream operating companies from raising debt in the domestic market. Downstream investments through internal accruals are permissible, subject to provisions of para 4.6.4

W.e.f. April 1st, 2011, The guidelines have been comprehensively simplified and rationalised. Companies have now been classified into only two categories – 'companies owned *or* controlled by foreign investors' and 'companies owned *and* controlled by Indian residents'. The earlier categorisation of *'investing companies', 'operating companies'* and *'investing-cum-operating companies'* has been done away with.

(c) *Additional conditions*

The full details about the foreign investment including ownership details etc. in Indian company(s) and information about the control of the company(s) would be furnished by the Company(s) to the Government of India at the time of seeking approval.

In any sector/activity, where Government approval is required for foreign investment and in cases where there are any *inter-se* agreements between/amongst share-holders which have an effect on the appointment of the Board of Directors or on the exercise of voting rights or of creating voting rights disproportionate to shareholding or any incidental matter thereof, such agreements will have to be informed to the approving authority. The approving authority will consider such *inter-se* agreements for determining ownership and control when considering the case for granting approval for foreign investment.

In all sectors attracting sectoral caps, the balance equity *i.e.* beyond the sectoral foreign investment cap, would specifically be beneficially owned by/held with/in the hands of resident Indian citizens and Indian companies, owned and controlled by resident Indian citizens.

In the Information and Broadcasting (I & B) and Defence sectors where the sectoral cap is less than 49%, the company would need to be 'owned **and** controlled' by resident Indian citizens and Indian companies, which are owned and controlled by resident Indian citizens.

For this purpose, the equity held by the largest Indian shareholder would have to be *at least* 51% of the total equity, excluding the equity held by Public Sector Banks and Public Financial Institutions, as defined in Section 4A of the Companies Act, 1956. The term 'largest Indian shareholder', used in this clause, will include any or a combination of the following:

(I) In the case of an individual shareholder:

(*aa*) The individual shareholder;

(*bb*) A relative of the shareholder within the meaning of Section 6 of the Companies Act, 1956;

(*cc*) A company/group of companies in which the individual shareholder/ HUF to which he belongs has management and controlling interest.

(II) In the case of an Indian company:

(*aa*) The Indian company;

(*bb*) A group of Indian companies under the same management and ownership control.

For the purpose of this Clause, "Indian company" shall be a company which must have a resident Indian or a relative as defined under Section 6 of the Companies Act, 1956/HUF, either singly or in combination holding at least 51% of the shares. However, it is provided that, in case of a combination of all or any of the entities mentioned above, each of the parties shall have entered into a legally binding agreement to act as a single unit in managing the matters of the applicant company.

If a declaration is made by persons as per section 187C of the Indian Companies Act about a beneficial interest being held by a non resident entity, then even though the investment may be made by a resident Indian citizen, the same shall be counted as foreign investment.

The above mentioned policy and the methodology would be applicable for determining the total foreign investment in all sectors, excepting in sectors where it is governed specifically under any statutes or rules there under. The above methodology of determining direct and indirect foreign investment therefore does not apply to the Insurance Sector which will continue to be governed by the relevant Regulation. Any foreign investment already made in accordance with the guidelines in existence prior to February 13, 2009 (date of issue of Press Note 2 of 2009) would not require any modification to conform to these guidelines. All other investments, past and future, would come under the ambit of these new guidelines.

FDI Guidelines under Press Notes 2, 3 and 4 (2009) (source: http://www.indlawnews.com/)

The Department of Industrial Policy and Promotion (DIPP) has, in the course of the last month, issued a series of press notes outlining the revised Foreign Direct Investment (FDI) guidelines announced by the Cabinet Committee on Economic Affairs (CCEA). Press Notes 2 and 3, dealing with calculations of foreign investment in downstream entities and requirement for Foreign Investment Promotion Board (FIPB) approval in relation to transfer of ownership or control in sectoral cap companies, were issued on 13th February 09. These press notes raised certain issues regarding the clarity of their content. In response to some of these, Press Note 4 was issued on 26th February; however, confusion is still present and the guidelines leave much to be desired. While there are both supporters and detractors of the content of these guidelines, the latter put forth well founded doubts and concerns that need to be addressed.

Calculation of Foreign Equity

The PNs have replaced the conventional proportionate method of computing foreign indirect equity by the parameter of beneficial ownership and control of entities at each stage of investment. As per Cl. 2.6 of PN 3, foreign investment shall include all types of foreign investments *i.e.* FDI, investment by FIIs, NRIs, ADRs, GDRs and convertible preference shares. This is in contravention to previous policies. As a result, several foreign investment compliant Indian companies may now be in breach of sectoral caps, especially in the telecom and banking sectors, and will probably have to seek clarifications from the FIPB on their holdings.

By the current approach, even if multiple unrelated foreign investors cumulatively hold more than 50% in an Indian company, the company will now be treated as foreign investor. Hence any investment by such an Indian Company in equity would be treated entirely as a foreign investment, rather than a proportional investment. The problem with this is that while this is a legitimate policy mechanism of dealing with a single foreign investor who owns a majority of an Indian company, there are a number of board-driven Indian institutional companies which have attracted foreign investment which will be treated in the same way. Thus, there will now be no difference, for instance, between a foreign company's subsidiary (e.g. Hindustan Unilever) and an Indian company that has majority ownership in foreign hands (e.g. ICICI) though these hands are not related.

Downstream Investment

PN 4 seeks to clarify compliance with foreign investment norms in terms of downstream investments by Indian companies that may have foreign investment. Although the language of the Press Note is not entirely clear as regards its scope, the first paragraph refers to the guiding principle, which is that downstream investment by companies owned or controlled by non-resident entities would require to follow the same norms as a direct foreign investment. In other words, it applies only to Indian investing companies that may be either owned (more than 50%) or otherwise controlled (in terms of power to appoint a majority of directors) by foreign companies. However, where Indian investing companies carry foreign investment to an extent that is less than 50% and where control is with the Indian owners, then investment by that company will be treated as domestic investment. Hence, Indian investing companies with minority foreign ownership may indirectly be able to invest in sectors that are otherwise not open for foreign investment, such as the multi-brand retail sector.

According to the recent clarification by the government on PN 4 on downstream investments by foreign owned or controlled companies, clearance requirements for such investments have been done away with for some types of companies (refer below) subject to foreign investment caps in that sector.

This leads to a situation where, in a field in which foreign investment is regulated by way of sectoral caps, a foreign investor could take a direct equity stake to the fullest extent of the permitted sectoral cap (say 49%), and the balance beneficial interest could be taken through one or more Indian companies where the foreign investor holds not more than 50 per cent equity. In such a scenario, the foreign investor effectively owns a large stake in a domestic company, in contravention of sectoral norms, and this is treated as legitimate even in sensitive sectors where caps exist in the first place, to protect national interests.

Clearance requirements

Historically, an Indian company with foreign investment required approval from the FIPB before it could make further downstream investments. This onerous requirement seems to have been done away with; the new guidelines in PN 4 provide procedural relief on the approval requirements. A foreign owned or controlled Indian company that either runs a business, or runs a business and also invests in other companies down the line will no longer require prior clearance from the FIPB, subject to sectoral caps and other conditions. They only need to notify the FIPB, DIPP and Secretariat for Industrial Assistance (SIA) about their investment within 30 days of downstream investment.

However, foreign owned or controlled Indian companies that are only investment companies, or companies that neither operate nor invest at the moment but could undertake either activity subsequently, still need prior FIPB approval. The aim of this change is clear to facilitate easier FDI entry in the country; the terms investing company have been defined to exclude companies holding investment for trading of holdings/securities which mean that there is a distinction between investing companies making strategic investment and those making portfolio investment, and excludes the latter from scope of definition. So the guidelines are not explicit on the treatment of past investment. This aspect needs to be clarified with the DIPP since the guidelines are done away with the historical policy guideline.

Wholly Owned Subsidiary

Another major oversight seen in the DIPPs approach is that in treating the entire holding by an Indian company owned or controlled by foreign investors, an exception is made as regards investment in wholly owned subsidiaries. The foreign equity stake in a wholly owned subsidiary would be regarded as a mirror image of the level of foreign equity stake in the parent company. This leads to an anomalous situation, where a 51% foreign-owned Indian company invests in a wholly owned subsidiary (thereby owning 100% equity stake in that subsidiary), but as per the Press notes the foreign holding in the subsidiary would be regarded as only 51%. Taking this example further, if the 51% foreign owned Indian company gives 5% of the subsidiary's equity to another investor, and now owns 95% of the subsidiary, the foreign investment in the subsidiary would now become 95%. This clearly becomes a disincentive for foreign investors to share their holdings with other Indian investors.

Overall Arguments and Conclusion

The norms appear to be liberal on the issue of what constitutes FDI: a company with less than 50% foreign holding is deemed Indian. The latest norms are clearly meant to incentivize FDI and cross-border flow of funds, given the domestic resource-crunch at present. The advantages of FDI are that it accelerates growth, with added spillovers of technology, skills and knowledge on to the domestic economy. As seen, a company with more than 50% of the equity interest in it beneficially owned by resident Indian citizens and companies is deemed Indian. Also, a company with majority of Indian directors will be seen as Indian controlled. This gives enough scope for cascading investment via a series of multi-layered investments and holding-company structures. Given the added benefits of FDI, these norms seem attractive. FDI would improve efficiency by entering sectors with high entry barriers and reduce monopolistic distortions.

However, the benefits of FDI do not take away from the fact that certain sectors are too important and strategic to allow foreign control in these sectors. As explained above, the new regime makes it very plausible for Indian companies in these sectors to be effectively owned by foreigners in breach of sectoral caps, but on paper (as per the rules) it would be an Indian company.

Further, the enticing investment incentives will not yield results in the current global recession. Lastly, one cannot assume that even if there is investment of foreign funds, automatic gainful spillovers will occur. In sum, the point is that the new guidelines for FDI need to be thoroughly reconsidered while PN 4 clarified some doubts that arose with PN2 and PN3, there are still areas that seem to reflect bad policy. It would be more fruitful to do away with the plethora of delays and policy glitches involved for foreign investors to set up projects, rather than making our policy rules round-about, and corporate structure vulnerable.

FDI rules: press notes bring up new issues (source: www.livemint.com)

The ministry of commerce and industry has issued a series of press notes outlining the revised foreign direct investment (FDI) guidelines announced by the cabinet committee on economic affairs. Press Notes 2 and 3, dealing with calculations of foreign investment in downstream entities and requirement for Foreign Investment Promotion Board (FIPB) approval in relation to transfer of ownership or control in sectoral cap companies, were issued on 11 February.

These press notes have raised certain issues, including in relation to downstream investment by Indian companies having minority foreign holding. In response to some of these issues, Press Note 4 was issued on 26 February.

This article seeks to deal with what emerges out of the press notes.

FDI policy

Under the FDI policy before the 11 February press note, foreign investment was allowed in an Indian company under the automatic route (that is, without prior approvals) in almost all sectors except: (*a*) certain prohibited sectors such as gambling and betting, the lottery business, atomic energy, retail trading (except single-brand retail) or (*b*) where prior government approval is specifically required.

The issue of the method of computation of sectoral caps has been engaging the attention of the government and the controversy and confusion of an operating and holding company owes its genesis to this issue. In essence, the government was taking a stand that regardless of the quantum of foreign investment in an Indian company (ICO), an investment by an ICO in a downstream operating company (DCO) would require FIPB approval, even if the DCO operates in the automatic sector. In fact, FIPB has been giving approvals with retrospective effect for such investments, subject to the requirement of compounding by the Reserve Bank of India.

Press Note 2 of 2009

Under Press Note 2 of 2009, foreign investment in an Indian company shall include all types of foreign investment, namely FDI, by non-resident Indians (NRIs), portfolio investment by foreign institutional investors (FIIs)/NRIs, American depository receipts (ADRs)/global depository receipts (GDRs), foreign currency convertible bonds (FCCBs), convertible preference shares/convertible debentures. This note provides for a framework for calculation of total foreign investment (direct and indirect) in Indian companies, which is based on ownership and control of such firms.

According to the new FDI policy, Indian companies (which are owned and controlled by Indian resident citizens directly or through Indian companies) will be considered "pure" Indian companies. Accordingly, any downstream investments made by such companies will not be considered as having any flow-through foreign investment (compared with a view in the earlier regime of having pro rata foreign investment). However, this methodology for computation of foreign investment does not apply to sectors that are governed specifically by a separate statute such as the insurance sector.

If, however, there is an Indian company that is either foreign-owned or controlled (as opposed to owned *and* controlled); the downstream investment therein will be subject to sectoral caps. For example, if a foreign company owns 55% in an ICO and the ICO has made an investment in a DCO of 75%, foreign investment in the DCO would be considered as 75% (earlier, it would have been considered at 55% of 75%).

Press Note 3 of 2009

This press note applies to all cases involving transfer of ownership or control from Indian resident citizens to non-resident entities in sectors/activities that either have an FDI cap or require prior FIPB approval. In these sectors, FIPB approval will now be required for transfer of ownership or control of Indian companies either directly to foreign entities or to an Indian company set up with foreign investment and which is owned or controlled by non-resident entities, irrespective of whether such a transfer is taking place through merger, amalgamation, acquisition, etc. This effectively means a step back in the liberalization process, where prior FIPB approval is now required even in cases that did not require such approvals earlier. It is important to realize this press note is not talking about downstream investment, but investment in an Indian company per se.

Press Note 4 of 2009

This press note seeks to clarify compliance with foreign investment norms compared with downstream investments. Although the language in the operating part of the press note is not very clear, the introductory paragraph suggests that it is restricted to downstream investments by an ICO if the ICO is owned or controlled by non-resident entities, as opposed to downstream investment by ICOs that are owned and controlled by residents. It categorizes such ICOs (foreign-owned or foreign-controlled ICOs) into three baskets:

- *Only operating companies:* sectoral caps and conditionalities to be complied with.
- *Operating-cum-investment companies:* In such cases, the DCO would have to comply with the relevant sectoral caps and conditionalities.
- *Investment companies:* If the ICO is an investment company (*i.e.* neither an operating company nor an operating-cum-investment company), foreign investment in the ICO will require FIPB approval regardless of the amount or extent of foreign investment. Further, the DCO will have to comply with conditionalities and sector caps.

There are some additional conditions also prescribed in relation to downstream investment by an ICO in a DCO, if the ICO is an operating-cum-investing company, or just an investment company. Two of the conditions are procedural and require certain intimations of downstream investment within 30 days of investment and certain board resolutions to be submitted. The two other conditions are substantive and require compliance with certain pricing guidelines as well as the ICO being required to bring funds from abroad and not borrow domestically for downstream investments.

The implications

The key principle emerging from Press Note 2 is that as long as an Indian company is owned and controlled ultimately by resident Indians, foreign investment in the Indian company would be ignored in relation to downstream investments made by the Indian company.

While the purpose of this press note is purportedly to simplify matters, it has several implications, some of which are as under (for the purpose of explanation, a foreign company investing in an ICO is being referred to as FCO):

1. The concept of indirect foreign investment now needs to be looked at vis-à-vis whether the ICO is owned and controlled by Indian citizens/ultimately Indian-controlled companies. If so, a downstream investment is not considered to be FDI even if there is investment of an FCO in the ICO, as long as the investment of the FCO is below 50%. If that is the case, it appears that if the ICO invests in a DCO, even if the DCO is functioning in a sectoral cap segment, that should be irrelevant and the sectoral cap, therefore, should not have any relevance. For example, if the ICO makes an investment in a hitherto FDI-restricted sector, multi-brand retail, for example, on a plain reading of Press Note 2, that should not be violative of FDI norms. The reason is that an ICO investment will be deemed not to be a foreign investment, not even proportionate. Press Note 4 seems to clearly support this interpretation implicitly, because the restrictions envisaged are only for foreign-owned or foreign-controlled resident ICOs.
2. For determining foreign ownership/control, the wording is "owned or controlled" as distinct from "owned and controlled", which is the situation described in Point 1 vis-à-vis an ICO being considered a "pure" Indian company. In other words, if an ICO is owned more than 50% by several unconnected foreign entities, then the question arises as to whether it is to be considered as not being exempt from downstream sectoral caps. On a plain reading, the answer appears to be that investment by an ICO in such cases would be subject to sectoral caps, although one understands that this matter is under review, given that this may not be the intent.
3. The press note seems to deal with more than 50% Indian ownership or more than 50% foreign ownership. It does not deal with a situation of a 50:50 joint venture.

4. An important issue is whether this press note has dealt with the controversy of operating and holding companies. While it does not expressly do so, it seems clear that if an ICO is an Indian-owned and controlled company, then the issue of downstream investment requiring FIPB approval does not arise because it is not considered to have any foreign investment in the first place. Here again, Press Note 4 seems to support this proposition implicitly, because even in that, the conditionalities of government approval seem to be linked only with foreign-owned ICOs.
5. The issue of control being defined as the ability to appoint a majority of the members of the board of directors may not always be the appropriate benchmark for control. For example, in the case of private equity investment with significant veto rights, but without the power to appoint a majority of the board, it would not be construed as foreign control, but at the same time would put significant fetters on the ICO. Perhaps what the government had in mind is "positive" control, as distinct from "negative" control.
6. The unification of the categories of foreign investment brings up other issues:
   - In the case of ADRs or GDRs, voting rights are not exercised by foreign investors, but the investments are included.
   - FII investment is very volatile. Hence, the inclusion of that in foreign investment has its own set of issues. In fact, in order to compute the level of FII investment, the date of 31 March has been prescribed. Therefore, if a sectoral cap is to be computed today, the FII investment as on 31 March 2008 would be looked at, which could be significantly higher given the huge FII pull-out that has happened. Clearly, a tricky issue and one would think that one will hear much more about this in the days to come.

Additional issues

The contents of Press Note 4 have already been explained above, including vis-à-vis Press Note 2. A couple of additional issues:

- The way the press note is worded, it seems that if an ICO is Indian-owned and controlled with minority FCO interest, such FCO investment will be ignored vis-à-vis the sector in which the ICO can invest by way of downstream investment.
- Second, if the ICO has internal accruals, the ability of the ICO to use such internal accruals has not been dealt with by the press note. Logically it should be permitted to use such funds, but one wishes that the press note had clarified this issue expressly.

Summing up

While the intent of the press notes may be laudable, new issues have arisen, as discussed here, including a possibility that some sectoral caps have been made meaningless and potential downstream investment in restricted sectors has been probably made possible. In addition, some avoidable requirements of going back to FIPB have been reintroduced by Press Note 3 of 2009.

On a more macro basis, foreign entities are not likely to invest in Indian-owned and controlled companies simply because of the ability to make downstream investments by such Indian companies in restricted/prohibited sectors. Clearly, commercial reality will dictate that rather than regulatory "liberalization".

3. Downstream Investment by Indian Companies

The Policy for downstream investment by Indian companies seeks to lay down and clarify about compliance with the Foreign investment norms on entry route, conditionalities and sectoral caps. The 'guiding principle' is that downstream investment by companies 'owned' or 'controlled' by non resident entities would require to follow the same norms as a direct foreign investment *i.e.* only as much can be done by way of indirect foreign investment through downstream investment under this policy as can be done through direct foreign investment and what can be done directly can be done indirectly under same norms.

The Guidelines for calculation of total foreign investment, both direct and indirect in an Indian company, at every stage of investment, including downstream investment, have been detailed in paragraphs above mentioned, which enables determination of total foreign investment in any/all Indian Companies.

For the purpose of this chapter,—

(*i*) 'Operating Company' is an Indian company which is undertaking operations in various economic activities and sectors;

(*ii*) 'Downstream investment' means indirect foreign investment by one Indian company into another Indian company by way of subscription or acquisition.

Removal of the condition of prior approval, in case of joint ventures/technical collaboration in the 'same field': The DIPP in the Press Release on Circular 1 of 2011, expressed that "*there is a felt need to attract fresh investment and technology inflows into the country, as also to reduce the levels of State intervention in the commercial sphere. Keeping in view the above, Government has decided to abolish this condition. It is expected that this measure will promote the competitiveness of India as an investment destination and be instrumental in attracting higher levels of FDI and technology inflows into the country*".

This is a welcome measure, which was relaxed previously by way of Press Note 1 of 2005 and now removed.

Downstream investments: Foreign investment in Indian companies can be direct or indirect. Any non-resident investment in an Indian company is direct foreign investment. Indian company would have indirect foreign investment if the Indian investing company has foreign investment in it.

As per the Consolidated Circular, 'Downstream investment' means indirect foreign investment, by one Indian company, into another Indian company, by way of subscription or acquisition, made in accordance with guidelines and conditions provided under the Circular.

The test for computing indirect foreign investment is to see whether the Indian company is owned or controlled by nonresident entities. In case an Indian company is owned or controlled by a non-resident entity, the investment made by such an Indian company into another Indian company would be considered as indirect foreign investment.

Thus, the Companies have now been classified into only two categories – 'companies owned *or* controlled by foreign investors' and 'companies owned *and* controlled by Indian residents'. The earlier categorisation of *'investing companies', 'operating companies'* and *'investing-cum-*operating *companies'* has been done away with.

Though, the new guidelines are aimed to comprehensively simplify and rationalise downstream investment, by removing the complex structure of *'investing companies', 'operating companies'* and *'investing-cum-*operating *companies'*, the concept of '*operating-cum-investing/investing companies*' still finds a mention in the consolidated circular, while calculating the total foreign investment.

(a) Guidelines for downstream investment by Investing Indian Companies 'owned or controlled by non resident entities'

The Policy on downstream investment comprises policy for (*a*) only operating companies (*b*) operating-cum-investing companies (*c*) only investing companies as below:

(*i*) *Only operating companies:* Foreign investment in such companies would have to comply with the relevant sectoral conditions on entry route, conditionalities and caps with regard to the sectors in which such companies are operating.

(*ii*) *Operating-cum-investing companies:* Foreign investment into such companies would have to comply with the relevant sectoral conditions on entry route, conditionalities and caps with regard to the sectors in which such companies are operating. Further, the subject Indian companies into which downstream investments are made by such companies would have to comply with the relevant sectoral conditions on entry route, conditionalities and caps in regard of the sector in which the subject Indian companies are operating.

(*iii*) *Investing companies:* Foreign Investment in Investing Companies will require the prior Government/FIPB approval, regardless of the amount or extent of foreign investment. The Indian companies into which downstream investments are made by such investing companies would have to comply with the relevant sectoral conditions on entry route, conditionalities and caps in regard of the sector in which the subject Indian companies are operating.

For infusion of foreign investment into such companies which do not have any operations and also do not have any downstream investments, Government/ FIPB approval would be required, regardless of the amount or extent of foreign investment. Further, as and when such company commences business(s) or makes downstream investment it will have to comply with the relevant sectoral conditions on entry route, conditionalities and caps.

For Operating-cum- investing companies and investing companies and for other companies as per para given above, downstream investments can be made subject to the following conditions:

(*i*) Such company has to notify SIA, DIPP and FIPB of its downstream investment within 30 days of such investment even if capital instruments have not been allotted along with the modality of investment in new/ existing ventures (with/without expansion programme);

(*ii*) downstream investment by way of induction of foreign equity in an existing Indian Company to be duly supported by a resolution of the Board of Directors supporting the said induction as also a shareholders Agreement if any;

(*iii*) issue/transfer/pricing/valuation of shares shall be in accordance with applicable SEBI/RBI guidelines;

(*iv*) For the purpose of downstream investment, the operating cum investing companies and the investing companies would have to bring in requisite funds from abroad and not leverage funds from domestic market for such investments. This would, however, not preclude downstream operating companies to raise debt in the domestic market.

4. Entry Routes for Investment

Investments can be made by non-residents in the shares/fully, compulsorily and mandatorily convertible debentures/fully, compulsorily and mandatorily convertible preference shares of an Indian company, through two routes:

1. the Automatic Route; and
2. the Government Route

Under the Automatic Route, the foreign investor or the Indian company does not require any approval from the RBI or Government of India for the investment. Under the Government Route, prior approval of the Government of India through Foreign Investment Promotion Board (FIPB) is required. Proposals for foreign investment under Government route as laid down in the FDI policy from time to time, are considered by the Foreign Investment Promotion Board (FIPB) in Department of Economic Affairs (DEA), Ministry of Finance.

(a) Investment subjected to the 'Existing Venture/tie-up condition'

Investment would be subject to the 'Existing Venture/tie-up condition' as defined below:

1. *Conflict of Interest Clause:* With effect from January 12, 2005 the joint venture agreements are expected to include a *'conflict of interest'* clause to determine/safeguard the interests of joint venture partners in the event of one of the partners desiring to set up another joint venture or a wholly owned subsidiary in the same field of economic activity. The policy is, however, expected to protect the interest of the joint venture partner where the agreement had been entered prior to January 12, 2005;
2. *Onus of new venture justification:* Where a foreign investor has an existing joint venture/technology transfer/trademark agreement in the same field, prior to January 12, 2005, the proposal for fresh investment/ technology transfer/technology collaboration/trademark agreement in a new joint venture for technology transfer/technology collaboration/ trademark agreement would have to be under the Government approval route through FIPB/Project Approval Board. The onus to provide requisite justification that the new tie-up would not jeopardize the existing joint venture or technology transfer/trademark partner, would lie equally on the foreign investor/technology supplier and the Indian partner;
3. *Exempted Investments:* The following investments, however, will be exempt from the requirement of Government approval even though the foreign investor may be having a joint venture or technology transfer/ trademark agreement in the same filed:
   (*a*) Investments to be made by Venture Capital Fund registered with the Securities and Exchange Board of India (SEBI); or
   (*b*) Investments by Multinational Financial Institutions like Asian Development Bank (ADB), International Finance Corporation (IFC), Commonwealth Finance Corporation (CFC), Deutsche Entwicklungs Gescelschaft (DEG) etc.; or
   (*c*) Where in the existing joint venture, investment by either of the parties is less than 3 per cent; or
   (*d*) Where the existing joint venture/collaboration is defunct or sick; or
   (*e*) For issue of shares of an Indian company engaged in Information Technology sector or in the mining sector, if the existing joint venture or technology transfer/trade mark agreement of the person to whom the shares are to be issued are also in the Information Technology sector or in the mining sector for same area/mineral.

(b) Guidelines for transfer of ownership or control of Indian companies in sectors with caps from resident Indian citizens to non-resident entities in sectors with caps

In sectors with caps, including *inter-alia* defence production, air transport services, ground handling services, asset reconstruction companies, private sector banking, broadcasting, commodity exchanges, credit information companies, insurance, print media, telecommunications and satellites, *Government approval/ FIPB approval would be required in all cases where*:

(*i*) An Indian company is being established with foreign investment and is *owned* by a non-resident entity; or

(*ii*) An Indian company is being established with foreign investment and is *controlled* by a nonresident entity; or

(*iii*) The *control* of an existing Indian company, currently owned or controlled by resident Indian citizens and Indian companies, which are owned or controlled by resident Indian citizens, will be/is being transferred/passed on to a non-resident entity as a consequence of transfer of shares and/or fresh issue of shares to non-resident entities through amalgamation, merger/demerger, acquisition etc.; or

(*iv*) The *ownership* of an existing Indian company, currently owned or controlled by resident Indian citizens and Indian companies, which are owned or controlled by resident Indian citizens, will be/is being transferred/passed on to a non-resident entity as a consequence of transfer of shares and/or fresh issue of shares to non-resident entities through amalgamation, merger/demerger, acquisition etc.

It is clarified that these policy guidelines will not apply for sectors/activities where there are no foreign investment caps, that is, 100% foreign investment is permitted under the automatic route. It is also clarified that Foreign investment shall include all types of foreign investments *i.e.* FDI, investment by FIIs, NRIs, ADRs, GDRs, Foreign Currency Convertible Bonds (FCCB) and fully, mandatorily & compulsorily convertible preference shares/debentures, regardless of whether the said investments have been made under Schedule 1, 2, 3 and 6 of FEMA (Transfer or Issue of Security by Persons Resident Outside India) Regulations.

5. Caps on Investments

Investments can be made by non-residents in the capital of a resident entity only to the extent of the percentage of the total capital as provided/permitted in the FDI policy. Thus while investment are prohibited in some sectors/activities, there are restrictions/conditions/caps on the investment in certain other sector/ activities. The caps in various sector(s)/activity are detailed out in Chapter 5 of this new policy (see Chapter 6 for details).

6. Entry Conditions on Investment

Investments can be permitted to be made by non-residents in the capital of a resident entity in certain sectors/activity with entry conditions. These entry conditions would be applicable for investment only by non-resident entities. Such conditions may include norms for minimum capitalization, lock-in period, etc. The entry conditions in various sectors/activities are detailed in Chapter 5 of this new policy (see Chapter 6 for details).

7. Other Conditions on Investment besides Entry Conditions

Besides the entry conditions on foreign investment, the investment/investors need to confirm to all relevant sectoral laws, regulations, rules etc. The national security/internal security related conditions as contained in relevant statutes will also have to be complied with. The State Governments/Union Territories have regulations in relations to the subjects in their legislative domain. These conditions also have to be met/complied with.

8. Guidelines for Consideration of FDI Proposals by FIPB

The following guidelines are laid down to enable the FIPB to consider the proposals for FDI and formulate its recommendations:

(*i*) All applications should be put up before the FIPB by its Secretariat within 15 days and it should be ensured that comments of the administrative ministries are placed before the Board either prior to/or in the meeting of the Board;

(*ii*) Proposals should be considered by the Board keeping in view the time frame of thirty (30) days for communicating Government decision;

(*iii*) In cases in which either the proposal is not cleared or further information is required in order to obviate delays presentation by applicant in the meeting of the FIPB should be resorted to;

(*iv*) While considering cases and making recommendations, FIPB should keep in mind the sectoral requirements and the sectoral policies vis-à-vis the proposal(s);

(*v*) FIPB would consider each proposal in its totality.

The Board should examine the following while considering proposals submitted to it for consideration:

(*i*) whether the items of activity involve industrial licence or not and if so the considerations for grant of industrial licence must be gone into;

(*ii*) whether the proposal involves any export projection and if so the items of export and the projected destinations;

(*iii*) whether the proposal has any strategic or defence related considerations.

While considering proposals the following may be prioritised.

(*i*) Items falling in infrastructure sector;

(*ii*) Items which have an export potential;

(*iii*) Items which have large scale employment potential and especially for rural people;

(*iv*) Items which have a direct or backward linkage with agro business/farm sector;

(*v*) Items which have greater social relevance such as hospitals, human resource development, life saving drugs and equipment;

(*vi*) Proposals which result in induction of technology or infusion of capital.

The following should be especially considered during the scrutiny and consideration of proposals.

(*i*) The extent of foreign equity proposed to be held (keeping in view sectoral caps, if any);

(*ii*) Extent of equity from the point of view whether the proposed project would amount to a holding company/wholly owned subsidiary/a company with dominant foreign investment (*i.e.* 76% or more) joint venture;

(*iii*) Whether the proposed foreign equity is for setting up a new project (joint venture or otherwise) or whether it is for enlargement of foreign/NRI equity or whether it is for fresh induction of foreign equity/NRI equity in an existing Indian company;

(*iv*) In the case of fresh induction offerings/NRI equity and/or in cases of enlargement of foreign/NRI equity, in existing Indian companies whether there is a resolution of the Board of Directors supporting the said induction/enlargement of foreign/NRI equity and whether there is a shareholders agreement or not;

(*v*) In the case of induction of fresh equity in the existing Indian companies and/or enlargement of foreign equity in existing Indian companies, the reason why the proposal has been made and the modality for induction/enhancement (*i.e.* whether by increase of paid up capital/authorized capital, transfer of shares (hostile or otherwise) whether by rights issue, or by what modality;

(*vi*) Issue/transfer/pricing of shares will be as per SEBI/RBI guidelines;

(*vii*) Whether the activity is an industrial activity or a service activity or a combination of both;

(*vii*) Whether the items of activity involves any restriction by way of reservation for the Micro & Small Enterprises sector;

(*ix*) Whether there are any sectoral restrictions on the activity;

(*x*) Whether the proposal involves import of items which are either hazardous, banned or detrimental to environment (e.g. import of plastic scrap or recycled plastics).

As per this policy, no condition specific to the letter of approval issued to a foreign investor would be changed or additional condition imposed subsequent to the issue of a letter of approval. This would not prohibit changes in general policies and, regulations applicable to the industrial sector.

9. Constitution of FIPB

FIPB comprises of the following Core Group of Secretaries to the Government of India:

(*i*) Secretary to Government, Department of Economic Affairs, Ministry of Finance – Chairperson;

(*ii*) Secretary to Government, Department of Industrial Policy & Promotion, Ministry of Commerce & Industry;

(*iii*) Secretary to Government, Department of Commerce, Ministry of Commerce & Industry;

(*iv*) Secretary to Government, Economic Relations, Ministry of External Affairs;

(*v*) Secretary to Government, Ministry of Overseas Indian Affairs.

The Board would be able to co-opt other Secretaries to the Central Government and top officials of financial institutions, banks and professional experts of Industry and Commerce, as and when necessary.

10. Approval Levels for Cases under Government Route

The following approval levels shall operate for proposals involving FDI under the Government route *i.e.* requiring prior Government approval:

(*i*) The Minister of Finance who is in-charge of FIPB would consider the recommendations of FIPB on proposals with total foreign equity inflow of and below ₹ 1200 crore;

(*ii*) The recommendations of FIPB on proposals with total foreign equity inflow of more than ₹ 1200 crore would be placed for consideration of CCEA. The FIPB Secretariat in DEA will process the recommendations of FIPB to obtain the approval of Minister of Finance and CCEA;

(*iii*) The CCEA would also consider the proposals which may be referred to it by the FIPB/the Minister of Finance (in-charge of FIPB).

11. Cases which do not require Fresh Approval

Companies may not require fresh prior approval of the Government *i.e.* Minister in-charge of FIPB/CCEA for bringing in additional foreign investment into the same entity, in the following cases:

(*i*) Cases of entities whose activities had earlier required prior approval of FIPB/CCFI/CCEA and who had, accordingly, earlier obtained prior approval of FIPB/CCFI/CCEA for their initial foreign investment but subsequently such activities/sectors have been placed under automatic route;

(*ii*) Cases of entities whose activities had sectoral caps earlier and who had, accordingly, earlier obtained prior approval of FIPB/CCFI/CCEA for their initial foreign investment but subsequently such caps were removed/increased and the activities placed under the automatic route, provided that such additional investment alongwith the initial/original investment does not exceed the sectoral caps; and

(*iii*) The cases of additional foreign investment into the same entity where prior approval of FIPB/CCFI/CCEA had been obtained earlier for the initial/original foreign investment due to requirements of Press Note 18/1998 or Press Note 1 of 2005 and prior approval of the Government under the FDI policy is not required for any other reason/purpose.

Appendix

Press Notes

Press Note No. 2 (2009 Series), dated 13-2-2009

Guidelines for Calculation of total Foreign Investment *i.e.* Direct and Indirect Foreign Investment in Indian Companies

Investment in Indian companies can be made both by non-resident as well as resident Indian entities. Any non-resident investment in an Indian company is direct foreign investment. Investment by resident Indian entities could again comprise of both resident and non-resident investment. Thus, such an Indian company would have indirect foreign investment if the Indian investing company has foreign investment in it. The indirect investment can be a cascading investment *i.e.* through multi-layered structure also.

2.0 The method of calculation of total foreign investment in an Indian company including indirect foreign investment through other Indian companies has been detailed out in entry 10 of Press Note 2 (2000), Press Note 1 (2006), Press Note 3 (2007) and entry 24 of Press Note 7 (2008). The methodology for some sectors is also separately contained in either sectoral regulations or rules and regulations under specific statutes. Essentially the present FDI guidelines provide for three different regimes for calculation of Indirect Foreign Equity.

2.1 Proportionate method is used in Telecom/Broadcasting sectors through Press Note 5 of 2005 (modifying Press Note 2 of 2000), Press Note 1 (2006) and Press Note 3 (2007).

2.2 Insurance: outlined in IRDA regulations (IRDA (Registration of Indian Insurance Companies) Regulations, 2000); and

2.3 In all other sectors, for an investing company in the infrastructure/ service sector attracting equity caps, indirect equity is calculated as was given in Press Note 2 of 2000: *Investing companies in infrastructure/service sectors (entry no. 10). This policy was reiterated by Press Note 4 of 2006 (Entry No. 18) which was modified by a Press release dated November 13, 2006 and Press Note 7(2008) (entry 24).* According to this, foreign investment in an investing company will not be set off against this cap where the foreign equity in the investing company does not exceed 49% and the Management of the investing company is with Indian owners. FIPB approval is required by Investing Companies for downstream investment.

3.0 Recognising the need to bring in clarity, uniformity, consistency and homogeneity into the exact methodology of calculation across sectors/activities for all direct and indirect foreign investment in Indian companies, Government of India now proposes to issue the following guidelines for calculation of direct and indirect foreign investment.

4.0 Definitions

4.1 For the purpose of computation of indirect Foreign investment, Foreign Investment in Indian company shall include all types of foreign investments *i.e.* FDI, investment by FIIs (holding as on March 31), NRIs, ADRs, GDRs, Foreign Currency Convertible Bonds (FCCB) and convertible preference shares, convertible Currency Debentures regardless of whether the said investments have been made under Schedule 1, 2, 3 and 6 of FEMA (Transfer or Issue of Security by Persons Resident Outside India) Regulations.

4.2 The term 'Resident Indian Citizen' shall be interpreted in line with the definition of 'person resident in India' as per FEMA, 1999, read in conjunction with the Indian Citizenship Act.

4.3 A 'non resident entity' means a 'person resident outside India' as defined under FEMA 1999.

4.4 The term 'Indian Company' means a company registered or incorporated in India as per the Indian Companies Act, 1956.

4.5 'Investing Company' means an Indian Company making equity/ preference/CCD investment into another Indian Company.

4.6 Holding Company would have the same meaning as defined in Indian Companies Act 1956.

5.0 Guidelines for calculation of total foreign investment *i.e.* direct and indirect foreign investment in an Indian company

5.1 Counting the Direct Foreign Investment

5.1.1. All investment directly by a non-resident entity into the Indian company would be counted towards foreign investment.

5.2 Counting of indirect foreign Investment

5.2.1 The foreign investment through the investing Indian company would not be considered for calculation of the indirect foreign investment in case of Indian companies which are 'owned and controlled' by resident Indian citizens and/or Indian Companies which are owned and controlled by resident Indian citizens.

For this purpose, an Indian company may be taken as being:

- **"owned"** by resident Indian citizens and Indian companies, which are owned and controlled by resident Indian citizens, if more than 50% of the equity interest in it is beneficially owned by resident Indian citizens and Indian companies, which are owned and controlled ultimately by resident Indian citizens;

and

- **"controlled"** by resident Indian citizens and Indian companies, which are owned and controlled by resident Indian citizens, if the resident

Indian citizens and Indian companies, which are owned and controlled by resident Indian citizens, have the power to appoint a majority of its directors.

5.2.2 For cases where condition 5.2.1 above is not satisfied or if the investing company is owned or controlled by 'non resident entities', the entire investment by the investing company into the subject Indian Company would be considered as indirect foreign investment,

5.2.2.1 Provided that, as an exception, the indirect foreign investment in only the 100% owned subsidiaries of operating-cum-investing/investing companies, will be limited to the foreign investment in the operating-cum-investing/investing company. For the purposes of explanation, it is clarified that this exception is being made since the downstream investment of a 100% owned subsidiary of the holding company is akin to investment made by the holding company and the downstream investment should be a mirror image of the holding company.

5.2.2.2 For the above purpose, an Indian company may be taken as being:

- **"owned"** by 'non resident entities', if more than 50% of the equity interest in it is beneficially owned by non-residents
- **"controlled"** by 'non resident entities', if non-residents have the power to appoint a majority of its directors

5.2.2.3 Illustration

To illustrate, if the indirect foreign investment is being calculated for Company A which has investment through an investing company B having foreign investment, the following would be the method of calculation:

(*i*) where Company B has foreign investment less than 50%- Company A would not be taken as having any indirect foreign investment through Company B.

(*ii*) where Company B has foreign investment of say 75% and:

(*a*) invests 26% in Company A, the entire 26% investment by Company B would be treated as indirect foreign investment in Company A;

(*b*) Invests 80% in Company A, the indirect foreign investment in Company A would be taken as 80%

(*c*) where Company A is a wholly owned subsidiary of Company B (*i.e.* Company B owns 100% shares of Company A), then only 75% would be treated as indirect foreign equity and the balance 25% would be treated as resident held equity. The indirect foreign equity in Company A would be computed in the ratio of 75: 25 in the total investment of Company B in Company A.

5.3 The total foreign investment would be the sum total of direct and indirect foreign investment.

5.4 The above methodology of calculation would apply at every stage of investment in Indian Companies and thus to each and every Indian Company.

5.5 Additional Conditions

5.5.1 The full details about the foreign investment including ownership details etc. in Indian company(s) and information about the control of the company(s) would be furnished by the Company(s) to the Government of India at the time of seeking approval.

5.5.2 In any sector/activity, where Government approval is required for foreign investment and in cases where there are any *inter-se* agreements between/ amongst share-holders which have an effect on the appointment of the Board of Directors or on the exercise of voting rights or of creating voting rights disproportionate to shareholding or any incidental matter thereof, such agreements will have to be informed to the approving authority. The approving authority will consider for determining ownership and control such *inter-se* agreements when considering the case for granting approval for foreign investment.

5.5.3 In all sectors attracting sectoral caps, the balance equity *i.e.* beyond the sectoral foreign investment cap, would specifically be beneficially owned by/held with/in the hands of resident Indian citizens and Indian companies, owned and controlled by resident Indian citizens.

5.5.4 In the I& B and Defense sectors where the sectoral cap is less than 49%, the company would need to be 'owned and controlled' by resident Indian citizens and Indian companies, which are owned and controlled by resident Indian citizens.

5.5.4.1 For this purpose, the equity held by the largest Indian shareholder would have to be at least 51% of the total equity, excluding the equity held by Public Sector Banks and Public Financial Institutions, as defined in Section 4A of the Companies Act, 1956. The term 'largest Indian shareholder', used in this clause, will include any or a combination of the following:

(*i*) In the case of an individual shareholder,—

(*a*) The individual shareholder,

(*b*) A relative of the shareholder within the meaning of Section 6 of the Companies Act, 1956.

(*c*) A company/group of companies in which the individual shareholder/ HUF to which he belongs has management and controlling interest.

(*ii*) In the case of an Indian company,—

(*a*) The Indian company

(*b*) A group of Indian companies under the same management and ownership control.

5.5.4.2 For the purpose of this Clause, "Indian company" shall be a company which must have a resident Indian or a relative as defined under Section 6 of the Companies Act, 1956/HUF, either singly or in combination holding at least 51% of the shares.

5.5.4.3 Provided that, in case of a combination of all or any of the entities mentioned in Sub-Clauses (*i*) and (*ii*) of clause 5.5.4.1 above, each of the parties shall have entered into a legally binding agreement to act as a single unit in managing the matters of the applicant company.

5.5.5 If a declaration is made by persons as per section 187C of the Indian Companies Act about a beneficial interest being held by a non resident entity, then even though the investment may be made by a resident Indian citizen, the same shall be counted as foreign investment.

6.0 The above mentioned policy and the methodology would be applicable for determining the total foreign investment in all sectors, excepting in sectors where it is governed specifically under any statutes or rules thereunder. Thus, for the present purposes this methodology will not be applicable in the Insurance Sector where it will continue to be governed by the relevant Regulation.

7.0 Policy for downstream investment by investing companies

Based on the above methodology for calculation of total foreign investment in Indian companies, the policy on downstream investment-*i.e.* for only operating companies, operating-cum-investing companies, investing companies and for holding companies without any downstream investment and operations would be notified separately in amendment to Press Note 3 of 1997, Press Note 9 of 1999, entry 10 under Press Note 2 of 2000, entry 18 under Press Note 4 of 2006 as amended by the Press release dated 13th November, 2006, and entry 24 of Press Note 7 (2008).

8.0 Any foreign investment already made in accordance with the guidelines in existence prior to issue of this Press Note would not require any modification to conform with these guidelines. All other investments, past and future, would come under the ambit of these new guidelines.

8.1 Any violation of these guidelines and noncompliance would be a violation under FEMA 1999 and would lead to action under the relevant regulations under the Act.

9.0 Entry 10 under Press Note 2(2000), entry 18 under Press Note 4 (2006), as amended by the Press Release dated 13th November, 2006 and entry 24 under Press Note 7 (2008) stand deleted.

10.0 The relevant entry pertaining to calculation of foreign equity of the applicant company under paragraph 2(*c*) of Press Note 1 of 2006 and paragraph 2.A.(*ii*) of Press Note 3 of 2007 stand deleted.

11.0 These guidelines will be effective from the date of issue of this Press Note.

Press Note No. 3 (2009 Series), dated 13-2-2010

Guidelines for Transfer of Ownership or Control of Indian Companies in Sectors with caps from Resident Indian Citizens to Non-resident Entities

At present, the transfer of shares from residents to non-residents, including acquisition of shares in an existing company, is on the automatic route, subject to the sectoral policy on FDI. Concerns have been raised on recent acquisitions of certain Indian companies by non-resident entities in sectors with caps. Accordingly, guidelines for transfer of ownership or control of Indian companies in sectors with caps from resident Indian citizens to non-resident entities have been formulated and are enumerated below.

2.0 Definitions

2.1 The term 'Resident Indian Citizen' shall be interpreted in line with the definition of 'person resident in India' as per FEMA, 1999, read in conjunction with the Indian Citizenship Act.

2.2 A 'non resident entity' means a 'person resident outside India' as defined under FEMA 1999.

2.3 The term 'Indian Company' means a company registered or incorporated in India as per the Indian Companies Act, 1956.

2.4 For the purpose of these guidelines, an Indian company may be taken as being:

- **"owned"** by resident Indian citizens and Indian companies, which are owned and controlled by resident Indian citizens, if more than 50% of the equity interest in it is beneficially owned by resident Indian citizens and Indian companies, which are owned and controlled ultimately by resident Indian citizens;
- **"controlled"** by resident Indian citizens and Indian companies, which are owned and controlled by resident Indian citizens, if the resident Indian citizens and Indian companies, which are owned and controlled by resident Indian citizens, have the power to appoint a majority of its directors.

2.5 Further, for the above purpose, an Indian company may be taken as being:

- **"owned"** by 'non resident entities', if more than 50% of the equity interest in it is beneficially owned by non-residents
- **"controlled"** by 'non resident entities', if non-residents have the power to appoint a majority of its directors.

2.6 Foreign investment shall include all types of foreign investments *i.e.* FDI, investment by FIIs, NRIs, ADRs, GDRs, Foreign Currency Convertible Bonds (FCCB) and convertible preference shares, regardless of whether the said investments have been made under Schedule 1, 2, 3 and 6 of FEMA (Transfer or Issue of Security by Persons Resident Outside India) Regulations.

3.0 Guidelines for transfer of ownership or control of Indian companies in sectors with caps from resident Indian citizens to non-resident entities in sectors with caps

3.1 In sectors with caps, including *inter alia* defence production, air transport services, ground handling services, asset reconstruction companies, private sector banking, broadcasting, commodity exchanges, credit information companies, insurance, print media, telecommunications and satellites, Government approval/ FIPB approval would be required in all cases where:

3.1.1 An Indian company is being established with foreign investment and is owned by a non-resident entity or

3.1.2 An Indian company is being established with foreign investment and is controlled by a non-resident entity or

3.1.3 The control of an existing Indian company, currently owned or controlled by resident Indian citizens and Indian companies, which are owned or controlled by resident Indian citizens, will be/is being transferred/passed on to a non-resident entity as a consequence of transfer of shares to non-resident entities through amalgamation, merger, acquisition etc. or

3.1.4 The ownership of an existing Indian company, currently owned or controlled by resident Indian citizens and Indian companies, which are owned or controlled by resident Indian citizens, will be/is being transferred/passed on to a non-resident entity as a consequence of transfer of shares to non-resident entities through amalgamation, merger, acquisition etc.

3.2 It is clarified that these guidelines will not apply for sectors/activities where there are no foreign investment caps, that is, 100% foreign investment is permitted under the automatic route.

4.0 These guidelines will issue in modification of paragraph 2(*e*) of Press Note 4 of 2006 and will be effective from the date of issue of this Press Note. FDI policy announced vide Annex to Press Note 7 (2008) dated 16th June, 2008 stands amplified to the above extent.

Press Note No. 4 (2009 Series), dated 25-2-2009

Clarificatory guidelines on downstream investment by Indian Companies

The Policy for downstream investment by Indian companies seeks to lay down and clarify about compliance with the Foreign investment norms on entry route, conditionalities and sectoral caps. The 'guiding principle' is that downstream investment by companies 'owned' or 'controlled' by non resident entities would require to follow the same norms as a direct foreign investment i.e. only as much can be done by way of indirect foreign investment through downstream investment in terms of Press Note 2 (2009 series) as can be done through direct foreign investment and what can be done directly can be done indirectly under same norms.

2.0 The Guidelines for calculation of total foreign investment, both direct and indirect in an Indian company, at every stage of investment, including downstream investment, have been detailed in Press Note 2 of 2009 which enables determination of total foreign investment in any/all Indian Companies.

3.0 Definitions

3.1 The term 'Indian Company' means a company registered or incorporated in India as per the Indian Companies Act, 1956

3.2 'Operating Company' is an Indian company which is undertaking operations in various economic activities and sectors.

3.3 'Downstream investment' means indirect foreign investment by one Indian company into another Indian company by way of subscription or acquisition in terms of Press Note 2 of 2009. Para 5.2 of the said Press Note provides the guidelines for calculation of indirect foreign investment with conditions specified in para 5.5.

3.4 'Investing Company' means an Indian Company holding only investments in another Indian company, directly or indirectly, other than for trading of such holdings/securities.

3.5 'Foreign Investment' would have the same meaning as in Press Note 2 (2009 series).

4.0 Guidelines for downstream investment by Investing Indian Companies 'owned or controlled by non resident entities' as per Press Note 2 of 2009

Recognizing the need to bring in clarity into the Policy for downstream investment by investing Indian companies, the Government of India now proposes to clarify the policy in this regard.

4.1 The Policy on downstream investment comprises policy for (*a*) only operating companies (*b*) operating-cum-investing companies (*c*) only investing companies.

4.2 The Policy in this regard will be as below:

4.2.1 Only operating companies: Foreign investment in such companies would have to comply with the relevant sectoral conditions on entry route, conditionalities and caps with regard to the sectors in which such companies are operating.

4.2.2 Operating-cum-investing companies: Foreign investment into such companies would have to comply with the relevant sectoral conditions on entry route, conditionalities and caps with regard to the sectors in which such companies are operating. Further, the subject Indian companies into which downstream investments are made by such companies would have to comply with the relevant sectoral conditions on entry route, conditionalities and caps in regard of the sector in which the subject Indian companies are operating.

4.2.3 Investing companies: Foreign Investment in Investing Companies will require the prior Government/FIPB approval, regardless of the amount or extent of foreign investment. The Indian companies into which downstream investments are made by such investing companies would have to comply with the relevant sectoral conditions on entry route, conditionalities and caps in regard of the sector in which the subject Indian companies are operating.

5.0 For companies which do not have any operations and also do not have any downstream investments, for infusion of foreign investment into such companies, Government/FIPB approval would be required, regardless of the amount or extent of foreign investment. Further, as and when such company commences business(s) or makes downstream investment it will have to comply with the relevant sectoral conditions on entry route, conditionalities and caps.

6.0 For Operating-cum- investing companies and investing companies (Para 4.2.2, 4.2.3) and for companies as per para 5.0 above, downstream investments can be made subject to the following conditions:

(*a*) Such company is to notify SIA, DIPP and FIPB of its downstream investment within 30 days of such investment even if equity shares/ CCPS/CCD have not been allotted along with the modality of investment in new/existing ventures (with/without expansion programme);

(*b*) downstream investment by way of induction of foreign equity in an existing Indian Company to be duly supported by a resolution of the Board of Directors supporting the said induction as also a shareholders Agreement if any;

(*c*) issue/transfer/pricing/valuation of shares shall be in accordance with applicable SEBI/RBI guidelines;

(*d*) Investing companies would have to bring in requisite funds from abroad and not leverage funds from domestic market for such investments. This would, however, not preclude downstream operating companies to raise debt in the domestic market.

5.0 Para 11 of Press Note 3 of 1997 and Press Note 9 of 1999 stand deleted. These guidelines will be effective from the date of issue of this Press Note. FDI Policy announced *vide* Annex to Press Note 7 (2008), dated June 16, 2008 stands amplified to the above extent.

Press Note No. 18 (1998 Series), dated 14-12-1998

Guidelines pertaining to approval of foreign/technical collaborations under the automatic route with previous ventures/tie-up in India

1. The Government have reviewed the present Guidelines relating to approval of foreign/technical collaborations under the automatic route and after careful consideration it has been decided that foreign financial/technical collaborators with previous ventures/tie-up in India would be subjected to the following guidelines:

I. Automatic route for FDI and/or technology collaboration would not be available to those who have or had any previous joint venture or technology transfer/trade-mark agreement in the same or allied field in India. RBI, therefore, have to stipulate necessary declaration before applications for the automatic route are taken on record.

II. Investors of Technology to the suppliers of the above category therefore will have to necessarily seek the FIPB/PAB approval route for joint ventures or the technology transfer agreements (including trade-mark) giving detailed circumstances in which they find it necessary to set-up a new joint venture/enter into new technology transfer (including trade-mark).

III. The onus is clearly on such investors/technology suppliers to provide the requisite justification as also proof to the satisfaction of FIPB/PAB that the new proposal would not in any way jeopardize the interests of the existing joint venture or technology/trade-mark partner or other stakeholders. It will be at the sole discretion of FIPB/PAB to either approve the application with or without conditions or reject in toto duly recording the reasons for doing so.

2. The above procedure will form part of the approval procedures contained in the "Manual on Industrial Policy & Procedures in India" published by SIA, Ministry of Industries, Government of India, which shall stand clarified accordingly in respect of foreign/technical collaborators with previous joint ventures/tie-up in India.

Press Note No. 1 (2005 Series), dated 12-1-2005

Guidelines pertaining to approval of foreign/technical collaborations under the automatic route with previous ventures/tie-up in India.

The Government has reviewed the guidelines notified vide Press Note 18 (1998 series) which stipulated approval of the Government for new proposals for foreign investment/technical collaboration where the foreign investor has or had any previous joint venture or technology transfer/trademark agreement in the same or allied field in India.

2. New proposals for foreign investment/technical collaboration would henceforth be allowed under the automatic route, subject to sectoral policies, as per the following guidelines:

(*i*) Prior approval of the Government would be required only in cases where the foreign investor has an existing joint venture or technoldgy transfer/trademark agreement in the 'same' field. The onus to provide requisite justification as also proof to the satisfaction of the Government that the new proposal would or would not in any way jeopardize the interests of the existing joint venture or technology/trademark partner or other stakeholders would lie equally on the foreign investor/technology supplier and the Indian partner.

(*ii*) Even in cases where the foreign investor has a joint venture or technology transfer/trademark agreement in the 'same' field prior approval of the Government will not be required in the following cases:

(*a*) Investments to be made by Venture Capital Funds registered with the Security and Exchange Board of India (SEBI); or

(*b*) where in the existing joint-venture investment by either of the parties is less than 3%; or

(*c*) where the existing venture/collaboration is defunct or sick.

(*iii*) In so far as joint ventures to be entered into after the date of this Press Note are concerned, the joint venture agreement may embody a 'conflict of interest' clause to safeguard the interests of joint venture partners in the event of one of the partners desiring to set up another joint venture or a wholly owned subsidiary in the 'same' field of economic activity.

3. These guidelines would come into force with immediate effect.

Chapter 6

POLICY ON ROUTE, CAPS AND ENTRY CONDITIONS

SYNOPSIS

1. Prohibition on Investment in India

FDI is prohibited in the following activities/sectors:

(*i*) Retail Trading (except single brand product retailing);

(*ii*) Atomic Energy;

(*iii*) Lottery Business including Government/private lottery, online lotteries, etc.;

(*iv*) Gambling and Betting including casinos etc.;

(*v*) Business of chit fund;

(*vi*) Nidhi company;

(*vii*) Trading in Transferable Development Rights (TDRs);

(*viii*) Real Estate Business or Construction of Farm Houses;

(*ix*) Activities/sectors not opened to private sector investment.

Besides foreign investment in any form, foreign technology collaboration in any form including licensing for franchise, trademark, brand name, management contract is also completely prohibited for Lottery Business and Gambling and Betting activities.

2. Agriculture

(a) Agriculture & Animal Husbandry

100% FDI is allowed under automatic route in Floriculture, Horticulture, Development of Seeds, Animal Husbandry, Pisciculture, Aquaculture and Cultivation of Vegetables & Mushrooms under controlled conditions and services related to agro and allied sectors. *Besides this, FDI is not allowed in any other agricultural sector/activity.*

For companies dealing with development of transgenic seeds/vegetables, the following conditions apply:

(*i*) When dealing with genetically modified seeds or planting material the company shall comply with safety requirements in accordance with laws enacted under the Environment (Protection) Act on the genetically modified organisms.

(*ii*) Any import of genetically modified materials if required shall be subject to the conditions laid down vide Notifications issued under Foreign Trade (Development and Regulation) Act, 1992.

(*iii*) The company shall comply with any other Law, Regulation or Policy governing genetically modified material in force from time to time.

(*iv*) Undertaking of business activities involving the use of genetically engineered cells and material shall be subject to the receipt of approvals from Genetic Engineering Approval Committee (GEAC) and Review Committee on Genetic Manipulation (RCGM).

(*v*) Import of materials shall be in accordance with National Seeds Policy.

Clarification on the coverage of "controlled conditions" for FDI in Agriculture, Animal Husbandry etc {*Para 5.2.1.1*(*vi*)}**:** The term is relevant because FDI is permitted only under '*controlled conditions*' under specified sub-sectors within the "Agriculture and Animal Husbandry" sector. A number of queries had been received from stakeholders with regard to the coverage of this term. The coverage/scope of the term 'controlled conditions' has now been separately defined in respect of 'animal husbandry', 'development of seeds', 'pisciculture and aquaculture' and 'floriculture/horticulture/cultivation of vegetables and mushrooms'. It is expected that this would lead to adequate clarity on FDI in this sector. (Circular 2 of 2010 as on September 30, 2010).

The term "under controlled conditions" covers the following:

1. 'Cultivation under controlled conditions' for the categories of Floriculture, Horticulture, Cultivation of vegetables and Mushrooms is the practice of cultivation wherein rainfall, temperature, solar radiation, air humidity and culture medium are controlled artificially. Control in these parameters may be effected through protected cultivation under green houses, net houses, polyhouses or any other improved infrastructure facilities where microclimatic conditions are regulated anthropogenically;
2. Development of seeds will be considered to be 'under controlled conditions' when seed farms/laboratories use tissue culture or any other micro-propagation techniques for development and multiplication of seeds/planting material. Seed development in the case of anthuriums, orchids and other ornamental crops in green houses/net houses/poly houses is also be included in this category.
3. In case of Animal Husbandry, scope of the term 'under controlled conditions' includes –
    - Rearing of animals under intensive farming systems with stall-feeding. Intensive farming system will require climate systems (ventilation, temperature/humidity management), health care and nutrition, herd registering/pedigree recording, use of machinery, waste management systems.
    - Poultry breeding farms and hatcheries where microclimate is controlled through advanced technologies like incubators, ventilation systems etc.
4. In the case of pisciculture and aquaculture, 'under controlled conditions' includes—
    - Aquariums
    - Hatcheries where eggs are artificially fertilized and fry are hatched and incubated in an enclosed environment with artificial climate control.

W.e.f. April 1st, 2011, in the agriculture sector, FDI will now be permitted in the development and production of seeds and planting material, without the stipulation of having to do so under 'controlled conditions'.

5. *Inclusion of 'apiculture', under controlled conditions, under the agricultural activities permitted for FDI (FDI Circular of 30-9-2011)*: FDI has been allowed up to 100% under the automatic route in apiculture under controlled conditions. Apiculture is an important agro-based industry and has the potential of bringing in high economic returns with comparatively low levels of investment. Being a decentralized activity, it does not bring pressure on land and can flourish as a household activity in villages. The activity has the potential of large scale income generation with some infusion of capital and technology. This liberalization would

not only provide the desired thrust to the sector but would also bring in international best practices to upgrade the product and the methods of production.

(*b*) *Tea Plantation*

100% FDI is allowed in the Tea sector including tea plantations under Government route subject to the conditions of:

(*a*) Compulsory divestment of 26% equity of the company in favour of an Indian partner/Indian public within a period of 5 years;

(*b*) Prior approval of the State Government concerned in case of any future land use change.

Besides the above, FDI is not allowed in any other plantation sector/activity.

3. Industry

(*a*) *Mining*

100% FDI is allowed under the automatic route in Mining and Exploration of metal and non-metal ores including diamond, gold, silver and precious ores but excluding titanium bearing minerals and its ores; subject to the Mines and Minerals (Development & Regulation) Act, 1957.

Clarification on the concept of value-addition in case of mining and mineral separation of Titanium bearing minerals {*Para 5.2.3.3.2*(*ii*)}: This is relevant because FDI for separation of Titanium bearing minerals and ores is subject to the setting up of value-addition facilities in India. It has been clarified that the objective of the policy is to ensure that raw material available in the country is utilized for setting up downstream industries and the technology available internationally is available for setting up such industries within the country. Thus, if with the technology transfer, the objective of the FDI policy can be achieved, the conditions stipulated in regard of setting up value addition facilities shall be deemed to be fulfilled. (Circular 2 of 2010 as on September 30, 2010).

(*b*) *Coal and Lignite*

(*a*) 100% FDI is allowed under the automatic route in Coal & Lignite mining for captive consumption by power projects, iron & steel and cement units and other eligible activities permitted under and subject to the provisions of Coal Mines (Nationalization) Act, 1973.

(*b*) 100% FDI is allowed for setting up coal processing plants like washeries subject to the condition that the company shall not do coal mining and shall not sell washed coal or sized coal from its coal processing plants in the open market and shall supply the washed or sized coal to those parties who are supplying raw coal to coal processing plants for washing or sizing.

(c) Mining and mineral separation of titanium bearing minerals and ores, its value addition and integrated activities

India has large reserves of beach sand minerals in the coastal stretches around the country. Titanium bearing minerals viz. Ilmenite, rutile and leucoxene, and Zirconium bearing minerals including zircon are some of the beach sand minerals which have been classified as "prescribed substances" under the Atomic Energy Act, 1962. Under the Industrial Policy Statement, 1991, mining and production of minerals classified as "prescribed substances" and specified in the Schedule to the Atomic Energy (Control of Production and Use) Order, 1953 were included in the list of industries reserved for the public sector.

Vide Resolution No. 8/1(1)/97-PSU/1422, dated 6th October, 1998 issued by the Department of Atomic Energy laying down the policy for exploitation of beach sand minerals, private participation including Foreign Direct Investment (FDI), was permitted in mining and production of Titanium ores (Ilmenite, Rutile and Leucoxene) and Zirconium minerals (Zircon). Vide Notification No. S.O. 61(E), dated 18-1-2006, the Department of Atomic Energy re-notified the list of "prescribed substances" under the Atomic Energy Act, 1962. Titanium bearing ores and concentrates (Ilmenite, Rutile and Leucoxene) and Zirconium, its alloys and compounds and minerals/concentrates including Zircon, were removed from the list of "prescribed substances".

FDI up to 100% is allowed under Government route in mining and mineral separation of titanium bearing minerals & ores, its value addition and integrated activities subject to sectoral regulations and the Mines and Minerals (Development and Regulation Act, 1957).

FDI for separation of titanium bearing minerals & ores will be subject to the following additional conditions viz:

(A) value addition facilities are set up within India along with transfer of technology;

(B) disposal of tailings during the mineral separation shall be carried out in accordance with regulations framed by the Atomic Energy Regulatory Board such as Atomic Energy (Radiation Protection) Rules, 2004 and the Atomic Energy (Safe Disposal of Radioactive Wastes) Rules, 1987.

FDI will not be allowed in mining of "prescribed substances" listed in the Notification No. S.O. 61(E), dated 18-1-2006 issued by the Department of Atomic Energy.

4. Manufacturing

(a) Manufacture of items reserved for production in Micro and Small Enterprises (MSEs)

Any industrial undertaking which is not a Micro or Small Scale Enterprise, but manufactures items reserved for the MSE sector would require Government route where foreign investment is more than 24% in the equity capital. Such an undertaking would also require an Industrial License under the Industries (Development & Regulation) Act 1951, for such manufacture. The issue of Industrial License is subject to a few general conditions and the specific condition that the Industrial Undertaking shall undertake to export a minimum of 50% of the new or additional annual production of the MSE reserved items to be achieved within a maximum period of three years. The export obligation would be applicable from the date of commencement of commercial production and in accordance with the provisions of section 11 of the Micro, Small and Medium Enterprises Development Act 2006. As per section 11 of MSMED Act, 2006, for facilitating promotion and development of micro and small enterprise, the Central Government or a State Government may notify preference policies in respect of procurement of goods and services, produced and provided by micro and small enterprise, by its Ministries, departments or its aided institutions and public sector enterprises. This is valid only for Micro and Small Enterprises and not for Medium Enterprises.

(b) Alcohol — Distillation & Brewing

100% FDI is allowed under the automatic route.

(c) Cigars & Cigarettes Manufacture

100% FDI is allowed under Government route and subject to the obtaining of Industrial licence under the Industries (Development & Regulation) Act, 1951.

Incorporation of Press Note 2 of 2010 relating to the prohibition on manufacture of cigarettes etc. {*Para 5.1*}: The manufacturing of 'cigars, cheroots, cigarillos and cigarettes, of tobacco or of tobacco substitutes', in which FDI had been prohibited earlier this year, has now been formally included in the list of sectors/activities in which FDI is prohibited. (Circular 2 of 2010 as on September 30, 2010).

(d) Coffee & Rubber processing and warehousing

100% FDI is allowed under the automatic route.

(e) Defence Industry

FDI is permissible up to 26%, under Government route subject to Industrial license under the Industries (Development & Regulation) Act, 1951 and the following conditions:

(*i*) Licence applications will be considered and licences given by the Department of Industrial Policy & Promotion, Ministry of Commerce & Industry, in consultation with Ministry of Defence.

(*ii*) Cases involving FDI will be considered by the FIPB and licences given by the Department of Industrial Policy & Promotion in consultation with Ministry of Defence.

(*iii*) The applicant should be an Indian company/partnership firm.

(*iv*) The management of the applicant company/partnership should be in Indian hands with majority representation on the Board as well as the Chief Executives of the company/partnership firm being resident Indians.

(*v*) Full particulars of the Directors and the Chief Executives should be furnished along with the applications.

(*vi*) The Government reserves the right to verify the antecedents of the foreign collaborators and domestic promoters including their financial standing and credentials in the world market. Preference would be given to original equipment manufacturers or design establishments, and companies having a good track record of past supplies to Armed Forces, Space and Atomic energy sections and having an established R&D base.

(*vii*) There would be no minimum capitalization for the FDI. A proper assessment, however, needs to be done by the management of the applicant company depending upon the product and the technology. The licensing authority would satisfy itself about the adequacy of the net worth of the foreign investor taking into account the category of weapons and equipment that are proposed to be manufactured.

(*viii*) There would be a three-year lock-in period for transfer of equity from one foreign investor to another foreign investor (including NRIs & erstwhile OCBs with 60% or more NRI stake) and such transfer would be subject to prior approval of the FIPB and the Government.

(*ix*) The Ministry of Defence is not in a position to give purchase guarantee for products to be manufactured. However, the planned acquisition programme for such equipment and overall requirements would be made available to the extent possible.

(*x*) The capacity norms for production will be provided in the licence based on the application as well as the recommendations of the Ministry of Defence, which will look into existing capacities of similar and allied products.

(*xi*) Import of equipment for pre-production activity including development of prototype by the applicant company would be permitted.

(*xii*) Adequate safety and security procedures would need to be put in place by the licensee once the licence is granted and production commences. These would be subject to verification by authorized Government agencies.

(*xiii*) The standards and testing procedures for equipment to be produced under licence from foreign collaborators or from indigenous R & D will have to be provided by the licensee to the Government nominated quality assurance agency under appropriate confidentiality clause. The nominated quality assurance agency would inspect the finished product and would conduct surveillance and audit of the Quality Assurance Procedures of the licensee. Self-certification would be permitted by the

Ministry of Defence on case to case basis, which may involve either individual items, or group of items manufactured by the licensee. Such permission would be for a fixed period and subject to renewals.

(*xiv*) Purchase preference and price preference may be given to the Public Sector organizations as per guidelines of the Department of Public Enterprises.

(*xv*) Arms and ammunition produced by the private manufacturers will be primarily sold to the Ministry of Defence. These items may also be sold to other Government entities under the control of the Ministry of Home Affairs and State Governments with the prior approval of the Ministry of Defence. No such item should be sold within the country to any other person or entity. The export of manufactured items would be subject to policy and guidelines as applicable to Ordnance Factories and Defence Public Sector Undertakings. Non-lethal items would be permitted for sale to persons/entities other than the Central of State Governments with the prior approval of the Ministry of Defence. Licensee would also need to institute a verifiable system of removal of all goods out of their factories. Violation of these provisions may lead to cancellation of the licence.

(*xvi*) Government decision on applications to FIPB for FDI in defence industry sector will be normally communicated within a time frame of 10 weeks from the date of acknowledgement.

(f) Drugs & Pharmaceuticals including those involving use of recombinant technology

100% FDI is allowed under the automatic route.

Press Note No. 3 (2011 Series), dated 8-11-2011

Review of the Policy on Foreign Direct Investment in Pharmaceuticals Sector — Insertion of a New Paragraph 6.2.25 to Circular 2 of 2011, dated 30-9-2011

1. Present Position

Foreign Direct Investment (FDI), up to 100%, under the automatic route, is permitted in the pharmaceuticals sector.

2. Revised Position

The Government of India has reviewed the extant policy on FDI and decided as under:

(*i*) FDI, up to 100%, under the automatic route, would continue to be permitted for greenfield investments in the pharmaceuticals sector.

(*ii*) FDI, up to 100%, would be permitted for brownfield investments (*i.e.*, investments in existing companies), in the pharmaceuticals sector, under the Government approval route.

3. Accordingly, the following amendment is made in *'Circular 2 of 2011-Consolidated FDI Policy'*, dated 30-9-2011, issued by the Department of Industrial Policy & Promotion:

Insertion of a new paragraph 6.2.25:

A new paragraph (6.2.25) is inserted as below:

6.2.25	**Pharmaceuticals**		
6.2.25.1	Greenfield	100%	Automatic
6.2.25.2	Existing companies	100%	Government

4. The above decision will take immediate effect. It would be reviewed after a period of six months.

(g) Hazardous chemicals viz. hydrocyanic acid and its derivatives; phosgene and its derivatives; and isocyanates and di-isocyanates of hydrocarbon

100% FDI is allowed under the automatic route and subject to the obtaining of Industrial licence under the Industries (Development & Regulation) Act, 1951.

(h) Industrial Explosives

100% FDI is allowed under the automatic route and subject to the obtaining of Industrial licence under the Industries (Development & Regulation) Act, 1951 and regulations under Explosives Act, 1898.

5. Power

(a) Electric Generation, Transmission, Distribution and Trading

FDI upto 100% is permitted under automatic route for:

(*i*) Generation and transmission of electric energy produced in-hydro electric, coal/lignite based thermal, oil based thermal and gas based thermal power plants.

(*ii*) Non-Conventional Energy Generation and Distribution.

(*iii*) Distribution of electric energy to households, industrial, commercial and other users; and

(*iv*) Power Trading.

The above would be subject to the provisions of the Electricity Act, 2003. Further, (*i*) to (*iii*) above do not include generation, transmission and distribution of electricity produced in atomic power plant/atomic energy since private investment in this sector/activity is prohibited and is reserved for public sector.

6. Services Sector

(a) Advertising and Films

100% FDI under the automatic route is allowed in Advertising sector. 100% FDI under the automatic route is allowed in Film Industry including film financing, production, distribution, exhibition, marketing and associated activities related to film industry.

(b) Civil Aviation Sector

The Civil Aviation sector includes Airports, Scheduled and Non-Scheduled domestic passenger airlines, Helicopter services/Seaplane services, Ground Handling Services, Maintenance and Repair organizations; Flying training institutes; and Technical training institutions.

For the purposes of the Civil Aviation sector:

(*i*) "Airport" means a landing and taking off area for aircrafts, usually with runways and aircraft maintenance and passenger facilities and includes aerodrome as defined in clause (2) of section 2 of the Aircraft Act, 1934;

(*ii*) "Aerodrome" means any definite or limited ground or water area intended to be used, either wholly or in part, for the landing or departure of aircraft, and includes all buildings, sheds, vessels, piers and other structures thereon or pertaining thereto;

(*iii*) "Air transport service" means a service for the transport by air of persons, mails or any other thing, animate or inanimate, for any kind of remuneration whatsoever, whether such service consists of a single flight or series of flights;

(*v*) "Air Transport Undertaking" means an undertaking whose business includes the carriage by air of passengers or cargo for hire or reward;

(*v*) "Aircraft component" means any part, the soundness and correct functioning of which, when fitted to an aircraft, is essential to the continued airworthiness or safety of the aircraft and includes any item of equipment;

(*vi*) "Helicopter" means a heavier-than -air aircraft supported in flight by the reactions of the air on one or more power driven rotors on substantially vertical axis;

(*vii*) "Scheduled air transport service", means an air transport service undertaken between the same two or more places and operated according to a published time table or with flights so regular or frequent that they constitute a recognizably systematic series, each flight being open to use by members of the public;

(*viii*) "Non-Scheduled Air Transport service" means any service which is not a scheduled air transport service and will include Chartered and Cargo airlines;

(*ix*) Chartered" and "Cargo" airlines would mean such airlines which meet the conditions as given in the Civil Aviation Requirements issued by the Ministry of Civil Aviation;

(*x*) "Seaplane" means an aeroplane capable normally of taking off from and alighting solely on water;

(*xi*) "Ground Handling" means (*i*) ramp handling , (*ii*) traffic handling both of which shall include the activities as specified by the Ministry of Civil Aviation through the Aeronautical Information Circulars from time to time, and (*iii*) any other activity specified by the Central Government to be a part of either ramp handling or traffic handling.

7. Policy for FDI in Civil Aviation sector

(a) Airports

(*a*) Greenfield projects- FDI upto 100% is allowed under the automatic route.

(*b*) Existing projects- FDI upto 100% is allowed. The investment upto 74% is under the automatic route and beyond 74% under the Government route.

(b) Air Transport Services

(*a*) Air Transport Services would include Domestic Scheduled Passenger Airlines; Non-Scheduled Airlines; Chartered Airlines; Cargo Airlines; helicopter and seaplane services.

(*b*) No foreign airlines would be allowed to participate directly or indirectly in the equity of an Air Transport Undertaking engaged in operating Scheduled, Non-Scheduled, and Chartered airlines.

(*c*) Foreign airlines are allowed to participate in the equity of companies operating Cargo airlines, helicopter and seaplane services.

(c) FDI ceilings in Air Transport Services

(*a*) Scheduled Air Transport Service/Domestic Scheduled Passenger Airline - FDI up to 49% and investment by Non-resident Indians (NRI) up to 100% allowed on the automatic route.

(*b*) Non-Scheduled Air Transport Service/Non-Scheduled airlines, Chartered airlines, and Cargo airlines- FDI up to 74% and investment by Non-resident Indians (NRI) up to 100% allowed. FDI in on the automatic route upto 49% and on the Government route beyond 49% and upto 74%.

(*c*) Helicopter services/seaplane services requiring DGCA approval- FDI up to 100% allowed on the automatic route.

(d) FDI ceilings in other services under Civil Aviation sector:

(*a*) Ground Handling Services- FDI up to 74% and investment by Non-resident Indians (NRI) up to 100% allowed. FDI under the automatic route upto 49% and through the Government route beyond 49% and upto 74%. This will be subject to sectoral regulations and security clearance.

(*b*) Maintenance and Repair organizations; flying training institutes; and technical training institutions - FDI up to 100% allowed on the automatic route.

The policy for FDI in the Civil Aviation Sector would be subject to the Aircraft Rules, 1934 as amended from time to time, Civil Aviation Requirements, and Aeronautical Information Circulars as notified by the Ministry of Civil Aviation.

8. Asset Reconstruction Companies

'Asset Reconstruction Company' (ARC) means a company registered with the Reserve Bank of India under Section 3 of the Securitisation and Reconstruction of Financial Assets and Enforcement of Security Interest Act, 2002 (SARFAESI Act).

Persons resident outside India, other than Foreign Institutional Investors (FIIs), can invest in the equity capital of Asset Reconstruction Companies (ARCs) registered with Reserve Bank only under the Government Route. Automatic Route is not available for such investment. Such investments have to be strictly in the nature of FDI. Investments by FIIs are not permitted in the equity capital of ARCs and FDI is restricted to 49 per cent of the paid-up capital of the ARC. 5.16.3 However, FIIs registered with SEBI can invest in the Security Receipts (SRs) issued by ARCs registered with Reserve Bank. FIIs can invest upto 49 per cent of each tranche of scheme of SRs, subject to the condition that investment by a single FII in each tranche of SRs shall not exceed 10 per cent of the issue.

Any individual investment of more than 10% would be subject to provisions of section 3(3)(*f*) of Securitization and Reconstruction of Financial Assets and Enforcement of Security Interest Act, 2002. As per section 3(3)(*f*) of SARFAESI Act, 2002, The Reserve Bank may, for the purpose of considering the application for registration of a securitisation company or reconstruction company to commence or carry on the business of securitisation or asset reconstruction, as the case may be, require to be satisfied, by an inspection of records or books of such securitisation company or reconstruction company, or otherwise, that a sponsor, is not a holding company of the securitisation company or reconstruction company, as the case may be, or, does not otherwise hold any controlling interest in such securitisation company or reconstruction company.

9. Banking-Private sector

FDI limit in Private Sector Banks is 74 % including investment by FIIs. This will include FDI investment under the Portfolio Investment Scheme (PIS) by FIIs, NRIs and shares acquired prior to September 16, 2003 by erstwhile OCBs, and continue to include IPOs, Private placements, GDR/ADRs and acquisition of shares from existing shareholders. FDI as above upto 49% is under the automatic route and beyond that upto 74% on the Government route.

The aggregate foreign investment in a private bank from all sources will be allowed up to a maximum of 74 per cent of the paid up capital of the Bank. At all times, at least 26 per cent of the paid up capital will have to be held by residents, except in regard to a wholly-owned subsidiary of a foreign bank.

The stipulations as above will be applicable to all investments in existing private sector banks also. The permissible limits under portfolio investment schemes through stock exchanges for FIIs and NRIs will be as follows:

(*i*) In the case of FIIs, as hitherto, individual FII holding is restricted to 10 per cent of the total paid-up capital, aggregate limit for all FIIs cannot exceed 24 per cent of the total paid-up capital, which can be raised to 49 per cent of the total paid-up capital by the bank concerned through a resolution by its Board of Directors followed by a special resolution to that effect by its General Body:

(*a*) Thus, the FII investment limit will continue to be within 49 per cent of the total paid-up capital.

(*b*) In the case of NRIs, as hitherto, individual holding is restricted to 5 per cent of the total paid-up capital both on repatriation and non-repatriation basis and aggregate limit cannot exceed 10 per cent of the total paid-up capital both on repatriation and non-repatriation basis. However, NRI holding can be allowed up to 24 per cent of the total paid-up capital both on repatriation and non-repatriation basis provided the banking company passes a special resolution to that effect in the General Body.

(*c*) Applications for foreign direct investment (FDI route) in private banks having joint venture/subsidiary in insurance sector may be addressed to the Reserve Bank of India (RBI) for consideration in consultation with the Insurance Regulatory and Development Authority (IRDA) in order to ensure that the 26 per cent limit of foreign shareholding applicable for the insurance sector is not being breached.

(*d*) Transfer of shares under FDI from residents to non-residents will continue to require approval of RBI and FIPB.

(*e*) The policies and procedures prescribed from time to time by RBI and other institutions such as SEBI, Department of Company Affairs (now Ministry of Corporate Affairs) and IRDA on these matters will continue to apply.

(*f*) RBI guidelines relating to acquisition by purchase or otherwise of shares of a private bank, if such acquisition results in any person owning or controlling 5 per cent or more of the paid up capital of the private bank will apply to foreign investors as well.

(*ii*) Setting up of a subsidiary by foreign banks:

(*a*) Foreign banks will be permitted to either have branches or subsidiaries but not both.

(*b*) Foreign banks regulated by banking supervisory authority in the home country and meeting Reserve Bank's licensing criteria will be allowed to hold 100 per cent paid up capital to enable them to set up a wholly-owned subsidiary in India.

(*c*) A foreign bank may operate in India through only one of the three channels viz., (*i*) branches (*ii*) a wholly-owned subsidiary and (*iii*) a subsidiary with aggregate foreign investment up to a maximum of 74 per cent in a private bank.

(*d*) A foreign bank will be permitted to establish a wholly-owned subsidiary either through conversion of existing branches into a subsidiary or through a fresh banking license. A foreign bank will be permitted to establish a subsidiary through acquisition of shares of an existing private sector bank provided at least 26 per cent of the paid capital of the private sector bank is held by residents at all times consistent with para (*i*)(*b*) above.

(*e*) A subsidiary of a foreign bank will be subject to the licensing requirements and conditions broadly consistent with those for new private sector banks.

(*f*) Guidelines for setting up a wholly-owned subsidiary of a foreign bank will be issued separately by RBI.

(*g*) All applications by a foreign bank for setting up a subsidiary or for conversion of their existing branches to subsidiary in India will have to be made to the RBI.

(*iii*) At present there is a limit of ten per cent on voting rights in respect of banking companies, and this should be noted by potential investor. Any change in the ceiling can be brought about only after final policy decisions and appropriate Parliamentary approvals.

10. Banking-Public Sector

FDI and Portfolio Investment in nationalized Banks are subject to overall statutory limit of 20% under Government route as per section 3(2D) of the Banking Companies (Acquisition & Transfer of Undertakings) Acts 1970/80. The same ceiling is also applicable to the State Bank of India and its associate Banks.

11. Broadcasting

(1) Terrestrial Broadcasting FM (FM Radio)

Foreign investment, including FDI, NRI and PIO investments and portfolio investments are permitted up to 20% equity for FM Radio's Broadcasting Services with prior approval of the Government subject to such terms and conditions as specified from time to time by Ministry of Information and Broadcasting for grant of permission for setting up of FM Radio Stations.

Notification of the revised limit of 26% for foreign investment in Terrestrial Broadcasting/FM radio (FDI Circular of 30.9.2011): The foreign investment limit for FM radio has been enhanced to 26% from the earlier 20%. This change ensures conformity of the foreign investment limit in this sector with other similar activities in the Information & Broadcasting sector.

(2) Cable Network

Foreign investment, including FDI, NRI and PIO investments and portfolio investments are permitted up to 49% for Cable Networks under Government route subject to Cable Television Network Rules, 1994 and other conditions as specified from time to time by Ministry of Information and Broadcasting.

(3) Direct-to-Home

Foreign investment, including FDI, NRI and PIO investments and portfolio investments are permitted up to 49% for Direct to Home under Government route. Within the limit of 49%, FDI will not exceed 20%. This will be subject to such guidelines/terms and conditions as specified from time to time by Ministry of Information and Broadcasting.

(4) Headend-In-The-Sky (HITS) Broadcasting Service

(*i*) Headend-in-the-Sky (HITS) Broadcasting Service refers to the multichannel downlinking and distribution of television programme in C-Band or Ku Band wherein all the pay channels are downlinked at a central facility (Hub/teleport) and again uplinked to a satellite after encryption of channel. At the cable headend these encrypted pay channels are downlinked using a single satellite antenna, transmodulated and sent to the subscribers by using a land based transmission system comprising of infrastructure of cable/optical fibres network.

(*ii*) The total direct and indirect foreign investment including portfolio and foreign direct investment in HITS shall not exceed 74%. FDI upto 49% would be on automatic route and beyond that under government route.

(*iii*) This will be subject to such guidelines/terms and conditions as specified from time to time by Ministry of Information and Broadcasting.

(5) Setting up hardware facilities such as up-linking, HUB etc.:

(*i*) FDI policy in the Up-linking of TV Channels is as under:

(*a*) Foreign investment of FDI and FII up to 49% would be permitted under the Government route for setting up Up-linking HUB/ Teleports;

(*b*) FDI up to 100% would be allowed under the Government route for Up linking a Non-News & Current Affairs TV Channel;

(*c*) Foreign investment of FDI and FII up to 26% would be permitted under the Government route for Up-linking a News & Current Affairs TV Channel subject to the condition that the portfolio investment from FII/NRI shall not be "persons acting in concert" with FDI investors, as defined in the SEBI (Substantial Acquisition of Shares and Takeovers) Regulations, 1997.

(*ii*) The above will be further subject to the condition that the Company permitted to uplink the channel shall certify the continued compliance of this requirement through the Company Secretary at the end of each financial year.

(*iii*) FDI for Up-linking TV Channels will be subject to compliance with the Up-linking Policy notified by the Ministry of Information & Broadcasting from time to time.

12. Business Services

100% FDI under the automatic route is allowed in Data processing, software development and computer consultancy services; Software supply services; Business and management consultancy services, Market Research Services, Technical testing& Analysis services.

13. Commodity Exchanges

Futures trading in commodities are regulated under the Forward Contracts (Regulation) Act, 1952. Commodity Exchanges, like Stock Exchanges, are infrastructure companies in the commodity futures market. With a view to infuse globally acceptable best practices, modern management skills and latest technology, it was decided to allow foreign investment in Commodity Exchanges. For the purposes of this chapter,—

(*i*) "Commodity Exchange" is a recognized association under the provisions of the Forward Contracts (Regulation) Act, 1952, as amended from time to time, to provide exchange platform for trading in forward contracts in commodities.

(*ii*) "recognized association" means an association to which recognition for the time being has been granted by the Central Government under Section 6 of the Forward Contracts (Regulation) Act, 1952

(*iii*) "Association" means anybody of individuals, whether incorporated or not, constituted for the purposes of regulating and controlling the business of the sale or purchase of any goods and commodity derivative.

(*iv*) "Forward contract" means a contract for the delivery of goods and which is not a ready delivery contract.

(*v*) "Commodity derivative" means—

- a contract for delivery of goods, which is not a ready delivery contract; or
- a contract for differences which derives its value from prices or indices of prices of such underlying goods or activities, services, rights, interests and events, as may be notified in consultation with the Forward Markets Commission by the Central Government, but does not include securities.

Policy for foreign investment in Commodity Exchanges:

(*i*) There is composite ceiling of 49% for foreign investment under Government route as follows:

(*a*) Investment upto 26% as Foreign Direct Investment (FDI) under the FDI Scheme incorporated as Schedule 1 under regulation 5 (1) of the Foreign Exchange Management (Transfer or Issue of Security By a Person Resident Outside India) Regulations, 2000 (FEMA Regulations).

(*b*) Investment upto 23% by registered FII under the Portfolio Investment Scheme incorporated as Schedule 2 under Regulation 5(2) of the FEMA Regulations.

(*ii*) FII purchases shall be restricted to secondary market only.

(*iii*) No foreign investor/entity, including persons acting in concert, will hold more than 5% of the equity in these companies.

Policy for FDI in Commodity Exchanges (FDI Circular 10.4.2012): At present, foreign investment, within a composite (FDI & FII) cap of 49%, under the Government approval route-*i.e.* through the Foreign Investment Promotion Board (FIPB)-is permitted in commodity exchanges. Within this overall limit of 49%, investment by Registered FIIs, under the Portfolio Investment Scheme (PIS) is limited to 23% and investment under the FDI Scheme is limited to 26%. It has now been decided to liberalise the policy and to mandate the requirement of Government approval only for FDI component of the investment. Such investment by FIIs, in commodity exchanges, will, therefore, no longer require Government approval. This change aligns the policy for foreign investment in commodity exchanges, with that of other infrastructure companies in the securities markets, such as stock exchanges, depositories and clearing corporations.

14. Construction and maintenance

100% FDI is allowed under the automatic route in Construction and maintenance of-roads, rail-beds, bridges, tunnels, pipelines, ropeways, runways, waterways & water reservoirs, hydroelectric projects, power plants and industrial plants. 100 % FDI is allowed under the automatic route in construction and maintenance of Roads and highways offered on BOT basis including collection of toll. 100 % FDI is allowed under the automatic route in construction and maintenance of Rural Drinking Water Supply Projects, Package Water Treatment Plants, Rain and Rain Water Harvesting Structures, Waste-Water Recycling and Re-Use Techniques and Facilities, Rain-Water Re-Charging and Re-Use Techniques of Ground Water.

15. Ports and Harbours

100% FDI is allowed under the automatic route for:

(*i*) Leasing of existing assets of ports

(*ii*) Construction/creation and maintenance of assets such as-container terminals bulk/break bulk/multipurpose and specialized cargo berths, warehousing, container freight stations, storage facilities and tank farms, cranage/handling equipment, setting up of captive power plants, dry docking and ship repair facilities.

(*iii*) Leasing of equipment for port handling and leasing of floating crafts.

(*iv*) Captive facilities for port based industries.

FDI upto 100% is permitted on the automatic route for **Mass Rapid Transport Systems** in all Metropolitan Cities including associated commercial development of real estate. The conditions at para (given below) 5.23.1, 5.23.2 and 5.23.3 of this policy would not apply.

16. Development of Townships, Housing, Built-up infrastructure and Construction Development projects

FDI up to 100% under the automatic route in townships, housing, built-up infrastructure and construction-development projects (which would include, but not be restricted to, housing, commercial premises, hotels, resorts, hospitals, educational institutions, recreational facilities, city and regional level infrastructure) is allowed subject to the following guidelines (para 5.23.1):

Minimum area to be developed under each project would be as under:

(*i*) In case of development of serviced housing plots, a minimum land area of 10 hectares;

(*ii*) In case of construction-development projects, a minimum built-up area of 50,000 sq.mts;

(*iii*) In case of a combination project, any one of the above two conditions would suffice.

The investment would further be subject to the following conditions (para 5.23.2):

(*i*) Minimum capitalization of US$10 million for wholly owned subsidiaries and US$ 5 million for joint ventures with Indian partners. The funds would have to be brought in within six months of commencement of business of the Company.

(*ii*) Original investment cannot be repatriated before a period of three years from completion of minimum capitalization. However, the investor may be permitted to exit earlier with prior approval of the Government through the FIPB.

Clarification of the terms 'original investment' and 'lock-in period' in case of minimum capitalization of construction development projects {*Para 5.2.13.2*(*3*)}**:** It has been clarified that the term "Original investment" means the entire amount brought in as FDI. It has further been clarified that the lock-in-period of three years will be applied from the date of receipt of each installment/tranche of FDI or from the date of completion of minimum capitalization, whichever is later. This was necessary as a number of queries had been received in regard to the coverage of these terms. (Circular 2 of 2010 as on September 30, 2010).

As per para 5.23.3, at least 50% of the project must be developed within a period of five years from the date of obtaining all statutory clearances. The investor/investee company would not be permitted to sell undeveloped plots. For the purpose of these guidelines, "undeveloped plots" will mean where roads, water supply, street lighting, drainage, sewerage, and other conveniences, as applicable under prescribed regulations, have not been made available. It will be necessary that the investor provides this infrastructure and obtains the completion certificate from the concerned local body/service agency before he would be allowed to dispose of serviced housing plots.

The project shall conform to the norms and standards, including land use requirements and provision of community amenities and common facilities, as laid down in the applicable building control regulations, bye-laws, rules, and other regulations of the State Government/Municipal/Local Body concerned (para 5.23.4).

The investor/investee company shall be responsible for obtaining all necessary approvals, including those of the building/layout plans, developing internal and peripheral areas and other infrastructure facilities, payment of development, external development and other charges and complying with all other requirements as prescribed under applicable rules/bye-laws/regulations of the State Government/Municipal/Local Body concerned. The State Government/ Municipal/Local Body concerned, which approves the building/development plans, would monitor compliance of the above conditions by the developer. The conditions as at paras 5.23.1, 5.23.2 and 5.23.3 would not apply to Hotels & Tourism, Hospitals and SEZ's. For investment by NRIs, the conditions at paras 5.23.1, 5.23.2 and 5.23.3 would not apply. 100% FDI is allowed under the automatic route in development of Special Economic Zones (SEZ) without the conditionalities at paras 5.23.1, 5.23.2 and 5.23.3 above. This will be subject to the provisions of Special Economic Zones Act, 2005 and the SEZ Policy of the Department of Commerce.

FDI is not allowed in Real Estate Business.

Exemption of construction-development activities in the education sector and in old-age homes, from the general conditionalities in the construction-development sector (FDI Circular of 30-9-2011): FDI into construction development activities in the education sector and in respect of old-age homes has been exempted from the conditionalities imposed on FDI in the construction development sector in general *i.e.,* minimum area and built-up area requirement; minimum capitalization requirement; and lock-in period. These conditionalities perhaps posed a constraint to FDI coming into these areas since educational institutions like schools, colleges, universities etc. as well as old-age homes have their own special requirements which do not necessarily fit these conditionalities. This step should augment the educational infrastructure in the country and bring it up to global standards. Similarly, with growing urbanisation, there is an increasing demand for old-age homes to cater to the needs of senior citizens. The physical infrastructure in this area also is short of the requirements. Hence, it has also been decided to exempt old-age homes also from the general conditionalities applicable to the construction development sector.

17. Courier services for carrying packages, parcels and other items which do not come within the ambit of the Indian Post Office Act, 1898

100% FDI is allowed under the Government route. This will be subject to existing Law *i.e.* Indian Post Office Act, 1898 and exclusion of activity relating to the distribution of letters.

18. Credit Information Companies (CIC)

Foreign investment in Credit Information Companies is subject to the Credit Information Companies (Regulation) Act, 2005. Foreign investment consisting of FDI and FII upto 49% is permitted under the Government route, subject to regulatory clearance from RBI. Investment by a registered FII under the Portfolio Investment Scheme would be permitted up to 24% only in the CICs listed at the Stock Exchanges, within the overall limit of 49% for foreign investment. Such FII investment would be permitted subject to the conditions that:

(*a*) No single entity should directly or indirectly hold more than 10% equity.

(*b*) Any acquisition in excess of 1% will have to be reported to RBI as a mandatory requirement; and

(*c*) FIIs investing in CICs shall not seek a representation on the Board of Directors based upon their shareholding.

19. Health and Medical Services

100% FDI is allowed under the automatic route.

20. Hotels and Tourism related Industry

100% Foreign Investment is allowed under automatic route. The terms hotel includes restaurants, beach resorts and other tourism complexes providing accommodation and/or catering and food facilities to tourists. The term tourism related industry includes:

(*i*) Travel agencies, tour operating agencies and tourist transport operating agencies.

(*ii*) Units providing facilities for cultural, adventure and wildlife experience to tourists.

(*iii*) Surface, air and water transport facilities for tourists.

(*iv*) Convention/seminar units and organizations.

21. Industrial Parks - both setting up and already established Industrial Parks

FDI up to 100% is permitted under the automatic route in Industrial Parks. FDI up to 100% on the automatic route is allowed in Construction development projects, etc. prescribing therein, inter-alia, the conditions for minimum capitalization, minimum area requirements and lock-in of original investment as per para 5.23 above.

For the purposes of this chapter:

(*i*) "Industrial Park" is a project in which quality infrastructure in the form of plots of developed land or built up space or a combination with common facilities, is developed and made available to all the allottee units for the purposes of industrial activity.

(*ii*) "Infrastructure" refers to facilities required for functioning of units located in the Industrial Park and includes roads (including approach roads), water supply and sewerage, common effluent treatment facility, telecom network, generation and distribution of power, air conditioning.

(*iii*) "Common Facilities" refer to the facilities available for all the units located in the industrial park, and include facilities of power, roads (including approach roads), water supply and sewerage, common effluent treatment, common testing, telecom services, air conditioning, common facility buildings, industrial canteens, convention/conference halls, parking, travel desks, security service, first aid center, ambulance and other safety services, training facilities and such other facilities meant for common use of the units located in the Industrial Park.

(*iv*) "Allocable area" in the Industrial Park means—

(*a*) in the case of plots of developed land- the net site area available for allocation to the units, excluding the area for common facilities.

(*b*) in the case of built up space- the floor area and built up space utilized for providing common facilities.

(*c*) in the case of a combination of developed land and built-up space- the net site and floor area available for allocation to the units excluding the site area and built up space utilized for providing common facilities.

(*v*) "Industrial Activity" means manufacturing, electricity, gas and water supply, post and telecommunications, software publishing, consultancy and supply, data processing, database activities and distribution of electronic content, other computer related activities, Research and experimental development on natural sciences and engineering, Business and management consultancy activities and Architectural, engineering and other technical activities.

FDI up to 100% under the automatic route is allowed both in setting up new and in established industrial parks and would not be subject to the conditionalities applicable for construction development projects etc. spelt out in Para 5.23 above provided the Industrial Parks meet with the under-mentioned conditions:

(*i*) it would comprise of a minimum of 10 units and no single unit shall occupy more than 50% of the allocable area;

(*ii*) the minimum percentage of the area to be allocated for industrial activity shall not be less than 66% of the total allocable area.

Inclusion of 'basic and applied R&D on bio-technology pharmaceutical sciences/life sciences', as an 'industrial activity', under industrial parks (FDI Circular of 30.9.2011): FDI, up to 100%, under the automatic route, is permitted in existing and new industrial parks. Under the existing regime, industrial parks cover specified sectors.

The coverage has been expanded to specifically include research and development in bio-technology, pharmaceutical and life sciences, given the urgent need to augment research and development infrastructure in these areas as also expand the production facilities.

22. Insurance

FDI up to 26% in the Insurance sector, as prescribed in the Insurance Act, 1999, is allowed under the automatic route. This will be subject to the condition that Companies bringing in FDI shall obtain necessary license from the Insurance Regulatory & Development Authority for undertaking insurance activities.

23. Infrastructure Company in the Securities Market

Foreign investment is permitted in infrastructure companies in Securities Markets, namely, stock exchanges, depositories and clearing corporations, in compliance with SEBI Regulations and subject to the following conditions:

(*a*) There is a composite ceiling of 49 per cent for Foreign Investment, with a FDI limit of 26 per cent and an FII limit of 23 per cent of the paid-up capital;

(*b*) FDI will be allowed under the Government route; and

(*c*) FII can invest only through purchases in the secondary market.

24. Non-Banking Finance Companies (NBFC)

100% foreign investment in NBFC is allowed under the automatic route in the following activities:

(*i*) Merchant Banking

(*ii*) Under Writing

(*iii*) Portfolio Management Services

(*iv*) Investment Advisory Services

(*v*) Financial Consultancy

(*vi*) Stock Broking

(*vii*) Asset Management

(*viii*) Venture Capital

(*ix*) Custodian Services

(*x*) Factoring

(*xi*) Credit Rating Agencies

(*xii*) Leasing & Finance

(*xiii*) Housing Finance

(*xiv*) Forex Broking

(*xv*) Credit Card Business

(*xvi*) Money Changing Business

(*xvii*) Micro Credit

(*xviii*) Rural Credit

Investment would be subject to the following minimum capitalisation norms:

(*i*) US $0.5 million for foreign capital upto 51% to be brought upfront.

(*ii*) US $5 million for foreign capital more than 51% and upto 75% to be brought upfront.

(*iii*) US $50 million for foreign capital more than 75% out of which US$7.5 million to be brought upfront and the balance in 24 months.

(*iv*) 100% foreign owned NBFCs with a minimum capitalisation of US$50 million can set up step down subsidiaries for specific NBFC activities, without any restriction on number of operating subsidiaries and without bringing in additional capital.

Clarification that 100% foreign owned NBFCs, with a minimum capitalization of $ 50 million, can set up subsidiaries for specific NBFC activities, without bringing additional capital towards minimum capitalization {*Para 5.2.18.2(iv)*}**:** The need for this clarification had arisen as requests had been received for clarifying whether such downstream subsidiaries were independently required to meet conditions relating to minimum capitalization. (Circular 2 of 2010 as on September 30, 2010).

Non Banking Finance Companies (NBFC) — clarification on 'leasing' (FDI Circular of 10.4.2012): It has been clarified that the activity of 'leasing and finance', which is one among the eighteen NBFC activities, where induction of FDI is permitted, covers only 'financial leases' and not 'operating leases'. This provision intends to clarify the coverage of the term 'leasing and finance', insofar as the NBFC sector is concerned.

(*v*) Joint Venture operating NBFCs that have 75% or less than 75% foreign investment can also set up subsidiaries for undertaking other NBFC activities, subject to the subsidiaries also complying with the applicable minimum capitalisation norm mentioned in (*i*), (*ii*) and (*iii*) above and (*vi*) below.

(*vi*) Non-Fund based activities: US $0.5 million for all permitted non-fund based NBFCs irrespective of the level of foreign investment subject to the following condition:

It would not be permissible for such a company to set up any subsidiary for any other activity, nor can it participate in any equity of an NBFC holding/operating company.

Note: The following activities would be classified as Non-Fund Based activities:

(*a*) Investment Advisory Services

(*b*) Financial Consultancy

(*c*) Forex Broking

(*d*) Money Changing Business

(*e*) Credit Rating Agencies

(*vii*) This will be subject to compliance with the guidelines of RBI.

Credit Card business includes issuance, sales, marketing & design of various payment products such as credit cards, charge cards, debit cards, stored value cards, smart card, value added cards etc.

25. Venture Capital Fund (VCF)

A Foreign Venture Capital Investor (FVCI) may contribute upto 100% of the capital of an Indian Venture Capital Undertaking and may also set up a domestic asset management company to manage the fund. All such investments can be made under automatic route in terms of Schedule 6 to Notification No. FEMA, 2000. A SEBI registered FVCI can also invest in domestic venture capital fund registered under the SEBI (Venture Capital Fund) Regulations, 1996. Such investments would also be subject to RBI regulations and FDI policy. However, in case the entity undertaking venture capital fund activity is a Trust registered under the Indian Trust Act, 1882, foreign investment would be permitted under the Government route. FVCIs are also allowed to invest in other companies subject to FDI Regulations. The NBFC will have to comply with the guidelines of the RBI.

26. Petroleum & Natural Gas Sector

FDI up to 100% under the automatic route is permitted in exploration activities of oil and natural gas fields, infrastructure related to marketing of petroleum products, actual trading and marketing of petroleum products, petroleum product pipelines, natural gas/LNG pipelines, market study and formulation and Petroleum refining in the private sector. This will be subject to the existing sectoral policy and regulatory framework in the oil marketing sector and the policy of the Government on private participation in exploration of oil and the discovered fields of national oil companies. FDI up to 49% is permitted under the Government route in petroleum refining by the Public Sector Undertakings (PSU). This should not involve any divestment or dilution of domestic equity in the existing PSUs.

27. Print Media

Publishing of Newspaper and periodicals dealing with news and current affairs: Foreign investment, including FDI and investment by NRIs/PIOs/FII, up to 26%, is permitted under the Government route. Publication of Indian editions of foreign magazines dealing with news and current affairs:

(*i*) Foreign investment, including FDI and investment by NRIs/PIOs/FII, up to 26%, is permitted under the Government route.

(*ii*) 'Magazine', for the purpose of these guidelines, will be defined as a periodical publication, brought out on non-daily basis, containing public news or comments on public news.

(*iii*) Foreign investment would also be subject to the Guidelines for Publication of Indian editions of foreign magazines dealing with news and current affairs issued by the Ministry of Information & Broadcasting on 4.12.2008.

Publishing/printing of Scientific and Technical Magazines/specialty journals/periodicals: 100% FDI is permitted under the Government route. This will also be subject to compliance with the legal framework as applicable and guidelines issued in this regard from time to time by Ministry of Information and Broadcasting.

Publication of facsimile edition of foreign newspapers:

(*i*) FDI up to 100% is permitted under Government route in publication of facsimile edition of foreign newspapers provided the FDI is by the owner of the original foreign newspapers whose facsimile edition is proposed to be brought out in India.

(*ii*) Publication of facsimile edition of foreign newspapers can be undertaken only by an entity incorporated or registered in India under the provisions of the Companies Act, 1956.

(*iii*) Publication of facsimile edition of foreign newspaper would also be subject to the Guidelines for publication of newspapers and periodicals dealing with news and current affairs and publication of facsimile edition of foreign newspapers issued by Ministry of Information & Broadcasting on 31-3-2006, as amended from time to time.

28. Research and Development Services excluding basic Research and setting of R&D/academic institutions which would award degrees/diplomas/certificates

100% FDI is allowed under the automatic route.

29. Security Agencies in Private sector

The 'Private Security Agencies (Regulation) Act, 2005' regulates the operations of private security agencies. Under Section 6(2) of the above Act, "A company, firm or an association of persons shall not be considered for issue of a licence under this Act, if, it is not registered in India, or is having a proprietor or a majority shareholder, partner or director, who is not a citizen of India". As such, under the provisions of this Act:

- a foreign company cannot be considered for a license under the Act
- only a firm registered in India can be eligible for a license
- to be eligible for a license under the Act, a firm cannot have a foreign director/partner
- majority shareholder cannot be a foreigner *i.e.* foreign shareholding would be restricted to a maximum of 49% under the Government route.

30. Satellites — Establishment and operation

FDI upto 74% is allowed under Government route. This will be subject to the sectoral guidelines of Department of Space/ISRO.

31. Storage and Warehouse Services

100% FDI is allowed under the automatic route in Storage and Warehousing including warehousing of agricultural products with refrigeration (cold storage).

32. Telecommunication

Telecom services: Foreign Direct Investment limit in telecom services is 74 percent subject to the following conditions:

(*i*) This is applicable in case of Basic, Cellular, Unified Access Services, National/International Long Distance, V-Sat, Public Mobile Radio Trunked Services (PMRTS), Global Mobile Personal Communications Services (GMPCS) and other value added Services.

(*ii*) Both direct and indirect foreign investment in the licensee company shall be counted for the purpose of FDI ceiling. Foreign Investment shall include investment by Foreign Institutional Investors (FIIs), Non-resident Indians (NRIs), Foreign Currency Convertible Bonds (FCCBs), American Depository Receipts (ADRs), Global Depository Receipts (GDRs) and convertible preference shares held by foreign entity. In any case, the `Indian' shareholding will not be less than 26 percent.

(*iii*) FDI up to 49 percent is on the automatic route and beyond that on the Government route. FDI in the licensee company/Indian promoters/ investment companies including their holding companies shall require approval of the Foreign Investment Promotion Board (FIPB) if it has a bearing on the overall ceiling of 74 percent. While approving the investment proposals, FIPB shall take note that investment is not coming from countries of concern and/or unfriendly entities.

(*iv*) The investment approval by FIPB shall envisage the conditionality that Company would adhere to licence Agreement.

(*v*) FDI shall be subject to laws of India and not the laws of the foreign country/countries.

Security Conditions:

(*i*) The Chief Officer In-charge of technical network operations and the Chief Security Officer should be a resident Indian citizen.

(*ii*) Details of infrastructure/network diagram (technical details of the network) could be provided on a need basis only to telecom equipment suppliers/manufacturers and the affiliate/parents of the licensee company. Clearance from the licensor (Department of Telecommunications) would be required if such information is to be provided to anybody else.

(*iii*) For security reasons, domestic traffic of such entities as may be identified/specified by the licensor shall not be hauled/routed to any place outside India.

(*iv*) The licensee company shall take adequate and timely measures to ensure that the information transacted through a network by the subscribers is secure and protected.

(*v*) The officers/officials of the licensee companies dealing with the lawful interception of messages will be resident Indian citizens.

(*vi*) The majority Directors on the Board of the company shall be Indian citizens.

(*vii*) The positions of the Chairman, Managing Director, Chief Executive Officer (CEO) and/or Chief Financial Officer (CFO), if held by foreign nationals, would require to be security vetted by Ministry of Home Affairs (MHA). Security vetting shall be required periodically on yearly basis. In case something adverse is found during the security vetting, the direction of MHA shall be binding on the licensee.

(*viii*) The Company shall not transfer the following to any person/place outside India:—

(*a*) Any accounting information relating to subscriber (except for international roaming/billing) (Note: it does not restrict a statutorily required disclosure of financial nature); and

(*b*) User information (except pertaining to foreign subscribers using Indian Operator's network while roaming).

(*ix*) The Company must provide traceable identity of their subscribers. However, in case of providing service to roaming subscriber of foreign Companies, the Indian Company shall endeavour to obtain traceable identity of roaming subscribers from the foreign company as a part of its roaming agreement.

(*x*) On request of the licensor or any other agency authorised by the licensor, the telecom service provider should be able to provide the geographical location of any subscriber (BTS location) at a given point of time.

(*xi*) The Remote Access (RA) to Network would be provided only to approved location(s) abroad through approved location(s) in India. The approval for location(s) would be given by the Licensor (DOT) in consultation with the Security Agencies (IB).

(*xii*) Under no circumstances, should any RA to the suppliers/manufacturers and affiliate(s) be enabled to access Lawful Interception System (LIS), Lawful Interception Monitoring (LIM), Call contents of the traffic and any such sensitive sector/data, which the licensor may notify from time to time.

(*xiii*) The licensee company is not allowed to use remote access facility for monitoring of content.

(*xiv*) Suitable technical device should be made available at Indian end to the designated security agency/licensor in which a mirror image of the remote access information is available on line for monitoring purposes.

(*xv*) Complete audit trail of the remote access activities pertaining to the network operated in India should be maintained for a period of six months and provided on request to the licensor or any other agency authorised by the licensor.

(*xvi*) The telecom service providers should ensure that necessary provision (hardware/software) is available in their equipment for doing the Lawful interception and monitoring from a centralized location.

(*xvii*) The telecom service providers should familiarize/train Vigilance Technical Monitoring (VTM)/security agency officers/officials in respect of relevant operations/features of their systems.

(*xviii*) It shall be open to the licensor to restrict the Licensee Company from operating in any sensitive area from the National Security angle.

(*xix*) In order to maintain the privacy of voice and data, monitoring shall only be upon authorisation by the Union Home Secretary or Home Secretaries of the States/Union Territories.

(*xx*) For monitoring traffic, the licensee company shall provide access of their network and other facilities as well as to books of accounts to the security agencies.

(*xxi*) The aforesaid Security Conditions shall be applicable to all the licensee companies operating telecom services covered under this circular irrespective of the level of FDI.

(*xxii*) Other Service Providers (OSPs), providing services like Call Centres, Business Process Outsourcing (BPO), tele-marketing, tele-education, etc, and are registered with DoT as OSP. Such OSPs operate the service using the telecom infrastructure provided by licensed telecom service providers and 100% FDI is permitted for OSPs. As the security conditions are applicable to all licensed telecom service providers, the security conditions mentioned above shall not be separately enforced on OSPs.

The conditions at above para shall also be applicable to the companies operating telecom service(s) with the FDI cap of 49%. All the telecom service providers shall submit a compliance report on the aforesaid conditions to the licensor on 1st day of July and January on six monthly basis.

FDI upto 74% is allowed in following activities:

(*a*) ISP with gateways

(*b*) ISP's not providing gateways *i.e.* without gate-ways (both for satellite and marine cables)

Note.—The new guidelines of August 24, 2007 Department of Telecommunications provide for new ISP licenses with FDI upto 74%.

(*c*) Radio paging

(*d*) End-to-End bandwidth

(*i*) FDI upto 49% would be allowed under the automatic route and above that under the Government route.

(*ii*) This will be subject to licensing and security requirements notified by the Department of Telecommunications.

FDI upto 100% is allowed for the following activities:

(*a*) Infrastructure provider providing dark fibre, right of way, duct space, tower (IP Category I)

(*b*) Electronic Mail

(*c*) Voice Mail

(*i*) The investment upto 49% is under the automatic route and beyond 49% under the Government route.

(*ii*) This will be subject to the condition that such companies will divest 26% of their equity in favour of Indian public in 5 years, if these companies are listed in other parts of the world.

(*iii*) This will be subject to licensing and security requirements notified by the Department of Telecommunications.

33. Trading

100% FDI is permitted under the automatic route for trading companies for the following activities:

Cash & Carry trading Wholesale Trading/Wholesale Trading: Cash & Carry Wholesale trading/Wholesale trading, would mean sale of goods/merchandise to retailers, industrial, commercial, institutional or other professional business users or to other wholesalers and related subordinated service providers. Wholesale trading would, accordingly, be sales for the purpose of trade, business and profession, as opposed to sales for the purpose of personal consumption. The yardstick to determine whether the sale is wholesale or not would be the type of customers to whom the sale is made and not the size and volume of sales. Wholesale trading would include resale, processing and thereafter sale, bulk imports with export/ex-bonded warehouse business sales and B2B e-Commerce.

Guidelines for Cash & Carry Wholesale Trading/Wholesale Trading (WT):

(*a*) For undertaking WT, requisite licenses/registration/permits, as specified under the relevant Acts/Regulations/Rules/Orders of the State Government/Government Body/Government Authority/Local Self-Government Body under that State Government should be obtained.

(*b*) Except in case of sales to Government, sales made by the wholesaler would be considered as 'cash & carry wholesale trading/wholesale trading' with valid business customers, only when WT are made to the following entities:

(I) Entities holding sales tax/VAT registration/service tax/excise duty registration; or

(II) Entities holding trade licenses *i.e.* a license/registration certificate/membership certificate/registration under Shops and Establishment Act, issued by a Government Authority/Government Body/Local Self-Government Authority, reflecting that the entity/person holding the license/registration certificate/membership certificate, as the case may be, is itself/himself/herself engaged in a business involving commercial activity; or

(III) Entities holding permits/license etc. for undertaking retail trade (like tehbazari and similar license for hawkers) from Government Authorities/Local Self Government Bodies; or

(IV) Institutions having certificate of incorporation or registration as a society or registration as public trust for their self consumption.

Note: *An Entity to whom WT is made, may fulfill any one of the 4 conditions.*

(*c*) Full records indicating all the details of such sales like name of entity, kind of entity, registration/license/permit etc. number, amount of sale etc. should be maintained on a day to day basis.

(*d*) WT of goods would be permitted among companies of the same group. However, such WT to group companies taken together should not exceed 25% of the total turnover of the wholesale venture and the wholesale made to the group companies should be for their internal use only.

Removal of the condition that 'wholesale trading made to Group companies should be for internal use only' in the guidelines for Cash & Carry Wholesale Trading {*Para 5.2.24.1.2(d)*}**:** This change has been made in response to requests for simplification of the guidelines received from stakeholders. (Circular 2 of 2010 as on September 30, 2010).

(*e*) WT can be undertaken as per normal business practice, including extending credit facilities subject to applicable regulations.

(*f*) A Wholesale/Cash & carry trader cannot open retail shops to sell to the consumer directly.

34. Trading for exports

(*a*) *E-commerce activities*

E-commerce activities refer to the activity of buying and selling by a company through the e-commerce platform. Such companies would engage only in Business to Business (B2B) e-commerce and not in retail trading, inter-alia implying that existing restrictions on FDI in domestic trading would be applicable to e-commerce as well. 100% FDI is permitted under the Government route for trading companies for the following activities:

(*i*) Trading of items sourced from small scale sector.

(*ii*) Test marketing of such items for which a company has approval for manufacture, provided such test marketing facility will be for a period of two years, and investment in setting up manufacturing facility commences simultaneously with test marketing.

(*b*) *Single Brand product trading*

FDI up to 51%, under the Government route is allowed in retail trade of 'Single Brand' products. This is, *inter alia*, aimed at attracting investments in production and marketing, improving the availability of such goods for the consumer, encouraging increased sourcing of goods from India, and enhancing competitiveness of Indian enterprises through access to global designs, technologies and management practices. FDI up to 51% in retail trade of 'Single Brand' products would be subject to the following conditions:

(*a*) Products to be sold should be of a 'Single Brand' only.

(*b*) Products should be sold under the same brand internationally *i.e.* products should be sold under the same brand in one or more countries other than India.

(*c*) 'Single Brand' product-retailing would cover only products which are branded during manufacturing.

Application seeking permission of the Government for FDI in retail trade of 'Single Brand' products would be made to the Secretariat for Industrial Assistance (SIA) in the Department of Industrial Policy & Promotion. The application would specifically indicate the product/product categories which are proposed to be sold under a 'Single Brand'. Any addition to the product/product categories to be sold under 'Single Brand' would require a fresh approval of the Government.

Applications would be processed in the Department of Industrial Policy & Promotion, to determine whether the products proposed to be sold satisfy the notified guidelines, before being considered by the FIPB for Government approval.

AP (DIR Series 2011-12) Circular No. 67, dated 13-1-2012

Foreign Investment in Single — Brand Retail Trading — Amendment to the Foreign Direct Investment (FDI) Scheme

1. Attention of Authorised Dealers Category-I (AD Category-I) banks is invited to the Foreign Exchange Management (Transfer or Issue of Security by a Person Resident Outside India) Regulations, 2000, notified *vide* Notification No. FEMA 20/2000-RB, dated May 3, 2000, as amended from time to time. In terms of Schedule 1 of the Notification, FDI up to 51 per cent is permitted in Single Brand product trading under Government route of FDI Scheme.

2. The extant FDI policy has since been reviewed and it has now been decided that FDI up to 100 per cent would be permitted in Single Brand product trading under the Government route subject to the terms and conditions as stipulated in Press Note No. 1 (2012 Series), dated January 10, 2012 issued by Department of Industrial Policy & Promotion, Ministry of Commerce & Industry, Government of India.

3. A copy of Press Note No. 1 (2012 Series) dated January 10, 2012 is issued in this regard.

4. AD Category-I banks may bring the contents of the circular to the notice of their customers/constituents concerned.

5. Necessary amendments to Foreign Exchange Management (Transfer or Issue of Security by a Person Resident outside India) Regulations, 2000 (Notification No. FEMA 20/2000-RB, dated May 3, 2000) are being notified separately.

6. The directions contained in this circular have been issued under sections 10(4) and 11(1) of the Foreign Exchange Management Act, 1999 (42 of 1999) and are without prejudice to permissions/approvals, if any, required under any other law.

Press Note No. 1 (2012 Series) D/o IPP File No. 5/12/2010-FC-1, dated 10-1-2012

Review of the policy on Foreign Direct Investment- liberalization of the policy in Single-Brand Retail Trading

1.0 Present Position

Foreign Direct Investment (FDI), in retail trade, is prohibited except in single brand product retail trading, in which FDI, up to 51% is permitted, subject to conditions specified under paragraph 6.2.16.4 of 'Circular 2 of 2011-Consolidated FDI Policy'.

2.0 Revised Position

The Government of India has reviewed the extant policy on FDI and decided that FDI, up to 100%, under the government approval route, would be permitted in Single-Brand Product Retail Trading, subject to specified conditions, as indicated in paragraph 3.0 below.

3.0 Accordingly, the following amendment is made in *'Circular* 2 *of 2011- Consolidated FDI Policy',* dated 30.09.2011, issued by the Department of Industrial Policy & Promotion:

3.1 Paragraph 6.2.16.4 is substituted with the following:

6.2.16.4	**Single Brand product retail trading**	100%	Government
	(1) Foreign Investment in Single Brand product retail trading is aimed at attracting investments in production and marketing, improving the availability of such goods for the consumer, encouraging increased sourcing of goods from India, and enhancing competitiveness of Indian enterprises through access to global designs, technologies and management practices. (2) FDI in Single Brand product retail trading would be subject to the following conditions: (*a*) Products to be sold should be of a 'Single Brand' only. (*b*) Products should be sold under the same brand internationally i.e. products should be sold under the same brand in one or more countries other than India. (*c*) 'Single Brand' product-retail trading would cover only products which are branded during manufacturing. (*d*) The foreign investor should be the owner of the brand. (*e*) In respect of proposals involving FDI beyond 51%, mandatory sourcing of at least 30% of the value of products sold would have to be done from Indian 'small industries/village and cottage industries, artisans and craftsmen'. 'Small industries' would be defined as industries which have a total investment in plant & machinery not exceeding US $ 1.00 million. This valuation refers to the value at the time of installation, without providing for depreciation. Further, if at any point in time, this valuation is exceeded, the industry shall not qualify as a 'small industry' for this purpose. The compliance of this condition will be ensured through self-certification by the company, to be subsequently checked, by statutory auditors, from the duly certified accounts, which the company will be required to maintain. (3) Application seeking permission of the Government for FDI in retail trade of 'Single Brand' products would be made to the Secretariat for Industrial Assistance (SIA) in the Department of Industrial Policy & Promotion. The application would specifically indicate the product/product categories which are proposed to be sold under a 'Single Brand'. Any addition to the product/product categories to be sold under 'Single Brand' would require a fresh approval of the Government.		

6.2.16.4	**Single Brand product retail trading**	100%	Government
	(4) Applications would be processed in the Department of Industrial Policy & Promotion, to determine whether the products proposed to be sold satisfy the notified guidelines, before being considered by the FIPB for Government approval.		

4.0 The above decision will take immediate effect.

5.0 The above provisions will be incorporated in the next Circular on Consolidated FDI Policy to be issued on 31-3-2012.

(c) *Transport and Transport Support Services*

100% FDI under the automatic route is allowed for:

(*i*) Pipeline transport, ocean and water transport, inland water transport.

(d) *Transport Support Services*

(*i*) Support services to land transport like operation of highway bridges, toll roads, and vehicular tunnels.

(*ii*) Support services to water transport like operation and maintenance of piers, loading and discharging of vessels.

(*iii*) Services incidental to transport like cargo handling incidental to land, water and air transport

(*iv*) Rental and leasing of — motor vehicles without operator for passenger transport and freight transport, refrigerated/cold transport.

(*v*) Renting of transport equipment without operator, of other transport equipment.

In sectors/Activities not listed above, FDI is permitted upto 100% on the automatic route subject to applicable laws/sectoral rules/regulations.

Other General Clarifications *vide* Circular 2 of 2010 as on September 30, 2010:

- **Clarification that Minimum Capitalization includes share premium received along with face value of the shares only when it is received by the company upon issue of the shares to the non-resident investors** {*Para 5.2.25.2 – Note below*}: This is relevant in sectors such as NBFC and construction development where "minimum capitalization" requirements have been stipulated. This clarification is expected to bring in requisite clarity on the issues of inclusion of share premium within minimum capitalization and on the circumstances under which such share premium can be counted towards minimum capitalization.
- **Amendment of Note below the definition of 'Capital' to allow for FDI in partly-paid shares and warrants through the Government route** {*Para 2.1.5*}: At present, capital is defined as "equity shares, fully, compulsorily and mandatorily convertible preference shares, fully compulsorily and mandatorily convertible debentures". This clarification,

allowing for FDI in partly-paid shares and warrants, through the Government route, is intended to bring in consistency with extant practice.

- **Changes in the paragraphs relating to issue price of shares and addition of a paragraph on share-swaps, consistent with extant instructions** {*Paras 3.4.2 and 3.5.6*}: The latter has been included as a number of cases of share swaps are now being considered under the Government approval route. Prior to this, the issue of share swaps had not been explicitly mentioned under the FDI policy. This is expected to bring in clarity on the aspect of share swaps requiring approval of Government.

Chapter 7

REMITTANCE, REPORTING AND VIOLATION

SYNOPSIS

1. Remittance and Repatriation

(a) Remittance of sale proceeds/Remittance on winding up/Liquidation of Companies:

(*i*) Sale proceeds of shares and securities and their remittance is 'remittance of asset' governed by the Foreign Exchange Management (Remittance of Assets) Regulations, 2000 under FEMA.

(*ii*) AD Category I bank can allow the remittance of sale proceeds of a security (net of applicable taxes) to the seller of shares resident outside India, provided the security has been held on repatriation basis, the sale of security has been made in accordance with the prescribed guidelines and NOC/tax clearance certificate from the Income Tax Department has been produced.

(*iii*) *Remittance on winding up/liquidation of Companies:* AD Category I banks have been allowed to remit winding up proceeds of companies in India, which are under liquidation, subject to payment of applicable taxes. Liquidation may be subject to any order issued by the court winding up the company or the official liquidator in case of voluntary winding up under the provisions of the Companies Act, 1956. AD Category I banks shall allow the remittance provided the applicant submits:

(*a*) No objection or Tax clearance certificate from Income Tax Department for the remittance.

(*b*) Auditor's certificate confirming that all liabilities in India have been either fully paid or adequately provided for.

(*c*) Auditor's certificate to the effect that the winding up is in accordance with the provisions of the Companies Act, 1956.

(*d*) In case of winding up otherwise than by a court, an auditor's certificate to the effect that there are no legal proceedings pending in any court in India against the applicant or the company under liquidation and there is no legal impediment in permitting the remittance.

(b) Repatriation of Dividend

Dividends are freely repatriable without any restrictions (net after Tax deduction at source or Dividend Distribution Tax, if any, as the case may be). The repatriation is governed by the provisions of the Foreign Exchange Management (Current Account Transactions) Rules, 2000 (see chapter 8 for details), as amended from time to time.

(*c*) *Repatriation of Interest*

Interest on fully, mandatorily & compulsorily convertible debentures is also freely repatriable without any restrictions (net of applicable taxes). The repatriation is governed by the provisions of the Foreign Exchange Management (Current Account Transactions) Rules, 2000 (see chapter 8 for details), as amended from time to time.

2. Reporting of FDI

(*a*) *Reporting of Inflow*

(*i*) An Indian company receiving investment from outside India for issuing shares/convertible debentures/preference shares under the FDI Scheme, should report the details of the amount of consideration to the Regional Office concerned of the Reserve Bank not later than 30 days from the date of receipt in the Advance Reporting Form enclosed as Annex-5 of this policy.

(*ii*) Indian companies are required to report the details of the receipt of the amount of consideration for issue of shares/convertible debentures, through an AD Category I bank, together with a copy/ies of the FIRC/s evidencing the receipt of the remittance along with the KYC report (enclosed as Annex-6 of this policy) on the non-resident investor from the overseas bank remitting the amount. The report would be acknowledged by the Regional Office concerned, which will allot a Unique Identification Number (UIN) for the amount reported.

(*b*) *Reporting of issue of shares*

(*i*) After issue of shares (including bonus and shares issued on rights basis and shares issued under ESOP)/fully, mandatorily & compulsorily convertible debentures/fully, mandatorily & compulsorily convertible preference shares, the Indian company has to file Form FC-GPR, enclosed in Annex-1 of this policy, not later than 30 days from the date of issue of shares.

(*ii*) Part A of Form FC-GPR has to be duly filled up and signed by Managing Director/Director/Secretary of the Company and submitted to the Authorized Dealer of the company, who will forward it to the Reserve Bank. The following documents have to be submitted along with Part A:

(*a*) A certificate from the Company Secretary of the company certifying that:

(A) all the requirements of the Companies Act, 1956 have been complied with;

(B) terms and conditions of the Government's approval, if any, have been complied with;

(C) the company is eligible to issue shares under these Regulations; and

(D) the company has all original certificates issued by authorized dealers in India evidencing receipt of amount of consideration.

For companies with paid up capital with less than ₹ 5 crore, the above mentioned certificate can be given by a practicing company secretary.

(*b*) A certificate from Statutory Auditor or Chartered Accountant indicating the manner of arriving at the price of the shares issued to the persons resident outside India.

(*c*) The report of receipt of consideration as well as Form FC-GPR have to be submitted by the AD Category I bank to the Regional Office concerned of the Reserve Bank under whose jurisdiction the registered office of the company is situated.

(*d*) Part B of Form FC-GPR should be filed on an annual basis by the Indian company, directly with the Reserve Bank 6. This is an annual return to be submitted by 31st of July every year, pertaining to all investments by way of direct/portfolio investments/reinvested earnings/other capital in the Indian company made during the previous years (i.e. the information in Part B submitted by 31st July will pertain to all the investments made in the previous years up to March 31). The details of the investments to be reported would include all foreign investments made into the company which is outstanding as on the balance sheet date. The details of overseas investments in the company both under direct/portfolio investment may be separately indicated.

(*e*) Issue of bonus/rights shares or stock options to persons resident outside India directly or on amalgamation/merger/demerger with an existing Indian company, as well as issue of shares on conversion of ECB/royalty/lumpsum technical know-how fee/import of capital goods by units in SEZs has to be reported in Form FC-GPR.

(c) *Reporting of transfer of shares*

Reporting of transfer of shares between residents and non-residents and vice-versa is to be done in Form FC-TRS (Annex 7 of this policy). The Form FC-TRS should be submitted to the AD Category I bank, within 60 days from the date of receipt of the amount of consideration. The onus of submission of the Form FC-TRS within the given timeframe would be on the transferor/transferee, resident in India. The AD Category I bank, would forward the same to its link office. The link office would consolidate the Form FC-TRS and submit a monthly report to the Reserve Bank.

(d) *Reporting of Non-Cash*

Details of issue of shares against conversion of ECB has to be reported to the Regional Office concerned of the RBI, as indicated below:

(*i*) In case of **full conversion** of ECB into equity, the company shall report the conversion in Form FC-GPR to the Regional Office concerned of the Reserve Bank as well as in Form ECB-2 to the Department of Statistics and Information Management (DSIM), Reserve Bank of India, Bandra-Kurla Complex, Mumbai – 400 051, within seven working days from the close of month to which it relates. The words "ECB wholly converted to equity" shall be clearly indicated on top of the Form ECB-2. Once reported, filing of Form ECB 2 in the subsequent months is not necessary.

(*ii*) In case of **partial conversion** of ECB, the company shall report the converted portion in Form FC-GPR to the Regional Office concerned as well as in Form ECB-2 clearly differentiating the converted portion from the non-converted portion. The words "ECB partially converted to equity" shall be indicated on top of the Form ECB-2. In the subsequent months, the outstanding balance of ECB shall be reported in Form ECB-2 to DSIM.

(*e*) *Reporting of FCCB/ADR/GDR Issues*

The Indian company issuing ADRs/GDRs has to furnish to the Reserve Bank, full details of such issue in the Form enclosed as Annex-8 of this policy, within 30 days from the date of closing of the issue. The company should also furnish a quarterly return in the Form enclosed as Annex 9 of this policy, to the Reserve Bank within 15 days of the close of the calendar quarter. The quarterly return has to be submitted till the entire amount raised through ADR/GDR mechanism is either repatriated to India or utilized abroad as per the extant Reserve Bank guidelines.

3. Adherence to Guidelines/orders and Consequences of Violation

FDI is a capital account transaction and thus any violation of FDI regulations are covered by the penal provisions of the FEMA. Reserve Bank of India administers the FEMA and Directorate of Enforcement under the Ministry of Finance is the authority for the enforcement of FEMA. The Directorate takes up investigation in any contravention of FEMA.

(*a*) *Penalties*

(*i*) If a person violates/contravenes any FDI Regulations, by way of breach/ non-adherence/noncompliance/contravention of any rule, regulation, notification, press note, press release, circular, direction or order issued in exercise of the powers under FEMA or contravenes any conditions subject to which an authorization is issued by the Government of India/FIPB/Reserve Bank of India, he shall, upon adjudication, be liable to a penalty up to thrice the sum involved in such contraventions where such amount is quantifiable, or up to two lakh Rupees where the amount is not quantifiable, and where such contraventions is a continuing one, further penalty which may extend to five thousand Rupees for every day after the first day during which the contraventions continues.

(*ii*) Where a person committing a contravention of any provisions of this Act or of any rule, direction or order made there under is a company (company means any body corporate and includes a firm or other association of individuals as defined in the Companies Act), every person who, at the time the contravention was committed, was in charge of, and was responsible to, the company for the conduct of the business of the company as well as the company, shall be deemed to be guilty of the contravention and shall be liable to be proceeded against and punished accordingly.

(*iii*) Any Adjudicating Authority adjudging any contraventions, may, if he thinks fit in addition to any penalty which he may impose for such contravention direct that any currency, security or any other money or property in respect of which the contravention has taken place shall be confiscated to the Central Government.

(*b*) *Adjudication and Appeals*

(*i*) For the purpose of adjudication of any contravention of FEMA, the Ministry of Finance as per the provisions contained in the Foreign Exchange Management (Adjudication Proceedings and Appeal) Rules, 2000 appoints officers of the Central Government as the Adjudicating Authorities for holding an enquiry in the manner prescribed. A reasonable opportunity has to be given to the person alleged to have committed contraventions against whom a complaint has been made for being heard before imposing any penalty.

(*ii*) The Central Government may appoint as per the provisions contained in the Foreign Exchange Management (Adjudication Proceedings and Appeal) Rules, 2000, an Appealing Authority/Appellate Tribunal to hear appeals against the orders of the adjudicating authority.

(*c*) *Compounding Proceedings*

Under the Foreign Exchange (Compounding Proceedings) Rules, 2000, the Central Government may appoint 'Compounding Authority' an officer either from Enforcement Directorate or Reserve Bank of India for any person contravening any provisions of the FEMA. The Compounding Authorities are authorized to compound the amount involved in the contravention to the Act made by the person. *No contravention shall be compounded unless the amount involved in such contravention is quantifiable.* Any second or subsequent contravention committed after the expiry of a period of three years from the date on which the contravention was previously compounded shall be deemed to be a first contravention. The Compounding Authority may call for any information, record or any other documents relevant to the compounding proceedings. The Compounding Authority shall pass an order of compounding after affording an opportunity of being heard to all the concerns as expeditiously as possible and not later than 180 days from the date of application made to the Compounding Authority. Compounding Authority shall issue order specifying the provisions of the Act or of the rules, directions, requisitions or orders made there under in respect of which contravention has taken place along with details of the alleged contraventions.

Case Study: TKM Exporters of New Delhi are engaged in Export Business. It made certain exports, but failed to realize and repatriate to India the foreign exchange due on its exports. The Adjudicating Authority imposed a penalty under the provisions of Foreign Exchange Management Act, 1999 (FEMA). Being aggrieved by this penalty, the said exporter seeks your advice as to the authority to which appeal can be made and the time limit for making such appeals. You are required to advise on the matter.

Recommendations: Sections 17 and 19 of FEMA, 1999 provide for appeals against orders of Adjudicating Authority. If Adjudicating Authority is Assistant Director of the Enforcement or Deputy Director of Enforcement, appeal will lie to Special Director (Appeals). Further appeal shall lie with Appellate Tribunal for Foreign Exchange. However, if the Adjudicating Authority is senior to the Assistant Director of Enforcement or Deputy Director of Enforcement, then the appeal shall lie directly to the Appellate Tribunal.

(*d*) *Appeal to Special Director (Appeals)*

Appeal against order of Assistant Director of Enforcement or Deputy Director of Enforcement can be filed with Special Director (Appeals) under Section 17 within 45 days from the date on which the copy of the order made by the Adjudicating Authority is received by the aggrieved person. The Special Director (Appeals) can condone the delay in filing the appeal if he is satisfied that there were sufficient cause for not filing the appeal within the stipulated time. Special Director (Appeals) will hear the parties and then pass his order. Copy of the order shall be sent to the concerned parties and the Adjudicating Authority.

(*e*) *Appeal to Appellate Tribunal*

Appeal against the order of Adjudicating Authority being senior to Assistant Director of Enforcement or Deputy Director of Enforcement or against the order of Special Director (Appeals) can be made to the Appellate Tribunal for Foreign Exchange under section 19 of FEMA within 45 days from the date on which the copy of the order made by such Adjudicating Authority or Special Director (Appeals) is received by the aggrieved person. In this case also, the delay can be condoned by the Appellate Tribunal. In case of an appeal against the order imposing penalty, the appellant has to deposit the amount of such penalty with the authority prescribed by the Central Government. However, the Appellate Tribunal may waive such deposit to mitigate the likely hardship that may be caused to the appellant. After hearing of the appeal, the Appellate Tribunal shall pass a reasoned order.

It may be noted that the Tribunal is the final fact finding authority and no appeal lies against the facts determined by the Tribunal.

Case Study: Mr. Guilt an Indian National realizes that a penalty may be imposed upon him for violation of the provisions of the Foreign Exchange Management Act, 1999. He therefore desires to compound his offences. Advise Mr. Guilt about the process and procedure of compounding of the offence.

Recommendations: Sections 15 of Foreign Exchange Management Act, 1999 (FEMA) authorizes the Reserve Bank of India and Enforcement Directorate to compound contravention on an application made by any person who has committed contravention. The process and procedure of compounding is as under:

- An application for compounding of a contravention under the FEMA may be submitted to the compounding authority either on being advised of a contravention or either through a memorandum or suomoto on being made or becoming aware of the contravention. The application should be as per format in the Foreign Exchange (Compounding proceeding) Rules.
- Application for compounding in prescribed form together with a copy of the memorandum wherever applicable with the prescribed fee has to be submitted with relevant facts and supporting documents to the compounding authority.
- The compounding authority may call for any information/record or any other documents relevant to the compounding proceedings.
- Where additional information/documents are called for, such information shall be submitted within thirty days or such additional period as may be given by the compounding authority from the date of the said letter. In case the contravener fails to submit additional information/document called for within the specified period, the application for compounding will be liable for rejection.
- On receipt of the application for compounding, the proceeding would be concluded and the order issued by the compounding authority within 180 days from the date of the receipt of the application for compounding.
- The sum for which contravention has been compounded shall be paid within 15 days from the date of order of compounding.
- The payment towards application fee and the sum for which contravention has been compounded shall be paid by demand draft in favour of compounding authority.

Thus Mr. Guilt will have to follow the above procedure for compounding his offences.

Appendix 1

Foreign Exchange Management (Remittance of Assets) Regulations, 2000

Notification No. GSR 396(E) [FEMA 13/2000-RB], dated 3-5-2000[1]

Regulation *Page No.*

In exercise of the powers conferred by section 47 of the Foreign Exchange Management Act, 1999 (42 of 1999), the Reserve Bank makes the following regulations in respect of remittance outside India by a person whether resident outside India or not, of assets in India, namely:—

1. Short title and commencement.—(1) These regulations may be called the Foreign Exchange Management (Remittance of Assets) Regulations, 2000.

(2) They shall come into force on the 1st day of June, 2000.

2. Definitions.—In these regulations, unless the context requires otherwise,—

(*i*) "Act" means the Foreign Exchange Management Act, 1999 (42 of 1999);

(*ii*) "authorised dealer" means a person authorised as an authorised dealer under sub-section (1) of section 10 of the Act;

[2][(*iii*) 'Non-Resident Indian (NRI)' means a person resident outside India who is a citizen of India;]

[3][(*iv*)] "Person of Indian Origin (PIO)" means a citizen of any country other than Bangladesh or Pakistan, if—

(*a*) he at any time held Indian passport; or

(*b*) he or either of his parents or any of his grand-parents was a citizen of India by virtue of the Constitution of India or the Citizenship Act, 1955 (57 of 1955); or

(*c*) the person is a spouse of an Indian citizen or a person referred to in sub-clause (*a*) or (*b*);

---

1 Published in the Gazette of India, Extraordinary No. 249, dated 4-5-2000, Part II, section 3(*i*).

2 Inserted by Foreign Exchange Management (Remittance of Assets) (Amendment) Regulations, 2002, w.e.f. 13-5-2002.

3 Renumbered by Foreign Exchange Management (Remittance of Assets) (Amendment) Regulations, 2002, w.e.f. 13-5-2002.

[1][(*v*)] "Remittance of asset" means remittance outside India of funds representing a deposit with a bank or a firm or a company, provident fund balance or superannuation benefits, amount of claim or maturity proceeds of Insurance policy, sale proceeds of shares, securities, immovable property or any other asset held in India in accordance with the provisions of the Act or rules or regulations made thereunder;

[2][(*vi*)] the words and expressions used but not defined in these regulations shall have the same meanings respectively assigned to them in the Act.

3. Prohibition on Remittance outside India of assets held in India.—Save as otherwise provided in the Act or rules or regulations made or issued thereunder, no person whether resident in India or not, shall make remittance of any asset held in India by him or by any other person:

Provided that the Reserve Bank may, for sufficient reasons, permit any person to make remittance of any asset held in India by him or by any other person.

4. Permission for remittance of assets in certain cases[3].—[4][(1) A person specified in sub-regulations (2) and (3) may make remittance of assets through an authorised dealer, to the extent specified in those sub-regulations.]

(2) A citizen of foreign state, not being a citizen of Nepal or Bhutan or a person of Indian origin (PIO), who—

(*i*) has retired from an employment in India, or

(*ii*) has inherited the assets from a person referred to in sub-section (5) of section 6 of the Act; or

(*iii*) is a widow resident outside India and has inherited assets of her deceased husband who was an Indian citizen resident in India, may remit an amount, not exceeding [5][[6][US $ 1,000,000 (US Dollar One million only)] per [7][financial], year on production of,—

---

1 Renumbered by Foreign Exchange Management (Remittance of Assets) (Amendment) Regulations, 2002, w.e.f. 13-5-2002.

2 *Ibid.*

3 In terms of AP (DIR Series) Circular No. 65, dated 31-5-2007, AD Category-I banks are permitted to remit out of assets of Indian companies which are being liquidated under the provisions of the Companies Act, 1956 subject to the specified conditions.

4 Substituted by the Foreign Exchange Management (Remittance of Assets) (Amendment) Regulations, 2002, w.e.f. 13-5-2002 for the following:

"(1) A person specified in sub-regulation (2) may make remittance of assets through an authorised dealer, to the extent specified in that sub-regulation."

5 Substituted for "₹ 20 lakhs per calendar year" by the Foreign Exchange Management (Remittance of Assets) (Amendment) Regulations, 2002, w.e.f. 13-5-2002.

6 Substituted for "US $ 1,00,000 (US Dollar One Lakh only)" by the Foreign Exchange Management (Remittance of Assets) (Second Amendment) Regulations, 2003, w.e.f. 8-7-2003.

7 Substituted for the word "calendar" *vide* Foreign Exchange Management (Remittance of Assets) (Amendment) Regulations, 2007 w.r.e.f. 16-11-2006 [Notification No. FEMA 152/2007-RB, dated 15-5-2007).

[1][(*a*) documentary evidence in support of acquisition, inheritance or legacy of assets by the remitter, and]

(*b*) [2][an undertaking by the remitter and certificate from a Chartered Accountant in the format prescribed by the Central Board of Direct Taxes, Ministry of Finance, Government of India in their Circular No. 10/2002, dated October 9, 2000:]

Provided that for the purpose of arriving at annual ceiling of remittance under sub-regulation (2), the funds representing sale proceeds of shares and immovable property owned or held by the citizen of foreign state on repatriation basis in accordance with the Foreign Exchange Management (Acquisition and Transfer of Immovable Property in India) Regulations, 2000 and Foreign Exchange Management (Transfer of Indian Security by a Person Resident Outside India) Regulations, 2000 made under the Act, shall not be included:

Provided further that where the remittance is made in more than one instalment, the remittance of all instalments shall be made through the same authorised dealer.

(*iv*) had come to India for studies/training and has completed his studies/training, may remit the balance available in his account, provided such balance represents funds derived out of remittances received from abroad through normal banking channels or rupee proceeds of foreign exchange brought by such person and sold to an authorised dealer or out of stipend/scholarship received from the Government or any Organisation in India.

[3][(3) A Non-Resident Indian (NRI)/Person of Indian Origin (PIO) may remit

---

1 Substituted by the Foreign Exchange Management (Remittance of Assets) (Second Amendment) Regulations, 2003, w.e.f. 8-7-2003 for the following:

"(*a*) documentary evidence in support of acquisition of assets by the remitter; and"

2 Substituted for the following *vide* Foreign Exchange Management (Remittance of Assets) (Amendment) Regulations, 2007 w.r.e.f. 16-11-2006 [Notification No. FEMA 152/2007-RB, dated 15-5-2007):

"a Tax clearance/no objection certificate from the income-tax authority for the remittance:"

3 Substituted by the Foreign Exchange Management (Remittance of Assets) (Amendment) Regulations, 2004, w.e.f. 29-6-2004 [FEMA 119/2004-RB] for the following:

"(3) A non-resident Indian (NRI)/person of Indian origin (PIO) may remit an amount, not exceeding US $ 1,000,000 (US Dollar one million only) per calendar year, out of the balances held in NRO accounts/sale proceeds of assets/the assets in India acquired by him by way of inheritance/legacy, on production of the documents detailed in sub-regulation (2)(*a*) and (*b*):

Provided that in respect of remittance of sale proceeds of immovable property, the property/sale proceeds were held/retained as deposits cumulatively for a minimum period of 10 years:

Provided further that where the remittance is made in more than one instalment, the remittance of all instalments shall be made through the same authorised dealer." →→

an amount, not exceeding US$ 1,000,000 (US Dollar One million only) per [1][financial] year,

(*i*) Out of the balances held in NRO accounts/sale proceeds of assets/the assets in India acquired by him by way of inheritance/legacy on production of:

(*a*) documentary evidence in support of acquisition, inheritance or legacy of assets by the remitter, and

(*b*) [2][an undertaking by the remitter and certificate from a Chartered Accountant in the format prescribed by the Central Board of Direct Taxes, Ministry of Finance, Government of India in their Circular No. 10/2202, dated October 9, 2002.]

(*ii*) Under a deed of settlement made by either of his parents or a close relative (as defined in section 6 of the Companies Act, 1956) and the settlement taking effect on the death of the settler, on production of:

(*a*) the original deed of settlement; and

(*b*) [3][an undertaking by the remitter and certificate from a Chartered Accountant in the format prescribed by the Central Board of Direct Taxes, Ministry of Finance, Government of India in their Circular No. 10/2002, dated October 9, 2002:]

[4][* * *]

→ → Earlier it was substituted by the Foreign Exchange Management (Remittance of Assets) (Second Amendment) Regulations, 2003, w.e.f. 8-7-2003 for the following:

[1]"(3) A Non-resident Indian (NRI)/Person of Indian Origin (PIO), may remit an amount, not exceeding US$ 1,00,000 (US Dollar One lakh only) per calendar year, out of the assets in India acquired by him by way of inheritance/legacy on production of:—

(*a*) documentary evidence in support of the inheritance/legacy, and

(*b*) a Tax clearance/no objection certificate from the Income-Tax authority for the remittance.

Provided that where the remittance is made in more than one instalment, the remittance of all instalments shall be made through the same authorised dealer."

1 Inserted by the Foreign Exchange Management (Remittance of Assets) (Amendment) Regulations, 2002, w.e.f. 13-5-2002.

1 Substituted for the word "calendar" *vide* Foreign Exchange Management (Remittance of Assets) (Amendment) Regulations, 2007 w.r.e.f. 16-11-2006 [Notification No. FEMA 152/2007-RB, dated 15-5-2007).

2 Substituted for the following *vide* Foreign Exchange Management (Remittance of Assets) (Amendment) Regulations, 2007 w.r.e.f. 16-11-2006 [Notification No. FEMA 152/2007-RB, dated 15-5-2007):

"a Tax clearance/no objection certificate from the income-tax authority for the remittance:"

3 Substituted for the following, *ibid*:

"a Tax clearance/no objection certificate from the income-tax authority for the remittance:"

4 First proviso omitted by FEM (Remittance of Assets) (Amendment) Regulations, 2007, w.r.e.f. 16-11-2006. [Notification No. FEMA 152/2007-RBI, dated 15-5-2007]. Prior to omission, first proviso read as under: → →

Provided [1][* * *] that where the remittance under clauses (*i*) and (*ii*) is made in more than one instalment, the remittance of all instalments shall be made through the same Authorised Dealer.]

[2][(4) An authorised dealer in India may, without approval from Reserve Bank, effect remittance of assets made by a person eligible under sub-regulation (2) or sub-regulation (3) as the case may be and also allow remittance out of the assets of Indian companies under liquidation under the provisions of the Companies Act, 1956 , subject to the following conditions:

(*i*) Authorised Dealer shall ensure that the remittance is in compliance with the order issued by a court in India/order issued by the official liquidator or the liquidator in the case of voluntary winding up; and

(*ii*) no remittance shall be allowed unless the applicant submits:—

(*a*) No objection or Tax clearance certificate from Income Tax authority for the remittance.

(*b*) Auditor's certificate confirming that all liabilities in India have been either fully paid or adequately provided for.

(*c*) Auditor's certificate to the effect that the winding up is in accordance with the provisions of the Companies Act, 1956.

(*d*) In case of winding up otherwise than by a court, an auditor's certificate to the effect that there is no legal proceedings pending in any court in India against the applicant or the company under liquidation and there is no legal impediment in permitting the remittance.]

5. Permission to an Indian entity to remit funds in certain cases.—An entity in India may remit the amount being its contribution towards the provident fund/superannuation/pension fund in respect of the expatriate staff in its employment who are resident in India but not permanently resident therein.

→ → "Provided that in respect of remittance of sale proceeds of immovable property (acquired other than by way of inheritance/legacy/settlement), the property/sale proceeds were held/retained as eligible investments cumulatively for a minimum period of 10 years".

1 The word "further" omitted, *ibid.*

2 Substituted *vide* Foreign Exchange Management (Remittance of Assets) (Second Amendment) Regulations, 2007, w.r.e.f. 31.5.2007 [FEMA 161/2007-RB, dated 18.9.2007]. Before substitution sub-regulation (4) read as under:

"(4) An authorised dealer in India may, without approval from Reserve Bank, effect remittance of assets made by a person eligible under sub-regulation (2) or sub-regulation (3) as the case may be."

Note: The above sub-regulation (4) was earlier substituted *vide* Foreign Exchange Management (Remittance of Assets) (Amendment) Regulations, 2002 w.e.f 13.5.2002 for the following sub-regulation (3):

"(3) An authorised dealer in India may, without approval from Reserve Bank, effect remittance of assets made by a person eligible under sub-regulation (2)."

Explanation.—For the purpose of this regulation,—

(*a*) "expatriate staff" means a person whose provident/superannuation/ pension fund is maintained outside India by his principal employer outside India;

(*b*) "not permanently resident" means a person resident in India for employment of a specified duration (irrespective of length thereof) or for a specific job or assignment, the duration of which does not exceed three years.

6. Reserve Bank's prior permission in certain cases.—(1) A person who desires to make a remittance of assets in the following cases, may apply to the Reserve Bank, namely:—

[1][(*i*) Remittance exceeding US $ 1,000,000 (US Dollar one million only) per [2][financial] year—

(*a*) on account of legacy, bequest or inheritance to a citizen of foreign State, permanently resident outside India; and

(*b*) by a non-resident Indian (NRI)/person of Indian origin (PIO), out of the balances held in NRO accounts/sale proceeds of assets/the assets in India acquired by way of inheritance/legacy;]

(*ii*) remittance to a person resident outside India on the ground that hardship will be caused to such a person if remittance from India is not made;

(*iii*) remittance of winding up proceeds of a branch/office [3][other than project office] in India of a person resident outside India:

Provided that the application is supported by the following documents, namely:—

(A) copy of the Reserve Bank's permission for establishing the branch/office in India;

(B) Auditor's certificate,—

---

1 Substituted by the Foreign Exchange Management (Remittance of Assets) (Second Amendment) Regulations, 2003, w.e.f. 8-7-2003 for the following:

[(*i*) Remittance exceeding US $ 1,00,000 (US Dollar One lakh only) per calendar year on account of legacy, bequest or inheritance to a citizen of foreign state permanently resident outside India;]

Earlier it was substituted by the Foreign Exchange Management (Remittance of Assets) (Amendment) Regulations, 2002, w.e.f. 13-5-2002 for the following:

"(*i*) in Form LEG annexed to this regulation for remittance on account of legacy, bequest or inheritance to a citizen of foreign state permanently resident outside India;"

2 Substituted for the word "calendar" *vide* Foreign Exchange Management (Remittance of Assets) (Amendment) Regulations, 2007 w.r.e.f. 16-11-2006 [Notification No. FEMA 152/2007-RB, dated 15-5-2007).

3 Inserted by Foreign Exchange Management (Remittance of Assets) (Amendment) Regulations, 2003, w.e.f. 2-7-2003 [FEMA 96/2003].

(*i*) indicating the manner in which the remittable amount has been arrived and supported by a statement of assets and liabilities of the applicant, and indicating the manner of disposal of assets;

(*ii*) confirming that all liabilities in India including arrears of gratuity and other benefits to employees, etc. of the branch/office have been either fully met or adequately provided for;

(*iii*) confirming that no income accruing from sources outside India (including proceeds of exports) has remained unrepatriated to India;

[1][(C) no-objection or tax clearance certificate from income-tax authority for the remittance;

(D) confirmation from the applicant that no legal proceedings in any Court in India are pending and there is no legal impediment to the remittance; and

(E) a report from the Registrar of Companies regarding compliance with the provisions of the Companies Act, 1956, in case of winding up of the office in India.]

(2) On consideration of the application made under sub-regulation (1), the Reserve Bank may permit the remittance, subject to such terms and conditions as it deem necessary.

LEG[2]

[*See* regulation 6]

Application for remittance of legacies, bequests or inheritances to beneficiaries resident outside India

Instructions

1. The application should be completed and submitted through an authorised dealer through whom the remittance is sought to be made to the office of Reserve Bank under whose jurisdiction the applicant resides.

Documentation

2. Certified copy of the probate together with a copy of the Will annexed thereto, or letters of administration or succession certificate, as the case may be, in respect of the Indian assets of the deceased person.

---

1 Substituted by the Foreign Exchange Management (Remittance of Assets) (Amendment) Regulations, 2009, w.e.f. 23-11-2009 for the following:

"(C) no-objection or Tax clearance certificate from Income-tax authority for the remittance; and

(D) confirmation from the applicant that no legal proceedings in any court in India are pending and there is no legal impediment to the remittance."

2 Form LEG not required now with substitution of Regulation 6(1).

3. Tax Clearance/No Objection Certificate from the Income-tax authorities to show that no liabilities are outstanding in respect of the state of the deceased person on account of Income-tax, Wealth-tax, Capital Gains tax, etc.
4. A statement of Indian assets of the deceased person, indicating the form in which they are held. The number and date of Reserve Bank's approval for holding or acquiring shares of Indian companies and immovable property should be indicated, wherever applicable.
5. A certificate from a Chartered Accountant showing how the remittable amount has been arrived at and that all liabilities of the estate in India have been met or adequately provided for.

1. Particulars of the deceased person: 1.
   (*i*) Name (*i*)
   (*ii*) Nationality (*ii*)
   (*iii*) Country of permanent residence at the time of death (*iii*)
   (*iv*) Date and place of demise (*iv*)
   (*v*) Whether the deceased was residing in India at any time during his life time, if so, state period (*v*)
2. Particulars of the beneficiary/ies 2.
   (*i*) Name/s (*i*)
   (*ii*) Nationality/ies (*ii*)
   (*iii*) Country/ies of permanent residence (*iii*)
3. Whether the deceased person had made any investments in India, if so, details as under: 3.
   (*i*) Investments made on non-repatriation basis (*i*)
   (*ii*) Investments made with repatriation benefits (*ii*)
4. Amount of remittance applied for 4.

I/We hereby declare that the particulars given above and the documents submitted herewith are true and correct to the best of my/our knowledge and belief. I/We also declare that I/We have not made any application to any other office of the Reserve Bank of India for the same purpose.

Place ....

Date .... (Signature/s of Applicant)

Appendix 2

Foreign Exchange Management (Adjudication Proceedings and Appeal) Rules, 2000

[*Notification No. GSR 382(E), dated 3-5-2000*][1]

In exercise of the powers conferred by section 46 read with sub-section (1) of section 16, sub-section (3) of section 17 and sub-section (2) of section 19 of the Foreign Exchange Management Act, 1999 (42 of 1999), the Central Government hereby makes the following rules for holding enquiry for the purpose of imposing penalty and appeals under Chapter V of the said Act, namely:—

1. Short title and commencement.—(1) These rules may be called the Foreign Exchange Management (Adjudication Proceedings and Appeal) Rules, 2000.

(2) They shall come into force on the 1st day of June, 2000.

2. Definitions.—In these rules, unless the context otherwise requires,—

(*a*) "Act" means the Foreign Exchange Management Act, 1999 (42 of 1999);

(*b*) "Adjudicating Authority" means an officer appointed by the Central Government under sub-section (1) of section 16 of the Act;

(*c*) "applicant" means an aggrieved person who makes an appeal before Special Director (Appeals) or Appellate Tribunal, as the case may be;

(*d*) "Appellate Tribunal" means the Appellate Tribunal for Foreign Exchange established under section 18 of the Act;

(*e*) "Form" means form appended to these rules;

(*f*) "Section" means a section of the Act;

---

1 Published in the Gazette of India, Extraordinary No. 249, dated 4-5-2000, Part II, section 3(*i*).

(*g*) "Special Director (Appeals)" means Special Director (Appeals) appointed by the Central Government under sub-section (1) of section 17 of the Act;

(*h*) all other words and expressions used in these rules and not defined but defined in the Act, shall have the meaning respectively assigned to them in the Act.

3. Appointment of Adjudicating Authority.—The Central Government may, by an order published in the Official Gazette, appoint as many officers of the Central Government as it may think fit, as the Adjudicating Authorities for holding inquiry under the provisions of Chapter IV of the Act.

4. Holding of inquiry.—(1) For the purpose of adjudicating under section 13 of the Act whether any person has committed any contravention as specified in that section of the Act, the Adjudicating Authority shall, issue a notice to such person requiring him to show cause within such period as may be specified in the notice (being not less than ten days from the date of service thereof) why an inquiry should not be held against him.

(2) Every notice under sub-rule (1) to any such person shall indicate the nature of contravention alleged to have been committed by him.

(3) After considering the cause, if any, shown by such person, the Adjudicating Authority is of the opinion that an inquiry should be held, he shall issue a notice fixing a date for the appearance of that person either personally or through his legal practitioner or a chartered accountant duly authorised by him.

(4) On the date fixed, the Adjudicating Authority shall explain to the person proceeded against or his legal practitioner or the chartered accountant, as the case may be, the contravention, alleged to have been committed by such person indicating the provisions of the Act or of rules, regulations, notifications, direction or orders or any condition subject to which an authorisation is issued by the Reserve Bank of India in respect of which contravention is alleged to have taken place.

(5) The Adjudicating Authority shall, then, give an opportunity to such person to produce such documents or evidence as he may consider relevant to the inquiry and if necessary, the hearing may be adjourned to a future date and in taking such evidence the Adjudicating Authority shall not be bound to observe the provisions of the Indian Evidence Act, 1872 (1 of 1872).

(6) While holding an inquiry under this rule the Adjudicating Authority shall have the power to summon and enforce attendance of any person acquainted with the facts and circumstances of the case to give evidence or to produce any document which in the opinion of the Adjudicating Authority may be useful for or relevant to the subject-matter of the inquiry.

(7) If any person fails, neglects or refuses to appear as required by sub-rule (3) before the Adjudicating Authority, the Adjudicating Authority may proceed

with the adjudication proceedings in the absence of such person after recording the reasons for doing so.

(8) If, upon consideration of the evidence produced before the Adjudicating Authority, the Adjudicating Authority is satisfied that the person has committed the contravention, he may, by order in writing, impose such penalty as he thinks fit, in accordance with the provisions of section 13 of the Act.

(9) Every order made under sub-rule (8) of rule 4 shall specify the provisions of the Act or of the rules, regulations, notifications, direction or orders or any condition subject to which an authorisation is issued by the Reserve Bank of India in respect of which contravention has taken place and shall contain [1][* * *] reasons for such decisions.

(10) Every order made under sub-rule (8) shall be dated and signed by the Adjudicating Authority.

(11) A copy of the order made under sub-rule (8) of rule 4 shall be supplied free of charge to the person against whom the order is made and all other copies of proceedings shall be supplied to him on payment of copying fee @ ₹ 2 per page.

(12) The copying fee referred to in sub-rule (11) shall be paid in cash or in the form of demand draft in favour of the Adjudicating Authority.

5. Appeal to Special Director (Appeal) — Form of appeal.—(1) Every appeal presented to the Special Director (Appeals) under section 17 of the Act shall be in the Form I signed by the applicant. The appeal shall be filed in triplicate and accompanied by three copies of the order appealed against. Every appeal shall be accompanied by a fee of Rupees five thousand in the form of cash or demand draft payable in favour of the Special Director (Appeal).

(2) The appeal shall set forth concisely and under distinct heads the grounds of objection to the order appealed against without any argument of narrative and such grounds shall be numbered consecutively; and shall specify the address for service at which notice or other processes may be served on the applicant, the date on which the order appealed against was served on the applicant.

(3) Whether the appeal is presented after the expiry of the period of forty-five days referred to in sub-section (3) of section 17, it shall be accompanied by a petition, in triplicate, duly verified and supported by the documents, if any, relied upon by the applicant, showing cause how the applicant had been prevented from preferring the appeal within the said period of forty-five days.

(4) Any notice required to be served on the applicant shall be served on him in the manner specified in rule 9 at the address for service specified in the appeal.

---

1 The word "brief" omitted by the Foreign Exchange Management (Adjudication Proceedings and Appeal) Amendment Rules, 2005, w.e.f. 27-7-2005.

6. Procedure before Special Director (Appeals).—(1) On receipt of an appeal under rule 5, the Special Director (Appeals) shall send a copy of the appeal, together with a copy of the order appealed against, to the Director of Enforcement.

(2) The Special Director (Appeals) shall, then, issue notices to the applicant and the Director of Enforcement fixing a date for hearing of the appeal.

(3) On the date fixed for hearing of the appeal or any other day to which the hearing of the appeal may be adjourned, the applicant as well as the presenting officer of the Directorate of Enforcement shall be heard.

(4) Where on the date fixed, or any other day to which the hearing of the appeal may be adjourned, the applicant or the presenting officer fail to appear when the appeal is called for hearing, the Special Director (Appeals) may decide the appeal on the merits of the case [1][within one hundred and eighty days from the date of such appeal].

7. Contents of the order in appeal.—(1) The order of Special Director (Appeals) shall be in writing and shall state briefly the grounds for the decision.

(2) The order referred to in sub-rule (1) shall be signed by the Special Director (Appeal) hearing the appeal.

8. Representation of party.—Any applicant who has filed an appeal before the Special Director (Appeals) under section 17 of the Act, may appoint a legal practitioner or a chartered accountant to appear and plead and act on his behalf before the Special Director (Appeal) under the Act.

9. Service of notices, requisitions or orders.—A notice, requisition or an order issued under these rules shall be served on any person in the following manner, that is to say,—

(*a*) by delivering or tendering the notice or requisition or order to that person or his duly authorised person,

(*b*) by sending the notice or requisition or order to him by registered post with acknowledgement due to the address of his place of residence or his last known place or residence or the place where he carried on, or last carried on, business or personally works or last worked for gain, or

(*c*) by affixing it on the outer door or some other conspicuous part of the premises in which the person resides or is known to have last resided or carried on business or personally works or last worked for gain and that written report thereof should be witnesses by two persons; or

(*d*) if the notice or requisition or order cannot be served under clause (*a*) or clause (*b*) or clause (*c*), by publishing in a leading newspaper (both in vernacular and in English) having wide circulation of area or jurisdiction

---

1 Inserted by the Foreign Exchange Management (Adjudication Proceedings and Appeal) Amendment Rules, 2005, w.e.f. 27-7-2005.

in which the person resides or is known to have last resided or carried on business or personally works or last worked for gain.

10. Appeal to the Appellate Tribunal — Form of appeal.—(1) Every appeal presented to the Appellate Tribunal under section 19 of the Act shall be in Form II signed by the applicant. The appeal shall be sent in triplicate and accompanied by three copies of the order appealed against. Every appeal shall be accompanied by a fee of rupees ten thousand in the form of cash or demand draft payable in favour of the Registrar, Appellate Tribunal for Foreign Exchange, New Delhi:

Provided that the applicant shall deposit the amount of penalty imposed by the Adjudicating Authority or the Special Director (Appeals) as the case may be, to such authority as may be notified under the first proviso to section 19 of the Act:

Provided further that where in a particular case, the Appellate Tribunal is of the opinion that the deposit of such penalty would cause undue hardship to such person, the Appellate Tribunal may dispense with such deposit subject to such conditions as it may deem fit to impose so as to safeguard the realisation of penalty.

(2) The appeal shall set forth concisely and under distinct heads the grounds of objection to the order appealed against without any argument of narrative and such grounds shall be numbered consecutively; and shall specify the address for service at which notice or other processes may be served on the applicant, the date on which the order appealed against was served on the applicant; and the sum imposed by way of penalty under section 13 and the amount of fee prescribed in sub-rule (1) has been deposited or not.

(3) Where the appeal is presented after the expiry of the period of forty-five days referred to in sub-section (2) of section 19, it shall be accompanied by a petition, in triplicate, duly verified and supported by the documents, if any, relied upon by the applicant, showing cause how the applicant had been prevented from preferring the appeal within the said period of forty-five days.

(4) Any notice required to be served on the applicant shall be served on him in the manner prescribed in rule 14 at the address for service specified in the appeal.

11. Procedure before Appellate Tribunal.—(1) On receipt of an appeal under rule 10, the Appellate Tribunal shall send a copy of the appeal, together with a copy of the order appealed against, to the Director of Enforcement.

(2) The Appellate Tribunal shall, then, issue notices to the applicant and the Director of Enforcement fixing a date for hearing of the appeal.

(3) On the date fixed for hearing of the appeal, or any other day to which the hearing of the appeal may be adjourned, the applicant as well as the presenting officer of the Directorate of Enforcement shall be heard.

(4) Where on the date fixed, or any other day to which the hearing of the appeal may be adjourned, the applicant or the presenting officer fail to appear when the appeal is called on for hearing, the Appellate Tribunal may decide the appeal on the merits of the case.

12. Contents of the order in appeal.—(1) The order of Appellate Tribunal shall be in writing and shall state briefly the grounds for the decision.

(2) The order referred to in sub-rule (1) shall be signed by the Chairman or Member of the Appellate Tribunal hearing the appeal.

13. Representation of party.—Any applicant who has filed an appeal before the Appellate Tribunal under section 19 of the Act may appoint a legal practitioner or a chartered accountant to appear and plead and act on his behalf before the Special Director (Appeal) under the Act.

14. Service of notices, requisitions or orders.—A notice, requisition or an order issued under these rules shall be served on any person in the following manner, that is to say,—

(*a*) by delivering or tendering the notice or requisition or order to that person or his duly authorised person;

(*b*) by sending the notice or requisition or order to him by registered post with acknowledgement due to the address of his place of residence or his last known place or residence or the place where he carried on, or last carried on, business or personally works or last worked for gain; or

(*c*) by affixing it on the outer door or some other conspicuous part of the premises in which the person resides or is known to have last resided or carried on business or personally works or last worked for gain and that written report thereof should be witnesses by two persons; or

(*d*) if the notice or requisition or order cannot be served under clause (*a*) or clause (*b*) or clause (*c*), by publishing in a leading newspaper (both in vernacular and in English) having wide circulation of area or jurisdiction in which the person resides or is known to have last resided or carried on business or personally works or last worked for gain.

Form I

(*See* rule 5)

Form of Appeal

From ....

(Mention the name and address of the applicant here)

To

The Special Director (Appeals)

(Address)

Sir,

The applicant named above, begs to prefer this appeal under section 17 of the Foreign Exchange Management Act, 1999, against order No. ..... dated .... passed by the Adjudicating Authority under the said Act on the following facts and grounds.

Facts

(Mention briefly the facts of the case here. Enclose copy of the order passed by the Adjudicating Authority and copies of other relevant documents, if any)

Grounds

(Mention here the grounds on which the appeal is made)

Prayer

In the light of what is stated above, the applicant prays that he/she it may be granted the following relief.

Relief sought

(Specify the relief sought)

The fee of ₹ ...... for this appeal has been deposited in ...... *vide* receipt No. ...... dated ......

Place

Date (Signature of the applicant or his authorised representative)

List of Documents attached: (Signature of the applicant or his authorised representative)

Form II

(*See* rule 10)

Form of Appeal

From ....

(Mention the name and address of the applicant here)

To

The Registrar
Appellate Tribunal for Foreign Exchange
(Address)

Sir,

The applicant named above, begs to prefer this appeal under section 17 of the Foreign Exchange Management Act, 1999, against order No. ..... dated .... passed by the Adjudicating Authority under the said Act on the following facts and grounds.

Facts

(Mention briefly the facts of the case here. Enclose copy of the order passed by the Adjudicating Authority and copies of other relevant documents, if any)

Grounds

(Mention here the grounds on which the appeal is made)

Prayer

In the light of what is stated above, the applicant prays that he/she it may be granted the following relief.

Relief sought

(Specify the relief sought)

1. The fee of ₹ ...... for this appeal has been deposited in ...... *vide* receipt No. ...... dated ......

2. The amount of penalty imposed by Adjudicating Authority or Special Director (Appeals), as the case may be, ₹ ...... for this appeal has been deposited in .... *vide* receipt No. .... dated ....

Place

Date

(Signature of the applicant or his authorised representative)

List of Documents attached:

(Signature of the applicant or his authorised representative)

Appendix 3

Foreign Exchange (Compounding Proceedings) Rules, 2000[1]

[Notification No. GSR 383(E), dated 3-5-2000][2]

In exercise of the powers conferred by section 46 read with sub-section (1) of section 15 of the Foreign Exchange Management Act, 1999 (42 of 1999) the Central Government hereby makes the following rules relating to compounding contraventions under Chapter IV of the said Act, namely:—

1. Short title and commencement.—(1) These rules may be called the Foreign Exchange (Compounding Proceedings) Rules, 2000.

(2) They shall come into force on the 1st day of June, 2000.

2. Definitions.—In these rules, unless the context otherwise requires,—

(*a*) "Act" means the Foreign Exchange Management Act, 1999 (42 of 1999);

(*b*) "Authorised Officer" means an officer authorised under sub-rule (1) of rule 3;

(*c*) "applicant" means a person who makes an application under section 15(1) of the Act to the compounding authority;

(*d*) "Compounding Order" means an order issued under sub-section (1) of section 15 of the Act;

(*e*) "Form" means a form appended to these rules;

(*f*) "Section" means a section of the Act;

(*g*) all other words and expressions used in these rules and not defined but defined in the Act, shall have the meaning respectively assigned to them in the Act.

---

1 Published in the Gazette of India, Extraordinary No. 249, dated 4-5-2000, Part II, section 3(*i*).

2 For 'Compounding Process' at RBI level refer AP (DIR Series) Circular No. 56, dated 28-6-2010 which has been issued in supersession of AP (DIR Series) Circular No. 31, dated 1-2-2005.

3. "Compounding Authority" means the person authorised by the Central Government under sub-section (1) of section 15 of the Act, namely:—

(*a*) An officer of the Enforcement Directorate not below the rank of Deputy Director or Deputy Legal Adviser (DLA).

(*b*) An officer of the Reserve Bank of India not below the rank of the Assistant General Manager.

4. Power of Reserve Bank to compound contravention.—[1][(1) If any person contravenes any provisions of the Foreign Exchange Management Act, 1999 (42 of 1999) except clause (*a*) of section 3 of that Act:—]

(*a*) in case where the sum involved in such contravention is [2][ten lakhs] rupees or below, by the Assistant General Manager of the Reserve Bank of India;

(*b*) in case where the sum involved in such contravention is more than rupees [3][ten lakhs] but less than rupees [4][forty lakhs], by the Deputy General Manager of Reserve Bank of India;

(*c*) in case where the sum involved in the contravention is rupees [5][forty lakhs] or more but less than rupees [6][hundred lakhs[7]] by the General Manager of Reserve Bank of India;

(*d*) in case the sum involved in such contravention is rupees [8][one hundred lakhs] or more, by the Chief General Manager of the Reserve Bank of India:

Provided further that no contravention shall be compounded unless the amount involved in such contravention is quantifiable.

(2) Nothing contained in sub-section (1) shall apply to a contravention committed by any person within a period of three years from the date on which a similar contravention committed by him was compounded under these rules.

---

1 Substituted by the Foreign Exchange Management (Compounding Proceedings) (Amendment) Rules, 2004, w.e.f. 13-9-2004 for the following:

"(1) If any person contravenes any of the provisions of section 7, or section 8 or section 9 or Third Schedule to the Foreign Exchange (Current Account Transaction) Rules, 2000 notified by GSR No. 381(E), dated 3-5-2000, such contraventions may be compounded:—"

2 Substituted for the words "five lakhs" by the Foreign Exchange (Compounding Proceedings) (Amendment) Rules, 2008 [Notification No. G.S.R. 613 (E), dated 27.8.2008].

3 Substituted for the words "five lakhs" by the Foreign Exchange (Compounding Proceedings) (Amendment) Rules, 2008 [Notification No. G.S.R. 613 (E), dated 27.8.2008].

4 Substituted for the words "twenty lakhs" by the Foreign Exchange (Compounding Proceedings) (Amendment) Rules, 2008 [Notification No. G.S.R. 613 (E), dated 27.8.2008].

5 Substituted for the words "twenty lakhs" by the Foreign Exchange (Compounding Proceedings) (Amendment) Rules, 2008 [Notification No. G.S.R. 613 (E), dated 27.8.2008].

6 Substituted for the words "fifty lakhs" by the Foreign Exchange (Compounding Proceedings) (Amendment) Rules, 2008 [Notification No. G.S.R. 613 (E), dated 27.8.2008].

7 The correct wordings should have been 'one hundred lakhs'.

8 Substituted for the words "fifty lakhs" by the Foreign Exchange (Compounding Proceedings) (Amendment) Rules, 2008 [Notification No. G.S.R. 613 (E), dated 27.8.2008].

Explanation.—For the purposes of this rule, any second or subsequent contravention committed after the expiry of a period of three years from the date on which the contravention was previously compounded shall be deemed to be a first contravention.

(3) Every officer specified under sub-rule (1) of rule 4 of the Reserve Bank of India shall exercise the powers to compound any contravention subject to the direction, control and supervision of the Governor of the Reserve Bank of India.

(4) Every application for compounding any contravention under this rule shall be made in Form to the Reserve Bank of India, Exchange Control Department, Central Office, Mumbai along with a fee of ₹ 5,000 by Demand Draft in favour of compounding authority.

5. The power of Enforcement Directorate to compound contraventions.—[1][If any person contravenes provisions of section 3(*a*) of the Foreign Exchange Management Act:—]

(*a*) in case where the sum involved in such contravention is five lakhs rupees or below, by the Deputy Director of the Directorate of Enforcement;

(*b*) in case where the sum involved in such contravention is more than rupees five lakhs but less than rupees ten lakhs, by the Additional Director of the Directorate of Enforcement;

(*c*) in case where the sum involved in the contravention is rupees ten lakhs or more but less than fifty lakhs rupees by the Special Director of the Directorate of Enforcement;

(*d*) in case where the sum involved in the contravention is rupees fifty lakhs or more but less than one crore rupees by Special Director with Deputy Legal Adviser of the Directorate of Enforcement;

(*e*) in case the sum involved in such contravention is one crore rupees or more, by the Director of Enforcement with Special Director of the Enforcement Directorate:

Provided further that no contravention shall be compounded unless the amount involved in such contravention is quantifiable.

(2) Nothing contained in sub-section (1) shall apply to a contravention committed by any person within a period of three years from the date on which a similar contravention committed by him was compounded under these rules.

Explanation.—For the purposes of this rule, any second or subsequent contravention committed after the expiry of a period of three years from the date

---

1 Substituted by the Foreign Exchange Management (Compounding Proceedings) (Amendment) Rules, 2004, w.e.f. 13-9-2004 for the following:

"(1) If any person contravenes any of the provisions of sections other than section 7 or section 8 or section 9 or Third Schedule to the Foreign Exchange (Current Account Transactions) Rules, 2000 notified *vide* GSR No. 381(E), dated 3-5-2000, such contravention may be compounded:"

on which the contravention was previously compounded shall be deemed to be a first contravention.

(3) Every officer of the Directorate of Enforcement specified under sub-rule (1) of this rule shall exercise the powers to compound any contravention subject to the direction, control and supervision of the Director of Enforcement.

(4) Every application for compounding any contravention under this rule shall be made in Form to the Director, Directorate of Enforcement, New Delhi along with a fee of ₹ 5,000 by Demand Draft in favour of the compounding authority.

6. Where any contravention is compounded before the adjudication of any contravention under section 16, no inquiry shall be held for adjudication of such contravention in relation to such contravention against the person in relation to whom the contravention is so compounded.

7. Where the compounding of any contravention is made after making of a complaint under sub-section (3) of section 16, such compounding shall be brought by the authority specified in rule 4 or rule 5 in writing, to the notice of the Adjudicating Authority and on such notice of the compounding of the contravention being given, the person in relation to whom the contravention is so compounded shall be discharged.

8. Procedure for compounding.—(1) The Compounding Authority may call for any information, record or any other documents relevant to the compounding proceedings.

(2) The Compounding Authority shall pass an order of compounding after affording an opportunity of being heard to all the concerned as expeditiously as possible and not latter than 180 days from the date of application.

[1][**9. Payment of amount compounded.**—The sum for which the contravention is compounded as specified in the order of compounding under sub-rule (2) of rule 8, shall be paid by demand draft in favour of the Compounding Authority within fifteen days from the date of the order of compounding of such contravention.]

10. In case a person fails to pay the sum compounded in accordance with rule 9 within the time specified in that rule, he shall be deemed to have never made an application for compounding of any contravention under these rules and the provisions of the Act for contravention shall apply to him.

11. No contravention shall be compounded if an appeal has been filed under section 17 or section 19 of the Act.

---

1 Substituted by the Foreign Exchange Management (Compounding Proceedings) (Amendment) Rules, 2002, w.e.f. 22-10-2002 for the following:

"*9. Payment of amount compounded.*—Where a contravention has been compounded under rule 8(2) the sum involved in such contravention shall be deposited within fifteen days from the date of the order of compounding of such contravention by demand draft in favour of the Compounding Authority."

12. Contents of the order of the Compounding Authority.—(1) Every order shall specify the provisions of the Act or of the rules, directions, requisitions or orders made thereunder in respect of which contravention has taken place along with details of the alleged contravention.

(2) Every such order shall be dated and signed by the Compounding Authority under his seal.

13. Copy of the order.—One copy of the order made under rule 8(2) shall be supplied to the applicant and the Adjudicating Authority as the case may be.

Form

(*See* rule 4 or 5)

(To be filled in duplicate and shall be accompanied by certified copy of the Memorandum issued)

1. Name of the applicant:
   (in block letters)
2. Full address of the applicant:
3. Whether the applicant is resident
   in India or resident outside India
   [Please refer to section 2(*v*) of the Act]:
4. Name of the Adjudicating Authority
   before whom the case is pending:
5. Nature of the contravention (according
   to sub-section (1) of section 13):
6. Brief facts of the case:
7. Details of fee for application
   of compounding:
8. Any other information relevant to
   the case:

I/We declare that the particulars given above are true and correct to the best of my/our knowledge and belief and that I/We am/are willing to accept any direction/order of the Compounding Authority in connection with compounding of my/our case.

Dated ......

(Signature of Applicant)

Master Circular No. 8/2011-12 (Updated as on 20-1-2012), dated 1-7-2011

Master Circular on Compounding of Contraventions under FEMA, 1999

The compounding of contraventions under Foreign Exchange Management Act (FEMA), 1999 is a voluntary process by which an applicant can seek compounding of an admitted contravention of any provision of FEMA, 1999 under section 13(1) of the FEMA, 1999.

2. This Master Circular consolidates the existing instructions on the subject of "Compounding of Contraventions under FEMA, 1999" at one place. The list of underlying circulars/notifications, consolidated in this Master Circular, is furnished in the Appendix.

3. This Master Circular is being issued with a sunset clause of one year. This circular will stand withdrawn on July 1, 2012 and be replaced by an updated Master Circular on the subject.

1 General

1.1 If any person contravenes any provision of FEMA, 1999, or contravenes any rule, regulation, notification, direction or order issued in exercise of the powers under this Act, or contravenes any condition subject to which an authorization is issued by the Reserve Bank, he shall, upon adjudication, be liable to a penalty up to thrice the sum involved in such contravention where the amount is quantifiable or up to Rupees Two lakh, where the amount is not quantifiable and where the contravention is a continuing one, further penalty which may extend to Rupees Five thousand for every day after the first day during which the contravention continues (Section 13(1), Chapter IV of FEMA, 1999). In terms of rule 4 of the Foreign Exchange (Compounding Proceedings) Rules, 2000, the powers to compound the contraventions have been prescribed for compounding authorities with regard to the sum involved in such contravention and no contravention shall be compounded unless the amount involved in the contravention is quantifiable.

1.2 Foreign Exchange (Compounding Proceedings) Rules, 2000 have been framed and published by the Government of India empowering the Reserve Bank to compound contraventions under FEMA, 1999. The provisions of section 15 of FEMA, 1999 permit compounding of contraventions and empower the Compounding Authority to compound any contravention as defined under section 13 of the Act on an application made by the person committing such contravention either before or after the institution of adjudication proceedings.

1.3 The Government of India has, in consultation with the Reserve Bank placed the responsibility of administering compounding of contraventions with the Reserve Bank, except contraventions under section 3(*a*) of FEMA, 1999. Accordingly, the procedure for compounding of contraventions under FEMA, 1999 has been framed with a view to provide comfort to the citizens and corporate community by minimizing transaction costs, while taking severe view of willful, *mala fide* and fraudulent transactions.

2. Compounding Powers

2.1 The compounding powers of the Reserve Bank and the Directorate of Enforcement (DoE), respectively, are as under:

(*a*) Reserve Bank has been empowered to compound the contraventions of all the sections of FEMA, 1999, except clause (*a*) of section 3 of the Act, ibid.

(*b*) Directorate of Enforcement would exercise powers of compounding under clause (*a*) of section 3 of FEMA, 1999 (dealing essentially with Hawala transactions).

2.2 For effective implementation of compounding process under FEMA, 1999, the Reserve Bank has framed the procedure for compounding of contraventions. Once a contravention has been compounded by the Compounding Authority, no proceeding or further proceeding will be initiated or continued, as the case may be, against the contravener.

3. Delegation of Powers

3.1 As a measure of customer service and in order to facilitate the operational convenience, it has been decided to delegate the powers to the Regional Offices of the Reserve Bank of India mentioned below to compound the contraventions of FEMA involving (*i*) delay in reporting of inward remittance, (*ii*) delay in filing of form FC-GPR after allotment of shares and (*iii*) delay in issue of shares beyond 180 days (*viz.*paragraphs 9(1)(A), 9(1)(B) and 8, respectively, of the Schedule I to the Foreign Exchange Management (Transfer or Issue of Security by a Person Resident Outside India) Regulations, 2000, notified *vide*Notification No. FEMA 20/2000-RB, dated 3rd May 2000 and as amended from time to time:

(*a*) **Paragraphs 9(1)(A) and 9(1)(B) of Schedule I to FEMA 20/2000-RB, dated May 3, 2000** — Bhopal, Bhubaneshwar, Chandigarh, Guwahati, Jaipur, Jammu, Kanpur, Kochi, Patna and Panaji for amount of contravention below Rupees One hundred lakh only (₹1,00,00,000).

(*b*) **Paragraphs 9(1)(A), 9(1)(B) and 8 of Schedule I to FEMA 20/2000-RB, dated May 3, 2000** — Ahmedabad, Bangalore, Chennai, Hyderabad, Kolkata, Mumbai and New Delhi for amount of contravention without any limit.

4. Process of Compounding

4.1 An application for compounding of a contravention under FEMA, 1999 may be submitted to the Compounding Authority (CA) on being advised of a contravention under FEMA, 1999, either through a memorandum or *suo moto* on being made or on becoming aware of the contravention. The format of the application is appended to the Foreign Exchange (Compounding Proceedings) Rules, 2000 (Annex-I).

4.2 Along with the application in the prescribed format, the applicant may also furnish the details as per the enclosed Annexes (Annex-II) relating to Foreign Direct Investment, External Commercial Borrowings, Overseas Direct Investment and Branch Office/Liaison Office, as applicable, along with an undertaking that they are not under investigation of any agency such as DOE, CBI, etc., a copy of the Memorandum of Association and latest audited balance sheet while applying for compounding of contraventions under FEMA, 1999.

4.3 All applications for compounding whether on the advice of the Regional Office concerned or *suo moto*, relating to the contraventions mentioned at para 3 (*a*) and (*b*) above and up to the amount of contravention stated therein, may be submitted by the companies falling under the jurisdiction of the aforesaid Regional Offices directly to the Regional Office concerned, together with the prescribed fee of ₹5000 by way of a demand draft drawn in favour of "Reserve Bank of India" and payable at the concerned Regional Office. Applications for compounding of all other contraventions together with the prescribed fee of ₹5000 by way of a demand draft drawn in favour of "Reserve Bank of India" and payable at Mumbai may be submitted to: The Compounding Authority, [Cell for Effective implementation of FEMA (CEFA)], Foreign Exchange Department, 5th floor, Amar Building, Sir P.M. Road, Fort, Mumbai-400001.

4.4 On receipt of the application for compounding, the proceedings would be concluded and order issued by the CA within 180 days from the date of the receipt of the application for compounding. The time limit for this purpose would be reckoned from the date of receipt of the completed application for compounding by the Reserve Bank. The CA may call for any information, record or any other documents relevant to the compounding proceedings and will hold the proceedings. The Compounding Order will be passed by the CA after affording the contravener and others concerned, an opportunity of being heard.

4.5 The application will be examined based on the documents and submissions made in the application, in terms of sub rule (1) of rule (4) of the Foreign Exchange (Compounding Proceedings) Rules, 2000 and assess whether the contravention is compoundable and if so, the amount of contravention is accordingly quantified.

4.6 The nature of contravention is ascertained keeping in view, *inter alia*, the following indicative points:

(*a*) whether the contravention is technical and/or minor in nature and needs only an administrative cautionary advice;

(*b*) whether the contravention is serious in nature and warrants compounding of the contravention; and

(*c*) whether the contravention, prima facie, involves money-laundering, national and security concerns involving serious infringement of the regulatory framework.

However, the Reserve Bank reserves the right to classify the contraventions as stated above and neither the contravener nor others have any right to classify any contravention as technical *suo moto*.

4.7 The disposal of the compounding application is made by issue of a Compounding Order specifying the provisions of FEMA, 1999 or any rule, regulation, notification, direction or order issued in exercise of the powers under FEMA, 1999, in respect of which contravention has taken place.

4.8 The CA may call for any additional information, record or any other document relevant to the compounding proceedings. Such additional information/documents are required to be submitted within the period as may be specified by the CA and the application may be rejected if such information/ documents are not submitted within the prescribed time.

4.9 Where there is sufficient cause for further investigation, the Reserve Bank may refer the matter to the Directorate of Enforcement for further investigation and necessary action under FEMA, 1999, as deemed fit or to the Anti- Money Laundering Authority instituted under the Prevention of Money Laundering Act (PMLA), 2002 or to any other agencies, as deemed fit. Such applications will be disposed of by returning the application to the applicant.

5. Scope and Manner of Compounding

5.1 The CA will exercise jurisdiction in respect of the contraventions alleged to have been committed in relation to any of the provisions of the FEMA, 1999, or any rule, regulation, notification, direction or order issued in exercise of the powers under FEMA, 1999.

5.2 The CA will form an opinion on the basis of the application, together with the documents submitted and on the basis of submissions made during the personal hearing on the nature of the contravention.

5.3 The application for compounding will be disposed of on merits, upon consideration of the records and submissions and at the absolute discretion of the CA. The following factors, which are only indicative, may be taken into consideration for the purpose of passing the Compounding Order and for arriving at the quantum of sum on payment of which contravention shall be compounded:

(*i*) the amount of gain of unfair advantage, wherever quantifiable, made as a result of the contravention;

(*ii*) the amount of loss caused to any authority/agency/exchequer as a result of the contravention;

(*iii*) economic benefits accruing to the contravener from delayed compliance or compliance avoided;

(*iv*) the repetitive nature of the contravention, the track record and/or history of noncompliance of the contravener;

(*v*) contravener's conduct in undertaking the transaction and disclosure of full facts in the application and submissions made during the personal hearing; and

(*vi*) any other factor considered relevant and appropriate.

6. Issue of the Compounding Order

6.1 An opportunity for personal hearing is given to the applicant for further submission of documents in person in support of the application within a specified period. If the contravener or its authorized representative fails to appear in person or make any submissions before the CA for personal hearing, the CA may proceed with the processing of the compounding application on the basis of information and documents available in the application for compounding.

6.2 The Compounding Authority will pass a compounding order on the basis of the averments made in the application as well as other documents and submissions made in this context by the contravener during the personal hearings, if any.

6.3 Where the compounding of any contravention is made after making of a complaint under sub-section (3) of section 16 of FEMA, 1999 as the case may be, one copy of the compounding order made under sub rule (2) of Rule 8 of Foreign Exchange (Compounding Proceedings) Rules, 2000 will be provided to the applicant (the contravener) and also to the Adjudicating Authority.

7. Post-compounding procedure

7.1 The sum for which the contravention is compounded as specified in the order of compounding under sub-rule (2) of Rule 8 of Foreign Exchange (Compounding Proceedings) Rules, 2000 is payable by way of a demand draft in favour of the "Reserve Bank of India" within fifteen days from the date of the order of compounding of such contravention. The demand draft has to be deposited in the manner as directed in the compounding order.

7.2 The provisions of the Rules do not confer any right on the contravener, after a compounding order is passed, to seek to withdraw the order or to hold the compounding order as void or request a review of the order passed by the CA.

7.3 In case of failure to pay the sum compounded within the time specified in the compounding order, it shall be deemed in terms of Rule 10 of the Foreign Exchange (Compounding Proceedings) Rules, 2000, that the contravener had never made an application for compounding of any contravention under these Rules.

7.4 On realization of the demand draft for the sum for which contravention is compounded, a certificate in this regard shall be issued by the Reserve Bank subject to the specified conditions, if any, in the order.

7.5 In respect of the contraventions of FEMA, 1999 (as defined in section 13 of the FEMA, 1999), which are not compounded by the Compounding Authority, other relevant provisions of FEMA, 1999, shall apply.

8. Pre-requisites for compounding process

8.1 In respect of a contravention committed by any person within a period of three years from the date on which a similar contravention committed by him was compounded under the Compounding Rules, such contraventions would not be compounded. Such contravention would be dealt with under relevant provisions of the FEMA, 1999 for contravention. Any second or subsequent contravention committed after the expiry of a period of three years from the date on which the contravention was previously compounded shall be deemed to be a first contravention.

8.2 Contraventions relating to any transaction where proper approvals or permission from the Government or statutory authority concerned, as the case may be, have not been obtained, such contraventions would not be compounded unless the required approvals are obtained from the authorities concerned.

8.3 Cases of contravention, such as, those having a money laundering angle, national security concern and/or involving serious infringements of the regulatory framework or where the contravener fails to pay the sum for which contravention was compounded within the specified period in terms of the compounding order, shall be referred to the Directorate of Enforcement for further investigation and necessary action under FEMA, 1999 or to the authority instituted for implementation of the Prevention of Money Laundering Act 2002, (PMLA) or to any other agencies, for necessary action, as deemed fit.

8.4 The Reserve Bank generally advises the persons concerned of their choice and option to make an application for compounding as and when such contraventions come to its notice. The facts constituting such contraventions will be brought to the notice of the Directorate of Enforcement in case no application for compounding is made within the time indicated by the Reserve Bank.

Annexure I

FDI

Details to be furnished along with application for compounding of contravention relating to Foreign Direct Investment in India

- Name of the applicant
- Date of incorporation
- Nature of activities undertaken
- Brief particulars about the foreign investor
- Details of foreign inward remittances received by Applicant Company from date of incorporation till date

Table A

Sl. No.	Name of Remitter	Total Amount (INR)	Date of Receipt	Reported to RBI on*	Delay if any
	Total				
* date of reporting to RBI and not AD					

Table B

Name of Investor	Date of allotment of shares	Number of shares allotted	Amount for which shares allotted	Date of reporting to RBI*	Delay if any
	Total				

Table C

In case there is excess share application money

Sl. No	Name of Remitter	Total Amount (INR)	Date of Receipt	Excess share application money	Date of refund of share application money	Amount in forex	RBI approval letter and date
	Total						

Table D

Authorised Capital

SI. No.	Date	Authorised Capital	With effect from	Date of Board meeting	Date of filing with ROC

A = B+C

Please give supporting documents

Table A- Copies of FIRC with date stamp of receipt at RBI

Table B- Copies of FCGPR with date stamp of receipt at RBI

Table C - letter seeking refund/allotment of shares- approval letter from RBI A2 form

- Copies of Balance Sheet during the period of receipt of share application money and allotment of shares
- Nature of contravention and reasons for the contravention

Annexure II

ECB

Details to be furnished along with application for compounding of contravention relating to External Commercial Borrowing

- Name of the applicant
- Date of incorporation
- Nature of activities undertaken
- Brief particulars about the foreign lender
- Is the applicant an eligible borrower?
- Is the lender eligible lender?
- Is the lender an equity holder?
- What is the level of his holding at the time of loan agreement?

Details of ECB

- Date of Loan agreement
- Amount in Foreign Currency and Indian Rupee
- Rate of interest
- Period of loan
- Repayment particulars
- **Details of draw down** Date of draw down Amount in Foreign Currency Amount in INR
- Details of LRN Number- application and receipt
- Details of ECB 2 returns submitted; Period of return: Date of submission

- Details of Utilization of ECB in Foreign Currency and Indian Rupee
- Nature of contravention and reasons for the contravention
- All supporting documents may be submitted

Annexure III

ODI

Details to be furnished along with application for compounding of contravention relating to Overseas Investment

- Name of the applicant
- Date of incorporation
- Nature of activities undertaken
- Name of Overseas entity
- Date of incorporation of overseas entity
- Nature of activities under taken by overseas entity
- Nature of entity - WOS/JV
- Details of remittance sent- Date of remittance; Amount in FCY and in INR
- Details of other financial Commitment
- Details of UIN applied and received
- Date of receipt of share certificate
- Approval of other regulators if required
- Details of APRs submitted: For the period ended; date of submission
- Nature of contravention and reasons for the contravention
- All supporting documents may be submitted

Annexure IV

Branch Office/Liaison Office

Details to be furnished along with application for compounding of contravention relating to Branch/Liaison Office in India

- Name of the applicant
- Date of incorporation
- Date of approval for opening of Liaison Office/Branch Office
- Validity period of the approval
- Nature of activities under taken
- Income and expenditure of the LO/BO
- Dates of submission of Annual activity Certificates
- Nature of contravention and reasons for the contravention
- All supporting documents may be submitted

Appendix

List of Rules/AP (DIR Series) Circulars consolidated in the Master Circular Compounding of contraventions of FEMA, 1999

Rules Sl. No.	Rules No.	Date
1	Foreign Exchange (Compounding Proceedings) Rules, 2000	May 3, 2000
2	Foreign Exchange (Compounding Proceedings) Rules, 2002 (Amendment)	November 2, 2002
3	Foreign Exchange (Compounding Proceedings) Rules, 2004 (Amendment)	September 13, 2004
4	Foreign Exchange (Compounding Proceedings) Rules, 2004 (Amendment)	August 27, 2008

AP (DIR Series) Circular No. 56, dated June 28, 2010.

AP (DIR Series) Circular No. 57, dated December 13, 2011.

AP (DIR Series 2011-12) Circular No. 57, dated 13-12-2011

Foreign Exchange (Compounding Proceedings) Rules, 2000 — Compounding of Contraventions under FEMA, 1999

Attention of all the Authorised Dealer Category-I (AD Category-I) banks and their constituents is invited to AP (DIR Series) Circular No. 56, dated 28-6-2010 and the Foreign Exchange (Compounding Proceedings) Rules, 2000 notified by the Government of India *vide* GSR. No. 383(E), dated 3-5-2000, as amended from time to time.

2. As a measure of customer service and in order to facilitate the operational convenience, it has been decided to delegate the powers to the Regional Offices of the Reserve Bank of India mentioned below to compound the contraventions of FEMA involving (*i*) delay in reporting of inward remittance, (*ii*) delay in filing of form FC-GPR after allotment of shares and (*iii*) delay in issue of shares beyond 180 days (*viz.* paragraphs 9(1)(A), 9(1)(B) and 8, respectively, of the Schedule I to the Foreign Exchange Management (Transfer or Issue of Security by a Person Resident Outside India) Regulations, 2000, notified *vide* Notification No. FEMA 20/2000-RB, dated 3rd May 2000 and as amended from time to time:

(*a*) **Paragraphs 9(1)(A) and 9(1)(B) of Schedule I to FEMA 20/2000-RB, dated 3-5-2000** — Bhopal, Bhubaneshwar, Chandigarh, Guwahati, Jaipur, Jammu, Kanpur, Kochi, Patna and Panaji for amount of contravention below Rupees One hundred lakh only (₹1,00,00,000).

(*b*) **Paragraphs 9(1)(A), 9(1)(B) and 8 of Schedule I to FEMA 20/2000-RB, dated 3-5-2000** — Ahmedabad, Bangalore, Chennai, Hyderabad, Kolkata, Mumbai and New Delhi for amount of contravention without any limit.

The Compounding Authorities attached to these Regional Offices of the Foreign Exchange Department have been authorised to compound such cases at their level(s) within the financial powers as per the Foreign Exchange (Compounding Proceedings) Rules, 2000. Accordingly, all applications for compounding whether received on the advice of the Regional Office concerned or *suo moto,* relating to the contraventions mentioned at (*a*) and (*b*) above and up to the amount of contravention stated therein, may be submitted by the companies falling under the jurisdiction of the aforesaid Regional Offices directly to the Regional Office concerned, together with the prescribed fee and other relevant documents. All other applications may be submitted to the Compounding Authority, Cell for Effective implementation of FEMA (CEFA), Foreign Exchange Department, 5th floor, Amar Building, Sir P.M. Road, Fort, Mumbai-400001, as hitherto. The prescribed fee of ₹5,000 (Rupees Five thousand only) may be paid by way of a demand draft drawn in favour of "Reserve Bank of India" and payable at the Regional Office where the application is being submitted and at Mumbai if the application is submitted at CEFA, Mumbai.

3. In terms of sub-rule (1) to Rule 8 of Foreign Exchange (Compounding Proceedings) Rules, 2000, the Compounding Authority may call for any information, record or any other documents relevant to the compounding proceedings. It has been observed that there is no uniformity in submitting the required details with supporting documents along with the compounding application. This results in avoidable correspondence between Reserve Bank and the applicant. It has, therefore been decided that along with the application in the prescribed format, the applicant may also furnish the details as per the enclosed Annexes relating to Foreign Direct Investment, External Commercial Borrowings, Overseas Direct Investment and Branch Office/Liaison Office, as applicable, along with an undertaking that they are not under investigation of any agency such as DOE, CBI, etc., a copy of the Memorandum of Association and latest audited balance sheet while applying for compounding of contraventions under FEMA, 1999.

4. Authorised Dealers may bring the contents of this circular to the notice of their constituents and customers concerned.

5. The directions contained in this circular have been issued under sections 10(4) and 11(1) of the Foreign Exchange Management Act, 1999 (42 of 1999).

Annexures

(*same as reproduced under RBI's Master Circular, dated 1-7-2011, above*)

Appendix 4

FC-GPR

(*To be filed by the company through its Authorised Dealer Category-I bank with the Regional Office of the RBI under whose jurisdiction the Registered Office of the company making the declaration is situated as and when shares/convertible debentures are issued to the foreign investor, along with the documents mentioned in item No. 4 of the undertaking enclosed to this Form*)

Permanent Account Number (PAN) of the investee company given by the Income Tax Department	
Date of issue of shares/ convertible debentures	

No.	Particulars	(In Block Letters)
1.	Name	
	Address of the Registered Office	
	State	
	Registration No. given by Registrar of Companies	
	Whether existing company or new company (strike off whichever is not applicable)	Existing company/ New company
	If existing company, give registration number allotted by RBI for FDI, if any	
	Telephone	
	Fax	
	e-mail	
2.	Description of the main business activity NIC Code	
	Location of the project and NIC code for the district where the project is located	
	Percentage of FDI allowed as per FDI policy	
	State whether FDI is allowed under Automatic Route or Approval Route (strike out whichever is not applicable)	Automatic Route/Approval Route

<table>
<tr><td>3</td><td colspan="2">Details of the foreign investor/collaborator*</td></tr>
<tr><td></td><td>Name
Address
Country
Constitution/Nature of the investing Entity
[Specify whether
1. Individual
2. Company
3. FII
4. FVCI
5. Foreign Trust
6. Private Equity Fund
7. Pension/Provident Fund
8. Sovereign Wealth Fund (SWF)[1]
9. Partnership/Proprietorship Firm
10. Financial Institution
11. NRIs/PIO
12. Others (please specify)]
Date of incorporation
* If there is more than one foreign investor/collaborator, separate Annex may be included for items 3 and 4 of the Form.</td><td></td></tr>
<tr><td>4</td><td colspan="2">Particulars of Shares/Convertible Debentures Issued</td></tr>
<tr><td>(a)</td><td colspan="2">Nature and date of issue</td></tr>
</table>

	Nature of issue	*Date of issue*	*Number of shares/ convertible debentures*
01	IPO/FPO		
02	Preferential allotment/ private placement		
03	Rights		
04	Bonus		
05	Conversion of ECB		
06	Conversion of royalty (including lump sum payments)		

1 SWF means a Government investment vehicle which is funded by foreign exchange assets, and which manages those assets separately from the official reserves of the monetary authorities.

07	Conversion against import of capital goods by units in SEZ		
08	ESOPs		
09	Share Swap		
10	Others (please specify)		
	Total		

(*b*) Type of security issued

No.	Nature of security	Number	Maturity	Face value	Premium	Issue Price per share	Amount of inflow*
01	Equity						
02	Compulsorily Convertible Debentures						
03	Compulsorily Convertible Preference shares						
04	Others (please specify)						
	Total						

(*i*) In case the issue price is greater than the face value please give break up of the premium received.

(*ii*) * In case the issue is against conversion of ECB or royalty or against import of capital goods by units in SEZ, a Chartered Accountant's Certificate certifying the amount outstanding on the date of conversion

(*c*)	**Break up of premium**	**Amount**
	Control Premium	
	Non competition fee	
	Others@	
	Total	

@ ***please specify the nature***

(*d*)	**Total inflow** (in Rupees) on account of issue of shares/convertible debentures to non-residents (including premium, if any) vide (*i*) Remittance through AD:	

	(*ii*) Debit to NRE/FCNR A/c with Bank________ (*iii*) Others (please specify) Date of reporting of (i) and (ii) above to RBI under Para 9(1) A of Schedule I to Notification No. FEMA 20/2000-RB, dated 3-5-2000, as amended from time to time.	
(*e*)	**Disclosure of fair value of shares issued****	
	We are a listed company and the market value of a share as on date of the issue is*	
	We are an un-listed company and the fair value of a share is*	

** ***before issue of shares*** * (***Please indicate as applicable***)

5. Post issue pattern of shareholding

Investor category			*Equity*			*Compulsorily convertible Preference Shares/ Debentures*		
			No. of shares	Amount (Face Value) ₹	%	No. of shares	Amount (Face Value) ₹	%
(*a*)	Non-Resident							
	01	Individuals						
	02	Companies						
	03	FIIs						
	04	FVCIs						
	05	Foreign Trusts						
	06	Private Equity Funds						
	07	Pension/Provident Funds						
	08	Sovereign Wealth Funds						
	09	Partnership/ Proprietorship Firms						
	10	Financial Institutions						
	11	NRIs/PIO						
	12	Others (please specify)						
	Sub Total							
(*b*)	Resident							
Total								

Declaration to be Filed by the Authorised Representative of the Indian Company: (*Delete whichever is not applicable and authenticate*)

We hereby declare that:

1. We comply with the procedure for issue of shares/convertible debentures as laid down under the FDI scheme as indicated in Notification No. FEMA 20/2000-RB, dated 3-5-2000, as amended from time to time.

2. The investment is within the sectoral cap/statutory ceiling permissible under the Automatic Route of RBI and we fulfill all the conditions laid down for investments under the Automatic Route namely (strike off whichever is not applicable).

~~(*a*) Foreign entity/entities (other than individuals), to whom we have issued shares have existing joint venture or technology transfer or trade mark agreement in India in the same field and Conditions stipulated at Para 4.2 of Consolidated FDI policy Circular of Government of India have been complied with.~~

OR

Foreign entity/entities—(other than individuals), to whom we have issued shares do not have any existing joint venture or technology transfer or trade mark agreement in India in the same field. For the purpose of the 'same' field, 4 digit NIC 1987 code would be relevant.

(*b*) We are not an Industrial Undertaking manufacturing items reserved for small sector.

OR

We are an Industrial Undertaking manufacturing items reserved for small sector and the investment limit of 24% of paid-up capital has been observed/requisite approvals have been obtained.

(*c*) Shares issued on rights basis to non-residents are in conformity with Regulation 6 of the RBI Notification No FEMA 20/2000-RB, dated 3-5-2000, as amended from time to time.

OR

Shares issued are bonus.

OR

Shares have been issued under a scheme of merger and amalgamation of two or more Indian companies or reconstruction by way of de-merger or otherwise of an Indian company, duly approved by a court in India.

OR

Shares are issued under ESOP and the conditions regarding this issue have been satisfied.

3. Shares have been issued in terms of SIA/FIPB approval No._ dated

4. We enclose the following documents in compliance with Paragraph 9 (1) (B) of Schedule 1 to Notification No. FEMA 20/2000-RB, dated 3-5-2000:

(*i*) A certificate from our Company Secretary certifying that

(*a*) all the requirements of the Companies Act, 1956 have been complied with;

(*b*) terms and conditions of the Government approval, if any, have been complied with;

(*c*) the company is eligible to issue shares under these Regulations; and

(*d*) the company has all original certificates issued by authorised dealers in India evidencing receipt of amount of consideration in accordance with paragraph 8 of Schedule 1 to Notification No. FEMA 20/2000-RB, dated 3-5-2000.

(*ii*) A certificate from Statutory Auditors/SEBI registered Category I Merchant Banker/Chartered Accountant indicating the manner of arriving at the price of the shares issued to the persons resident outside India.

5. Unique Identification Numbers given for all the remittances received as consideration for issue of shares/convertible debentures (details as above), by Reserve Bank.

R														

(Signature of the Applicant)*:____________________

(Name in Block Letters):____________________

(Designation of the signatory):____________________

Place:

Date:

(* To be signed by Managing Director/Director/Secretary of the Company)

Certificate to be Filed by the Company Secretary[1] of the Indian Company Accepting the Investment

(*As per Para 9* (*1*) (*B*) (*i*) *of Schedule 1 to Notification No. FEMA 20/2000-RB, dated 3-5-2000*)

In respect of the abovementioned details, we certify the following:

1. All the requirements of the Companies Act, 1956 have been complied with.

---

1 If the company doesn't have a full time Company Secretary, a certificate from a practicing Company Secretary may be submitted.

2. Terms and conditions of the Government approval, if any, have been complied with.

3. The company is eligible to issue shares/convertible debentures under these Regulations.

4. The company has all original certificates issued by AD Category-I banks in India, evidencing receipt of amount of consideration in accordance with paragraph 8 of Schedule 1 to Notification No. FEMA 20/2000-RB, dated 3-5-2000.

(Name and Signature of the Company Secretary) (Seal)

For Use of the Reserve Bank Only

Registration Number for the FC-GPR:

R													

Unique Identification Number allotted to the Company at the time of reporting receipt of remittance

R													

AP (DIR Series 2011-12) Circular No. 98, dated 30-3-2012

Discontinuation of Supplying Printed GR Forms by Reserve Bank

1. Attention of Authorised Dealer Category-I banks is invited to AP (DIR Series) Circular No. 60, dated March 26, 2009, in terms of which GR forms were made available on-line on the Reserve Bank's website www.rbi.org.in. The facility of purchasing printed GR forms from the Regional Offices of Reserve Bank was also allowed to continue for one year.

2. With the advent of technology and penetration of internet access, the need for printing and supplying of GR forms by Reserve Bank does not exist any more. It has therefore, been decided to discontinue supplying/selling printed GR forms across the counter by Regional Offices of Reserve Bank. Therefore, with effect from July 1, 2012, GR forms shall be available only online at Reserve Bank's website www.rbi.org.in at the following link:

"Notification-> FEMA -> Forms -> For Printing of GR Form"

3. While downloading the GR forms, the exporter may ensure to use 'Legal' size paper *i.e.* 8.5 * 14 inches. Further, both the printer (printing preference) and paper size in the page setup option have to be set to legal size before printing. The GR number will be automatically allotted when the document goes to the print queue.

4. AD Category-I banks may bring the contents of this circular to the notice of their constituents and customers concerned.

5. The directions contained in this circular have been issued under sections 10(4) and 11(1) of the Foreign Exchange Management Act, 1999 (42 of 1999) and are without prejudice to permissions/approvals, if any, required under any other law.

Appendix 5

Report by the Indian Company Receiving Amount of Consideration for Issue of Shares/Convertible Debentures under the FDI Scheme

(*To be filed by the company through its Authorised Dealer Category-I bank, with the Regional Office of the Reserve Bank under whose jurisdiction the Registered Office of the company making the declaration is situated, not later than 30 days from the date of receipt of the amount of consideration, as specified in para 9 (I) (A) of Schedule I to Notification No. FEMA 20/2000- RB, dated 3-5-2000*)

Permanent Account Number (PAN) of the investee company given by the IT Department	

No.	Particulars	(In Block Letters)	
1.	Name of the Indian company Address of the Registered Office		
	Fax		
	Telephone		
	e-mail		
2	**Details of the foreign investor/collaborator**		
	Name Address Country		
3.	Date of receipt of funds		
4.	Amount	In foreign currency	In Indian Rupees
5.	Whether investment is under Automatic Route or Approval Route If Approval Route, give details (ref. no. of approval and date)	Automatic Route/Approval Route	
6.	Name of the AD through whom the remittance is received		
7.	Address of the AD		

A Copy of the FIRC evidencing the receipt of consideration for issue of shares/convertible debentures as above is enclosed.

(Authorised signatory of the investee company) (Stamp)	(Authorised signatory of the AD) (Stamp)

For Use of the Reserve Bank Only

Unique Identification Number for the remittance received:														

Appendix 6

Know Your Customer (KYC) form in Respect of the Non-Resident Investor

Registered Name of the Remitter/Investor (Name, if the investor is an Individual)	
Registration Number (Unique Identification Number* in case remitter is an Individual)	
Registered Address (Permanent Address if remitter Individual)	
Name of the Remitter's Bank	
Remitter's Bank Account No.	
Period of banking relationship with the remitter	

* Passport No., Social Security No, or any Unique No. certifying the *bona fides* of the remitter as prevalent in the remitter's country

We confirm that all the information furnished above is true and accurate as provided by the overseas remitting bank of the non-resident investor.

(Signature of the Authorised Official of the AD bank receiving the remittance)

Date: Stamp:

Place:

Appendix 7

Form FC-TRS

Declaration regarding transfer of shares/compulsorily and mandatorily convertible preference shares (CMCPS)/debentures by way of sale from resident to non resident/non-resident to resident

(to be submitted to the designated AD branch in quadruplicate within 60 days from the date of receipt of funds)

The following documents are enclosed

For sale of shares/compulsorily and mandatorily convertible preference shares/debentures by a person resident in India

(*i*) Consent Letter duly signed by the seller and buyer or their duly appointed agent and in the latter case the Power of Attorney Document.

(*ii*) The shareholding pattern of the investee company after the acquisition of shares by a person resident outside India.

(*iii*) Certificate indicating fair value of shares from a Chartered Accountant.

(*iv*) Copy of Broker's note if sale is made on Stock Exchange.

(*v*) Declaration from the buyer to the effect that he is eligible to acquire shares/compulsorily and mandatorily convertible preference shares/debentures under FDI policy and the existing sectoral limits and Pricing Guidelines have been complied with.

(*vi*) Declaration from the FII/sub account to the effect that the individual FII/Sub account ceiling as prescribed has not been breached.

Additional documents in respect of sale of shares/compulsorily and mandatorily convertible preference shares/debentures by a person resident outside India

(*vii*) If the sellers are NRIs/OCBs, the copies of RBI approvals, if applicable, evidencing the shares held by them on repatriation/non-repatriation basis.

(*viii*) No Objection/Tax Clearance Certificate from Income Tax Authority/Chartered Account.

1	**Name of the company**	
	Address (including e-mail, telephone Number, Fax no)	
	Activity	
	NIC Code No.	
2	**Whether FDI is allowed under Automatic route**	
	Sectoral Cap under FDI Policy	

3	**Nature of transaction** (*Strike out whichever is not applicable*)	Transfer from resident to non resident/Transfer from non resident to resident
4	**Name of the buyer**	
	Constitution/Nature of the investing Entity Specify whether 1. Individual 2. Company 3. FII 4. FVCI 5. Foreign Trust 6. Private Equity Fund 7. Pension/Provident Fund 8. Sovereign Wealth Fund (SWFπ) 9. Partnership/Proprietorship firm 10. Financial Institution 11. NRIs/PIOs 12. Others	
	Date and Place of Incorporation	
	Address of the buyer (*including e-mail, telephone number. Fax no.*)	
5	**Name of the seller**	
	Constitution/Nature of the disinvesting entity Specify whether 1. Individual 2. Company 3. FII 4. FVCI 5. Foreign Trust 6. Private Equity Fund 7. Pension/Provident Fund 8. Sovereign Wealth Fund (SWF∏) 9. Partnership/Proprietorship firm 10. Financial Institution 11. NRIs/PIOs 12. others	
	Date and Place of Incorporation	
	Address of the seller (*including e-mail, telephone Number Fax no*)	

<table>
<tr><td>6</td><td colspan="2">Particulars of earlier Reserve Bank/FIPB approvals</td><td colspan="4"></td></tr>
<tr><td>7</td><td colspan="6">Details regarding shares/compulsorily and mandatorily convertible preference shares (CMCPS)/debentures to be transferred</td></tr>
<tr><td></td><td>Date of the transaction</td><td>Number of shares CMCPS/ debentures</td><td>Face value in ₹</td><td>Negotiated Price for the transfer**in ₹</td><td>Amount of considera tion in ₹</td></tr>
<tr><td rowspan="3">8</td><td rowspan="3">Foreign Investments in the company</td><td></td><td colspan="2">No. of shares</td><td>Percentage</td></tr>
<tr><td>Before the transfer</td><td colspan="2"></td><td></td></tr>
<tr><td>After the transfer</td><td colspan="2"></td><td></td></tr>
<tr><td rowspan="7">9</td><td>Where the shares/CMCPS/debentur es are listed on Stock Exchange</td><td colspan="4"></td></tr>
<tr><td>Name of the Stock exchange</td><td colspan="4"></td></tr>
<tr><td>Price Quoted on the Stock exchange</td><td colspan="4"></td></tr>
<tr><td>Where the shares/ CMCPS/debentures are Unlisted</td><td colspan="4"></td></tr>
<tr><td>Price as per Valuation guidelines*</td><td colspan="4"></td></tr>
<tr><td>Price as per Chartered Accountants */** Valuation report (CA Certificate to be attached)</td><td colspan="4"></td></tr>
</table>

Declaration by the transferor/transferee

I/We hereby declare that:

(*i*) The particulars given above are true and correct to the best of my/our knowledge and belief.

(*ii*) I/We, was/were holding the shares compulsorily and mandatorily convertible preference shares/debentures as per FDI Policy under FERA/FEMA Regulations on repatriation/non repatriation basis.

(*iii*) I/We, am/are eligible to acquire the shares compulsorily and mandatorily convertible preference shares/debentures of the company in terms of the FDI Policy. It is not a transfer relating to shares compulsorily and mandatorily convertible preference shares/debentures of a company engaged in financial services sector or a sector where general permission is not available.

(*iv*) The Sectoral limit under the FDI Policy and the pricing guidelines have been adhered to.

Signature of the Declarant or his duly authorised agent

Date:

Note:

In respect of the transfer of shares/compulsorily and mandatorily convertible preference shares/compulsorily and mandatorily convertible debentures from resident to non resident the declaration has to be signed by the non resident buyer, and in respect of the transfer of shares/compulsorily and mandatorily convertible preference shares/compulsorily and mandatorily convertible debentures from non-resident to resident the declaration has to be signed by the non- resident seller.

Certificate by the AD Branch

It is certified that the application is complete in all respects.

The receipt/payment for the transaction are in accordance with FEMA Regulations/Reserve Bank guidelines.

Signature

Name and Designation of the Officer

Date: Name of the AD Branch

AD Branch Code

π SWF means a Government investment vehicle which is funded by foreign exchange assets, and which manages those assets separately from the official reserves of the monetary authorities.

Π SWF means a Government investment vehicle which is funded by foreign exchange assets, and which manages those assets separately from the official reserves of the monetary authorities.

Appendix 8

Form DR

[Refer to paragraph 4(2) of Schedule 1]

Return to be filed by an Indian Company who has arranged issue of GDR/ADR

Instructions

The Form should be completed and submitted to the Reserve Bank of India, Foreign Investment Division, Central Office, Mumbai.

1. Name of the Company
2. Address of Registered Office
3. Address for Correspondence
4. Existing Business (please give the NIC Code of the activity in which the company is predominantly engaged)
5. Details of the purpose for which GDRs/ADRs have been raised. If funds are deployed for overseas investment, details thereof
6. Name and address of the Depository abroad
7. Name and address of the Lead Manager/Investment/Merchant Banker
8. Name and address of the Sub-Managers to the issue
9. Name and address of the Indian Custodians
10. Details of FIPB approval (please quote the relevant NIC Code if the GDRs/ADRs are being issued under the Automatic Route)
11. Whether any overall sectoral cap for foreign investment is applicable. If yes, please give details

12. Details of the Equity Capital	Before Issue	After Issue
(*a*) Authorised Capital		
(*b*) Issued and Paid-up Capital		
(*i*) Held by persons Resident in India		

(*ii*) Held by foreign investors other than FIIs/NRIs/PIOs/OCBs (a list of After Issue foreign investors holding more than 10 percent of the paid-up capital and number of shares held by each of them should be furnished)

(*iii*) Held by NRIs/PIOs/OCBs

(*iv*) Held by FIIs

Total Equity held by non-residents

(*c*) Percentage of equity held by non-residents to total paid-up capital

13. Whether issue was on private placement basis. If yes, please give details of the investors and GDRs/ADRs issued to each of them

14. Number of GDRs/ADRs issued

15. Ratio of GDRs/ADRs to underlying shares

16. Issue Related Expenses

(*a*) Fee paid/payable to Merchant Bankers/ Lead Manager

(*i*) Amount (in US$)

(*ii*) Amount as percentage to the total issue

(*b*) Other expenses

17. Whether funds are kept abroad. If yes, name and address of the bank

18. Details of the listing arrangement

Name of Stock Exchange

Date of commencement of trading

19. The date on which GDRs/ADRs issue was launched

20. Amount raised (in US $)

21. Amount repatriated (in US $)

Certified that all the conditions laid down by Government of India and Reserve Bank of India have been complied with.

Sd	Sd
Chartered Accountant	Authorised Signatory of the Company

Appendix 9

Form DR - Quarterly

[Refer to paragraph 4(3) of Schedule 1]

Quarterly Return

(to be submitted to the Reserve Bank of India, Foreign Investment Division, Central Office, Mumbai)

1. Name of the Company
2. Address
3. GDR/ADR issue launched on
4. Total No. of GDRs/ADRs issued
5. Total amount raised
6. Total interest earned till end of quarter
7. Issue expenses and commission etc.
8. Amount repatriated
9. Balance kept abroad - Details
   (*i*) Banks Deposits
   (*ii*) Treasury Bills
   (*iii*) Others (please specify)
10. No. of GDRs/ADRs still outstanding
11. Company's share price at the end of the quarter
12. GDRs/ADRs price quoted on overseas stock exchange as at the end of the quarter

Certified that the funds raised through GDRs/ADRs have not been invested in stock market or real estate.

Sd	Sd
Chartered Accountant	Authorised Signatory of the Company

Appendix 10

Section 195 of the Income Tax Act, 1961

195. Other sums

[1][(1) Any person responsible for paying to a non-resident, not being a company, or to a foreign company, any interest [2][(*not being interest referred to in section 194LB or section 194LC*)] or any other sum chargeable under the provisions of this Act (not being income chargeable under the head "Salaries" [3][* * *]) shall, at the time of credit of such income to the account of the payee or at the time of payment thereof in cash or by the issue of a cheque or draft or by any other mode, whichever is earlier, deduct income-tax thereon at the rates in force:

[4][Provided that in the case of interest payable by the Government or a public sector bank within the meaning of clause (23D) of section 10 or a public financial institution within the meaning of that clause, deduction of tax shall be made only at the time of payment thereof in cash or by the issue of a cheque or draft or by any other mode:]

[5][Provided further that no such deduction shall be made in respect of any dividends referred to in section 115-O.]

Explanation [6][*1*].—For the purposes of this section, where any interest or other sum as aforesaid is credited to any account, whether called "Interest Payable Account" or "Suspense Account" or by any other name, in the books of account of the person liable to pay such income, such crediting shall be deemed to be credit of such income to the account of the payee and the provisions of this section shall apply accordingly.]

[7][*Explanation 2.—For the removal of doubts, it is hereby clarified that the obligation to comply with sub-section (1) and to make deduction thereunder applies and shall be deemed to have always applied and extends and shall be deemed to have always extended to all persons, resident or non-resident, whether or not the non-resident person has—*

(i) *a residence or place of business or business connection in India; or*

(ii) *any other presence in any manner whatsoever in India.*]

(2) Where the person responsible for paying any such sum chargeable under this Act [8][(other than salary)] to a non-resident considers that the whole of such sum would not be income chargeable in the case of the recipient, he may make an

---

1 Substituted by the Finance Act, 1987, w.e.f. 1-6-1987.

2 Being inserted by the Finance Bill, 2012, ***w.e.f. 1-4-2012***. Earlier, the words "(not being interest on securities)" were omitted by the Finance Act, 2003, w.e.f. 1-6-2003.

3 The words "or dividends" omitted by the Finance (No. 2) Act, 1991, w.e.f. 1-10-1991.

4 Inserted by the Direct Tax Laws (Second Amendment) Act, 1989, w.r.e.f. 1-6-1987.

5 Inserted by the Finance Act, 2003, w.e.f. 1-4-2003.

6 Being renumbered as *Explanation* 1 by the Finance Bill, 2012, ***w.r.e.f. 1-4-1962***.

7 Being inserted by the Finance Bill, 2012, ***w.r.e.f. 1-4-1962***.

8 Substituted for "(other than interest on securities and salary)" by the Finance Act, 2003, w.e.f. 1-6-2003.

application to the [1][Assessing] Officer to determine, [2][by general or special order], the appropriate proportion of such sum so chargeable, and upon such determination, tax shall be deducted under sub-section (1) only on that proportion of the sum which is so chargeable:

[3][(3) Subject to rules made under sub-section (5), any person entitled to receive any interest or other sum on which income-tax has to be deducted under sub-section (1) may make an application in the prescribed form to the [4][Assessing] Officer for the grant of a certificate authorising him to receive such interest or other sum without deduction of tax under that sub-section, and where any such certificate is granted, every person responsible for paying such interest or other sum to the person to whom such certificate is granted shall, so long as the certificate is in force, make payment of such interest or other sum without deducting tax thereon under sub-section (1).

(4) A certificate granted under sub-section (3) shall remain in force till the expiry of the period specified therein or, if it is cancelled by the [5][Assessing] Officer before the expiry of such period, till such cancellation.

(5) The Board may, having regard to the convenience of assessees and the interests of revenue, by notification in the Official Gazette, make rules[6] specifying the cases in which, and the circumstances under which, an application may be made for the grant of a certificate under sub-section (3) and the conditions subject to which such certificate may be granted and providing for all other matters connected therewith.]

[7][(6) The person referred to in sub-section (1) shall furnish the information relating to payment of any sum in such form and manner as may be prescribed[8] by the Board.]

[9][(*7*) *Notwithstanding anything contained in sub-section* (*1*) *and sub-section* (*2*), *the Board may, by notification in the Official Gazette, specify a class of persons or cases, where the person responsible for paying to a non-resident, not being a company, or to a foreign company, any sum, whether or not chargeable under the provisions of this Act, shall make an application to the Assessing Officer to determine, by general or special order, the appropriate proportion of sum chargeable, and upon such determination, tax shall be deducted under sub-section* (*1*) *on that proportion of the sum which is so chargeable*.]

---

1 Substituted for "Income-tax" by the Direct Tax Laws (Amendment) Act, 1987, w.e.f. 1-4-1988.

2 Substituted for "in the prescribed manner" by the Finance Act, 1988, w.r.e.f. 1-3-1988.

3 Inserted by the Finance Act, 1970, w.e.f. 1-4-1970.

4 Substituted for "Income-tax" by the Direct Tax Laws (Amendment) Act, 1987, w.e.f. 1-4-1988.

5 *Ibid.*

6 **See** rule 29B and Form Nos. 15C and 15D.

7 Inserted by the Finance Act, 2008, w.e.f. 1-4-2008.

8 **See** rule 37BB and Form Nos. 15CA and 15CB.

9 Being inserted by the Finance Bill, 2012, ***w.e.f. 1-7-2012***.

Appendix 11

Rule 37BB of Income-tax Rules, 1962

[1][**37BB. Furnishing of information under sub-section (6) of section 195**

(1) The information under sub-section (6) of section 195 shall be furnished by the person responsible for making the payment to a non-resident, not being a company, or to a foreign company, after obtaining a certificate from an accountant as defined in the Explanation to section 288 of the Income-tax Act, 1961.

(2) The information to be furnished under sub-section (6) of section 195 shall be in Form No. 15CA and shall be verified in the manner indicated therein and the certificate from an accountant referred to in sub-rule (1) shall be obtained in Form No. 15CB.

(3) The information in Form No. 15CA shall be furnished electronically to the website designated by the Income-tax Department and thereafter signed printout of the said form shall be submitted prior to remitting the payment.

(4) The Director-General of Income-tax (Systems) shall specify the procedures, formats and standards for ensuring secure capture, transmission of data and shall also be responsible for the day-to-day administration in relation to furnishing the information in the manner specified.]

1 Inserted by the Income-tax (Seventh Amendment) Rules, 2009, w.e.f. 1-7-2009.

Appendix 12

Forms 15CA & 15CB

Income-Tax Department	**FORM No. 15CA**[1] (See rule 37BB) **Information to be furnished under sub-section (6) of section 195 of the Income-tax Act, 1961 relating to remittance of payments to a non-resident or to a foreign company**	**Ack. No.**

PART A	GENERAL			
INFORMATION : REMITTER	Name of Remitter (Person responsible for making payment u/s 195 of Income-tax Act, 1961)			PAN of Remitter
	Flat/Door/Block No.	Name of Premises/ Building/Village		TAN of Remitter
	Road/Street/Post Office	Area/Locality		Status- Write 1 if company, Write 2 if firm, and write 3 if others ____ In case of company-If domestic, write '1' and if other than domestic, write '2' ____
	Town/City/ District	State	Pin code	
	Principal Place of Business			
	Email Address	(STD code)-Phone Number ( )		
		Area Code	AO Type / Range Code / AO No	
INFORMATION : RECIPIENT OF REMITTANCE	Name of recipient of Remittance			PAN of recipient of Remittance
	Complete Address:			Country to which remittance is made:
				Status- Write 1 if company, write 2 if firm, and write 3 if others
				In case of company- If domestic, write '1' and if other than domestic, write '2'

1 Inserted by the Income-tax (Seventh Amendment) Rules, 2009, w.e.f. 1-7-2009.

	Principal Place of Business		
	Email Address	(ISD code)-Phone Number ( )	

INFORMATION : ACCOUNTANT			
	(a)	Name of the Accountant* signing the certificate	
	(b)	Name of the proprietorship/ firm of the Accountant	
	(c)	Address	
	(d)	Registration no. of the Accountant	
	(e)	Date of Certificate : (DD/MM/YYYY)	**Certificate No:

* Accountant (other than an employee) shall have the same meaning as defined in the Explanation to section 288 of Income-tax Act, 1961.

** Please fill the serial number as mentioned in the certificate of the accountant.

For Office Use Only	For Office Use Only Receipt No. Date Seal and Signature of receiving official

PART B		PARTICULARS OF REMITTANCE AND TDS (as per certificate of the Accountant)		
PARTICULARS OF REMITTANCE AND TDS	1.	Country to which remittance is made	Country:	Currency:
	2.	Amount of remittance	In foreign currency	In Indian ₹
	3.	Name of the bank	Branch of the bank	
	4.	BSR Code of the bank branch (7 digit)		
	5.	Proposed date of remittance	(DD/MM/YYYY)	
	6.	Amount of TDS	In foreign currency	In Indian ₹
	7.	Rate of TDS	As per Income-tax Act (%) ☐	As per DTAA (%) ☐
	8.	Actual amount of remittance after TDS	In foreign currency	In Indian ₹
	9.	Date of deduction of tax at source	(DD/MM/YYYY)	
	10.	Nature of remittance as per agreement/ document		
	11.	In case the remittance is net of taxes, whether tax payable has been grossed up?	(Tick) ☐ ☐ Yes ☐ No	
	12.	If the remittance is for royalties, fee for technical services, interest, dividend, etc., please indicate:—	(Tick) ☐ ☐ Yes ☐ No	
		(a) The clause of the relevant DTAA under which the remittance is covered along with reasons	Clause of DTAA	
		(b) Rate of TDS required to be deducted in terms of such clause of the applicable DTAA	As per DTAA (%) ☐	
		(c) In case TDS is made at a lower rate than the rate prescribed under DTAA, reasons thereof		

	13.	In case remittance is for supply of articles or things (e.g. plant, machinery, equipment etc.), please indicate,	(Tick) ☑ ☐ Yes ☐ No	
		(a) Whether the recipient of remittance has any permanent establishment (PE) in India through which the beneficiary of the remittance is directly or indirectly carrying on such activity of supply of articles or things?	(Tick) ☑ ☐ Yes ☐ No	
		(b) Whether such remittance is attributable to or connected with such permanent establishment	(Tick) ☑ ☐ Yes ☐ No	
		(c) If the reply to Item no. (b) above is 'yes', the amount of income comprised in such remittance which is liable to tax.		
		(d) If not, the reasons in brief thereof.		
	14.	In case the remittance is on account of business income, please indicate:-	(Tick) ☑ ☐ Yes ☐ No	
		(a) Whether such income is liable to tax in India	(Tick) ☑ ☐ Yes ☐ No	
		(b) If so, the basis of arriving at the rate of deduction of tax.		
		(c) If not, the reasons thereof.		
	15.	In case any order u/s 195(2)/ 195(3)/ 197 of Income-tax Act has been obtained from the Assessing Officer, details thereof:	(Tick) ☑ ☐ Yes ☐ No	
		(a) Name and Designation of the Assessing Officer who issued the order/ certificate		
		(b) Date of the order/ certificate	(DD/MM/YYYY)	
		(c) Specify whether u/s 195(2)/ 195(3)/ 197 of I T Act	☐	
	16.	In case of any other remittance, if tax is not deducted at source for any reason, details thereof.		

Verification

I/We, ... (full name in block letters), son/daughter of .... solemnly declare that the information given above is true to the best of my/our knowledge and belief and no relevant information has been concealed. I/We certify that a certificate has been obtained from an accountant, particulars of which are given in this Form, certifying the amount, nature and correctness of deduction of tax at source. In a case where it is found that the tax actually deductible on the amount of remittance has not been deducted or after deduction has not been paid or not paid in full. I/we undertake to pay the amount of tax not deducted or not paid, as the case may be along with interest due. I/We shall also be subject to the provisions of penalty for the said default as per the provisions of the Income-tax Act, 1961. I/We further undertake to submit the requisite documents for enabling the Income-tax Authorities to determine the nature and amount of income of the recipient of the above remittance as well as documents required for determining my/our liability under the Income-tax Act as a person responsible for deduction of tax at source. I/We further declare that I/we am/are furnishing this information in my/our capacity as .... and I/we am/are also competent to sign the return of income as per provisions of section 140 of the Income-tax Act, 1961 and verify it.

Place Date Sign here

[1]FORM No. 15CB

(See rule 37BB)

Certificate of an accountant*

I/We have examined the agreement (wherever applicable) between Mr./Ms./M/s. .... and Mr./Ms./M/s. .... requiring the (remitters) (beneficiary) above remittance as well as the relevant documents and books of account required for ascertaining the nature of remittance and for determining the rate of deduction of tax at source as per provisions of sub-section (6) of section 195. We hereby certify the following:—

A	Name and address of the beneficiary of the remittance			
B	1.	Country to which remittance is made	Country:	Currency:
	2.	Amount of remittance	In foreign currency	In Indian ₹
	3.	Name of the bank	Branch of the bank	
	4.	BSR Code of the bank branch (7 digit)	☐☐☐☐☐☐☐	
	5.	Proposed date of remittance	(DD/MM/YYYY)	
	6.	Amount of TDS	In foreign currency	In Indian ₹
	7.	Rate of TDS	As per Income-tax Act (%) ☐	As per DTAA (%)☐
	8.	Actual amount of remittance after TDS	In foreign currency	In Indian ₹
	9.	Date of deduction of tax at source	(DD/MM/YYYY)	
	10.	Nature of remittance as per agreement/ document		
	11.	In case the remittance is net of taxes, whether tax payable has been grossed up? If so computation thereof may be indicated.	(Tick) ☑ ☐ Yes ☐ No	
	12.	If the remittance is for royalties, fee for technical services, interest, dividend, etc, please indicate:—	(Tick) ☑ ☐ Yes ☐ No	
		(a) The clause of the relevant DTAA under which the remittance is covered along with reasons	Clause of DTAA	
		(b) Rate of TDS required to be deducted in terms of such clause of the applicable DTAA	As per DTAA (%)	
		(c) In case TDS is made at a lower rate than the rate prescribed under DTAA, reasons thereof		
	13.	In case remittance is for supply of articles or things (e.g. plant, machinery, equipment etc.), please indicate,	(Tick) ☑ ☐ Yes ☐ No	
		(a) Whether the recipient of remittance has any permanent establishment (PE) in India through which the beneficiary of the remittance is directly or indirectly carrying on such activity of supply of articles or things?	(Tick) ☑ ☐ Yes ☐ No	
		(b) Whether such remittance is attributable to or connected with such permanent establishment	(Tick) ☑ ☐ Yes ☐ No	
		(c) If the reply to Item no (b) above is 'yes', the amount of income comprised in such remittance which is liable to tax.	Amount	
		(d) If not, the reasons in brief thereof.		

1 Inserted by the Income-tax (Seventh Amendment) Rules, 2009, w.e.f. 1-7-2009.

	14.	In case the remittance is on account of business income, please indicate:—	(Tick) ☑ ☐ Yes ☐ No	
		(a) Whether such income is liable to tax in India	(Tick) ☑ ☐ Yes ☐ No	
		(b) If so, the basis of arriving at the rate of deduction of tax.		
		(c) If not, the reasons thereof.		
	15.	In case any order u/s 195(2)/195(3)/197 of Income-tax Act has been obtained from the Assessing Officer, details thereof:	(Tick) ☑ ☐ Yes ☐ No	
		(a) Name and Designation of the Assessing officer who issued the order/certificate		
		(b) Date of the order/certificate	(DD/MM/YYYY)	
		(c) Specify whether u/s 195(2)/195(3)/ 197 of Income-tax Act		
	16.	In case of any other remittance, if tax is not deducted at source for any reason, details thereof.		

(Attach separate sheet duly authenticated wherever necessary)

**Certificate No.: ☐☐☐☐☐

Signature:

Date:

Name:

Place:

Name of the proprietorship/firm

Address:

Registration number:

* (To be signed and verified by an accountant (other than an employee) as defined in the Explanation to section 288 of the Income-tax Act, 1961).

** Certificate number is an internal reference number to be given by the Accountant.

Appendix 13

Procedure for furnishing information under section 195(6) of the Income-tax Act, 1961 read with rule 37BB of the Income-tax Rules, 1962

1. General

- Form 15CA should be used for furnishing information of remittances in e-mode in accordance with the provisions of section 195(6) of the Income-tax Act, 1961. The information should be furnished after obtaining a certificate in Form 15CB from an accountant as defined in the *Explanation* to section 288 of the Income-tax Act, 1961. The print out Form 15CA should be signed and submitted to the Reserve Bank of India/authorized dealer prior to remitting the payment.
- The Form should be furnished at the website of the Tax Information Network www.tin-nsdl.com.
- Fields marked with (*) are mandatory.
- Select the values from the drop down wherever provided.
- Each transaction detail should be filled in separately.

2. Guidelines for Part A of Form 15CA:

Remitter:

- Permanent Account Number (PAN) and Tax Deduction and collection Account Number (TAN) allotted by the Income Tax Department should be mentioned. TAN is mandatory in cases where-
    - o tax has been deducted or will be deducted at source;
    - o the remitter has obtained an order under section 195(2) of the Income-tax Act from the Assessing Officer.
- In case an invalid PAN and/or TAN is filled in by the remitter, the Form will not be generated.
- In case the remitter does not have a TAN, it is mandatory to quote PAN of the remitter.
- PAN of the remitter should invariably be given. However, the same is mandatory if status of entity is Company or Firm. If PAN is not given in such cases, the remitter will not be allowed to generate the Form.
- Details in at least two address fields for remitter should be mentioned.
- Name of the entity should be mentioned in the "Name of remitter" field.

No value is to be provided in Area code, AO type, Range code & AO number. The fields will be entered by the system after validating the PAN and/or TAN.

- Email id and mobile no., if any, should be provided.

3. Recipient of remittance:

- Complete address of recipient of remittance, separated by coma, should be provided.
- PAN, allotted by the Indian Income Tax Department should be mentioned.
- If status of entity is "company", then provide type of company i.e., "domestic" or "other than domestic".
- In the field "Principal Place of Business", the country of tax residence of the recipient of the remittance should be mentioned.

4. Information for accountant

- Enter name of the Chartered Accountant in the field "Name of the accountant".
- Details in at least two address fields should be mentioned.
- Date of certificate should not be a future date.
- Registration no. should be numeric.
- Details of accountant are not required if point no. 15 is selected i.e. any order u/s 195 (2)/195 (3)/197 of the Income-tax Act has been obtained from Assessing Officer.
- Certificate number is an alphanumeric field.

5. Guidelines for PART B of the Form (Particulars of Remittance and TDS)

- Provide the values as per the accountant certificate obtained in Form 15CB.
- In case name of the country is not available in drop down list, select value "other" from the drop down and provide name of the country.
- In case currency name is not available in drop down then select value "other" from the drop down and provide name of the currency.
- Proposed date of remittance should be current date or a future date.
- Amount of TDS should be less than amount of remittance.
- Actual amount of remittance after TDS should be less than amount of remittance.
- BSR code of the bank through which the remittance is made should be mentioned.

- Rate of TDS as per DTAA (if applicable) should be mentioned upto two decimal places.
- Amount should be mentioned upto 2 decimal places.
- Select any one out of fields 12, 13, 14 and 16. One form is to be filled for one type of remittance.
- Details of "responsible person" should be mentioned for verification.
- If **no** tax has been deducted then value "0.00" should be mentioned in "Amount of TDS" field (foreign currency and Indian ₹)
- Value for "rate of deduction as per the Income-tax Act" should be "0.00" if **no** tax has been deducted and "amount of TDS in Indian and foreign currency" should be "0.00".

6. Generation of Form 15CA

- After filling up the information, click "submit". On submission of details if system shows any errors, rectify and re-submit the form.
- A confirmation screen with all the data filled by the user will be displayed. The same can be either confirmed or edited.
- On confirmation, a filled up Form 15CA with an acknowledgement number will be displayed. Print out of the Form should be taken, signed and submitted prior to remitting the payment.
- Form 15CA can be re-printed by selecting the re-print option. For re-printing, please enter "acknowledgement no.", "PAN" and/or "TAN" mentioned in the Form.

Chapter 8
CURRENT ACCOUNT TRANSACTIONS

SYNOPSIS

1. Current Account Transactions — Meaning

S. No.	*Points Considered*	*Explanation*
1.	***Governing Rules***	Foreign Exchange Management (Current Account Transactions) Rules, 2000. (*Issued vide Notification No. GSR 381(E), dated 3-5-2000*)
2.	***Meaning of Current Account Transaction***	"Current account transaction" means a transaction other than a capital account transaction and without prejudice to the generality of the foregoing such transaction includes: (*i*) payments due in connection with foreign trade, other current business, services, and short-term banking and credit facilities in the ordinary course of business, (*ii*) payments due as interest on loans and as net income from investments,

S. No.	*Points Considered*	*Explanation*
		(*iii*) remittances for living expenses of parents, spouse and children residing abroad, and (*iv*) expenses in connection with foreign travel, education and medical care of parents, spouse and children. (*Source: Section 2(j) of FEMA, 1999*)
3.	***Meaning of 'Drawal'*** (*of foreign exchange*)	(*i*) The term "drawal" means drawal of foreign exchange from an authorised person and includes opening of Letter of Credit or use of International Credit Card or International Debit Card or ATM Card or any other thing by whatever name called which has the effect of creating foreign exchange liability. [*Source: Rule 2*(*b*)] (*ii*) Since "drawal" of foreign exchange includes use of International Credit Cards (ICC), International Debit Cards (IDC), ATM cards, etc. and in terms of section 2(*h*) of FEMA, 1999 "currency", *inter-alia*, includes ICC and also Reserve Bank, *vide* its Notification No. FEMA 15/2000-RB, dated 3rd May, 2000, has notified ATM Cards and Debit Cards as "currency"; therefore, all Rules, Regulations made and Directions issued under FEMA, 1999 shall apply to the use of ICC, IDC and ATM Cards.
4.	***Current Account Transactions and Section 5 of FEMA, 1999***	Dealing with current account transactions Section 5 of FEMA, 1999 states that any person may sell or draw foreign exchange to or from an authorised person if such sale or drawal is a current account transaction. *However, the Central Government may, in public interest and in consultation with the Reserve Bank, impose such reasonable restrictions for current account transactions as may be prescribed.* *Note.*—(*i*) Central Government has placed reasonable restrictions by framing Current Account Transactions Rules. In terms of the said Rules, drawal of exchange for certain categories of transactions as listed in Schedule I is expressly prohibited. Exchange facilities for transactions

S. No.	*Points Considered*	*Explanation*
		included in Schedule II to the rules may be permitted by the authorised dealers provided the applicant has secured the approval from the Ministry/Department of Government of India as specified therein. In respect of transactions included in Schedule III, prior approval of the Reserve Bank would be required for remittance exceeding specified values. The release of foreign exchange upto the threshold values specified in Schedule III stands delegated to Authorised Dealers. (*ii*) All applications for release of exchange as prescribed in Schedule III to the Rules should be referred to the Regional Office of the Foreign Exchange Department of the Reserve Bank, under whose jurisdiction the applicant is functioning/ residing.

2. Current Account Transactions — Prohibited Transactions

S. No.	*Points Considered*	*Explanation*
1.	***Governing Rules***	Foreign Exchange Management (Current Account Transactions) Rules, 2000. (*Issued vide Notification No. GSR 381(E), dated 3-5-2000*)
2.	***Prohibited Transactions***	No person can draw foreign exchange: (*a*) for undertaking transactions specified in Schedule I (refer point 3 below); or (*b*) for travel to Nepal and/or Bhutan; or (*c*) for undertaking transactions with a person resident in Nepal or Bhutan. However, this prohibition may be exempted by RBI by issuing special or general order. (*Source: Rule 3*)
3.	***Prohibited Transactions specified in Schedule I***	The prohibited transaction as per Schedule I are: 1. Remittance out of lottery winnings. 2. Remittance of income from racing/riding, etc., or any other hobby. 3. Remittance for purchase of lottery tickets, banned/proscribed magazines, football pools, sweepstakes, etc.

S. No.	*Points Considered*	*Explanation*
		Note.—(*i*) In terms of AP (DIR Series) Circular No. 2, dated 22-7-2001 AD banks have been advised not to allow any remittance towards participation in lottery schemes/lottery like schemes functioning under different names like money circulation scheme, remittances for the purpose of securing prize money/awards etc. Therefore, individuals in India who are advised by certain overseas organisations that they have won prizes in lotteries etc. and they should arrange to remit some amount in US Dollars, as fees, **cannot get the remittances made on this account**. (*ii*) Further, in terms of AP (DIR Series) Circular No. 49, dated 4-6-2002, it is clarified that prohibition on such payments include payment not only by a resident by use of cash/draft/credit card/ debit card etc. but also payments made by non-residents on behalf of residents. As such any person resident in India effecting/remitting such payment directly/ indirectly would make himself/ herself liable to be proceeded against the contravention of FEMA, 1999. 4. Payment of commission on exports made towards equity investment in Joint Ventures/Wholly Owned Subsidiaries abroad of Indian companies. 5. Remittance of dividend by any company to which the requirement of dividend balancing is applicable. *Note.*—In terms of DIPP Press Note No. 7 (2000 Series), dated 14.7.2000, the requirement of dividend balancing is not applicable w.e.f. 14-7-2000. Earlier, this was applicable in respect of 22 specified consumer goods Industries. 6. Payment of commission on exports under Rupee State Credit Route, except commission upto 10% of invoice value of exports of tea and tobacco.

S. No.	*Points Considered*	*Explanation*
		7. Payment related to "Call Back Services" of telephones *Note.*—Under "Call Back Services" of telephones, the person who receives the telephone call, pays the telephone call charges. 8. Remittance of interest income on funds held in Non-resident Special Rupee Scheme (Account) Scheme.

3. Current Account Transactions — Transactions requiring Prior Approval of Ministry/Department of Government of India

S. No.	*Points Considered*	*Explanation*
1.	***Governing Rules***	Foreign Exchange Management (Current Account Transactions) Rules, 2000. (*Issued vide Notification No. GSR 381(E), dated 3-5-2000*)
2.	***Transactions requiring Prior approval of Government of India***	In case of transactions included in Schedule II no person shall draw foreign exchange without prior approval of the Government of India ***Note:*** (*i*) The above restriction is not applicable where the payment is made out of funds held in **Resident Foreign Currency (RFC) Account** of the remitter, or. (*ii*) The above restriction is also not applicable where the payment is made out of funds held in **EEFC Account** of the remitter (*except items 10* and 11 of Schedule II*). * Reference to item 10 is redundant and needs to be rectified as this item stands omitted from Schedule II.
3.	***Transactions included in Schedule II requiring Prior approval of Ministry/ Department of Government of India***	Transactions included in Schedule II are as under:

S. No.	*Purpose of Remittance*	*Ministry/ Department of Government of India whose approval is required*
1.	Cultural Tours.	Ministry of Human Reso-

S. No.	*Points Considered*	*Explanation*		
				urces Development (Department of Education and Culture)
		2.	Advertisement in foreign print media for the purposes other than promotion of tourism, foreign investments and international bidding (exceeding US $ 10,000) by a State Government and its Public Sector Undertakings.	Ministry of Finance (Department of Economic Affairs)
		3.	Remittance of freight of vessel chartered by a PSU.	Ministry of Surface Transport (Chartering Wing)
		4.	Payment of import through ocean transport by a Government Department or a PSU on c.i.f. basis (*i.e.* other than f.o.b. and f.a.s. basis).	Ministry of Surface Transport (Chartering Wing)
		5.	Multi-modal transport operators making remittance to their agents abroad.	Registration Certificate from the Director General of Shipping.
		6.	Remittance of hiring charges of transponders by—	

S. No.	Points Considered	Explanation		
			(*a*) TV Channels (*b*) Internet service providers	(*a*) Ministry of Information and Broadcasting (*b*) Ministry of Communication and Information Technology
		7.	Remittance of container detention charges exceeding the rate prescribed by Director General of Shipping.	Ministry of Surface Transport (Director General of Shipping)
		8.	[1][*Omitted*]	
		9.	Remittance of prize money/sponsorship of sports activity abroad by a person other than International/National/State Level sports bodies, if the amount involved exceeds US $ 1,00,000.	Ministry of Human Resource Development (Department of Youth Affairs and Sports)
		10.	[2][*Omitted*]	

---

1 Omitted by the Foreign Exchange Management (Current Account Transactions) (Amendment) Rules, 2010, w.r.e.f. 16-12-2009 [Also refer AP (DIR Series) Circular No. 52, dated 13.5.2010]. Prior to its omission, the entry read as under:

"8. Remittances under technical collaboration agreements where payment of royalty exceeds 5% on local sales and 8% on exports and lump-sum payment exceeds US$ 2 million. — Ministry of Industry and Commerce"

2 Omitted by the Foreign Exchange Management (Current Account Transactions) (Amendment) Rules, 2004, w.e.f. 13-9-2004. Prior to omission it read as under:

"10. Payment for securing Insurance for health from a company abroad. — Ministry of Finance (Insurance Division)"

S. No.	*Points Considered*	*Explanation*		
		11.	Remittance for membership of P&I Club.	Ministry of Finance (Insurance Division)

4. Current Account Transactions — Transactions requiring Prior Approval of RBI

<table>
<tr><th>S. No.</th><th>Points Considered</th><th>Explanation</th></tr>
<tr><td>1.</td><td>Governing Rules</td><td>Foreign Exchange Management (Current Account Transactions) Rules, 2000.
(Issued vide Notification No. GSR 38(E), dated 3-5-2000)</td></tr>
<tr><td>2.</td><td>Transactions requiring Prior approval of Reserve Bank</td><td>In case of transactions included in Schedule III no person shall draw foreign exchange without prior approval of the RBI.
Note: (i) The above restriction is not applicable where the payment is made out of funds held in Resident Foreign Currency (RFC) Account of the remitter, or.
(ii) The above restriction is also not applicable where the payment is made out of funds held in EEFC Account of the remitter (except items 3, 4, 11, 16 and 17).</td></tr>
<tr><td>3.</td><td>Transactions included in Schedule III requiring Prior approval of Reserve Bank</td><td>Transactions included in Schedule III are as under:
<table>
<tr><th>S. No.</th><th>Details</th></tr>
<tr><td>1.</td><td>[Omitted]</td></tr>
<tr><td>2.</td><td>Release of exchange exceeding US $ 10,000 or its equivalent in one financial year, for one or more private visits to any country (except Nepal and Bhutan).</td></tr>
<tr><td>3.</td><td>Gift remittance exceeding US$ 5,000 per financial year per remitter or donor other than resident individual.
Note: This entry is effective from 20-12-2006.</td></tr>
<tr><td>4.</td><td>(i) Donation exceeding US$ 5,000 per financial year per remitter or donor other than resident individual;</td></tr>
</table>
</td></tr>
</table>

S. No.	*Points Considered*	*Explanation*	
			(*ii*) Donations by corporate, exceeding one per cent of their foreign exchange earnings during the previous three financial years or US$ 5,000,000, whichever is less, for,— (*a*) creation of Chairs in reputed educational institutes; (*b*) to funds (not being an investment fund) promoted by educational institutes; and (*c*) to a technical institution or body or association in the field of activity of the donor company. *Explanation*.—For the purposes of item numbers 3 and 4, remittance of gift and donation by resident individuals are subsumed under the Liberalised Remittance Scheme. *Note*.—This entry is effective from 30-4-2007.
		5.	Exchange facilities exceeding [US $ 1,00,000] for persons going abroad for employment.
		6.	Exchange facilities for emigration exceeding US $ 1,00,000 or amount prescribed by country of emigration.
		7.	Remittance for maintenance of close relatives abroad,— (*i*) exceeding net salary (after deduction of taxes, contribution to provident fund and other deductions) of a person who is resident but not permanently resident in India and (*a*) is a citizen of a foreign State other than Pakistan; or (*b*) is a citizen of India, who is on deputation to the office

S. No.	Points Considered		Explanation
			or branch or subsidiary or joint venture in India of such foreign company; (*ii*) Exceeding US $ 1,00,000 per year per recipient, in all other cases. *Explanation.*—For the purpose of this item, a person resident in India on account of his employment or deputation of a specified duration (irrespective of length thereof) or for a specific job or assignment; the duration of which does not exceed three years is a resident but not permanently resident.
		8.	Release of foreign exchange, exceeding US $ 25,000 to a person, irrespective of period of stay, for business travel, or attending a conference or specialised training or for maintenance expenses of a patient going abroad for medical treatment or check-up abroad, or for accompanying as attendant to a patient going abroad for medical treatment/check-up.
		9.	Release of exchange for meeting expenses for medical treatment abroad exceeding the estimate from the doctor in India or hospital/doctor abroad.
		10.	Release of exchange for studies abroad exceeding the estimate from the institution abroad or US $ 1,00,000, per academic year whichever is higher.
		11.	Commission, per transaction, to agents abroad for sale of residential flats or commercial plots in India exceeding USD 25,000 or 5% of the inward remittance, whichever is more.
		12-14.	[*Omitted*]
		15.	Remittances exceeding US$ 10,000,000 per project, for any

<table>
<tr><th>S. No.</th><th>Points Considered</th><th>Explanation</th></tr>
<tr><td></td><td></td><td>
<table>
<tr><td></td><td>consultancy services in respect of infra-structure projects and US$ 1,000,000 per project for other consultancy services procured from outside India.
Explanation.—For the purposes of this item number 'infra-structure project' is those related to—
(i) Power,
(ii) Telecommunication,
(iii) Railways,
(iv) Roads including bridges,
(v) Sea port and airport,
(vi) Industrial parks, and
(vii) Urban infrastructure (water supply, sanitation and sewage).
Note: This entry is effective from 30-4-2007. Also refer AP (DIR Series) Circular No. 46, dated 30-4-2007.</td></tr>
<tr><td>16.</td><td>[Omitted]</td></tr>
<tr><td>17.</td><td>Remittance exceeding 5 per cent of the investment brought into India or USD 100,000, whichever is higher, by an entity in India by way of reimbursement of pre-incorporation expenses.
Note.—AD Category I banks are permitted to allow drawal of foreign exchange by an entity in India by way of reimburse-mint of pre-incorporation expenses up to the limit mentioned above, on the basis of certification from statutory auditors.
(AP (DIR Series) Circular No. 47, dated 30.4.2007)</td></tr>
<tr><td>18.</td><td>[Omitted]</td></tr>
</table>
</td></tr>
<tr><td>4.</td><td>Referring of Applications to RO of RBI</td><td>All applications for release of exchange as prescribed in Schedule III to the Rules should be referred to the Regional Office of the Foreign Exchange Department of the Reserve Bank, under whose jurisdiction the applicant is functioning/residing.</td></tr>
</table>

S. No.	Points Considered	Explanation
5.	***Disposal Mechanism at RBI to clear Applications relating to release of Foreign Exchange exceeding USD 10,000 for Private Visits***	(*i*) ADs are required to obtain prior permission of the Reserve Bank to release foreign exchange exceeding USD 10,000 in one calendar year, for one or more private visits to any country, except Nepal and Bhutan (*refer AP* (*DIR Series*) *Circular No. 51, dated 18-11-2002*). (*ii*) With a view to ensuring that applications received in the Regional Offices of the Reserve Bank, in this regard, are disposed of **on the same day**, a Nodal Officer has been nominated in each Regional Office. Annexure to AP (DIR Series) Circular No. 31, 18-10-2002 (further modified by AP (DIR Series) Circular No. 79, dated 17-2-2003) contains name, telephone number, fax number and e-mail address of the Nodal Officer for each of the Regional Offices. ADs may forward applications for release of foreign exchange exceeding USD 10,000 for private visits to the Regional Office by either fax or e-mail. (*iii*) In case of any difficulty Chief General Manager, Exchange Control Department (now Foreign Exchange Department), Reserve Bank of India, Central Office, Mumbai may be contacted on telephone or fax.

5. Current Account Transactions — Release of Foreign Exchange by Authorised Dealers

S. No.	Points Considered	Explanation
1.	***Governing Rules***	Foreign Exchange Management (Current Account Transactions) Rules, 2000. (*Issued vide Notification No. GSR 381*(*E*)*, dated 3-5-2000*)
2.	***Permissible Current Account Transactions which may be undertaken by the freely by the Authorised Dealers***	(*i*) Section 5 of FEMA, 1999, as already stated, permits any person to sell or draw foreign exchange to or from an authorised dealer if such sale or withdrawal is a current account transaction. At the same time proviso to section 5 empowers

<table>
<tr><th>S. No.</th><th>Points Considered</th><th>Explanation</th></tr>
<tr><td></td><td></td><td>Government of India, in public interest and in consultation with the Reserve Bank to impose reasonable restrictions on certain current account transactions. Accordingly, certain current account transactions have been prohibited in terms of Rule 3 (including Schedule I transactions), certain other transactions either require approval of Ministry/ Department of Government of India (Schedule II transactions) or approval of RBI (Schedule III transactions).
(ii) In respect all other current account transactions which are not as per clause (i) above, remittances may be permitted by the authorised dealers without any monetary/percentage ceilings subject to the compliance with the provisions of section 10(5) of FEMA, 1999. Even in case of transactions included in Schedule III, remittances may be permitted by the authorised dealers upto the ceilings prescribed in that Schedule.</td></tr>
<tr><td>3.</td><td>Release of Foreign Exchange by AD banks for certain Current Account Transactions without seeking prior approval of RBI/Government Department</td><td>These transactions are given below:
<table>
<tr><th>Current Account Transaction</th><th>Permissible Foreign Exchange which may be released by AD Banks without approval</th></tr>
<tr><td>1. Studies abroad</td><td>Foreign exchange for studies abroad may be released up to the estimate from the institu-tion abroad or US $ 1,00,000, per academic year whichever is higher.</td></tr>
<tr><td>2. Private visit to any country (other than Nepal and Bhutan)</td><td>Foreign exchange for one or more private visits abroad may be released up to US $ 10,000 or its equivalent in one financial year (earlier calendar year).</td></tr>
</table></td></tr>
</table>

S. No.	***Points Considered***	***Explanation***	
			Cost of pre-paid telephone cards issued by overseas organisations and collected in Indian Rupees may not be adjusted in the travellers' entitlement of foreign exchange for private visit. Similar treatment may be given to the cost of passes/tickets collected in Indian Rupees. [*AP* (*DIR Series*) *Circular No. 54, dated 25-11-2002*] ***Note:*** Foreign exchange is not permitted to be released for visits to Nepal and Bhutan. Indian currency without any limit (except currency notes of denomination ₹500 and above) may be carried while visiting these countries.
		3. Medical treatment abroad (including of a person)	(*i*) Foreign exchange for meeting expenses in respect of medical treatment abroad may be released up to the estimate from the doctor in India or hospital/doctor abroad. (*ii*) US$ 1,00,000 or its equivalent may be released on the basis of a self declaration, without insisting on any estimate from a hospital/doctor. [*AP* (*DIR Series*) *Circular No. 3, dated 17-7-2003*]

S. No.	***Points Considered***	***Explanation***	
			Note: Foreign exchange as above may also be released in case of a person who has fallen sick after proceeding abroad. [*Master Circular No. 1/2010-11, dated 1-7-2010*]
		4. (*i*) Maintenance expenses of a patient going abroad for medical treatment/ check-up; or (*ii*) Maintenance expenses of the person accompanying as attendant to a patient going abroad for medical treatment/check-up.	Foreign exchange may be released up to US$ 25,000 to the person concerned irrespective of his period of stay abroad.
		5. Employment abroad	Foreign exchange up to US$ 1,00,000 may be released to persons going abroad for employment.
		6. Emigration	Foreign exchange up to US$ 1,00,000 or amount prescribed by the country of emigration may be released on production of emigration visa.
		7. Maintenance of close relatives abroad	Foreign exchange for maintenance of close relatives abroad may be released as under: (*i*) In case of a person who is resident but

S. No.	*Points Considered*	*Explanation*	
			not permanently resident in India and • is a citizen of a foreign State (other than Pakistan); or • is a citizen of India, who is on deputation to the office or branch or subsidiary or joint venture in India of the foreign company in which he is employed foreign exchange up to net salary (after deduction of taxes, contribution to provident fund and other deductions) may be released. *Explanation.*—For the purpose of this item, a person resident in India on account of his employment or deputation of a specified duration (irrespective of length thereof) or for a specific job or assignment, the duration of which does not exceed three years **is a resident but not permanently resident.** (*ii*) In all other cases up to US $ 1,00,000 per year per recipient.
		8. Gifts remittance	(*i*) Foreign exchange may be released up to US$ 5,000 per financial year per remitter or donor other than resident individual.

S. No.	Points Considered	Explanation	
			(*ii*) In case of **resident individual** since gift remittance is subsumed under the Liberalised Remittance Scheme, foreign exchange may be released up to US$ 2,00,000 per financial year.
		9. Donations	In respect of donations following limits are applicable: (*i*) Foreign exchange may be released up to US$ 5,000 per financial year per remitter or donor other than resident individual. (*ii*) In case of **resident individual** since remittance on account of donation is subsumed under the Liberalised Remittance Scheme, foreign exchange may be released up to US$ 2,00,000 per financial year. (*iii*) In case of corporates if the donation is for specified purposes, foreign exchange may be released up to one per cent of their foreign exchange earnings during the previous three financial years or US$ 5,000,000, whichever is less. The specified purposes are: (*a*) creation of Chairs in reputed educational institutes; (*b*) donation to funds (not being an investment fund) promoted by educational institutes; and

S. No.	*Points Considered*	*Explanation*	
			(*c*) donation to a technical institution or body or association in the field of activity of the donor company. ***Note:*** As per AP (DIR Series) Circular No. 45, dated 30.4.2007, in case the remittances for donations by corporates are not meant for specified purposes (*but exceeds the limit of US$ 5,000*), such applications shall be forwarded to the Chief General Manager, Reserve Bank of India, Central Office, Foreign Exchange Department, Foreign Investments Division (EPD), Central Office Building, Mumbai-400 001, mentioning the following details: (*a*) details of foreign exchange earning of the corporate concerned during the last 3 years; (*b*) brief background of the company's activities; (*c*) purpose of the donation; and (*d*) likely benefits to the corporate.
		10. Business travel/attending conference or specialised training	Foreign exchange may be released up to US$ 25,000 to the person concerned irrespective of his period of stay abroad.

S. No.	*Points Considered*	*Explanation*	
		11. Payment of Royalty and lump sum fee under Technical Collaboration Agreements	AD Category-I banks are authorised to permit drawal of foreign exchange by persons for payment of royalty and lump-sum payment under technical collaboration agreements without the approval of Ministry of Commerce and Industry, Government of India. This is so because item 8 of Schedule II to the FEM (Current Account Transactions) Rules, 2000 stands omitted w.r.e.f. 16-12-2009. [*AP* (*DIR Series*) *Circular No. 52, dated 13-5-2010*][1]
		12. Commission to agents abroad for sale of residential flats or commercial plots in India	Foreign exchange per transaction up to US$ 25,000 or 5% of the inward remittance, which-ever is more may be released. [*Also refer AP* (*DIR Series*) *Circular No. 76, dated 24-2-2004*].
		13. Any consultancy service procured from outside India except Indian companies executing infrastructure projects	Foreign exchange up to US $ 10,00,000 (one million) per project may be released.
		13A. Consultancy service procured from outside India by Indian companies	AD Category - I banks are permitted to allow remittances up to USD 10 million per project, after verifying the *bona fides* of the transaction.

S. No.	*Points Considered*	*Explanation*	
		executing infrastructure projects. *Note*: Infrastructure projects are those projects which are related to (*i*) power, (*ii*) telecom-munication, (*iii*) railways, (*iv*) roads including bridges, (*v*) sea port and airport, (*vi*) industrial parks, and (*vii*) urban infrastructure (water supply, sanitation and sewage projects).	***Note:*** In all other cases, the existing limit of USD 1 million, per project, (as indicated against 13 above) for any consultancy service procured from outside India, will continue. (*AP* (*DIR Series*) *Circular No. 46, dated 30.4.2007*)
		14. Remittance by an entity in India by way of reimbursement of pre-incorporation expenses.	Foreign exchange upto 5 per cent of the investment brought into India or USD 100,000, whichever is higher, may be released by AD Category-I banks on the basis of certification from statutory auditors. [*AP* (*DIR Series*) *Circular No. 47, dated 30-4-2007*]
		15. Payment for securing insurance for health from a company abroad	Foreign exchange may be released as per the requirement in this respect. ***Note:*** The condition of obtaining prior approval from Ministry of Finance (Insurance Division) has been removed. [*AP* (*DIR*

S. No.	*Points Considered*	*Explanation*	
			Series) *Circular No. 76, dated 24-2-2004*].
		16. Remittance by artistes *e.g.*, wrestler, dancer, entertainer, etc.	Foreign exchange may be released as per the requirement in this respect. ***Note:*** The condition of obtaining prior approval from RBI is not applicable. [*AP* (*DIR Series*) *Circular No. 76, dated 24-2-2004*]
		17. Remittance for advertisement on foreign television	Foreign exchange may be released as per the requirement in this respect. ***Note:*** The condition of obtaining prior approval from RBI is not applicable. [*AP* (*DIR Series*) *Circular No. 76, dated 24-2-2004*]
		18. Remittance towards cost of advertisement in print media, radio etc. outside India or on internet (except PSU)	Foreign exchange may be released as per the requirement [*AP* (*DIR Series*) *Circular No. 54, dated 25-11-2002*]
		19. Short-term credit to overseas offices of Indian companies	Foreign exchange may be released as per the requirement. ***Note:*** The condition of obtaining prior approval from RBI is not applicable. [*AP* (*DIR Series*) *Circular No. 76, dated 24-2-2004*].
		20. Remittance for use/purchase of trademark or franchise in India.	Foreign exchange may be released freely for **use/ purchase** of trademark or franchise in India. **Note:** Earlier both use and purchase of trademark/ franchise in India required

<table>
<tr><th>S. No.</th><th>Points Considered</th><th colspan="2">Explanation</th></tr>
<tr><td></td><td></td><td></td><td>approval of RBI. However, now there is no restriction. [AP (DIR Series) Circular No. 76, dated 24-2-2004, Notification No. GSR 412(E), dated 10-7-2006 and AP (DIR Series) Circular No. 14, dated 28-11-2006].</td></tr>
<tr><td></td><td></td><td>21. Remittance of prize money/ sponsorship of sports activity abroad by a person other than International/ National/State Level sports bodies.</td><td>Foreign exchange to the extent of US $ 1,00,000 may be released.</td></tr>
<tr><td></td><td></td><td>22. Remittance of container detention charges</td><td>Foreign exchange up to the rate prescribed by the Director General of Shipping may be released.</td></tr>
<tr><td>4.</td><td>Remittances for Tour Arrangements, etc. and opening of Foreign Currency Accounts in the name of Agents in India</td><td colspan="2">(i) Remittance at the request of travellers: Authorised dealers may remit foreign exchange upto a reasonable limit, at the request of a traveller towards his hotel accommodation, tour arrangements, etc., in the countries proposed to be visited by him, provided it is out of the foreign exchange purchased by the traveller from an authorized person (including exchange drawn for private travel abroad) in accordance with the Rules, Regulations and Directions in force.
(ii) Remittance at the request of agents: Authorised dealers may effect remittances at the request of agents in India who have tie up arrangements with hotels/agents, etc., abroad for providing hotel accommodation or making other tour arrangements for travellers from India, provided the authorised dealer is satisfied that</td></tr>
</table>

S. No.	*Points Considered*	*Explanation*
		the remittance is being made out of the foreign exchange purchased by the concerned traveller from an authorised person (including exchange drawn for private travel abroad) in accordance with the Rules, Regulations and Directions in force. **(*iii*) *Foreign currency accounts in the name of agents in India:*** Authorised dealer may open foreign currency accounts in the name of agents in India who have tie up arrangements with hotels/agents, etc., abroad for providing hotel accommodation or making other tour arrangements for travellers from India provided: (*a*) the credits to the account are by way of depositing • collections made in foreign exchange from travellers and • refunds received from outside India on account of cancellation of bookings/tour arrangements, etc., and (*b*) the debits in foreign exchange are for making payments towards hotel accommodation, tour arrangements, etc., outside India, in accordance with clause (*ii*) above. **(*iv*) *Permission to tour operators:*** Authorised dealer may allow tour operators to remit the cost of rail/road/water trans-portation charges outside India without any prior approval from the Reserve Bank, net of commission/mark up, due to the agent. The sale of passes/ticket in India can be made either against the payment in Indian Rupees or in foreign exchange released for visits abroad. The cost of passes/tickets collected in Indian Rupees need not be adjusted in the travellers' entitlement of foreign exchange for private visit. **(*v*) *Provisions regarding consolidated tours arranged by travel agents in India:*** In respect of consolidated tours arranged by travel agents in India for foreign tourists visiting India and

S. No.	*Points Considered*	*Explanation*
		neighbouring countries like Nepal, Bangladesh, Sri Lanka, etc., against advance payments/ reimbursement through an authorised dealer, part of the foreign exchange received in India against such consolidated tour arrangement, may require to be remitted from India to these countries for services rendered by travel agents and hoteliers in the neighbouring countries. Authorised dealers may allow such remittances after verifying that the amount being remitted to the neighbouring countries (inclusive of remittances, if any, already made against the tour) does not exceed the amount actually remitted to India and the country of residence of the beneficiary is not Pakistan. (*Source: AP* (*DIR Series*) *Circular No. 54, dated 25.11.2002*).
5.	***Opening of Trading Office/ Non-Trading Office/ Branch Office/ Representative Office Abroad-Remittance thereof and Reporting***	ADs have been permitting the Indian companies to open Trading Office/Non-Trading Office/ Branch Office/Representative Office abroad and allowing remittance for initial expenses and recurring expenses for maintenance of such office abroad. *Reporting:* (*i*) The authorised dealers are required to obtain from the applicants a statement in Form ORR where remittance is allowed from EEFC Account. (*ii*) Earlier they were required to submit copies of such statements to the Regional Office of Reserve Bank after adding their certification thereon along with the monthly statement in Form ORA. *On a review, it has been decided to discontinue forwarding the statement in Form ORR to Reserve Bank. It has also been decided that statement in Form ORA should be submitted to the Regional Office of Reserve Bank on half-yearly basis instead of on a monthly basis by the authorised dealers.* (*Source: AP* (*DIR Series*) *Circular No. 39, dated 20.4.2002*)
6.	***Payments of collected***	Authorised dealers may allow cable operators or collection agents in India of overseas TV media

S. No.	*Points Considered*	*Explanation*
	Subscription to Overseas TV Media Company	companies, to remit subscription collected from subscribers in India/advertisement charges collected from the advertisers who are eligible to advertise on overseas TV channels without any prior permission from the Reserve Bank. (*Source: AP* (*DIR Series*) *Circular No. 54, dated 25-11-2002*)
7.	***Bids in Foreign Currency for Projects to be executed in India***	Persons resident in India are permitted to incur liability in foreign exchange and to make or receive payments in foreign exchange in respect of global bids for projects to be executed in India. As a simplification procedure there is no need to insist upon prior approval of the concerned Administrative Ministry for the International Competitive Bidding (ICB), because now prior permission of Administrative Ministry/authorization from Central Government is not necessary for ICB and accordingly, authorised dealers may sell foreign exchange to the concerned resident Indian company which has been awarded the contract. (*Source: AP* (*DIR Series*) *Circular No. 54, dated 25.11.2002 as modified by AP* (*DIR Series*) *Circular No. 39, dated 28-4-2008*)
8.	***Sale of Overseas Telephone Cards***	Authorised Dealers may allow agents in India of the overseas organisa-tions issuing pre-paid telephone cards to remit the sale proceeds of such cards, net of their commission, to the issuers of the telephone cards. The cost of such cards collected in Indian Rupees **need not** be adjusted in the travellers' entitlement of foreign exchange for private visit. (*Source: AP* (*DIR Series*) *Circular No. 54, dated 25.11.2002*)
9.	***Supply of Goods by a 100% EOU/EPZ Unit to another such Unit against Foreign Exchange***	100% EOUs and units in EPZs have been permitted to sell goods manufactured by them to other 100% EOUs/EPZ units against payment in foreign exchange. Authorised dealers may sell foreign exchange to the buyer units to make payment for such transactions. ***Note***: The above provisions will also apply, *mutatis mutandis*, to supply of computer services

S. No.	*Points Considered*	*Explanation*
		and hardware by one unit in Software Technology Park (STP)/Electronic Hardware Technology Park (EHTP) to another unit in STP/EHTP against payment in foreign exchange. (*Source: AP* (*DIR Series*) *Circular No. 54, dated 25-11-2002*)
10.	***Supply of goods by 100% EOUs/Units in EPZs, EHTPs and STPs to units in DTA against Foreign Exchange***	(*i*) If the concerned authorities permit 100% Export Oriented Units (EOUs), units in Export Processing Zones (EPZs), Electronic Hardware Technology Parks (EHTPs) and Software Technology Parks (STPs) to sell goods to buyers in Domestic Tariff Area (DTA) against payment in free foreign exchange, authorised dealers may sell foreign exchange to the buyers of such goods in DTA, without prior approval of the Reserve Bank. (*Source: AP* (*DIR Series*) *Circular No. 54, dated 25.11.2002*) (*ii*) The above facility of making payment in foreign exchange by units in DTA is also extended in case goods are supplied to such units by units in Special Economic Zones (SEZs). In other words units in DTA can purchase foreign exchange for this purpose also. (*Source: AP* (*DIR Series*) *Circular No. 105, dated 16.6.2003*)
11.	***Payment of fees in Foreign Currency — Embassy affiliated Educational Institutions***	Authorised dealers may sell foreign exchange towards payment of fees to Schools/Educational Institutions under the administrative control of foreign embassies. (*Source: AP* (*DIR Series*) *Circular No. 54, dated 25.11.2002*)
12.	***Remittances for purchase of Websites***	Authorised dealers are permitted to allow remittance if they are satisfied that the website is being sold unconditionally and the remitter is purchasing it for developing it for his present/future business and *not for the purpose of adding further members to the chain.* For this purpose authorised dealers should satisfy themselves about the *bona fides* of the overseas company and/or the operators and the scheme, through proper documents.

S. No.	*Points Considered*	*Explanation*
		Precaution to be taken by AD banks: Many such schemes involving purchase of websites, offer earnings in US Dollars and/or in other foreign currency, on incremental basis, depending on the number of new clients/ customers added to the chain, thereby making the operation of such schemes akin to money circulation. Therefore, authorised dealers should not allow remittances to operators of such schemes and/or to any other overseas company carrying on such types of activities. (*Source: AP (DIR Series) Circular No. 22, dated 7.12.2000*)
13.	***Payment to non-whole time (non-resident) Director visiting India***	An Indian company is permitted to make payment in rupees towards sitting fees or commission or remuneration and travel expenses to and from and within India to its **non-whole time director** who is resident outside India and is on a visit to India for the company's work. ***Note:*** Appointment of a foreign national as a director on the board of directors of an Indian company does not require approval of Reserve Bank. (*Source: RBI Press Release, dated 2.8.2005*)
14.	***Payment towards Cash Calls for the purpose of Oil exploration in India***	AD Category-I banks are permitted to allow payment towards cash calls to the Operator for the purpose of oil exploration in India, either by credit to the foreign currency or Rupee account in India as approved by the Reserve Bank wherever applicable, or by remittance overseas, subject to the specified conditions. ***Note:*** For the purpose of exploration of oil and natural gas in India, agreements are signed between the Ministry of Petroleum and Natural Gas with various consortia, both inland and foreign. These oil fields are explored by one of the members of the consortium known as the 'Operator'. The expenditure incurred by the Operator is reimbursed by the members of the consortium as per the production sharing agreement and is termed as Cash Calls. Earlier, the payment to Operators towards Cash Calls

S. No.	*Points Considered*	*Explanation*
		required prior approval of the Reserve Bank but the same has now been relaxed. *Specified conditions of remittance:* These are as under: (*i*) AD Category-I bank should ensure that the demand made by the Operator for payment towards cash calls is as per the production sharing agreement, a copy of which may be obtained by it and kept on record; (*ii*) AD Category-I bank should obtain No Objection Certificate from the Income Tax Department/Tax paid challans/Chartered Accountant's certificate and Undertaking as per AP (DIR Series) Circular No. 56, dated November 26, 2002, wherever applicable; and (*iii*) The AD Category-I bank is satisfied about the *bona fides* of the transaction as stipulated under section 10(5) of FEMA, 1999. (*Source: AP* (*DIR Series*) *Circular No. 61, dated 24.5.2007*)
15.	***Sale of Exchange by AD Banks***	***Release foreign exchange for travel purposes:*** (*i*) Authorised Persons may release foreign exchange for **travel purposes** on the basis of a declaration given by the traveller regarding the amount of foreign exchange availed of during the financial year. ***Note:*** In case of issue of travellers' cheques, the traveller should sign the cheques in the presence of an authorized official and the purchaser's acknowledgement for receipt of the travellers cheques should be held on record. (*ii*) Out of the overall foreign exchange being sold to a traveller, exchange in the form of foreign currency notes and coins may be sold up to the limit indicated below: • *Travellers proceeding to countries other than Iraq, Libya, Islamic Republic of Iran, Russian Federation and other Republics of Commonwealth of Independent States:* Not exceeding US$ 3000 [earlier/US $ 2000] or its equivalent.

S. No.	*Points Considered*	*Explanation*
		• *Travellers proceeding to Iraq or Libya:* Not exceeding US$ 5000 or its equivalent. • *Travellers proceeding to Islamic Republic of Iran, Russian Federation and other Republics of Common-wealth of Independent States:* Full exchange may be released (*Source: Master Circular 1/2010-11, dated 1-7-2010. Also refer AP (DIR Series) Circular No. 50 [AP (FL Series) Circular No. 7], dated 4-5-2010*)
16.	***Advance Remittance***	AD banks are permitted to allow advance remittance for import of services. However, where the amount exceeds USD 500,000 or its equivalent, a guarantee from a bank of International repute situated outside India or a guarantee from an authorized dealer in India, if such a guarantee is issued against the counter-guarantee of a bank of International repute situated outside India, should be obtained from the overseas beneficiary. ***Note:*** The authorized dealer should follow up to ensure that the beneficiary of the advance remittance has fulfilled his obligations under the contract or agreement with the remitter in India. (*Source: Master Circular 1/2010-11, dated 1-7-2010.*)

6. Liberalised Remittance Scheme of US$ 2,00,000 for Resident Individuals

S. No.	*Points Considered*	*Explanation*
1.	***Governing Circulars***	AP (DIR Series) Circular No. 64, dated 4.2.2004; No. 80, dated 18.3.2004; No. 38, dated 31.3.2005; No. 24, dated 20-12-2006, No. 51, dated 8.5.2007; No. 9, dated 26.9.2007 and No. 36, dated 4.4.2008.
2.	***Scheme in Brief***	Under this Scheme, authorized dealers may freely allow remittances by individuals upto USD 2,00,000 per financial year[2] (April-March) for any permissible current or capital account transactions or a combination of both. Resident individuals are free to acquire and hold

S. No.	*Points Considered*	*Explanation*
		immovable property or shares or any other asset outside India without prior approval of the Reserve Bank. Individuals can also open, maintain and hold foreign currency accounts with a bank outside India for making remittances under the Scheme without prior approval of the Reserve Bank. The foreign currency accounts may be used for putting through all transactions connected with or arising from remittances eligible under this Scheme. *Not Permissible Transactions:* All transactions which are otherwise not permissible under FEMA and those in the nature of remittance for margins or margin calls to overseas exchanges/ overseas counterparty are not allowed under the Scheme [*AP* (*DIR Series*) *Circular No. 51, dated 8.5.2007*].
3.	***Eligibility***	**All resident individuals including minors**[3] are eligible to avail of the facility under the scheme. Further, remittances under the facility can be consolidated in respect of family members subject to individual family members complying with the terms and conditions of the Scheme[4]. ***Note:*** The facility **is not** available to corporates, partnership firms, HUF, Trusts, etc.
4.	***Purpose of the Liberalised Scheme***	1. This facility is available for making remittance up to USD 2,00,000 per financial year (April-March) for any current or capital account transac-tions or a combination of both. 2. Under this facility, resident individuals are free to acquire and hold immovable property or shares or any other asset outside India without prior approval of the Reserve Bank. Individuals will also be able to open, maintain and hold foreign currency accounts with a bank outside India for making remittances under the scheme without prior approval of Reserve Bank. The foreign currency account may be used for putting through all transactions connected with or arising from remittances eligible under this scheme.

S. No.	*Points Considered*	*Explanation*
		3. Limit of USD 2,00,000 under the Scheme includes remittances towards gift and donation by a resident individual. 4. Investment by resident individual in overseas companies would be subsumed under the Scheme of USD 2,00,000. The requirement of 10 per cent reciprocal shareholding in the listed Indian companies by such overseas companies has been dispensed with. 5. The facility under the scheme is in addition to those already available for private travel, business travel, (except gift remittances and donations), studies, medical treatment, etc as described in Schedule III of FEM (Current Account Transactions) Rules, 2000. ***Note:*** As per Master Circular 1/2010-11, dated 1.7.2010 (Para A-13), the facility under Liberalised Remittance Scheme can also be extended for the following purposes: • Remittances under the Scheme can be used for purchasing objects of art subject to the provisions of other applicable laws such as the extant Foreign Trade Policy of the Government of India. • The Scheme can also be used for remittance of funds for acquisition of ESOPs. The Scheme is in addition to acquisition of ESOPs linked to ADR/GDR and acquisition of qualification shares. • A resident individual can invest in units of Mutual Funds, Venture Funds, unrated debt securities, promissory notes, etc. under this Scheme. Further, the resident can invest in such securities out of the bank account opened abroad under the Scheme. • An individual who has availed of a loan abroad while a non resident can repay the same on return to India under the Scheme as a resident. • The Scheme can be used for outward remittance in the form of a DD either in

S. No.	Points Considered	Explanation
		the resident individual's own name or in the name of beneficiary with whom he intends putting through the permissible transactions at the time of private visit abroad, can be effected, against self declaration of the remitter in the format prescribed. **6. The remittance facility under the scheme is not available for the following**: *(i)* Remittance for any purpose specifically prohibited under Schedule-I (like purchase of lottery tickets/sweep stakes, proscribed magazines, etc.) or any item restricted under Schedule II of FEM (Current Account Transactions) Rules, 2000. *(ii)* Remittances for those transactions which are in the nature of remittance for margins or margin calls to overseas exchanges/overseas counterparty [*AP* (*DIR Series*) *Circular No. 51, dated 8.5.2007*]. *(iii)* Remittances made directly or indirectly to Bhutan, Nepal, Mauritius or Pakistan. *(iv)* Remittances made directly or indirectly to countries identified by the Financial Action Task Force (FATF) as "non co-operative countries and territories" viz Cook Islands, Egypt, Guatemala, Indonesia, Myanmar, Nauru, Nigeria, Philippines and Ukraine. ***Note:*** AD banks are advised to keep a record of "non co-operative countries and territories" and update the list from time to time and may also for the purpose access the website www.fatf-gafi.org to obtain the latest list of such countries. [*AP* (*DIR Series*) *Circular No. 38, dated 31-3-2005*] *(v)* Remittances directly or indirectly to those individuals and entities identified as posing significant risk of committing acts of terrorism as advised separately by the Reserve Bank to the banks. ***Note:*** As per AP (DIR Series) Circular No. 24, dated 20-12-2006 the existing facility of release

S. No.	*Points Considered*	*Explanation*
		of exchange by Authorised Persons up to USD 10,000 or its equivalent in one calendar year on a declaration basis for one or more private visits to any country (except Nepal and Bhutan) will continue to be available on a self-declaration basis. However, the facility would be now available on a financial year (April-March) basis.
5.	***Remittance Procedure under the Scheme***	***Requirements in case of remitter:*** Following are the requirements to be complied with by the remitter: 1. To avail of this facility, the individual will have to designate a branch of an AD through which all the remittances under the scheme will be made. 2. The resident individual seeking to make the remittance should furnish an **application letter cum declaration** in the prescribed format regarding the purpose of the remittance and declaration that the funds belong to the remitter and will not be used for the purposes as detailed above. 3. It is mandatory to have PAN to make remittances under the Scheme[5]. ***Requirements in case of ADs:*** Following are the requirements to be complied with by the Authorised Dealers: 1. While allowing the facility to resident individuals, Authorised Dealers are required to ensure that the "**Know Your Customer**" Guidelines have been implemented in respect of these accounts. They should also comply with the **Anti-Money Laundering Rules** in force while allowing the facility. 2. The applicants should have maintained the bank account with the bank for a minimum period of one year prior to the remittance. If the applicant seeking to make the remittance is a new customer of the bank, Authorised Dealers should carry out due diligence on the opening, operation and maintenance of the account. Further the AD should obtain bank statement for the

S. No.	*Points Considered*	*Explanation*
		previous year from the applicant to satisfy themselves regarding the source of funds. If such a bank statement is not available, copies of the latest Income Tax Assessment Order or Return filed by the applicant may be obtained. 3. The AD should ensure that the payment is received out of funds belonging to the person seeking to make the remittance, by a cheque drawn on the applicant's bank account or by debit to his account or by Demand Draft/Pay Order. 4. Banks should not extend any kind of credit facilities to resident individuals to facilitate remittances under the Scheme [*AP* (*DIR Series*) *Circular No. 51, dated 8.5.2007*]. 5. Authorised dealer should certify that the remittance is not being made directly or indirectly by/or to ineligible entities and that the remittances are made in accordance with the applicable instructions.
6.	***Reporting of the Transactions***	(*i*) The remittances made under this Scheme will be reported in the R-Return in the normal course. The ADs may also prepare and keep on record dummy Form A2, in respect of remittances exceeding USD 5000. (*ii*) As per AP (DIR Series) Circular No. 36, dated 4.4.2008, beginning from April 2008, AD Category-I banks are required to furnish the information relating to remittances made under 'Liberalised Remittance Scheme' on **monthly** basis[6], in the prescribed format to the Chief General Manager-in-Charge, Foreign Exchange Department, (FID-EPD), Reserve Bank of India, Central Office, 11th Floor, Central Office Building, Mumbai-400 001. The statement should reach RBI on or before fifth of the following month to which it relates. AP (DIR Series) Circular No. 24, dated 20.12.2006 requires that a soft copy

S. No.	***Points Considered***	***Explanation***
		of the statement (in Excel format) may also be sent by e-mail (fedcofid@rbi.org.in). (*iii*) As per Master Circular No. 1/2010-11, dated 1.7.2010, the statement in the revised format should be forwarded through Online Returns Filing System (ORFS) for which purpose all the AD category-I banks have been given user ID and password by the Reserve Bank.
7.	***Soliciting Deposits under "Liberalised Remittance Scheme"***: *Disclosure Requirements*	(*i*) A number of foreign banks operating in India as well as Indian banks have been soliciting foreign currency deposits from residents under the captioned Scheme through advertisements for placing the same at certain interest rates at overseas centers or on behalf of overseas mutual funds. These advertisements, however, do not contain appropriate disclosures to guide potential depositors. (*ii*) It has, therefore, been decided by the Reserve Bank, in public interest, that all banks, both Indian and foreign, including those not having an operational presence in India, should seek prior approval from RBI for the schemes being marketed by them in India to residents either for soliciting foreign currency deposits for their foreign/overseas branches or for acting as agents for overseas mutual funds or any other foreign financial services company. The applications in this regard may be addressed to the CGM, DBOD, RBI, C.O., Centre-1, World Trade Center, Cuffe Parade, Mumbai. Following information should be furnished in the application: • Name of the bank and location of its head office (and local offices, if applicable) with its full address; • The identity of the primary bank supervisory authority responsible for the supervision of the bank's head office;

S. No.	*Points Considered*	*Explanation*
		• Long term rating given by an internationally acceptable rating agency such as Moody's or Standard and Poor; • Full details of the scheme being marketed. ***Note:*** The above instructions do not restrict the freedom of resident individual from investing in permissible capital account transactions under the Scheme. [*Source: AP (DIR Series) Circulars No. 80, dated 18-3-2004, No. 24, dated 20-12-2006 and No. 51, dated 8-5-2007*]

AP (DIR Series 2011-12) Circular No. 90, dated 6-3-2012

6.1 Liberalised Remittance Scheme for Resident Individuals — Clarification dated 6-3-2012

1. Attention of Authorised Dealer Category-I (AD Category-I) banks is invited to AP (DIR Series) Circular No. 64, dated February 4, 2004, as amended form time to time, AP (DIR Series) Circular No. 24, dated December 20, 2006, AP (DIR Series) Circular No. 9, dated September 26, 2007, AP (DIR Series) Circular No. 51, dated May 8, 2007 and AP (DIR Series) Circular No. 32, dated October 10, 2011 on the Liberalised Remittance Scheme for Resident Individuals (the Scheme).

2. In this regard, it is clarified that:

(*i*) The facility is available to all resident individuals including minors. In case of remitter being a minor, the LRS declaration form should be countersigned by the minor's natural guardian. Accordingly, the modified LRS application-*cum*-declaration form is enclosed (Annexure).

(*ii*) Remittances under the facility can be consolidated in respect of family members subject to individual family members complying with the terms and conditions of the scheme; and

(*iii*) Remittances under the scheme can be used for purchasing objects of art subject to the provisions of other applicable laws such as the extant Foreign Trade Policy of the Government of India.

3. All other terms and conditions mentioned in the afore-mentioned Circulars shall remain unchanged.

4. AD - Category I banks may bring the contents of this circular to the notice of their constituents and customers concerned.

5. The directions contained in this Circular have been issued under sections 10(4) and 11(1) of the Foreign Exchange Management Act, 1999 (42 of 1999) and is without prejudice to permissions/approvals, if any, required under any other law.

Annexure

Application-*cum*-Declaration for purchase of foreign exchange under the Liberalised Remittance Scheme of USD 200,000 for Resident individuals

(To be completed by the applicant)

I. Details of the applicant

(*a*) Name ....

(*b*) Address.............................

(*c*) Account No.........................

(*d*) PAN..............................

II. Details of the foreign exchange required

1. Amount (Specify currency)..................................
2. Purpose ....

III. Source of funds: ....

IV. Nature of instrument

Draft............................

Direct remittance...........

V. Details of the remittance made under the Scheme in the financial year (April- March) 20__ – 20__

Date :.................

Amount :............

VI. Details of the Beneficiary

1. Name ....
2. Address ....
3. Country ....

4*. Name and address of the bank..........................

5*. Account No..

(* Required only when the remittance is to be directly credited to the bank account of the beneficiary)

This is to authorize you to debit my account and effect the foreign exchange remittance/issue a draft as detailed above (strike out whichever is not applicable).

Declaration

I, ...(Name), hereby declare that the total amount of foreign exchange purchased from or remitted through, all sources in India during the financial year as per item No. V of the Application, including utilisation of the said limit on account of loan extended or gift made in rupees credited to NRO account of non-resident close relative(s), is within the limit of USD 200,000/- (US Dollar Two hundred thousand only), which is the limit prescribed by the Reserve Bank for the purpose and certify that the source of funds for making the said remittance belongs to me and will not be used for prohibited purposes.

Signature of the applicant

(Name)

Signature of the natural guardian of the applicant @

(Name)

@ Where the applicant is minor, the application should be countersigned by minor's natural guardian

Certificate by the Authorised Dealer

This is to certify that the remittance is not being made by/to ineligible entities and that the remittance is in conformity with the instructions issued by the Reserve Bank from time to time under the Scheme.

Name and designation of the authorised official:

Place:

Signature:

Date:

Stamp and Seal

7. Current Account Transactions — Documentation and Procedure for Payment in Rupees

S. No.	*Points Considered*	*Explanation*
1.	***Governing Rules***	Foreign Exchange Management (Current Account Transactions) Rules, 2000. (*Issued vide Notification No. GSR 381(E), dated 3-5-2000*)
2.	***RBI not to prescribe Documents***	(*i*) The Reserve Bank will not, generally, prescribe the documents which should be verified by the authorized dealers while releasing foreign exchange. In this connection, attention of authorized dealers is drawn to sub-section (5) of section 10 of the FEMA, 1999 which provides that an authorized person shall require that person to make such a ***declaration*** and to give such ***information*** as will reasonably satisfy him that the transaction will not involve and is not designed for the purpose of any contravention or evasion of the provisions of the Act or any rule, regulation, notification, direction or order issued there under. (*ii*) Authorized dealers are also required to keep on record any information/documentation, on the basis of which the transaction was

S. No.	*Points Considered*	*Explanation*
		undertaken, for verification by the Reserve Bank. In case the applicant refuses to comply with any such requirement or makes unsatisfactory compliance therewith, the authorized person shall refuse in writing to undertake the transaction and shall, if he has reasons to believe that any contravention/ evasion is contemplated by the person, report the matter to Reserve Bank. (*iii*) Authorised Dealers have specifically been advised that they may release foreign exchange up to USD 100,000 each for employment, emigration, maintenance of close relatives, education and medical treatment abroad without insisting on any supporting documents but on the basis of self declaration incorporating certain basic details of the transactions and submission of Form A2. In addition, the existing facility of release of exchange by Authorised Persons up to USD 10,000 or its equivalent in one financial year for one or more private visits to any country (except Nepal and Bhutan) will continue to be available on a self declaration basis. (*Source: Master Circular 1/2010-11, dated 1.7.2010*)
3.	***Form A2 required for Non-import Transactions***	(*i*) With a view to simplify the procedures and documentation formalities in respect of non-import remittances, Reserve Bank, in consultation with FEDAI, has modified Form A-2 to incorporate the application form and the declaration in terms of Section 10(5) of FEMA, 1999. The customer will be required to submit only this form in respect of permissible transactions pertaining to individuals up to a limit of USD 5000. The AD will fill up the reverse of the form which contains purpose-wise codes. (*ii*) As regards other transactions, apart from Form A2, the AD may call for additional information and documents as may be

S. No.	Points Considered	Explanation
		required. In respect of regular corporate customers, the bank may like to obtain one-time declaration under FEMA. (*Source: AP (DIR Series) Circular 77, dated 13.3.2004*)
4.	***Retention of Form A2***	The form A2 relating to sale of foreign exchange should be retained for a period of one year by the authorised dealers, together with the related documents, for the purpose of verification by their Internal Auditors. ***Note:*** Instead of obtaining such A2 forms for remittance applications for miscellaneous non-trade current account transactions of value less than USD 5,000, ADs may obtain simplified Application-cum-Declaration form (Form A2).
5.	***Onus in case of self declaration***	In cases where the remittances are allowed on the basis of self declaration, the onus of furnishing the correct details in the application will remain with the applicant who has certified the details relating to the purpose of such remittance. (*Source: Master Circular 1/2010-11, dated 1.7.2010*).
6.	***Procedure for Payment in Rupees towards purchase of Foreign Exchange***	Authorised dealers may accept payment in cash upto ₹50,000 against sale of foreign exchange for travel abroad (for private visit or for any other purpose). Wherever the sale of foreign exchange exceeds the amount equivalent to ₹50,000, the payment must be received only by: (*i*) Crossed cheque drawn on the applicant's bank account, or (*ii*) Crossed cheque drawn on the bank account of the firm/company sponsoring the visit of the applicant, or (*iii*) Banker's Cheque/Pay Order/Demand Draft, or (*iv*) Debit cards/credit cards/prepaid cards. In case of use of this mode following conditions should be fulfilled: • KYC/AML guidelines are complied with;

S. No.	Points Considered	Explanation
		• sale of foreign currency/issue of foreign currency travellers' cheques is within the prescribed limits (credit/prepaid cards); • the purchaser of foreign currency/ foreign currency travellers' cheque and the credit/debit/prepaid card holder is one and the same person. ***Note***: Where the rupee equivalent of foreign exchange drawn exceeds ₹50,000 either for any single drawal or more than one drawal reckoned together for a single journey/visit, it should be paid by cheque or draft. (*Source: AP (DIR Series) Circular No. 19, dated 30-10-2000 (Para A.10 of the Annexure) read alongwith AP (DIR Series) Circular No. 40 [AP (FL Series) Circular No. 3], dated 10-12-2008*).
7.	***Endorsement on Passport***	It is not mandatory for authorized dealers to endorse the amount of foreign exchange sold for travel abroad on the passport of the traveller. However, if requested by the traveller, they may record under their stamp, date and signature, details of foreign exchange sold for travel. (*Source: Master Circular 1/2010-11, dated 1.7.2010*).
8.	***Income-tax Clearance***	Remittances to non-residents will be allowed to be made by the authorized dealers on production of an undertaking by the remitter and a Certificate from a Chartered Accountant in the formats prescribed by the Central Board of Direct Taxes, Ministry of Finance, Government of India in their Circular No. 10/2002, dated October 9, 2002 as referred to in AP (DIR Series) Circular No. 56, dated 26-11-2002. As clarified vide AP (DIR Series) Circular No. 3, dated 19.7.2007, similar procedure of obtaining undertaking and certificate is to be adopted when remittances in the nature of trade transactions such as import payments are made by the non-residents.

AP (DIR Series 2011-12) Circular No. 82, dated 21-2-2012

7.1 Release of Foreign Exchange for Imports — Further Liberalisation

1. Attention of all the Authorised Dealers (ADs) in foreign exchange is invited to the AP (DIR Series) Circular No. 106, dated June 19, 2003 in terms of which applications by persons, firms and companies for making payments, exceeding USD 500 or its equivalent towards imports into India must be made in Form A-1.

2. Based on suggestions received from the various stake holders, the said limit has been reviewed and it has been decided as a measure of liberalization to raise the above limit for foreign exchange remittance towards imports without any documentation formalities, from USD 500 or its equivalent to USD 5000 or its equivalent, with immediate effect.

3. It is clarified that the ADs need not obtain any document, including Form A-1, except a simple letter from the applicant containing the basic information *viz.,* the name and the address of the applicant, name and address of the beneficiary, amount to be remitted and the purpose of remittance, as long as the exchange being purchased is for a current account transaction (and is not included in the Schedules I and II of the Foreign Exchange Management (Current Account Transactions) Rules, 2000 framed by Government of India *vide* Notification No. GSR 381(E), dated May 3, 2000, as amended from time to time, the amount does not exceed USD 5000 or its equivalent and the payment is made by a cheque drawn on the applicant's bank account or by a Demand Draft.

4. Authorised Dealers may bring the contents of this circular to the notice of their constituents and customers concerned.

5. The directions contained in this circular have been issued under sections 10(4) and 11(1) of the Foreign Exchange Management Act, 1999 (42 of 1999) and are without prejudice to permissions/approvals, if any, required under any other law.

8. Foreign Technology Transfer/Foreign Technical Collaboration and Payment of Royalty; Payment for use of Foreign Trademarks and Brand Name

S. No.	*Points Considered*	*Explanation*
1.	*Governing Provisions*	Foreign Exchange Management (Current Account Transactions) Rules, 2000 *issued vide Notification No. GSR 381(E), dated 3-5-2000 and* clarifications issued by Government of India and RBI from time to time.
2.	*General Policy*	For promoting technological capability and competitiveness of the Indian industry, acquisition of foreign technology is encouraged through foreign technology collaboration

S. No.	*Points Considered*	*Explanation*
		agreements. Induction of know-how through such collaborations is permitted either through automatic route or with prior Government approval.
3.	***Lump-sum/Royalty Payment for Foreign Technology Collaboration under Automatic Route***	AD Category-I banks are authorised to permit drawal of foreign exchange by persons for payment of royalty and lump-sum payment under technical collaboration agreements without the approval of Ministry of Commerce and Industry, Government of India. This is so because item 8 of Schedule II to the FEM (Current Account Transactions) Rules, 2000 stands omitted w.r.e.f. 16-12-2009. [*AP (DIR Series) Circular No. 52, dated 13-5-2010*] It may be noted that the Government of India, after reviewing the extant policy with regard to liberalization of foreign technology agreement decided to permit, with immediate effect, payments for royalty, lump sum fee for transfer of technology and payments for use of trademark/ brand name on the automatic route. Accordingly, Government of India issued a Press Note on 16-12-2009 and hence, the above liberalization shall be deemed to have come into force with retrospective effect, i.e., from 16-12-2009. ***Prior Position:*** *Earlier release of foreign exchange in excess of 5% on local sales and 8% on exports and lump sum payment exceeding US$ 2 million required prior approval of Ministry of Industry and Commerce. In this respect it may be noted that AP (DIR Series) Circular No. 5, dated 21-7-2003 removed the applicability of restriction on the duration of royalty payment. Further, AP (DIR Series) Circular No. 76, dated 24-2-2004 removed the condition of obtaining RBI approval in case technical collaboration agreement was not registered with the Reserve Bank.* *Even prior to above liberalisation, only wholly owned subsidiaries were permitted to make payment of royalty up to 8% on exports and 5% on domestic sales to their offshore parent*

S. No.	*Points Considered*	*Explanation*
		companies on the automatic route without any restriction on the duration of the royalty payments. Royalty payments by other companies were allowed for a period not exceeding seven years from the date of commencement of commercial production or ten years from the date of agreement, whichever was earlier.
4.	***Method of Calculating Royalty***	The royalty will be calculated on the basis of the net ex-factory sale price of the product, exclusive of excise duties, minus the cost of the standard bought-out components and the landed cost of imported components, irrespective of the source of procurement, including ocean freight, insurance, custom duties, etc.
5.	***Payment of Royalty for use of Trademarks and Brand Name***	Payment of royalty for use of trademarks and brand name of the foreign collaborator without technology transfer is allowed under automatic route i.e. without any approval of the Government of India (Press Note 8 (2009 Series), dated 16-12-2009). ***Prior Position:*** *Earlier, where no technology transfer was involved, royalty up to 2% on exports and 1% on domestic sales was allowed under automatic route on use of trade- marks and brand names of the foreign collaborator. Payment exceeding above limit required approval of the Government of India.* ***Note:*** With the omission of Item No. 16 from Schedule III by the FEM (Current Account Transactions) (Amendment) Rules, 2006, w.e.f. 10-7-2006 [Notification No. GSR 412(E) dated 10-7-2006] the approval of RBI for remittance towards purchase of trademark or franchise in India is no longer required.
6.	***Standard Conditions***	Following standard conditions should be attached to the Technology Agreements: 1. (*a*) The royalty will be calculated on the basis of the net ex-factory sale price of the product, exclusive of excise duties, minus the cost of the standard bought-out components and the landed cost of imported components, irrespective of the source of procurement, including ocean freight,

S. No.	Points Considered	Explanation
		insurance, custom duties, etc. The payment of royalty will be restricted to the licensed capacity plus 25% in excess thereof for such items requiring industrial licence or on such capacity as specified in the approval letter. This restriction will not apply to items not requiring industrial licence. In case of production in excess of this quantum, approval of Government would have to be obtained regarding the terms of payment of royalty in respect of such excess production. 1. (*b*) No minimum guaranteed royalty would be allowed. 2. The lump sum shall be paid in three instalments as indicated below, unless otherwise stipulated in the approval letter:— • First 1/3rd after the approval for collaboration proposal is obtained from the Reserve Bank of India and collaboration agreement is filed with the Authorised Dealer in Foreign Exchange • Second 1/3rd on delivery of know-how documentation • Third and final 1/3rd on commencement of commercial production, or four years after the proposal is approved by the Reserve Bank of India and agreement is filed with the Authorised Dealer in Foreign Exchange, whichever is earlier. The lump sum can be paid in more than three instalments, subject to completion of activities as specified above. 3. All remittances to the foreign collaborator shall be made as per the exchange rates prevailing on the date of remittance. 4. The applications for remittances may be made to the Authorised Dealer in Form A2 with the under noted documents: • A "No Objection" certificate issued by the Income Tax authorities in the standard form or a copy of the certificate issued by the designated bank, regarding the payment of tax where tax has been paid at a flat rate of

S. No.	*Points Considered*	*Explanation*
		30% to the designated bank or a declaration in terms of Sec.266 of Income Tax Act. • A declaration by the applicant to the effect that the proposed remittance is strictly in accordance with the terms and conditions of the collaboration approved by RBI/ Government. 5. The agreement shall be subject to Indian Laws. 6. A copy of the foreign technology transfer agreement signed by both the parties may be furnished to the following authorities:— (*a*) Administrative Ministry/Department (*b*) Department of Scientific and Industrial Research, Technology Bhavan, New Delhi 110 016. (*c*) Concerned Regional Office of Exchange Control Department, RBI. ***Note:*** Under the present dispensation when registration of technology agreement with RBI is not required, it is doubtful whether the copy of agreement needs to be submitted to the RBI. (*d*) Authorised Dealer designated to service the agreement 8. All payments made under the foreign investment and technology transfer including Rupee payments (if any) to be made in connection with engagement/deputation of foreign technical personnel such as passage fare, living expenses etc. of foreign technicians, would be liable for the levy of cess under the Research and Development Cess Act, 1986 and the Indian company while making such payments should pay the cess prescribed under the Act.
7.	***Payment of Lump-sum/Royalty through Capitalisation***	General permission is available for issue of shares against lump-sum technical know-how fee/royalty, under automatic route or SIA/FIPB route, subject to pricing guidelines of Reserve Bank/SEBI and compliance with applicable tax laws. After issue of equity/preference shares by conversion of lump-sum fee or royalty, the details thereof shall be reported in form FC-GPR

S. No.	*Points Considered*	*Explanation*
		to the concerned Regional Office of Reserve Bank. (*Source: AP (DIR Series) Circular No. 15, dated 1-10-2004*)
8.	***Requirement of Government Approval if Automatic Route not available***	Royalty payment in the following cases requires prior Govt. approval (through Project Approval Board (PAB) when only technical collaboration is proposed and through FIPB where both financial & technical collaboration are proposed): (*a*) Sectors/activities which are not on the automatic route for FDI, or (*b*) Proposals not meeting any of the parameters for automatic approval.
9.	***Procedure for Government Approval***	(*i*) As already stated proposals for foreign technology collaboration not covered under the automatic route are considered by the Project Approval Board (PAB) in the Department of Industrial Policy and Promotion. (*ii*) Application in such cases should be submitted in Form FC-IL to the Secretariat for Industrial Assistance. Proposals where both financial & technical collaboration are proposed, application is to be submitted to FIPB. No fee is payable.
10.	***Prohibition on Foreign Technical Collaboration***	It is clarified vide Press Note 5 (2002 Series) dated 5-7-2002 that both foreign investment and **foreign technology collaboration** in any form are completely prohibited in the lottery business, gambling and betting sector.

Royalty under Income Tax Act, 1961: Explanation 2 to Section 9(1)(*vi*) states that, "For the purposes of this clause, "royalty" means consideration (including any lump sum consideration but excluding any consideration which would be the income of the recipient chargeable under the head "Capital gains") for—

(*i*) the transfer of all or any rights (including the granting of a licence) in respect of a patent, invention, model, design, secret formula or process or trade mark or similar property;

(*ii*) the imparting of any information concerning the working of, or the use of, a patent, invention, model, design, secret formula or process or trade mark or similar property;

(*iii*) the use of any patent, invention, model, design, secret formula or process or trade mark or similar property;

(*iv*) the imparting of any information concerning technical, industrial, commercial or scientific knowledge, experience or skill;

(*v*) (*va*) the use or right to use any industrial, commercial or scientific equipment but not including the amounts referred to in section 44BB;

(*vi*) the transfer of all or any rights (including the granting of a licence) in respect of any copyright, literary, artistic or scientific work including films or video tapes for use in connection with television or tapes for use in connection with radio broadcasting, but not including consideration for the sale, distribution or exhibition of cinematographic films; or

(*vii*) the rendering of any services in connection with the activities referred to in sub-clauses (*i*) to [(*iv*), (*iva*) and] (*v*)."

Explanations 4, 5 and 6 are being inserted by the Finance Bill, 2012, w.r.e.f. 1-6-1976 as under:

'Explanation 4.—For the removal of doubts, it is hereby clarified that the transfer of all or any rights in respect of any right, property or information includes and has always included transfer of all or any right for use or right to use a computer software (including granting of a licence) irrespective of the medium through which such right is transferred.

Explanation 5.—For the removal of doubts, it is hereby clarified that the royalty includes and has always included consideration in respect of any right, property or information, whether or not—

(a) the possession or control of such right, property or information is with the payer;

(b) such right, property or information is used directly by the payer;

(c) the location of such right, property or information is in India.

Explanation 6.—For the removal of doubts, it is hereby clarified that the expression "process includes and shall be deemed to have always included transmission by satellite (including up-linking, amplification, conversion for down-linking of any signal), cable, optic fibre or by any other similar technology, whether or not such process is secret;'.

Fees for Technical Services under Income Tax Act, 1961: Explanation 2 to section 9(1)(vii) states that, "For the purposes of this clause, "fees for technical services" means any consideration (including any lump sum consideration) for the rendering of any managerial, technical or consultancy services (including the provision of services of technical or other personnel) but does not include consideration for any construction, assembly, mining or like project undertaken by the recipient or consideration which would be income of the recipient chargeable under the head "Salaries".

Author's Opinion: The word used as per that RBI Circular is "components". In author's opinion a distinction lies in between two words namely, "components" and "raw materials". While "component" means a part of the finished good, "raw material" means the substance from which finished goods are manufactured or produced. To be more precise, in my opinion, while "raw material" are the indispensable part of the finished goods without which these cannot be brought into being, the "components" are those parts which are used as only auxiliary for finished goods. For instance, while cooking oil (raw material) is essential for preparing french fries (finished goods), salt (component) is only auxiliary to prepare french fries (finished goods). Thus, if it can be said that only "raw materials" were purchased and not the "components", the deduction for "standard bought out components" may not be required

Case Study: Mr. G., an Indian national desires to obtain Foreign Exchange on current account transactions for the following purposes:

(*i*) Payment of commission on exports made towards equity investment in wholly owned subsidiary abroad of an Indian Company.

(*ii*) Remittance of hiring charges of transponder.

(*iii*) Remittance for use of trade mark in India.

Advise G whether he can obtain Foreign Exchange and, if so, under what conditions?

Recommendation: Under Section 5 of Foreign Exchange Management Act, 1999, certain rules have been framed for drawal of foreign exchange on current account. According to the said rules, drawal of foreign exchange for certain transactions is prohibited. In respect of certain transactions drawal of foreign exchange is permissible with the prior approval of Central Government. In respect of some of the transaction, prior permission of RBI is sufficient for drawal of foreign exchange:

(*i*) In respect of item No.1 *i.e.* Payment of Commission on exports made towards equity investment in wholly owned subsidiary abroad of an Indian company is prohibited.

(*ii*) Drawal of foreign exchange for remittance of hiring charges of transponder, can be made with the prior approval of the Central Government.

(*iii*) So far as remittance for use of Trade Mark in India is concerned, the necessary foreign exchange can be obtained with the prior permission of the Reserve Bank of India.

In the case of (*ii*) & (*iii*) above, approval of concerned authority is not required if the payment is made out of funds held in Resident Foreign Currency (RFC) Account or Exchange Earner's Foreign Currency (EEFC) Account of the remitter. Further foreign Exchange can be drawn only from an authorised person.

Case Study: Mr. Ramesh is an exporter of goods and services. Explain briefly his duties under Foreign Exchange Management Act, 1999 with regard to the following:

(*i*) Furnishing of information relating to such exports.

(*ii*) Realisation and repatriation of foreign exchange on such exports.

Recommendation: Duty of every exporter of goods and services under FEMA, 1999:

(*i*) *Furnishing of Information:* Every exporter of goods is required the furnish to RBI or other prescribed authority a declaration containing true and correct material particulars, including the amount representing full export value. If full exportable value is not ascertainable at the time of export due to prevailing market conditions, the exporter shall indicate the amount he expects to share indicate the amount he expects to receive on sale of goods in a market outside India. The exporter of goods shall also furnish to RBI such other information as may be required by RBI for the purpose of ensuring realization of export proceeds by such exporter [section 7(*i*)].

RBI can direct any exporter to comply with prescribed requirements to ensure that full export value of the goods or such reduced value of the goods as RBI determines, is received without delay [section 7(2)]. Every exporter of services shall furnish to RBI or other prescribed authority a declaration containing true and correct material particulars in relation to payment of such services [section 7(3)].

(*ii*) *Realisation and repatriation of foreign exchange:* Where any amount of foreign exchange is due or has accrued to any resident in India, such person shall take all reasonable steps to realize and repatriate to India the foreign exchange within such period and in such manner as may be specified by RBI (section 8). Mr. Ramesh as an exporter of goods and services must comply with the requirements of section 7 and 8 of FEMA, 1999 and also with the requirements under Foreign Exchange Management (Export of Goods and Services) Regulations, 2000.

Case Study: Mr. Sane, an Indian National desires to obtain Foreign Exchange for the following purposes:

(*i*) Remittance of US Dollar 50,000 out of winnings on a lottery ticket.

(*ii*) US Dollar 1,00,000 for sending a cultural troupe on a tour of U.S.A.

(*iii*) US Dollar 50,000 for meeting the expenses of his business tour to Europe.

Advise him whether he can get Foreign Exchange and if so, under what conditions?

Recommendations: Under provisions of section 5 of the Foreign Exchange Management Act, 1999 certain Rules have been made for drawal of Foreign Exchange for Current Account transactions. As per these Rules, Foreign Exchange for some of the Current Account transactions is prohibited. As regards some other Current Account transactions, Foreign Exchange can be drawn with prior permission of the Central Government while in case of some Current Account transactions, prior permission of Reserve Bank of India is required.

(*i*) In respect of item No. (*i*), *i.e.*, remittance out of lottery winnings, such remittance is prohibited and the same is included in First Schedule to the Foreign Exchange Management (Current Account Transactions) Rules, 2000. Hence Mr. Sane cannot withdraw Foreign Exchange for this purpose.

(*ii*) Foreign Exchange for meeting expenses of cultural tour can be withdrawn by any person after obtaining permission from Government of India, Ministry of Human Resources Development, (Department of Education and Culture) as prescribed in Second Schedule to the Foreign Exchange Management (Current Account Transactions) Rules, 2000. Hence, in respect of item (*ii*), Mr. Sane can withdraw the Foreign Exchange after obtaining such permission.

(*iii*) The type of payment as envisaged in Item No. (*iii*) is covered under third Schedule to the Foreign Exchange Management (Current Account Transactions).

In all the cases, where remittance of Foreign Exchange is allowed, either by general or specific permission, the remitter has to obtain the Foreign Exchange from an Authorised Person as defined in Section 2(c) read with section 10 of the to the Foreign Exchange Management Act, 1999.

Case Study: Mr. Atul, an Indian National desires to obtain Foreign Exchange for the following purposes:

1. Remittance of US Dollar 10,000 for payment for goods purchased from a party situated in Nepal.
2. US Dollar 10,000 for remitting as commission to his agent in U.S.A. for sale of commercial plot situated near Bangalore, consideration in respect of which was received by Mr. Atul by way of foreign currency inward remittance amounting to US Dollar 1,00,000.

Advise him, if he can get the Foreign Exchange and under what conditions.

*Recommendation:*Under provisions of section 5 of the Foreign Exchange Management Act, 1999 certain Rules have been made for drawal of Foreign Exchange for Current Account transactions. As per these Rules, drawal of Foreign Exchange for some of the Current Account transactions is prohibited. As regards some other Current Account transactions, Foreign Exchange can be drawn with prior permission of the Central Government while in case of some

Current Account transactions prior permission of Reserve Bank of India is required.

In respect of item (1), i.e. remittance to Nepal, such remittance is prohibited and the same is included in First Schedule to the Foreign Exchange Management (Current Account Transactions) Rules, 2000. Hence Mr. Atul cannot withdraw Foreign Exchange for this purpose.

The type of payment as envisaged in item (2) is covered under Third Schedule to the Foreign Exchange Management (Current Account Transactions) Rules, 2000 and for withdrawing foreign Exchange exceeding 5% (five percent) of the inward remittance as commission to agent abroad for sale of commercial plot in India Mr. Atul will require the prior permission of the Reserve Bank of India. Current Account Transactions have been liberalized by RBI, Foreign Exchange Department with effect from 24.02.2004 vide A.P. (DIR Series) Circular No.76 dated 24.02.2004. Now authorized persons (authorized dealers) are authorized to allow freely such remittances ((i.e.) commission to agents abroad for sale of commercial plots) up to USD 25000 or 5 per cent of inward remittance per transaction, whichever is higher. As the amount to be remitted is only USD 10,000, authorized person (authorized dealer) may be approached for permission.

Case Study: Mr. F, an Indian National desires to obtain foreign exchange for the following purposes:

(*i*) Payment of US $10,000 as commission on exports under Rupee State Credit Route.

(*ii*) US $ 30,000 for a business trip to U.K.

(*iii*) Remittance of US $ 2,00,000 for payment as prize money to the winning team in a Hockey Tournament to be held in Australia.

Advise him, if he can get the Foreign Exchange and under what condition.

Recommendations: Under provisions of section 5 of the Foreign Exchange Management Act, 1999 certain Rules have been made for drawal of Foreign Exchange for Current Account transactions. As per these Rules, Foreign Exchange for some of the Current Account transactions in prohibited. As regards some other Current Account transactions, Foreign Exchange can be drawn with prior permission of the Central Government while in case of some Current Account transactions, prior permission of Reserve Bank of India is required:

(*i*) In respect of item No. (*i*), *i.e.*, payment of commission on exports under Rupee State Credit Route, such payment is prohibited and the same is included in First Schedule to the Foreign Exchange Management (Current Account Transactions) Rules, 2000.

(*ii*) Foreign Exchange for business trip upto US$ 25,000 can be obtained by any person. If a person wants to exceed this limit, then prior permission of Reserve Bank of India is required as per Third Schedule to the Foreign Exchange Management (Current Account Transactions) Rules, 2000. In respect of item (ii), since the amount involved is more than US $ 25,000, Mr. F can obtain the foreign exchange after getting the permission of Reserve Bank of India.

(*iii*) The type of payment as envisaged in item No.(*iii*) is covered under Second Schedule to the Foreign Exchange Management (Current Account Transactions) Rules, 2000 and for remitting of prize money exceeding US$ 1,00,000 for sports activity abroad other than International, National or State level body will require the prior permission of the Central Government. (Ministry of Human Resource Development – Department of Youth Affairs and Sports). Since the amount involved in item No. (*iii*) of the question is more than US$ 1,00,000 and Mr. F is not an International, National or State level body, he has to obtain the permission of the Central Government before remitting the prize money of US$ 2,00,000.

In all the cases, where remittance of Foreign Exchange is allowed, either by general or specific permission, the remitter has to obtain the Foreign Exchange from an Authorised Person as defined in Section 2(*c*) read with section 10 of the to the Foreign Exchange Management Act, 1999.

AP (DIR Series 2011-12) Circular No. 65, dated 12-1-2012

Export of Goods and Services — Forwarder's Cargo Receipt

1. Attention of Authorized Dealers is invited to AP (DIR Series) Circular No. 27, dated March 2, 2001, in terms of which they may accept Forwarder's Cargo Receipts (FCR) issued by IATA approved agents, in lieu of bill of lading, for negotiation/collection of shipping documents, in respect of export transactions backed by letters of credit, only if the relative letter of credit specifically provides for negotiation of this document in lieu of bill of lading and also if the relative sale contract with the overseas buyer provides that FCR may be accepted in lieu of bill of lading as a shipping document.

2. It has now been decided that authorized dealers may accept Forwarder's Cargo Receipts (FCR) issued by IATA approved agents, in lieu of bill of lading, for negotiation/collection of shipping documents, in respect of export transactions backed by letters of credit, if the relative letter of credit specifically provides for negotiation of this document in lieu of bill of lading even if the relative sale contract with the overseas buyer does not provide for acceptance of FCR as a shipping document, in lieu of bill of lading.

3. Further, authorized dealers may, at their discretion, also accept FCR issued by shipping companies of repute/IATA approved agents (in lieu of bill of lading), for purchase/discount/collection of shipping documents even in cases, where export transactions are not backed by letters of credit, provided their 'relative sale contract' with overseas buyer provides for acceptance of FCR as a shipping document in lieu of bill of lading. However, the acceptance of such FCR for purchase/discount would purely be the credit decision of the bank concerned who, among others, should satisfy itself about the bona fides of the transaction and the track record of the overseas buyer and the Indian supplier since FCRs are not negotiable documents. It would be advisable for the exporters to ensure due diligence on the overseas buyer, in such cases.

4. Authorized dealers may bring the contents of this circular to the notice of their constituents and customers concerned.

5. The directions contained in this circular have been issued under Section 10(4) and Section 11(1) of the Foreign Exchange Management Act, 1999 (42 of 1999) and are without prejudice to permissions/approvals, if any, required under any other law.

AP (DIR Series 2011-12) Circular No. 81, dated 21-2-2012

Export of Goods and Services — Receipt of Advance Payment for Export of Goods Involving Shipment (Manufacture and Ship) Beyond One Year

1. Attention of Authorised Dealer Category-I (AD Category I) banks is invited to the sub-regulation (2) of Regulation 16 of the Foreign Exchange Management (Export of Goods and Services) Regulations, 2000, notified *vide* Notification No.FEMA.23/RB-2000, dated 3rd May, 2000, as amended from time to time, in terms of which prior approval of the Reserve Bank is required to be obtained by an exporter for receipt of advance where the export agreement provides for shipment of goods extending beyond the period of one year from the date of receipt of advance payment.

2. With a view to liberalizing the procedure, it has been decided to permit AD Category-I banks to allow exporters to receive advance payment for export of goods which would take more than one year to manufacture and ship and where the 'export agreement' provides for shipment of goods extending beyond the period of one year from the date of receipt of advance payment subject to the following conditions:—

(*i*) the KYC and due diligence exercise has been done by the AD Category-I bank for the overseas buyer;

(*ii*) compliance with the Anti-Money Laundering standards has been ensured;

(*iii*) the AD Category-I bank should ensure that export advance received by the exporter should be utilized to execute export and not for any other purpose *i.e.*, the transaction is a *bona fide* transaction;

(*iv*) progress payment, if any, should be received directly from the overseas buyer strictly in terms of the contract;

(*v*) the rate of interest, if any, payable on the advance payment shall not exceed London Inter-Bank Offered Rate (LIBOR) + 100 basis points;

(*vi*) there should be no instance of refund exceeding 10% of the advance payment received in the last three years;

(*vii*) the documents covering the shipment should be routed through the same authorised dealer bank; and

(*viii*) in the event of the exporter's inability to make the shipment, partly or fully, no remittance towards refund of unutilized portion of advance payment or towards payment of interest should be made without the prior approval of the Reserve Bank.

3. Necessary amendments to the Foreign Exchange Management (Export of Goods and Services) Regulations, 2000, wherever necessary, are being issued separately.

4. AD Category-I banks may bring the contents of this circular to the notice of their constituents and customers concerned.

5. The directions contained in this circular have been issued under sections 10(4) and 11(1) of the Foreign Exchange Management Act, 1999 (42 of 1999) and are without prejudice to permissions/approvals, if any, required under any law.

AP (DIR Series 2011-12) Circular No. 83, dated 27-2-2012

Import of Gold on Loan Basis — Tenor of Loan and Opening of Standby Letter of Credit

1. Attention of Authorised Dealer Category-I (AD Category-I) banks is invited to the AP (DIR Series) Circular No. 34, dated February 18, 2005, in terms of which the maximum tenor of gold loan was notified as 240 days consisting of 60 days for manufacture and exports +180 days for fixing the price and repayment of gold loan as per the Foreign Trade Policy 2004-2009 of the Government of India and that the tenor of the Standby Letter of Credit (SBLC), for import of gold on loan basis, where ever required, should be in line with the aforesaid tenor of gold loan.

2. Attention of the AD Category-I banks is also invited to para 4A 23.2 and para 4A 23.3 of the Hand Book of Procedures (HBP) Vol. I of the Foreign Trade Policy (FTP) 2009-14 which states that, "the export has to be completed within a maximum period of 90 days from the date of release of gold on loan basis", and that, "the exporter shall have flexibility to fix the price and repay gold loan within 180 days from date of export". Accordingly, the maximum tenor of gold loan becomes 270 days at present (*i.e.*, 90 days for manufacture and export + 180 days for fixing the price and repayment) as per FTP 2009-14.

3. AD Category-I Banks may, accordingly, note to comply that (*i*) the maximum period of gold loan shall be as per the Foreign Trade Policy 2009-14 or as notified by the Government of India from time to time, in this regard and (*ii*) the tenor of SBLC, for import of gold on loan basis, where ever required, should also be in line with the tenor of gold loan.

4. All the other terms and conditions of the AP (DIR Series) Circular No. 34, dated February 18, 2005 shall remain changed.

5. AD Category-I banks may bring the contents of this circular to the notice of their constituents and customers concerned.

6. The directions contained in this circular have been issued under Section 10(4) and Section 11(1) of the Foreign Exchange Management Act (FEMA), 1999 (42 of 1999) and are without prejudice to permissions/approvals, if any, required under any other law.

AP (DIR Series 2011-12) Circular No. 102, dated 2-4-2012

Use of International Debit Cards/Store Value Cards/Charge Cards/Smart Cards by Resident Indians While on a Visit outside India

1. Attention of all Authorised Persons, who are authorised to issue foreign currency pre-paid cards to resident Indians visiting outside India, is invited to Para B(5) of the AP (DIR Series) Circular No. 46, dated June 14, 2005, in terms of which the use of such cards is limited to permissible current account transactions and subject to the prescribed limits under the Foreign Exchange Management (Current Account Transactions) Rules, 2000, as amended from time to time.

2. As per the practice followed by issuers, resident Indians who purchase their travel cards, are permitted refund of the unutilised foreign exchange balance only after 10 days from the date of last transaction and accordingly, this condition is stated in the "user guide". Since these cards are expected to act as substitutes for cash/Travellers Cheques, the facilities available to the user will have to be similar.

3. Accordingly, all such Authorised Persons shall redeem the unutilized balance outstanding in the cards immediately upon request by the resident Indians to whom the cards are issued subject to retention of:—

(*a*) The amounts that are authorised and remain unclaimed/not settled by the acquirers as of the date of redemption till the completion of the respective settlement cycle;

(*b*) A small balance not exceeding US$ 100, for meeting any pipeline transactions till the completion of the respective settlement cycle; and

(*c*) Transaction fees/service tax payable in India in Rupees.

For the amounts that are authorised but unclaimed/not settled by the acquirer, the issuer of such cards can hold such amounts until such transactions are processed/settled by the acquirers within the prescribed settlement timeframe.

4. All the other instructions contained in the above circular dated June 14, 2005, as amended from time to time, shall remain unchanged.

5. Authorised Persons may bring the contents of this circular to the notice of their constituents and customers concerned.

6. The directions contained in this circular have been issued under Sections 10(4) and 11(1) of the Foreign Exchange Management Act, 1999 (42 of 1999) and are without prejudice to permissions/approvals, if any, required under any other law.

AP (DIR Series) Circular No. 80, dated 15-2-2012

Export of Goods and Services — Simplification and Revision of SOFTEX Procedure

1. Attention of the Authorised Dealers is invited to Regulation 6 of the Notification No. FEMA 23/2000-RB, dated May 3, 2000 *viz.* Foreign Exchange Management (Export of Goods and Services) Regulations, 2000, as amended by the Notification No. FEMA 36/2001-RB, dated February 2, 2001, in terms of which designated officials of the Ministry of Information Technology, Government of India at the Software Technology Parks of India (STPIs) or at Free Trade Zones (FTZs) or Export Processing Zones (EPZs) or Special Economic Zones (SEZs), had been authorised to certify exports declared through SOFTEX Forms.

2. Considering the spurt in the volume of software exports from India in recent times, the complexity of work contracts involved, the voluminous nature of contract agreements and the duration involved in execution of each contract as well as the time-consuming process involved in the certification of SOFTEX forms, the matter was revisited and a revised procedure, given herein below, has now been finalised in consultation with the stakeholders involved.

3. As per the revised procedure, a software exporter, whose annual turnover is at least ₹1000 crore or who files at least 600 SOFTEX forms annually, will be eligible to submit a statement in excel format as per Annexure A, giving all particulars alongwith **quadruplicate** set of SOFTEX form to the nearest STPI. STPI will then verify the details and decide on a percentage sample check of the documents in details. Software companies will submit all the documents on demand to STPI within 30 days of their advice or any reasonable/extended time at the discretion of the Director, STPI, at the request from the exporter. STPI will thus certify the statement and SOFTEX forms in bulk on the **"Top Sheet"** regarding the values etc. and will thereafter forward the first **copy** of the revised SOFTEX format to the concerned Regional Office of RBI, the **duplicate copy** alongwith bulk statement in excel format to Authorised Dealers for negotiation/collection/settlement, the **third copy** to the exporter and the **last copy** will be retained by STPI for its own record. Under the revised procedure, the exporters, however, will have to provide information about all the invoices **including the ones lesser than US$25000**, in the bulk statement in excel format. [The revised procedure for submission of the Softex form and other relevant documents are detailed in the **Annex**.]

4. The new procedure will be effective initially in STPI Bangalore, Hyderabad, Chennai, Pune and Mumbai with effect from April 01, 2012. Based on the success in these centers, it would be adopted by all the STPIs and SEZ/EPZ/100% EOU/EHTP/DTA units by June 2012.

5. Authorised Dealers may bring the contents of this circular to the notice of their constituents concerned.

6. The directions contained in this circular have been issued under Section 10(4) and Section 11(1) of the Foreign Exchange Management Act, 1999 (42 of 1999) and are without prejudice to permissions/approvals, if any, required under any other law.

Annexure

1. Revised Procedure: Reporting of Software exports to STPI

A. ***Periodicity*** - Monthly

B. ***Time period*** - Not later than 30 days from the close of the month in which the invoice is raised

C. ***Applicability*** - Software exporters with annual turnover in excess of ₹1,000 crore or submitting at least 600 Softex forms annually.

D. ***Softex Number*** - Softex number shall be allocated/issued centrally by RBI once a year based on the requirements of exporter which can be about 200,000 numbers to be used by large exporters for the year for all locations. If the softex numbers are exhausted, the exporter can apply again to RBI for allotment of number. Exporters can use the allocated Softex number either for each invoice or for a group of invoices **with same currency** of a particular customer. **Softex number** would be the control number for identifying any of the export transaction.

E. ***Details of information*** - As per the template in **Annexure A,** which will broadly cover information as under

(*i*) Name and Address of the Exporter

(*ii*) Letter of permission number and date

(*iii*) Name of authorized data com service provider

(*iv*) Import Export Code number

(*v*) Software Export Declaration

(*vi*) Details of Export of Software during the period

(*a*) Period of submission *i.e.* Month name

(*b*) SOFTEX Number

(*c*) Name of Client

(*d*) Address of Client

(*e*) Country of Export

(*f*) Invoice Number

(*g*) Invoice Date

(*h*) Project Code or Contract or Agreement or PO & Date

(*i*) Type of Software Exported

(*j*) Invoice Currency

(*k*) Offshore Invoice value

(*vii*) Details of billings on account of Royalty on Software Packages/products exported as per **Annexure B**

(*a*) Period of submission *i.e.*, Month name

(*b*) SOFTEX Number

(*c*) Name of Client

(*d*) Address of Client

(*e*) Country of Export

(*f*) Invoice Number

(*g*) Invoice Date

(*h*) Unique internal Project Code or Contract/Agreement/PO Date

(*i*) Invoice Currency

(*j*) Offshore Invoice value

(*k*) Details of Software Package(s)/product(s) exported

(*l*) Royalty agreement details

1. % age and amount of royalty
2. Period of Royalty agreement
3. Mode of realisation of Royalty value
4. Calculation of Royalty amount

(*viii*) The Authorized dealer's name should be given in Section A of individual bulk statement itself along with email id **(Annexure A & B)**. If there are multiple ADs, then exporter may provide full details - *i.e.*, Details such as bank name, address and Authorized Dealer code plus

(*a*) Details of Letter of Credit (L/C) facility availed by the exporter

(*b*) Details of Bank Guarantee taken by the exporter

(*c*) Details of the Bank Accounts into which the transfer/remittance are received

(*ix*) Email id of the Exporter shall be specified to which the attested Bulk Softex statement will be sent

F. ***Soft copy Submission*** - Software Exports Declaration in summary excel sheet with above details.

G. ***Hard copy submission*** - Covering letter along with summary sheet declarations and Annexure copies in quadruplicate. Copies of Softex forms, Invoices, SoW, MSA or any other document are not required to be submitted along with summary.

H. ***Additional Information*** - At the request of STPI, software exporter need to submit additional details about selected sample invoices within 30 days of the request or any reasonable extended time at the discretion of the Director, STPI at the request from the exporter.

I. ***Time Period for additional Information*** - STPI would do sample audit periodically but not during the period beyond six months, to make the records concurrent with the filing of the Softex. This however, doesn't stop the regulator from asking old records as per FEMA.

J. STPI will send the attested Bulk Softex statement in hardcopy to software exporter and soft copy to RBI, Regional Office, Authorized Dealer and Exporter with **password protection** (to be provided by STPI)

K. Authorized Dealer will upload this information in their systems for further processing

L. Authorized Dealer will settle the Softex using AD internal control number based on details provided by Exporter on collections as per Annexure C

2. Reporting of Software export Realizations to Authorized Dealer (AD)

Software Exporters can have collection account overseas or get credit directly in the bank accounts maintained in India, where individual invoices raised on customers are collected. After meeting "onsite" branch expenses, as permitted by FEMA, net amount will be remitted to India. This would also include 100% realization of offsite exports.

A. **Periodicity** - Quarterly

B. **Applicability** - Software exporters with annual turnover in excess of ₹1,000 crore or submitting in excess of 600 Softex forms annually.

C. **Details of information** - As per **Annexure C**, which will cover information as under

(*i*) Name and Address of the Exporter

(*ii*) Import Export Code number

(*iii*) Details of invoice wise collections (**Attachment A**)

(*a*) SOFTEX Number

(*b*) Name of Customer

(*c*) Invoice Number

(*d*) Invoice Date

(*e*) Invoice Currency

(*f*) Offshore Invoice value

(*g*) Offshore Invoice value realized

(*h*) Date of Realization of exports proceeds

(*i*) Name of the Bank

(*j*) Country of the Bank

(*iv*) Details of Foreign Currency Inward Remittance in India (**Attachment B**). Authorized Dealers will give a control number for this Attachment B, which shall be used by them to settle all the softex forms in Attachment A

(*a*) Inward remittance in India from overseas bank accounts

1. Name and address of the Authorized Dealer at which the amount has been received
2. Inward remittance details like FIRC number, date, amount and foreign currency
3. Name and address of the Overseas bank from which remittance has been effected

(*b*) Direct Inward remittance in India from customers against exports of software

1. Name and address of the Authorized Dealer at which the amount has been received
2. Inward remittance details like FIRC number, date, amount and foreign currency
3. Name and address of the Customer from which remittance has been received

(*v*) ***Documentation:*** FIRCs to be given to AD for endorsement along with above details

(*vi*) Software exporters will furnish the credit notes to AD for invoices which have already been certified by STPI and settle the respective Softex forms.

3. Online Submission of Periodic Software Exports Declaration

STPI is in the process of computerizing the submission of Softex form. STPI would be required to ensure that the computerisation of the Softex forms and the populating of the data must be compatible to **'Softex Card Design'** as detailed in **Annexure E** and be able to generate a report in **'ENC file format'** as detailed in **Annexure D**

N.B. In the event of full computerisation at the STPIs, the exporters will upload their bulk statement to the STPI system which will be verified and certified by the STPI and the certified information will flow to RBI, Regional Office, Exporter as well as AD online. The data will eventually flow to DSIM, RBI for record with a copy retained at STPI.

Annexure A

Format of Softex Forms submitted in bulk Summery Sheet

Section A

Name and address of Exporter		*Period from and to*	
Letter of Permission (LOP) No. (STP/EHTP/SEZ/EPZ/100% EOU/DTA/Unit)		Date of LOP issued	
Name of Authorised Datacom Service Provider		IEC Code	xxxxxxxxx
Name and Address of Authorised Dealer/Bank		Authorized Dealer Code	xxxxxxx xxxxxxx

Section B

List of invoices for offshore export value through datacom link

Period of invoices raised from _______ to _______

Sl. No.	Softex No.	Name of the Client	Address of the Client	Country	Currency	Invoice Number	Invoice Date (DD/MM/YY)	Internal project code/ Contract/ Agreement No. & date	Type of S/W Exported	Offshore Export Value in Foreign Currency (INVOICE_AMT)

Section C

Declaration by Exporter

I/We hereby declare that I/we am/are the seller of the software in respect of which this declaration is made and that the particulars given above are true and that the value to be received from the buyer represents the export value contracted and declared above. I/we also declare that the software has been developed and exported by using authorised and legitimate datacom links.

I/We undertake that I/we will deliver to the bank named above the foreign exchange representing the full value of the software exported as above on or before .... (*i.e.,* within six months from the date of invoice/date of last invoice raised during a month), in the manner specified in the Regulations made under the Foreign Exchange Management Act, 1999.

Place

Date

Name | Stamp | ....

Designation | Signature of Exporter

Space for use of the competent authority (*i.e.,* STPI/EPZ/SEZ) on behalf of Ministry of Communications & Information Technology.

Certified that the software described above was actually transmitted and the export value declared by the exporter has been found to be in order and accepted by us.

Annexure B

Format of Softex Forms submitted in bulk for royalty receipt

Summary Sheet

Section A

Name and address of Exporter		*Period from and to*	
Latter of Permission (LOP) No. (STP/EHTP/SEZ/EPZ/100% EOU/DTA Unit)		Date of LOP issued	
Name of Authorised		IEC Code	xxxxxxxxx
Name and address of Authorised Dealer/Bank		Authorized Dealer Code	xxxxxxx xxxxxxx

Section B

List of Invoices for offshore export value through datacom link

Details of invoices of Royalty on software Packages/products exported during the Period raised from .... to ....

Sl. No.	*SOFTEX No*	*Name of Client*	*Address of Client*	*Country*	*Currency*	*Invoice Number*	*Invoice Date (DD/MM/YYY)*	*Unique Internal Project code/Contract/Agreement/PO Date*	*Offshore Export value in Invoice currency*	*Type of software Exported*	*Details of Software Packages/Products exported*				*Mode of realization of Royalty value*	*Calculation of Royalty amount*
											GR/SDF/PP/SOFTEX Form No. on which exports were declared	*Date of Export*	*Royalty agreement details*			
													% age and amount of royalty	*Period of Royalty agreement*		

Section C

Declaration by Exporter

I/We hereby declare that I/we am/are the seller of the software in respect of which this declaration is mode and that the particulars given above are true and that the value of be received from the buyer represent the export value contracted and declared above. I/we also declare that the software has been developed and exported by using authorised and legitimate datacom links.

I/We undertake that I/we will deliver to the bank named above the foreign exchange representing the full value of the software exported as above on or before .... (*i.e.* within six months from the date of invoice/date of last invoice raised during a month), in the manner specified in the Regulations made under the Foreign Exchange Management Act, 1999.

Place

Date Stamp

Name ....

Designation Signature of Exporter

Space for use of the component authority (*i.e.* STP/EPZ/SEZ) on behalf of Ministry of Communications & Information Technology

Certified that the software described above was actually transmitted and the export value declared by the exporter has been issued to be in order and accepted by us.

Place

Date Stamp

Name ....

Designation (Signature of the Designated Official of STP/EPZ/SEZ on behalf of Ministry of Communications & Information Technology)

Annexure C

Declaration of Realisation against Software Export Reported for the Quarter Ended.____________

1.	Name and Address of the Exporter	
2.	Import Export Code;	
3.	Details of collections by Invoices in respective collections account	As per Attachment A
4.	Details of Foreign Inward Remittances against software exports	As per Attachment B

We hereby declare that we are the seller of the software in respect of which this declaration is made out and the particulars given above and the enclosed Annexures A and B are true. We also declare that the software has been developed and exported, by using authorized and legitimate datacom links.

We undertake that where full value of software exports are not realized within the prescribed time period, we shall notify the same and seek necessary approvals for delayed remittance as per the Foreign Exchange Management Act, 1999.

Place:

Date :

Signature of the Exporter

Name:

Designation

Attachment A

Details of Invoices for export of software against which export sales proceeds were realized during the Quarter ended _________

Sl. No.	SOFTEX No	Name of Client	Invoice Number	Invoice Date	Invoice Currency	Offshore Invoice value	Offshore Invoice value realized	Date of realization of export proceeds	Name of the bank	Country of the Bank
	Referring to the SOFTEX number used while submitting the periodic declaration									

Attachment B

Details of Aggregate Foreign Inward Remittances during the Quarter ended

[I] Inward remittance from overseas bank accounts

Sl No	Name of address of the Authorised Dealer	Date of inward remittance	Foreign Currency	Amount of inward remittance in Rupees	Name and address of the Overseas bank from which remittance has been effected

[II] Direct inward remittance against exports of software

Sl No	Name of address of the Authorised Dealer	Date of inward remittance	Foreign Currency	Amount of inward remittance in Rupees	Name and address of the Customer from which remittance has been received

The remittance from our overseas bank accounts to our Indian bank accounts are on need basis after payment of expenses to foreign currency

- Annexure D

ENC File format

Field	*Format*	*Default Width*
A.D. Code (Uniform Code 1)	Char(7)	7
Fortnight end Date	YYYYMMDD	8
Date of Negotiation	YYYYMMDD	8
Bill Number	Char (7) *e.g.* N000001	7
Importer Exporter Code	Char(10)	10
GR/PP/SOFTEX Form Number	Char (8) *e.g.* AA000001	8
Shipping Bill Number (inclusive of 4 digit port code in case of EDI transactions	Char (11)	11
Shipping Bill Date	YYYYMMDD	8
Custom Serial Number	Char(10)	10
Currency	Char(3)	3
Invoice Value	Num. (10)	10
Country of Destination	Char(2)	2

Field	*Format*	*Default Width*
Field	Format	Default Width
Invoice Value	Num. (10)	10
Country of Destination	Char(2)	2

Chapter 9
CAPITAL ACCOUNT TRANSACTIONS

1. Capital Account Transactions Regulations

S. No.	Points Considered	Explanation
1.	***Governing Regulations***	Foreign Exchange Management (Permissible Capital Account Transactions) Regulations, 2000. (*Issued vide Notification No. GSR 384(E), dated 3-5-2000 [FEMA 1/2000-RB]*)
2.	***Meaning of Capital Account Transactions***	'Capital Account Transaction' means a transaction which alters the assets or liabilities, including contingent liabilities, outside India of persons resident in India or assets or liabilities in India of persons resident outside India, and includes transactions referred to in sub-section (3) of section 6 (refer S. No. 3). (*Source: Section 2(e) of FEMA, 1999*)
3.	***Capital Account Transactions included in Section 6(3) of FEMA, 1999***	Sub-section (3) of Section 6 specifies the following transactions as 'capital account transactions': (*a*) transfer or issue of any foreign security by a person resident in India; (*b*) transfer or issue of any security by a person resident outside India; (*c*) transfer or issue of any security or foreign security by any branch, office or agency in India of a person resident outside India; (*d*) any borrowing or lending in foreign exchange in whatever form or by whatever name called;

S. No.	*Points Considered*	*Explanation*
		(*e*) any borrowing or lending in rupees in whatever form or by whatever name called between a person resident in India and a person resident outside India; (*f*) deposits between persons resident in India and persons resident outside India; (*g*) export, import or holding of currency or currency notes; (*h*) transfer of immovable property outside India, other than a lease not exceeding five years, by a person resident in India; (*i*) acquisition or transfer of immovable property in India, other than a lease not exceeding five years, by a person resident outside India; (*j*) giving of a guarantee or surety in respect of any debt, obligation or other liability incurred,— (*i*) by a person resident in India and owed to a person resident outside India; or (*ii*) by a person resident outside India. *Note.*—Reserve Bank of India is empowered to prohibit, restrict or regulate the above transactions by regulations framed under the FEMA, 1999.
4.	***Meaning of 'Drawal' of Foreign Exchange***	The term "Drawal" means drawal of foreign exchange from an authorised person and includes opening of Letter of Credit or use of International Credit Card or International Debit Card or ATM card or any other thing by whatever name called which has the effect of creating foreign exchange liability. [*Source: Regulation 2*(*b*)]
5.	***General Prohibition on Capital Account Transactions***	In respect of any capital account transaction, there is general prohibition to undertake/sell/draw foreign exchange to or from an authorised person except what is provided under FEMA, 1999 or the rules or regulations issued thereunder.

S. No.	Points Considered	Explanation
6.	***Non-resident Persons not permitted to invest in certain Prohibited Transactions***	Persons resident outside India are not permitted to make investment in any company/firm/ proprietary concern/entity which is engaged or proposes to engage in: • the business of chit fund or Nidhi Company, or • agricultural or plantation activities, or • real estate business, or construction of farm houses (excluding development of townships, construction of residential/ commercial premises, roads or bridges), or • trading in Transferable Development Rights (TDRs). *Note.*—Rule 2(*d*) defines "TDRs" to mean certificates issued in respect of category of land acquired for public purpose either by Central or State Government in consideration of surrender of land by the owner without monetary compensation, which are transferable in part or whole.
7.	***Permissible Capital Account Transactions***	Permissible capital account transactions have been classified according to whether a person is resident in India or outside India. To regulate these transactions RBI has framed different Regulations following which a person may sell or draw foreign exchange to or from an authorised person.
8.	***Transactions of a person resident in India***	*Classes of capital account transactions of persons resident in India are as under:* (*a*) Investment by a person resident in India in foreign securities. (*b*) Foreign currency loans raised in India and abroad by a person resident in India. (*c*) Transfer of immovable property outside India by a person resident in India. (*d*) Guarantees issued by a person resident in India in favour of a person resident outside India. (*e*) Export, import and holding of currency/ currency notes.

S. No.	*Points Considered*	*Explanation*
		(*f*) Loans and overdrafts (borrowings) by a person resident in India from a person resident outside India. (*g*) Maintenance of foreign currency accounts in India and outside India by a person resident in India. (*h*) Taking out of insurance policy by a person resident in India from an insurance company outside India. (*i*) Loans and overdrafts by a person resident in India to a person resident outside India. (*j*) Remittance outside India of capital assets of a person resident in India. (*k*) Sale and purchase of foreign exchange derivatives in India and abroad and commodity derivatives abroad by a person resident in India. (*Source: Schedule I to the Regulations*)
9.	***General permission to draw foreign exchange upto US$ 2,00,000***	In respect of capital account transactions specified in Schedule I, a resident individual has been granted general permission to draw foreign exchange not exceeding US$ 2,00,000[1] per financial year (April-March), subject to the specified conditions. Accordingly, a scheme known as *'Liberalised Remittance Scheme of US$ 2,00,000 for Resident Individuals'* has been made operational *vide* AP (DIR Series) Circular No. 64, dated 4-2-2004, as amended[2] from time to time. *Note.*—'Liberalised Remittance Scheme' is applicable in respect of current account transactions also.

---

1 Enhanced from USD 1,00,000 per financial year *vide* AP (DIR Series) Circular No. 9, dated 26-9-2007. Earlier the limits under the 'Liberalised Remittance Scheme' were raised as under:

(*i*) raised upto USD 1,00,000 per financial year (from USD 50,000 per financial year) *vide* AP (DIR Series) Circular No. 51, dated 8-5-2007.

(*ii*) raised upto USD 50,000 per financial year (from USD 25,000 per calendar year) *vide* AP (DIR Series) Circular No. 24, dated 20-12-2006.

2 Refer AP (DIR Series) Circular No. 80, dated 18-3-2004, No. 38, dated 31-3-2005, No. 24, dated 20-12-2006, No. 51, dated 8-5-2007 and No. 9, dated 26-9-2007.

S. No.	***Points Considered***	***Explanation***
10.	***Transactions of a person resident outside India***	*Classes of capital account transactions of persons resident outside India are as under:* (*a*) Investment in India by a person resident outside India, that is to say,— (*i*) issue of security by a body corporate or an entity in India and investment therein by a person resident outside India; and (*ii*) investment by way of contribution by a person resident outside India to the capital of a firm or a proprietorship concern or an association of persons in India. (*b*) Acquisition and transfer of immovable property in India by a person resident outside India. (*c*) Guarantee by a person resident outside India in favour of, or on behalf of, a person resident in India. (*d*) Import and export of currency/currency notes into/from India by a person resident outside India. (*e*) Deposits between a person resident in India and a person resident outside India. (*f*) Foreign currency accounts in India of a person resident outside India. (*g*) Remittance outside India of capital assets in India of a person resident outside India. (*Source: Schedule II to the Regulations*)
11.	***Permission to Persons Resident in India***	In terms of Section 6(4) of FEMA, 1999, a person resident in India may hold, own, transfer or invest in foreign currency, foreign security or any immovable property situated outside India if such currency, security or property was acquired, held or owned by such person when he was resident outside India or inherited from a person who was resident outside India.

S. No.	*Points Considered*	*Explanation*
12.	***Permission to Persons Resident outside India***	(*i*) In terms of Section 6(5) of FEMA, 1999, a person resident outside India may hold, own, transfer or invest in Indian currency, security or any immovable property situated in India if such currency, security or property was acquired, held or owned by such person when he was resident in India or inherited from a person who was resident in India. (*ii*) Section 6(6) of FEMA, 1999, empowers Reserve Bank to prohibit, restrict, or regulate the establishment of a branch, office or other place of business in India by a non-resident person, for carrying on any activity relating to such branch, office or other place of business through regulations framed in this respect.
13.	***Permissible Method of making Payment for Investment***	Following modes of payment have been permitted for making investment: • remittance from abroad through normal banking channels; and • debit to an account of the investor maintained with an authorised person in India.
14.	***Furnishing of Declaration***	In respect of a capital account transaction any person who sells or draws foreign exchange to or from an authorised person is required to furnish a declaration to the Reserve Bank. For the form of the declaration and the time within which the same is to be furnished, the regulation relevant to the transaction is to be referred by the person concerned. *Note.*—Authorised persons (*i.e.* AD banks etc.) are under an obligation to complete the documentation/secure information from the person concerned in terms of section 10(5) of FEMA, 1999 before undertaking any transaction in foreign exchange with that person.

2. Immovable Property — Acquisition and Transfer in India

S. No.	*Points Considered*	*Explanation*
1.	***Governing Regulations***	Foreign Exchange Management (Acquisition and Transfer of Immovable Property in India) Regulations, 2000. (*Issued vide Notification No. GSR 407(E) [FEMA 21/2000-RB] dated 3-5-2000*)
2.	***Acquisition and Transfer of Immovable Property by a non-resident Indian Citizen (NRI)***	***Acquisition of Property:*** An Indian citizen resident outside India (NRI) is permitted to acquire by way of purchase immovable property in India other than agricultural property/plantation/farm house by paying the purchase price: • out of funds received in India through normal banking channels by way of inward remittance; or • out of funds held in any non-resident account. *Note*: Payment of purchase price is not permitted to be made either by traveller's cheque or by foreign currency notes or by any other mode except those specifically permitted. ***Transfer of Property:*** Such a person is permitted to transfer: • any immovable property (other than agricultural or plantation property or farm house) to a person resident outside India who is a citizen of India or to a person of Indian origin resident outside India or a person resident in India. • agricultural land/plantation property/farm house only to Indian citizens permanently residing in India.
3.	***Acquisition and Transfer of Immovable Property by a Person of Indian Origin (PIO)***	***Acquisition of Property:*** A PIO resident outside India is permitted to acquire immovable property in India (other than agricultural property/plantation/farm house) in the following manner: • by way of purchase through paying the purchase price: ○ out of funds received in India by way of inward remittance; or

S. No.	Points Considered	Explanation
		° out of funds held in any non-resident account. *Note*: Payment of purchase price is not permitted to be made either by traveller's cheque or by foreign currency notes or by any other mode except those specifically permitted. • by way of gift from a person resident in India or an Indian citizen resident outside India or a PIO. • by way of inheritance from a person resident in India or a person resident outside India who had acquired such property as per the provisions of the foreign exchange law in force or as per the present regulations at the time of acquisition of the property. ***Transfer of Property:*** A PIO is permitted to transfer:— (*a*) any immoveable property including residential or commercial property (but excluding agricultural land/plantation property/farmhouse in India) in the following manner: • by way of sale to a person resident in India. • by way of gift to a person resident in India or a non-resident Indian citizen or a PIO. (*b*) any agricultural land/plantation property/ farmhouse in India by way of sale or gift to an Indian citizen resident in India. (*Source: Regulation 4*)
4.	***Purchase/Sale of Immovable Property by Foreign Embassies/Diplomats/ Consulate General***	Foreign Embassies/Diplomats/Consulate General in India are permitted to purchase or sell immovable property in India (other than agricultural land/plantation property/farm house) on the following conditions: (*i*) *Clearance from MEA:* Clearance from Ministry of External Affairs is obtained for such purchase/sale; and

S. No.	*Points Considered*	*Explanation*
		(*ii*) *Payment of consideration in case of acquisition:* In case of acquisition of immovable property the consideration shall be paid out of funds remitted from abroad through banking channel. (*Source: Regulation 5A*)
5.	***Acquisition/Mortgage of Property for carrying on a Permitted Activity***	***Acquisition:*** A non-resident person who has established a branch, office or other place of business, (excluding a liaison office) in India for carrying on his business activity with requisite approvals (*vide FEM* (*Establishment in India of Branch or Office or Other Place of Business*) *Regulations, 2000*) is permitted to acquire an immovable property in India which is necessary for or incidental to carrying on such activity subject to the following: • For such acquisition it is a must that all applicable laws, rules, regulations or directions for the time being in force are duly complied with. • The entity/concerned person is required to file a declaration in the **form IPI 2** with the Reserve Bank, within ninety days from the date of such acquisition. ***Transfer by way of Mortgage:*** The non-resident mentioned at clause (*i*) above is permitted to transfer by way of mortgage the said immovable property to an authorised dealer as a security for the purpose of borrowing funds from it. (*Source: Regulation 5*)
6.	***Repatriation of Sale Proceeds when NRI/PIO sells his Immovable Property in India***	Where a non-resident Indian citizen or a PIO sells his immovable property in India (other than agricultural land/farm house/plantation property), the authorised dealer is permitted to allow repatriation of sale proceeds outside India subject to the following conditions: (*i*) *Property was acquired validly:* Such immovable property was acquired as per the foreign exchange law in force at the time of acquisition or the provisions of the present Regulations;

S. No.	Points Considered	Explanation
		(*ii*) *Repatriable amount:* The amount to be repatriated should not exceed: • the amount which was paid for acquisition of the immovable property in foreign exchange (such foreign exchange being received through normal banking channels or out of funds held in Foreign Currency Non-Resident Account); or • the foreign currency equivalent as on the date of payment, of the amount paid where such payment was made from the funds held in Non-Resident External account for acquisition of the property. *Note:* In terms of AP (DIR Series) Circular No. 101, dated 5-5-2003 authorised dealers are permitted to allow repatriation of sale proceeds of residential accommodation purchased by NRIs/PIOs out of funds raised through housing loans from the authorised dealers/housing finance institutions to the extent such loan/s are repaid by them out of foreign inward remittances or by debit to their NRE/FCNR accounts. This is so because such repayments of rupee loans in foreign exchange are treated as equivalent to foreign exchange received. (*iii*) *Repatriation in the case of residential property:* In the case of residential property, the repatriation of sale proceeds is restricted to only two such properties. *Note:* In terms of AP (DIR Series) Circular No. 35, dated 1-11-2002, the RBI has removed the existing lock-in-period of three years for repatriation of the sale proceeds of immovable property in respect of clauses (*i*), (*ii*) and (*iii*) (*cf.* Notification No. 65/2002-RB, dated 29-6-2002). Accordingly, the authorised dealers

S. No.	*Points Considered*	*Explanation*
		may allow remittance of sales proceeds irrespective of the period for which the property was held. The sale proceeds allowed to be repatriated should, however, not exceed the foreign exchange brought in to acquire the property. (*Source: Regulation 6*)
7.	***Refund of purchase consideration***	Refund of application/earnest money/purchase consideration made by the house building agencies/seller on account of non-allotment of flat/plot/cancellation of bookings/deals for purchase of residential/commercial property, together with interest, if any (net of income tax payable thereon) may be allowed by the Authorised Dealers by way of credit to NRE/FCNR (B) account, provided the original payment was made out of NRE/FCNR (B) account of the account holder or remittance from outside India through normal banking channels and the Authorised Dealer is satisfied about the *bonafides* of the transaction. (*Source: Master Circular No. 15/2010-11, dated 1-7-2010*)
8.	***Immovable property acquired by way of inheritance/legacy/out of Rupee funds***[1]	(*i*) A Non-Resident Indian (NRI)/Person of Indian Origin (PIO) may remit an amount, not exceeding US $ 1,000,000 (US Dollar One million only) per financial year out of the balances held in NRO accounts/sale proceeds of assets by way of purchase/the assets in India acquired by him by way of inheritance/legacy/ out of Rupee funds. This is subject to production of documentary evidence in support of acquisition, inheritance or legacy of assets by the remitter, and a tax clearance/no objection certificate from the Income Tax

1 As per Master Circular No. 15/2010-11, dated 1-7-2010. Also refer FEM (Remittance of Assets) Regulations, 2000. The restriction of lock-in period of 10 years for remittance of sale proceeds of immovable property has been dispensed with vide AP (DIR Series) Circular No. 12, dated 16-11-2006. Earlier, the restriction of lock-in-period was made inapplicable where the immovable property was acquired by way of inheritance/legacy/settlement *vide* AP (DIR Series) Circular No. 62, dated 31-1-2004.

S. No.	*Points Considered*	*Explanation*
		Authority for the remittance. Remittances exceeding US $ 1,000,000 (US Dollar One million only) in any financial year requires prior permission of the Reserve Bank. (*ii*) In cases of deed of settlement made by either of his parents or a close relative (as defined in Section 6 of the Companies Act, 1956) and the settlement taking effect on the death of the settler, the original deed of settlement and a tax clearance/No objection certificate from the Income-Tax Authority should be produced for the remittance. *Note:* Where the remittance as above is made in more than one instalment, the remittance of all such installments shall be made through the same Authorised Dealer. (*iii*) AD-Category I banks may furnish, on a quarterly basis, a statement on the number of applicants and total amount remitted, as per the prescribed proforma, to the Chief General Manager-in-Charge, Foreign Exchange Department, Foreign Investments Division (NRFAD), Reserve Bank of India, Central Office, Mumbai-400001 within 10 days of the reporting quarter. A soft copy of the statement may be sent by e-mail. (*As per AP* (*DIR Series*) *Circular No. 12, dated 16-11-2006*)
9.	***Prohibition on Acquisition or Transfer of Immovable Property in India by Citizens of certain Countries***	Citizens of Pakistan, Bangladesh, Sri Lanka, Afghanistan, China, Iran, Nepal or Bhutan (whether resident in India or outside India) are prohibited to acquire or transfer immovable property in India, (other than lease, not exceeding five years) unless they have obtained prior permission of the RBI. (*Source: Regulation 7*)
10.	***Acquisition or Transfer of Immovable Property by Foreign Nationals of non-Indian origin***	***Restricted Acquisition:*** (*i*) Foreign nationals of non-Indian origin resident outside India are not permitted to acquire any immovable property in India unless such property is acquired by way of inheritance from a person who was

S. No.	*Points Considered*	*Explanation*
		resident in India. However, they can acquire or transfer immovable property in India, on lease, not exceeding five years without the prior permission of the Reserve Bank. (*ii*) Foreign Nationals of non-Indian origin, other than a citizen of Pakistan, Bangladesh, Sri Lanka, Afghanistan, China, Iran, Nepal or Bhutan, can acquire immovable property in India on becoming resident in India in terms of Section 2(*v*) of the Foreign Exchange Management Act, 1999. In this connection, he has to satisfy the condition of period of stay. The type of visa granted should clearly indicate the intention to stay in India for an uncertain period to determine his residential status in terms of section 2(*v*) FEMA, 1999[1]. ***Restricted Transfer:*** Foreign nationals of non-Indian origin who have acquired immovable property in India by way of inheritance with the specific approval of the Reserve Bank or have purchased the immovable property with the specific approval of the Reserve Bank cannot transfer such property without the prior permission of the Reserve Bank. (*Source: Master Circular No. 15/2010-11, dated 1-7-2010*)

Liberalisation of conversion of imported capital goods/machinery and pre-operative/pre-incorporation expenses to equity instruments (FDI Circular of 30.9.2011): Conversion of imported capital goods/machinery and pre-operative/pre-incorporation expenses to equity instruments had been permitted in the last Circular on FDI policy, effective 1 April, 2011. It was stipulated that such conversions must be made within a period of 180 days of the date of shipment of capital goods/machinery or retention of advance against equity and that payments made through third parties would not be allowed. This conveyed the sense that the onus of conversion is on the investor with no allowance for the FIPB process involved. This has been clarified through the present amendment, under which the time limit for making applications for such conversions will be 180 days. Further, payments for pre-operative/incorporation expenses can now be made directly by the foreign

1 As per Press Release, dated 1-2-2009 issued by Government of India.

investor to the company or through a bank account, opened by the foreign investor, as provided under the FEMA regulations.

FDI Circular of 10.4.2012 Clarification: At present, conversion to equity is permitted for import of capital goods/machinery/equipment (including second-hand machinery). It has been represented before Government that the Indian capital goods sector, including the machine tools industry, construction machinery and textile machinery, has been suffering because of import of cheaper second hand machinery, which is often sub-standard. With a view to incentivising machinery embodying state-of-the-art technology, compliant with international standards, in terms of being green, clean and energy efficient, second-hand machinery has now been excluded from the purview of this provision.

3. Immovable Property — Acquisition and Transfer outside India

S. No.	***Points Considered***	***Explanation***
1.	***Governing Regulations***	Foreign Exchange Management (Acquisition and Transfer of Immovable Property Outside India) Regulations, 2000. (*Issued vide Notification No. GSR 390(E) [FEMA 7/2000-RB] dated 3-5-2000*)
2.	***General Prohibition on acquisition/transfer of Immovable Property Outside India***	It is generally prohibited for a person resident in India to acquire or transfer any immovable property situated outside India except where such acquisition or transfer is permitted by FEMA, 1999 or the Regulations made thereunder or where RBI has accorded general or special permission in this respect. ***Exemption to General Prohibition:*** General prohibition is not applicable in the following cases: (*i*) where a foreign national resident in India holds immovable property outside India; (*ii*) where a person resident in India acquired the immovable property outside India on or before 8-7-1947 and the same is continued to be held by him with the permission of the RBI. (*Source: Regulations 3 and 4*)
3.	***Permitted Cases of Acquisition of Immovable***	***Permitted cases of acquisition:*** (*i*) Acquisition of immovable property outside India ***by way of gift or inheritance***—

S. No.	*Points Considered*	*Explanation*
	Property outside India by a person resident in India	• from a person who acquired the property when he was resident outside India or from a person who inherited the property from a person resident outside India; • from a person resident in India who acquired the property on or before 8-7-1947 and is validly holding it with the permission of RBI. (*ii*) Acquisition of immovable property outside India ***by way of purchase*** from balances held in Resident Foreign Currency (RFC) Account. *Note:* Under the above two cases persons resident in India are generally permitted to acquire immovable property outside India. (*Source: Regulation 5*)
4.	***Permitted Cases of Transfer of Immovable Property outside India***	Any person who has acquired property in the permitted manner as indicated under S. No. 3 above is permitted to transfer the same ***by way of gift*** to his close relative (*i.e.* husband, wife, brother or sister or any of his lineal ascendant or descendant) who is a person resident in India. (*Source: Regulation 5*)
5.	***Acquisition of Property outside India by a Company Incorporated in India***	An Indian company having overseas offices may be permitted by the RBI, on an application made to it, to acquire immovable property outside India for the purpose of its business or the residential purposes of its staff members. (*Source: Regulation 5*) *Note:* Application Form in this respect has been prescribed by AP (DIR) Series Circular No. 71, dated 13-1-2003. The same may be submitted to the Chief General Manager, Reserve Bank of India, Central Office, Exchange Control Department, Trade Division (Exports), Amar Building, Mumbai through the authorised dealer.
6.	***Permissible Remittances by AD Category-I Banks for acquiring***	As a matter of liberalisation, AD Category-I Banks have been permitted by the Reserve Bank to allow limited remittances on behalf of an Indian company having overseas offices for

S. No.	*Points Considered*	*Explanation*
	Immovable Property outside India	acquiring immovable property outside India for its business and for residential purpose of its staff. The limited remittances are not to exceed the limits meant for initial and recurring expenses that may be allowed for the purpose of normal business operations of the branch or office or representative abroad of an Indian entity under FEM (Foreign Currency Accounts by a Person Resident in India) Regulations, 2000. ***Note:*** Current permissible limits for 'initial and recurring expenses' meant for the purpose of normal business operations of the branch or office or representative abroad of an Indian entity are as under: (*a*) *Remittances for initial expenses:* Up to 15% of the average annual sales/income or turnover during the last two financial years or up to 25% of the net worth, whichever is higher. (*b*) *Remittances for recurring expenses*: Up to 10% of the average annual sales/income or turnover during the last two financial years. (*Source: AP* (*DIR Series*) *Circular No. 18, dated 4-12-2006*)

AP (*DIR Series 2011-12*) *Circular No. 79, dated 15-2-2012*

3.1 Purchase of Immovable Property in India — Reporting Requirement

1. Attention of Authorised Dealer Category-I banks is invited to Regulation 5 of Notification No. FEMA 21/2000-RB *viz.* Foreign Exchange Management (Acquisition and Transfer of Immovable Property in India), Regulations, 2000 dated May 3, 2000, as amended from time to time. In terms of the above Regulation, when a person resident outside India, who has established in India in accordance with the Foreign Exchange Management (Establishment in India of Branch or Office or other Place of Business) Regulations, 2000, a branch, office or other place of business, excluding a liaison office, acquires any immovable property in India in accordance with the provision of said regulation, the said person has to file with the Reserve Bank a declaration in the form IPI annexed to those regulations, not later than ninety days from the date of such acquisition. As the form is required to be submitted by such persons only, the form is suitably amended to reflect the position.

2. It is clarified that the extant regulations do not prescribe any reporting requirements for transactions where a person resident outside India who is a citizen of India **or** a Person of Indian Origin (PIO) as defined in Regulation 2(c) of Notification No. FEMA 21/2000-RB, *ibid,* acquire/s immovable property in India in accordance with the said provisions of the aforesaid Notification. Form IPI has been, accordingly, amended for greater clarity.

3. Authorised Dealer Category-I banks may bring the contents of this circular to the notice of their constituents and customers concerned.

4. The directions contained in this circular have been issued under sections 10(4) and 11(1) of the Foreign Exchange Management Act (FEMA), 1999 (42 of 1999) and are without prejudice to permissions/approvals, if any, required under any other law.

Annexure

FORM IPI

(*See* Regulation 5)

Declaration of immovable property acquired in India by a person resident outside India who has established in India a branch, office or other place of business, excluding a liaison office

Instructions:

1. The declaration should be completed in duplicate and submitted directly to the Chief General Manager, Foreign Exchange Department, (Foreign Investment Division), Reserve Bank of India , Central Office , Mumbai-400 001 within 90 days from the date of acquisition of the immovable property.
2. This form is not to be submitted by a person resident outside India who is a citizen of India **or** a Person of Indian Origin (PIO) acquiring immovable property in India under General Permission in accordance with Regulations 3 and 4 of Notification No. FEMA 21/2000-RB, dated May 3, 2000.

Documentation: Certified copies of letter of approval from Reserve Bank obtained under section 6(6) of FEMA, 1999 (42 of 1999).

1		Full name and address of the acquirer who has acquired the immovable property	
2	(*a*)	Description of immovable property	(*a*)
	(*b*)	Details of its exact location stating the name of the state, town and municipal/survey number, etc	(*b*)
3	(*a*)	Purpose for which the immovable property has been acquired	(*a*)
	(*b*)	Number and date of Reserve Bank's permission , if any	(*b*)
4		Date of acquisition of the immovable property	
5	(*a*)	How the immovable property was acquired *i.e.* whether by way of purchase or lease	(*a*)
	(*b*)	Name, citizenship and address of the seller/lessor	(*b*)
	(*c*)	Amount of purchase price and sources of funds	(*c*)

I/We hereby declare that—

(*a*) the particulars given above are true and correct to the best of my/our knowledge and belief;

(*b*) no portion of the said property has been leased/rented to, or is otherwise being allowed to be used by, any other party.

Encls: ....

(Signature of Authorised official)

Stamp

Place: .... Name: ....

Date: .... Designation: ....

Case Study: Mr. Amit, a citizen of India, left India for employment in Australia on 1st June, 2007. Mr. Amit purchased a flat at New Delhi for ₹15 lakhs in September, 2008. His brother, Mr. Sumit employed in New Delhi, also purchased a flat in the same building in September, 2008 for ₹15 lakhs. Mr. Sumit's flat was financed by a loan from a housing finance company and the loan was guaranteed by Mr. Amit. Examine with reference to the provisions of Foreign Exchange Management Act, 1999, whether purchase of flat and guarantee by Mr. Amit are capital account transactions and whether these transactions are permissible.

Recommendation: A "capital account transaction" means a transaction which alters the assets or liabilities, including contingent liabilities, outside India of persons resident in India or assets or liabilities in India of persons resident outside India. It also includes following transactions referred to in sub-section (3) of Section 6 of Foreign Exchange Management Act 1999:

(*a*) Acquisition or transfer of immovable property in India, other than a lease not exceeding five years, by a person resident outside India;

(*b*) Giving of a guarantee or surety in respect of any debt, obligation or other liability incurred.

Thus purchase of flat at New Delhi and giving of guarantee would be considered as capital account transactions.

A capital account transaction is not permissible, unless otherwise provided in the Act, Rules or Regulations made there under, or with the general or special permission of Reserve Bank of India.

In the case referred, Mr. Amit left India for employment in Australia on 1st June 2007. Therefore, he becomes a person resident outside India from June 2007.

The purchase of flat by Mr. Amit is a capital account transaction. This is permissible in accordance with the regulation framed in this behalf *i.e.* The Foreign Exchange Management (Acquisition and Transfer of Immovable Property in India) Regulation, 2000. The Foreign Exchange Management (Acquisition and Transfer of Immovable property In India) Regulation, 2000 imposes restrictions on a person resident outside India from acquiring immovable property in India provided he fulfills both the following conditions:

(*a*) the person resident outside India is citizen of India; and

(*b*) the immovable property acquired in India is not agricultural/plantation or farmhouse.

Therefore the purchase of flat by Mr. Amit is permissible under FEMA.

Guarantee involves a long term commitment which alters the assets and liabilities of a person and therefore it is considered as a "capital account transaction' and thus restricted under FEMA. Accordingly Mr. Amit can give a guarantee to the housing finance company in respect of purchase of flat by Mr. Sumit with the permission of Reserve Bank of India.

Case Study: Explain the restrictions, if any, under Foreign Exchange Management Act, 1999 in respect of the following issue and transfer of shares:

(*i*) Issue of Equity Shares of ₹1 crore at face value accounting for 45 percent of post-issue capital to non-resident Indians in U.S.A. on non-repatriation basis. The shares are issued by M/s ABC Knitwear Limited to finance the modernization of its plant.

(*ii*) A Non-resident Indian, who is holding Equity shares in M/s DEF Textiles Limited, proposes to sell some shares to another Non-resident Indian for a consideration of ₹50 lakhs and also transfer shares of face value of ₹25 lakhs to a person resident in India by way of Gift.

Recommendation: Issue of equity shares to NRI's and transfer of shares by NRIs are capital account transactions. RBI may in consultation with the Central Government specify any class or classes of transactions which are permissible (Section 6(2)(*a*).

According to Regulation 3(1) of the Foreign Exchange Management (Permissible capital Account Transactions) Regulations, 2000 issued by RBI, Investment in India by a person resident outside India is a permissible capital account transactions (Schedule II).

Further RBI is empowered under Section 6(3)(b) to prohibit, restrict or regulate, by regulations, transfer or issue of any security by a person resident outside India. In exercise of these powers RBI issued Foreign Exchange Management (Transfer or issue of security by a person resident outside India) Regulations 2000.

According to Regulation 5(3)(*ii*) of the said regulations a NRI may purchase shares of an Indian Company which is not engaged in Print Media Sector on non-repatriation basis without any limit (para 2 of Schedule 4). The shares may be issued by the company either by public issue or private placement. The only condition is that the amount of consideration for purchase of shares shall be paid by way of inward remittance through normal banking channels from abroad or out of funds held in NRE/FCNR/NRO/NRSR/N&NR account maintained with an authorized dealer or as the case may be with an authorised bank in India (Para 3 of Schedule 4).

Transfer of shares of an Indian Company by a person resident outside India: Regulation 9(2)(*ii*) of Foreign Exchange Management (Transfer or issue of security by a person resident outside India) Regulations, 2000 permits NRI to transfer by way of sale the shares held by him to another NRI. Further according to Regulation 9(2)(*iii*) a person resident outside India may transfer any security held by him, to a person resident in India by way of gift. There are no restrictions in this regard. Hence the proposed sale of shares to NRI and transfer to a persons resident in India by way of gift are permissible under FEMA. Indian company can issue the above shares and record in its books the above transfer (Regulation 4).

Case Study: State whether there are any restrictions in respect of the following transactions:

(*i*) Drawal of Foreign Exchange for payments due on account of amortisation of loans in ordinary course of business.

(*ii*) Purchase by a person resident outside India of shares of a company in India engaged in plantation activities.

Recommendations:

(*i*) Amortisation of Loans:

Under provisions of FEMA, 1999 subject to Foreign Exchange Management (Permissible Capital Account Transactions) Regulations, 2000 as amended by Foreign Exchange Management (Permissible Capital Account Transactions) (Amendment) Regulations, 2004 all capital account transactions are prohibited unless permitted by proviso to section 6(2) of FEMA. The proviso specifically permits drawal of foreign exchange for payments due on account of amortisation of loans in ordinary course of business. Hence, there is no restriction in FEMA in this regard.

(*ii*) Purchase of Shares of Company engaged in Plantation activities:

According to Section 6(2) of FEMA, 1999 the Reserve Bank of India is empowered to specify in consultation with the Central Government, the classes of capital account transactions which are permissible and the limits upto which the foreign exchange shall be admissible for such transactions. Foreign Exchange Management (Permissible Capital Account Transactions) Regulations, 2000 completely prohibits certain capital account transactions. One such transaction is foreign investment in India in any company, firm or proprietary concern engaged in or proposed to be engaged in agriculture or plantation activities. Hence, purchase by a person resident outside India of shares of a company in India engaged in plantation activities in not permissible.

AP (DIR Series 2011-12) Circular No. 66, dated 13-1-2012

4. Revision of Scheme for Investment by Qualified Foreign Investors in Equity Shares and in Rupee Denominated Units of Domestic Mutual Funds

1. Attention of Authorised Dealers Category-I (AD Category-I) banks is invited to AP (DIR Series) Circular No. 8, dated August 9, 2011 and AP (DIR Series) Circular No. 42, dated November 3, 2011 in terms of which Qualified Foreign Investors (QFIs as defined therein to mean non-resident investors, other than SEBI registered FIIs and SEBI registered FVCIs, who meet the KYC requirements of SEBI) are allowed to invest in rupee denominated units of domestic Mutual Funds subject to the terms and conditions mentioned therein.

(I) Scheme for Investment by Qualified Foreign Investors in equity shares

2. It has now been decided to allow QFIs to purchase on repatriation basis equity shares of Indian companies subject the following terms and conditions:

(*i*) ***Eligible instruments and eligible transactions*** - QFIs shall be permitted to invest through SEBI registered Depository Participants (DPs) only in equity shares of listed Indian companies through recognized brokers on recognized stock exchanges in India as well as in equity shares of Indian companies which are offered to public in India in terms of the relevant and applicable SEBI guidelines/regulations. QFIs shall also be permitted to acquire equity shares by way of rights shares, bonus shares or equity shares on account of stock split/consolidation or equity shares on account of amalgamation, demerger or such corporate actions subject to the investment limits as prescribed in para 2 (*iv*) below.

QFIs shall be allowed to sell the equity shares so acquired by way of sale

(*a*) Through recognized brokers on recognized stock exchanges in India; or

(*b*) In an open offer in accordance with the SEBI (Substantial Acquisition of Shares and Takeovers) Regulations, 2011; or

(*c*) In an open offer in accordance with the SEBI (Delisting of Securities) Guidelines, 2009; or

(*d*) Through buyback of shares by a listed Indian company in accordance with the SEBI (Buyback) Regulations, 1998.

(*ii*) ***Mode of payment/repatriation*** - For QFI investments under this scheme a separate single rupee pool bank account would be maintained by the DP with an AD Category- I bank in India for QFI investments under this scheme. The DP will purchase equity at the instruction of the respective QFIs within five working days (including the date of credit of funds to the single rupee pool bank account by way of foreign inward remittances through normal banking channels) failing which the funds would be immediately repatriated back to the QFI's designated overseas bank account. The sale proceeds of the equity shares will also be received in this single rupee pool bank account of the DP and shall be repatriated to the designated overseas bank account of the QFI within five working days (including the date of credit of funds to the single rupee pool bank account by way of sale of equity shares) of having been received in the single rupee pool bank account of the DP. Within these five working days, the sale proceeds of the existing investment can be also utilized for fresh purchases of equity shares under this scheme, if so instructed by the QFI. Dividend payments on equity shares held by QFIs can either be directly remitted to the designated overseas bank accounts of the QFIs or credited to the single rupee pool bank account. In case dividend payments are credited to the single rupee pool bank account they shall be remitted to the designated overseas bank accounts of the QFIs within five working days (including the day of credit of such funds to the single rupee pool bank account). Within these five working days, the dividend payments can be also utilized for fresh purchases of equity shares under this scheme, if so instructed by the QFI.

(*iii*) ***Demat accounts*** - QFIs would be allowed to open a dedicated demat account with a DP in India for investment in equity shares under the scheme. The QFIs would however not be allowed to open any bank account in India.

(*iv*) ***Limits*** - The individual and aggregate investment limits for the QFIs shall be 5% and 10% respectively of the paid up capital of an Indian company. These limits shall be over and above the FII and NRI investment ceilings prescribed under the Portfolio Investment Scheme for foreign investment in India. Further, wherever there are composite sectoral caps under the extant FDI policy, these limits for QFI investment in equity shares shall also be within such overall FDI sectoral caps. The onus of monitoring and compliance of these limits shall remain jointly and severally with the respective QFIs, DPs and the respective Indian companies (receiving such investment).

(*v*) ***Eligibility*** - Only QFIs from jurisdictions which are FATF compliant and with which SEBI has signed MOUs under the IOSCO framework will be eligible to invest in equity shares under this scheme.

(*vi*) ***KYC*** - DPs will ensure KYC of the QFIs as per the norms prescribed by SEBI.

(*vii*) ***Permissible currencies*** - QFIs will remit foreign inward remittance through normal banking channel in any permitted currency (freely convertible) directly into single rupee pool bank account of the DP maintained with AD Category-I bank.

(*viii*) ***Pricing*** - The pricing of all eligible transactions and investment in all eligible instruments by QFIs under this scheme shall be in accordance with the relevant and applicable SEBI guidelines only.

(*ix*) ***Reporting*** - In addition to the reporting to SEBI as may be prescribed by them, DPs will also ensure reporting to the Reserve Bank of India in a manner and format as prescribed by the Reserve Bank of India from time to time.

(II) Scheme for Investment by Qualified Foreign Investors in Rupee Denominated Units of Domestic Mutual Funds

3. QFI investment in rupee denominated units of Domestic Mutual Funds under the Direct Route

On a further review it has been decided to modify the time period for which funds (by way of foreign inward remittance through normal banking channels from QFIs as well as by way of credit of redemption proceeds of the units of domestic Mutual Funds by QFIs in India) can be kept in the single rupee pool bank account of the DP under the scheme for investment by QFIs in units of domestic Mutual Funds (as per the terms and conditions specified in AP (DIR Series) Circular No.8, dated August 9, 2011 and AP (DIR Series) Circular No.42, dated November 3, 2011) to five working days (including the day of credit of funds received by way of foreign inward remittance through normal banking channels from QFIs as well as by way of credit of redemption proceeds of the units of domestic Mutual Funds by QFIs in India). It has also been decided to allow credit of dividend payments to QFIs on account of units of mutual funds held by them to the single rupee pool bank account subject to the condition that in case dividend payments are credited to the single rupee pool bank account they shall be remitted to the designated overseas bank accounts of the QFIs within five working days (including the day of credit of such funds to the single rupee pool bank account). Within these five working days, the dividend payments can be also utilized for fresh purchases of units of domestic mutual funds under this scheme, if so instructed by the QFI.

4. AD Category-I banks may bring the contents of the circular to the notice of their customers/constituents concerned.

5. Necessary amendments to Foreign Exchange Management (Transfer or Issue of Security by a Person Resident outside India) Regulations, 2000 (Notification No. FEMA 20/2000-RB, dated May 3, 2000)and Foreign Exchange Management (Deposit) Regulations, 2000 (Notification No. FEMA 5/2000-RB, dated May 3, 2000) are being notified separately.

6. The directions contained in this circular have been issued under sections 10(4) and 11(1) of the Foreign Exchange Management Act, 1999 (42 of 1999) and are without prejudice to permissions/approvals, if any, required under any other law.

Chapter 10

EXTERNAL COMMERCIAL BORROWINGS

1. External Commercial Borrowings (under Automatic Route)

S. No.	***Points Considered***	***Explanation***
1.	***Governing Regulations***	Foreign Exchange Management (Borrowing or Lending in Foreign Exchange) Regulations, 2000. (*Issued vide Notification No. GSR 386(E)* [*FEMA 3/2000-RB*] *dated 3-5-2000*)
2.	***Nature of External Commercial Borrowings (ECBs)***	ECBs are commercial loans in nature comprising bank loans, buyers'/suppliers' credit, securitised instruments like floating rate notes (FRNs)/fixed rate bonds (FRBs) availed from non-resident lenders. They should have minimum average maturity of 3 years. External commercial borrowings (ECBs) in foreign exchange have been permitted to be availed either under 'Automatic Route' or 'Approval Route'. In case a particular ECB cannot be availed under 'Automatic Route' the borrower shall resort to 'Approval Route'. **This Table contains the *modus operandi* of availing ECB under 'Automatic Route'.** *Notes:* (*i*) Schedule I to the Regulations read along with AP (DIR) Series Circular No. 5, dated 1-8-2005[1] contains the *modus operandi* of availing ECB under 'Automatic Route'.

1 Also refer AP (DIR Series) Circular No. 15, dated 4-11-2005; 23, dated 23-1-2006; 34, dated 12-5-2006; 17 dated 4-12-2006; 44 dated 30-4-2007; 60 dated 21-5-2007; 4, dated 7-5-2007; 10, dated 26-9-200743, dated 29-5-2008; 46, dated 2-6-2008; 1, dated 11-7-2008; 16, dated 22-9-2008; 20, dated 8-10-2008; 26, dated 22-10-2008; 46, dated 2.1.2009; 64, dated 24-4-2009 and 71, dated 30.6.2009.

S. No.	*Points Considered*	*Explanation*
		(*ii*) Under 'Automatic Route' there is no need to seek permission from the RBI for raising external commercial borrowings.
3.	***Borrowers Eligible to raise ECBs***	(*i*) ***Corporates*** which have been registered and incorporated under the Companies Act (except financial intermediaries such as banks, financial institutions (FIs), housing finance companies and NBFCs). (*ii*) ***Non-Government Organisations (NGOs)*** which are engaged in micro finance activities. Such NGOs— (*a*) should have a *satisfactory borrowing relationship* for at least 3 years with a scheduled commercial bank authorised to deal in foreign exchange; and (*b*) should obtain a *certificate of due diligence on 'fit and proper' status* of the board/ committee of management of the borrowing entity from the designated Authorised Dealer (AD). (*iii*) ***Units in Special Economic Zones (SEZs)*** are allowed to raise ECB for their own requirements. Therefore, they cannot transfer or on lend ECB funds to sister concerns or any unit in Domestic Tariff Area. (*iv*) In terms of AP (DIR Series) Circular No. 46, dated 2-1-2009 corporates in the Hotels, Hospitals and Software sectors are permitted to avail of ECB up to USD 100 million per financial year, for foreign currency and/or Rupee capital expenditure for permissible end-use. The proceeds of the ECBs should not be used for acquisition of land[1]. **(v) Infrastructure Finance Companies (IFCs) (a separate category of NBFCs classified by RBI as IFC)[2]:** may avail ECBs under automatic route for on-lending to the infrastructure sector,

1 Earlier, entities in the services sector viz. Hotels, Hospitals and Software sector were allowed to avail of ECB up to USD 100 million per financial year for import of capital goods, under the Approval Route, vide AP (DIR Series) Circular No. 46, dated 2.6.2008.

2 As per AP (DIR Series) Circular No. 51, dated 11-5-2010. Also refer AP (DIR Series) Circular No. 39, dated 2-3-2010.

S. No.	*Points Considered*	*Explanation*
		subject to the compliance with the following conditions: • compliance with the norms prescribed in the DNBS Circular No. DNBS.PD.CC No. 168/03.02.089/2009-10, dated February 12, 2010; • hedging of the currency risk in full; and • the total outstanding ECBs including the proposed ECB not exceeding 50 per cent of the Owned Funds. Designated Authorized Dealer banks should ensure compliance with the extant norms while certifying the ECB application. ***Note:*** Proposed ECBs (including the outstanding ECBs) by IFCs above 50 per cent of their owned funds would require the approval of the Reserve Bank and therefore, will be considered under the **approval route**
4.	***Borrowers NOT Eligible to raise ECBs***	Individuals, Trusts and Non-Profit making Organisations (NPOs) are not eligible to raise ECBs.
5.	***Recognised Lenders***	(I) ***Internationally recognised sources*** such as: (*i*) international banks, (*ii*) international capital markets, (*iii*) multilateral financial institutions (such as IFC, ADB, CDC etc.,), (*iv*) export credit agencies, (*v*) suppliers of equipment, (*vi*) foreign collaborators; and (*vii*) foreign equity holders (other than erstwhile OCBs). To be eligible as "recognized lender" they require minimum equity holding in the borrower's company as under: • *where ECB is up to USD 5 million* – minimum equity of 25% held directly by the lender,

S. No.	*Points Considered*	*Explanation*
		• *where ECB is more than USD 5 million* – minimum equity of 25% held directly by the lender and debt-equity ratio not exceeding 4:1 (i.e. the proposed ECB should not exceed four times of the direct foreign equity holding). (II) ***Overseas organisations*** may provide ECBs to NGOs engaged in micro finance activities subject to furnishing of a certificate of due diligence from an overseas bank (which in turn is subject to regulation of host-country regulator and adheres to Financial Action Task Force (FATF) guidelines) to the designated AD. Such a certificate should comprise the following: • that the lender maintains an account with the bank for at least a period of two years, • that the lending entity is organised as per the local law and is held in good esteem by the business/local community; and • that there is no criminal action pending against it. (III) ***Individual lenders*** may also provide ECBs to NGOs engaged in micro finance activities subject to obtaining a certificate of due diligence from an overseas bank indicating that the lender maintains an account with the bank for at least a period of two years. Other evidence/documents such as audited statement of account and income tax return which the overseas lender may furnish need to be certified and forwarded by the overseas bank. *Note: In-eligible Individual lenders:* Individual lenders from countries wherein banks are not required to adhere to Know Your Customer (KYC) guidelines are not permitted to extend ECBs. ***Note:*** In terms of AP (DIR Series) Circular No. 34, dated 12-5-06 OCBs, in view of their de-recognition cannot be considered as recognised lenders.

S. No.	*Points Considered*	*Explanation*
6.	***Amount of ECB and Maturity requirements***	***Amount of ECB:*** *In case of Corporates:* The maximum amount of ECB which can be raised by a corporate is USD 500 million during a financial year. The proceeds are permitted to be utilized for Rupee expenditure and/or foreign currency expenditure for permissible end-uses[1]. ***Note*:** Refer S. No. 6A for enhanced amount of ECB for Corporates. *In case of NGOs engaged in micro finance activities:* Such NGOs can raise ECB up to USD 5 million during a financial year. However AD bank must ensure that at the time of draw down the forex exposure of the borrower is hedged. ***Maturity requirements:*** (*i*) *ECB up to USD 20 million or equivalent:* Minimum average maturity must be three years. Such ECBs can have call/put option provided the minimum average maturity of 3 years is complied before exercising call/put option. (*ii*) *ECB above USD 20 million and up to USD 500 million or equivalent:* Minimum average maturity must be five years. (*iii*) *ECB in excess of USD 100 million for Rupee expenditure:* In this case minimum average maturity period should be of seven years[2]. However, this condition is not applicable in case ECB proceeds are meant for Rupee capital expenditure in infrastructure sector[3].
6A.	***Enhanced Amount of ECB for Corporates*** (*with the Approval of RBI*)	Corporates can now avail, over and above the existing limit of USD 500 million under the automatic route, ECB of an **additional amount of USD 250 million** with average maturity of more than 10 years under the approval route, during a financial year.

1 *Vide* AP (DIR Series) Circular No. 26, dated 22-10-2008.
2 *Vide* AP (DIR Series) Circular No. 16, dated 22-9-2008.
3 *Vide* AP (DIR Series) Circular No. 26, dated 22-10-2008.

S. No.	*Points Considered*	*Explanation*
		Notes: (*i*) Other ECB criteria such as end-use, all-in-cost ceiling, recognised lender, etc. need to be complied with. (*ii*) Prepayment and call/put options are not permissible for such ECB up to a period of 10 years. (*Source: AP* (*DIR Series*) *Circular No. 17, dated 4-12-2006*)
7.	*Applicable All-in-cost Ceilings*	**All-in-cost ceilings** depend upon 'average maturity period' of ECB and are linked to '6 months LIBOR'. Present ceilings[1] *vide* AP (DIR Series) Circular No. 26, dated 22.10.2008 are as under: (*i*) *Where average maturity period is three years but maximum up to five years:* 300 basis points over 6 months LIBOR* (*ii*) *Where average maturity period is more than five years:* 500 basis points over 6 months LIBOR* ***Notes:*** (*a*) *Inclusion in 'All-in-cost ceilings':* Rate of interest, other fees and expenses in foreign currency. (*b*) *All-in-cost ceilings do not include:* Commitment fee, pre-payment fee, and fees payable in Indian Rupees and also the payment of withholding tax in Indian Rupees. * For the respective currency of borrowing or applicable benchmark.

---

1 Earlier, all-in-cost ceilings effective from time to time were as under:

Average Maturity Period	**All-in-Cost ceilings over 6 Months LIBOR***			
	Vide AP (DIR Series) Circular No. 5, dated 1-8-2005	*Vide* AP (DIR Series) Circular No. 60, dated 21-5-2007	*Vide* AP (DIR Series) Circular No. 43, dated 29-5-2008	*Vide* AP (DIR Series) Circular No. 16, dated 2-9-2008
Three years and up to five years	200 bps	150 bps	200 bps	200 bps
More than five years and up to seven years	350 bps	250 bps	350 bps	350 bps
More than seven years				450 bps
*for the respective currency of borrowing or applicable benchmark				

S. No.	***Points Considered***	***Explanation***
8.	***End-use of ECBs***	ECBs have been permitted to be utilized for Rupee expenditure and/or foreign currency expenditure[1] as under: ***(i) For Investment purpose:*** ECBs can be utilised for investment purpose (such as import of capital goods, new projects, modernization/ expansion of existing production units) in real sector in India. The real sector comprises industrial sector including small and medium enterprises (SME) and infrastructure sector. ***Note:*** *Infrastructure sector*[2] is defined as (*i*) power, (*ii*) telecommunication, (*iii*) railways, (*iv*) road including bridges, (*v*) sea port and airport (*vi*) industrial parks, (*vii*) urban infrastructure (water supply, sanitation and sewage projects), (*viii*) mining, exploration and refining, and (*ix*) cold storage or cold room facility, including for farm level pre-cooling, for preservation or storage of agricultural and allied produce, marine products and meat. ***(ii) For development of Special Economic Zone (SEZ):*** ECBs can be availed by units in the SEZ for their own requirements. However, SEZ developers are also allowed to avail of ECB for providing infrastructure facilities, as defined in the ECB policy, within the SEZ, but only under Approval route[3]. ***Note:*** ECB shall not be permissible for development of integrated township and commercial real estate within the SEZ. ***(iii) For overseas direct investment:*** ECBs can be utilised for overseas direct investment in Joint Ventures (JV)/Wholly Owned Subsidiaries (WOS) subject to the existing guidelines on Indian Direct Investment in JV/WOS abroad.

1 *Vide* AP (DIR Series) Circular No. 26, dated 22-10-2008. For earlier position regarding utilization of ECB proceeds for foreign currency expenditure and/or rupee expenditure, refer AP (DIR Series) Circular No. 4, dated 7-8-2007 and AP (DIR Series) Circular No. 43, dated 29-5-2008.

2 Revised definition *vide* AP (DIR Series) Circular No. 20, dated 8-10-2008 and 38, dated 2-3-2010.

3 *Vide* AP (DIR Series) Circular No. 71, dated 30-6-2009.

S. No.	*Points Considered*	*Explanation*
		(*iv*) ***For obtaining License/Permit for 3G Spectrum**:* In terms of AP (DIR Series) Circular No. 26, dated 22.10.2008, ECB proceeds can be utilized for making payment towards acquiring license/permit for 3G Spectrum. (*v*) ***For making payment towards Spectrum allocation:*** In terms of AP (DIR Series) Circular No. 19, dated 9-12-2009, eligible borrowers in the telecommunication sector are permitted to avail of ECB for the purpose of payment for Spectrum allocation. *Note:* As per AP (DIR Series) Circular No. 28, dated 25-1-2010, payment for spectrum allocation may initially be met out of Rupee resources by the successful bidders, to be refinanced with a long-term ECB. However, this is permissible only under the **approval route**. For details, refer 'Approval Route' Table II. (*vi*) ***Other Utilisations of ECBs:*** ECBs are permitted to be utilised in the first stage acquisition of shares in the disinvestment process and also in the mandatory second stage offer to the public under the Government's disinvest-ment programme of PSU shares. (*vii*) ***Utilisation of ECB in case of NGOs***: NGOs engaged in micro finance activities may utilise ECB proceeds for lending to self-help groups (SHGs) or for micro-credit or for *bona fide* micro finance activity including capacity building. *Note 1:* In terms of AP (DIR Series) Circular No. 04, dated 7.8.2007, following directions are applicable with immediate effect: (*i*) ECB of **more than USD 20 million** per borrower company per financial year would be permitted only for **foreign currency expenditure** for permissible end-uses of ECB. Accordingly, borrowers raising ECB of more than USD 20 million shall park the ECB

1 Earlier the limit was USD 20 million, permitted *vide* AP (DIR Series) Circular No. 4, dated 7-8-2007.

S. No.	*Points Considered*	*Explanation*
		proceeds overseas for use as foreign currency expenditures for permissible end-uses and shall not remit the funds to India. (*ii*) Similarly, ECB **up to USD 20 million** per borrowing company per financial year would be permitted for foreign currency expenditures for permissible end-uses under the Automatic Route and these funds shall be parked overseas and not be remitted to India. ***Note 2***: As regards **Rupee expenditure,** AP (DIR Series) Circular No. 43, dated 29.5.2008 provides the following directions: (*i*) In case, a borrower (not belonging to infrastructure sector) proposes to avail ECB up to USD 50 million[1] for **Rupee expenditure** for permissible end-uses, he would require prior approval of the Reserve Bank under the Approval Route. However, such funds shall be continued to be parked overseas until actual requirement in India. (*ii*) Borrowers in infrastructure sector may avail ECB up to USD 100 million for **Rupee expenditure** for permissible end-uses under the Approval Route.
		Purposes for which Utilisation of ECB is Not Permitted: (*a*) ECB proceeds are not to be utilised for on-lending or investment in capital market or acquiring a company (or a part thereof) in India by a corporate. (*b*) ECB proceeds are not permitted to be utilised in 'real estate'. *However, the term 'real estate' excludes development of integrated township, as defined in Press Note 3 (2002 Series) dated January 04, 2002, issued by DIPP, Ministry of Commerce & Industry*[1]. Accordingly, corporates, engaged

1 The exemption to 'development of integrated township' has been restored vide AP (DIR Series) Circular No. 46, dated 2-1-2009 for the purpose of availing ECB. The exemption obtained valid till June 2009 and later on extended to December, 2009 (Ref: AP (DIR Series) Circular No. 71, dated 30-6-2009). On a review, it is further extended till 31st December, 2010 (Ref: AP (DIR Series) Circular No. 19, dated 9-12-2009). Earlier, *vide* AP ➜ ➜

S. No.	*Points Considered*	*Explanation*
		in the development of integrated township, are permitted to avail of ECB under the **Approval Route** for development of integrated township. (*c*) ECB proceeds are not permitted to be utilised for working capital, general corporate purpose and repayment of existing Rupee loans.
9.	*Guarantees etc. for ECBs*	Subject to the 'Note' below, issuance of guarantee, standby letter of credit, letter of undertaking or letter of comfort by banks, financial institutions and NBFCs relating to ECB are not permitted. *Note*: As a measure of rationalization, in terms of AP (DIR Series) Circular No. 1, dated 11-7-2008 AD Category-I banks have been allowed to convey 'no objection' under FEMA, 1999 for issue of corporate or personal guarantees in favour of overseas lender/security trustee, for securing ECB to be raised by the borrower subject to certain conditions. For details refer heading 'Security' under S. No. 10.
10.	*Security*	Choice of security that may be offered to the lender/supplier rests with the borrowing entity. In terms of AP (DIR Series) Circular No. 1, dated 11-7-2008, AD Category-I banks have been allowed to convey **'no objection'** under FEMA, 1999 for creation of charge on immovable assets, financial securities and issue of corporate or personal guarantees in favour of overseas lender/security trustee, for securing ECB to be raised by the borrower[1]. However, before according 'no objection' the AD Category-I banks may ensure and satisfy themselves:

→ → (DIR Series) Circular No. 60, dated 21-5-2007, this exemption was withdrawn and accordingly, utilisation of ECB proceeds were not permissible even for 'development of integrated township' besides real estate.

1 Earlier, proposals for creation of charge on immovable assets, financial securities and issue of corporate or personal guarantees, on behalf of the borrower in favour of the overseas lender, to secure the ECB under automatic/approval route, were considered by the Reserve Bank.

S. No.	*Points Considered*	*Explanation*
		(*i*) that the underlying ECB is strictly in compliance with the extant ECB guidelines; (*ii*) that there exists a security clause in the Loan Agreement requiring the borrower to create charge on immovable assets/ financial securities/furnish corporate or personal guarantee; (*iii*) that the loan agreement has been signed by both the lender and the borrower; and (*iv*) that the borrower has obtained Loan Registration Number (LRN) from the RBI. **Other Applicable Conditions for conveying 'No Objection' under FEMA, 1999** (*1*) *For Creation of Charge on Immovable Assets:* AD Category-I banks may convey their 'no objection' under FEMA, 1999 for creation of charge on immovable assets either in favour of the lender or the security trustee, subject to the following conditions: • 'No objection' shall be granted only to a resident ECB borrower. • The period of such charge on immovable assets has to be co-terminus with the maturity of the underlying ECB. • Such 'no objection' should not be construed as a permission to acquire immovable asset (property) in India, by the overseas lender/security trustee. • In the event of enforcement/invocation of the charge, the immovable asset (property) will have to be sold only to a person resident in India and the sale proceeds shall be repatriated to liquidate the outstanding ECB. (*2*) *For Creation of Charge over Financial Securities:* AD Category-I banks may convey their 'no objection' under FEMA, 1999 to the resident ECB borrower for pledge of shares of the borrowing company held by promoters as well as in domestic associate companies of the borrower to secure the ECB subject to the following conditions :

S. No.	*Points Considered*	*Explanation*
		• The period of such pledge shall be co-terminus with the maturity of the underlying ECB. • In case of invocation of pledge, transfer shall be in accordance with the extant FDI policy. • A certificate from the Statutory Auditor of the company that the ECB proceeds have been utilized or will be utilized for the permitted end-use. (*3*) *For Issue of Corporate or Personal Guarantee:* The 'no objection' to the resident ECB borrower for issue of corporate or personal guarantee under FEMA, 1999 may be conveyed by AD Category-I banks subject to: • obtaining of Board Resolution for issue of corporate guarantee from the company issuing such guarantees, specifying names of the officials authorised to execute such guarantees on behalf of the company or in individual capacity. • obtaining of specific requests from individuals to issue personal guarantee indicating details of the ECB. • ensuring that the period of such corporate or personal guarantee is co-terminus with the maturity of the underlying ECB. ***Note:*** AD Category-I banks may invariably specify that the **'no objection'** is issued from the foreign exchange angle under the provisions of FEMA, 1999 and should not be construed as an approval by any other statutory authority or Government under any other laws/regulations. If further approval or permission is required from any other regulatory/statutory authority or Government under the relevant laws/regulations, the applicant should take the approval of the authority concerned before undertaking the transaction. Further, the 'no objection' should not be construed as regularizing or validating any irregularities, contravention or other lapses, if

S. No.	*Points Considered*	*Explanation*
		any, under the provisions of FEMA or any other laws or regulations.
11.	***Parking of ECB proceeds overseas and Investment in Liquid Assets***	ECB proceeds are permitted to be parked overseas until actual requirement in India. *Investment of ECB proceeds parked overseas:* The proceeds parked overseas can be invested in the liquid assets but should be invested in such a way that the investments can be liquidated as and when funds are required by the borrower in India. The liquid assets for investment purpose are: • deposits or Certificate of Deposit or other products offered by banks rated not less than AA(-) by Standard and Poor/Fitch IBCA or Aa3 by Moody's; • deposits with overseas branch of an authorised dealer in India; and • Treasury bills and other monetary instruments of one year maturity having minimum rating as indicated above. *Further Liberalisation:* In terms of AP (DIR Series) Circular No. 26, dated 22-10-2008, besides keeping the ECB proceeds as above, they can also be kept as under till their actual utilisation for permissible end-uses: (*i*) keep the funds with the overseas branches/subsidiaries of Indian banks abroad; or (*ii*) remit the funds to India for credit to the Rupee accounts with AD Category I banks in India. However, as hitherto, the rupee funds will not be permitted to be used for investment in capital markets, real estate or for inter-corporate lending.
12.	***Prepayment of ECB up to USD 500 million***	Such prepayment may be allowed by ADs subject to compliance with the stipulated minimum average maturity period as applicable to the loan. No prior approval of RBI is required in this respect. ***Note:*** The enhanced prepayment of ECB upto USD 500 million (as against the earlier limit of

S. No.	***Points Considered***	***Explanation***
		USD 400 million) has been permitted in terms of AP (DIR Series) Circular No. 10, dated 26-9-2007. Prior to the above enhancement, the ECB prepayment limits were raised as under: (*i*) prepayment upto USD 400 million (as against the limit of USD 300 million): *permitted vide AP (DIR Series) Circular No. 44, dated 30.4.2007;* (*ii*) pre-payment upto USD 300 million (as against the limit of USD 200 million): *permitted vide AP (DIR Series) Circular No. 17, dated 04.12.2006.*
13.	***Refinance of existing ECB by raising fresh ECB***	Refinancing of existing ECB by raising fresh ECB at lower cost is permitted subject to the condition that the outstanding maturity of the original loan is maintained.
14.	***Debt Servicing***	The designated AD is permitted to make remittances of instalments of principal, interest and other charges in conformity with ECB guidelines.
15.	***Procedure for raising ECB***	Borrower may after complying with ECB guidelines and without prior approval of RBI enter into loan agreement with recognised lender for raising ECB under Automatic Route. In this respect following points are noteworthy: • The borrower should comply with the reporting arrangement. • The borrower must obtain a loan Registration Number (LRN) from the Reserve Bank before drawing down the ECB. • It is the responsibility of borrower to ensure that ECB raised/utilised are in conformity with the ECB guidelines and the Reserve Bank regulations/ directions/circulars. • Any contravention of the ECB guidelines will be viewed seriously and may invite penal action. • The designated AD is also required to ensure that raising/utilisation of ECB is in compliance with ECB guidelines at the time of certification.

S. No.	*Points Considered*	*Explanation*
16.	***Changes permissible by AD category-I Banks***	In terms of AP (DIR Series) Circular No. 33, dated 9-02-2010, AD category-I banks have been delegated powers to approve the following requests from the ECB borrowers, subject to specified conditions: ***(i) Changes/modifications in the drawdown/ repayment schedule***: Designated AD Category-I banks may approve changes/modifications in the drawdown/ repayment schedule of the ECBs already availed, both under the approval and the automatic routes, subject to the condition that **the average maturity period, as declared while obtaining the LRN, is maintained**. The changes in the drawdown/repayment schedule should be promptly reported to the DSIM, Reserve Bank in Form 83. However, any elongation/rollover in the repayment on expiry of the original maturity of the ECB would require the prior approval of the Reserve Bank. ***(ii) Changes in the currency of borrowing:*** Designated AD Category-I banks may allow changes in the currency of borrowing, if so desired, by the borrower company, in respect of ECBs availed of both under the automatic and the approval routes, subject to all other terms and conditions of the ECB remaining unchanged. Designated AD banks should, however, ensure that the proposed currency of borrowing is freely convertible. ***(iii) Change of the AD bank:*** Designated AD Category-I banks may allow change of the existing designated AD bank by the borrower company for effecting its transactions pertaining to the ECBs subject to No-Objection Certificate (NOC) from the existing designated AD bank and after due diligence. ***(iv) Changes in the name of the Borrower Company:*** Designated AD Category-I banks may allow changes in the name of the borrower company subject to production of supporting documents evidencing the change in the name from the Registrar of Companies.

S. No.	*Points Considered*	*Explanation*
17.	***ECB Policy regarding Corporates under Investigation***	Those corporates, which have violated the extant ECB policy and are under investigation by Reserve Bank and/or by Directorate of Enforcement, will not be allowed to access the Automatic route for ECB. Any request by such corporates for ECB will be examined under the Approval route. (*Source*: *AP* (*DIR Series*) *Circular No. 71, dated 30-6-2009*)
18.	***Reporting Arrangements***	***(i) Submission of Form 83:*** Borrowers are required to submit Form 83, in duplicate, certified by the Company Secretary (CS) or Chartered Accountant (CA) to the designated AD. One copy is to be forwarded by the designated AD to the Director, Balance of Payments Statistics Division, Department of Statistical Analysis and Computer Services (DESACS), Reserve Bank of India, Bandra-Kurla Complex, Mumbai-400 051 for allotment of loan registration number. *Note:* The borrower can draw-down the Loan only after obtaining the loan registration number from DESACS, RBI. ***(ii) Submission of ECB-2 Return:*** Borrowers are required to submit ECB-2 Return certified by the designated AD on monthly basis so as to reach DESACS, RBI within seven working days from the close of month to which it relates. ***(iii) No Need to submit copy of loan agreement:*** With a view to simplify the procedure, submission of copy of loan agreement is dispensed with.

2. External Commercial Borrowings (under Approval Route)

S. No.	*Points Considered*	*Explanation*
1.	***Governing Regulations***	Foreign Exchange Management (Borrowing or Lending in Foreign Exchange) Regulations, 2000. (*Issued vide Notification No. GSR 386*(*E*) [*FEMA 3/2000-RB*], *dated 3-5-2000*)

S. No.	*Points Considered*	*Explanation*
2.	***Nature of External Commercial Borrowings (ECBs)***	ECBs are commercial loans in nature comprising bank loans, buyers'/suppliers' credit, securitised instruments like floating rate notes (FRNs)/fixed rate bonds (FRBs) availed from non-resident lenders. They should have minimum average maturity of 3 years. External commercial borrowings (ECBs) in foreign exchange have been permitted to be availed either under 'Automatic Route' or 'Approval Route'. Where parameters relating to Automatic Route are not applicable in a particular case or where the borrowing entity is doubtful whether it can avail ECB under Automatic Route though apparently the case might be classifiable under this Route, the borrower shall resort to avail ECB under the 'Approval Route'. **This Table contains the *modus operandi* of availing ECB under 'Approval Route'.** *Notes:* (*i*) Schedule II to the Regulations read along with AP (DIR) Series Circular No. 5, dated 1-8-2005 contains the *modus operandi* of availing ECB under 'Approval Route'. (*ii*) Further changes in the ECB policy relating to 'Approval Route' have been made vide AP (DIR Series) Circular Nos. 15, dated 4-11-2005; 23, dated 23-1-2006; 34, dated 12-5-2006; 17 dated 4-12-2006; 44 dated 30-4-2007; 60 dated 21-5-2007 4 dated 7-8-2007; 10, dated 26-9-2007; 43, dated 29-5-2008; 46, dated 2-6-2008; 1, dated 11-7-2008; 16, dated 22-9-2008; 20, dated 8-10-2008; 26, dated 22-10-2008; 46, dated 2.1.2009; 64, dated 24-4-2009 and 71, dated 30.6.2009.
3.	***Empowered Committee***	RBI has set up an Empowered Committee to consider proposals coming under the Approval Route.
4.	***Borrowers Eligible to raise ECBs***	(*i*) ***Corporates*** which have been registered and incorporated under the Companies Act. (*ii*) ***Financial institutions*** dealing exclusively with infrastructure or export finance such as IDFC, IL&FS, Power Finance Corporation

S. No.	*Points Considered*	*Explanation*
		(PFC), Power Trading Corporation, IRCON and EXIM Bank. *Note:* In terms of AP (DIR Series) Circular No. 15, dated 4-11-2005 *Special Purpose Vehicles (SPVs) or any other entity*, notified by the Reserve Bank, set up to finance infrastructure companies/projects exclusively will also be treated as financial institutions. It is clarified that ECB by such entities will be considered under the Approval Route on a case by case basis. ***(iii) Banks and financial institutions*** which had participated in the textile or steel sector restructuring package as approved by the Government. The quantum of ECB shall be limited to the extent of their investment in the package and assessment by RBI based on prudential norms. It may be noted that any ECB availed for this purpose so far shall be deducted from the entitlement. ***(iv) Cases falling outside the purview of the automatic route in respect of limits and maturity period*** *i.e.* where the quantum of ECB exceeds US$ 500 or where the average maturity period is less than three years. ***(v) Non-banking Financial Companies (NBFCs):*** NBFCs are permitted to raise ECBs with minimum average maturity of 5 years from multilateral financial institutions, reputable regional financial institutions, official export credit agencies and international banks to finance import of infrastructure equipment for leasing to infrastructure projects. ***(vi) Infrastructure Finance Companies (IFCs) (a separate category of NBFCs classified by RBI as IFC):***[1] IFCs are permitted to avail of ECBs for on-lending to the infrastructure sector. As per the revised instructions, for availment of ECB, IFCs would require the approval of the Reserve Bank where the total

1 As per AP (DIR Series) Circular No. 39, dated 2-3-2010 read with AP (DIR Series) Circular No. 51, dated 11-5-2010.

S. No.	Points Considered	Explanation
		outstanding ECBs including the proposed ECB exceed 50 per cent of their Owned Funds, and therefore, under such circumstances, their proposals will be considered under approval route, subject to the compliance with the following conditions: • compliance with the norms prescribed in the DNBS Circular No. DNBS.PD.CC No. 168/03.02.089/2009-10, dated February 12, 2010; • hedging of the currency risk in full; Designated Authorized Dealer banks should ensure compliance with the extant norms while certifying the ECB application. *Note:* Proposals for ECBs (including the outstanding ECBs) by IFCs not exceeding 50 per cent of their owned funds are permitted to be considered under the **automatic route.** ***(vii) Foreign Currency Convertible Bonds (FCCB) by housing finance companies:*** HFCs must satisfy the following minimum criteria: • the *minimum net worth* of the financial intermediary during the previous three years shall not be less than ₹500 crore, • a listing on the BSE or NSE, • minimum size of FCCB should be USD 100 million, • the applicant should submit the purpose/ plan of utilization of funds. ***(viii) Multi-State Co-operative Societies engaged in Manufacturing Activities:*** In terms of AP (DIR Series) Circular No. 23, dated 23-1-2006, these Co-operative societies are permitted to raise ECB under the 'Approval Route' provided they are financially solvent and submit their up-to-date audited balance sheet. ***(ix) SEZ Developers:*** In terms of AP (DIR Series) Circular No. 71, dated 30.6.2009, SEZ developers are allowed to avail of ECB for providing infrastructure facilities, as defined in the ECB policy, within the SEZ.

S. No.	*Points Considered*	*Explanation*
		(x) ***Entities in the services sectors viz., Hotels, Hospitals and Software:*** In terms of AP (DIR Series) Circular No. 8, dated 12.8.2010, corporates in the Hotel, Hospital and Software sectors are permitted to avail of ECB **beyond USD 100 million** under the Approval Route, for foreign currency and/or Rupee capital expenditure for permissible end-uses. The proceeds of the ECB should not be used for acquisition of land. ***Note:*** ECB upto USD 100 million can be availed by the above entities in the Hotel, Hospital and Software sectors, under the automatic route.
5.	***Recognised Lenders***	ECB can be raised by the eligible borrowers from **internationally recognised sources** like: (*i*) international banks, (*ii*) international capital markets, (*iii*) multilateral financial institutions (such as IFC, ADB, CDC etc.,), (*iv*) export credit agencies, (*v*) suppliers of equipment, (*vi*) foreign collaborators and (*vii*) foreign equity holders (other than erstwhile OCBs): In this case, Approval Route is applicable under circumstances where the minimum equity held directly by the foreign equity lender is 25 per cent **but debt-equity ratio exceeds 4:1** (*i.e.* the proposed ECB exceeds four times the direct foreign equity holding).
6.	***Amount and Maturity***	(1) All such cases shall be considered under Approval Route where: • the minimum average maturity is less than three years; or • the ECB amount exceeds USD 500 million or equivalent.[1]

1 In terms of AP (DIR Series) Circular No. 26, dated 22-10-2008, ECB up to USD 500 million per borrower per financial is permitted for Rupee expenditure for permissible end-uses under the Automatic Route. Further, the requirement of minimum average maturity period of seven years* for ECB of more than USD 100 million for Rupee capital expenditure by the →→

S. No.	*Points Considered*	*Explanation*
		(2) In terms of AP (DIR Series) Circular No. 17, dated 4-12-2006, over and above the existing limit of USD 500 million under the automatic route, corporates can avail ECB of an **additional amount of USD 250 million** with average maturity of more than 10 years under the approval route, during a financial year. *Notes:* (*i*) Other ECB criteria such as end-use, all-in-cost ceiling, recognised lender, etc. need to be complied with. (*ii*) Prepayment and call/put options are not permissible for such ECB up to a period of 10 years.
7.	***Applicable All-in-cost ceilings***	In terms of AP (DIR Series) Circular No. 19, dated 9-12-2009, the existing relaxation[1] in the all-in-cost ceilings stands withdrawn with effect from January 1, 2010. Accordingly, the all-in-cost ceilings under the approval route for the ECBs, where Loan Agreements have been signed on or after January 1, 2010 will be as under: (*i*) *Where average maturity period is three years but maximum up to five years:* 300 basis points over 6 months LIBOR* (*ii*) *Where average maturity period is more than five years:* 500 basis points over 6 months LIBOR* Eligible borrowers proposing to avail of ECB after December 31, 2009, where the Loan Agreement has been signed on or before December 31, 2009 and where the all-in-cost exceed the above ceilings, should furnish a copy of the Loan Agreement. Such proposals

→ → borrowers in the infrastructure sector has been dispensed with.

*Earlier *vide* AP (DIR Series) Circular No. 16, dated 22-9-2008, it was prescribed that ECBs in excess of USD 100 million for Rupee expenditure should have a minimum average maturity period of 7 years.

1 Till December 31, 2009, the requirement of all-in-cost ceilings on ECB under approval route was dispensed with. [*Ref: AP (DIR Series) Circular No. 46, dated 2-1-2009 read with Circular No. 64, dated 28-4-2009*]

S. No.	Points Considered	Explanation
		would continue to be considered under the approval route. *Notes:* (*a*) All-in-cost ceilings depend upon 'average maturity period' of ECB and are linked to '6 months LIBOR'. (*b*) *Inclusion in 'All-in-cost ceilings':* Rate of interest, other fees and expenses in foreign currency. (*c*) *All-in-cost ceilings do not include:* Commitment fee, pre-payment fee, and fees payable in Indian Rupees and also the payment of withholding tax in Indian Rupees. * *For the respective currency of borrowing or applicable benchmark.*
8.	***End-use of ECBs***	ECBs have been permitted to be utilised as under: ***(i) For Investment purpose:*** ECBs can be utilised for investment purpose (such as import of capital goods, new projects, moderniza-tion/expansion of existing production units) in real sector in India. The real sector comprises industrial sector including small and medium enterprises (SME) and infrastructure sector. ***Note***: *Infrastructure sector*[1] is defined as (*i*) power, (*ii*) telecom-munication, (*iii*) railways, (*iv*) road including bridges, (*v*) sea port and airport, (*vi*) industrial parks, (*vii*) urban infrastructure (water supply, sanitation and sewage projects), (*viii*) mining, exploration and refining and (*ix*) cold storage or cold room facility, including for farm level pre-cooling, for preservation or storage of agricultural and allied produce, marine products and meat. ***(ii) For development of Special Economic Zone (SEZ):*** SEZ developers are allowed to avail of ECB for providing infrastructure facilities, as defined in the ECB policy, within the SEZ[2].

1 Revised definition *vide* AP (DIR Series) Circular No. 20, dated 8-10-2008.

2 *Vide* AP (DIR Series) Circular No. 71, dated 30-6-2009.

S. No.	*Points Considered*	*Explanation*
		Note: ECB shall not be permissible for development of integrated township and commercial real estate within the SEZ.
		(iii) For overseas direct investment: ECBs can be utilised for overseas direct investment in Joint Ventures (JV)/Wholly Owned Subsidiaries (WOS) subject to the existing guidelines on Indian Direct Investment in JV/WOS abroad.
		(iv) For obtaining License/Permit for 3G Spectrum: In terms of AP (DIR Series) Circular No. 26, dated 22-10-2008, ECB proceeds can be utilized for making payment towards acquiring license/permit for 3G Spectrum.
		(v) For making payment towards Spectrum allocation: In terms of AP (DIR Series) Circular No. 19, dated 9-12-2009, eligible borrowers in the telecommunication sector are permitted to avail of ECB for the purpose of payment for Spectrum allocation. It may be noted that AP (DIR Series) Circular No. 28, dated 25-1-2010 grants permission to the successful bidders to make payment for spectrum allocation initially out of Rupee resources. Thereafter, it may be refinanced with a long-term ECB, subject to the following conditions: • The ECB should be raised within 12 months from the date of payment of the final installment to the Government; • The designated AD - Category I bank should monitor the end-use of funds;

1 The exemption to 'development of integrated township' has been restored *vide* AP (DIR Series) Circular No. 46, dated 2.1.2009 for the purpose of availing ECB The exemption obtained valid till June 2009 and later on extended to December, 2009 (Ref: AP (DIR Series) Circular No. 71, dated 30-6-2009). On a review, it is further extended till 31st December, 2010 (Ref: AP (DIR Series) Circular No. 19, dated 9.12.2009). Earlier, *vide* AP (DIR Series) Circular No. 60, dated 21-5-2007, this exemption was withdrawn and accordingly, utilisation of ECB proceeds were not permissible even for 'development of integrated township' besides real estate.

2 As per AP (DIR Series) Circular No. 71, dated 30-6-2009.

S. No.	*Points Considered*	*Explanation*
		• Banks in India will not be permitted to provide any form of guarantees; and • All other conditions of ECB, such as eligible borrower, recognized lender, all-in-cost, average maturity, etc, should be complied with. The above one-time relaxation in the end-use conditions of the ECB policy has been made with a view that a large outlay of funds is involved and the same is required to be paid directly to the Government within a limited period of time. ***Note:*** Where the eligible borrowers in the telecommunications sector propose to fund the payment for Spectrum allocation directly out of the proceeds of the ECBs, they may continue to avail of the ECBs under the automatic route as per the extant policy. **(*vi*) *For development of integrated township:*** In terms of AP (DIR Series) Circular No. 46, dated 2-1-2009 corporates, engaged in the development of integrated township, as defined in Press Note 3 (2002 Series) dated January 4, 2002, issued by DIPP, Ministry of Commerce & Industry, are permitted to avail and utilise ECB proceeds for development of integrated township. This permission, earlier available till *December 2009* (*vide AP* (*DIR Series*) *Circular No. 71, dated 30-6-2009*) *now stands extended to December 31, 2010* [*Refer AP* (*DIR Series*) *Circular No. 19, dated 9-12-2009*]. ***Note:*** Integrated township includes housing, commercial premises, hotels, resorts, city and regional level urban infrastructure facilities such as roads and bridges, mass rapid transit systems and manufacture of building materials. Development of land and providing allied infrastructure forms an integrated part of township's development. The minimum area to be developed should be 100 acres for which norms and standards are to be followed as per local bye-laws/rules. In the absence of such

S. No.	Points Considered	Explanation
		bye-laws/rules, a minimum of two thousand dwelling units for about ten thousand population will need to be developed. **(*vii*) *Other Utilisations of ECBs:*** ECBs are permitted to be utilised in the first stage acquisition of shares in the disinvestment process and also in the mandatory second stage offer to the public under the Government's disinvestment programme of PSU shares. **Purposes for which Utilisation of ECB is Not Permitted:** (*a*) ECB proceeds are not to be utilised for on-lending or investment in capital market or acquiring a company (or a part thereof) in India by a corporate except for banks and financial institutions mentioned under clauses (*ii*) and (*iii*) against '*Borrowers Eligible to raise ECB*'. (*b*) ECB proceeds are not permitted to be utilised in 'real estate'. *However, the term 'real estate' excludes development of integra-ted township, as defined in Press Note 3 (2002 Series) dated January 4, 2002, issued by DIPP, Ministry of Commerce & Industry*[1]. (*c*) ECB proceeds are not permitted to be utilised for working capital, general]corporate purpose and repayment of existing Rupee loans. (*d*) ECB shall not be permissible for development of integrated township and commercial real estate within the SEZ[2].
9.	***Guarantees etc. for ECBs***	Subject to the 'Note' below, normally issuance of guarantee, standby letter of credit, letter of undertaking or letter of comfort by banks, financial institutions and NBFCs relating to ECB is not permitted. However in the following exceptional cases issuing of guarantees etc. will be considered: (*i*) *Cases of Small and Medium Enterprises:* Applications for issuing guarantee/standby

S. No.	*Points Considered*	*Explanation*
		letter of credit or letter of comfort by banks, financial institutions relating to ECB in the case of SME will be considered on merit subject to prudential norms. (*ii*) *Cases of Textile Companies:* As permitted by AP (DIR Series) Circular No., dated (DIR Series) Circular No. 15, dated 4-11-2005 banks will be allowed to issue guarantees, standby letters of credit, letters of undertaking or letters of comfort in respect of ECB by textile companies for modernization or expansion of their textile units. Such applications will be considered under the Approval Route subject to prudential norms. ***Note:*** As a measure of rationalization, in terms of AP (DIR Series) Circular No. 1, dated 11-7-2008 AD Category-I banks have been allowed to convey **'no objection'** under FEMA, 1999 for issue of corporate or personal guarantees in favour of overseas lender/ security trustee, for securing ECB to be raised by the borrower subject to certain conditions. For details refer heading 'Security' under S. No. 10.
10.	***Security***	Choice of security that may be offered to the lender/supplier rests with the borrowing entity. In terms of AP (DIR Series) Circular No. 1, dated 11-7-2008, AD Category-I banks have been allowed to convey **'no objection'** under FEMA, 1999 for creation of charge on immovable assets, financial securities and issue of corporate or personal guarantees in favour of overseas lender/security trustee, for securing ECB to be raised by the borrower[1]. However, before according 'no objection' the AD Category-I banks may ensure and satisfy themselves:

1 Earlier, proposals for creation of charge on immovable assets, financial securities and issue of corporate or personal guarantees, on behalf of the borrower in favour of the overseas lender, to secure the ECB under automatic/approval route, were considered by the Reserve Bank.

S. No.	*Points Considered*	*Explanation*
		(*i*) that the underlying ECB is strictly in compliance with the extant ECB guidelines; (*ii*) that there exists a security clause in the Loan Agreement requiring the borrower to create charge on immovable assets/ financial securities/furnish corporate or personal guarantee; (*iii*) that the loan agreement has been signed by both the lender and the borrower; and (*iv*) that the borrower has obtained Loan Registration Number (LRN) from the RBI. **Other Applicable Conditions for conveying 'No Objection' under FEMA, 1999** (*1*) *For Creation of Charge on Immovable Assets:* AD Category-I banks may convey their 'no objection' under FEMA, 1999 for creation of charge on immovable assets either in favour of the lender or the security trustee, subject to the following conditions: • 'No objection' shall be granted only to a resident ECB borrower. • The period of such charge on immovable assets has to be co-terminus with the maturity of the underlying ECB. • Such 'no objection' should not be construed as a permission to acquire immovable asset (property) in India, by the overseas lender/security trustee. • In the event of enforcement/invocation of the charge, the immovable asset (property) will have to be sold only to a person resident in India and the sale proceeds shall be repatriated to liquidate the outstanding ECB. (*2*) *For Creation of Charge over Financial Securities:* AD Category-I banks may convey their 'no objection' under FEMA, 1999 to the

S. No.	*Points Considered*	*Explanation*
		resident ECB borrower for pledge of shares of the borrowing company held by promoters as well as in domestic associate companies of the borrower to secure the ECB subject to the following conditions: • The period of such pledge shall be co-terminus with the maturity of the underlying ECB. • In case of invocation of pledge, transfer shall be in accordance with the extant FDI policy. • A certificate from the Statutory Auditor of the company that the ECB proceeds have been utilized or will be utilized for the permitted end-use. (3) *For Issue of Corporate or Personal Guarantee:* The 'no objection' to the resident ECB borrower for issue of corporate or personal guarantee under FEMA, 1999 may be conveyed by AD Category-I banks subject to: • obtaining of Board Resolution for issue of corporate guarantee from the company issuing such guarantees, specifying names of the officials authorised to execute such guarantees on behalf of the company or in individual capacity. • obtaining of specific requests from individuals to issue personal guarantee indicating details of the ECB. • ensuring that the period of such corporate or personal guarantee is co-terminus with the maturity of the underlying ECB. ***Note:*** AD Category-I banks may invariably specify that the **'no objection'** is issued from the foreign exchange angle under the provisions of FEMA, 1999 and should not be construed as an approval by any other statutory authority or Government under any other laws/ regulations. If further approval or permission is required from any other regulatory/statutory

S. No.	*Points Considered*	*Explanation*
		authority or Government under the relevant laws/regulations, the applicant should take the approval of the authority concerned before undertaking the transaction. Further, the 'no objection' should not be construed as regularizing or validating any irregularities, contravention or other lapses, if any, under the provisions of FEMA or any other laws or regulations.
11.	***Parking of ECB proceeds Overseas and Investment in Liquid Assets***	ECB proceeds are permitted to be parked overseas until actual requirement in India. *Investment of ECB proceeds parked overseas:* The proceeds parked overseas can be invested in the liquid assets but should be invested in such a way that the investments can be liquidated as and when funds are required by the borrower in India. The liquid assets for investment purpose are: • deposits or Certificate of Deposit or other products offered by banks rated not less than AA(-) by Standard and Poor/Fitch IBCA or Aa3 by Moody's; • deposits with overseas branch of an authorised dealer in India; and • Treasury bills and other monetary instruments of one year maturity having minimum rating as indicated above. *Further Liberalisation:* In terms of AP (DIR Series) Circular No. 26, dated 22-10-2008, besides keeping the ECB proceeds as above, they can also be kept as under till their actual utilisation for permissible end-uses: (*i*) keep the funds with the overseas branches/subsidiaries of Indian banks abroad; or (*ii*) remit the funds to India for credit to the Rupee accounts with AD Category I banks in India. However, as hitherto, the rupee funds will not be permitted to be used for investment in capital markets, real estate or for inter-corporate lending.

S. No.	*Points Considered*	*Explanation*
11A.	***Permission to Take-out Financing Arrangement through ECB***	Keeping in view the special funding needs of the infrastructure sector, permission has been granted for take-out financing arrangement through ECB, **under the approval route**, for refinancing of Rupee loans availed of from the domestic banks by eligible borrowers in the **sea port and airport, roads including bridges and power sectors** for the development of new projects, subject to the following conditions: • The corporate developing the infrastructure project should have a tripartite agreement with domestic banks and overseas recognized lenders for either a **conditional** or **unconditional** take-out of the loan within three years of the scheduled Commercial Operation Date (COD). The scheduled date of occurrence of the take-out should be clearly mentioned in the agreement. • The loan should have a minimum average maturity period of seven years. • The domestic bank financing the infrastructure project should comply with the extant prudential norms relating to take-out financing. • The fee payable, if any, to the overseas lender until the take-out shall not exceed 100 bps per annum. • On take-out, the residual loan agreed to be taken- out by the overseas lender would be considered as ECB and the loan should be designated in a convertible foreign currency and all extant norms relating to ECB should be complied with. • Domestic banks/Financial Institutions will not be permitted to guarantee the take-out finance. • The domestic bank will not be allowed to carry any obligation on its balance sheet after the occurrence of the take-out event.

S. No.	*Points Considered*	*Explanation*
		• Reporting arrangement as prescribed under the ECB policy should be adhered to. Eligible borrowers may, accordingly, apply to the Reserve Bank for necessary approval before entering into take-out finance arrangement. (*Source: AP (DIR Series) Circular No. 4, dated 22.7.2010*)
12.	***Prepayment of ECB***	(*i*) *Not exceeding USD 500 million*: Such prepayment may be allowed by ADs without prior approval of RBI subject to compliance with the stipulated minimum average maturity period as applicable to the loan. ***Note:*** The limit of USD 500 million has been enhanced from USD 300 million *vide* AP (DIR Series) Circular No. 10, dated 26-9-2007. Prior to the above enhancement, the ECB prepayment limits were raised as under: (*i*) prepayment upto USD 400 million (as against the limit of USD 300 million): *permitted vide AP (DIR Series) Circular No. 44, dated 30.4.2007*; (*ii*) prepayment upto USD 300 million (as against the limit of USD 200 million): *permitted vide AP (DIR Series) Circular No. 17, dated 04.12.2006.* (*ii*) *Exceeding USD 500 million:* Such prepayment would be considered by the Reserve Bank under the Approval Route.
13.	***Refinance of existing ECB by raising fresh ECB***	Refinancing of existing ECB by raising fresh ECB at lower cost is permitted subject to the condition that the outstanding maturity of the original loan is maintained.
14.	***Debt Servicing***	The designated AD is permitted to make remittances of instalments of principal, interest and other charges in conformity with ECB guidelines.

S. No.	*Points Considered*	*Explanation*
15.	***Procedure for raising ECB***	Applicants may submit an application in form ECB through designated AD to the RBI along with necessary documents. In this respect Chief General Manager, Foreign Exchange Department, Central Office, External Commercial Borrowings Division, Mumbai-400 001 may be approached.
16.	***Changes permissible by AD category-I Banks***	In terms of AP (DIR Series) Circular No. 33, dated 9-02-2010, AD category-I banks have been delegated powers to approve the following requests from the ECB borrowers, subject to specified conditions: ***(i) Changes/modifications in the drawdown/repayment schedule***: Designated AD Category-I banks may approve changes/ modifications in the drawdown/repayment schedule of the ECBs already availed, both under the approval and the automatic routes, subject to the condition that **the average maturity period, as declared while obtaining the LRN, is maintained**. The changes in the drawdown/ repayment schedule should be promptly reported to the DSIM, Reserve Bank in Form 83. However, any elongation/rollover in the repayment on expiry of the original maturity of the ECB would require the prior approval of the Reserve Bank. ***(ii) Changes in the currency of borrowing:*** Designated AD Category-I banks may allow changes in the currency of borrowing, if so desired, by the borrower company, in respect of ECBs availed of both under the automatic and the approval routes, subject to all other terms and conditions of the ECB remaining unchanged. Designated AD banks should, however, ensure that the proposed currency of borrowing is freely convertible. ***(iii) Change of the AD bank:*** Designated AD Category-I banks may allow change of the existing designated AD bank by the borrower company for effecting its transactions pertaining to the ECBs subject to No-Objection

S. No.	*Points Considered*	*Explanation*
		Certificate (NOC) from the existing designated AD bank and after due diligence. ***(iv) Changes in the name of the Borrower Company:*** Designated AD Category-I banks may allow changes in the name of the borrower company subject to production of supporting documents evidencing the change in the name from the Registrar of Companies.
17.	***ECB Policy regarding Corporates under Investigation***	Those corporates, which have violated the extant ECB policy and are under investigation by Reserve Bank and/or by Directorate of Enforcement, will not be allowed to access the Automatic route for ECB. Any request by such corporates for ECB will be examined under the Approval route. **(Source:** AP (DIR Series) Circular No. 71, dated 30.6.2009)
18.	***Reporting Arrangements***	***(i) Submission of Form 83:*** Borrowers are required to submit Form 83, in duplicate, certified by the Company Secretary (CS) or Chartered Accountant (CA) to the designated AD. One copy is to be forwarded by the designated AD to the Director, Balance of Payments Statistics Division, Department of Statistical Analysis and Computer Services (DESACS), Reserve Bank of India, Bandra-Kurla Complex, Mumbai-400 051 for allotment of loan registration number. *Note:* The borrower can draw-down the loan only after obtaining the loan registration number from DESACS, RBI. ***(ii) Submission of ECB-2 Return:*** Borrowers are required to submit ECB-2 Return certified by the designated AD on monthly basis so as to reach DESACS, RBI within seven working days from the close of month to which it relates. ***(iii) No need to submit copy of loan agreement:*** With a view to simplify the procedure, submission of copy of loan agreement is dispensed with.

S. No.	*Points Considered*	*Explanation*
19.	***Structured Obligations***	In order to enable corporates to raise resources domestically and hedge exchange rate risks, domestic rupee denominated structured obligations are permitted by the Government to be credit enhanced by international banks/ international financial institutions/joint venture partners. In view of the growing needs of funds in the infrastructure sector, the RBI, after reviewing the existing norms, has put in place *vide* AP (DIR Series) Circular No. 40, dated 2-3-2010, a comprehensive policy framework on **credit enhancement to domestic debt** as indicated below: According to the comprehensive policy framework, the facility of credit enhancement by eligible non-resident entities may be extended to domestic debt raised through issue of capital market instruments, such as debentures and bonds, by Indian companies engaged exclusively in the development of infrastructure and by the Infrastructure Finance Companies (IFCs), which have been classified as such by the Reserve Bank in terms of the guidelines contained in the circular DNBS.PD. CC No. 168/03.02.089/2009-10, dated February 12, 2010, subject to the following conditions: 1. credit enhancement will be permitted to be provided by multilateral/regional financial institutions and Government owned development financial institutions; 2. the underlying debt instrument should have a minimum average maturity of seven years; 3. prepayment and call/put options would not be permissible for such capital market instruments up to an average maturity period of 7 years;

<table>
<tr><th>S. No.</th><th>Points Considered</th><th>Explanation</th></tr>
<tr><td></td><td></td><td>4. guarantee fee and other costs in connection with credit enhancement will be restricted to a maximum 2 per cent of the principal amount involved;
5. on invocation of the credit enhancement, if the guarantor meets the liability and if the same is permissible to be repaid in foreign currency to the eligible non-resident entity, the all-in-cost ceilings, as applicable to the relevant maturity period of the Trade Credit/ECBs, would apply to the novated loan. Presently, the all-in-cost ceilings, depending on the average maturity period, are applicable as follows:

Average maturity period of the loan on invocation — All-in-cost ceilings over 6 month Libor*
Up to 3 years — 200 basis points
Three years and up to five years — 300 basis points
More than five years — 500 basis points
*for the respective currency of borrowing or applicable benchmark

6. In case of default and if the loan is serviced in Indian Rupees, the applicable rate of interest would be the coupon of the bonds or 250 bps over the prevailing secondary market yield of 5 years Government of India security, as on the date of novation, whichever is higher;
7. IFCs proposing to avail of the credit enhancement facility should comply with the eligibility criteria and prudential norms laid down in the circular DNBS.PD.CC No. 168/03.02.089/2009-10, dated February 12, 2010 and in case the novated loan is designated in foreign currency, the IFC should hedge the entire foreign currency exposure; and
8. The reporting arrangements as applicable to the ECBs would be applicable to the novated loans.</td></tr>
</table>

3. External Commercial Borrowings (Other Residual Aspects)

S. No.	*Points Considered*	*Explanation*
1.	***Governing Regulations/ Circular***	Foreign Exchange Management (Borrowing or Lending in Foreign Exchange) Regulations, 2000 read along with different AP (DIR Series) Circular issued from time to time by the RBI.
2.	***Conversion of ECB into Equity and Reporting Arrangement*** *(permitted vide AP (DIR) Series Circular No.15, dated 1-10-2004)*	***Conversion of ECB into equity*** Such conversion is permitted subject to the following conditions: (*i*) *Adherence to norms for foreign equity:* The activity of the company is covered under the Automatic Route for FDI or else Government approval for foreign equity in the company has been obtained. (*ii*) *Adherence to Sectoral Cap:* The foreign equity after such conversion of debt into equity is within the sectoral cap, if any. (*iii*) *Pricing of shares*: The pricing is as per SEBI guidelines in the case of listed companies and as per erstwhile CCI regulations in the case of unlisted companies. *Note:* Import payables, deemed as ECB, are not eligible for conversion into equity/ preference shares. ***Reporting Arrangement*** Conversion of ECB into equity may be reported to the RBI as follows: (*i*) *In case of full conversion of ECB into equity:* Borrowers are required to report full conversion: • in the form FC-GPR to the concerned Regional Office of the Reserve Bank; and • in the form ECB-2 to the Deptt. of Statistical Analysis and Computer Services (DESACS), RBI (to be submitted within seven working days from the close of month to which it relates).

S. No.	Points Considered	Explanation
		Notes: (*a*) Form FC-GPR is required to be submitted within 30 days from the date of issue of shares as per Schedule I to FEM (Transfer or Issue of Security by a Person resident outside India) Regulations, 2000. (*b*) The words "ECB wholly converted to equity" should be clearly indicated on top of the ECB-2 form. (*c*) Once reported, filing of ECB-2 in the subsequent months is not necessary. (*ii*) *In case of partial conversion of ECB into equity*: Borrowers are required to report the converted portion: • in the form FC-GPR to the concerned Regional Office of the RBI; and • in the form ECB-2 to the DESACS, RBI clearly differentiating the converted portion from the unconverted portion. *Notes:* (*a*) The words "ECB partially converted to equity" should be indicated on top of the ECB-2 form. (*b*) In subsequent months, the outstanding portion of ECB should be reported in ECB-2 form to DESACS.
3.	***ECB under erstwhile USD 5 Million Scheme-Elongation of Repayment Period*** (*Permitted vide AP* (*DIR Series) Circular No. 82, dated 1-4-2004*)	Designated ADs are permitted to approve elongation of repayment period for loans raised under the erstwhile USD 5 Million Scheme, provided there is a consent letter from the overseas lender for such re-schedulement without any additional cost. ***Reporting Arrangement*** Such approval with existing and revised repayment schedule along with the Loan Key/Loan Registration Number should be

S. No.	Points Considered	Explanation
		initially communicated to the CGM, Foreign Exchange Department, RBI, ECB Division, Mumbai within seven days of approval and subsequently in ECB-2.
4.	***Crystallisation of ECB Liability*** *(permitted vide AP (DIR) Series Circular No.41, dated 29-4-2002)*	In case, guarantees provided by ADs for ECB raised by corporates in India are invoked and ADs desire to crystallise their foreign exchange liability arising out of such guarantees into Rupees, they may make an application to the CGM, Foreign Exchange Department, ECB Division, RBI, Mumbai, giving the following details in full: • name of the borrower; • amount raised; • maturity; • circumstances leading to invocation of guarantee/letter of comfort; • date of default; • its impact on the liabilities of the overseas branch of the AD concerned; and • other relevant factors.
5.	***ECB by Units in Special Economic Zones (SEZ)*** *(permitted vide AP (DIR) Series Circular No.29, dated 18-10-2003)*	Units in SEZ are permitted to raise ECB subject to the following conditions : • ECB is raised for their own requirement, and • They shall not transfer or on-lend any borrowed funds to their sister concern or any other unit in Domestic Tariff Area (DTA).

AP (DIR Series) Circular No. 40, dated 2-3-2010

External Commercial Borrowings (ECB) Policy – Structured Obligations

Attention of Authorised Dealer Category I (AD Category I) banks is invited to Notification No.FEMA 29/2000-RB, dated September 26, 2000 viz. Payment to person resident outside India on invocation of guarantee, A.P. (DIR Series) Circular No. 28, dated March 30, 2001 and A.P. (DIR Series) Circular No. 5, dated August 1, 2005 relating to External Commercial Borrowings (ECB).

2. Borrowing and lending of Indian Rupees between two persons resident in India does not attract the provisions of the Foreign Exchange Management Act,

1999. In case where a Rupee loan is granted against the guarantee provided by a person resident outside India, there is no transaction involving foreign exchange until the guarantee is invoked and the non-resident guarantor is required to meet the liability under the guarantee. The Reserve Bank *vide* Notification No. FEMA 29/2000-RB, dated September 26, 2000 has granted general permission to a person resident in India, being a principal debtor, to make payment to a person resident outside India, who has met the liability under a guarantee.

3. As per the extant policy, domestic Rupee denominated structured obligations have been permitted to be credit enhanced by non-resident entities under the approval route. In view of the growing needs of funds in the infrastructure sector, the existing norms have been reviewed and it has been decided to put in place a comprehensive policy framework on credit enhancement to domestic debt as indicated below:

4. It has since been decided that the facility of credit enhancement by eligible non-resident entities may be extended to domestic debt raised through issue of capital market instruments, such as debentures and bonds, by Indian companies engaged exclusively in the development of infrastructure and by the Infrastructure Finance Companies (IFCs), which have been classified as such by the Reserve Bank in terms of the guidelines contained in the circular DNBS.PD. CC No. 168/03.02.089/ 009-10, dated February 12, 2010, subject to the following conditions:

(*i*) credit enhancement will be permitted to be provided by multilateral/ regional financial institutions and Government owned development financial institutions;

(*ii*) the underlying debt instrument should have a minimum average maturity of seven years;

(*iii*) prepayment and call/put options would not be permissible for such capital market instruments up to an average maturity period of 7 years;

(*iv*) guarantee fee and other costs in connection with credit enhancement will be restricted to a maximum 2 per cent of the principal amount involved;

(*v*) on invocation of the credit enhancement, if the guarantor meets the liability and if the same is permissible to be repaid in foreign currency to the eligible non-resident entity, the all-in-cost ceilings, as applicable to the relevant maturity period of the Trade Credit/ECBs, would apply to the novated loan. Presently, the all-in-cost ceilings, depending on the average maturity period, are applicable as follows:

Average maturity period of the loan on invocation	**All-in-cost ceilings over 6 month Libor***
Up to 3 years	200 basis points
Three years and up to five years	300 basis points
More than five years	500 basis points
*for the respective currency of borrowing or applicable benchmark	

(*vi*) In case of default and if the loan is serviced in Indian Rupees, the applicable rate of interest would be the coupon of the bonds or 250 bps over the prevailing secondary market yield of 5 years Government of India security, as on the date of novation, whichever is higher;

(*vii*) IFCs proposing to avail of the credit enhancement facility should comply with the eligibilitycriteria and prudential norms laid down in the circular DNBS.PD.CC No. 168/03.02.089/2009-10, dated February 12, 2010 and in case the novated loan is designated in foreign currency, the IFC should hedge the entire foreign currency exposure; and

(*viii*) The reporting arrangements as applicable to the ECBs would be applicable to the novated loans.

5. Necessary amendments to the Foreign Exchange Management (Borrowing or Lending in Foreign Exchange) Regulations, 2000 dated May 3, 2000 are being issued separately wherever necessary.

6. AD Category I banks may bring the contents of this circular to the notice of their constituents and customers concerned.

7. The directions contained in this circular have been issued under sections 10(4) and 11(1) of the Foreign Exchange Management Act, 1999 (42 of 1999) and is without prejudice to permissions/approvals, if any, required under any other law.

AP (DIR Series 2011-12) Circular No. 99, dated 30-3-2012

External Commercial Borrowings (ECB) Policy — Review of All-In-Cost Ceiling

1. Attention of Authorized Dealer Category-I (AD Category-I) banks is invited to AP (DIR Series) Circular No. 51, dated November 23, 2011 relating to External Commercial Borrowings.

2. Considering the developments in the global financial markets and the fact that borrowers were experiencing difficulties in raising ECBs within the existing all-in-cost ceiling, the all-in-cost ceiling for ECBs with average maturity of three and up to five years was enhanced to 6 months LIBOR + 350 bps with effect from November 23, 2011 and was subject to review on March 31, 2012. On a review, it has been decided to continue with the enhanced all-in-cost ceiling for a further period of six months in respect of ECBs as under:

Average Maturity Period	All-in-cost over 6 month LIBOR*
Three years and up to five years	350 bps
More than five years	500 bps
* for the respective currency of borrowing or applicable benchmark	

3. The all-in-cost ceiling is applicable up to September 30, 2012 and subject to review thereafter. All other aspects of ECB policy remain unchanged.

4. AD Category-I banks may bring the contents of this circular to the notice of their constituents and customers.

5. The directions contained in this circular have been issued under sections 10(4) and 11(1) of the Foreign Exchange Management Act, 1999 (42 of 1999) and are without prejudice to permissions/approvals, if any, required under any other law.

AP (DIR Series 2011-12) Circular No. 100, dated 30-3-2012

Trade Credits for Imports into India — Review of All-In-Cost Ceiling

1. Attention of Authorized Dealer Category-I (AD Category-I) banks is invited to AP (DIR Series) Circular No. 44, dated November 15, 2011 relating to the all-in-cost ceiling of Trade Credits for imports into India.

2. Considering the developments in the global financial markets and the fact that domestic importers were experiencing difficulties in raising trade credit within the existing all-in-cost ceiling, the all-in-cost ceiling for trade credit was enhanced to 6 months LIBOR + 350 bps with effect from November 15, 2011 and was subject to review on March 31, 2012. On a review, it has been decided to continue with the enhanced all-in-cost ceiling for Trade Credits for a further period of six months as under:

Maturity Period	All-in-cost over 6 month LIBOR*
Upto one year	350 bps
More than one year and upto three years	

* for the respective currency of credit or applicable benchmark

The all-in-cost ceiling will include arranger fee, upfront fee, management fee, handling/processing charges, out of pocket and legal expenses, if any.

3. The all-in-cost ceiling is applicable up to September 30, 2012 and subject to review thereafter. All other aspects of Trade Credit policy remain unchanged.

4. AD Category - I banks may bring the contents of this circular to the notice of their constituents and customers.

5. The directions contained in this circular have been issued under sections 10(4) and 11(1) of the Foreign Exchange Management Act, 1999 (42 of 1999) and are without prejudice to permissions/approvals, if any, required under any other law.

AP (DIR Series 2011-12) Circular No. 64, dated 5-1-2012

**External Commercial Borrowings (ECB) —
Revised Average Maturity Guidelines, etc.**

Attention of Authorized Dealer Category-I (AD Category-I) banks is invited to the Foreign Exchange Management (Borrowing or Lending in Foreign Exchange) Regulations, 2000, notified *vide* Notification No. FEMA 3/2000-RB, dated May 3, 2000, amended from time to time, Foreign Exchange Management

(Transfer or Issue of any Foreign Security) (Amendment) Regulations, 2004 issued *vide* Notification No.FEMA.120/RB-2004, dated July 7, 2004, as amended from time to time, AP (DIR Series) Circular No. 5, dated August 1, 2005, as amended from time to time, AP (DIR Series) Circular No. 17, dated December 4, 2006, AP (DIR Series) Circular No. 1, dated July 04, 2011 and AP (DIR Series) Circular No. 27, dated September 23, 2011 relating to the External Commercial Borrowings (ECB).

2. The ECB limit for eligible borrowers under the automatic route was enhanced to USD 750 million or equivalent per financial year per borrower for permissible end-uses under the automatic route *vide* AP (DIR Series) Circular No. 27, dated September 23, 2011. Consequent to the enhancement in limits, the revised average maturity guidelines under the automatic route are as follows:—

(*a*) ECB up to USD 20 million or equivalent in a financial year with minimum average maturity of three years; and

(*b*) ECB above USD 20 million and up to USD 750 million or equivalent with minimum average maturity of five years.

3. Accordingly, the requirement of average maturity period, prepayment and call/put options specified *vide* AP (DIR Series) Circular No.17, dated December 4, 2006 (for additional amount of USD 250 million) has been dispensed with.

4. It is also clarified that the eligible borrowers under the automatic route can raise Foreign Currency Convertible Bonds (FCCBs) up to USD 750 million or equivalent per financial year for permissible end-uses. Similarly, corporates in specified service sectors, *viz.*, hotel, hospital and software, can raise FCCBs up to USD 200 million or equivalent for permissible end-uses during a financial year subject to the condition that the proceeds of the ECB should not be used for acquisition of land.

5. *Vide* para 2(*viii*) of AP (DIR Series) Circular No. 01, dated July 04, 2011, ECB/FCCB availed of for the purpose of refinancing the existing outstanding FCCB were to be reckoned as part of the limit of USD 500 million available under the automatic route as per the extant norms. Consequent to the enhancement in the limits under the automatic route, it is clarified that the ECB/FCCB availed of for the purpose of refinancing the existing outstanding FCCB will be reckoned as part of the limit of USD 750 million available under the automatic route as per the extant norms.

6. All other aspects of the ECB policy, such as eligible borrower, recognised lender, all-in-cost, end-use, prepayment, refinancing of existing ECB and reporting arrangements shall remain unchanged.

7. Necessary amendments to the Foreign Exchange Management (Borrowing or Lending in Foreign Exchange) Regulations, 2000, dated May 3, 2000 and Foreign Exchange Management (Transfer or Issue of any Foreign Security) (Amendment) Regulations, 2004, dated July 7, 2004 are being issued separately wherever necessary.

8. AD Category-I banks may bring the contents of this circular to the notice of their constituents and customers.

9. The directions contained in this circular have been issued under sections 10(4) and 11(1) of the Foreign Exchange Management Act, 1999 (42 of 1999) and are without prejudice to permissions/approvals, if any, required under any other law.

AP (DIR Series 2011-12) Circular No. 70, dated 25-1-2012

External Commercial Borrowings (ECB) Policy — Infrastructure Finance Companies (IFCs)

1. Attention of Authorized Dealer Category-I (AD Category-I) banks is invited to AP (DIR Series) Circular No. 5, dated August 1, 2005, amended from time to time and AP (DIR Series) Circular No. 51, dated May 11, 2010 relating to External Commercial Borrowings (ECBs). As per the extant guidelines, Non-Banking Finance Companies (NBFCs) categorized as Infrastructure Finance Companies (IFCs) by the Reserve Bank and complying with the norms prescribed in the DNBS Circular DNBS.PD.CC.No.168/03.02.089/2009-10, dated February 12, 2010 are permitted to avail of ECBs, including the outstanding ECBs, up to 50 per cent of their owned funds under the automatic route. ECBs by IFCs above 50 per cent of their owned funds are being considered under the approval route. The permitted end-use should be for on-lending to the infrastructure sector, as defined under the extant ECB policy. IFCs should also hedge their currency risk in full.

2. It has now been decided that the designated AD Category – I banks should certify the leverage ratio (*i.e.* outside liabilities/owned funds) of IFCs desirous of availing ECBs under the approval route while forwarding such proposals to the Reserve Bank of India.

3. All other aspects of the ECB policy, such as eligible borrower, recognised lender, maximum permissible limit under the automatic route, average maturity, all-in-cost, end-use, prepayment, refinancing of existing ECB and reporting arrangements shall remain unchanged.

4. AD Category - I banks may bring the contents of this circular to the notice of their constituents and customers.

5. The directions contained in this circular have been issued under sections 10(4) and 11(1) of the Foreign Exchange Management Act, 1999 (42 of 1999) and are without prejudice to permissions/approvals, if any, required under any other law.

AP (DIR Series 2011-12) Circular No. 85, dated 29-2-2012

External Commercial Borrowings (ECB) for Infrastructure Facilities within National Manufacturing Investment Zone (NMIZ)

1. Attention of Authorized Dealer Category-I (AD Category-I) banks is invited to the Foreign Exchange Management (Borrowing or Lending in Foreign Exchange) Regulations, 2000, notified *vide* Notification No. FEMA 3/2000-RB, dated May 3, 2000, as amended from time to time and AP (DIR Series) Circular No. 5, dated August 1, 2005, as amended from time to time.

2. As per the extant guidelines, availing of ECB is permissible for the infrastructure sector, which is defined to include (*i*) power, (*ii*) telecommunication, (*iii*) railways, (*iv*) road including bridges, (*v*) sea port and airport, (*vi*) industrial parks, (*vii*) urban infrastructure (water supply, sanitation and sewage projects), (*viii*) mining, refining and exploration and (*ix*) cold storage or cold room facility, including for farm level pre cooling, for preservation or storage of agricultural and allied produce, marine products and meat. Developers of SEZ were also allowed to provide such infrastructure facilities within the SEZ.

3. Keeping in view the infrastructural needs of the proposed National Manufacturing Investment Zones (NMIZs), it has now been decided to allow developers of NMIZ also to avail of ECB under the "approval route" for providing infrastructure facilities within the NMIZ, as indicated above.

4. The modifications to the ECB policy will come into force with immediate effect. All other aspects of the ECB policy, such as, recognised lender, average maturity, all-in-cost, prepayment, refinancing of existing ECB and reporting arrangements shall remain unchanged.

5. AD Category - I banks may bring the contents of this circular to the notice of their constituents and customers.

6. The directions contained in this circular have been issued under sections 10(4) and 11(1) of the Foreign Exchange Management Act, 1999 (42 of 1999) and are without prejudice to permissions/approvals, if any, required under any other law.

AP (DIR Series 2011-12) Circular No. 69, dated 25-1-2012

External Commercial Borrowings — Simplification of Procedure (Part I)

1. Attention of Authorized Dealer Category-I (AD Category-I) banks is invited to the Foreign Exchange Management (Borrowing or Lending in Foreign Exchange) Regulations, 2000, notified *vide* Notification No. FEMA 3/2000-RB, dated May 3, 2000 and the AP (DIR Series) Circular No. 5, dated August 1, 2005 relating to the External Commercial Borrowings (ECB), as amended from time to time.

2. As per the extant ECB procedures any request for cancellation of Loan Registration Number (LRN) given by the Department of Statistics and Information Management (DSIM), Reserve Bank of India or change in permissible end-use for an existing ECB is required to be referred by the AD Category-I bank to the Foreign Exchange Department, Central Office, Reserve Bank of India for necessary approval.

3. As a measure of simplification of the existing procedures, it has been decided to delegate powers to the designated AD category-I banks to approve the following requests from the ECB borrowers, subject to specified conditions:

(*a*) ***Cancellation of LRN:*** The designated AD Category-I bank may directly approach DSIM for cancellation of LRN for ECBs availed, both under the automatic and approval routes, subject to fulfilment of the following conditions:—

(*i*) no draw down for the said LRN has taken place; and

(*ii*) the monthly ECB-2 returns till date in respect of the LRN have been submitted to DSIM.

(*b*) ***Change in the end-use of ECB proceeds:*** The designated AD Category-I bank may approve requests from ECB borrowers for change in end-use in respect of ECBs availed under the automatic route, subject to the following conditions:—

(*i*) the proposed end-use is permissible under the automatic route as per the extant ECB guidelines;

(*ii*) there is no change in the other terms and conditions of the ECB;

(*iii*) the ECB is in compliance with the extant guidelines; and

(*iv*) the monthly ECB-2 returns till date in respect of the LRN have been submitted to DSIM.

The AD Category–I bank shall continue to monitor the utilization of end-use proceeds and changes in the end-use should be promptly reported to DSIM, RBI in Form 83. However, change in the end-use of ECBs availed under the approval route will continue to be referred to the Foreign Exchange Department, Central Office, Reserve Bank of India, as hitherto.

4. The above modifications to the ECB guidelines will come into force with immediate effect. All other aspects of the ECB policy, such as, USD 750 million limit per company per financial year under the automatic route, eligible borrower, recognized lender, end-use, all-in-cost ceiling, average maturity period, prepayment, refinancing of existing ECB and reporting arrangements shall remain unchanged.

5. AD Category–I banks may bring the contents of this circular to the notice of their constituents and customers concerned.

6. The directions contained in this circular have been issued under sections 10(4) and 11(1) of the Foreign Exchange Management Act, 1999 (42 of 1999) and are without prejudice to permissions/approvals, if any, required under any other law.

AP (DIR Series 2011-12) Circular No. 75, dated 7-2-2012

External Commercial Borrowings — Simplification of Procedure (Part II)

1. Attention of Authorized Dealer Category-I (AD Category-I) banks is invited to the Foreign Exchange Management (Borrowing or Lending in Foreign Exchange) Regulations, 2000, notified *vide* Notification No. FEMA 3/2000-RB, dated May 3, 2000, AP (DIR Series) Circular No. 5, dated August 1, 2005 relating to the External Commercial Borrowings (ECB), as amended from time to time and AP (DIR Series) Circular No. 33, dated February 09, 2010.

2. As per the extant ECB procedures, requests for reduction in the amount of ECB, changes in the drawdown schedule where the original average maturity period is not maintained and reduction in the all-in-cost of the ECB after obtaining the Loan Registration Number (LRN) is required to be referred by the AD Category-I bank to the Foreign Exchange Department, Central Office, Reserve Bank of India for necessary approval.

3. As a measure of simplification of the existing procedures, it has been decided to delegate powers to the designated AD category-I banks to approve the following requests from the ECB borrowers, subject to specified conditions:

(*a*) ***Reduction in amount of ECB:*** The designated AD Category-I bank may approve requests from ECB borrowers for reduction in loan amount in respect of ECBs availed under the automatic route, subject to ensuring the following conditions:—

(*i*) the consent of the lender for reduction in loan amount has been obtained;

(*ii*) the average maturity period of the ECB is maintained;

(*iii*) the monthly ECB-2 returns in respect of the LRN have been submitted to the Department of Statistics and Information Management (DSIM); and

(*iv*) there is no change in the other terms and conditions of the ECB.

(*b*) ***Changes/modifications in the drawdown schedule when original average maturity period is not maintained:*** As per the extant procedures, Designated AD Category-I banks have been delegated powers to approve changes/modifications in the drawdown/repayment schedule of the ECBs already availed, both under the approval and the automatic routes, subject to the condition that the average maturity period, as declared while obtaining the LRN, is maintained.

It has now been decided that the designated AD Category-I bank may approve requests from ECB borrowers for changes/modifications in the drawdown schedule resulting in the original average maturity period undergoing change in respect of ECBs availed both under the automatic and approval routes, subject to ensuring the following conditions:—

(*i*) there are no changes/modifications in the repayment schedule of the ECB;

(*ii*) the average maturity period of the ECB is reduced as against the original average maturity period stated in the Form 83 at the time of obtaining the LRN;

(*iii*) such reduced average maturity period complies with the stipulated minimum average maturity period as per the extant ECB guidelines;

(*iv*) the change in all-in-cost is only due to the change in the average maturity period and the ECB complies with the extant guidelines; and (*v*) the monthly ECB-2 returns in respect of the LRN have been submitted to DSIM.

Any elongation/rollover in the repayment, on expiry of the original maturity, of the ECB, would however, continue to require the prior approval of the Reserve Bank.

(*c*) ***Reduction in the all-in-cost of ECB:*** The designated AD Category-I bank may approve requests from ECB borrowers for reduction in all-in-cost, in respect of ECBs availed both under the automatic and approval routes, subject to ensuring the following conditions:—

(*i*) the consent of the lender has been obtained and there are no other changes in the terms and conditions of the ECB; and

(*ii*) the monthly ECB-2 returns in respect of the LRN have been submitted to DSIM.

4. The designated AD Category-I bank should ensure that the ECBs continue to comply with the extant guidelines while exercising their delegated powers and changes are promptly reported to the Department of Statistics and Information Management (DSIM), Reserve Bank of India in Form 83.

5. The above modifications to the ECB guidelines will come into force with immediate effect. All other aspects of the ECB policy, such as, USD 750 million limit per company per financial year under the automatic route, eligible borrower, recognized lender, end-use, all-in-cost ceiling, average maturity period, prepayment, refinancing of existing ECB and reporting arrangements shall remain unchanged.

6. AD Category-I banks may bring the contents of this circular to the notice of their constituents and customers concerned.

7. The directions contained in this circular have been issued under sections 10(4) and 11(1) of the Foreign Exchange Management Act, 1999 (42 of 1999) and are without prejudice to permissions/approvals, if any, required under any other law.

Introduction of Provisions on 'Pledging of Shares' and Opening of Non-Interest Bearing Escrow Accounts, Subject to Specified Conditions (FDI Circular, dated 30-9-2011)

The policy has been amended to provide for pledge of shares of an Indian company which has raised external commercial borrowings, or that of its associate resident companies for the purpose of securing the ECB raised by the borrowing company, subject to conditions. The policy also now provides for opening and maintaining AD Category-I banks without the prior approval of RBI, non-interest bearing Escrow accounts in Indian Rupees in India, on behalf of non-residents, towards payment of share purchase consideration and/or for keeping securities to facilitate FDI transactions, subject to the terms and conditions specified by RBI. This will streamline the process for bringing in FDI and provide the investors with options.

AP (DIR Series 2011-12) Circular No. 112, dated 20-4-2012

External Commercial Borrowings (ECB) Policy — Refinancing/Rescheduling of ECB

Attention of Authorized Dealer Category-I (AD Category-I) banks is invited to the Foreign Exchange Management (Borrowing or Lending in Foreign Exchange) Regulations, 2000, notified vide Notification No. FEMA 3/2000-RB, dated May 3, 2000 and AP (DIR Series) Circular No. 5 dated August 1, 2005, as amended from time to time.

2. As per the extant guidelines, existing ECB may be refinanced by raising a fresh ECB, subject to the condition that the fresh ECB is raised at a lower all-in-cost.

3. On a review, it has been decided that the borrowers desirous of refinancing/rescheduling an existing ECB can raise fresh ECB at a higher all-in-cost under the approval route subject to the condition that the enhanced all-in-cost does not exceed the all-in-cost ceiling prescribed as per the extant guidelines.

4. The modifications to the ECB policy will come into force with immediate effect and will be subject to review. All other aspects of ECB policy remain unchanged.

5. Necessary amendments to the Foreign Exchange Management (Borrowing or Lending in Foreign Exchange) Regulations, 2000, dated May 3, 2000 are being issued separately wherever necessary.

6. AD Category - I banks may bring the contents of this circular to the notice of their constituents and customers concerned.

7. The directions contained in this circular have been issued under sections 10(4) and 11(1) of the Foreign Exchange Management Act, 1999 (42 of 1999) and are without prejudice to permissions/ approvals, if any, required under any other law.

AP (DIR Series 2011-12) Circular No. 111, dated 20-4-2012

Liberalisation and Rationalisation of External Commercial Borrowings (ECB) Policy

Attention of Authorized Dealer Category-I (AD Category-I) banks is invited to the Foreign Exchange Management (Borrowing or Lending in Foreign Exchange) Regulations, 2000, notified vide Notification No. FEMA 3/2000-RB dated May 3, 2000 and AP (DIR Series) Circular No. 5 dated August 1, 2005, as amended from time to time, relating to External Commercial Borrowings.

2. On a review of the policy related to ECB and keeping in view the announcements made in the Union Budget for the Year 2012-13, it has been decided to further rationalize and liberalize the extant guidelines as under:—

(*i*) *Enhancement of Refinancing limit for Power Sector* - Indian companies in the power sector will be allowed to utilise 40 per cent of the fresh ECB raised towards refinancing of the Rupee loan/s availed by them from the domestic banking system, under the approval route, subject to the condition that at least 60 per cent of the fresh ECB proposed to be raised should be utilised for fresh capital expenditure for infrastructure project(s). All other terms and conditions relating to refinancing of Rupee loans mentioned in A.P. (DIR Series) Circular No. 25 dated September 23, 2011 remain unchanged.

(*ii*) *ECB for Maintenance and Operation of Toll systems for Roads and Highways* - ECBs would also be allowed for capital expenditure under the automatic route for the purpose of maintenance and operations of toll systems for roads and highways provided they form part of the original project.

3. The modifications to the ECB policy will come into force with immediate effect. All other aspects of the ECB policy, such as, maximum permissible limit under the automatic route, eligible borrower, recognised lender, average maturity, all-in-cost, prepayment, refinancing of existing ECB and reporting arrangements shall remain unchanged.

4. AD Category-I banks may bring the contents of this circular to the notice of their constituents and customers.

5. The directions contained in this circular have been issued under sections 10(4) and 11(1) of the Foreign Exchange Management Act, 1999 (42 of 1999) and are without prejudice to permissions/approvals, if any, required under any other law.

Chapter 11

ESTABLISHMENT OF BRANCH OR OFFICE OR OTHER PLACE OF BUSINESS IN INDIA

S. No.	*Points Considered*	*Explanation*
1.	***Governing Regulations***	Foreign Exchange Management (Establishment in India of Branch or Office or Other Place of Business) Regulations, 2000. (*Issued vide Notification No. GSR 408*(*E*) [*FEMA 22/2000-RB*] *dated 3-5-2000*)
2.	***General Prohibition on Establishing Branch/Office in India***	It is not permitted to a person resident outside India to establish in India a branch or a liaison office or any other place of business without seeking prior approval from the Reserve Bank. However, opening of Project Office under specified circumstances has been brought under general permission of RBI. (*Source: Regulation 3*)
3.	***Prohibition on Citizens of certain Countries***	It is specifically prohibited for a citizen of Pakistan, Bangladesh, Sri Lanka, Afghanistan, Iran or China, to establish in India, a branch or a liaison office or a project office or any other place of business. All these citizens need prior permission of the Reserve Bank. (*Source: Regulation 4*)

S. No.	*Points Considered*	*Explanation*
3A.	***Prohibition on Partnership/Proprietary concerns set up abroad***	Partnership/Proprietary concerns set up abroad are not allowed to establish Branch/Liaison Offices. (*Source: Master Circular 11/2010-11, dated 1-7-2010*)
3B.	***Permission for Liaison Office in case of Entities from Nepal***	Entities from Nepal are allowed to establish only Liaison Offices in India. (*Source: Master Circular 11/2010-11, dated 1-7-2010*)
4.	***Meaning of Branch Office and Liaison Office***	Regulation 2 defines a Branch Office (BO) and a Liaison Office (LO) as under: ***Branch Office:*** A branch office takes its meaning from Section 2(9) of the Companies Act, 1956. Accordingly, a "branch office" in relation to a company means — (*a*) any establishment described as a branch by the company; or (*b*) any establishment carrying on either the same or substantially the same activity as that carried on by the head office of the company; or (*c*) any establishment engaged in any production, processing or manufacture, but does not include any establishment specified in any order made by the Central Government under section 8. ***Liaison Office:*** A liaison office means a place of business to act as a channel of communication between the principal place of business or Head Office and entities in India. It is not permitted to undertake any commercial/trading/ industrial activity, directly or indirectly, and should maintain itself out of inward remittances received from abroad through normal banking channel.

S. No.	*Points Considered*	*Explanation*
5.	***Eligibility Criteria for Establishment of Branch / Liaison Office in India***	An application from a foreign entity to establish Branch/Liaison Office in India is considered on the basis of two criteria viz, basic and additional: ***Basic criteria*** • *Reserve Bank Route* – Principal business of the foreign entity falls under sectors where 100 per cent foreign direct investment (FDI) is permissible under the automatic route. • *Government Route* – Principal business of the foreign entity falls under the sectors where 100 per cent FDI is not permissible under the automatic route. Applications from entities falling under this category are considered by the Reserve Bank, in consultation with the Government of India, Ministry of Finance. ***Additional criteria*** • *Track Record* o For Branch Office – a profit making track record during the immediately preceding five financial years in the home country. o For Liaison Office – a profit making track record during the immediately preceding three financial years in the home country. • *Net Worth* [total of paid-up capital and free reserves, less intangible assets as per the latest Audited Balance Sheet or Account Statement certified by a Certified Public Accountant or any Registered Accounts Practitioner by whatever name]. o For Branch Office – not less than USD 100,000 or its equivalent.

S. No.	*Points Considered*	*Explanation*
		o For Liaison Office – not less than USD 50,000 or its equivalent. ***Letter of Comfort from Applicants not satisfying the eligibility criteria and are subsidiaries of other companies:*** Applicants that do not satisfy the eligibility criteria and are subsidiaries of other companies may submit a Letter of Comfort from their parent company as per Annex D to AP (DIR Series) Circular No. 23, dated 30-12-2009, subject to the condition that the parent company satisfies the eligibility criteria as prescribed. (*Source: AP* (*DIR Series*) *Circular No. 23, dated 30-12-2009*)
6.	***Application (Form FNC) and Documentation***	Applications in Form FNC [Annex C to AP (DIR Series) Circular No. 23, dated 30-12-2009], duly completed in all respects and signed by the authorized signatory of the foreign entity in the home country may be submitted along with the Letter of Comfort, wherever applicable (Annex D to AP (DIR Series) Circular No. 23, dated 30-12-2009), to the designated AD Category-I (i.e. an AD Category-I bank identified by the applicant with whom they intend to pursue banking relations) for onward transmission to the Chief General Manager-in-Charge, Reserve Bank of India, Foreign Exchange Department, Foreign Investment Division, Central Office, Fort, Mumbai-400 001, along with their comments and recommendations and the prescribed documents (vide item (*viii*) of Form FNC), as stated below: • Copy of the Certificate of Incorporation/Registration attested by the Notary Public in the country of registration. [If the original Certificate is in a language other than in English, the

S. No.	*Points Considered*	*Explanation*
		same may be translated into English and notarized as above and cross verified/attested by the Indian Embassy/Consulate in the home country]. • Latest Audited Balance sheet of the applicant company. [If the applicants' home country laws/regulations do not insist on auditing of accounts, an Account Statement certified by a Certified Public Accountant (CPA) or any Registered Accounts Practitioner by any name, clearly showing the net worth may be submitted] • Bankers' Report from the applicant's banker in the host country/ country of registration showing the number of years the applicant has had banking relations with that bank. The designated AD Category-I bank should exercise due diligence in respect of the applicant's background, antecedents of the promoter, nature and location of activity, sources of funds, etc. and also ensure compliance with the KYC norms before forwarding the application together with their comments/ recommendations to the Reserve Bank (refer AP (DIR Series) Circular No. 24, dated 30-12-2009. ***Note:*** As stated Para 3 of AP (DIR Series) Circular No. 23, dated 30-12-2009, applications from foreign banks and insurance companies will continue to be directly received and examined by the Department of Banking Operations and Development (DBOD), Reserve Bank, Central Office and the Insurance Regulatory and Development Authority (IRDA), respectively. (*Source: AP* (*DIR Series*) *Circular No. 23, dated 30-12-2009*)

S. No.	*Points Considered*	*Explanation*
7.	*Allotment of UIN*	In order to provide a uniform framework, a Unique Identification Number (UIN) would be allotted to both, the existing as well as the new BOs/LOs. The UIN will have to be quoted in all references to the Reserve Bank by the BO/LO and the designated AD Category-I bank. Consequent upon delegation of powers from February 01, 2010 vide AP (DIR Series) Circular No. 24, dated 30-12-2009, existing BO/LO will also have to necessarily approach the Reserve Bank through their designated AD Category -I bank for their requests/references. (*Source: AP* (*DIR Series*) *Circular No. 23, dated 30-12-2009*)
8.	*Obtaining of PAN*	The BOs/LOs shall obtain Permanent Account Number (PAN) from the Income Tax Authorities on setting up of their office in India and report the same in the Annual Activity Certificate. (*Source: AP* (*DIR Series*) *Circular No. 23, dated 30-12-2009*)
9.	*Permitted activities of a Branch Office/Liaison Office*	Permitted activities for a Branch/Liaison Office in India would be as under: ***Branch Office:*** • Export/import of goods. • Rendering professional or consultancy services. • Carrying out research work, in which the parent company is engaged. • Promoting technical or financial collaborations between Indian companies and parent or overseas group company. • Representing the parent company in India and acting as buying/ selling agent in India. • Rendering services in Information Technology and development of software in India.

S. No.	*Points Considered*	*Explanation*
		• Rendering technical support to the products supplied by parent/group companies. • Foreign airline/shipping company. ***Note:*** Normally, the Branch Office should be engaged in the activity in which the parent company is engaged. (*ii*) Retail trading activities of any nature is not allowed for a Branch Office in India[1]. (*iii*) A Branch Office is not allowed to carry out manufacturing or processing activities in India, directly or indirectly[2]. ***Liaison Office:*** • Representing the parent company/ group companies in India. • Promoting export/import from/to India. • Promoting technical/financial collaborations between parent/ group companies and companies in India. • Acting as a communication channel between the parent company and Indian companies. (*Source: AP* (*DIR Series*) *Circular No. 23, dated 30-12-2009*)
10.	***Submission of Annual Activity Certificate***	Earlier, BO/LOs were required to submit Annual Activity Certificate from their Auditors to the Central Office/Regional Office of the Reserve Bank, certifying that the BO/LO had carried out only those activities which were approved by the Reserve Bank. With effect from **February 01, 2010**, the Annual Activity Certificate (AAC) from the Auditors, as at end of March 31, along with the audited Balance Sheet may be submitted on or before September 30 of that year (*earlier*

1 As per Master Circular 11/2010-11, dated 1-7-2010.

2 As per Master Circular 11/2010-11, dated 1-7-2010.

S. No.	*Points Considered*	*Explanation*
		required to be submitted on or before April 30) to the designated AD Category-I bank and a copy thereof to the Directorate General of Income Tax (International Taxation), Drum Shape Building, I.P. Estate, New Delhi 110002, by the following entities: (*a*) In case of a sole BO/LO, by the BO/LO concerned; (*b*) In case of multiple BO/LOs, a combined Annual Activity Certificate in respect of all the Offices in India by the Nodal Office of the BOs/LOs. *Clarification:* It is clarified that in case the annual accounts of the LO/ BO are finalized with reference to a date other than March 31, the AAC along with the audited Balance Sheet may be submitted within six months from the due date of the Balance Sheet. The designated AD Category-I bank shall scrutinize the Annual Activity Certificate and ensure that the activities undertaken by the BO/LO are being carried out in accordance with the terms and conditions of the approval given by the Reserve Bank. In the event of any adverse findings being reported by the Auditor or noticed by the designated AD Category -I bank, the same should be reported immediately by the designated AD Category–I bank to the respective Regional Office of the Reserve Bank in respect of LOs and to the Central Office of the Reserve Bank in the case of BOs, along with the copy of the Annual Activity Certificate and their comments thereon. (*Source: AP* (*DIR Series*) *Circular No. 24, dated 30-12-2009 read alongwith AP* (*DIR Series*) *Circular No. 6, dated 9-8-2010*)

<table>
<tr><th>S. No.</th><th>Points Considered</th><th>Explanation</th></tr>
<tr><td>11.</td><td>Applications for additional offices or undertaking additional activities</td><td>In this respect following points as mentioned in Annex B(ii) to AP (DIR Series) Circular No. 23, dated 30-12-2009 are to be noted:<ul><li>Requests for establishing additional BO/LOs may be submitted to the Reserve Bank in the same manner, as indicated in Annex A (refer paragraphs 18.4 and 18.5).</li><li>Fresh FNC form, duly signed by the authorized signatory of the foreign entity in the home country should be submitted. However, the documents mentioned in form FNC need not be resubmitted, if there are no changes to the documents already submitted earlier.</li><li>If the number of Offices exceeds 4 (i.e. one BO/LO in each zone viz; East, West, North and South), the applicant has to justify the need for additional office/s.</li><li>The applicant may identify one of its Offices in India as the Nodal Office, which will coordinate the activities of all of its Offices in India.</li></ul>Requests for undertaking activities in addition to what has been permitted initially by the Reserve Bank may be submitted through the designated AD Category-I bank to the Chief General Manager-in-Charge, Reserve Bank of India, Foreign Exchange Department, Foreign Investment Division, Central Office, Mumbai, justifying the need with comments of the designated AD Category-I bank.</td></tr>
<tr><td>12.</td><td>Extension of validity of the approval of Liaison Offices</td><td>In this respect following points as mentioned in Annex B(iii) to AP (DIR Series) Circular No. 23, dated 30-12-2009 are to be noted:</td></tr>
</table>

S. No.	*Points Considered*	*Explanation*
		• Requests on letter head of LO for extension of time for continuance of LOs [*other than those from entities in the Insurance sector, banks, NBFCs and Construction and Development sectors (excluding infrastructure development companies*)] may be submitted to the AD Category-I bank concerned under whose jurisdiction the LO/Nodal Office is located before the expiry of the validity of the approval. • Applications from foreign banks and insurance companies will continue to be directly received and examined by the Department of Banking Operations and Development, Reserve Bank and Insurance Regulatory and Development Authority (IRDA) respectively, as hitherto. • No extension would be considered for LOs of entities which are NBFCs and those engaged in Construction and Development sectors (excluding infrastructure development companies). Upon expiry of the validity period, these entities have to either close down or be converted into a Joint Venture (JV)/Wholly Owned Subsidiary (WOS), in conformity with the extant FDI policy. ***Authorisation to designated AD Category-I banks for extension of validity period:*** In terms of AP (DIR Series) Circular No. 24, dated 30-12-2009, the designated AD Category-I bank may, with effect from **February 01, 2010**, extend the validity period of LO/s for a period of **3 years** from the date of expiry of the original approval/extension granted by the Reserve Bank, if the

S. No.	*Points Considered*	*Explanation*
		applicant has complied with the following and the application is otherwise in order. • The LO has submitted the Annual Activity Certificates for the previous years (initially, for existing LO, the designated AD Category-I banks may obtain confirmation from the Regional Office concerned about timely submission of the Certificate for previous years); and • The account of the LO maintained with the designated AD Category-I bank is being operated in accordance with the terms and conditions stipulated in the approval. AS advised by RBI, such extension may be granted, as expeditiously as possible, say within a period of one month from the receipt of the request under intimation to the Regional Office concerned and to the Chief General Manager-in-Charge, Foreign Exchange Department, Reserve Bank of India, Central Office, Mumbai-400 001, as the case may be, quoting the reference number of the original approval letter and the UIN. *Note:* As already mentioned, in the case of LOs of banks and entities engaged in insurance business, the application has to be directly submitted to the Department of Banking Operations and Development, Reserve Bank of India and Insurance Regulatory and Development Authority (IRDA), respectively as stipulated by them, as hitherto. Further, no extension would be considered for LOs of entities which are NBFCs and those engaged in Construction and Development sectors (excluding infrastructure development). Upon expiry of the validity period, these entities have to either close down or be converted into a Joint Venture (JV)/

S. No.	*Points Considered*	*Explanation*
		Wholly Owned Subsidiary (WOS), in conformity with the extant Foreign Direct Investment policy.
13.	***Rejection of an application***	The Reserve Bank or the Government of India, as the case may be, reserves the right to reject an application for non-fulfillment of any other condition/s not specifically referred to in the Annexes to the AP (DIR Series) Circular No. 23, dated 30-12-2009, fulfillment of which, in the opinion of the Reserve Bank/the Government of India, is necessary for grant of such permission or in the public interest. The Reserve Bank or the Government of India, as the case may be, also reserves the right to verify/examine the activities of the BO/LO of the foreign entities established in India and to withdraw the permission already granted, after due notice, if the circumstances so warrant or due to changes in the policy. (*Source: AP* (*DIR Series*) *Circular No. 23, dated 30-12-2009*)
14.	***Winding up of Branch/ Liaison Offices***	Requests for closure of the BO/LO and allowing the remittance of winding up proceeds of BO/LO may be submitted to the designated AD Category-I bank by the BO/LO or their Nodal Office, as the case may be. In terms of AP (DIR Series) Circular No. 24, dated 30-12-2009, the work related to closure of Branch/Liaison Offices, hitherto being done by the Reserve Bank (Central Office in the case of Branch Offices and Regional Office in the case of Liaison Offices), shall be handled by the designated AD Category-I bank with effect from **February 01, 2010**. The closure formalities in respect of BO/LO are to be dealt with in accordance with Regulation 6(1)(*iii*) of FEM

S. No.	*Points Considered*	*Explanation*
		(Remittance of Assets) Regulations 2000, as amended from time to time. In terms of the aforementioned Regulation, following documents are required to bc obtained by the designated AD Category-I bank, while considering the closure of the BO/LO and permitting the remittance of winding up proceeds: (A) Copy of the Reserve Bank's permission/approval from the sectoral regulator(s) for establishing the BO/LO. (B) Auditor's certificate— (*i*) indicating the manner in which the remittable amount has been arrived at and supported by a statement of assets and liabilities of the applicant, and indicating the manner of disposal of assets; (*ii*) confirming that all liabilities in India including arrears of gratuity and other benefits to employees, etc., of the Office have been either fully met or adequately provided for; and (*iii*) confirming that no income accruing from sources outside India (including proceeds of exports) has remained un-repatriated to India. (C) No-objection/Tax Clearance Certificate from Income-Tax authority for the remittance/s. (D) Confirmation from the applicant/ parent company that no legal proceedings in any Court in India are pending and there is no legal impediment to the remittance. (E) A report from the Registrar of Companies regarding compliance

S. No.	*Points Considered*	*Explanation*
		with the provisions of the Companies Act, 1956, in case of winding up of the Office in India. In addition to the above, any other document/s, specified by the Reserve Bank while granting approval may be obtained and verified. The designated AD Category-I banks may also ensure that the BO/LOs had filed their respective **Annual Activity Certificates** with the Reserve Bank for the previous years, in respect of the existing Branch/Liaison Offices. Confirmation about the same may be obtained from the Central Office of the Reserve Bank in the case of BOs and from the Regional Office concerned in the case of LOs. On receipt of the documents as mentioned above, the AD Category-I bank may, after satisfying themselves about the *bonafides*, allow closure of the Office by closing the account maintained with them and remit the proceeds to the overseas entity. ***Reporting:*** Closure of such BO/LO should be reported by the designated AD Category-I bank to the Reserve Bank (the Regional Office concerned for LOs and Central Office for BOs), along with a declaration stating that all the necessary documents submitted by the BO/LO have been scrutinized and found to be in order. If the documents are not found in order, the AD Category-I bank may forward the application to the Reserve Bank, with their observations, for necessary action. ***Retaining of documents:*** All the documents relating to the BO/LO operations may be retained by the AD Category-I bank for verification by the internal auditors of the AD/inspecting officers of the Reserve Bank.

S. No.	*Points Considered*	*Explanation*
		Reference to the RBI: Cases which are not covered under the delegated powers will continue to be referred to the Reserve Bank, by the designated AD Category-I bank. *Note:* Designated Authorised Dealers may allow remittance of winding up proceeds in respect of Offices of banks and insurance companies, after obtaining copies of closure permission from the sectoral regulators along with the documents mentioned above.
15.	***Parking of temporary surplus funds in fixed deposits***	One of the conditions of the approval for establishing branch/liaison office in India pertains to the permissible credits and debits to the bank account in India of the resident outside India. Reserve Bank has been receiving requests from some branches/offices to allow branch/project/ liaison offices in India of foreign firms/ companies for keeping temporary surplus funds lying in their non-interest bearing account in term deposits with any Authorised Dealer. Accordingly, Authorised Dealers have been permitted by RBI to open term deposit account for a period not exceeding 6 months in favour of a branch/ office of a person resident outside India provided the Authorised Dealer is satisfied that the term deposit is out of temporary surplus funds and the branch/office furnishes an undertaking that the maturity proceeds of the term deposit will be utilised for their business in India within 3 months of maturity. *Note:* Such facility of keeping funds in fixed deposits should not be extended to shipping/airline companies. (*Source: AP* (*DIR Series*) *Circular No. 3, dated 6-7-2002*)

S. No.	*Points Considered*	*Explanation*
16.	***Remittance of Profit of a Branch***	A branch office established by a non-resident person after seeking approval from RBI is permitted to remit profit outside India net of applicable Indian taxes on production of following documents to the satisfaction of authorised dealer remitting the funds: (*a*) certified copy of the audited balance-sheet and profit and loss account for the relevant year; (*b*) a Chartered Accountant's certificate certifying,— (*i*) the manner of arriving at the remittable profit, (*ii*) that the entire remittable profit has been earned by undertaking the permitted activities, and (*iii*) that the profit does not include any profit on revaluation of the assets of the branch. (*Source: Regulation 7*)
17.	***Transfer of Assets of Liaison/Branch Office***	Transfer of assets of Liaison/Branch Office to subsidiaries or other Liaison/ Branch Offices is allowed with specific approval of the Central Office of RBI. (*Source: Master Circular 11/2010-11, dated 1-7-2010*)
17A.	**Acquisition of Property**	Branch/Project Offices of a foreign entity, excluding a Liaison Office are permitted to acquire property for their own use and to carry out permitted/incidental activities but not for leasing or renting out the property. However, entities from Pakistan, Bangladesh, Sri Lanka, Afghanistan, Iran, Bhutan or China are not allowed to acquire immovable property in India even for a Branch Office. These entities are allowed to lease such property for a period not exceeding five years. (*Source: Master Circular 11/2010-11, dated 1-7-2010*)

S. No.	*Points Considered*	*Explanation*
17B.	**Opening of non-interest bearing INR current accounts in India**	Branch/Liaison/Project Offices are allowed to open non-interest bearing INR current accounts in India. Such Offices are required to approach their Authorised Dealers for opening the accounts. (*Source: Master Circular 11/2010-11, dated 1-7-2010*)
18.	**Opening of Branches by Foreign Banks**	Foreign banks do not require separate approval under FEMA, for opening branch office in India. Such banks are, however, required to obtain necessary approval under the provisions of the Banking Regulation Act, 1949, from Department of Banking Operations & Development, Reserve Bank. (*Source: Regulation 3 read with Master Circular 11/2010-11, dated 1-7-2010*)
19.	***No prior Approval of RBI in case of establishment of a Unit in SEZ***	In case a company desires to establish a branch or unit in Special Economic Zone (SEZ) for manufacturing activities or for provision of services, no prior approval of RBI is required for such establishment, if the following conditions are satisfied: (*i*) such units belong to those sectors where full foreign direct investment (*i.e.* 100% FDI) is permitted. (*ii*) such units comply with part XI of the Companies Act incorporating Sections 592 to 602. ***Note:*** Part XI of the Companies Act, 1956 contains provisions as to establishment of places of business In India by companies Incorporated outside India I.e. foreign companies. (*iii*) such units function on a stand-alone basis. ***Note:*** "Stand alone basis" means such branch offices would be isolated and restricted to the

S. No.	*Points Considered*	*Explanation*
		Special Economic Zone alone. Thus, no business activity/ transaction will be allowed outside the SEZ in India including with branches/ subsidiaries of its parent office in India. (*iv*) in the event of winding-up of business and for remittance of winding-up proceeds, the branch or unit shall approach an authorised dealer in foreign exchange with the following documents listed in regulation 6(1)(*iii*) of FEM (Remittance of Assets) Regulations, 2000: (*a*) Auditor's certificate,— • indicating the manner of calculating the remittable amount duly supported by a statement of assets and liabilities of the applicant, and also indicating the manner of disposal of assets; • confirming that all liabilities in India including arrears of gratuity and other benefits to employees, etc. of the branch/office have been either fully met or adequately provided for; • confirming that no income accruing from sources outside India (including proceeds of exports) has remained un-repatriated to India.

S. No.	*Points Considered*	*Explanation*
		(*b*) NOC or Tax clearance certificate from Income-tax authority for the remittance; and (*c*) confirmation from the applicant that no legal proceedings in any court in India are pending and there is no legal impediment to the remittance. (*d*) A report from the registrar of companies regarding companies with the provisions of the Companies Act, 1956, in case of winding up of the office in India. (*Source: Regulation 3 and AP* (*DIR Series*) *Circular No. 58, dated 16-1-2004*)
20.	***No prior Approval of RBI in case of establishment of a Liaison Office by an Insurance Company***	In case an insurance company desires to establish a Liaison Office in India, no approval of RBI shall be necessary if such insurance company has obtained approval from the Insurance Regulatory and Development Authority (IRDA). However, the general permission shall be subject to the terms and conditions indicated below and other conditions that may be stipulated by the IRDA from time to time. *Note:* General Permission granted under FEMA 1999 to the foreign insurance company for establishing a liaison office in India is without prejudice to the permissions and approvals, if any, which may be taken by such company under any other law in force. ***Terms and Conditions applicable to the General Permission*** As per AP (DIR Series) Circular No. 39, dated 25-4-2005 following terms and conditions are applicable in case an

S. No.	*Points Considered*	*Explanation*
		overseas insurance company avails general permission for opening its Liaison Office in India: (*i*) *Not to carry on any other activity/new activity or any activity of a trading, commercial or industrial nature:* The Liaison Office in India shall not carry on any activity other than the one for which approval has been granted. Similarly, it shall not, without the prior permission of IRDA/RBI, undertake any new activity or carry on by itself or in partnership or by otherwise associating with others, any activity of a trading, commercial or industrial nature other than the activity for which the approval has been granted by the IRDA/RBI. (*ii*) *Not permitted to enter into any business contracts:* The Liaison Office in India shall not enter into any business contracts in its own name without prior permission of IRDA/RBI. (*iii*) *Not permitted to charge any commission/fess or receive remuneration or earn income:* The Liaison Office in India is not permitted to charge any commission/fees or receive any other remuneration or earn any other income for liaison activities/ services, consultancy services or any other services rendered by it in India, either directly or indirectly, unless approved by the IRDA. (*iv*) *Expenses to be met exclusively from inward remittances:* The entire expenses of the Liaison Office in India will be met

S. No.	*Points Considered*	*Explanation*
		exclusively out of the funds received from abroad through normal banking channels. (*v*) *Not permitted to borrow/lend money or accept deposits:* The Liaison Office in India shall not borrow any money from or lend any money to any person in India nor shall it accept deposits in India. (*vi*) *Not permitted to acquire/hold/ transfer/dispose of any immovable property in India:* The Liaison Office, in India shall not acquire, hold, transfer or dispose of any immovable property in India (except by way of lease for a period not exceeding five years) without obtaining prior permission of RBI under the FEM (Acquisition and Transfer of Immovable Property in India) Regulations, 2000. (*vii*) *Submission of Auditor's Certificate on annual basis:* The Liaison Office in India is required to furnish to the IRDA, on an annual basis, a certificate from the auditor that it has complied with the stipulated terms and conditions of IRDA/RBI and that all the expenses are being met through approved means. (*viii*) *Closure of Liaison Office:* Where Liaison Offices have been established with the approval of IRDA/RBI, their closure will be allowed by IRDA under intimation to RBI. (*ix*) *Not to render any consultancy/ other services:* The Liaison Office in India shall not render any consultancy or any other services

S. No.	*Points Considered*	*Explanation*
		directly/ indirectly by charging or otherwise any fees for such services. (*x*) *No signing/commitment powers:* The Liaison Office in India will not have any signing/commitment powers, except which are required for normal functioning of the office, on behalf of the Head Office. (*xi*) *Permission to open a 'Head Office Account':* The Foreign Insurance Company is permitted to open a 'head office account' in the books of their Liaison Office/s in India, subject to the conditions that: • the credits to the account should represent the funds received from Head Office through normal banking channels for meeting the expenses of the Liaison Office; and • the debits to the account would be raised only for meeting the local expenses of the Liaison Office. (*xiii*) *Verification of activities/affairs:* The activities/affairs of the Liaison Offices may be verified/examined by IRDA/RBI/Government of India by carrying out a scrutiny as and when found necessary. (*xiii*) *Indian legal system to be obeyed in strict sense:* The Liaison office in India shall have to strictly obey and respect the laws in force in India and there shall be no compromise or excuse for the ignorance of the Indian legal system in any manner. (*Source: Regulation 3 and AP (DIR Series) Circular No. 39, dated 25-4-2005*)

S. No.	***Points Considered***	***Explanation***
21.	***No prior Approval of RBI in case of Establishment of Project Office under Specific Circumstances***	Effective from 2nd July 2003, Reserve Bank has granted general permission to a foreign entity for setting up a Project Office in India if the foreign entity has secured from an Indian company a contract to execute a project in India. Other conditions to be fulfilled in this respect are: (*a*) the project is funded by inward remittance from abroad; or (*b*) the project is funded by a bilateral or multilateral International Finance Agency like World Bank or IMF or similar other body; or (*c*) the project has been cleared by an appropriate authority; or (*d*) a company or entity in India awarding the contract has been granted Term Loan by a Public Financial Institution as defined in Section 4A of the Companies Act, 1956 (*refer Note* (*iv*) *below*) or a bank in India for the project. ***Notes:*** **(*i*)** A Project Office so established in India is permitted to undertake or carry on only those activities which are relating and incidental to execution of the project and no other activity. **(*ii*)** Where general permission, as above, is available the Project Office need not submit application in FNC 1. **(*iii*)** Any Project Office not falling under the general permission may approach the respective Regional Office under whose jurisdiction it is situated for necessary approvals. **(*iv*)** Section 4A of the Companies Act, 1956 specifies the following financial institutions as Public Financial Institutions:

S. No.	*Points Considered*	*Explanation*
		(*i*) ICICI Ltd., (*ii*) IFCI Ltd., (*iii*) IDBI; (*iv*) LIC; (*v*) UTI; (*vi*) IDFC Ltd. Further, the Central Government may notify such other institution as public financial institution if it is established by any Central Act or not less than 51% of the paid up share capital of such institution is held or controlled by the Central Government. ***Opening of Foreign Currency Account:*** The Project Office so established in India by the foreign entity may be permitted by the concerned Authorised Dealer to open **non-interest** bearing Foreign Currency Account without seeking prior approval of Reserve Bank. Such account shall be opened subject to the following conditions: (*i*) *Project office established under general/specific permission:* The Project Office must have been established in India, with the general/ specific permission of Reserve Bank, having the requisite approval from the concerned Project Sanctioning Authority; (*ii*) *Provision for payment in foreign currency:* The project sanctioning contract specifically provides for payment in foreign currency; (*iii*) *Single Foreign Currency Account:* Each Project has only one Foreign Currency Account. (*iv*) *Permissible debits and credits:* The permissible debits and credits in the account shall be as under:

S. No.	*Points Considered*	*Explanation*
		• **Debits:** Payment of project related expenditure. • **Credits:** (*a*) Foreign currency receipts from the Project Sanctioning Authority, and (*b*) Remittances from parent/group company abroad or bilateral/multilateral international financing agency. (*v*) *Responsibility of the Authorised Dealer:* The Authorised Dealer opening Foreign Currency Account for a Project Office shall be solely responsible for ensuring that: • only approved debits and credits are allowed in such account • the account is subjected to 100 percent scrutiny by its concurrent auditor. (*vi*) *Closure of the Account:* The Foreign Currency account may be closed at the completion of the Project. *Note:* In terms of AP (DIR Series) Circular No. 2, dated 31.7.2008, AD Category-I banks are allowed to open an additional foreign currency account for each Project Office (established under the general/specific approval of Reserve Bank) subject to the same terms and conditions as applicable to the existing foreign currency account provided that both the foreign currency accounts are maintained with the same AD Category-I bank. ***Treatment with the Foreign Currency Account in case of Dispute:*** In case any dispute arises between the Project Office and the project sanctioning authority or other Government/Non-Government agencies etc., the balance held in such foreign currency account shall be

S. No.	*Points Considered*	*Explanation*
		converted into INR and credited to a special account which shall be dealt with as per the settlement of the dispute. ***Intermittent Remittance:*** The concerned AD bank's branch may, without seeking necessary approval from Reserve Bank, permit intermittent remittances by Project Offices pending winding up/completion of the project if the branch is satisfied with the bona-fides of the transaction and subject to the following conditions: (*i*) *Project Office Submits Auditors'/Chartered Accountants' Certificate* to the effect that sufficient provisions have been made to meet the liabilities in India including Income-tax etc. (*ii*) *Project Office submits an undertaking* that such remittance will, in no way, affect the completion of the Project and that any shortfall of funds for meeting any liability in India will be met by inward remittance. ***Furnishing of Report:*** The foreign company establishing a Project Office in India is required to furnish a report through the concerned AD branch, within two months of such establishment, to the concerned Regional Office of Reserve Bank under whose jurisdiction the Project Office is set up, comprising the following details: (*a*) Name and address of the Foreign Company; (*b*) Reference Number and date of letter issued by the Indian company awarding the contract to execute a project in India; (*c*) Particulars of authority awarding the projects/contract;

S. No.	*Points Considered*	*Explanation*
		(*d*) Total amount of contract; (*e*) Address/e-mail address/telephone no./fax no. and tenure of the Project Office; (*f*) Brief details of the Project undertaken; (*g*) AD branch with whom the foreign currency account has been opened and the foreign currency in which the account is opened, (*h*) An undertaking to the effect that the Project Office is eligible to avail of the General Permission under Regulation 5(*ii*) showing the reason thereof. ***Submission of CA Certificate:*** The Project Office shall submit to the AD branch an annual Certificate from a Chartered Accountant which will: • show the Project Status; and • certify that the accounts of the Project Office have been audited and the activities undertaken are in conformity with the General/Specific permission given by the Reserve Bank. ***Inter Project transfer of Funds not allowed without permission:*** Without prior permission of the concerned Regional Office of the Reserve Bank under whose jurisdiction the Project Office is situated, there will be no inter-project transfer of funds. ***Parking of temporary surplus funds in fixed deposits:*** Please refer details stated against. ***Remittance of surplus on winding up/completion of the Project:*** By amending the provisions of Regulation 6(*iii*) of FEM (Remittance of Assets) Regulations, 2000 (*vide Notification No.*

S. No.	*Points Considered*	*Explanation*
		FEMA 96/2003-RB, dated 2-7-2003), RBI has granted general permission to foreign entities to remit the surplus on winding up/completion of Projects. Authorised Dealers may allow such remittances on receipt of requests from their respective constituents subject to the production of following documents: (*a*) certified copy of the final audited Project accounts; (*b*) a Chartered Accountant's certificate showing the manner of arriving at the remittable surplus; (*c*) income-tax assessment order or either documentary evidence showing payment of income-tax and other applicable taxes, or a Chartered Accountant's certificate stating that sufficient funds have been set aside for meeting all Indian tax liabilities; and (*d*) auditor's certificate stating that no statutory liabilities in respect of the Project are outstanding. (*Source: Regulation 5 as well as 7 and AP* (*DIR Series*) *Circular No. 44, dated 17-5-2005*)

AP (*DIR Series 2011-12*) *Circular No. 88, dated 1-3-2012*

Clarification on Establishment of Branch Offices (BO)/Liaison Offices (LO) in India by Foreign Entities — Delegation of Powers

1. Attention of Authorised Dealer Category-I (AD Category-I) banks is invited to AP (DIR Series) Circular No. 24, dated December 30, 2009 in terms of which powers have been delegated to the AD Category-I bank regarding submission of Annual Activity Certificate by BO/LOs, extension of the validity period of LOs and closure of BO/LOs of foreign entities in India.

2. In the AP (DIR Series) Circular mentioned above, powers as regards the transfer of assets of LO/BO to others have not been delegated. It is, therefore, clarified that transfer of assets of Liaison/Branch Office to subsidiaries or other LO/BO or any other entity is permitted only with the specific approval of the Central Office of the Foreign Exchange Department, Reserve Bank of India.

3. All the other instructions of AP (DIR Series) Circular No. 24, dated December 30, 2009 shall remain unchanged.

4. AD Category-I banks may bring the contents of this circular to the notice of their constituents and customers concerned.

5. The directions contained in this circular have been issued under sections 10(4) and 11(1) of the Foreign Exchange Management Act, 1999 (42 of 1999) and is without prejudice to permissions/approvals, if any, required under any other law.

Appendix 1
THE FOREIGN EXCHANGE MANAGEMENT ACT, 1999

SYNOPSIS

(*Arrangement of Sections*)

CHAPTER I

Preliminary

CHAPTER II

Regulation and Management of Foreign Exchange

CHAPTER III

Authorised person

CHAPTER IV

Contravention and Penalties

CHAPTER V

Adjudication and Appeal

THE FOREIGN EXCHANGE MANAGEMENT ACT, 1999

(42 of 1999)

An Act

to consolidate and amend the law relating to foreign exchange with the objective of facilitating external trade and payments and for promoting the orderly development and maintenance of foreign exchange market in India

BE it enacted by Parliament in the Fiftieth Year of the Republic of India as follows:—

CHAPTER I

Preliminary

1. Short title, extent, application and commencement

(1) This Act may be called the Foreign Exchange Management Act, 1999.

(2) It extends to the whole of India.

(3) It shall also apply to all branches, offices and agencies outside India owned or controlled by a person resident in India and also to any contravention thereunder committed outside India by any person to whom this Act applies.

(4) It shall come into force on such date as the Central Government may, by notification in the Official Gazette,[1] appoint:

Provided that different dates may be appointed for different provisions of this Act and any reference in any such provision to the commencement of this Act shall be construed as a reference to the coming into force of that provision.

COMMENTS

The Parliament has enacted the Foreign Exchange Management Act, 1999 to replace the Foreign Exchange Regulation Act, 1973.

The object of the Act is enumerated in the Statement of Objects and Reasons which are reproduced below:

"1. The Foreign Exchange Regulation Act, 1973 was reviewed in 1993 and several amendments were enacted as part of the on-going process of economic liberalisation relating to foreign investments and foreign trade for closer interaction with the world economy. At that stage, the Central Government decided that a further review of the Foreign Exchange Regulation Act would be

---

1 W.e.f. 1-6-2000, *vide* Notification No. GSR 371(E), dated 1-5-2000.

undertaken in the light of subsequent developments and experience in relation to foreign trade and investment. It was subsequently felt that a better course would be to repeal the existing Foreign Exchange Regulation Act and enact a new legislation. Reserve Bank of India was accordingly asked to undertake a fresh exercise and suggest a new legislation. A Task Force constituted for this purpose submitted its report in 1994 recommending substantial changes in the existing Act.

2. Significant developments have taken place since 1993 such as substantial increase in our foreign exchange reserves, growth in foreign trade, rationalisation of tariffs, current account convertibility, liberalisation of Indian investments abroad, increased access to external commercial borrowings by Indian corporates and participation of foreign institutional investors in our stock markets.

3. Taking into consideration the above facts a Bill to repeal and replace the Foreign Exchange Regulation Act, 1973 was introduced in Lok Sabha on 4th August, 1998. The said Bill was referred to the Standing Committee on Finance, which submitted its report to the House on 23rd December, 1998 with certain modifications and suggestions. Before any decision could be taken by the Central Government on the recommendations of the Standing Committee on Finance, the 12th Lok Sabha was dissolved. Due to the dissolution of the Lok Sabha the Bill also lapsed.

4. After incorporating certain modifications and suggestions of the Standing Committee on Finance, the Central Government has decided to introduce the Foreign Exchange Management Bill and repeal the Foreign Exchange Regulation Act, 1973. The provisions of the Bill aim at consolidating and amending the law relating to foreign exchange with the objective of facilitating external trade and payments and for promoting the orderly development and maintenance of foreign exchange markets in India.

5. The notes on clauses explain in detail various provisions contained in the Bill."

The Act extends to the whole of India and will also apply to all branches, offices and agencies outside India owned or controlled by a person resident in India. It will also be applicable to any contravention committed outside India by any person to whom this Act is applicable.

It will come into force on a date to be notified by the Central Government and different dates may be appointed for different provisions of the Act. Government has notified 1st June, 2000 as the date on which the Act will come into force *vide* Notification No. 371(E), dated 1-5-2000 placed in Annexure III.

2. Definitions

In this Act, unless the context otherwise requires,—

(*a*) "Adjudicating Authority" means an officer authorised under sub-section (1) of section 16;

(*b*) "Appellate Tribunal" means the Appellate Tribunal for Foreign Exchange established under section 18;

(*c*) "authorised person" means an authorised dealer, money changer, off-shore banking unit or any other person for the time being authorised under sub-section (1) of section 10 to deal in foreign exchange or foreign securities;

(*d*) "Bench" means a Bench of the Appellate Tribunal;

(*e*) "capital account transaction" means a transaction which alters the assets or liabilities, including contingent liabilities, outside India of persons resident in India or assets or liabilities in India of persons resident outside India, and includes transactions referred to in sub-section (3) of section 6;

(*f*) "Chairperson" means the Chairperson of the Appellate Tribunal;

(*g*) "chartered accountant" shall have the meaning assigned to it in clause (*b*) of sub-section (1) of section 2 of the Chartered Accountants Act, 1949 (38 of 1949);

(*h*) "currency" includes all currency notes, postal notes, postal orders, money orders, cheques, drafts, travellers cheques, letters of credit, bills of exchange and promissory notes, credit cards or such other similar instruments, as may be notified by the Reserve Bank;

COMMENTS

Debit cards, ATM cards or any other instrument by whatever name called that can be used to create a financial liability have been notified as currency: Notification GSR 402(E), dated 3-5-2000, w.e.f. 1-6-2000.

(*i*) "currency notes" means and includes cash in the form of coins and bank notes;

(*j*) "current account transaction" means a transaction other than a capital account transaction and without prejudice to the generality of the foregoing such transaction includes,—

(*i*) payments due in connection with foreign trade, other current business, services, and short-term banking and credit facilities in the ordinary course of business, (*ii*) payments due as interest on loans and as net income from investments,

(*iii*) remittances for living expenses of parents, spouse and children residing abroad, and

(*iv*) expenses in connection with foreign travel, education and medical care of parents, spouse and children;

(*k*) "Director of Enforcement" means the Director of Enforcement appointed under sub-section (1) of section 36;

(*l*) "export", with its grammatical variations and cognate expressions, means,—

(*i*) the taking out of India to a place outside India any goods,

(*ii*) provision of services from India to any person outside India;

(*m*) "foreign currency" means any currency other than Indian currency;

(*n*) "foreign exchange" means foreign currency and includes,—

(*i*) deposits, credits and balances payable in any foreign currency,

(*ii*) drafts, travellers cheques, letters of credit or bills of exchange, expressed or drawn in Indian currency but payable in any foreign currency,

(*iii*) drafts, travellers cheques, letters of credit or bills of exchange drawn by banks, institutions or persons outside India, but payable in Indian currency;

(*o*) "foreign security" means any security, in the form of shares, stocks, bonds, debentures or any other instrument denominated or expressed in foreign currency and includes securities expressed in foreign currency, but where redemption or any form of return such as interest or dividends is payable in Indian currency;

(*p*) "import", with its grammatical variations and cognate expressions, means bringing into India any goods or services;

(*q*) "Indian currency" means currency which is expressed or drawn in Indian rupees but does not include special bank notes and special one rupee notes issued under section 28A of the Reserve Bank of India Act, 1934 (2 of 1934);

(*r*) "legal practitioner" shall have the meaning assigned to it in clause (*i*) of sub-section (1) of section 2 of the Advocates Act, 1961 (25 of 1961);

(*s*) "Member" means a Member of the Appellate Tribunal and includes the Chairperson thereof;

(*t*) "notify" means to notify in the Official Gazette and the expression "notification" shall be construed accordingly;

(*u*) "person" includes—

(*i*) an individual,

(*ii*) a Hindu undivided family,

(*iii*) a company,

(*iv*) a firm,

(*v*) an association of persons or a body of individuals, whether incorporated or not,

(*vi*) every artificial juridical person, not falling within any of the preceding sub-clauses, and

(*vii*) any agency, office or branch owned or controlled by such person;

(*v*) "person resident in India" means—

(*i*) a person residing in India for more than one hundred and eighty-two days during the course of the preceding financial year but does not include—

(A) a person who has gone out of India or who stays outside India, in either case—

(*a*) for or on taking up employment outside India, or

(*b*) for carrying on outside India a business or vocation outside India, or

(*c*) for any other purpose, in such circumstances as would indicate his intention to stay outside India for an uncertain period;

(B) a person who has come to or stays in India, in either case, otherwise than—

(*a*) for or on taking up employment in India, or

(*b*) for carrying on in India a business or vocation in India, or

(*c*) for any other purpose, in such circumstances as would indicate his intention to stay in India for an uncertain period;

(*ii*) any person or body corporate registered or incorporated in India,

(*iii*) an office, branch or agency in India owned or controlled by a person resident outside India,

(*iv*) an office, branch or agency outside India owned or controlled by a person resident in India;

(*w*) "person resident outside India" means a person who is not resident in India;

(*x*) "prescribed" means prescribed by rules made under this Act;

(*y*) "repatriate to India" means bringing into India the realised foreign exchange and—

(*i*) the selling of such foreign exchange to an authorised person in India in exchange for rupees; or

(*ii*) the holding of realised amount in an account with an authorised person in India to the extent notified by the Reserve Bank,

and includes use of the realised amount for discharge of a debt or liability denominated in foreign exchange and the expression "repatriation" shall be construed accordingly;

(*z*) "Reserve Bank" means the Reserve Bank of India constituted under sub-section (1) of section 3 of the Reserve Bank of India Act, 1934 (2 of 1934);

(*za*) "security" means shares, stocks, bonds and debentures, Government securities as defined in the Public Debt Act, 1944 (18 of 1944), savings certificates to which the Government Savings Certificates Act, 1959 (46 of 1959) applies, deposit receipts in respect of deposits of securities and units of the Unit Trust of India established under sub-section (1) of section 3 of the Unit Trust of India Act, 1963 (52 of 1963) or of any mutual fund and includes certificates of title to securities, but does not include bills of exchange or promissory notes other than Government promissory notes or any other instruments which may be notified by the Reserve Bank as security for the purposes of this Act;

(*zb*) "service" means service of any description which is made available to potential users and includes the provision of facilities in connection with banking, financing, insurance, medical assistance, legal assistance, chit fund, real estate, transport, processing, supply of electrical or other energy, boarding or lodging or both, entertainment, amusement or the purveying of news or other information, but does not include the rendering of any service free of charge or under a contract of personal service;

(*zc*) "Special Director (Appeals)" means an officer appointed under section 17;

(*zd*) "specify" means to specify by regulations made under this Act and the expression "specified" shall be construed accordingly;

(*ze*) "transfer" includes sale, purchase, exchange, mortgage, pledge, gift, loan or any other form of transfer of right, title, possession or lien.

COMMENTS

Section 2 defines thirty-one important terms and expressions used in the Act.

CHAPTER II

Regulation and Management of Foreign Exchange

3. Dealing in foreign exchange, etc.

Save as otherwise provided in this Act, rules or regulations made thereunder, or with the general or special permission of the Reserve Bank, no person shall—

(*a*) deal in or transfer any foreign exchange or foreign security to any person not being an authorised person;

(*b*) make any payment to or for the credit of any person resident outside India in any manner;

(*c*) receive otherwise through an authorised person, any payment by order or on behalf of any person resident outside India in any manner.

Explanation.—For the purpose of this clause, where any person in, or resident in, India receives any payment by order or on behalf of any person resident outside India through any other person (including an authorised person) without a corresponding inward remittance from any place outside India, then, such person shall be deemed to have received such payment otherwise than through an authorised person;

(*d*) enter into any financial transaction in India as consideration for or in association with acquisition or creation or transfer of a right to acquire, any asset outside India by any person.

Explanation.—For the purpose of this clause, "financial transaction" means making any payment to, or for the credit of any person, or receiving any payment for, by order or on behalf of any person, or drawing, issuing or negotiating any bill of exchange or promissory note, or transferring any security or acknowledging any debt.

COMMENTS

This section prohibits dealings in foreign exchange except through an authorised person. It lays down restrictions on dealings in foreign exchange and provides that:

(*a*) no person will deal in or transfer foreign exchange or foreign security to any person who is not an authorised person as defined in section 2(*c*);

(*b*) no person will make any payment to any person resident outside India or to the credit of any such person;

(*c*) no person will receive any payment from or on behalf of any person resident outside India otherwise through an authorised person.

Explanation to clause (*c*) of section 3 further provides that in case any person receives any payment by order or on behalf of any person resident outside India through any other person and even through an authorised person, without a corresponding inward remittance from any place outside India, then receipt of such payment shall be deemed to be otherwise than through an authorised person;

(*d*) no person will enter into a financial transaction in India which is as consideration or is associated with the acquisition or creation or transfer of any asset outside India by any person.

Explanation to clause (*d*) defines the financial transaction as under:

Explanation.—For the purpose of this clause, "financial transaction" means making any payment to, or for the credit of any person, or receiving any payment for, by order or on behalf of any person, or drawing, issuing or negotiating any bill of exchange or promissory note, or transferring any security or acknowledging any debt.

However, RBI is empowered to give general or special permission to any one for dealing in foreign exchange.

Notifications issued under section 3.—Refer Annexure III for text of notifications issued under this section.

4. Holding of foreign exchange, etc.

Save as otherwise provided in this Act, no person resident in India shall acquire, hold, own, possess or transfer any foreign exchange, foreign security or any immovable property situated outside India.

COMMENTS

This section restrains any person resident in India from acquiring, holding, owning, possessing or transferring any foreign exchange, foreign security or any immovable property situated outside India except as specifically provided in the Act.

The terms "foreign exchange" and "foreign security" are defined in sections 2(*n*) and 2(*o*) respectively.

5. Current account transactions

Any person may sell or draw foreign exchange to or from an authorised person if such sale or drawal is a current account transaction:

Provided that the Central Government may, in public interest and in consultation with the Reserve Bank, impose such reasonable restrictions for current account transactions as may be prescribed.

COMMENTS

"Current account transaction" has been defined under section 2(*j*). Any person is free to buy or sell foreign exchange from an authorised person if such transaction is a current account transaction. However, the Central Government may, in consultation with the Reserve Bank of India impose such restrictions on current account transactions as may be considered reasonable.

Rules framed under section 5.—Central Government has, in exercise of the powers conferred under section 46, framed the Foreign Exchange Management (Current Account Transactions) Rules, 2000.

6. Capital account transactions

(1) Subject to the provisions of sub-section (2), any person may sell or draw foreign exchange to or from an authorised person for a capital account transaction.

(2) The Reserve Bank may, in consultation with the Central Government, specify—

(*a*) any class or classes of capital account transactions which are permissible;

(*b*) the limit up to which foreign exchange shall be admissible for such transactions:

Provided that the Reserve Bank shall not impose any restriction on the drawal of foreign exchange for payments due on account of amortization of loans or for depreciation of direct investments in the ordinary course of business.

(3) Without prejudice to the generality of the provisions of sub-section (2), the Reserve Bank may, by regulations prohibit, restrict or regulate the following,—

(*a*) transfer or issue of any foreign security by a person resident in India;

(*b*) transfer or issue of any security by a person resident outside India;

(*c*) transfer or issue of any security or foreign security by any branch, office or agency in India of a person resident outside India;

(*d*) any borrowing or lending in foreign exchange in whatever form or by whatever name called;

(*e*) any borrowing or lending in rupees in whatever form or by whatever name called between a person resident in India and a person resident outside India;

(*f*) deposits between persons resident in India and persons resident outside India;

(*g*) export, import or holding of currency or currency notes;

(*h*) transfer of immovable property outside India, other than a lease not exceeding five years, by a person resident in India;

(*i*) acquisition or transfer of immovable property in India, other than a lease not exceeding five years, by a person resident outside India;

(*j*) giving of a guarantee or surety in respect of any debt, obligation or other liability incurred,—

(*i*) by a person resident in India and owed to a person resident outside India; or

(*ii*) by a person resident outside India.

(4) A person resident in India may hold, own, transfer or invest in foreign currency, foreign security or any immovable property situated outside India if such currency, security or property was acquired, held or owned by such person when he was resident outside India or inherited from a person who was resident outside India.

(5) A person resident outside India may hold, own, transfer or invest in Indian currency, security or any immovable property situated in India if such currency, security or property was acquired, held or owned by such person when he was resident in India or inherited from a person who was resident in India.

(6) Without prejudice to the provisions of this section, the Reserve Bank may by regulation prohibit, restrict, or regulate establishment in India of a branch, office or other place of business by a person resident outside India, for carrying on any activity relating to such branch, office or other place of business.

COMMENTS

This section allows a person to draw or sell foreign exchange from or to an authorised person for a capital account transaction.

Sub-section (2) lays down that the RBI may, in consultation with the Central Government permit any class or classes of capital account transactions and also lay down the limit upto which foreign exchange shall be admissible for such capital account transactions.

However, the Act requires that RBI shall not impose any restriction on the drawal of foreign exchange for payments due on account of amortization of loans or for depreciation of direct investments in the ordinary course of business.

Sub-section (3) allows RBI, to prohibit, restrict or regulate by regulations framed under the Act the transactions specified below:

(*a*) transfer or issue of any foreign security by a person resident in India;

(*b*) transfer or issue of any security by a person resident outside India;

(*c*) transfer or issue of any security or foreign security by any branch, office or agency in India of a person resident outside India;

(*d*) any borrowing or lending in foreign exchange in whatever form or by whatever name called;

(*e*) any borrowing or lending in rupees in whatever form or by whatever name called between a person resident in India and a person resident outside India;

(*f*) deposits between persons resident in India and persons resident outside India;

(*g*) export, import or holding of currency or currency notes;

(*h*) transfer of immovable property outside India, other than a lease not exceeding five years, by a person resident in India;

(*i*) acquisition or transfer of immovable property in India, other than a lease not exceeding five years, by a person resident outside India;

(*j*) giving of a guarantee or surety in respect of any debt, obligation or other liability incurred,—

(*i*) by a person resident in India and owed to a person resident outside India; or

(*ii*) by a person resident outside India.

While sub-section (4) allows a person resident in India to hold, own, transfer or invest in foreign currency, foreign security or any immovable property situated outside India if the same was transacted when he was resident outside India or is inherited from a person who was resident outside India, sub-section (5) allows a person resident outside India to hold, own, transfer or invest in Indian currency, etc. situated in India if the same was transacted by him when he was resident in India or is inherited from a person who was resident in India.

Sub-section (6) gives the powers to the RBI to prohibit, restrict or regulate the establishing of a branch office or other place of business by a person resident outside India in India. Such restrictions, etc. may be imposed through regulations.

Regulations framed under section 6.—Reserve Bank of India has, in exercise of the powers conferred under section 47 framed the following Regulations:—

(*a*) Foreign Exchange Management (Permissible Capital Account Transactions) Regulations, 2000 under sub-section (2);

(*b*) Foreign Exchange Management (Issue of Security in India by a branch, office or agency of a person resident outside India) Regulations, 2000 under sub-section (3)(*c*);

(*c*) Foreign Exchange Management (Borrowing or lending in foreign exchange) Regulations, 2000 under sub-section (3)(*d*);

(*d*) Foreign Exchange Management (Borrowing and lending in rupees) Regulations, 2000 under sub-section (3)(*e*);

(*e*) Foreign Exchange Management (Deposit) Regulations, 2000 under sub-section 3(*f*);

(*f*) Foreign Exchange Management (Export and Import of Currency) Regulations, 2000 under sub-section (3)(*g*);

(*g*) Foreign Exchange Management (Acquisition and transfer of immovable property outside India) Regulations, 2000 under sub-section 3(*h*);

(*h*) Foreign Exchange Management (Guarantees) Regulations, 2000 under sub-section (3)(*j*);

(*i*) Foreign Exchange Management (Transfer or issue of security by a person resident outside India) Regulations, 2000 placed in division 3A;

(*j*) Foreign Exchange Management (Acquisition and transfer of immovable property in India) Regulations, 2000 under sub-section (3)(*i*), placed in division 3A;

(*k*) Foreign Exchange Management (Establishment in India of branch or office or other place of business) Regulations, 2000 under sub-section (6);

(*l*) Foreign Exchange Management (Transfer or issue of any foreign security) (Amendment) Regulations, 2004 under sub-section (3)(*a*);

(*m*) Foreign Exchange Management (Offshore Banking Unit) Regulations, 2002;

(*n*) Foreign Exchange Management (Withdrawal of General Permission to Overseas Corporate Bodies (OCBs)] Regulations, 2003.

7. Export of goods and services

(1) Every exporter of goods shall—

(*a*) furnish to the Reserve Bank or to such other authority a declaration in such form and in such manner as may be specified, containing true and correct material particulars, including the amount representing the full export value or, if the full export value of the goods is not ascertainable at the time of export, the value which the exporter, having regard to the prevailing market conditions, expects to receive on the sale of the goods in a market outside India;

(*b*) furnish to the Reserve Bank such other information as may be required by the Reserve Bank for the purpose of ensuring the realisation of the export proceeds by such exporter.

(2) The Reserve Bank may, for the purpose of ensuring that the full export value of the goods or such reduced value of the goods as the Reserve Bank determines, having regard to the prevailing market conditions, is received without any delay, direct any exporter to comply with such requirements as it deems fit.

(3) Every exporter of services shall furnish to the Reserve Bank or to such other authorities a declaration in such form and in such manner as may be specified, containing the true and correct material particulars in relation to payment for such services.

COMMENTS

This section deals with export of goods and services.

Every exporter is required to furnish to the RBI or any other authority, as may be specified, a declaration, the form and manner of which will be specified, containing true and correct material particulars including the amount representing the full export value, and where such amount cannot be determined at the stage of export, the value which the exporter expects to receive subject to the prevailing market conditions.

Further, RBI may require the exporter to furnish such other information as it may deem necessary for ensuring the realisation of the export proceeds.

RBI may also direct any exporter to comply with such requirements as it may deem fit for ensuring that the export value of the goods is received without any delay.

In case of services also, the exporter is required to give a declaration to RBI or any other authority, in such form as may be specified, giving true and correct particulars in relation to payment for such services.

Regulations framed under section 7.—Reserve Bank of India has, in exercise of the powers conferred by section 47, framed the—

(*a*) Foreign Exchange Management (Export of goods and services) Regulations, 2000 under sub-sections (1)(*a*) and (3).

(*b*) Foreign Exchange Management (Offshore Banking Unit) Regulations, 2002.

8. Realisation and repatriation of foreign exchange

Save as otherwise provided in this Act, where any amount of foreign exchange is due or has accrued to any person resident in India such person shall take all reasonable steps to realise and repatriate to India such foreign exchange within such period and in such manner as may be specified by the Reserve Bank.

COMMENTS

This section casts the responsibility on the persons resident in India who have any amount of foreign exchange due or accrued in their favour to get the same realised and repatriated to India within the period and in the manner specified by RBI.

Regulations framed under section 8.—Reserve Bank of India, in exercise of the powers conferred by section 47 has framed the—

(*a*) Foreign Exchange Management (Realisation, repatriation and Surrender of Foreign Exchange) Regulations, 2000 under this section.

(*b*) Foreign Exchange Management (Offshore Banking Unit) Regulations, 2002.

9. Exemption from realisation and repatriation in certain cases

The provisions of sections 4 and 8 shall not apply to the following, namely:—

(*a*) possession of foreign currency or foreign coins by any person up to such limit as the Reserve Bank may specify;

(*b*) foreign currency account held or operated by such person or class of persons and the limit up to which the Reserve Bank may specify;

(*c*) foreign exchange acquired or received before the 8th day of July, 1947 or any income arising or accruing thereon which is held outside India by any person in pursuance of a general or special permission granted by the Reserve Bank;

(*d*) foreign exchange held by a person resident in India up to such limit as the Reserve Bank may specify, if such foreign exchange was acquired by way of gift or inheritance from a person referred to in clause (*c*), including any income arising therefrom;

(*e*) foreign exchange acquired from employment, business, trade, vocation, services, honorarium, gifts, inheritance or any other legitimate means up to such limit as the Reserve Bank may specify; and

(*f*) such other receipts in foreign exchange as the Reserve Bank may specify.

COMMENTS

The provisions of section 4 relating to holding of foreign exchange and the provisions of section 8 relating to realisation and repatriation of foreign exchange will not apply to the following cases:

(*a*) possession of foreign currency or foreign coins by any person up to such limit as the Reserve Bank may specify;

(*b*) foreign currency account held or operated by such person or class of persons and the limit up to which the Reserve Bank may specify;

(*c*) foreign exchange acquired or received before the 8th day of July, 1947 or any income arising or accruing thereon which is held outside India by any person in pursuance of a general or special permission granted by the Reserve Bank;

(*d*) foreign exchange held by a person resident in India up to such limit as the Reserve Bank may specify, if such foreign exchange was acquired by way of gift or inheritance from a person referred to in clause (*c*), including any income arising therefrom;

(*e*) foreign exchange acquired from employment, business, trade, vocation, services, honorarium, gifts, inheritance or any other legitimate means up to such limit as the Reserve Bank may specify; and

(*f*) such other receipts in foreign exchange as the Reserve Bank may specify.

Regulations under section 9.—Reserve Bank of India has, in exercise of the powers conferred under section 47, framed the—

(*a*) Foreign Exchange Management (Foreign Currency Accounts by a person resident in India) Regulations, 2000 under this section.

(*b*) Foreign Exchange Management (Possession and retention of foreign currency) Regulations, 2000 under clauses (*a*) and (*e*) of this section.

(*c*) Foreign Exchange Management (Offshore Banking Unit) Regulations, 2002.

CHAPTER III

Authorised person

10. Authorised person

(1) The Reserve Bank may, on an application made to it in this behalf, authorise any person to be known as authorised person to deal in foreign exchange or in foreign securities, as an authorised dealer, money changer or off-shore banking unit or in any other manner as it deems fit.

(2) An authorisation under this section shall be in writing and shall be subject to the conditions laid down therein.

(3) An authorisation granted under sub-section (1) may be revoked by the Reserve Bank at any time if the Reserve Bank is satisfied that—

(*a*) it is in public interest so to do; or

(*b*) the authorised person has failed to comply with the condition subject to which the authorisation was granted or has contravened any of the provisions of the Act or any rule, regulation, notification, direction or order made thereunder:

Provided that no such authorisation shall be revoked on any ground referred to in clause (*b*) unless the authorised person has been given a reasonable opportunity of making a representation in the matter.

(4) An authorised person shall, in all his dealings in foreign exchange or foreign security comply with such general or special directions or orders as the Reserve Bank may, from time to time, think fit to give, and, except with the previous permission of the Reserve Bank, an authorised person shall not engage in any transaction involving any foreign exchange or foreign security which is not in conformity with the terms of his authorisation under this section.

(5) An authorised person shall, before undertaking any transaction in foreign exchange on behalf of any person, require that person to make such declaration and to give such information as will reasonably satisfy him that the transaction will not involve, and is not designed for the purpose of any contravention or evasion of the provisions of this Act or of any rule, regulation, notification, direction or order made thereunder, and where the said person refuses to comply with any such requirement or makes only unsatisfactory compliance therewith, the authorised person shall refuse in writing to undertake the transaction and shall, if he has reason to believe that any such contravention or evasion as aforesaid is contemplated by the person, report the matter to the Reserve Bank.

(6) Any person, other than an authorised person, who has acquired or purchased foreign exchange for any purpose mentioned in the declaration made by him to authorised person under sub-section (5) does not use it for such purpose or does not surrender it to authorised person within the specified period or uses the foreign exchange so acquired or purchased for any other purpose for which purchase or acquisition of foreign exchange is not permissible under the provisions of the Act or the rules or regulations or direction or order made thereunder shall be deemed to have committed contravention of the provisions of the Act for the purpose of this section.

COMMENTS

Chapter III deals with the "authorised person". Section 10 provides that the RBI may authorise, in writing, subject to conditions as may be specified, any person who has made an application to it to act as an authorised person and to deal in foreign exchange or in foreign securities or in both, or act as an authorised dealer, money changer or off-share banking unit.

Sub-section (3) empowers RBI to revoke the authorisation granted if it is satisfied that:

(*a*) it is in public interest; or

(*b*) the authorised person has failed to comply with the conditions specified in the authorisation or has contravened the provisions of the Act, or any rule, regulation, notification, direction or order made thereunder. However the authorised person will be given a reasonable opportunity of making representation.

RBI may give general or special directions from time to time as it may think fit to be complied with by the authorised persons while dealing in foreign exchange or foreign security. In case any transaction involving foreign exchange or foreign security is not in conformity with the terms of the authorisation, the authorised person will seek prior permission of the RBI.

In case the authorised person is going to deal in foreign exchange on behalf of any person, it is obligatory upon him to take a declaration and also require such person to furnish such information as will satisfy him that the transaction will not contravene any provisions of the Act or any rules, regulations, notifications, etc. issued thereunder. In case the person refuses to comply with the requirements or makes unsatisfactory compliance, the authorised person may refuse, in writing, to undertake the transaction and where he has reason to believe that such person is contemplating such contravention or evasion, he may report the same to the RBI.

Where the person who has purchased the foreign exchange for any purpose as has been stated by him in the declaration but he does not use it for such purpose or does not surrender the balance to the authorised person or uses it for some other purpose which is not permissible under the Act or the rules, regulations, orders, etc. notified thereunder he will be deemed to have contravened the provisions of the Act for the purpose of section 10.

Regulations framed under section 10.—Reserve Bank of India has, in exercise of the powers conferred under section 47, framed the Foreign Exchange Management (Realisation, repatriation and surrender of foreign exchange) Regulations, 2000 under this section.

11. Reserve Bank's powers to issue directions to authorised person

(1) The Reserve Bank may, for the purpose of securing compliance with the provisions of this Act and of any rules, regulations, notifications or directions

made thereunder, give to the authorised persons any direction in regard to making of payment or the doing or desist from doing any act relating to foreign exchange or foreign security.

(2) The Reserve Bank may, for the purpose of ensuring the compliance with the provisions of this Act or of any rule, regulation, notification, direction, or order made thereunder, direct any authorised person to furnish such information, in such manner, as it deems fit.

(3) Where any authorised person contravenes any direction given by the Reserve Bank under this Act or fails to file any return as directed by the Reserve Bank, the Reserve Bank may, after giving reasonable opportunity of being heard, impose on the authorised person a penalty which may extend to ten thousand rupees and in the case of continuing contravention with an additional penalty which may extend to two thousand rupees for every day during which such contravention continues.

COMMENTS

The RBI is empowered under this section to issue such directions to the authorised persons as it may deem fit. The directions may be with regard to the making of payment or doing or desist from doing any act relating to foreign exchange or foreign security. RBI may further require the authorised person to furnish information in such manner, it may deem fit to ensure the compliance of the provisions of the Act, rules, notifications, etc.

In case the authorised person contravenes any directions issued by the RBI or fails to file any return as directed by RBI, RBI may, after giving an opportunity of being heard, impose penalty on the authorised person which may extend to ten thousand rupees and in the case of a continuing contravention upto two thousand rupees for every day during which such contravention continues.

12. Power of Reserve Bank to inspect authorised person

(1) The Reserve Bank may, at any time, cause an inspection to be made, by any officer of the Reserve Bank specially authorised in writing by the Reserve Bank in this behalf, of the business of any authorised person as may appear to it to be necessary or expedient for the purpose of—

(*a*) verifying the correctness of any statement, information or particulars furnished to the Reserve Bank;

(*b*) obtaining any information or particulars which such authorised person has failed to furnish on being called upon to do so;

(*c*) securing compliance with the provisions of this Act or of any rules, regulations, directions or orders made thereunder.

(2) It shall be the duty of every authorised person, and where such person is a company or a firm, every director, partner or other officer of such company or

firm, as the case may be, to produce to any officer making an inspection under sub-section (1), such books, accounts and other documents in his custody or power and to furnish any statement or information relating to the affairs of such person, company or firm as the said officer may require within such time and in such manner as the said officer may direct.

COMMENTS

This section gives the powers to the Reserve Bank to inspect the authorised persons. According to it, RBI may appoint any officer, in writing, to inspect the business of any authorised person. Such inspection may be for the purpose of:

(*a*) verifying the correctness of any statement, information or particulars furnished to the Reserve Bank;

(*b*) obtaining any information or particulars which such authorised person has failed to furnish on being called upon to do so;

(*c*) securing compliance with the provisions of this Act or of any rules, regulations, directions or orders made thereunder.

Sub-section (2) imposes the liability on the authorised person and in the case of a company or a firm, on every director, partner or officer of such company to furnish all the books of account as well as all other information in such manner as may be directed by such officer.

CHAPTER IV

Contravention and Penalties

13. Penalties

(1) If any person contravenes any provision of this Act, or contravenes any rule, regulation, notification, direction or order issued in exercise of the powers under this Act, or contravenes any condition subject to which an authorisation is issued by the Reserve Bank, he shall, upon adjudication, be liable to a penalty up to thrice the sum involved in such contravention where such amount is quantifiable, or up to two lakh rupees where the amount is not quantifiable, and where such contravention is a continuing one, further penalty which may extend to five thousand rupees for every day after the first day during which the contravention continues.

(2) Any Adjudicating Authority adjudging any contravention under sub-section (1), may, if he thinks fit in addition to any penalty which he may impose for such contravention direct that any currency, security or any other money or property in respect of which the contravention has taken place shall be confiscated to the Central Government and further direct that the foreign exchange holdings, if any of the persons committing the contraventions or any part thereof, shall be brought back into India or shall be retained outside India in accordance with the directions made in this behalf.

Explanation.—For the purposes of this sub-section, "property" in respect of which contravention has taken place, shall include—

(*a*) deposits in a bank, where the said property is converted into such deposits;

(*b*) Indian currency, where the said property is converted into that currency; and

(*c*) any other property which has resulted out of the conversion of that property.

COMMENTS

If any person—

(*a*) contravenes any provision of the Act, or

(*b*) contravenes any rule, regulation, notification, etc. issued under the Act, or

(*c*) contravenes any condition subject to which an authorisation is issued by the RBI,

he will be liable to penalty, on adjudication, upto thrice the sum involved in such contravention if the amount is quantifiable, and in case it is not quantifiable upto two lakh rupees, and where the contravention is a continuing one, further penalty of upto ₹5,000 for every day after the first day during which the fault continues.

Further, the adjudicating authority may direct that any currency, security or any other money or property be confiscated to the government and further direct that the foreign exchange holdings of the person committing the contravention be brought back to India or may be retained outside India in accordance with the directions.

Property for the purpose of sub-section (2) includes:

(*a*) deposits in a bank, where the said property is converted into such deposits;

(*b*) Indian currency, where the said property is converted into that currency; and

(*c*) any other property which has resulted out of the conversion of that property.

14. Enforcement of the orders of adjudicating authority

(1) Subject to the provisions of sub-section (2) of section 19, if any person fails to make full payment of the penalty imposed on him under section 13 within a period of ninety days from the date on which the notice for payment of such penalty is served on him, he shall be liable to civil imprisonment under this section.

(2) No order for the arrest and detention in civil prison of a defaulter shall be made unless the Adjudicating Authority has issued and served a notice upon the defaulter calling upon him to appear before him on the date specified in the notice and to show cause why he should not be committed to the civil prison, and unless the Adjudicating Authority, for reasons in writing, is satisfied.

(*a*) that the defaulter, with the object or effect of obstructing the recovery of penalty, has after the issue of notice by the Adjudicating Authority, dishonestly transferred, concealed, or removed any part of his property, or

(*b*) that the defaulter has, or has had since the issuing of notice by the Adjudicating Authority, the means to pay the arrears or some substantial part thereof and refuses or neglects or has refused or neglected to pay the same.

(3) Notwithstanding anything contained in sub-section (1), a warrant for the arrest of the defaulter may be issued by the Adjudicating Authority if the Adjudicating Authority is satisfied, by affidavit or otherwise, that with the object or effect of delaying the execution of the certificate the defaulter is likely to abscond or leave the local limits of the jurisdiction of the Adjudicating Authority.

(4) Where appearance is not made pursuant to a notice issued and served under sub-section (1), the Adjudicating Authority may issue a warrant for the arrest of the defaulter.

(5) A warrant of arrest issued by the Adjudicating Authority under sub-section (3) or sub-section (4) may also be executed by any other Adjudicating Authority within whose jurisdiction the defaulter may for the time being be found.

(6) Every person arrested in pursuance of a warrant of arrest under this section shall be brought before the Adjudicating Authority issuing the warrant as soon as practicable and in any event within twenty-four hours of his arrest (exclusive of the time required for the journey):

Provided that, if the defaulter pays the amount entered in the warrant of arrest as due and the costs of the arrest to the officer arresting him such officer shall at once release him.

Explanation.—For the purposes of this sub-section, where the defaulter is a Hindu undivided family, the *karta* thereof shall be deemed to be the defaulter.

(7) When a defaulter appears before the Adjudicating Authority pursuant to a notice to show cause or is brought before the Adjudicating Authority under this section, the Adjudicating Authority shall give the defaulter an opportunity showing cause why he should not be committed to the civil prison.

(8) Pending the conclusion of the inquiry, the Adjudicating Authority may, in his discretion, order the defaulter to be detained in the custody of such officer as the Adjudicating Authority may think fit or release him on his furnishing the

security to the satisfaction of the Adjudicating Authority for his appearance as and when required.

(9) Upon the conclusion of the inquiry, the Adjudicating Authority may make an order for the detention of the defaulter in the civil prison and shall in that event cause him to be arrested if he is not already under arrest:

Provided that in order to give a defaulter an opportunity of satisfying the arrears, the Adjudicating Authority may, before making the order of detention, leave the defaulter in the custody of the officer arresting him or of any other officer for a specified period not exceeding fifteen days, or release him on his furnishing security to the satisfaction of the Adjudicating Authority for his appearance at the expiration of the specified period if the arrears are not satisfied.

(10) When the Adjudicating Authority does not make an order of detention under sub-section (9), he shall, if the defaulter is under arrest, direct his release.

(11) Every person detained in the civil prison in execution of the certificate may be so detained,—

(*a*) where the certificate is for a demand of an amount exceeding rupees one crore — up to three years, and

(*b*) in any other case — up to six months:

Provided that he shall be released from such detention on the amount mentioned in the warrant for his detention being paid to the officer-in-charge of the civil prison.

(12) A defaulter released from detention under this section shall not, merely by reason of his release, be discharged from his liability for the arrears but he shall not be liable to be arrested under the certificate in execution of which he was detained in the civil prison.

(13) A detention order may be executed at any place in India in the manner provided for the execution of warrant of arrest under the Code of Criminal Procedure, 1973 (2 of 1974).

COMMENTS

Where the person fails to make the full payment of penalty within ninety days from the date on which the notice for payment of penalty is served on him, he will be liable to civil imprisonment.

The order for arrest and detention of the defaulter will be made only after the adjudicating authority has issued a notice asking the defaulter to appear before the authority on the specified date and to show cause as to why such an order should not be passed against him. The adjudicating authority should be satisfied:

(*a*) that the defaulter, with the object or effect of obstructing the recovery of penalty, has after the issue of notice by the

Adjudicating Authority, dishonestly transferred, concealed, or removed any part of his property, or

(*b*) that the defaulter has, or has had since the issuing of notice by the Adjudicating Authority, the means to pay the arrears or some substantial part thereof and refuses or neglects or has refused or neglected to pay the same.

The adjudicating authority is empowered to issue a warrant for the arrest of the defaulter where there is fear of his absconding or leaving the local limits of the jurisdiction of the authority. Arrest warrant may also be issued where the defaulter fails to appear before the adjudicating authority once the notice has been issued and served under sub-section (1) of this section. The warrant may be executed by any other adjudicating authority where the defaulter is found in its jurisdiction.

The arrested defaulter is required to be brought before the warrant issuing authority within twenty-four hours of his arrest excluding the time taken in the journey. However, if the defaulter pays the amount mentioned in the warrant of arrest plus the costs of arrest to the officer who has come to arrest, he will be released immediately.

Karta would be deemed to be the defaulter in the case of a Hindu undivided family.

The defaulter will be given an opportunity to show cause why he should not be put in detention in a civil prison. The Adjudicating Authority has been empowered to either order the detention of the defaulter pending the conclusion of the inquiry or release him on his furnishing a reasonable security for his appearance. On the completion of the inquiry the defaulter may be put into a civil prison but the Adjudicating Authority may before making the order of detention put the defaulter in the custody of the arresting officer or any other officer with a view to giving the defaulter to make good the arrears. Such order will not be for a period of more than fifteen days. The defaulter may also be released on his furnishing a security to the satisfaction of the adjudicating authority.

If the adjudicating authority does not issue an order of arrest, the defaulter, if under arrest will be released forthwith.

The defaulter will be put into a civil prison:

(*a*) upto three years — where the demand is for over Rupees one crore; and

(*b*) upto six months — in any other case.

However, the defaulter will be released where he pays the amount due to the officer-in-charge of the prison.

The defaulter though released, will not be discharged from his liability for the arrears. The detention order may be executed at any place in India in the similar manner as adopted for execution of warrant of arrest under the Code of Criminal Procedure, 1973.

15. Power to compound contravention

(1) Any contravention under section 13 may, on an application made by the person committing such contravention, be compounded within one hundred and eighty days from the date of receipt of application by the Director of Enforcement or such other officers of the Directorate of Enforcement and officers of the Reserve Bank as may be authorised in this behalf by the Central Government in such manner as may be prescribed.

(2) Where a contravention has been compounded under sub-section (1), no proceeding or further proceeding, as the case may be, shall be initiated or continued, as the case may be, against the person committing such contravention under that section, in respect of the contravention so compounded.

COMMENTS

The Director of Enforcement or such other officers of Directorate of Enforcement or officers of RBI, authorised by the Central Government, may accept the application of the defaulter for compounding within one hundred and eighty days from the date of receipt of application. Where the contravention has been compounded, the defaulter shall not be proceeded further for such contravention.

Rules framed under section 15.—Central Government has, in exercise of the powers conferred under section 46, framed the Foreign Exchange Management (Compounding Proceedings) Rules, 2000.

CHAPTER V

Adjudication and Appeal

16. Appointment of Adjudicating Authority

(1) For the purpose of adjudication under section 13, the Central Government may, by an order published in the Official Gazette, appoint as many officers of the Central Government as it may think fit, as the Adjudicating Authorities for holding an inquiry in the manner prescribed after giving the person alleged to have committed contravention under section 13, against whom a complaint has been made under sub-section (3) (hereinafter in this section referred to as the said person) a reasonable opportunity of being heard for the purpose of imposing any penalty:

Provided that where the Adjudicating Authority is of opinion that the said person is likely to abscond or is likely to evade in any manner, the payment of penalty, if levied, it may direct the said person to furnish a bond or guarantee for such amount and subject to such conditions as it may deem fit.

(2) The Central Government shall, while appointing the Adjudicating Authorities under sub-section (1), also specify in the order published in the Official Gazette their respective jurisdictions.

(3) No Adjudicating Authority shall hold an enquiry under sub-section (1) except upon a complaint in writing made by any officer authorised by a general or special order by the Central Government.

(4) The said person may appear either in person or take the assistance of a legal practitioner or a chartered accountant of his choice for presenting his case before the Adjudicating Authority.

(5) Every Adjudicating Authority shall have the same powers of a civil court which are conferred on the Appellate Tribunal under sub-section (2) of section 28 and—

(*a*) all proceedings before it shall be deemed to be judicial proceedings within the meaning of sections 193 and 228 of the Indian Penal Code, 1860 (45 of 1860);

(*b*) shall be deemed to be a civil court for the purposes of sections 345 and 346 of the Code of Criminal Procedure, 1973 (2 of 1974).

(6) Every Adjudicating Authority shall deal with the complaint under sub-section (2)[1] as expeditiously as possible and endeavor shall be made to dispose off the complaint finally within one year from the date of receipt of the complaint:

Provided that where the complaint cannot be disposed off within the said period, the Adjudicating Authority shall record periodically the reasons in writing for not disposing off the complaint within the said period.

COMMENTS

The Central Government may appoint any number of its officers as adjudicating authorities for the purpose of holding inquiry under section 13. The Central Government will also specify the jurisdiction of such authorities.

The adjudicating authority will hold an enquiry only upon a written complaint by any officer authorised by a general or special order of the Central Government. The person alleged to have committed the contravention will be given a reasonable opportunity of being heard. He may take the assistance of a legal practitioner or a chartered accountant to present his case before the adjudicating authority.

The adjudicating authority will have the same powers as are given to the Appellate Tribunal under section 28(2). All the proceedings before it shall be deemed to be judicial proceedings within the meaning of sections 193 and 228 of the Indian Penal Code and it will be deemed to be a civil

1 *Sic.* Should be sub-section (3).

court for the purposes of sections 345 and 346 of the Code of Criminal Procedure.

The adjudicating authority will deal with the enquiry expeditiously and try to complete the same finally within one year and where there is delay in the same it will record periodically, in writing, the reasons for the delay.

Notifications under section 16.—Refer Annexure III for text of notifications issued under this section defining the jurisdiction of various adjudicating authorities.

Rules framed under section 16.—Central Government has, in exercise of the powers conferred under section 46, framed the Foreign Exchange Management (Adjudication Proceedings and Appeal) Rules, 2000.

17. Appeal to Special Director (Appeals)

(1) The Central Government shall, by notification, appoint one or more Special Directors (Appeals) to hear appeals against the orders of the Adjudicating Authorities under this section and shall also specify in the said notification the matter and places in relation to which the Special Director (Appeals) may exercise jurisdiction.

(2) Any person aggrieved by an order made by the Adjudicating Authority, being an Assistant Director of Enforcement or a Deputy Director of Enforcement, may prefer an appeal to the Special Director (Appeals)

(3) Every appeal under sub-section (1) shall be filed within forty-five days from the date on which the copy of the order made by the Adjudicating Authority is received by the aggrieved person and it shall be in such form, verified in such manner and be accompanied by such fee as may be prescribed:

Provided that the Special Director (Appeals) may entertain an appeal after the expiry of the said period of forty-five days, if he is satisfied that there was sufficient cause for not filing it within that period.

(4) On receipt of an appeal under sub-section (1), the Special Director (Appeals) may after giving the parties to the appeal an opportunity of being heard, pass such order thereon as he thinks fit confirming, modifying or setting aside the order appealed against.

(5) The Special Director (Appeals) shall send a copy of every order made by him to the parties to appeal and to the concerned Adjudicating Authority.

(6) The Special Director (Appeals) shall have the same powers of a civil court which are conferred on the Appellate Tribunal under sub-section (2) of section 28 and—

(*a*) all proceedings before him shall be deemed to be judicial proceedings within the meaning of sections 193 and 228 of the Indian Penal Code, 1860 (45 of 1860);

(*b*) shall be deemed to be a civil court for the purposes of sections 345 and 346 of the Code of Criminal Procedure, 1973 (2 of 1974).

COMMENTS

The Central Government will appoint Special Director (Appeals) to hear appeals against the order of the adjudicating authority. The Government will also specify the matters and also the jurisdiction of such Special Director (Appeals).

Any person aggrieved by the order of the adjudicating authority may prefer an appeal within 45 days of the receipt of the order and it shall be in such form, verified in such manner and be accompanied by such fee as may be prescribed. The Special Director (Appeals) may, entertain the appeal after the forty-five day period if it is satisfied that there was sufficient cause for not filing the appeal within the period.

The Special Director (Appeals) may, after giving reasonable opportunity of being heard to both the parties pass such order as it may deem fit. Copy of the order will be sent to the parties to appeal as well as the adjudicating authority.

The Special Director (Appeals) will have the same powers as are given to the Appellate Tribunal under section 28(2). All the proceedings before him shall be deemed to be judicial proceedings within the meaning of sections 193 and 228 of the Indian Penal Code and it will be deemed to be a civil court for the purposes of sections 345 and 346 of the Code of Criminal Procedure, 1973.

Rules framed under section 17.—Central Government has, in exercise of powers conferred by section 46, framed the Foreign Exchange Management (Adjudication Proceedings and Appeal) Rules, 2000.

Appointment of Special Director (Appeals).—Central Government has, *vide* Notification No. 12/2002, dated 27-2-2002, appointed Mr. Anil Kumar Jain, Commissioner of Income-tax (Appeals) Delhi as the Special Director (Appeals) to hear appeals against the orders of the Adjudicating Authorities under all the zones of Directorate of Enforcement. The notification is placed in Annexure III.

18. Establishment of Appellate Tribunal

The Central Government shall, by notification, establish an Appellate Tribunal to be known as the Appellate Tribunal for Foreign Exchange to hear appeals against the orders of the Adjudicating Authorities and the Special Director (Appeals) under this Act.

COMMENTS

Central Government has established the Appellate Tribunal for Foreign Exchange at New Delhi *vide* Notification No. 531(E), dated 1-6-2000, reproduced in Annexure III.

The address of the Tribunal is as under:

The Appellate Tribunal for Foreign Exchange,

4th Floor,

B Wing,

Janpath Bhawan,

Janpath

New Delhi

Phone: 23714281

19. Appeal to Appellate Tribunal

(1) Save as provided in sub-section (2), the Central Government or any person aggrieved by an order made by an Adjudicating Authority other than those referred to in sub-section (1) of section 17, or the Special Director (Appeals), may prefer an appeal to the Appellate Tribunal:

Provided that any person appealing against the order of the Adjudicating Authority or the Special Director (Appeals) levying any penalty, shall while filing the appeal, deposit the amount of such penalty with such authority as may be notified by the Central Government:

Provided further that where in any particular case, the Appellate Tribunal is of the opinion that the deposit of such penalty would cause undue hardship to such person, the Appellate Tribunal may dispense with such deposit subject to such conditions as it may deem fit to impose so as to safeguard the realisation of penalty.

(2) Every appeal under sub-section (1) shall be filed within a period of forty-five days from the date on which a copy of the order made by the Adjudicating Authority or the Special Director (Appeals) is received by the aggrieved person or by the Central Government and it shall be in such form verified in such manner and be accompanied by such fee as may be prescribed:

Provided that the Appellate Tribunal may entertain an appeal after the expiry of the said period of forty-five days if it is satisfied that there was sufficient cause for not filing it within that period.

(3) On receipt of an appeal under sub-section (1), the Appellate Tribunal may, after giving the parties to the appeal an opportunity of being heard, pass such orders thereon as it thinks fit, confirming, modifying or setting aside the order appealed against.

(4) The Appellate Tribunal shall send a copy of every order made by it to the parties to the appeal and to the concerned Adjudicating Authority or the Special Director (Appeals) as the case may be.

(5) The appeal filed before the Appellate Tribunal under sub-section (1) shall be dealt with by it as expeditiously as possible and endeavour shall be made by it to dispose of the appeal finally within one hundred and eighty days from the date of receipt of the appeal:

Provided that where any appeal could not be disposed off within the said period of one hundred and eighty days, the Appellate Tribunal shall record its reasons in writing for not disposing off the appeal within the said period.

(6) The Appellate Tribunal may, for the purpose of examining the legality, propriety or correctness of any order made by the Adjudicating Authority under section 16 in relation to any proceeding, on its own motion or otherwise, call for the records of such proceedings and make such order in the case as it thinks fit.

COMMENTS

The Central Government will constitute the Appellate Tribunal for Foreign Exchange to hear appeals against the orders of the Special Director (Appeals) as well as appeals against the orders of the adjudicating authority on matters other than those specified in section 17. The Tribunal has been established at New Delhi.

The person appealing against the order has to deposit the amount of penalty, while filing the appeal, with such authority as may be notified by the Central Government. Deputy Director of the Directorate of Enforcement of the concerned zone has been authorised to accept the deposit of penalty *vide* Notification No. 537(E), dated 1-6-2000, reproduced in Annexure III. However, the Appellate Tribunal may waive this requirement if it is satisfied that it would cause undue hardship to such person.

The appeal has to be filed within forty-five days of the receipt of the order by the aggrieved person or by the Central Government and it has to be in such form, verified in such manner and be accompanied with such fee as may be prescribed. The Appellate Tribunal may, however accept the appeal even after the 45 days period where it is satisfied that there was sufficient cause for not filing the appeal within the period.

The Appellate Tribunal, after giving due opportunity of being heard to all the parties would pass its order confirming, modifying or setting aside the order appealed against. The Tribunal will take up all appeals expeditiously and try to dispose off the same within 180 days from the date of receipt of the appeal and where it cannot dispose off the appeal within the period, the Tribunal will record the reasons in writing. A copy of the order of the Appellate Tribunal will be given to the parties to the appeal as well as to the concerned adjudicating authority or the Special Director (Appeals), as the case may be.

The Appellate Tribunal is also empowered to examine the legality, propriety or correctness of any order of the adjudicating authority passed under section 16. It can on its own motion call for the records of any proceeding and make such order as it thinks fit.

Rules framed under section 19.—Central Government has, in exercise of the powers conferred by section 46, framed the Foreign Exchange Management (Adjudication Proceedings and Appeal) Rules, 2000.

20. Composition of Appellate Tribunal

(1) The Appellate Tribunal shall consist of a Chairperson and such number of Members as the Central Government may deem fit.

(2) Subject to the provisions of this Act,—

(*a*) the jurisdiction of the Appellate Tribunal may be exercised by Benches thereof;

(*b*) a Bench may be constituted by the Chairperson with one or more Members as the Chairperson may deem fit;

(*c*) the Benches of the Appellate Tribunal shall ordinarily sit at New Delhi and at such other places as the Central Government may, in consultation with the Chairperson, notify;

(*d*) the Central Government shall notify the areas in relation to which each Bench of the Appellate Tribunal may exercise jurisdiction.

(3) Notwithstanding anything contained in sub-section (2), the Chairperson may transfer a member from one Bench to another Bench.

(4) If at any stage of the hearing of any case or matter it appears to the Chairperson or a Member that the case or matter is of such a nature that it ought to be heard by a Bench consisting of two Members, the case or matter may be transferred by the Chairperson or, as the case may be, referred to him for transfer, to such Bench as the Chairperson may deem fit.

COMMENTS

The Appellate Tribunal will consist of a chairperson and such number of members as the Central Government may deem fit.

The benches of the Appellate Tribunal will exercise the jurisdiction of the Appellate Tribunal and they will normally sit at New Delhi and at other places as the Central Government may, in consultation with the chairperson notify.

The bench may consist of one or more members and the chairperson may transfer a member from one bench to another. The areas in relation to which the benches will exercise their jurisdiction will be notified by the Central Government.

Where a single member bench or the chairperson during the course of the proceedings feel that the case or matter is such that it should be heard by a bench of two members the chairperson may transfer the case to such a bench as he deems fit.

Constitution of Benches.—The chairperson of the Appellate Tribunal has constituted the following benches:

(*a*) Two single member Benches one consisting of the chairperson and the other consisting of a member, and

(*b*) One Division Bench consisting of the chairperson and the member.

The notification is reproduced in Annexure III.

21. Qualifications for appointment of Chairperson, member and 'Special Director (Appeals)

(1) A person shall not be qualified for appointment as the Chairperson or a Member unless he—

(*a*) in the case of Chairperson, is or has been, or is qualified to be, a Judge of a High Court; and

(*b*) in the case of a Member, is or has been, or is qualified to be, a District Judge.

(2) A person shall not be qualified for appointment as a Special Director (Appeals) unless he—

(*a*) has been a member of the Indian Legal Service and has held a post in Grade I of that Service; or

(*b*) has been a member of the Indian Revenue Service and has held a post equivalent to a Joint Secretary to the Government of India.

COMMENTS

The chairperson or any member of the Tribunal, to qualify for appointment must be—

(*a*) in the case of chairperson, be qualified to be a judge of a High Court or must be or have been a judge of a High Court, and

(*b*) in the case of a member, is or has been or be qualified to be a District Judge.

A person will not qualify to act as a Special Director (Appeals) unless he—

(*a*) has been a member of the Indian Legal Service and has held a post in Grade I of that Service; or (*b*) has been a member of the Indian Revenue Service and has held a post equivalent to a Joint Secretary to the Government of India.

22. Term of office

The Chairperson and every other Member shall hold office as such for a term of five years from the date on which he enters upon his office:

Provided that no Chairperson or other Member shall hold office as such after he has attained,—

(*a*) in the case of the Chairperson, the age of sixty-five years;

(*b*) in the case of any other Member, the age of sixty-two years.

COMMENTS

The chairperson and the members will hold office for a period of five years from the date on which they enter the office. The maximum age of chairperson will be sixty-five years and in case of members it will be sixty-two years.

23. Terms and conditions of service

The salary and allowances payable to and the other terms and conditions of service of the Chairperson, other Members and the Special Director (Appeals) shall be such as may be prescribed:

Provided that neither the salary and allowances nor the other terms and conditions of service of the Chairperson or a Member shall be varied to his disadvantage after appointment.

COMMENTS

The salary, allowances, etc. and the conditions of service of the chairperson, the members and the Special Director (Appeals) shall be prescribed. However none of the conditions, salary, etc. be modified during their period of appointments to their detriment.

Central Government has notified the Appellate Tribunal for Foreign Exchange (Recruitment, Salary and Allowances and other Conditions of Service of Chairperson and Members) Rules, 2000.

24. Vacancies

If, for reason other than temporary absence, any vacancy occurs in the office of the Chairperson or a Member, the Central Government shall appoint another person in accordance with the provisions of this Act to fill the vacancy and the proceedings may be continued before the Appellate Tribunal from the stage at which the vacancy is filled.

COMMENTS

The Central Government will fill the vacancies in the office of chairperson and the members in accordance with the provisions of the Act.

25. Resignation and removal

(1) The Chairperson or a Member may, by notice in writing under his hand addressed to the Central Government, resign his office:

Provided that the Chairperson or a Member shall, unless he is permitted by the Central Government to relinquish his office sooner, continue to hold office until the expiry of three months from the date of receipt of such notice or until a person duly appointed as his successor enters upon his office or until the expiry of term of office, whichever is the earliest.

(2) The Chairperson or a Member shall not be removed from his office except by an order by the Central Government on the ground of proved misbehaviour or incapacity after an inquiry made by such person as the President may appoint for this purpose in which the Chairperson or a Member concerned has been informed of the charges against him and given a reasonable opportunity of being heard in respect of such charges.

COMMENTS

The chairperson or any member may resign from the office by giving notice in writing to the Central Government. However, the chairperson or such member will continue in office for a period of three months or unless and until the successor takes his place or until the expiry of his term in office, whichever is earlier.

The Central Government may remove the chairperson or a member on the ground of proved misbehaviour or incapacity after an inquiry has been conducted by any person appointed by the President and after giving due opportunity of being heard to such person.

26. Member to act as Chairperson in certain circumstances

(1) In the event of the occurrence of any vacancy in the office of the Chairperson by reason of his death, resignation or otherwise, the senior-most member, shall act as the Chairperson until the date on which a new Chairperson, appointed in accordance with the provisions of this Act to fill such vacancy, enters upon his office.

(2) When the Chairperson is unable to discharge his functions owing to absence, illness or any other cause, the senior-most member, shall discharge the functions of the Chairperson until the date on which the Chairperson resumes his duties.

COMMENTS

The seniormost member of the Appellate Tribunal will act as the chairperson in the case of vacancy in the seat due to death or retirement or resignation of the chairperson. He will continue to hold office till the new chairperson joins his office. Similarly, where the chairperson is unable to discharge his functions owing to absence, illness, etc. the seniormost member will act as chairperson during such period.

27. Staff of Appellate Tribunal and Special Director (Appeals)

(1) The Central Government shall provide the Appellate Tribunal and the Special Director (Appeals) with such officers and employees as it may deem fit.

(2) The officers and employees of the Appellate Tribunal and office of the Special Director (Appeals) shall discharge their functions under the general superintendence of the Chairperson and the Special Director (Appeals), as the case may be.

(3) The salaries and allowances and other conditions of service of the officers and employees of the Appellate Tribunal and Office of the Special Director (Appeals) shall be such as may be prescribed.

COMMENTS

The Appellate Tribunal and the Special Director (Appeals) will be provided with the requisite staff who will work under the general superintendence of the Chairperson or the Special Director (Appeals), as the case may be.

28. Procedure and powers of Appellate Tribunal and Special Director (Appeals)

(1) The Appellate Tribunal and the Special Director (Appeals) shall not be bound by the procedure laid down by the Code of Civil Procedure, 1908 (5 of 1908), but shall be guided by the principles of natural justice and, subject to the other provisions of this Act, the Appellate Tribunal and the Special Director (Appeals) shall have powers to regulate its own procedure.

(2) The Appellate Tribunal and the Special Director (Appeals) shall have, for the purposes of discharging its functions under this Act, the same powers as are vested in a civil court under the Code of Civil Procedure, 1908 (5 of 1908) while trying a suit, in respect of the following matters, namely:—

(*a*) summoning and enforcing the attendance of any person and examining him on oath;

(*b*) requiring the discovery and production of documents;

(*c*) receiving evidence on affidavits;

(*d*) subject to the provisions of sections 123 and 124 of the Indian Evidence Act, 1872 (1 of 1872), requisitioning any public record or document or copy of such record or document from any office;

(*e*) issuing commissions for the examination of witnesses or documents;

(*f*) reviewing its decisions;

(*g*) dismissing a representation of default or deciding it *ex parte*;

(*h*) setting aside any order of dismissal of any representation for default or any order passed by it *ex parte*; and

(*i*) any other matter which may be prescribed by the Central Government.

(3) An order made by the Appellate Tribunal or the Special Director (Appeals) under this Act shall be executable by the Appellate Tribunal or the Special Director (Appeals) as a decree of civil court and, for this purpose, the Appellate Tribunal and the Special Director (Appeals) shall have all the powers of a civil court.

(4) Notwithstanding anything contained in sub-section (3), the Appellate Tribunal or the Special Director (Appeals) may transmit any order made by it to a civil court having local jurisdiction and such civil court shall execute the order as if it were a decree made by that court.

(5) All proceedings before the Appellate Tribunal and the Special Director (Appeals) shall be deemed to be judicial proceedings within the meaning of sections 193 and 228 of the Indian Penal Code, 1860 (45 of 1860) and the Appellate Tribunal shall be deemed to be a civil court for the purposes of sections 345 and 346 of the Code of Criminal Procedure, 1973 (2 of 1974).

COMMENTS

The Appellate Tribunal and the Special Director (Appeals) shall be guided by the principles of natural justice and shall not be bound by the procedure laid down in the Code of Civil Procedure, 1908. Both the authorities shall, subject to the provisions of this Act, have powers to regulate their own procedure.

The Appellate Tribunal and the Special Director (Appeals) will have the same powers as are vested in a civil court under the Code of Civil Procedure, 1908 while trying a suit, in respect of the following matters, namely—

(*a*) summoning and enforcing the attendance of any person and examining him on oath;

(*b*) requiring the discovery and production of documents;

(*c*) receiving evidence on affidavits;

(*d*) subject to the provisions of sections 123 and 124 of the Indian Evidence Act, 1872 (1 of 1872), requisitioning any public record or documents or copy of such record or document from any office;

(*e*) issuing commissions for the examination of witnesses or documents;

(*f*) reviewing its decisions;

(*g*) dismissing a representation of default or deciding it *ex parte*;

(*h*) setting aside any order of dismissal of any representation for default or any order passed by it *ex parte*; and

(*i*) any other matter which may be prescribed by the Central Government.

The orders made by the Appellate Tribunal or the Special Director (Appeals) under this Act will be executable as a decree of a civil court and both the authorities will be vested with the powers of a civil court. They may transmit any order made by them to a civil court having local jurisdiction and such civil court will execute the order as if it were a decree made by that court.

All the proceedings before the Appellate Tribunal and the Special Director (Appeals) will be deemed to be judicial proceedings within the meaning of sections 193 and 228 of the Indian Penal Code, 1860. Further the Appellate Tribunal will be deemed to be a civil court for the purposes of sections 345 and 346 of the Code of Criminal Procedure, 1973.

29. Distribution of business amongst Benches

Where Benches are constituted, the Chairperson may, from time to time, by notification, make provisions as to the distribution of the business of the Appellate Tribunal amongst the Benches and also provide for the matters which may be dealt with by each Bench.

COMMENTS

The chairperson may by notification distribute the business of the Appellate Tribunal among the benches and may also provide for matters which may be dealt with by each Bench.

30. Power of Chairperson to transfer cases

On the application of any of the parties and after notice to the parties, and after hearing such of them as he may desire to be heard, or on his own motion without such notice, the Chairperson may transfer any case pending before one Bench, for disposal, to any other Bench.

COMMENTS

The chairperson is empowered to transfer any case from one bench to another either on his own motion or on the application of any of the parties after giving notice to the parties and hearing them, if he so desires.

31. Decision to be by majority

If the Members of a Bench consisting of two Members differ in opinion on any point, they shall state the point or points on which they differ, and make a reference to the Chairperson who shall either hear the point or points himself or refer the case for hearing on such point or points by one or more of the other Members of the Appellate Tribunal and such point or points shall be decided according to the opinion of the majority of the Members of the Appellate Tribunal who have heard the case, including those who first heard it.

COMMENTS

Where a bench consisting of two members have difference of opinion on any point, they will state the point or points on which they differ and refer the same to the chairperson who may either hear himself or refer the same to other member or members of the Tribunal and the same will be decided by a majority of members including those who heard it first.

32. Right of appellant to take assistance of legal practitioner or Chartered Accountant and of Government, to appoint presenting officers

(1) A person preferring an appeal to the Appellate Tribunal or the Special Director (Appeals) under this Act may either appear in person or take the assistance of a legal practitioner or a Chartered Accountant of his choice to present his case before the Appellate Tribunal or the Special Director (Appeals), as the case may be.

(2) The Central Government may authorise one or more legal practitioners or a Chartered Accountants or any of its officers to act as presenting officers and every person so authorised may present the case with respect to any appeal before the Appellate Tribunal or the Special Director (Appeals), as the case may be.

COMMENTS

Person making an appeal to the Appellate Tribunal or the Special Director (Appeals) may appear in person or may take the assistance of a legal practitioner or a Chartered Accountant. At the same time, the Central Government may also appoint one or more legal practitioners or Chartered Accountants or any other officer to act as presenting officers before the Appellate Tribunal or the Special Director (Appeals), as the case may be.

33. Members, etc., to be public servants

The Chairperson, Members and other officers and employees of the Appellate Tribunal the Special Director (Appeals) and the Adjudicating Authority shall be deemed to be public servants within the meaning of section 21 of the Indian Penal Code, 1860 (45 of 1860).

COMMENTS

According to this section the Chairperson, Members, officers and other employees of the Appellate Tribunal and the Special Director (Appeals) and the Adjudicating Authority will be public servants within the meaning of section 21 of the Indian Penal Code.

34. Civil court not to have jurisdiction

No civil court shall have jurisdiction to entertain any suit or proceeding in respect of any matter which an Adjudicating Authority or the Appellate Tribunal or the Special Director (Appeals) is empowered by or under this Act to determine and no injunction shall be granted by any court or other authority in respect of any action taken or to be taken in pursuance of any power conferred by or under this Act.

COMMENTS

The civil court will not have any jurisdiction in respect of any matter under this Act which the Adjudicating Authority, Special Director (Appeals) or the Appellate Tribunal is empowered to determine. Further no court will grant injunction in respect of any action taken or to be taken under the Act.

35. Appeal to High Court

Any person aggrieved by any decision or order of the Appellate Tribunal may file an appeal to the High Court within sixty days from the date of communication of the decision or order of the Appellate Tribunal to him on any question of law arising out of such order:

Provided that the High Court may, if it is satisfied that the appellant was prevented by sufficient cause from filing the appeal within the said period, allow it to be filed within a further period not exceeding sixty days.

Explanation.—In this section "High Court" means—

(*a*) the High Court within the jurisdiction of which the aggrieved party ordinarily resides or carries on business or personally works for gain; and

(*b*) where the Central Government is the aggrieved party, the High Court within the jurisdiction of which the respondent, or in a case where there are more than one respondent, any of the respondents, ordinarily resides or carries on business or personally works for gain.

COMMENTS

Where a person is aggrieved by the order of the Appellate Tribunal he can file an appeal with the High Court within sixty days from the date of communication of the order to him on any question of law arising out of such order. The High Court may allow the person to file the appeal within a further period of sixty days if it is satisfied that the person was prevented by sufficient cause from filing the appeal.

High Court for section 35 means:

(*a*) the High Court within the jurisdiction of which the aggrieved party ordinarily resides or carries on business or personally works for gain; and

(*b*) where the Central Government is the aggrieved party, the High Court within the jurisdiction of which the respondent, or in a case where there are more than one respondent, any of the respondents, ordinarily resides or carries on business or personally works for gain.

CHAPTER VI

Directorate of Enforcement

36. Directorate of Enforcement

(1) The Central Government shall establish a Directorate of Enforcement with a Director and such other officers or class of officers as it thinks fit, who shall be called officers of Enforcement, for the purposes of this Act.

(2) Without prejudice to provisions of sub-section (1), the Central Government may authorise the Director of Enforcement or an Additional Director of Enforcement or a Special Director of Enforcement or a Deputy Director of Enforcement to appoint officers of Enforcement below the rank of an Assistant Director of Enforcement.

(3) Subject to such conditions and limitations as the Central Government may impose, an officer of Enforcement may exercise the powers and discharge the duties conferred or imposed on him under this Act.

COMMENTS

Section 36 requires the Central Government to establish a Directorate of Enforcement. The Directorate will comprise of a Director and such other officers as it may think fit. The Director of Enforcement or an Additional/ Special/Deputy Director of Enforcement may be authorised to appoint officers below the rank of an Assistant Director of Enforcement. The officers of Enforcement will exercise the powers and discharge the duties conferred on them.

The Central Government has established the Directorate of Enforcement with following officers as "Officers of Enforcement" for the purposes of this Act, namely:—

(*a*) Director of Enforcement;

(*b*) Special Director of Enforcement;

(*c*) Additional Director of Enforcement;

(*d*) Deputy Director of Enforcement;

(*e*) Deputy Legal Adviser;

(*f*) Assistant Director of Enforcement; and

(*g*) Assistant Legal Adviser.

vide Notification No. 534(E), dated 1-6-2000, reproduced in Annexure III.

The Director of Enforcement has been authorised to appoint the Chief Enforcement Officer, Enforcement Officer and Assistant Enforcement Officer *vide* Notification No. 536(E), dated 1-6-2000, reproduced in Annexure III. Central Government has notified that the officers holding office under the Foreign Exchange Regulation Act, 1973 as Chief

Enforcement Officers, Enforcement Officers and Assistant Enforcement Officers are appointed as 'Officers of Enforcement' under FEMA w.e.f. 1-6-2000. [Notification No. 797(E), dated 3-7-2003].

37. Power of search, seizure, etc.

(1) The Director of Enforcement and other officers of Enforcement not below the rank of an Assistant Director shall take up for investigation the contravention referred to in section 13.

(2) Without prejudice to the provisions of sub-section (1), the Central Government may also, by notification, authorise any officer or class of officers in the Central Government, State Government or the Reserve Bank, not below the rank of an Under Secretary to the Government of India to investigate any contravention referred to in section 13.

(3) The officers referred to in sub-section (1) shall exercise the like powers which are conferred on income-tax authorities under the Income-tax Act, 1961 (43 of 1961) and shall exercise such powers, subject to such limitations laid down under that Act.

COMMENTS

Investigation of contravention referred under section 13 will be conducted by the Director of Enforcement and other officers not below the rank of Assistant Director of Enforcement.

The officers will exercise the like powers which are conferred under the Income-tax Act, 1961 subject to the limitations laid down in that Act.

Officers not below the rank of Under Secretary in the Central Government, State Government or the Reserve Bank may also be authorised by notification, by the Central Government to investigate the contravention referred to in section 13.

38. Empowering other officers

(1) The Central Government may, by order and subject to such conditions and limitations as it thinks fit to impose, authorise any officer of customs or any central excise officer or any police officer or any other officer of the Central Government or a State Government to exercise such of the powers and discharge such of the duties of the Director of Enforcement or any other officer of Enforcement under this Act as may be stated in the order.

(2) The officers referred to in sub-section (1) shall exercise the like powers which are conferred on the income-tax authorities under the Income-tax Act, 1961 (43 of 1961), subject to such conditions and limitations as the Central Government may impose.

COMMENTS

The Central Government may also authorise any officer of customs or central excise or any police officer or any other officer of the Central

Government or a State Government, to exercise such of the powers and discharge such of the duties of the Director of Enforcement or the officers of Enforcement, as may be specified by the Central Government in the order.

Central Government has authorised officers of Customs and Central Excise not below the rank of Deputy Commissioner and Officers of the Directorate General of Revenue Intelligence not below the rank of Deputy Director to exercise powers conferred under the Act for the contravention regarding:

(*a*) export, import or holding of currency or currency notes [Section 6(3)(*g*)];

(*b*) failure to furnish to RBI or such other authority declaration regarding the export value of goods exported [Section 7(1)(*a*)].

[*Notification No. 21/2000, dated 26-12-2000*]

The officers will exercise the like powers which are conferred under the Income-tax Act, 1961 subject to the limitations laid down in that Act.

CHAPTER VII

Miscellaneous

39. Presumption as to documents in certain cases

Where any document—

(*i*) is produced or furnished by any person or has been seized from the custody or control of any person, in either case, under this Act or under any other law; or

(*ii*) has been received from any place outside India (duly authenticated by such authority or person and in such manner as may be prescribed) in the course of investigation of any contravention under this Act alleged to have been committed by any person,

and such document is tendered in any proceeding under this Act in evidence against him, or against him and any other person who is proceeded against jointly with him, the court or the adjudicating authority, as the case may be, shall—

(*a*) presume, unless the contrary is proved, that the signature and every other part of such document which purports to be in the handwriting of any particular person or which the court may reasonably assume to have been signed by, or to be in the handwriting of, any particular person, is in that person's handwriting and in the case of a document executed or attested, that it was executed or attested by the person by whom it purports to have been so executed or attested;

(*b*) admit the document in evidence notwithstanding that it is not duly stamped, if such document is otherwise admissible in evidence;

(*c*) in a case falling under clause (*i*), also presume, unless the contrary is proved, the truth of the contents of such document.

COMMENTS

Section 39 deals with documents which may be:

(*i*) produced or furnished by any person or are seized from the custody of any person, either under the Act or under any other law; or

(*ii*) received from any place outside India in the course of investigation of any contravention under the Act (such document should be duly authenticated by such authority or person in such manner as may be prescribed),

and such document is tendered in any proceeding as evidence against such person or against any other person who is proceeded against jointly with him, the court or adjudicating authority will:

(*a*) presume, unless the contrary is proved, that the signature and every part of the document which purports to be in the handwriting of any person or which the court may reasonably assume to have been signed or have been in the handwriting of such person and in case of document executed or attested, that it was executed or attested by the person by whom it purports to have been executed or attested; and also presume the truth of the contents of such documents;

(*b*) admit the document as evidence even if it is not adequately stamped, if such document is otherwise admissible in evidence.

Rules framed under section 39.—Central Government has, in exercise of the powers conferred under section 46, framed the Foreign Exchange Management (Authentication of Documents) Rules, 2000 under this section.

40. Suspension of operation of this Act

(1) If the Central Government is satisfied that circumstances have arisen rendering it necessary that any permission granted or restriction imposed by this Act should cease to be granted or imposed, or if it considers necessary or expedient so to do in public interest, the Central Government may, by notification, suspend or relax to such extent either indefinitely or for such period as may be notified, the operation of all or any of the provisions of this Act.

(2) Where the operation of any provision of this Act has under sub-section (1) been suspended or relaxed indefinitely, such suspension or relaxation may, at any time while this Act remains in force, be removed by the Central Government by notification.

(3) Every notification issued under this section shall be laid, as soon as may be after it is issued, before each House of Parliament, while it is in session, for a total period of thirty days which may be comprised in one session or in two or more successive sessions, and if, before the expiry of the session immediately following the session or the successive sessions aforesaid, both Houses agree in making any modification in the notification or both Houses agree that the notification should not be issued, the notification shall thereafter have effect only in such modified form or be of no effect, as the case may be; so, however, that any such modification or annulment shall be without prejudice to the validity of anything previously done under that notification.

COMMENTS

This section empowers the Central Government to suspend or relax, by notification, the operation of the Act where it is satisfied that there are such circumstances which necessitate that any permission granted or restriction imposed should cease to be granted or imposed. Every notification issued under this section shall be laid before each House of Parliament.

41. Power of Central Government to give directions

For the purposes of this Act, the Central Government may, from time to time, give to the Reserve Bank such general or special directions as it thinks fit and the Reserve Bank shall, in the discharge of its functions under this Act, comply with any such directions.

COMMENTS

The Central Government is empowered *vide* this section to issue directions to the RBI under the Act and RBI will comply with such directions.

42. Contravention by companies

(1) Where a person committing a contravention of any of the provisions of this Act or of any rule, direction or order made thereunder is a company, every person who, at the time the contravention was committed, was in charge of, and was responsible to, the company for the conduct of the business of the company as well as the company, shall be deemed to be guilty of the contravention and shall be liable to be proceeded against and punished accordingly:

Provided that nothing contained in this sub-section shall render any such person liable to punishment if he proves that the contravention took place without his knowledge or that he exercised due diligence to prevent such contravention.

(2) Notwithstanding anything contained in sub-section (1), where a contravention of any of the provisions of this Act or of any rule, direction or order made thereunder has been committed by a company and it is proved that the contravention has taken place with the consent or connivance of, or is

attributable to any neglect on the part of, any director, manager, secretary or other officer of the company, such director, manager, secretary or other officer shall also be deemed to be guilty of the contravention and shall be liable to be proceeded against and punished accordingly.

Explanation.— For the purposes of this section—

(*i*) "company" means any body corporate and includes a firm or other association of individuals; and

(*ii*) "director", in relation to a firm, means a partner in the firm.

COMMENTS

This section deals with the contravention by companies. In case a contravention is committed by a company, then every person who was in charge of and was responsible to the company for the conduct of its business will be deemed to be guilty of the contravention and will be liable to be proceeded against. However any such person is free to prove that the contravention took place without his knowledge or that he exercised due diligence to prevent such contravention.

Where it is proved that the contravention by the company took place with the consent or connivance of or due to the negligence of any director, manager, secretary or any other officer of the company, then such person will be deemed to be guilty of the contravention and be proceeded against.

Company means any body corporate and includes a firm or other associations of individuals, and director in relation to a firm, means a partner of the firm.

43. Death or insolvency in certain cases

Any right, obligation, liability, proceedings or appeal arising in relation to the provisions of section 13 shall not abate by reason of death or insolvency of the person liable under that section and upon such death or insolvency such rights and obligations shall devolve on the legal representative of such person or the official receiver or the official assignee, as the case may be:

Provided that a legal representative of the deceased shall be liable only to the extent of the inheritance or estate of the deceased.

COMMENTS

Death or insolvency of the person liable under section 13 will not abate any right, obligation, liability, proceedings or appeal arising in relation to section 13. The same will devolve upon the legal representative, who will be liable only to the extent of the inheritance, or the official receiver or official assignee, as the case may be.

44. Bar of legal proceedings

No suit, prosecution or other legal proceedings shall lie against the Central Government or the Reserve Bank or any officer of that Government or of the Reserve Bank or any other person exercising any power or discharging any functions or performing any duties under this Act, for anything in good faith done or intended to be done under this Act or any rule, regulation, notification, direction or order made thereunder.

45. Removal of difficulties

(1) If any difficulty arises in giving effect to the provisions of this Act, the Central Government may, by order, do anything not inconsistent with the provisions of this Act for the purpose of removing the difficulty:

Provided that no such order shall be made under this section after the expiry of two years from the commencement of this Act.

(2) Every order made under this section shall be laid, as soon as may be after it is made, before each House of Parliament.

COMMENTS

Refer to the Foreign Exchange Management (Removal of Difficulties) Order, 2000 placed at Annexure III.

46. Power to make rules

(1) The Central Government may, by notification, make rules to carry out the provisions of this Act.

(2) Without prejudice to the generality of the foregoing power, such rules may provide for,—

(*a*) the imposition of reasonable restrictions on current account transactions under section 5;

(*b*) the manner in which the contravention may be compounded under sub-section (1) of section 15;

(*c*) the manner of holding an inquiry by the Adjudicating Authorities under sub-section (1) of section 16;

(*d*) the form of appeal and fee for filing such appeal under sections 17 and 19;

(*e*) the salary and allowances payable to and the other terms and conditions of service of the Chairperson and other Members of the Appellate Tribunal and the Special Director (Appeals) under section 23;

(*f*) the salaries and allowances and other conditions of service of the officers and employees of the Appellate Tribunal and the Office of the Special Director (Appeals) under sub-section (3) of section 27;

(*g*) the additional matters in respect of which the Appellate Tribunal and the Special Director (Appeals) may exercise the powers of a civil court under clause (*i*) of sub-section (2) of section 28;

(*h*) the authority or person and the manner in which any documents may be authenticated under clause (*ii*) of section 39; and

(*i*) any other matter which is required to be, or may be prescribed.

COMMENTS

Section 46 empowers the Central Government to make rules, by notification, to carry out the provisions of the Act. The rules may provide for:

(*a*) the imposition of reasonable restrictions on current account transactions under section 5 — Foreign Exchange Management (Current Account Transactions) Rules, 2000;

(*b*) the manner in which the contravention may be compounded under sub-section (1) of section 15 — Foreign Exchange Management (Compounding Proceedings) Rules, 2000;

(*c*) the manner of holding an inquiry by the Adjudicating Authorities under sub-section (1) of section 16 — Foreign Exchange Management (Adjudication Proceedings and Appeal) Rules, 2000;

(*d*) the form of appeal and fee for filing such appeal under sections 17 and 19 — Foreign Exchange Management (Adjudication Proceedings and Appeal) Rules, 2000;

(*e*) the salary and allowances payable to and the other terms and conditions of service of the chairperson and other members of the Appellate Tribunal and the Special Director (Appeals) under section 23 — Appellate Tribunal for Foreign Exchange (Recruitment, Salary and Allowances and other conditions of Service of Chairperson and Members) Rules, 2000;

(*f*) the salaries and allowances and other conditions of service of the officers and employees of the Appellate Tribunal and the Office of the Special Director (Appeals) under sub-section (3) of section 27;

(*g*) the additional matters in respect of which the Appellate Tribunal and the Special Director (Appeals) may exercise the powers of a civil court under clause (*i*) of sub-section (2) of section 28;

(*h*) the authority or person and the manner in which any documents may be authenticated under clause (*ii*) of section 39 — Foreign Exchange (Authentication of Documents) Rules, 2000; and (*i*) any other matter which is required to be, or may be prescribed — Foreign Exchange Management (Encashment of Draft, Cheque, Instrument and Payment of Interest) Rules, 2000.

47. Power to make regulations

(1) The Reserve Bank may, by notification, make regulations, to carry out the provisions of this Act and the rules made thereunder.

(2) Without prejudice to the generality of the foregoing power, such regulations may provide for,—

(*a*) the permissible classes of capital account transactions, the limits of admissibility of foreign exchange for such transactions, and the prohibition, restriction or regulation of certain capital account transactions under section 6;

(*b*) the manner and the form in which the declaration is to be furnished under clause (*a*) of sub-section (1) of section 7;

(*c*) the period within which and the manner of repatriation of foreign exchange under section 8;

(*d*) the limit up to which any person may possess foreign currency or foreign coins under clause (*a*) of section 9;

(*e*) the class of persons and the limit up to which foreign currency account may be held or operated under clause (*b*) of section 9;

(*f*) the limit up to which foreign exchange acquired may be exempted under clause (*d*) of section 9;

(*g*) the limit up to which foreign exchange acquired may be retained under clause (*e*) of section 9;

(*h*) any other matter which is required to be, or may be, specified.

COMMENTS

Reserve Bank of India, is empowered by the provisions of section 47 to make regulations to carry out the provisions of the Act as well as the rules made thereunder. Such regulations may provide for:

(*a*) the permissible classes of capital account transactions, the limits of admissibility of foreign exchange for such transactions, and the prohibition, restriction or regulation of certain capital account transactions under section 6;

(*b*) the manner and the form in which the declaration is to be furnished under clause (*a*) of sub-section (1) of section 7;

(*c*) the period within which and the manner of repatriation of foreign exchange under section 8;

(*d*) the limit up to which any person may possess foreign currency or foreign coins under clause (*a*) of section 9;

(*e*) the class of persons and the limit up to which foreign currency account may be held or operated under clause (*b*) of section 9;

(*f*) the limit up to which foreign exchange acquired may be exempted under clause (*d*) of section 9;

(*g*) the limit up to which foreign exchange acquired may be retained under clause (*e*) of section 9;

(*h*) any other matter which is required to be, or may be, specified.

The following are the individual regulations framed by the Reserve Bank of India.

1. Foreign Exchange Management (Permissible Capital Account Transactions) Regulations, 2000.

2. Foreign Exchange Management (Issue of Security in India by a Branch, Office or Agency of a Person Resident outside India) Regulations, 2000.

3. Foreign Exchange Management (Borrowing or Lending in Foreign Exchange) Regulations, 2000.

4. Foreign Exchange Management (Borrowing and Lending in Rupees) Regulations, 2000.

5. Foreign Exchange Management (Deposit) Regulations, 2000.

6. Foreign Exchange Management (Export and Import of Currency) Regulations, 2000.

7. Foreign Exchange Management (Acquisition and Transfer of Immovable Property Outside India) Regulations, 2000.

8. Foreign Exchange Management (Guarantees) Regulations, 2000.

9. Foreign Exchange Management (Realisation, Repatriation and Surrender of Foreign Exchange) Regulations, 2000.

10. Foreign Exchange Management (Foreign Currency Accounts by a person resident in India) Regulations, 2000.

11. Foreign Exchange Management (Possession and Retention of Foreign Currency) Regulations, 2000.

12. Foreign Exchange Management (Insurance) Regulations, 2000.

13. Foreign Exchange Management (Remittance of Assets) Regulations, 2000.
14. Foreign Exchange Management (Manner of Receipt and Payment) Regulations, 2000.
15. Foreign Exchange Management (Transfer or Issue of Security by a Person Resident Outside India) Regulations, 2000.
16. Foreign Exchange Management (Acquisition and Transfer of Immovable Property in India) Regulations, 2000.
17. Foreign Exchange Management (Establishment in India of Branch or Office or other Place of Business) Regulations, 2000.
18. Foreign Exchange Management (Export of Goods and Services) Regulations, 2000.
19. Foreign Exchange Management (Investment in Firm or Proprietary Concern in India) Regulations, 2000.
20. Foreign Exchange Management (Foreign Exchange Derivative contracts) Regulations, 2000.
21. Foreign Exchange Management (Transfer or Issue of any Foreign Security) (Amendment) Regulations, 2004.
22. Foreign Exchange Management (Offshore Banking Unit) Regulations, 2002.
23. Foreign Exchange Management [Withdrawal of General Permission to Overseas Corporate Bodies (OCBs)] Regulations, 2003.

48. Rules and regulations to be laid before Parliament

Every rule and regulation made under this Act shall be laid, as soon as may be after it is made, before each House of Parliament, while it is in session, for a total period of thirty days which may be comprised in one session or in two or more successive sessions, and if, before the expiry of the session immediately following the session or the successive sessions aforesaid, both Houses agree in making any modification in the rule or regulation or both Houses agree that the rule or regulation should not be made, the rule or regulation shall thereafter have effect only in such modified form or be of no effect, as the case may be; so, however, that any such modification or annulment shall be without prejudice to the validity of anything previously done under that rule or regulation.

49. Repeal and saving

(1) The Foreign Exchange Regulation Act, 1973 (46 of 1973) is hereby repealed and the Appellate Board constituted under sub-section (1) of section 52 of the said Act (hereinafter referred to as the repealed Act) shall stand dissolved.

(2) On the dissolution of the said Appellate Board, the person appointed as Chairman of the Appellate Board and every other person appointed as Member and holding office as such immediately before such date shall vacate their respective offices and no such Chairman or other person shall be entitled to claim any compensation for the premature termination of the term of his office or of any contract of service.

(3) Notwithstanding anything contained in any other law for the time being in force, no court shall take cognizance of an offence under the repealed Act and no adjudicating officer shall take notice of any contravention under section 51 of the repealed Act after the expiry of a period of two years from the date of the commencement of this Act.

(4) Subject to the provisions of sub-section (3) all offences committed under the repealed Act shall continue to be governed by the provisions of the repealed Act as if that Act had not been repealed.

(5) Notwithstanding such repeal,—

(*a*) anything done or any action taken or purported to have been done or taken including any rule, notification, inspection, order or notice made or issued or any appointment, confirmation or declaration made or any licence, permission, authorization or exemption granted or any document or instrument executed or any direction given under the Act hereby repealed shall, in so far as it is not inconsistent with the provisions of this Act, be deemed to have been done or taken under the corresponding provisions of this Act;

(*b*) any appeal preferred to the Appellate Board under sub-section (2) of section 52 of the repealed Act but not disposed of before the commencement of this Act shall stand transferred to and shall be disposed of by the Appellate Tribunal constituted under this Act;

(*c*) every appeal from any decision or order of the Appellate Board under sub-section (3) or sub-section (4) of section 52 of the repealed Act shall, if not filed before the commencement of this Act, be filed before the High Court within a period of sixty days of such commencement:

Provided that the High Court may entertain such appeal after the expiry of the said period of sixty days if it is satisfied that the appellant was prevented by sufficient cause from filing the appeal within the said period.

(6) Save as otherwise provided in sub-section (3), the mention of particular matters in sub-sections (2), (4) and (5) shall not be held to prejudice or affect the general application of section 6 of the General Clauses Act, 1897 (10 of 1897) with regard to the effect of repeal.

COMMENTS

The Foreign Exchange Regulation Act, 1973 has been repealed by this Act and the Appellate Board constituted under it has been dissolved.

However all the offences committed under FERA would continue to be governed by the provisions of the repealed Act as if the Act had not been repealed.

Further, no court will take cognizance of an offence under the repealed FERA and no adjudicating officer will take notice of any contravention under section 51 after the expiry of two years from the date of commencement of the Act, *i.e.* w.e.f. 1-6-2002. Thus, the Foreign Exchange Regulation Act, 1973 stands repealed and the sun-set period too has expired.

Sub-section (5) provides that notwithstanding the repeal,

(*a*) anything done or any action taken including any rule, notification, inspection, order or notice or any appointment, confirmation or declaration made or any licence, permission, authorization or exemption granted or any document or instrument executed or any direction given under the repealed Act which is not inconsistent with the provisions of this Act, be deemed to have been done or taken under the corresponding provisions of this Act;

(*b*) any appeal made to the Appellate Board under section 52(2) of FERA but not disposed of before the commencement of this Act will be transferred and disposed of by the Appellate Tribunal;

(*c*) any appeal against the decision or order of Appellate Board under section 52(3) or 52(4) of FERA, if not filed before the commencement of this Act, be filed before the High Court within sixty days of commencement of this Act. However the High Court may entertain the appeal even after the expiry of the sixty days period if it is satisfied that there was sufficient cause which prevented the appellant from filing the appeal.

Annexure I

Provisions of the Income-tax Act, 1961 regarding search, seizure, etc.

[1][**132. Search and seizure**[2]

[3](1) Where the [4][Director General or Director] or the [5][Chief Commissioner or Commissioner] [6][or any such] [7][[8][Joint] Director] or [9][Joint] Commissioner as may be empowered in this behalf by the Board], in consequence of information in his possession, has reason to believe that—

(*a*) any person to whom a summons under sub-section (1) of section 37 of the Indian Income-tax Act, 1922 (11 of 1922), or under sub-section (1) of section 131 of this Act, or a notice under sub-section (4) of section 22 of the Indian Income-tax Act, 1922 (11 of 1922), or under sub-section (1) of section 142 of this Act was issued to produce, or cause to be produced, any books of account or other documents has omitted or failed to produce, or cause to be produced, such books of account or other documents as required by such summons or notice, or

(*b*) any person to whom a summons or notice as aforesaid has been or might be issued will not, or would not, produce or cause to be produced, any books of account or other documents which will be useful for, or relevant to, any proceeding under the Indian Income-tax Act, 1922 (11 of 1922), or under this Act, or

(*c*) any person is in possession of any money, bullion, jewellery or other valuable article or thing and such money, bullion, jewellery or other valuable article or thing represents either wholly or partly income or property [10][which has not been, or would not be disclosed] for the purposes of the Indian Income-tax Act, 1922 (11 of 1922) or this Act (hereinafter in this section referred to as the undisclosed income or property),

---

1 Substituted by the Income-tax (Amendment) Act, 1965, w.e.f. 12-3-1965. The Amendment Act also provided for a validating provision (section 6) for pre-1965 searches. Earlier, section 132 was substituted by the Finance Act, 1964, w.e.f. 1-4-1964.

2 **See** Instruction No. 1497, dated 13-1-1983.

3 **See** rule 112(2)(*a*) and Form No. 45.

4 Substituted for "Director of Inspection" by the Direct Tax Laws (Amendment) Act, 1987, w.e.f. 1-4-1988.

5 Substituted for "Commissioner", *ibid.*

6 Inserted by the Taxation Laws (Amendment) Act, 1975, w.e.f. 1-10-1975.

7 Substituted for "Deputy Director of Inspection" by the Direct Tax Laws (Amendment) Act, 1987, w.e.f. 1-4-1988.

8 Substituted for "Deputy" by the Finance (No. 2) Act, 1998, w.e.f. 1-10-1998.

9 Substituted for "Deputy" by the Finance (No. 2) Act, 1998, w.e.f. 1-10-1998, which was earlier substituted for "Inspecting Assistant" by the Direct Tax Laws (Amendment) Act, 1987, w.e.f. 1-4-1988.

10 Substituted for "which has not been disclosed" by the Taxation Laws (Amendment) Act, 1975, w.e.f. 1-10-1975.

[1][then,—

(A) the [2][Director General or Director] or the [3][Chief Commissioner or Commissioner], as the case may be, may authorise any [4][[5][Joint] Director], [6][Joint] Commissioner, [7][Assistant Director] [8][or Deputy Director], [9][Assistant Commissioner [10][or Deputy Commissioner] or Income-tax Officer], or

(B) such [11][[12][Joint] Director] or [13][Joint] Commissioner, as the case may be, may authorise any [14][Assistant Director] [15][or Deputy Director], [16][Assistant Commissioner [17][or Deputy Commissioner] or Income-tax Officer],

(the officer so authorised in all cases being hereinafter referred to as the authorised officer) to—]

(*i*) enter and search any [18][building, place, vessel, vehicle or aircraft] where he has reason to suspect that such books of account, other documents, money, bullion, jewellery or other valuable article or thing are kept;

---

1 Substituted for "he may authorise any Deputy Director of Inspection, Inspecting Assistant Commissioner, Assistant Director of Inspection or Income-tax Officer (hereinafter referred to as the authorised officer) to—" by the Taxation Laws (Amendment) Act, 1975, w.e.f. 1-10-1975.

2 Substituted for "Director of Inspection" by the Direct Tax Laws (Amendment) Act, 1987, w.e.f. 1-4-1988.

3 Substituted for "Commissioner", *ibid.*

4 Substituted for "Deputy Director of Inspection" by the Direct Tax Laws (Amendment) Act, 1987, w.e.f. 1-4-1988.

5 Substituted for "Deputy" by the Finance (No. 2) Act, 1998, w.e.f. 1-10-1998.

6 Substituted for "Deputy" by the Finance (No. 2) Act, 1998, w.e.f. 1-10-1998, which was earlier substituted for "Inspecting Assistant" by the Direct Tax Laws (Amendment) Act, 1987, w.e.f. 1-4-1988.

7 Substituted for "Assistant Director of Inspection" by the Direct Tax Laws (Amendment) Act, 1987, w.e.f. 1-4-1988.

8 Inserted by the Finance (No. 2) Act, 1998, w.e.f. 1-10-1998.

9 Substituted for "or Income-tax Officer" by the Direct Tax Laws (Amendment) Act, 1987 (as amended by the Finance Act, 1988), w.e.f. 1-4-1988.

10 Inserted by the Finance (No. 2) Act, 1998, w.e.f. 1-10-1998.

11 Substituted for "Deputy Director of Inspection" by the Direct Tax Laws (Amendment) Act, 1987 (as amended by the Finance Act, 1988), w.e.f. 1-4-1988.

12 Substituted for "Deputy" by the Finance (No. 2) Act, 1998, w.e.f. 1-10-1998.

13 Substituted for "Deputy" by the Finance (No. 2) Act, 1998, w.e.f. 1-10-1998, which was earlier substituted for "Inspecting Assistant" by the Direct Tax Laws (Amendment) Act, 1987, w.e.f. 1-4-1988.

14 Substituted for "Assistant Director of Inspection" by the Direct Tax Laws (Amendment) Act, 1987 (as amended by the Finance Act, 1988), w.e.f. 1-4-1988.

15 Inserted by the Finance (No. 2) Act, 1998, w.e.f. 1-10-1998.

16 Substituted for "or Income-tax Officer" by the Direct Tax Laws (Amendment) Act, 1987 (as amended by the Finance Act, 1988), w.e.f. 1-4-1988.

17 Inserted by the Finance (No. 2) Act, 1998, w.e.f. 1-10-1998.

18 Substituted for "building or place" by the Taxation Laws (Amendment) Act, 1975, w.e.f. 1-10-1975.

(*ii*) break open the lock of any door, box, locker, safe, almirah or other receptacle for exercising the powers conferred by clause (*i*) where the keys thereof are not available;

[1][(*iia*) search any person who has got out of, or is about to get into, or is in the building, place, vessel, vehicle or aircraft, if the authorised officer has reason to suspect that such person has secreted about his person any such books of account, other documents, money, bullion, jewellery or other valuable article or thing;]

[2][(*iib*) require any person who is found to be in possession or control of any books of account or other documents maintained in the form of electronic record as defined in clause (*t*) of sub-section (1) of section 2 of the Information Technology Act, 2000[3] (21 of 2000), to afford the authorised officer the necessary facility to inspect such books of account or other documents;]

(*iii*) seize any such books of account, other documents, money, bullion, jewellery or other valuable article or thing found as a result of such search:

[4][Provided that bullion, jewellery or other valuable article or thing, being stock-in-trade of the business, found as a result of such search shall not be seized but the authorized officer shall make a note or inventory of such stock-in-trade of the business;]

(*iv*) place marks of identification on any books of account or other documents or make or cause to be made extracts or copies therefrom;

(*v*) make a note or an inventory of any such money, bullion, jewellery or other valuable article or thing:

[5][Provided that where any building, place, vessel, vehicle or aircraft referred to in clause (*i*) is within the area of jurisdiction of any [6][Chief Commissioner or Commissioner], but such [7][Chief Commissioner or Commissioner] has no jurisdiction over the person referred to in clause (*a*) or clause (*b*) or clause (*c*), then, notwithstanding anything contained in section [8][120], it shall be competent for him to exercise the powers under this sub-section in all cases where he has

---

1 Inserted, *ibid.*

2 Inserted by the Finance Act, 2002, w.e.f. 1-6-2002.

3 For the provision, refer Bharat's Handbook to Direct Taxes.

4 Inserted by the Finance Act, 2003, w.e.f. 1-6-2003.

5 Inserted by the Taxation Laws (Amendment) Act, 1975, w.e.f. 1-10-1975. **See** rule 112(2)(*b*) and Form No. 45A.

6 Substituted for "Commissioner" by the Direct Tax Laws (Amendment) Act, 1987, w.e.f. 1-4-1988.

7 *Ibid.*

8 Substituted for "121" by the Direct Tax Laws (Amendment) Act, 1987 (as amended by the Finance Act, 1988) w.e.f. 1-4-1988.

reason to believe that any delay in getting the authorisation from the [1][Chief Commissioner or Commissioner] having jurisdiction over such person may be prejudicial to the interests of the revenue:]

[2][Provided further that where it is not possible or practicable to take physical possession of any valuable article or thing and remove it to a safe place due to its volume, weight or other physical characteristics or due to its being of a dangerous nature, the authorised officer may serve an order on the owner or the person who is in immediate possession or control thereof that he shall not remove, part with or otherwise deal with it, except with the previous permission of such authorised officer and such action of the authorised officer shall be deemed to be seizure of such valuable article or thing under clause (*iii*):]

[3][Provided also that nothing contained in the second proviso shall apply in case of any valuable article or thing, being stock-in-trade of the business.]

[4][(1A) Where any [5][Chief Commissioner or Commissioner], in consequence of information in his possession, has reason to suspect that any books of account, other documents, money, bullion, jewellery or other valuable article or thing in respect of which an officer has been authorised by the [6][Director General or Director] or any other [7][Chief Commissioner or Commissioner] or any such [8][[9][Joint] Director] or [10][Joint] Commissioner as may be empowered in this behalf by the Board to take action under clauses (*i*) to (*v*) of sub-section (1) are or is kept in any building, place, vessel, vehicle or aircraft not mentioned in the authorisation under sub-section (1), such [11][Chief Commissioner or Commissioner] may, notwithstanding anything contained in section [12][120], authorise the said officer to take action under any of the clauses aforesaid in respect of such building, place, vessel, vehicle or aircraft.]

---

1 Substituted for "Commissioner" by the Direct Tax Laws (Amendment) Act, 1987, w.e.f. 1-4-1988.

2 Inserted by the Finance Act, 1988, w.e.f. 1-4-1989.

3 Inserted by the Finance Act, 2003, w.e.f. 1-6-2003.

4 Inserted by the Taxation Laws (Amendment) Act, 1975, w.e.f. 1-10-1975. **See** rule 112(2)(*c*) and Form No. 45B.

5 Substituted for "Commissioner" by the Direct Tax Laws (Amendment) Act, 1987, w.e.f. 1-4-1988.

6 Substituted for "Director of Inspection" by the Direct Tax Laws (Amendment) Act, 1987, w.e.f. 1-4-1988.

7 Substituted for "Commissioner", *ibid.*

8 Substituted for "Deputy Director of Inspection", *ibid.*

9 Substituted for "Deputy" by the Finance (No. 2) Act, 1998, w.e.f. 1-10-1998.

10 Substituted for "Deputy" by the Finance (No. 2) Act, 1998, w.e.f. 1-10-1998, which was earlier substituted for "Inspecting Assistant" by the Direct Tax Laws (Amendment) Act, 1987, w.e.f. 1-4-1988.

11 Substituted for "Commissioner" by the Direct Tax Laws (Amendment) Act, 1987, w.e.f. 1-4-1988.

12 Substituted for "121" by the Direct Tax Laws (Amendment) Act, 1987 (as amended by the Finance Act, 1988), w.e.f. 1-4-1988.

(2) The authorised officer may requisition the services of any police officer or of any officer of the Central Government or of both, to assist him for all or any of the purposes specified in sub-section (1) [1][or sub-section (1A)] and it shall be the duty of every such officer to comply with such requisition.

(3) The authorised officer may, where it is not practicable to seize any such books of account, other documents, money, bullion, jewellery or other valuable article or thing, [2][for reasons other than those mentioned in the second proviso to sub-section (1),] serve an order on the owner or the person who is in immediate possession or control thereof that he shall not remove, part with or otherwise deal with it except with the previous permission of such officer and such officer may take such steps as may be necessary for ensuring compliance with this sub-section.

[3][*Explanation.*—For the removal of doubts, it is hereby declared that serving of an order as aforesaid under this sub-section shall not be deemed to be seizure of such books of account, other documents, money, bullion, jewellery or other valuable article or thing under clause (*iii*) of sub-section (1).]

(4) The authorised officer may, during the course of the search or seizure, examine on oath any person who is found to be in possession or control of any books of account, documents, money, bullion, jewellery or other valuable article or thing and any statement made by such person during such examination may thereafter be used in evidence in any proceeding under the Indian Income-tax Act, 1922 (11 of 1922), or under this Act.

[4][*Explanation.*—For the removal of doubts, it is hereby declared that the examination of any person under this sub-section may be not merely in respect of any books of account, other documents or assets found as a result of the search, but also in respect of all matters relevant for the purposes of any investigation connected with any proceeding under the Indian Income-tax Act, 1922 (11 of 1922), or under this Act.]

[5][(4A) Where any books of account, other documents, money, bullion, jewellery or other valuable article or thing are or is found in the possession or control of any person in the course of a search, it may be presumed—

(*i*) that such books of account, other documents, money, bullion, jewellery or other valuable article or thing belong or belongs to such person;

(*ii*) that the contents of such books of account and other documents are true; and

---

1 Inserted by the Taxation Laws (Amendment) Act, 1975, w.e.f. 1-10-1975.

2 Inserted by the Finance Act, 1988, w.e.f. 1-4-1989.

3 Inserted by the Direct Tax Laws (Amendment) Act, 1987, w.e.f. 1-4-1989.

4 Inserted by the Direct Tax Laws (Amendment) Act, 1987, w.e.f. 1-4-1989.

5 Inserted by the Taxation Laws (Amendment) Act, 1975, w.e.f. 1-10-1975. **See** rule 112(2)(*c*) and Form No. 45B.

(*iii*) that the signature and every other part of such books of account and other documents which purport to be in the handwriting of any particular person or which may reasonably be assumed to have been signed by, or to be in the handwriting of, any particular person, are in that person's handwriting, and in the case of a document stamped, executed or attested, that it was duly stamped and executed or attested by the person by whom it purports to have been so executed or attested.]

[(5) to (7) *Omitted by the Finance Act, 2002, w.e.f. 1-6-2002.*]

(8) The books of account or other documents seized under sub-section (1) [1][or sub-section (1A)] shall not be retained by the authorised officer for a period exceeding [2][thirty days from the date of the order of assessment [3][under section 153A or clause (*c*) of section 158BC]] unless the reasons for retaining the same are recorded by him in writing and the approval of the [4][Chief Commissioner, Commissioner, Director General or Director] for such retention is obtained:

Provided that the [5][Chief Commissioner, Commissioner, Director General or Director] shall not authorise the retention of the books of account and other documents for a period exceeding thirty days after all the proceedings under the Indian Income-tax Act, 1922 (11 of 1922), or this Act in respect of the years for which the books of account or other documents are relevant are completed.

[6][(8A) An order under sub-section (3) shall not be in force for a period exceeding sixty days from the date of the order.]

(9) The person from whose custody any books of account or other documents are seized under sub-section (1) [7][or sub-section (1A)] may make copies thereof, or take extracts therefrom, in the presence of the authorised officer or any other person empowered by him in this behalf, at such place and time as the authorised officer may appoint in this behalf.

[8][(9A) Where the authorised officer has no jurisdiction over the person referred to in clause (*a*) or clause (*b*) or clause (*c*) of sub-section (1), the books of account or other documents, or any money, bullion, jewellery or other valuable article or thing (hereafter in this section and in sections 132A and 132B referred to as assets) seized under that sub-section shall be handed over by the authorised officer to the Assessing Officer having jurisdiction over such person within a period of sixty days from the date on which the last of the authorisations for search was executed and thereupon the powers exercisable by the authorised

---

1 Inserted by the Taxation Laws (Amendment) Act, 1975, w.e.f. 1-10-1975.

2 Substituted for "one hundred and eighty days from the date of the seizure" by the Finance Act, 2002, w.e.f. 1-6-2002.

3 Substituted for "under clause (*c*) of section 158BC" by the Finance Act, 2003, w.e.f. 1-6-2003.

4 Substituted for "Chief Commissioner or Commissioner" by the Finance Act, 1997, w.e.f. 1-10-1996.

5 *Ibid.*

6 Substituted by the Finance Act, 2002, w.e.f. 1-6-2002.

7 Inserted by the Taxation Laws (Amendment) Act, 1975, w.e.f. 1-10-1975.

8 Substituted by the Finance Act, 2002, w.e.f. 1-6-2002.

officer under sub-section (8) or sub-section (9) shall be exercisable by such Assessing Officer.]

(10) If a person legally entitled to the books of account or other documents seized under sub-section (1) [1][or sub-section (1A)] objects for any reason to the approval given by the [2][Chief Commissioner, Commissioner, Director General or Director] under sub-section (8), he may make an application to the Board stating therein the reasons for such objection and requesting for the return of the books of account or other documents [3][and the Board may, after giving the applicant an opportunity of being heard, pass such orders as it thinks fit].

[*(11)*, *(11A)* & *(12) Omitted by the Finance Act, 2002, w.e.f. 1-6-2002.*]

[4][(13) The provisions of the Code of Criminal Procedure, 1973 (2 of 1974), relating to searches and seizure shall apply, so far as may be, to searches and seizure under sub-section (1) or sub-section (1A).]

[5](14) The Board may make rules in relation to any search or seizure under this section; in particular, and without prejudice to the generality of the foregoing power, such rules may provide for the procedure to be followed by the authorised officer—

(*i*) for obtaining ingress into [6][any building, place, vessel, vehicle or aircraft] to be searched where free ingress thereto is not available;

(*ii*) for ensuring safe custody of any books of account or other documents or assets seized.

[7][*Explanation 1.*—For the purposes of sub-section (9A), "execution of an authorisation for search" shall have the same meaning as assigned to it in Explanation 2 to section 158BE.]

Explanation 2.—In this section, the word "proceeding" means any proceeding in respect of any year, whether under the Indian Income-tax Act, 1922 (11 of 1922), or this Act, which may be pending on the date on which a search is authorised under this section or which may have been completed on or before such date and includes also all proceedings under this Act which may be commenced after such date in respect of any year.]

---

1 Inserted by the Taxation Laws (Amendment) Act, 1975, w.e.f. 1-10-1975.

2 Substituted for "Chief Commissioner or Commissioner" by the Finance Act, 1997, w.e.f. 1-10-1996.

3 Inserted by the Finance Act, 2002, w.e.f. 1-6-2002.

4 Substituted by the Taxation Laws (Amendment) Act, 1975, w.e.f. 1-10-1975.

5 **See** rules 112, 112A and 112B.

6 Substituted for "such building or place" by the Taxation Laws (Amendment) Act, 1975, w.e.f. 1-10-1975.

7 Substituted by the Finance Act, 2002, w.e.f. 1-6-2002.

[1][**132A. Powers to requisition books of account, etc.**[2]

(1) Where the [3][Director General or Director] or the [4][Chief Commissioner or Commissioner], in consequence of information in his possession, has reason to believe that—

(*a*) any person to whom a summons under sub-section (1) of section 37 of the Indian Income-tax Act, 1922 (11 of 1922), or under sub-section (1) of section 131 of this Act, or a notice under sub-section (4) of section 22 of the Indian Income-tax Act, 1922, or under sub-section (1) of section 142 of this Act was issued to produce, or cause to be produced, any books of account or other documents has omitted or failed to produce, or cause to be produced, such books of account or other documents, as required by such summons or notice and the said books of account or other documents have been taken into custody by any officer or authority under any other law for the time being in force, or

(*b*) any books of account or other documents will be useful for, or relevant to, any proceeding under the Indian Income-tax Act, 1922 (11 of 1922), or under this Act and any person to whom a summons or notice as aforesaid has been or might be issued will not, or would not, produce or cause to be produced, such books of account or other documents on the return of such books of account or other documents by any officer or authority by whom or which such books of account or other documents have been taken into custody under any other law for the time being in force, or

(*c*) any assets represent either wholly or partly income or property which has not been, or would not have been, disclosed for the purposes of the Indian Income-tax Act, 1922 (11 of 1922), or this Act by any person from whose possession or control such assets have been taken into custody by any officer or authority under any other law for the time being in force,

then, the [5][Director General or Director] or the [6][Chief Commissioner or Commissioner] may authorise any [7][[8][Joint] Director], [9][Joint] Commissioner,

---

1 Inserted by the Taxation Laws (Amendment) Act, 1975, w.e.f. 1-10-1975.

2 **See** rule 112D and Form No. 45C.

3 Substituted for "Director of Inspection" by the Direct Tax Laws (Amendment) Act, 1987, w.e.f. 1-4-1988.

4 Substituted for "Commissioner", *ibid.*

5 Substituted for "Director of Inspection" by the Direct Tax Laws (Amendment) Act, 1987, w.e.f. 1-4-1988

6 Substituted for "Commissioner", *ibid.*

7 Substituted for "Deputy Director of Inspection", *ibid.*

8 Substituted for "Deputy" by the Finance (No. 2) Act, 1998, w.e.f. 1-10-1998.

9 Substituted for "Deputy" by the Finance (No. 2) Act, 1998, w.e.f. 1-10-1998, which was earlier substituted for "Inspecting Assistant" by the Direct Tax Laws (Amendment) Act, 1987, w.e.f. 1-4-1988.

[1][Assistant Director] [2][or Deputy Director], [3][Assistant Commissioner [4][or Deputy Commissioner] or Income-tax Officer] (hereafter in this section and in sub-section (2) of section 278D referred to as the requisitioning officer) to require the officer or authority referred to in clause (*a*) or clause (*b*) or clause (*c*), as the case may be, to deliver such books of account, other documents or assets to the requisitioning officer.

(2) On a requisition being made under sub-section (1), the officer or authority referred to in clause (*a*) or clause (*b*) or clause (*c*), as the case may be, of that sub-section shall deliver the books of account, other documents or assets to the requisitioning officer either forthwith or when such officer or authority is of the opinion that it is no longer necessary to retain the same in his or its custody.

(3) Where any books of account, other documents or assets have been delivered to the requisitioning officer, the provisions of sub-sections (4A) to (14) (both inclusive) of section 132 and section 132B shall, so far as may be, apply as if such books of account, other documents or assets had been seized under sub-section (1) of section 132 by the requisitioning officer from the custody of the person referred to in clause (*a*) or clause (*b*) or clause (*c*), as the case may be, of sub-section (1) of this section and as if for the words "the authorised officer" occurring in any of the aforesaid sub-sections (4A) to (14), the words "the requisitioning officer" were substituted.]

[7][**132B. Application of seized or requisitioned assets**

(1) The assets seized under section 132 or requisitioned under section 132A may be dealt with in the following manner, namely:—

(*i*) the amount of any existing liability under this Act, the Wealth-tax Act, 1957 (27 of 1957), the Expenditure-tax Act, 1987 (35 of 1987), the Gift-tax Act, 1958 (18 of 1958) and the Interest-tax Act, 1974 (45 of 1974), and the amount of the liability determined on completion of the assessment [6][under section 153A and the assessment of the year relevant to the previous year in which search is initiated or requisition is made, or the amount of liability determined on completion of the assessment under Chapter XIV-B for the block period, as the case may be,] (including any penalty levied or interest payable in connection with such assessment) and in respect of which such person is in default or is deemed to be in default, may be recovered out of such assets:

---

1 Substituted for "Assistant Director of Inspection" by the Direct Tax Laws (Amendment) Act, 1987, w.e.f. 1-4-1988.

2 Inserted by the Finance (No. 2) Act, 1998, w.e.f. 1-10-1998.

3 Substituted for "or Income-tax Officer" by the Direct Tax Laws (Amendment) Act, 1987, (as amended by the Finance Act, 1988) w.e.f. 1-4-1988.

4 Inserted by the Finance (No. 2) Act, 1998, w.e.f. 1-10-1998.

5 Substituted by the Finance Act, 2002, w.e.f. 1-6-2002.

6 Substituted for "under Chapter XIVB for the block period" by the Finance Act, 2003, w.e.f. 1-6-2003.

[1][Provided that where the person concerned makes an application to the Assessing Officer within thirty days from the end of the month in which the asset was seized, for release of asset and the nature and source of acquisition of any such asset is explained] to the satisfaction of the Assessing Officer, the amount of any existing liability referred to in this clause may be recovered out of such asset and the remaining portion, if any, of the asset may be released, with the prior approval of the Chief Commissioner or Commissioner, to the person from whose custody the assets were seized:

Provided further that such asset or any portion thereof as is referred to in the first proviso shall be released within a period of one hundred and twenty days from the date on which the last of the authorisations for search under section 132 or for requisition under section 132A, as the case may be, was executed;

(*ii*) if the assets consist solely of money, or partly of money and partly of other assets, the Assessing Officer may apply such money in the discharge of the liabilities referred to in clause (*i*) and the assessee shall be discharged of such liability to the extent of the money so applied;

(*iii*) the assets other than money may also be applied for the discharge of any such liability referred to in clause (*i*) as remains undischarged and for this purpose such assets shall be deemed to be under distraint as if such distraint was effected by the Assessing Officer or, as the case may be, the Tax Recovery Officer under authorisation from the Chief Commissioner or Commissioner under sub-section (5) of section 226 and the Assessing Officer or, as the case may be, the Tax Recovery Officer may recover the amount of such liabilities by the sale of such assets and such sale shall be effected in the manner laid down in the Third Schedule.

(2) Nothing contained in sub-section (1) shall preclude the recovery of the amount of liabilities aforesaid by any other mode laid down in this Act.

(3) Any assets or proceeds thereof which remain after the liabilities referred to in clause (*i*) of sub-section (1) are discharged shall be forthwith made over or paid to the persons from whose custody the assets were seized.

(4) (*a*) The Central Government shall pay simple interest at the rate of [2][six per cent] per annum on the amount by which the aggregate amount of money seized under section 132 or requisitioned under section 132A, as reduced by the amount of money, if any, released under the first proviso to clause (*i*) of sub-section (1), and of the proceeds, if any, of the assets sold towards the discharge of the existing liability referred to in clause (*i*) of sub-section (1), exceeds the

---

1 Substituted for "Provided that where the nature and source of acquisition of any such asset is explained" by the Finance Act, 2003, w.e.f. 1-6-2003.

2 Substituted for "eight per cent" by the Taxation Laws (Amendment) Act, 2003, w.e.f. 8-9-2003.

aggregate of the amount required to meet the liabilities referred to in clause (*i*) of sub-section (1) of this section.

(*b*) Such interest shall run from the date immediately following the expiry of the period of one hundred and twenty days from the date on which the last of the authorisations for search under section 132 or requisition under section 132A was executed to the date of completion of the assessment [1][under section 153A or] under Chapter XIV-B.

Explanation.—In this section,—

(*i*) "block period" shall have the meaning assigned to it in clause (*a*) of section 158B;

(*ii*) "execution of an authorisation for search or requisition" shall have the same meaning as assigned to it in *Explanation* 2 to section 158BE.]

---

1 Inserted by the Finance Act, 2003, w.e.f. 1-6-2003.

Annexure II

Provisions of Allied enactments referred to in the Act

I. Section 2(1)(*b*) of the Chartered Accountants Act, 1949

[Referred in section 2(*g*)]

2. Interpretation.—(1) In this Act, unless there is anything repugnant in the subject or contcxt,—

* * *

(*b*) "chartered accountant" means a person who is a member of the Institute;

II. Section 2(1)(*i*) of the Advocates Act, 1961

[Referred in section 2(*q*)]

(*i*) "legal practitioner" means an advocate or vakil of any High Court, a pleader, mukhtar or revenue agent;

III. Section 21 of the Indian Penal Code, 1860

[Referred in section 33]

21. "Public Servant".—The words "Public Servant" denote a person falling under any of the descriptions hereinafter following, namely:—

First.—[*Repealed by the Adaptation of Laws Order, 1950*].

Second.—Every Commissioned Officer in the Military, Naval or Air Forces of India;

Third.—Every Judge including any person empowered by law to discharge whether by himself or as a member of any body of persons, any adjudicatory functions;

Fourth.—Every officer of a Court of Justice including a liquidator, receiver or commissioner whose duty it is, as such officer, to investigate or report on any matter of law or fact, or to make, authenticate, or keep any document, or to take charge or dispose of any property, or to execute any judicial process, or to administer any oath, or to interpret, or to preserve order in the Court, and every person specially authorized by a Court of Justice to perform any of such dates;

Fifth.—Every juryman, assessor, or member of a panchayat assisting a Court of Justice or public servant;

Sixth.—Every arbitrator or other person to whom any cause or matter has been referred for decision or report by any Court of Justice, or by any other competent public authority;

Seventh.—Every person who holds any office by virtue of which he is empowered to place or keep any person in confinement;

Eighth.—Every officer of the Government whose duty it is, as such officer, to prevent offences, to give information of offences, to bring offenders to justice, or to protect the public health, safety or convenience;

Ninth.—Every officer whose duty it is, as such officer, to take, receive, keep or expend any property on behalf of the Government, or to make any survey, assessment or contract on behalf of the Government, or to execute any revenue-process, or to investigate, or to report, on any matter affecting the pecuniary interests of the Government, or to make, authenticate or keep any document relating to the pecuniary interests of the Government, or to prevent the infraction of any law for the protection of the pecuniary interests of the Government;

Tenth.—Every officer whose duty it is, as such officer, to take, receive, keep or expend any property, to make any survey or assessment or to levy any rate or tax for any secular common purpose of any village, town or district, or to make, authenticate or keep any document for the ascertaining of the rights of the people of any village, town or district;

Eleventh.—Every person who holds any office in virtue of which he is empowered to prepare, publish, maintain or revise an electoral roll or to conduct an election or part of an election;

Twelfth.—Every person—

(*a*) in the service or pay of the Government or remunerated by fees or commission for the performance of any public duty by the Government;

(*b*) in the service or pay of a local authority, a corporation established by or under a Central, Provincial or State Act or a Government company as defined in section 617 of the Companies Act, 1956 (1 of 1956).

Illustration

A Municipal Commissioner is a public servant.

Explanation 1.—Persons falling under any of the above descriptions are public servants, whether appointed by the Government or not.

Explanation 2.—Wherever the words "public servant" occur, they shall be understood of every person who is in actual possession of the situation of a public servant, whatever legal defect there may be in his right to hold that situation.

Explanation 3.—The word "election" denotes an election for the purpose of selecting members of any legislative, municipal or other public authority, of whatever character, the method of selection to which is by, or under, any law prescribed as by election.

IV. Section 193 of the Indian Penal Code, 1860

[Referred in section 16(5), 17(6), 28(5)]

193. Punishment for false evidence.—Whoever intentionally gives false evidence in any stage of a judicial proceeding, or fabricates false evidence for the purpose of being used in any stage of a judicial proceeding, shall be punished with imprisonment of either description for a term which may extend to seven years, and shall also be liable to fine;

and whoever intentionally gives or fabricates false evidence in any other case, shall be punished with imprisonment of either description for a term which may extend to three years, and shall also be liable to fine.

Explanation 1.—A trial before a Court-martial is a judicial proceeding.

Explanation 2.—An investigation directed by law preliminary to a proceeding before a Court of Justice, is a stage of a judicial proceeding, though that investigation may not take place before a Court of Justice.

Illustration

A, in an enquiry before a Magistrate for the purpose of ascertaining whether *Z* ought to be committed for trial, makes on oath a statement which he knows to be false. As this enquiry is a stage of a judicial proceeding, *A* has given false evidence.

Explanation 3.—An investigation directed by a Court of Justice according to law, and conducted under the authority of a Court of Justice, is a stage of a judicial proceeding, though that investigation may not take place before a Court of Justice.

Illustration

A, in an enquiry before an officer deputed by a Court of Justice to ascertain on the spot the boundaries of land, makes on oath a statement which he knows to be false. As this enquiry is a stage of a judicial proceeding. *A* has given false evidence.

V. Section 228 of the Indian Penal Code, 1860

[Referred in section 16(5), 17(6), 28(5)]

228. Intentional insult or interruption to public servant sitting in judicial proceeding.—Whoever intentionally offers any insult, or causes any interruption to any public servant, while such public servant is sitting in any stage of a judicial proceeding, shall be punished with simple imprisonment for a term which may extend to six months, or with fine which may extend to one thousand rupees, or with both.

VI. Section 345 of the Code of Criminal Procedure, 1973

[Referred in section 16(5), 28(5)]

345. Procedure in certain cases of contempt.—(1) When any such offence as is described in section 175, section 178, section 179, section 180, or section 228 of the Indian Penal Code, (45 of 1860), is committed in the view or presence of any Civil, Criminal or Revenue Court, the Court may cause the offender to be detained in custody and may, at any time before the rising of the Court on the same day, take cognizance of the offence and, after giving the offender a reasonable opportunity of showing cause why he should not be punished under this section, or sentence the offender to fine not exceeding two hundred rupees, and, in default of payment of fine, to simple imprisonment for a term which may extend to one month, unless such fine be sooner paid.

(2) In every such case the Court shall record the facts constituting the offence, with the statement (if any) made by the offender, as well as the finding and sentence.

(3) If the offence is under section 228 of the Indian Penal Code (45 of 1860), the record shall show the nature and stage of the judicial proceeding in which the Court interrupted or insulted was sitting, and the nature of the interruption or insult.

VII. Section 346 of the Code of Criminal Procedure, 1973

[Referred in section 16(5), 17(6), 28(5)]

346. Procedure where Court considers that case should not be dealt with under section 345.—(1) If the Court in any case considers that a person accused of any of the offences referred to in section 345 and committed in its view or presence should be imprisoned otherwise than in default of payment of fine, or that a fine exceeding two hundred rupees should be imposed upon him, or such Court is for any other reason or opinion that the case should not be disposed of under section 345, such Court, after recording the facts constituting the offence and the statement of the accused as hereinbefore provided, may forward the case to a Magistrate having jurisdiction to try the same, and may require security to be given for the appearance of such person before such Magistrate, or if sufficient security is not given shall forward such person in custody to such Magistrate.

(2) The Magistrate to whom any case is forwarded under this section shall proceed to deal with, as far as may be, as if it were instituted on a police report.

VIII. Section 123 of the Indian Evidence Act, 1872

[Referred in section 28(2)(*d*)]

123. Evidence as to affairs of State.—No one shall be permitted to give any evidence derived from unpublished official records relating to any affairs of State, except with the permission of the officer at the head of the department concerned, who shall give or withhold such permission as he thinks fit.

IX. Section 124 of the Indian Evidence Act, 1872

[Referred in section 28(2)(*d*)]

124. Official communications.—No public officer shall be compelled to disclose communications, made to him in official confidence, when he considers that the public interest would suffer by the disclosure.

X. Section 6 of the General Clauses Act, 1897

[Referred in section 49(6)]

6. Effect of repeal.—Where this Act, or any Central Act or Regulation made after the commencement of this Act, repeals any enactment hitherto made or hereafter to be made, then, unless a different intention appears, the repeal shall not—

(*a*) revive anything not in force or existing at the time at which the repeal takes effect; or

(*b*) affect the previous operation of any enactment so repealed or anything duly done or suffered thereunder; or

(*c*) affect any right, privilege, obligation or liability acquired, accrued or incurred under any enactment so repealed; or

(*d*) affect any penalty, forfeiture or punishment incurred in respect of any offence committed against any enactment so repealed; or

(*e*) affect any investigation, legal proceeding or remedy in respect of any such right, privilege, obligation, liability, penalty, forfeiture or punishment as aforesaid;

and any such investigation, legal proceeding or remedy may be instituted, continued or enforced, and any such penalty, forfeiture or punishment may be imposed as if the repealing Act or Regulation had not been passed.

Annexure III

Notifications and Orders issued under FEMA

Notification issued under section 1

Notification No. GSR 371(E), dated 1-5-2000

In exercise of the powers conferred by sub-section (4) of section 1 of the Foreign Exchange Management Act, 1999 (42 of 1999), the Central Government hereby appoints the 1st day of June, 2000 as the date on which the said Act shall come into force.

Notification issued under section 2(*h*)

Notification No. GSR 402(E), dated 3-5-2000 [*FEMA 15/2000*]

In pursuance of clause (*h*) of section 2 of the Foreign Exchange Management Act, 1999 (42 of 1999), the Reserve Bank notifies debit cards, ATM cards or any other instrument by whatever name called that can be used to create a financial liability, as "currency".

They shall come into effect on the 1st day of June, 2000.

Notifications issued under section 3

I. Notification No. GSR 403(E), dated 3-5-2000 [*FEMA 16/2000*]

In pursuance of the provisions of section 3 of the Foreign Exchange Management Act, 1999 (42 of 1999), the Reserve Bank is pleased to permit—

(1) any person, to receive any payment—

(*a*) made in rupees by order or on behalf of a person resident outside India during his stay in India out of rupee funds provided by him by sale of foreign exchange to an authorised dealer or a money changer in India;

(*b*) made by means of a cheque drawn on a bank situated outside India or a bank draft or travellers cheque issued outside India;

(*c*) made in foreign currency notes directly from out of India;

subject to the condition that the foreign exchange received pursuant to clauses (*b*) and (*c*) shall be offered for sale or caused to be offered for sale to an authorised dealer or a money changer within seven days of receipt thereof;

(*d*) by means of postal order issued by a post office outside India or by a postal money order issued by such post office;

(2) a person resident in India, to make any payment in rupees—

(*i*) towards meeting expenses on account of boarding, lodging and services related thereto or travel to and from and within India of a person resident outside India who is on a visit to India;

(*ii*) to a person resident outside India, by means of a crossed cheque or a draft as consideration for purchase of gold or silver in any form imported by such person in accordance with the terms and conditions imposed under any order issued by the Central Government under the Foreign Trade (Development and Regulations) Act, 1992 or under any other law, rules or regulations for the time being in force;

[1][(2A) A person resident in India being the principal debtor, to make payment to a person resident outside India being a guarantor, such payment being by way of reimbursement of the payment made to the resident creditor by the non-resident guarantor under the guarantee furnished by him on behalf of the principal debtor:

Provided that the amount payable by way of reimbursement by the resident principal debtor shall not exceed the rupee equivalent of the amount paid by the non-resident guarantor under the guarantee:

Provided further that where the payment of the amount is made by the guarantor out of funds held in NRNR/NRO/NRSR account/s maintained with an authorised dealer in India, the amount paid by way of reimbursement shall not be remitted outside India or credited to NRE/FCNR account of the non-resident.]

(3) a company in or resident in India, to make payment in rupees to its [2][non-]whole time director who is resident outside India and is on a visit to India for the company's work and is entitled to payment of sitting fees or commission or remuneration, and travel expenses to and from and within India, in accordance with the provisions contained in the company's Memorandum of Association or Articles of Association or in any agreement entered into by it or in any resolution passed by the company in general meeting or by its Board of Directors, provided the requirements of any law, rules, regulations, directions applicable for making such payments are duly complied with.

They shall come into effect on the 1st day of June, 2000.

II. Notification No. GSR 404(E), dated 3-5-2000 [*FEMA 17/2000*]

In exercise of the powers conferred by section 3 of the Foreign Exchange Management Act, 1999 (42 of 1999), the Reserve Bank hereby directs that the prohibitions imposed by clauses (*b*), (*c*) and (*d*) of that section shall not apply to any transaction entered into in Indian rupees by or with:—

(*i*) a person who is a citizen of India, Nepal or Bhutan resident in Nepal or Bhutan;

---

1 Inserted by Notification No. FEMA/29/RB-2000, dated 26-9-2000.

2 Inserted by Notification No. FEMA/39/2001-RB, dated 27-2-2001, w.e.f. 27-2-2001.

(*ii*) a branch situated in Nepal or Bhutan of any business carried on by a company or a corporation incorporated under any law in force in India, Nepal or Bhutan;

(*iii*) a branch situated in Nepal or Bhutan of any business carried on as a partnership firm or otherwise, by a citizen of India, Nepal or Bhutan.

They shall come into effect on the 1st day of June, 2000.

III. Notification No. GSR 405(E), dated 3-5-2000 [FEMA 18/2000]

In pursuance of clause (*a*) of section 3 of Foreign Exchange Management Act, 1999 (42 of 1999), the Reserve Bank of India is pleased to permit any person to buy from any Post Office, in accordance with any law or rules made thereunder for the time being in force, any foreign exchange in the form of postal orders or money orders.

They shall come into effect on the 1st day of June, 2000.

Notifications issued under section 16(1)

I. Notification No. SO 535(E), dated 1-6-2000

In exercise of the powers conferred under sub-section (1) of section 16 of the Foreign Exchange Management Act, 1999 (42 of 1999), the Central Government hereby appoints the following officers as adjudicating authorities and their respective jurisdiction to hold an inquiry for the purpose of adjudication under section 13 of the said Act, namely:—

Sl. No.	Designation of adjudicating authorities	Jurisdiction
(1)	(2)	(3)
1.	Director	Cases involving an amount exceeding Rupees one crore falling under all the zones of the Directorate of Enforcement.
2.	Special Director of Enforcement-I, in the Headquarters at Delhi.	Cases involving an amount exceeding Rupees one crore falling under Chennai, Calcutta, Delhi, Jallandhar and Bangalore zones of the Directorate of Enforcement as may be assigned by the Director of Enforcement either by general or special order.
3.	Special Director of Enforcement-II in the Headquarters at Delhi.	
4.	Special Director of Enforcement-III at Mumbai.	Cases involving an amount exceeding Rupees one crore falling under Ahmedabad and Mumbai zones of the Directorate of Enforcement.

Sl. No.	Designation of adjudicating authorities	Jurisdiction
(1)	(2)	(3)
5.	Additional Director of Enforcement in the Headquarters at Delhi.	Cases involving an amount exceeding ₹75 lakhs but not more than ₹1 crore falling under all the zones of the Directorate of Enforcement.
6.	Deputy Directors of Enforcement of Ahmedabad/Bangalore /Chennai/Calcutta/ Delhi/Jallandhar/ Mumbai zones.	Cases involving an amount not exceeding ₹75 lakhs falling under the respective zones of the Directorate of Enforcement of such Deputy Director Enforcement or as may be assigned by the Director of Enforcement.

II. Notification No. 1155(E) [20/2000], dated 26-12-2000

In exercise of the powers conferred under sub-section (1) of section 16 of the Foreign Exchange Management Act, 1999 (42 of 1999), the Central Government hereby appoints the officers mentioned in column No. 2 of the Table below as adjudicating authorities to hold an inquiry for the purpose of adjudication in respect of contraventions of sections 6(3)(*g*) and 7(1)(*a*) of the said Act and their jurisdictions as mentioned in column No. 3 of the said Table:

Table

Sl. No.	Designation of adjudicating authorities	Jurisdiction
(1)	(2)	(3)
1.	Commissioner of Customs and Central Excise.	Cases within their territorial jurisdiction, involving an amount exceeding ₹1 crore.
2.	Additional Commissioner of Customs and Central Excise.	Cases within their territorial jurisdiction, involving an amount exceeding ₹75 lakhs, but not more than ₹1 crore.
3.	Joint Commissioner of Customs and Central Excise.	Cases within their territorial jurisdiction not exceeding ₹75 lakhs.

Notification issued under section 16(3)

Notification No. 1157(E) [22/2000], dated 26-12-2000

In exercise of the powers conferred under sub-section (3) of section 16 of the Foreign Exchange Management Act, 1999 (42 of 1999), the Central Government hereby authorises an officer not below the rank of Assistant Director of the Directorate of Enforcement to file complaint before the Adjudicating Authority appointed under sub-section (1) of that section for the purpose of holding inquiry under sub-section (1) of section 16 of the said Act.

Notification issued under section 17(1)

Notification No. 12/2002, dated 27-2-2002

Appointment of Special Director (Appeals)

In exercise of the powers conferred by sub-section (1) of section 17 of the Foreign Exchange Management Act, 1999 (42 of 1999), the Central Government hereby appoints Shri Anil Kumar Jain (Indian Revenue Service 1973), presently posted as the Commissioner of Income-tax (Appeals), Delhi, as the Special Director (Appeals) to hear appeals against the orders of the Adjudicating Authorities under the said Act, falling under all the Zones of the Directorate of Enforcement, the Department of Revenue, in addition to his existing duties with effect from the date of publication of this notification in the Official Gazette.

Notification issued under section 18

Notification No. SO 531(E), dated 1-6-2000

In exercise of the powers conferred by section 18 of the Foreign Exchange Management Act, 1999 (42 of 1999), the Central Government hereby establishes, with immediate effect, the Appellate Tribunal for Foreign Exchange at New Delhi.

Notification issued under section 19(1)

Notification No. SO 537(E), dated 1-6-2000

In exercise of the powers conferred under the proviso to sub-section (1) of section 19 of the Foreign Exchange Management Act, 1999 (42 of 1999), the Central Government hereby notifies the Deputy Director of the Directorate of Enforcement of the concerned Zone to accept the deposit of such penalty as imposed by the Adjudicating Authorities or the Special Director (Appeals) under the provisions of the Act.

Notification issued under section 20(2)(*b*)

Appellate Tribunal Benches

I. Constitution of Benches of Appellate Tribunal

Notification No. S.O. 320(E), dated 4-4-2001 as amended by Notification No. SO 472(E), dated 30-4-2002

In exercise of the powers conferred by clause (*b*) of sub-section (2) of section 20 and section 29 of the Foreign Exchange Management Act, 1999 (42 of 1999), the chairperson hereby constitutes the following Benches of the Appellate Tribunal, namely:—

(*a*) Two single member Benches one consisting of the chairperson and the other consisting of a member, and

(*b*) One Division Bench consisting of the chairperson and the member.

2. The Division Bench referred to in clause (*b*) above shall hear only such cases which in opinion of the chairperson or member involves substantial question of law or mixed question of law and fact which ought to be decided by the Division Bench. The chairperson or member hearing any case irrespective of valuation of the appeal may refer the case for hearing by a Division Bench.

II. Constitution of Benches of Appellate Tribunal

Notification No. SO 388(E), dated 23-3-2004

In exercise of the powers conferred by clause (*b*) of sub-section (2) of section 20 and section 29 of the Foreign Exchange Management Act, 1999 (42 of 1999), the Chairperson hereby constitutes the following Benches of the Appellate Tribunal, namely:—

(*a*) Single Member Benches, one Bench consisting of the Chairperson and other Benches consisting of a Member each; and

(*b*) Division Benches consisting of either the Chairperson with a Member or any two Members sitting jointly.

2. A Division Bench shall hear cases in which the amount of penalty exceeds rupees five lakhs, and all other cases shall be heard by a Single Member Bench. The distribution of work amongst Benches shall be done at times by the Chairperson.

Notification issued under section 36(1)

Notification No. SO 534(E), dated 1-6-2000

In exercise of the powers conferred under sub-section (1) of section 36 of the Foreign Exchange Management Act, 1999 (42 of 1999), the Central Government hereby establishes a Directorate called the Directorate of Enforcement with the following officers as "Officers of Enforcement" for the purposes of this Act, namely:—

(*a*) Director of Enforcement;

(*b*) Special Director of Enforcement;

(*c*) Additional Director of Enforcement;

(*d*) Deputy Director of Enforcement;

(*e*) Deputy Legal Adviser;

(*f*) Assistant Director of Enforcement; and

(*g*) Assistant Legal Adviser.

Notifications issued under section 36(2)

I. Notification No. SO 536(E), dated 1-6-2000

In exercise of the powers conferred under sub-section (2) of section 36 of the Foreign Exchange Management Act, 1999 (42 of 1999), the Central Government hereby authorities the Director of Enforcement to appoint the Chief Enforcement

Officer, Enforcement Officer and Assistant Enforcement Officer as officers of Enforcement.

II. Notification No. SO 797(E), dated 3-7-2003

In pursuance of the Central Government Notification bearing No. SO 536(E), dated 1-6-2000, issued under sub-section (2) of section 36 of the Foreign Exchange Management Act, 1999 (42 of 1999) and in exercise of the powers conferred by the said Notification, the persons holding office under the Foreign Exchange Regulation Act, 1973 (46 of 1973) as Chief Enforcement Officers, Enforcement Officers and Assistant Enforcement Officers are appointed as "Officers of Enforcement" with effect from the first day of June, 2000 for the purposes of the Foreign Exchange Management Act, 1999 (42 of 1999).

Notification issued under section 38(1)

Notification No. 21/2000, dated 26-12-2000

In exercise of the powers conferred under sub-section (1) of section 38 of the Foreign Exchange Management Act, 1999 (42 of 1999), the Central Government hereby authorises officers of the Customs and Central Excise, not below the rank of Deputy Commissioner and officers of the Directorate General of Revenue Intelligence not below the rank of Deputy Director, to exercise the powers conferred under the Act for the contravention referred to in clause (*g*) of sub-section (3) of section 6 and clause (*a*) of sub-section (1) of section 7 of the said Act in accordance with the provisions of section 38(1) of the said Act.

Notification issued under section 45

Foreign Exchange Management (Removal of Difficulties) Order, 2000

Notification No. SO 530(E), dated 1-6-2000

Whereas the Foreign Exchange Management Act, 1999 (42 of 1999) (hereafter referred to as the said Act) came into force on the 1st day of June, 2000;

AND WHEREAS the Foreign Exchange Regulation Act, 1973 (46 of 1973) has been repealed and the Appellate Board constituted under sub-section (1) of section 52 of the said Act (hereafter referred to as the repealed Act) stood dissolved as on 1st June, 2000;

AND WHEREAS any appeal preferred to the Appellate Board under sub-section (2) of section 52 of the Repealed Act but not disposed of before the 1st June, 2000 being the date on which the said Act came into force, shall stand transferred to and shall be disposed of by the Appellate Tribunal constituted under the said Act;

AND WHEREAS the Appellate Tribunal has been established section 18 of the said Act on the 1st June, 2000;

AND WHEREAS under sub-section (1) of section 20 of the said Act the Appellate Tribunal shall consist of a Chairperson and such number of Members as the Central Government may deem fit;

AND WHEREAS the Central Government has initiated measures for filling up the said posts in accordance with sections 20, 21 and 22 of the said Act and the affairs of the Appellate Tribunal are likely to come to standstill unless immediate action is taken to provide for any interim arrangement by way of filling up of the said posts on *ad hoc* basis;

NOW, THEREFORE, in exercise of the powers conferred by section 45 of the Foreign Exchange Management Act, 1999 (42 of 1999), the Central Government hereby makes the following Order, namely:—

1. Short title and commencement.—(1) This Order may be called the Foreign Exchange Management (Removal of Difficulties) Order, 2000.

(2) It shall come into force at once.

2. Appointment of Chairperson and Members of Appellate Tribunal on *ad hoc* basis.—Until a Chairperson and Members are appointed in accordance with the provisions of sections 20, 21 and 22 of the said Act, the Central Government shall appoint such person as it may deem fit on *ad hoc* basis to discharge functions of a Chairperson and Members of the Appellate Tribunal.

Notification issued under section 47(2)

Change in nomenclature of ECD as FED

Notification No. FEMA.123/2004-RB [*F. No. 1/23/EM/2000-Vol.III*], *dated 9-9-2004, referred to above*

In exercise of the powers conferred by clause (*h*) of sub-section (2) of section 47 of the Foreign Exchange Management Act, 1999 (42 of 1999) and pursuant to change of nomenclature of Exchange Control Department of Reserve Bank of India from "Exchange Control Department" to "Foreign Exchange Department", the Reserve Bank hereby notifies that with effect from January 31, 2004, the words "Exchange Control Department" and "ECD" appearing in the Regulations notified from time to time by Reserve Bank of India, shall be read as "Foreign Exchange Department" and "FED", respectively.

Notifications issued under section 49(3) & (4)

Notified Officers of Enforcement

I. Notification No. SO 308(E), dated 20-3-2003

Whereas the provisions of the Foreign Exchange Management Act, 1999 (42 of 1999) were brought into force *vide* GSR 371(E) published in the Gazette of India on 1st May, 2002 giving effect to the provisions of the said Act from 1st June, 2000;

And, whereas, the Central Government by an order published in the Gazette in exercise of the powers conferred under section 50 of Foreign Exchange Regulation Act, 1973 (repealed Act), read with sub-section (1) of section 4 and clause (*c*) of section 3 of the repealed Act appointed certain officers of the Central Government to adjudicate cases for contravention made on or before 31st May, 2002 of the provisions of the repealed Act;

Now, therefore, in exercise of the powers conferred under section 50, read with sub-section (1) of section 4 of the Foreign Exchange Regulation Act, 1973 (repealed Act) and sub-sections (3) and (4) of section 49 of the Foreign Exchange Management Act, 1999 (42 of 1999), the Central Government hereby appoints the following persons given in the table below as Officers of the Enforcement, namely:—

Sl. No.	Name and Designation of Officer
Delhi	
1.	Shri C.L. Mahar, Joint Commissioner of Customs & Central Excise
2.	Shri P.K. Dash, II, Additional Commissioner of Customs & Central Excise
3.	Shri A.K. Jyothishi, Additional Commissioner of Customs & Central Excise
4.	Shri R.K. Yadav, Additional Commissioner of Income-tax
5.	Shri N.P. Sinha, Additional Commissioner of Income-tax
6.	Shri Kirnwant Sahai, Additional Commissioner of Income-tax
7.	Shri Kunal Singh, Additional Commissioner of Income-tax
8.	Shri Pushkar Bhatnagar, Additional Commissioner of Income-tax
9.	Shri R.L. Meena, Additional Commissioner of Income-tax
10.	Shri H.B.S. Gill, Additional Commissioner of Income-tax
Kolkata	
1.	Shri R.C. Mahapatra, Additional Commissioner of Customs & Central Excise
2.	Shri T.K. Kar, Additional Commissioner of Customs & Central Excise
3.	Shri B.K. Singh, Joint Commissioner of Income-tax
4.	Shri Samir Mukhopadhyay, Additional Commissioner of Income-tax
5.	Shri R.B. Mishra, Joint Commissioner of Income-tax
Chennai	
1.	Shri P.A. Parumal, Additional Commissioner of Customs & Central Excise
2.	Shri B.S.V. Murthy, Additional Commissioner of Customs & Central Excise
3.	Shri K. Umesh, Additional Commissioner of Customs & Central Excise
4.	Shri C.P. Rao[1], Additional Commissioner of Customs & Central Excise
5.	Shri A.A. Khalkho, Additional Commissioner of Income-tax
6.	Shri J. Albert, Additional Commissioner of Income-tax
7.	Dr. I. Vijaya Kumar, Additional Commissioner of Income-tax

1 Corrected by Notification No. 1169(E), dated 29-9-2003.

Sl. No.	Name and Designation of Officer

Mumbai

1. Shri A.K. Pandey, Additional Commissioner of Customs & Central Excise
2. Shri R.L. Meena, Additional Commissioner of Customs & Central Excise
3. Shri R.S. Rautela, Additional Commissioner of Customs & Central Excise
4. Shri B. Bhattacharya, Additional Commissioner of Customs & Central Excise
5. Shri Ajay Dixit, Joint Commissioner of Customs & Central Excise
6. Shri Pawan Kumar Sinha, Joint Commissioner of Customs & Central Excise
7. Shri A.K. Mehra, Additional Commissioner of Customs & Central Excise
8. Shri D.D. Gupta, Additional Commissioner of Income-tax
9. Shri Bharat Tripathi, Additional Commissioner of Income-tax
10. Shri Hareshwar Sharma, Additional Commissioner of Income-tax
11. Shri Bharat Bhushan, Additional Commissioner of Income-tax
12. Shri Samar Bhadra, Joint Commissioner of Income-tax
13. Shri Samuel Darse, Joint Commissioner of Income-tax
14. Shri Anand Sharan Singh, Additional Commissioner of Income-tax
15. Shri Devadasan, Joint Commissioner of Income-tax

II. Notification No. SO 395(E), dated 31-3-2003

Whereas the provisions of the Foreign Exchange Management Act, 1999 (42 of 1999) were brought into force *vide* GSR 371(E) published in the Gazette of India on 1st May, 2000 giving effect to the provisions of the said Act from 1st June, 2000;

And, whereas the Central Government by an order published in the Gazette in exercise of the powers conferred under section 50 of Foreign Exchange Regulation Act, 1973 (Repealed Act) appointed certain officers of the Central Government to take action for contravention under section 51 of the repealed Act and also initiated certain actions under the provisions of the repealed Act;

And, whereas, the Central Government by an order published in the Official Gazette *vide* SO 308(E), dated 20th March, 2003 appointed certain officers as Officers of Enforcement to give continued effect for the action taken under paragraph 2 above.

Now, therefore, in exercise of the powers conferred under section 50 of the Foreign Exchange Regulation Act, 1973 (Repealed Act) read with section 5 of the Repealed Act and sub-sections (3) and (4) of section 49 of the Foreign Exchange Management Act, 1999 (42 of 1999), the Central Government authorises the persons mentioned in the Table below to function as Adjudicating Officers to adjudicate the cases of contravention of any of the provisions of the Repealed Act [other than section 13, clause (*a*) of section 18, sub-clause (*a*) of sub-section (1) of section 19] or any rule or direction or order made thereunder, such cases as may be assigned by the Directorate of Enforcement, namely:—

Sl. No.	Name and Designation of Officer
Delhi	
1.	Shri C.L. Mahar, Joint Commissioner of Customs & Central Excise
2.	Shri P.K. Dash, II, Additional Commissioner of Customs & Central Excise
3.	Shri A.K. Jyothishi, Additional Commissioner of Customs & Central Excise
4.	Shri R.K. Yadav, Additional Commissioner of Income-tax
5.	Shri N.P. Sinha, Additional Commissioner of Income-tax
6.	Shri Kirnwant Sahai, Additional Commissioner of Income-tax
7.	Shri Kunal Singh, Additional Commissioner of Income-tax
8.	Shri Pushkar Bhatnagar, Additional Commissioner of Income-tax
9.	Shri R.L. Meena, Additional Commissioner of Income-tax
10.	Shri H.B.S. Gill, Additional Commissioner of Income-tax
Kolkata	
1.	Shri R.C. Mahapatra, Additional Commissioner of Customs & Central Excise
2.	Shri T.K. Kar, Additional Commissioner of Customs & Central Excise
3.	Shri B.K. Singh, Joint Commissioner of Income-tax
4.	Shri Samir Mukhopadhyay, Additional Commissioner of Income-tax
5.	Shri R.B. Mishra, Joint Commissioner of Income-tax
Chennai	
1.	Shri P.A. Parumal, Additional Commissioner of Customs & Central Excise
2.	Shri B.S.V. Murthy, Additional Commissioner of Customs & Central Excise
3.	Shri K. Umesh, Additional Commissioner of Customs & Central Excise
4.	Shri C.P. Rao[1], Additional Commissioner of Customs & Central Excise
5.	Shri A.A. Khalkho, Additional Commissioner of Income-tax

1 Corrected by Notification No. 1170(E), dated 29-9-2003.

Sl. No.	Name and Designation of Officer
6.	Shri J. Albert, Additional Commissioner of Income-tax
7.	Dr. I. Vijaya Kumar, Additional Commissioner of Income-tax
Mumbai	
1.	Shri A.K. Pandey, Additional Commissioner of Customs & Central Excise
2.	Shri R.L. Meena, Additional Commissioner of Customs & Central Excise
3.	Shri R.S. Rautela, Additional Commissioner of Customs & Central Excise
4.	Shri B. Bhattacharya, Additional Commissioner of Customs & Central Excise
5.	Shri Ajay Dixit, Joint Commissioner of Customs & Central Excise
6.	Shri Pawan Kumar Sinha, Joint Commissioner of Customs & Central Excise
7.	Shri A.K. Mehra, Additional Commissioner of Customs & Central Excise
8.	Shri D.D. Gupta, Additional Commissioner of Income-tax
9.	Shri Bharat Tripathi, Additional Commissioner of Income-tax
10.	Shri Hareshwar Sharma, Additional Commissioner of Income-tax
11.	Shri Bharat Bhushan, Additional Commissioner of Income-tax
12.	Shri Samar Bhadra, Joint Commissioner of Income-tax
13.	Shri Samuel Darse, Joint Commissioner of Income-tax
14.	Shri Anand Sharan Singh, Additional Commissioner of Income-tax
15.	Shri Devadasan, Joint Commissioner of Income-tax

III. Notification No. SO 964(E), dated 25-8-2003

Whereas the provisions of the Foreign Exchange Management Act, 1999 (42 of 1999) were brought into force *vide* GSR 371(E) published in the Gazette of India on 1st May, 2000 giving effect to the provisions of the said Act from 1st June, 2000;

And, whereas the Central Government by an Order published in the Gazette in exercise of the powers conferred under section 50 of Foreign Exchange Regulation Act, 1973 (repealed Act) read with sub-section (1) of section 4 and clause (*e*) of section 3 of the repealed Act appointed certain officers of the Central Government to adjudicate cases for contravention made on or before 31st May, 2002 of the provisions of the repealed Act;

Now, therefore, in exercise of the powers conferred under section 50 read with sub-section (1) of section 4 of the Foreign Exchange Regulation Act, 1973 (repealed Act) and sub-sections (3) and (4) of section 49 of the Foreign Exchange Management Act, 1999 (42 of 1999), the Central Government hereby appoints the following persons given in the table below as Officers of the Enforcement, namely:—

Table

Sl. No.	*Name and Designation of Officer*
Delhi	
1.	Shri K. Srivastava, Commissioner, Directorate of Housing and Welfare, Customs & Central Excise
2.	Shri S.K.S. Somvanshi, Commissioner, Directorate of Publicity & Public Relation, Customs & Central Excise
3.	Shri V.K. Sharma, ADG, Directorate General of Audit, Customs & Central Excise
4.	Shri Suman Nayar, Commissioner, Directorate of O&M Services, Customs & Central Excise
5.	Ms. Rashida Hussain, ADG, Directorate General of Inspection, Customs & Central Excise
6.	Ms. Sheila Sangwan, ADG, National Academy of Customs, Excise & Narcotics
7.	Shri Sanjeev Sachdeva, ADG, Directorate General of Central Excise Intelligence
8.	Ms. Chitra Gaurilal, Commissioner, Directorate of Data Management, Customs & Central Excise
9.	Ms. Jasdeep V. Singh, Commissioner, Directorate of Preventive Operation, Customs & Central Excise
10.	Shri T. Prem Kumar, ADG, Directorate General Of Inspection, Customs & Central Excise
11.	Shri P.K. Mohanty, Additional Director General, Directorate General of Central Excise Intelligence
12.	Ms. Rani S. Nair, Commissioner of Income-tax
13.	Shri A.K. Singh, Commissioner of Income-tax
14.	Shri M.S. Kaushik, Commissioner of Income-tax
15.	Shri A.K. Tewari, Commissioner of Income-tax
16.	Shri Sushil Chandra, Commissioner of Income-tax
17.	Shri N.K. Sangwan, Commissioner of Income-tax
18.	Shri B.P. Meena, Commissioner of Income-tax
19.	Shri A. Bhaskar Reddy, Commissioner of Income-tax
20.	Shri S.S. Rathore, Commissioner of Income-tax
21.	Shri B.D. Gupta, Commissioner of Income-tax

Sl. No.	Name and Designation of Officer
22.	Shri Akhilesh Ranjan, Commissioner of Income-tax
23.	Shri Harsh Bardhan, Commissioner of Income-tax
24.	Shri Ashutosh Chandra, Commissioner of Income-tax
Mumbai	
1.	N. Sasidharan, Commissioner, Directorate of Valuation, Customs & Central Excise
2.	R.P. Raheja, ADG, Directorate General of Service Tax, Customs & Central Excise
3.	R.M. Ramchandani, ADG, Directorate General of Audit, Customs & Central Excise
4.	Deepak Shetty, ADG, Central Economic Intelligence
5.	Ms. K. Satpathy, ADG, Directorate General of Systems, Customs & Central Excise

IV. Notification No. SO. 986(E), dated 28-8-2003

Whereas the provisions of the Foreign Exchange Management Act, 1999 (42 of 1999) were brought into force *vide* GSR 371(E), published in the Gazette of India on 1st May, 2000 giving effect to the provisions of the said Act from 1st June, 2000;

And, whereas the Central Government by an Order published in the Gazette in exercise of the powers conferred under section 50 of Foreign Exchange Regulation Act, 1973 (repealed Act) appointed certain officers of the Central Government to take action for contravention under section 51 of the repealed Act and also initiated certain actions under the provisions of the repealed Act;

And, whereas, the Central Government by an order published in the Official Gazette *vide* S.O. 964(E), dated 25-8-2003 appointed certain officers as Officers of Enforcement to give continued effect from the action taken under paragraph 2 above.

Now, therefore in exercise of the powers conferred under section 50 of the Foreign Exchange Regulation Act, 1973 (repealed Act) read with section 5 of the repealed Act and sub-sections (3) and (4) of section 49 of the Foreign Exchange Management Act, 1999 (42 of 1999), the Central Government authorises the persons mentioned in the Table below to function as adjudicating officers to adjudicate the cases of contravention of any of the provisions of the repealed Act [other than section 13, clause (*a*) of section 18, sub-clause (*a*) of sub-section (1) of section 19] or any rule or direction or order made thereunder, such cases as may be assigned by the Directorate of Enforcement, namely:—

Table

Sl. No.	*Name and Designation of Officer*
Delhi	
1.	Shri K. Srivastava, Commissioner, Directorate of Housing and Welfare, Customs & Central Excise
2.	Shri S.K.S. Somvanshi, Commissioner, Directorate of Publicity & Public Relation, Customs & Central Excise
3.	Shri V.K. Sharma, ADG, Directorate General of Audit, Customs & Central Excise
4.	Shri Suman Nayar, Commissioner, Directorate of O&M Services, Customs & Central Excise
5.	Ms. Rashida Hussain, ADG, Directorate General of Inspection, Customs & Central Excise
6.	Ms. Sheila Sangwan, ADG, National Academy of Customs, Excise & Narcotics
7.	Shri Sanjeev Sachdeva, ADG, Directorate General of Central Excise Intelligence
8.	Ms. Chitra Gaurilal, Commissioner, Directorate of Data Management, Customs & Central Excise
9.	Ms. Jasdeep V. Singh, Commissioner, Directorate of Preventive Operation, Customs & Central Excise
10.	Shri T. Prem Kumar, ADG, Directorate General of Inspection, Customs & Central Excise
11.	Shri P.K. Mohanty, Additional Director General, Directorate General of Central Excise Intelligence
12.	Ms. Rani S. Nair, Commissioner of Income-tax
13.	Shri A.K. Singh, Commissioner of Income-tax
14.	Shri M.S. Kaushik, Commissioner of Income-tax
15.	Shri A.K. Tewari, Commissioner of Income-tax
16.	Shri Sushil Chandra, Commissioner of Income-tax
17.	Shri N.K. Sangwan, Commissioner of Income-tax
18.	Shri B.P. Meena, Commissioner of Income-tax
19.	Shri A. Bhaskar Reddy, Commissioner of Income-tax
20.	Shri S.S. Rathore, Commissioner of Income-tax
21.	Shri B.D. Gupta, Commissioner or Income-tax
22.	Shri Akhilesh Ranjan, Commissioner of Income-tax
23.	Shri Harsh Bardhan, Commissioner of Income-tax
24.	Shri Ashuotosh Chandra, Commissioner of Income-tax

Sl. No.	Name and Designation of Officer
Mumbai	
1.	Shri N. Sasidharan, Commissioner of Directorate of Valuation, Customs & Central Excise
2.	Shri R.P. Raheja, ADG, Directorate General of Service Tax, Customs & Central Excise
3.	Shri R.M. Ramchandani, ADG, Directorate General of Audit, Customs and Central Excise
4.	Shri Deepak Shetty, ADG, Central Economic Intelligence
5.	Ms. K. Satpathy, ADG, Directorate General of Systems, Customs & Central Excise

V. Notification No. SO 1394(E), dated 28-11-2003

Whereas the provisions of the Foreign Exchange Management Act, 1999 (42 of 1999) were brought into force *vide* GSR 371(E) published in the Gazette of India on 1st May, 2000 giving effect to the provisions of the said Act from 1st June, 2000;

And, whereas, the Central Government by an order published in the Gazette in exercise of the powers conferred under section 50 of Foreign Exchange Regulation Act, 1973 (Repealed Act) read with sub-section (1) of section 4 and clause (*e*) of section 3 of the repealed Act appointed certain officers of the Central Government to adjudicate cases for contravention made on or before 31st May, 2002 of the provisions of the repealed Act.

Now, therefore, in exercise of the powers conferred under section 50 read with sub-section (1) of section 4 of the Foreign Exchange Regulation Act, 1973 (Repealed Act) and sub-sections (3) and (4) of section 49 of the Foreign Exchange Management Act, 1999 (42 of 1999), the Central Government hereby appoints the following persons given in the Table below as Officers of the Enforcement, namely:—

Table

Sl. No.	Name and Designation of Officer
1.	Shri C.S. Parthasarthy, Additional Commissioner of Income Tax, Mumbai.
2.	Shri Shantam Bose, Additional Commissioner of Income Tax, Mumbai.

VI. Notification No. SO 1424(E), dated 16-12-2003

Whereas the provisions of the Foreign Exchange Management Act, 1999 (42 of 1999) were brought into force *vide* GSR 371(E) published in the Gazette of India on 1st May, 2000 giving effect to the provisions of the said Act from 1st June, 2000;

And, whereas the Central Government by an order published in the Gazette in exercise of the powers conferred under section 50 of Foreign Exchange Regulation Act, 1973 (Repealed Act) appointed certain officers of the Central Government to take action for contravention under section 51 of the Repealed Act and also initiated certain actions under the provisions of the Repealed Act;

And, whereas, the Central Government by an order published in the Official Gazette *vide* SO 1394(E), dated 28th November, 2003 appointed certain officers as Officers of Enforcement to give continued effect for the action taken under paragraph 2 above.

Now, therefore, in exercise of the powers conferred under section 50 of the Foreign Exchange Regulation Act, 1973 (Repealed Act) read with section 5 of the Repealed Act under sub-sections (3) and (4) of section 49 of the Foreign Exchange Management Act, 1999 (42 of 1999), the Central Government authorises the persons mentioned in the Table below to function as adjudicating officers to adjudicate the cases of contravention of any of the provisions of the Repealed Act [other than section 13, clause (*a*) of section 18, sub-clause (*a*) of sub-section (1) of section 19] or any rule or direction or order made thereunder, such cases as may be assigned by the Directorate of Enforcement, namely:—

Table

Sl. No.	Name and Designation of Officer
1.	Shri C.S. Parthasarthy, Additional Commissioner of Income Tax, Mumbai.
2.	Shri Shantam Bose, Additional Commissioner of Income Tax, Mumbai.

Notification issued under section 40 of Reserve Bank of India Act, 1934

Notification No. SO 235(E), dated 27-2-2002

In exercise of the powers conferred by section 40 of the Reserve Bank of India Act, 1934 (2 of 1934) and in supersession of the previous order of the Government of India in the Ministry of Finance (Department of the Economic Affairs) No. SO 140(E), dated 27th February, 1993, the Central Government hereby directs that on and from the 1st day of March, 2002, the Reserve Bank of India, shall,—

(*a*) sell to any authorised person at its offices in Bombay (Mumbai), Calcutta (Kolkata), Madras (Chennai) and New Delhi and at its branches in Ahmedabad, Bangalore, Hyderabad, Kanpur and Nagpur US dollars for delivery at New York or Euro for delivery at Frankfurt for meeting foreign currency payments only at a rate of Exchange expressed in terms of per ₹100 and calculated by that Bank with reference to the prevailing market rate within a margin of five per cent, on either side of such market rate;

(*b*) buy from any authorised person at its offices in Bombay (Mumbai), Calcutta (Kolkata), Madras (Chennai) and New Delhi and at its branches in Ahmedabad, Bangalore, Hyderabad, Kanpur and Nagpur US dollars for delivery at New York or Euro for delivery at Frankfurt at a rate of Exchange expressed in terms of per ₹100 and calculated by that Bank with reference to the prevailing market rate within a margin of five per cent, on either side of such market rate.

Appendix 2
CONSOLIDATED FDI POLICY

SYNOPSIS

Chapter 1

Intent and Objective

Chapter 2

Definitions

Chapter 3

General Conditions on FDI

Chapter 4

Calculation of Foreign Investment

Chapter 5

Foreign Investment Promotion Board (FIPB)

Chapter 6

Sector Specific Conditions on FDI

AGRICULTURE

MANUFACTURING

CONSOLIDATED FDI POLICY[1]

(Effective from April 10, 2012)

Circular 1 of 2012 D/o IPP F. No. 5(2)/2012-FC-I, dated 10-4-2012

Chapter 1

Intent and Objective

1.1 Intent and Objective

1.1.1 It is the intent and objective of the Government of India to attract and promote foreign direct investment in order to supplement domestic capital, technology and skills, for accelerated economic growth. Foreign Direct Investment, as distinguished from portfolio investment, has the connotation of establishing a 'lasting interest' in an enterprise that is resident in an economy other than that of the investor.

1.1.2 The Government has put in place a policy framework on Foreign Direct Investment, which is transparent, predictable and easily comprehensible. This framework is embodied in the Circular on Consolidated FDI Policy, which may be updated every year, to capture and keep pace with the regulatory changes, effected in the interregnum. The Department of Industrial Policy and Promotion (DIPP), Ministry of Commerce & Industry, Government of India makes policy pronouncements on FDI through Press Notes/Press Releases which are notified by the Reserve Bank of India as amendments to the Foreign Exchange Management (Transfer or Issue of Security by Persons Resident Outside India) Regulations, 2000 (notification No .FEMA 20/2000-RB dated May 3, 2000). These notifications take effect from the date of issue of Press Notes/Press Releases, unless specified otherwise therein. In case of any conflict, the relevant FEMA Notification will prevail. The procedural instructions are issued by the Reserve Bank of India *vide* AP DIR (series) Circulars. The regulatory framework, over a period of time, thus, consists of Acts, Regulations, Press Notes, Press Releases, Clarifications, etc.

1.1.3 The present consolidation subsumes and supersedes all Press Notes/ Press Releases/Clarifications/Circulars issued by DIPP, which were in force as on April 09, 2012, and reflects the FDI Policy as on April 10, 2012. This Circular accordingly will take effect from April 10, 2012. Reference to any statute or legislation made in this Circular shall include modifications, amendments or re-enactments thereof.

1.1.4 Notwithstanding the rescission of earlier Press Notes/Press Releases/ Clarifications/Circulars, anything done or any action taken or purported to have been done or taken under the rescinded Press Notes/Press Releases/ Clarifications/Circulars prior to April 10, 2012, shall, in so far as it is not inconsistent with those Press Notes/Press Releases/Clarifications/Circulars, be deemed to have been done or taken under the corresponding provisions of this circular and shall be valid and effective.

---

1 Issued by the Department of Industrial Policy and Promotion, Ministry of Commerce and Industry Government of India.

Chapter 2

Definitions

2.1 Definitions

2.1.1 'AD Category-I Bank' means a bank (Scheduled Commercial, State or Urban Cooperative) which is authorized under Section 10(1) of FEMA to undertake all current and capital account transactions according to the directions issued by the RBI from time to time.

2.1.2 'Authorized Bank' means a bank including a co-operative bank (other than an authorized dealer) authorized by the Reserve Bank to maintain an account of a person resident outside India

2.1.3 'Authorized Dealer' means a person authorized as an authorized dealer under sub-section (1) of section 10 of FEMA.

2.1.4 'Authorized Person' means an authorized dealer, money changer, offshore banking unit or any other person for the time being authorized under sub-section (*a*) of Section 10 of FEMA to deal in foreign exchange or foreign securities.

2.1.5 'Capital' means equity shares; fully, compulsorily & mandatorily convertible preference shares; fully, compulsorily & mandatorily convertible debentures. *Note:* Warrants and partly paid shares can be issued to person/(s) resident outside India only after approval through the Government route[1].

2.1.6 'Capital account transaction' means a transaction which alters the assets or liabilities, including contingent liabilities, outside India of persons resident in India or assets or liabilities in India of persons resident outside India, and includes transactions referred to in sub-section (3) of section 6 of FEMA.

2.1.7 A company is considered as "Controlled" by resident Indian citizens if the resident Indian citizens and Indian companies, which are owned and controlled by resident Indian citizens, have the power to appoint a majority of its directors in that company .

2.1.8 'Depository Receipt' (DR) means a negotiable security issued outside India by a Depository bank, on behalf of an Indian company, which represent the local Rupee denominated equity shares of the company held as deposit by a Custodian bank in India. DRs are traded on Stock Exchanges in the US, Singapore, Luxembourg, etc. DRs listed and traded in the US markets are known as American Depository Receipts (ADRs) and those listed and traded anywhere/elsewhere are known as Global Depository Receipts (GDRs).

2.1.9 'Erstwhile Overseas Corporate Body' (OCB) means a company, partnership firm, society and other corporate body owned directly or indirectly to the extent of at least sixty percent by non-resident Indian and includes overseas trust in which not less than sixty percent beneficial interest is held by non-resident Indian directly or indirectly but irrevocably and which was in existence

1 Review of FDI policy to include warrants and partly-paid shares is under consideration of the Government.

on the date of commencement of the Foreign Exchange Management (Withdrawal of General Permission to Overseas Corporate Bodies (OCBs)) Regulations, 2003 (the Regulations) and immediately prior to such commencement was eligible to undertake transactions pursuant to the general permission granted under the Regulations.

2.1.10 'Foreign Currency Convertible Bond'(FCCB) means a bond issued by an Indian company expressed in foreign currency, the principal and interest of which is payable in foreign currency. FCCBs are issued in accordance with the Foreign Currency Convertible Bonds and ordinary shares (through depository receipt mechanism) Scheme 1993 and subscribed by a non-resident entity in foreign currency and convertible into ordinary shares of the issuing company in any manner, either in whole, or in part.

2.1.11 'FDI' means investment by non-resident entity/person resident outside India in the capital of an Indian company under Schedule 1 of Foreign Exchange Management (Transfer or Issue of Security by a Person Resident Outside India) Regulations 2000 (Original notification is available athttp://rbi.org.in/Scripts/BS_FemaNotifications.aspx?Id=174. Subsequent amendment notifications are available at http://rbi.org.in/Scripts/BS_FemaNotifications.aspx)

2.1.12 'FEMA' means the Foreign Exchange Management Act 1999 (42 of 1999) (http://finmin.nic.in/law/index.asp).

2.1.13 'FIPB' means the Foreign Investment Promotion Board constituted by the Government of India.

2.1.14 'Foreign Institutional Investor'(FII) means an entity established or incorporated outside India which proposes to make investment in India and which is registered as a FII in accordance with the SEBI (FII) Regulations 1995.

2.1.15 'Foreign Venture Capital Investor' (FVCI) means an investor incorporated and established outside India, which is registered under the Securities and Exchange Board of India (Foreign Venture Capital Investor) Regulations, 2000 SEBI(FVCI) Regulations} and proposes to make investment in accordance with these Regulations

2.1.16 'Government route' means that investment in the capital of resident entities by non-resident entities can be made only with the prior approval of Government (FIPB, Department of Economic Affairs (DEA), Ministry of Finance or Department of Industrial Policy & Promotion, as the case may be).

2.1.17 'Holding Company' would have the same meaning as defined in Companies Act 1956.

2.1.18 'Indian Company' means a company incorporated in India under the Companies Act, 1956.

2.1.19 'Indian Venture Capital Undertaking' (IVCU) means an Indian company:—

(*i*) whose shares are not listed in a recognised stock exchange in India;

(*ii*) which is engaged in the business of providing services, production or manufacture of articles or things, but does not include such activities or sectors which are specified in the negative list by the SEBI, with approval of Central Government, by notification in the Official Gazette in this behalf.

2.1.20 'Investing Company' means an Indian Company holding only investments in other Indian company/(ies), directly or indirectly, other than for trading of such holdings/securities.

2.1.21 'Investment on repatriable basis' means investment, the sale proceeds of which, net of taxes, are eligible to be repatriated out of India and the expression 'investment on non-repatriable basis' shall be construed accordingly.

2.1.22 'Joint Venture' (JV) means an Indian entity incorporated in accordance with the laws and regulations in India in whose capital a non-resident entity makes an investment.

2.1.23 "Limited Liability Partnership" means a Limited Liability Partnership firm, formed and registered under the Limited Liability Partnership Act, 2008.

2.1.24 'Non resident entity' means a 'person resident outside India' as defined under FEMA.

2.1.25 'Non Resident Indian' (NRI) means an individual resident outside India who is a citizen of India or is a person of Indian origin.

2.1.26 A company is considered as 'Owned' by resident Indian citizens if more than 50% of the capital in it is beneficially owned by resident Indian citizens and/or Indian companies, which are ultimately owned and controlled by resident Indian citizens;

2.1.27 'Person' includes—

(*i*) an individual

(*ii*) a Hindu undivided family,

(*iii*) a company

(*iv*) a firm

(*v*) an association of persons or a body of individuals whether incorporated or not,

(*vi*) every artificial juridical person, not falling within any of the preceding sub-clauses, and

(*vii*) any agency, office, or branch owned or controlled by such person.

2.1.28 'Person of Indian Origin' (PIO) means a citizen of any country other than Bangladesh or Pakistan, if—

(*i*) he at any time held Indian Passport

(*ii*) he or either of his parents or any of his grandparents was a citizen of India by virtue of the Constitution of India or the Citizenship Act, 1955 (57 of 1955); or (*iii*) the person is a spouse of an Indian citizen or a person referred to in sub-clause (*i*) or (*ii*).

2.1.29 'Person resident in India' means—

(*i*) a person residing in India for more than one hundred and eighty-two days during the course of the preceding financial year but does not include—

(A) A person who has gone out of India or who stays outside India, in either case—

(*a*) for or on taking up employment outside India, or

(*b*) for carrying on outside India a business or vocation outside India, or

(*c*) for any other purpose, in such circumstances as would indicate his intention to stay outside India for an uncertain period;

(B) A person who has come to or stays in India, in either case, otherwise than—

(*a*) for or on taking up employment in India; or

(*b*) for carrying on in India a business or vocation in India, or

(*c*) for any other purpose, in such circumstances as would indicate his intention to stay in India for an uncertain period;

(*ii*) any person or body corporate registered or incorporated in India,

(*iii*) an office, branch or agency in India owned or controlled by a person resident outside India,

(*iv*) an office, branch or agency outside India owned or controlled by a person resident in India.

2.1.30 'Person resident outside India' means a person who is not a Person resident in India.

2.1.31 'Portfolio Investment Scheme' means the Portfolio Investment Scheme referred to in Schedules 2 & 3 of FEM (Transfer or Issue of Security by a Person Resident Outside India) Regulations, 2000.

2.1.32 'A Qualified Foreign Investor (QFI)' means a non-resident investor (other than SEBI registered FII and SEBI registered FVCI) who meets the KYC requirements of SEBI for the purpose of making investments in accordance with the regulations/orders/circulars of RBI/SEBI.

2.1.33 'RBI' means the Reserve Bank of India established under the Reserve Bank of India Act, 1934.

2.1.34 'Resident Entity' means 'Person resident in India' excluding an individual.

2.1.35 'Resident Indian Citizen' shall be interpreted in line with the definition of 'person resident in India' as per FEMA, 1999, read in conjunction with the Indian Citizenship Act, 1955.

2.1.36 'SEBI' means the Securities and Exchange Board of India established under the Securities and Exchange Board of India Act, 1992.

2.1.37 'SEZ' means a Special Economic Zone as defined in Special Economic Zone Act, 2005.

2.1.38 'SIA' means Secretariat of Industrial Assistance in DIPP, Ministry of Commerce & Industry, Government of India.

2.1.39 'Transferable Development Rights' (TDR) means certificates issued in respect of category of land acquired for public purposes either by the Central or State Government in consideration of surrender of land by the owner without monetary compensation, which are transferable in part or whole.

2.1.40 'Venture Capital Fund' (VCF) means a Fund established in the form of a Trust, a company including a body corporate and registered under Securities and Exchange Board of India (Venture Capital Fund) Regulations, 1996, which

(*i*) has a dedicated pool of capital;

(*ii*) raised in the manner specified under the Regulations; and

(*iii*) invests in accordance with the Regulations.

Chapter 3

General Conditions on FDI

3.1 Who Can Invest In India?

3.1.1 A non-resident entity (other than a citizen of Pakistan or an entity incorporated in Pakistan) can invest in India, subject to the FDI Policy. A citizen of Bangladesh or an entity incorporated in Bangladesh can invest only under the Government route.

3.1.2 NRIs resident in Nepal and Bhutan as well as citizens of Nepal and Bhutan are permitted to invest in the capital of Indian companies on repatriation basis, subject to the condition that the amount of consideration for such investment shall be paid only by way of inward remittance in free foreign exchange through normal banking channels.

3.1.3 OCBs have been derecognized as a class of investors in India with effect from September 16, 2003. Erstwhile OCBs which are incorporated outside India and are not under the adverse notice of RBI can make fresh investments under FDI Policy as incorporated non-resident entities, with the prior approval of Government of India if the investment is through Government route; and with the prior approval of RBI if the investment is through Automatic route.

3.1.4 (*i*) An FII may invest in the capital of an Indian Company under the Portfolio Investment Scheme which limits the individual holding of an FII to 10% of the capital of the company and the aggregate limit for FII investment to 24% of the capital of the company. This aggregate limit of 24% can be increased to the sectoral cap/statutory ceiling, as applicable, by the Indian Company concerned through a resolution by its Board of Directors followed by a special resolution to that effect by its General Body and subject to prior intimation to RBI. The aggregate FII investment, in the FDI and Portfolio Investment Scheme, should be within the above caps.

(*ii*) The Indian company which has issued shares to FIIs under the FDI Policy for which the payment has been received directly into company's account should report these figures separately under item no. 5 of Form FC-GPR (Annex-1).

(*iii*) A daily statement in respect of all transactions (except derivative trade) has to be submitted by the custodian bank in floppy/soft copy in the prescribed format directly to RBI.

3.1.5 Only SEBI registered FII and NRIs as per Schedules 2 and 3 respectively of Foreign Exchange Management (Transfer or Issue of Security by a Person Resident Outside India) Regulations, 2000, can invest/trade through a registered broker in the capital of Indian Companies on recognised Indian Stock Exchanges.

3.1.6 A SEBI registered Foreign Venture Capital Investor (FVCI) may contribute up to 100% of the capital of an Indian Venture Capital Undertaking (IVCU) and may also set up a domestic asset management company to manage the fund. All such investments can be made under the automatic route in terms of Schedule 6 to Notification No. FEMA 20. A SEBI registered FVCI can invest in a domestic venture capital fund registered under the SEBI (Venture Capital Fund) Regulations, 1996. Such investments would also be subject to the extant FEMA regulations and extant FDI policy including sectoral caps, etc. SEBI registered FVCIs are also allowed to invest under the FDI Scheme, as non-resident entities, in other companies, subject to FDI Policy and FEMA regulations.

Further, FVCIs are allowed to invest in the eligible securities (equity, equity linked instruments, debt, debt instruments, debentures of an IVCU or VCF, units of schemes/funds set up by a VCF) by way of private arrangement/purchase from a third party also, subject to terms and conditions as stipulated in Schedule 6 of Notification No. FEMA 20/2000-RB, dated May 3, 2000 as amended from time to time. It is also being clarified that SEBI registered FVCIs would also be allowed to invest in securities on a recognized stock exchange subject to the provisions of the SEBI (FVCI) Regulations, 2000, as amended from time to time, as well as the terms and conditions stipulated therein.

3.1.7 Qualified Foreign Investors (QFIs) investment in equity shares

3.1.7.1 QFIs are permitted to invest through SEBI registered Depository Participants (DPs) only in equity shares of listed Indian companies through recognized brokers on recognized stock exchanges in India as well as in equity shares of Indian companies which are offered to public in India in terms of the relevant and applicable SEBI guidelines/regulations. QFIs are also permitted to acquire equity shares by way of right shares, bonus shares or equity shares on account of stock split/consolidation or equity shares on account of amalgamation, demerger or such corporate actions subject to the prescribed investment limits. QFIs are allowed to sell the equity shares so acquired subject to the relevant SEBI guidelines.

3.1.7.2 The individual and aggregate investment limits for the QFIs shall be 5% and 10% respectively of the paid up capital of an Indian company. These limits shall be over and above the FII and NRI investment ceilings prescribed under the Portfolio Investment Scheme for foreign investment in India. Further, wherever there are composite sectoral caps under the extant FDI policy, these limits for QFI investment in equity shares shall also be within such overall FDI sectoral caps.

3.1.7.3 Dividend payments on equity shares held by QFIs can either be directly remitted to the designated overseas bank accounts of the QFIs or credited to the single rupee pool bank account. In case dividend payments are credited to the single rupee pool bank account they shall be remitted to the designated overseas bank accounts of the QFIs within five working days (including the day of credit of such funds to the single rupee pool bank account). Within these five working days, the dividend payments can be also utilized for fresh purchases of equity shares under this scheme, if so instructed by the QFI.

3.2 Entities into Which FDI Can Be Made

3.2.1 FDI in an Indian Company

Indian companies can issue capital against FDI.

3.2.2 FDI in Partnership Firm/Proprietary Concern

(*i*) A Non-Resident Indian (NRI) or a Person of Indian Origin (PIO) resident outside India can invest in the capital of a firm or a proprietary concern in India on non-repatriation basis provided:

(*a*) Amount is invested by inward remittance or out of NRE/FCNR(B)/NRO account maintained with Authorized Dealers/Authorized banks.

(*b*) The firm or proprietary concern is not engaged in any agricultural/plantation or real estate business or print media sector.

(*c*) Amount invested shall not be eligible for repatriation outside India.

(*ii*) Investments with repatriation option: NRIs/PIO may seek prior permission of Reserve Bank for investment in sole proprietorship concerns/partnership firms with repatriation option. The application will be decided in consultation with the Government of India.

(*iii*) Investment by non-residents other than NRIs/PIO: A person resident outside India other than NRIs/PIO may make an application and seek prior approval of Reserve Bank for making investment in the capital of a firm or a proprietorship concern or any association of persons in India. The application will be decided in consultation with the Government of India.

(*iv*) *Restrictions:* An NRI or PIO is not allowed to invest in a firm or proprietorship concern engaged in any agricultural/plantation activity or real estate business or print media.

3.2.3 *FDI in Venture Capital Fund (VCF)*

FVCIs are allowed to invest in Indian Venture Capital Undertakings (IVCUs)/Venture Capital Funds (VCFs)/other companies, as stated in paragraph 3.1.6 of this Circular. If a domestic VCF is set up as a trust, a person resident outside India (non-resident entity/individual including an NRI) can invest in such domestic VCF subject to approval of the FIPB. However, if a domestic VCF is set-up as an incorporated company under the Companies Act, 1956, then a person resident outside India (non-resident entity/individual including an NRI) can invest in such domestic VCF under the automatic route of FDI Scheme, subject to the pricing guidelines, reporting requirements, mode of payment, minimum capitalization norms, etc.

3.2.4 *FDI in Trusts*

FDI in Trusts other than VCF is not permitted.

3.2.5 *FDI in Limited Liability Partnerships (LLPs)*

FDI in LLPs is permitted, subject to the following conditions:

(*a*) FDI will be allowed, through the Government approval route, only in LLPs operating in sectors/activities where 100% FDI is allowed, through the automatic route and there are no FDI- linked performance conditions (such as 'Non Banking Finance Companies' or 'Development of Townships, Housing, Built-up infrastructure and Construction-development projects' etc.).

(*b*) LLPs with FDI will not be allowed to operate in agricultural/plantation activity, print media or real estate business.

(*c*) An Indian company, having FDI, will be permitted to make downstream investment in an LLP only if both-the company, as well as the LLP- are operating in sectors where 100% FDI is allowed, through the automatic route and there are no FDI-linked performance conditions.

(*d*) LLPs with FDI will not be eligible to make any downstream investments.

(*e*) Foreign Capital participation in LLPs will be allowed only by way of cash consideration, received by inward remittance, through normal banking channels or by debit to NRE/FCNR account of the person concerned, maintained with an authorized dealer/authorized bank.

(*f*) Investment in LLPs by Foreign Institutional Investors (FIIs) and Foreign Venture Capital Investors (FVCIs) will not be permitted. LLPs will also not be permitted to avail External Commercial Borrowings (ECBs).

(*g*) In case the LLP with FDI has a body corporate that is a designated partner or nominates an individual to act as a designated partner in accordance with the provisions of Section 7 of the LLP Act, 2008, such a body corporate should only be a company registered in India under the Companies Act, 1956 and not any other body, such as an LLP or a trust.

(*h*) For such LLPs, the designated partner "resident in India", as defined under the '*Explanation*' to Section 7(1) of the LLP Act, 2008, would also have to satisfy the definition of "person resident in India", as prescribed under Section 2(*v*)(*i*) of the Foreign Exchange Management Act, 1999.

(*i*) The designated partners will be responsible for compliance with all the above conditions and also liable for all penalties imposed on the LLP for their contravention, if any.

(*j*) Conversion of a company with FDI, into an LLP, will be allowed only if the above stipulations are met and with the prior approval of FIPB/Government.

3.2.6 FDI in other Entities

FDI in resident entities other than those mentioned above is not permitted.

3.3 Types of Instruments

3.3.1 Indian companies can issue equity shares, fully, compulsorily and mandatorily convertible debentures and fully, compulsorily and mandatorily convertible preference shares subject to pricing guidelines/valuation norms prescribed under FEMA Regulations. The price/conversion formula of convertible capital instruments should be determined upfront at the time of issue of the instruments. The price at the time of conversion should not in any case be lower than the fair value worked out, at the time of issuance of such instruments, in accordance with the extant FEMA regulations [the DCF method of valuation for the unlisted companies and valuation in terms of SEBI (ICDR) Regulations, for the listed companies].

3.3.2 Other types of Preference shares/Debentures *i.e.* non-convertible, optionally convertible or partially convertible for issue of which funds have been received on or after May 1, 2007 are considered as debt. Accordingly all norms applicable for ECBs relating to eligible borrowers, recognized lenders, amount and maturity, end-use stipulations, etc. shall apply. Since these instruments would be denominated in rupees, the rupee interest rate will be based on the swap equivalent of London Interbank Offered Rate (LIBOR) plus the spread as permissible for ECBs of corresponding maturity.

3.3.3 The inward remittance received by the Indian company *vide* issuance of DRs and FCCBs are treated as FDI and counted towards FDI.

3.3.4 Issue of shares by Indian Companies under FCCB/ADR/GDR

(*i*) Indian companies can raise foreign currency resources abroad through the issue of FCCB/DR (ADRs/GDRs), in accordance with the Scheme for issue of Foreign Currency Convertible Bonds and Ordinary Shares (Through Depository Receipt Mechanism) Scheme, 1993 and guidelines issued by the Government of India there under from time to time.

(*ii*) A company can issue ADRs/GDRs if it is eligible to issue shares to persons resident outside India under the FDI Policy. However, an Indian listed company, which is not eligible to raise funds from the Indian Capital Market including a company which has been restrained from accessing the securities market by the Securities and Exchange Board of India (SEBI) will not be eligible to issue ADRs/GDRs.

(*iii*) Unlisted companies, which have not yet accessed the ADR/GDR route for raising capital in the international market, would require prior or simultaneous listing in the domestic market, while seeking to issue such overseas instruments. Unlisted companies, which have already issued ADRs/GDRs in the international market, have to list in the domestic market on making profit or within three years of such issue of ADRs/GDRs, whichever is earlier. ADRs/GDRs are issued on the basis of the ratio worked out by the Indian company in consultation with the Lead Manager to the issue. The proceeds so raised have to be kept abroad till actually required in India. Pending repatriation or utilization of the proceeds, the Indian company can invest the funds in:—

(*a*) Deposits, Certificate of Deposits or other instruments offered by banks rated by Standard and Poor, Fitch, IBCA ,Moody's, etc. with rating not below the rating stipulated by Reserve Bank from time to time for the purpose;

(*b*) Deposits with branch/es of Indian Authorized Dealers outside India; and

(*c*) Treasury bills and other monetary instruments with a maturity or unexpired maturity of one year or less.

(*iv*) There are no end-use restrictions except for a ban on deployment/investment of such funds in real estate or the stock market. There is no monetary limit up to which an Indian company can raise ADRs/GDRs.

(*v*) The ADR/GDR proceeds can be utilized for first stage acquisition of shares in the disinvestment process of Public Sector Undertakings/ Enterprises and also in the mandatory second stage offer to the public in view of their strategic importance.

(*vi*) Voting rights on shares issued under the Scheme shall be as per the provisions of Companies Act, 1956 and in a manner in which restrictions on voting rights imposed on ADR/GDR issues shall be consistent with the Company Law provisions. Voting rights in the case of banking companies will continue to be in terms of the provisions of the Banking Regulation Act, 1949 and the instructions issued by the Reserve Bank from time to time, as applicable to all shareholders exercising voting rights.

(*vii*) Erstwhile OCBs who are not eligible to invest in India and entities prohibited from buying, selling or dealing in securities by SEBI will not be eligible to subscribe to ADRs/GDRs issued by Indian companies.

(*viii*) The pricing of ADR/GDR issues should be made at a price determined under the provisions of the Scheme of issue of Foreign Currency Convertible Bonds and Ordinary Shares (through Depository Receipt Mechanism) Scheme, 1993 and guidelines issued by the Government of India and directions issued by the Reserve Bank, from time to time.

(*ix*) The pricing of sponsored ADRs/GDRs would be determined under the provisions of the Scheme of issue of Foreign Currency Convertible Bonds and Ordinary Shares (Through Depository Receipt Mechanism) Scheme, 1993 and guidelines issued by the Government of India and directions issued by the Reserve Bank, from time to time.

3.3.5 (i) Two-way Fungibility Scheme: A limited two-way Fungibility scheme has been put in place by the Government of India for ADRs/GDRs. Under this Scheme, a stock broker in India, registered with SEBI, can purchase shares of an Indian company from the market for conversion into ADRs/GDRs based on instructions received from overseas investors. Re- issuance of ADRs/ GDRs would be permitted to the extent of ADRs/GDRs which have been redeemed into underlying shares and sold in the Indian market.

(ii) Sponsored ADR/GDR issue: An Indian company can also sponsor an issue of ADR/GDR. Under this mechanism, the company offers its resident shareholders a choice to submit their shares back to the company so that on the basis of such shares, ADRs/GDRs can be issued abroad. The proceeds of the ADR/GDR issue are remitted back to India and distributed among the resident investors who had offered their Rupee denominated shares for conversion. These proceeds can be kept in Resident Foreign Currency (Domestic) accounts in India by the resident shareholders who have tendered such shares for conversion into ADRs/GDRs.

3.4 Issue/Transfer of Shares

3.4.1 The capital instruments should be issued within 180 days from the date of receipt of the inward remittance received through normal banking channels including escrow account opened and maintained for the purpose or by debit to the NRE/FCNR (B) account of the non-resident investor. In case, the capital instruments are not issued within 180 days from the date of receipt of the inward remittance or date of debit to the NRE/FCNR (B) account, the amount of consideration so received should be refunded immediately to the non-resident investor by outward remittance through normal banking channels or by credit to the NRE/FCNR (B) account, as the case may be. Non-compliance with the above provision would be reckoned as a contravention under FEMA and would attract penal provisions. In exceptional cases, refund of the amount of consideration outstanding beyond a period of 180 days from the date of receipt may be considered by the RBI, on the merits of the case.

3.4.2 Issue price of shares

Price of shares issued to persons resident outside India under the FDI Policy, shall not be less than—

(*a*) the price worked out in accordance with the SEBI guidelines, as applicable, where the shares of the company is listed on any recognised stock exchange in India;

(*b*) the fair valuation of shares done by a SEBI registered Category-I Merchant Banker or a Chartered Accountant as per the discounted free cash flow method, where the shares of the company is not listed on any recognised stock exchange in India; and

(*c*) the price as applicable to transfer of shares from resident to non-resident as per the pricing guidelines laid down by the Reserve Bank from time to time, where the issue of shares is on preferential allotment.

3.4.3 Foreign Currency Account

Indian companies which are eligible to issue shares to persons resident outside India under the FDI Policy may be allowed to retain the share subscription amount in a Foreign Currency Account, with the prior approval of RBI.

3.4.4 Transfer of shares and convertible debentures

(*i*) Subject to FDI sectoral policy (relating to sectoral caps and entry routes), applicable laws and other conditionalities including security conditions, non-resident investors can also invest in Indian companies by purchasing/acquiring existing shares from Indian shareholders or from other non-resident shareholders. General permission has been granted to non-residents/NRIs for acquisition of shares by way of transfer subject to the following:

(*a*) A person resident outside India (other than NRI and erstwhile OCB) may transfer by way of sale or gift, the shares or convertible debentures to any person resident outside India (including NRIs).

(*b*) NRIs may transfer by way of sale or gift the shares or convertible debentures held by them to another NRI.

(*c*) A person resident outside India can transfer any security to a person resident in India by way of gift.

(*d*) A person resident outside India can sell the shares and convertible debentures of an Indian company on a recognized Stock Exchange in India through a stock broker registered with stock exchange or a merchant banker registered with SEBI.

(*e*) A person resident in India can transfer by way of sale, shares/ convertible debentures (including transfer of subscriber's shares), of an Indian company under private arrangement to a person resident outside India, subject to the guidelines given in para 3.4.5.2 and **Annex-2**.

(*f*) General permission is also available for transfer of shares/convertible debentures, by way of sale under private arrangement by a person resident outside India to a person resident in India, subject to the guidelines given in para 3.4.5.2 and **Annex-2**.

(*g*) The above General Permission also covers transfer by a resident to a non-resident of shares/convertible debentures of an Indian company, engaged in an activity earlier covered under the Government Route but now falling under Automatic Route, as well as transfer of shares by a non-resident to an Indian company under buyback and/or capital reduction scheme of the company.

(*h*) The Form FC-TRS should be submitted to the AD Category-I Bank, within 60 days from the date of receipt of the amount of consideration. The onus of submission of the Form FC-TRS within the given timeframe would be on the transferor/transferee, resident in India.

(*ii*) The sale consideration in respect of equity instruments purchased by a person resident outside India, remitted into India through normal banking channels, shall be subjected to a Know Your Customer (KYC) check by the remittance receiving AD Category-I bank at the time of receipt of funds. In case, the remittance receiving AD Category-I bank is different from the AD Category-I bank handling the transfer transaction, the KYC check should be carried out by the remittance receiving bank and the KYC report be submitted by the customer to the AD Category-I bank carrying out the transaction along with the Form FC-TRS.

(*iii*) ***Escrow:*** AD Category-I banks have been given general permission to open Escrow account and Special account of non-resident corporate for open offers/exit offers and delisting of shares. The relevant SEBI (SAST) Regulations or any other applicable SEBI Regulations/provisions of the Companies Act, 1956 will be applicable. AD Category-I banks have also been permitted to open and maintain, without prior approval of RBI, **non-interest bearing** Escrow accounts in Indian Rupees in India on behalf of residents and/or non-residents, towards payment of share purchase consideration and/or provide Escrow facilities for keeping securities to facilitate FDI transactions subject to the terms and conditions specified by RBI. SEBI authorised Depository Participants have also been permitted to open and maintain, without prior approval of RBI, Escrow accounts for securities subject to the terms and conditions as specified by RBI. In both cases, the Escrow agent shall necessarily be an AD Category- I bank or SEBI authorised Depository Participant (in case of securities' accounts). These facilities will be applicable for both issue of fresh shares to the non- residents as well as transfer of shares from/to the non- residents.

3.4.5 Prior permission of RBI in certain cases for transfer of capital instruments

3.4.5.1 Except cases mentioned in paragraph 3.4.5.2 below, the following cases require prior approval of RBI:

(*i*) Transfer of capital instruments from resident to non-residents by way of sale where:

(*a*) Transfer is at a price which falls outside the pricing guidelines specified by the Reserve Bank from time to time and the transaction does not fall under the exception given in para 3.4.5.2.

(*b*) Transfer of capital instruments by the non-resident acquirer involving deferment of payment of the amount of consideration. Further, in case approval is granted for a transaction, the same should be reported in Form FC-TRS, to an AD Category-I bank for necessary due diligence, within 60 days from the date of receipt of the full and final amount of consideration.

(*ii*) Transfer of any capital instrument, by way of gift by a person resident in India to a person resident outside India. While forwarding applications to Reserve Bank for approval for transfer of capital instruments by way of gift, the documents mentioned in **Annex-3** should be enclosed. Reserve Bank considers the following factors while processing such applications:

(*a*) The proposed transferee (donee) is eligible to hold such capital instruments under Schedules 1, 4 and 5 of Notification No. FEMA 20/2000-RB, dated May 3, 2000, as amended from time to time.

(*b*) The gift does not exceed 5 per cent of the paid-up capital of the Indian company/each series of debentures/each mutual fund scheme.

(*c*) The applicable sectoral cap limit in the Indian company is not breached.

(*d*) The transferor (donor) and the proposed transferee (donee) are close relatives as defined in Section 6 of the Companies Act, 1956, as amended from time to time. The current list is reproduced in Annex-4.

(*e*) The value of capital instruments to be transferred together with any capital instruments already transferred by the transferor, as gift, to any person residing outside India does not exceed the rupee equivalent of USD 50,000 during the financial year.

(*f*) Such other conditions as stipulated by Reserve Bank in public interest from time to time.

(*iii*) Transfer of shares from NRI to non-resident .

3.4.5.2 In the following cases, approval of RBI is not required:

A. Transfer of shares from a Non Resident to Resident under the FDI scheme where the pricing guidelines under FEMA, 1999 are not met provided that :—

(*i*) The original and resultant investment are in line with the extant FDI policy and FEMA regulations in terms of sectoral caps, conditionalities (such as minimum capitalization, etc.), reporting requirements, documentation, etc.;

(*ii*) The pricing for the transaction is compliant with the specific/explicit, extant and relevant SEBI regulations/guidelines (such as IPO, Book building, block deals, delisting, exit, open offer/substantial acquisition/ SEBI SAST, buy back); and (*iii*) Chartered Accountants Certificate to the effect that compliance with the relevant SEBI regulations/guidelines as indicated above is attached to the form FC-TRS to be filed with the AD bank.

B. Transfer of shares from Resident to Non Resident:

(*i*) **where the transfer of shares requires the prior approval of the FIPB** as per the extant FDI policy provided that :

(*a*) the requisite approval of the FIPB has been obtained; and

(*b*) the transfer of share adheres with the pricing guidelines and documentation requirements as specified by the Reserve Bank of India from time to time.

(*ii*) **where the transfer of shares attract SEBI (SAST) guidelines** subject to the adherence with the pricing guidelines and documentation requirements as specified by Reserve Bank of India from time to time.

(*iii*) **where the transfer of shares does not meet the pricing guidelines under the FEMA, 1999 provided that:—**

(*a*) The resultant FDI is in compliance with the extant FDI policy and FEMA regulations in terms of sectoral caps, conditionalities (such as minimum capitalization, etc.), reporting requirements, documentation etc.;

(*b*) The pricing for the transaction is compliant with the specific/explicit, extant and relevant SEBI regulations/guidelines (such as IPO, Book building, block deals, delisting, exit, open offer/substantial acquisition/SEBI SAST); and

(*c*) Chartered Accountants Certificate to the effect that compliance with the relevant SEBI regulations/guidelines as indicated above is attached to the form FC-TRS to be filed with the AD bank.

(*iv*) **where the investee company is in the financial sector provided that:**

(*a*) NOCs are obtained from the respective financial sector regulators/regulators of the investee company as well as transferor and transferee entities and such NOCs are filed along with the form FC-TRS with the AD bank; and

(*b*) The FDI policy and FEMA regulations in terms of sectoral caps, conditionalities (such as minimum capitalization, pricing, etc.), reporting requirements, documentation etc., are complied with.

3.4.6 Conversion of ECB/Lumpsum Fee/Royalty etc. into Equity

(*i*) Indian companies have been granted general permission for conversion of External Commercial Borrowings (ECB) (excluding those deemed as ECB) in convertible foreign currency into equity shares/fully compulsorily and mandatorily convertible preference shares, subject to the following conditions and reporting requirements.

(*a*) The activity of the company is covered under the Automatic Route for FDI or the company has obtained Government approval for foreign equity in the company;

(*b*) The foreign equity after conversion of ECB into equity is within the sectoral cap, if any;

(*c*) Pricing of shares is as per the provision of para 3.4.2 above;

(*d*) Compliance with the requirements prescribed under any other statute and regulation in force; and

(*e*) The conversion facility is available for ECBs availed under the Automatic or Government Route and is applicable to ECBs, due for payment or not, as well as secured/unsecured loans availed from non-resident collaborators.

(*ii*) General permission is also available for issue of shares/preference shares against lump sum technical know-how fee, royalty, subject to entry route, sectoral cap and pricing guidelines (as per the provision of para 3.4.2 above) and compliance with applicable tax laws.

(*iii*) Issue of equity shares under the FDI policy is allowed under the Government route for the following:

(I) import of capital goods/machinery/equipment (excluding second-hand machinery), subject to compliance with the following conditions:

(*a*) Any import of capital goods/machinery etc., made by a resident in India, has to be in accordance with the Export/Import Policy issued by Government of India/as defined by DGFT/FEMA provisions relating to imports.

(*b*) There is an independent valuation of the capital goods/machinery /equipments (including second-hand machinery) by a third party entity, preferably by an independent valuer from the country of import along with production of copies of documents/certificates issued by the customs authorities towards assessment of the fair-value of such imports.

(*c*) The application clearly indicating the beneficial ownership and identity of the Importer Company as well as overseas entity.

(*d*) Applications complete in all respects, for conversions of import payables for capital goods into FDI being made within 180 days from the date of shipment of goods.

(II) pre-operative/pre-incorporation expenses (including payments of rent etc.), subject to compliance with the following conditions:

(*a*) Submission of FIRC for remittance of funds by the overseas promoters for the expenditure incurred.

(*b*) Verification and certification of the pre-incorporation/pre-operative expenses by the statutory auditor.

(*c*) Payments should be made by the foreign investor to the company directly or through the bank account opened by the foreign investor as provided under FEMA Regulations.

(*d*) The applications, complete in all respects, for capitalization being made within the period of 180 days from the date of incorporation of the company

General conditions:

(*i*) All requests for conversion should be accompanied by a special resolution of the company.

(*ii*) Government's approval would be subject to pricing guidelines of RBI and appropriate tax clearance.

3.5 Specific Conditions in Certain Cases

3.5.1 Issue of Rights/Bonus Shares

FEMA provisions allow Indian companies to freely issue Rights/Bonus shares to existing non-resident shareholders, subject to adherence to sectoral cap, if any. However, such issue of bonus/rights shares has to be in accordance with other laws/statutes like the Companies Act, 1956, SEBI (Issue of Capital and Disclosure Requirements) Regulations, 2009 (in case of listed companies), etc. The offer on right basis to the persons resident outside India shall be:

(*a*) in the case of shares of a company listed on a recognized stock exchange in India, at a price as determined by the company;

(*b*) in the case of shares of a company not listed on a recognized stock exchange in India, at a price which is not less than the price at which the offer on right basis is made to resident shareholders.

3.5.2 Prior permission of RBI for Rights issue to erstwhile OCBs

OCBs have been de- recognised as a class of investors from September 16, 2003. Therefore companies desiring to issue rights share to such erstwhile OCBs will have to take specific prior permission from RBI. As such, entitlement of rights share is not automatically available to erstwhile OCBs. However bonus shares can be issued to erstwhile OCBs without the approval of RBI.

3.5.3 Additional allocation of rights share by residents to non-residents

Existing non- resident shareholders are allowed to apply for issue of additional shares/fully, compulsorily and mandatorily convertible debentures/ fully, compulsorily and mandatorily convertible preference shares over and above their rights share entitlements. The investee company can allot the additional rights share out of unsubscribed portion, subject to the condition that the overall issue of shares to non-residents in the total paid-up capital of the company does not exceed the sectoral cap.

3.5.4 Acquisition of shares under Scheme of Merger/Demerger/Amalgamation

Mergers/demergers/amalgamations of companies in India are usually governed by an order issued by a competent Court on the basis of the Scheme submitted by the companies undergoing merger/demerger/amalgamation. Once the scheme of merger or demerger or amalgamation of two or more Indian companies has been approved by a Court in India, the transferee company or new company is allowed to issue shares to the shareholders of the transferor company resident outside India, subject to the conditions that:

(*i*) the percentage of shareholding of persons resident outside India in the transferee or new company does not exceed the sectoral cap, and

(*ii*) the transferor company or the transferee or the new company is not engaged in activities which are prohibited under the FDI policy .

3.5.5 Issue of shares under Employees Stock Option Scheme (ESOPs)

(*i*) Listed Indian companies are allowed to issue shares under the Employees Stock Option Scheme (ESOPs), to its employees or employees of its joint venture or wholly owned subsidiary abroad, who are resident outside India, other than to the citizens of Pakistan. ESOPs can be issued to citizens of Bangladesh with the prior approval of FIPB. Shares under ESOPs can be issued directly or through a Trust subject to the condition that:

(*a*) The scheme has been drawn in terms of relevant regulations issued by the SEBI, and

(*b*) The face value of the shares to be allotted under the scheme to the non-resident employees does not exceed 5 per cent of the paid-up capital of the issuing company.

(*ii*) Unlisted companies have to follow the provisions of the Companies Act, 1956. The Indian company can issue ESOPs to employees who are resident outside India, other than to the citizens of Pakistan. ESOPs can be issued to the citizens of Bangladesh with the prior approval of the FIPB.

(*iii*) The issuing company is required to report (plain paper reporting) the details of granting of stock options under the scheme to non-resident employees to the Regional Office concerned of the Reserve Bank and thereafter the details of issue of shares subsequent to the exercise of such stock options within 30 days from the date of issue of shares in Form FC-GPR.

3.5.6 Share Swap

In cases of investment by way of swap of shares, irrespective of the amount, valuation of the shares will have to be made by a Category I Merchant Banker registered with SEBI or an Investment Banker outside India registered with the appropriate regulatory authority in the host country. Approval of the Foreign Investment Promotion Board (FIPB) will also be a prerequisite for investment by swap of shares.

3.5.7 Pledge of Shares

(A) A person being a promoter of a company registered in India (borrowing company), which has raised external commercial borrowings, may pledge the shares of the borrowing company or that of its associate resident companies for the purpose of securing the ECB raised by the borrowing company, provided that a no objection for the same is obtained from a bank which is an authorised dealer. The authorized dealer, shall issue the no objection for such a pledge after having satisfied itself that the external commercial borrowing is in line with the extant FEMA regulations for ECBs and that:

(*i*) the loan agreement has been signed by both the lender and the borrower,

(*ii*) there exists a security clause in the Loan Agreement requiring the borrower to create charge on financial securities, and

(*iii*) the borrower has obtained Loan Registration Number (LRN) from the Reserve Bank:

and the said pledge would be subject to the following conditions :

(*a*) the period of such pledge shall be co-terminus with the maturity of the underlying ECB;

(*b*) in case of invocation of pledge, transfer shall be in accordance with the extant FDI Policy and directions issued by the Reserve Bank;

(*c*) the Statutory Auditor has certified that the borrowing company will utilized/has utilized the proceeds of the ECB for the permitted end use/s only.

(B) Non-resident holding shares of an Indian company, can pledge these shares in favour of the AD bank in India to secure credit facilities being extended to the resident investee company for bonafide business purpose, subject to the following conditions:

(*i*) in case of invocation of pledge, transfer of shares should be in accordance with the FDI policy in vogue at the time of creation of pledge;

(*ii*) submission of a declaration/annual certificate from the statutory auditor of the investee company that the loan proceeds will be/have been utilized for the declared purpose;

(*iii*) the Indian company has to follow the relevant SEBI disclosure norms; and

(*iv*) pledge of shares in favour of the lender (bank) would be subject to Section 19 of the Banking Regulation Act, 1949.

(C) Non-resident holding shares of an Indian company, can pledge these shares in favour of an overseas bank to secure the credit facilities being extended to the non-resident investor/non- resident promoter of the Indian company or its overseas group company, subject to the following:

(*i*) loan is availed of only from an overseas bank;

(*ii*) loan is utilized for genuine business purposes overseas and not for any investments either directly or indirectly in India;

(*iii*) overseas investment should not result in any capital inflow into India;

(*iv*) in case of invocation of pledge, transfer should be in accordance with the FDI policy in vogue at the time of creation of pledge; and

(*v*) submission of a declaration/annual certificate from a Chartered Accountant/Certified Public Accountant of the non-resident borrower that the loan proceeds will be/have been utilized for the declared purpose.

3.6 Entry Routes for Investment

3.6.1 Investments can be made by non-residents in the equity shares/fully, compulsorily and mandatorily convertible debentures/fully, compulsorily and mandatorily convertible preference shares of an Indian company, through the Automatic Route or the Government Route. Under the Automatic Route, the non-resident investor or the Indian company does not require any approval from Government of India for the investment. Under the Government Route, prior approval of the Government of India is required. Proposals for foreign investment under Government route, are considered by FIPB.

3.6.2 Guidelines for establishment of Indian companies/transfer of ownership or control of Indian companies, from resident Indian citizens to non-resident entities, in sectors with caps

In sectors/activities with caps, including *inter-alia* defence production, air transport services, ground handling services, asset reconstruction companies, private sector banking, broadcasting, commodity exchanges, credit information companies, insurance, print media, telecommunications and satellites, Government approval/FIPB approval would be required in all cases where:

(*i*) An Indian company is being established with foreign investment and is owned by a non- resident entity or

(*ii*) An Indian company is being established with foreign investment and is controlled by a non- resident entity or

(*iii*) The control of an existing Indian company, currently owned or controlled by resident Indian citizens and Indian companies, which are owned or controlled by resident Indian citizens, will be/is being transferred/passed on to a non-resident entity as a consequence of transfer of shares and/or fresh issue of shares to non-resident entities through amalgamation, merger/demerger, acquisition etc. or

(*iv*) The ownership of an existing Indian company, currently owned or controlled by resident Indian citizens and Indian companies, which are owned or controlled by resident Indian citizens, will be/is being transferred/passed on to a non-resident entity as a consequence of transfer of shares and/or fresh issue of shares to non-resident entities through amalgamation, merger/demerger, acquisition etc.

(*v*) It is clarified that these guidelines will not apply to sectors/activities where there are no foreign investment caps, that is, 100% foreign investment is permitted under the automatic route.

(*vi*) It is also clarified that Foreign investment shall include all types of foreign investments *i.e.* FDI, investment by FIIs, NRIs, ADRs, GDRs, Foreign Currency Convertible Bonds (FCCB) and fully, mandatorily & compulsorily convertible preference shares/debentures, regardless of whether the said investments have been made under Schedule 1, 2, 3 and 6 of FEMA (Transfer or Issue of Security by Persons Resident Outside India) Regulations.

3.7 Caps on Investments

3.7.1 Investments can be made by non-residents in the capital of a resident entity only to the extent of the percentage of the total capital as specified in the FDI policy. The caps in various sector(s) are detailed in Chapter 6 of this circular.

3.8 Entry Conditions on Investment

3.8.1 Investments by non-residents can be permitted in the capital of a resident entity in certain sectors/activity with entry conditions. Such conditions may include norms for minimum capitalization, lock-in period, etc. The entry conditions in various sectors/activities are detailed in Chapter 6 of this circular.

3.9 Other Conditions on Investment besides Entry Conditions

3.9.1 Besides the entry conditions on foreign investment, the investment/ investors are required to comply with all relevant sectoral laws, regulations, rules, security conditions, and state/local laws/regulations.

3.10 Foreign Investment Into/Downstream Investment by Indian Companies

3.10.1 The Guidelines for calculation of total foreign investment, both direct and indirect in an Indian company, at every stage of investment, including downstream investment, have been detailed in Paragraph 4.1.

3.10.2 For the purpose of this chapter,

(*i*) 'Downstream investment' means indirect foreign investment, by one Indian company, into another Indian company, by way of subscription or acquisition, in terms of Paragraph 4.1. Paragraph 4.1.3 provides the guidelines for calculation of indirect foreign investment, with conditions specified in paragraph 4.1.3(*v*).

(*ii*) 'Foreign Investment' would have the same meaning as in Paragraph 4.1

3.10.3 Foreign investment into an Indian company engaged only in the activity of investing in the capital of other Indian company/ies (regardless of its ownership or control)

3.10.3.1 Foreign investment into an Indian company, engaged only in the activity of investing in the capital of other Indian company/ies, will require prior Government/FIPB approval, regardless of the amount or extent of foreign investment. Foreign investment into Non-Banking Finance Companies (NBFCs), carrying on activities approved for FDI, will be subject to the conditions specified in paragraph 6.2.24 of this Circular.

3.10.3.2 Those companies, which are Core Investment Companies (CICs), will have to additionally follow RBI's Regulatory Framework for CICs.

3.10.3.3 For infusion of foreign investment into an Indian company which does not have any operations and also does not have any downstream investments, Government/FIPB approval would be required, regardless of the amount or extent of foreign investment. Further, as and when such a company commences business(s) or makes downstream investment, it will have to comply with the relevant sectoral conditions on entry route, conditionalities and caps.

Note: Foreign investment into other Indian companies would be in accordance/compliance with the relevant sectoral conditions on entry route, conditionalities and caps.

3.10.4 Downstream investment by an Indian company which is owned and/or controlled by non resident entity/ies

3.10.4.1 Downstream investment by an Indian company, which is owned and/or controlled by non-resident entity/ies, into another Indian company, would be in accordance/compliance with the relevant sectoral conditions on entry route, conditionalities and caps, with regard to the sectors in which the latter Indian company is operating.

3.10.4.2 Downstream investments by Indian companies will be subject to the following conditions:

(*i*) Such a company is to notify SIA, DIPP and FIPB of its downstream investment in the form available at http://www.fipbindia.com within 30 days of such investment, even if capital instruments have not been allotted along with the modality of investment in new/existing ventures (with/without expansion programme);

(*ii*) downstream investment by way of induction of foreign equity in an existing Indian Company to be duly supported by a resolution of the Board of Directors as also a shareholders Agreement, if any;

(*iii*) issue/transfer/pricing/valuation of shares shall be in accordance with applicable SEBI/RBI guidelines;

(*iv*) For the purpose of downstream investment, the Indian companies making the downstream investments would have to bring in requisite funds from abroad and not leverage funds from the domestic market. This would, however, not preclude downstream companies, with operations, from raising debt in the domestic market. Downstream investments through internal accruals are permissible, subject to the provisions of paragraphs 3.10.3 and 3.10.4.1.

Chapter 4

Calculation of Foreign Investment

4.1 Total Foreign Investment *i.e.* Direct and Indirect Foreign Investment in Indian Companies

4.1.1 Investment in Indian companies can be made both by non-resident as well as resident Indian entities. Any non-resident investment in an Indian company is direct foreign investment. Investment by resident Indian entities could again comprise of both resident and non-resident investment. Thus, such an Indian company would have indirect foreign investment if the Indian investing company has foreign investment in it. The indirect investment can also be a cascading investment *i.e.* through multi-layered structure.

4.1.2 For the purpose of computation of indirect Foreign investment, Foreign Investment in Indian company shall include all types of foreign investments *i.e.* FDI; investment by FIIs (holding as on March 31); NRIs; ADRs; GDRs; Foreign Currency Convertible Bonds (FCCB); fully, compulsorily and mandatorily convertible preference shares and fully, compulsorily and mandatorily convertible Debentures regardless of whether the said investments have been made under Schedule 1, 2, 3 and 6 of FEM (Transfer or Issue of Security by Persons Resident Outside India) Regulations, 2000.

4.1.3 Guidelines for calculation of total foreign investment i.e. direct and indirect foreign investment in an Indian company

(*i*) *Counting the Direct Foreign Investment:* All investment directly by a non-resident entity into the Indian company would be counted towards foreign investment.

(*ii*) *Counting of indirect foreign Investment:*

(*a*) The foreign investment through the investing Indian company would not be considered for calculation of the indirect foreign investment in case of Indian companies which are 'owned **and** controlled' by resident Indian citizens and/or Indian Companies which are owned and controlled by resident Indian citizens .

(*b*) For cases where condition (*a*) above is not satisfied or if the investing company is owned **or** controlled by 'non resident entities', the entire investment by the investing company into the subject Indian Company would be considered as indirect foreign investment, provided that, as an exception, the indirect foreign investment in only the 100% owned subsidiaries of operating-cum-investing/ investing companies, will be limited to the foreign investment in the operating-cum-investing/investing company. This exception is made since the downstream investment of a 100% owned subsidiary of the holding company is akin to investment made by the holding company and the downstream investment should be a mirror image of the holding company. This exception, however, is strictly for those cases where the entire capital of the downstream subsidiary is owned by the holding company.

Illustration

To illustrate, if the indirect foreign investment is being calculated for Company X which has investment through an investing Company Y having foreign investment, the following would be the method of calculation:

(A) where Company Y has foreign investment less than 50%- Company X would not be taken as having any indirect foreign investment through Company Y.

(B) where Company Y has foreign investment of say 75% and:

(I) invests 26% in Company X, the entire 26% investment by Company Y would be treated as indirect foreign investment in Company X;

(II) Invests 80% in Company X, the indirect foreign investment in Company X would be taken as 80%

(III) where Company X is a wholly owned subsidiary of Company Y (*i.e.* Company Y owns 100% shares of Company X), then only 75% would be treated as indirect foreign equity and the balance 25% would be treated as resident held equity. The indirect foreign equity in Company X would be computed in the ratio of 75: 25 in the total investment of Company Y in Company X.

(*iii*) The total foreign investment would be the sum total of direct and indirect foreign investment.

(*iv*) The above methodology of calculation would apply at every stage of investment in Indian companies and thus to each and every Indian company.

(*v*) *Additional conditions:*

(*a*) The full details about the foreign investment including ownership details etc. in Indian company(s) and information about the control of the company(s) would be furnished by the Company(s) to the Government of India at the time of seeking approval.

(*b*) In any sector/activity, where Government approval is required for foreign investment and in cases where there are any *inter-se* agreements between/amongst share-holders which have an effect on the appointment of the Board of Directors or on the exercise of voting rights or of creating voting rights disproportionate to shareholding or any incidental matter thereof, such agreements will have to be informed to the approving authority. The approving authority will consider such *inter-se* agreements for determining ownership and control when considering the case for approval of foreign investment.

(*c*) In all sectors attracting sectoral caps, the balance equity *i.e.* beyond the sectoral foreign investment cap, would specifically be beneficially owned by/held with/in the hands of resident Indian citizens and Indian companies, owned and controlled by resident Indian citizens.

(*d*) In the I& B and Defence sectors where the sectoral cap is less than 49%, the company would need to be 'owned **and** controlled' by resident Indian citizens and Indian companies, which are owned and controlled by resident Indian citizens.

(A) For this purpose, the equity held by the largest Indian shareholder would have to be at least 51% of the total equity, excluding the equity held by Public Sector Banks and Public Financial Institutions, as defined in Section 4A of the Companies Act, 1956. The term 'largest Indian shareholder', used in this clause, will include any or a combination of the following:

(I) In the case of an individual shareholder,

(*aa*) The individual shareholder,

(*bb*) A relative of the shareholder within the meaning of Section 6 of the Companies Act, 1956.

(*cc*) A company/group of companies in which the individual shareholder/HUF to which he belongs has management and controlling interest.

(II) In the case of an Indian company,

(*aa*) The Indian company

(*bb*) A group of Indian companies under the same management and ownership control.

(B) For the purpose of this Clause, "Indian company" shall be a company which must have a resident Indian or a relative as defined under Section 6 of the Companies Act, 1956/HUF, either singly or in combination holding at least 51% of the shares.

(C) Provided that, in case of a combination of all or any of the entities mentioned in Sub- Clauses (I) and (II) of clause 4.1.3(*v*)(*d*)(A) above, each of the parties shall have entered into a legally binding agreement to act as a single unit in managing the matters of the applicant company.

(*e*) If a declaration is made by persons as per section 187C of the Indian Companies Act about a beneficial interest being held by a non resident entity, then even though the investment may be made by a resident Indian citizen, the same shall be counted as foreign investment.

4.1.4 The above mentioned policy and methodology would be applicable for determining the total foreign investment in all sectors, except in sectors where it is specified in a statute or rule there under. The above methodology of determining direct and indirect foreign investment therefore does not apply to the Insurance Sector which will continue to be governed by the relevant Regulation.

4.1.5 Any foreign investment already made in accordance with the guidelines in existence prior to February 13, 2009 (date of issue of Press Note 2 of 2009) would not require any modification to conform to these guidelines. All other investments, past and future, would come under the ambit of these new guidelines.

Chapter 5

Foreign Investment Promotion Board (FIPB)

5.1 Constitution of FIPB

5.1.1 FIPB comprises of the following Secretaries to the Government of India:

(*i*) Secretary to Government, Department of Economic Affairs, Ministry of Finance – Chairperson

(*ii*) Secretary to Government, Department of Industrial Policy & Promotion, Ministry of Commerce & Industry

(*iii*) Secretary to Government, Department of Commerce, Ministry of Commerce & Industry

(*iv*) Secretary to Government, Economic Relations, Ministry of External Affairs

(*v*) Secretary to Government, Ministry of Overseas Indian Affairs.

5.1.2 The Board would be able to co-opt other Secretaries to the Central Government and top officials of financial institutions, banks and professional experts of Industry and Commerce, as and when necessary.

5.2 Levels of Approvals for Cases under Government Route

5.2.1 The Minister of Finance who is in-charge of FIPB would consider the recommendations of FIPB on proposals with total foreign equity inflow of and below
₹1200 crore.

5.2.2 The recommendations of FIPB on proposals with total foreign equity inflow of more than ₹1200 crore would be placed for consideration of CCEA.

5.2.3 The CCEA would also consider the proposals which may be referred to it by the FIPB/the Minister of Finance (in-charge of FIPB).

5.3 Cases Which Do Not Require Fresh Approval

5.3.1 Companies may not require fresh prior approval of the Government *i.e.* Minister in- charge of FIPB/CCEA for bringing in additional foreign investment into the same entity, in the following cases:

(*i*) Entities the activities of which had earlier required prior approval of FIPB/CCFI/CCEA and which had, accordingly, earlier obtained prior approval of FIPB/CCFI/CCEA for their initial foreign investment but subsequently such activities/sectors have been placed under automatic route;

(*ii*) Entities the activities of which had sectoral caps earlier and which had, accordingly, earlier obtained prior approval of FIPB/CCFI/CCEA for their initial foreign investment but subsequently such caps were removed/increased and the activities placed under the automatic route; provided that such additional investment alongwith the initial/original investment does not exceed the sectoral caps; and

(*iii*) Additional foreign investment into the same entity where prior approval of FIPB/CCFI/CCEA had been obtained earlier for the initial/original foreign investment due to requirements of Press Note 18/1998 or Press Note 1 of 2005 and prior approval of the Government under the FDI policy is not required for any other reason/purpose.

5.4 Online Filing of Applications for FIPB/Government's Approval

5.4.1 Guidelines for e-filing of applications, filing of amendment applications and instructions to applicants are available at FIPB's website (http://finmin.nic.in/) and (http://www.fipbindia.com).

Chapter 6

Sector Specific Conditions on FDI

6.1 Prohibited Sectors

FDI is prohibited in:

(*a*) Retail Trading (except single brand product retailing)

(*b*) Lottery Business including Government/private lottery, online lotteries, etc.

(*c*) Gambling and Betting including casinos etc.

(*d*) Chit funds

(*e*) Nidhi company

(*f*) Trading in Transferable Development Rights (TDRs) (g) Real Estate Business or Construction of Farm Houses

(*h*) Manufacturing of Cigars, cheroots, cigarillos and cigarettes, of tobacco or of tobacco substitutes

(*i*) Activities/sectors not open to private sector investment *e.g.* Atomic Energy and Railway Transport (other than Mass Rapid Transport Systems).

Foreign technology collaboration in any form including licensing for franchise, trademark, brand name, management contract is also prohibited for Lottery Business and Gambling and Betting activities.

6.2 Permitted Sectors

In the following sectors/activities, FDI up to the limit indicated against each sector/activity is allowed, subject to applicable laws/regulations; security and other conditionalities. In sectors/activities not listed below, FDI is permitted upto 100% on the automatic route, subject to applicable laws/regulations; security and other conditionalities.

Wherever there is a requirement of minimum capitalization, it shall include share premium received along with the face value of the share, only when it is received by the company upon issue of the shares to the non-resident investor. Amount paid by the transferee during post-issue transfer of shares beyond the issue price of the share, cannot be taken into account while calculating minimum capitalization requirement;

Sl.No.	Sector/Activity	% of FDI Cap/Equity	Entry Route
	AGRICULTURE		
6.2.1	**Agriculture & Animal Husbandry**		
	(*a*) Floriculture, Horticulture, Apiculture and Cultivation of Vegetables & Mushrooms under controlled conditions; (*b*) Development and production of Seeds and planting material; (*c*) Animal Husbandry (including breeding of dogs), Pisciculture, Aquaculture, under controlled conditions; and (*d*) services related to agro and allied sectors *Note:* **Besides the above, FDI is not allowed in any other agricultural sector/activity**	100%	Automatic
6.2.1.1	**Other conditions:**		
	I. For companies dealing with development of transgenic seeds/vegetables, the following conditions apply: (*i*) When dealing with genetically modified seeds or planting material the company shall comply with safety requirements in accordance with laws enacted under the Environment (Protection) Act on the genetically modified organisms. (*ii*) Any import of genetically modified materials if required shall be subject to the conditions laid down *vide* Notifications issued under Foreign Trade (Development and Regulation) Act, 1992. (*iii*) The company shall comply with any other Law, Regulation or Policy governing genetically modified material in force from time to time. (*iv*) Undertaking of business activities involving the use of genetically engineered cells and material shall be subject to the receipt of approvals from Genetic Engineering Approval Committee (GEAC) and Review Committee on Genetic Manipulation (RCGM). (*v*) Import of materials shall be in accordance with National Seeds Policy.		

<table>
<tr><th>Sl.No.</th><th>Sector/Activity</th><th>% of FDI Cap/Equity</th><th>Entry Route</th></tr>
<tr><td></td><td colspan="3">II. The term "under controlled conditions" covers the following:
• 'Cultivation under controlled conditions' for the categories of Floriculture, Horticulture, Cultivation of vegetables and Mushrooms is the practice of cultivation wherein rainfall, temperature, solar radiation, air humidity and culture medium are controlled artificially. Control in these parameters may be effected through protected cultivation under green houses, net houses, poly houses or any other improved infrastructure facilities where micro-climatic conditions are regulated anthropogenically.
• In case of Animal Husbandry, scope of the term 'under controlled conditions' covers—
➢ Rearing of animals under intensive farming systems with stall-feeding. Intensive farming system will require climate systems (ventilation, temperature/humidity management), health care and nutrition, herd registering/pedigree recording, use of machinery, waste management systems.
➢ Poultry breeding farms and hatcheries where micro-climate is controlled through advanced technologies like incubators, ventilation systems etc.
• In the case of pisciculture and aquaculture, scope of the term 'under controlled conditions' covers—
➢ Aquariums
➢ Hatcheries where eggs are artificially fertilized and fry are hatched and incubated in an enclosed environment with artificial climate control.
• In the case of apiculture, scope of the term 'under controlled conditions' covers—
➢ Prodution of honey by bee-keeping, except in forest/wild, in designated spaces with control of temperatures and climatic factors like humidity and artificial feeding during lean seasons.</td></tr>
<tr><td>6.2.2</td><td colspan="3">Tea Plantation</td></tr>
<tr><td>6.2.2.1</td><td>Tea sector including tea plantations
Note: Besides the above, FDI is not allowed in any other plantation sector/activity</td><td>100%</td><td>Government</td></tr>
<tr><td>6.2.2.2</td><td colspan="3">Other conditions:</td></tr>
<tr><td></td><td colspan="3">(i) Compulsory divestment of 26% equity of the company in favour of an Indian partner/Indian public within a period of 5 years</td></tr>
</table>

Sl.No.	Sector/Activity	% of FDI Cap/Equity	Entry Route
	(*ii*) Prior approval of the State Government concerned in case of any future land use change.		
6.2.3	**Mining**		
6.2.3.1	**Mining and Exploration of metal and non-metal ores** including diamond, gold, silver and precious ores but excluding titanium bearing minerals and its ores; **subject to** the Mines and Minerals (Development & Regulation) Act, 1957.	100%	Automatic
6.2.3.2	**Coal and Lignite**		
	(1) Coal & Lignite mining for captive consumption by power projects, iron & steel and cement units and other eligible activities permitted under and **subject to** the provisions of Coal Mines (Nationalization) Act, 1973	100%	Automatic
	(2) Setting up coal processing plants like washeries **subject to** the condition that the company shall not do coal mining and shall not sell washed coal or sized coal from its coal processing plants in the open market and shall supply the washed or sized coal to those parties who are supplying raw coal to coal processing plants for washing or sizing.	100%	Automatic
6.2.3.3	**Mining and mineral separation of titanium bearing minerals and ores, its value addition and integrated activities**		
6.2.3.3.1	Mining and mineral separation of titanium bearing minerals & ores, its value addition and integrated activities **subject to** sectoral regulations and the Mines and Minerals	100%	Government

Sl.No.	Sector/Activity	% of FDI Cap/Equity	Entry Route
	(Development and Regulation Act 1957)		
6.2.3.3.2	***Other conditions:***		
	India has large reserves of beach sand minerals in the coastal stretches around the country. Titanium bearing minerals viz. Ilmenite, rutile and leucoxene, and Zirconium bearing minerals including zircon are some of the beach sand minerals which have been classified as "prescribed substances" under the Atomic Energy Act, 1962. Under the Industrial Policy Statement 1991, mining and production of minerals classified as "prescribed substances" and specified in the Schedule to the Atomic Energy (Control of Production and Use) Order, 1953 were included in the list of industries reserved for the public sector. *Vide* Resolution No. 8/1(1)/97-PSU/1422 dated 6th October 1998 issued by the Department of Atomic Energy laying down the policy for exploitation of beach sand minerals, private participation including Foreign Direct Investment (FDI), was permitted in mining and production of Titanium ores (Ilmenite, Rutile and Leucoxene) and Zirconium minerals (Zircon). *Vide* Notification No. S.O. 61(E), dated 18.1.2006, the Department of Atomic Energy re-notified the list of "prescribed substances" under the Atomic Energy Act 1962. Titanium bearing ores and concentrates (Ilmenite, Rutile and Leucoxene) and Zirconium, its alloys and compounds and minerals/concentrates including Zircon, were removed from the list of "prescribed substances". (*i*) FDI for separation of titanium bearing minerals & ores will be subject to the following additional conditions viz.: (A) value addition facilities are set up within India along with transfer of technology; (B) disposal of tailings during the mineral separation shall be carried out in accordance with regulations framed by the Atomic Energy Regulatory Board such as Atomic Energy (Radiation Protection) Rules, 2004 and the Atomic Energy (Safe Disposal of Radioactive Wastes) Rules, 1987. (*ii*) FDI will not be allowed in mining of "prescribed substances" listed in the Notification No. S.O. 61(E) dated 18.1.2006 issued by the Department of Atomic Energy. Clarification: (1) For titanium bearing ores such as Ilmenite, Leucoxene and Rutile, manufacture of titanium dioxide pigment and titanium sponge constitutes value addition. Ilmenite can be processed to produce 'Synthetic Rutile or Titanium Slag as an intermediate value added product.		

Sl.No.	Sector/Activity	% of FDI Cap/Equity	Entry Route
	(2) The objective is to ensure that the raw material available in the country is utilized for setting up downstream industries and the technology available internationally is also made available for setting up such industries within the country. Thus, if with the technology transfer, the objective of the FDI Policy can be achieved, the conditions prescribed at (i) (A) above shall be deemed to be fulfilled.		
6.2.4	**Petroleum & Natural Gas**		
6.2.4.1	Exploration activities of oil and natural gas fields, infrastructure related to marketing of petroleum products and natural gas, marketing of natural gas and petroleum products, petroleum product pipelines, natural gas/pipelines, LNG Regasification infrastructure, market study and formulation and Petroleum refining in the private sector, **subject to** the existing sectoral policy and regulatory framework in the oil marketing sector and the policy of the Government on private participation in exploration of oil and the discovered fields of national oil companies	100%	Automatic
6.2.4.2	Petroleum refining by the Public Sector Undertakings (PSU), without any disinvestment or dilution of domestic equity in the existing PSUs.	49%	Government
	MANUFACTURING		
6.2.5	**Manufacture of items reserved for production in Micro and Small Enterprises (MSEs)**		
6.2.5.1	FDI in MSEs (as defined under Micro, Small And Meduim Enterprises Development Act, 2006 (MSMED, Act 2006)) will be subject to the sectoral caps, entry routes and other relevant sectoral regulations. Any industrial undertaking which is not a Micro or		

Sl.No.	Sector/Activity	% of FDI Cap/Equity	Entry Route
	Small Scale Enterprise, but manufactures items reserved for the MSE sector would require Government route where foreign investment is more than 24% in the capital. Such an undertaking would also require an Industrial License under the Industries (Development & Regulation) Act 1951, for such manufacture. The issue of Industrial License is subject to a few general conditions and the specific condition that the Industrial Undertaking shall undertake to export a minimum of 50% of the new or additional annual production of the MSE reserved items to be achieved within a maximum period of three years. The export obligation would be applicable from the date of commencement of commercial production and in accordance with the provisions of section 11 of the Industries (Development & Regulation) Act 1951.		
6.2.6	**Defence**		
6.2.6.1	Defence Industry subject to Industrial license under the Industries (Development & Regulation) Act 1951	26%	Government
6.2.6.2	***Other conditions:***		
	(*i*) Licence applications will be considered and licences given by the Department of Industrial Policy & Promotion, Ministry of Commerce & Industry, in consultation with Ministry of Defence. (*ii*) The applicant should be an Indian company/partnership firm. (*iii*) The management of the applicant company/partnership should be in Indian hands with majority representation on the Board as well as the Chief Executives of the company/partnership firm being resident Indians. (*iv*) Full particulars of the Directors and the Chief Executives should be furnished along with the applications. (*v*) The Government reserves the right to verify the antecedents of the foreign collaborators and domestic promoters including their financial standing and credentials in the world market. Preference would be given to original equipment manufacturers or design establishments, and companies having a good track record of past supplies to Armed Forces, Space and Atomic energy sections and having an established R & D base. (*vi*) There would be no minimum capitalization for the FDI. A proper assessment, however, needs to be done by the management of the applicant company depending upon the		

Sl.No.	Sector/Activity	% of FDI Cap/Equity	Entry Route
	product and the technology. The licensing authority would satisfy itself about the adequacy of the net worth of the non-resident investor taking into account the category of weapons and equipment that are proposed to be manufactured. (*vii*) There would be a three-year lock-in period for transfer of equity from one non-resident investor to another non-resident investor (including NRIs & erstwhile OCBs with 60% or more NRI stake) and such transfer would be subject to prior approval of the Government. (*viii*) The Ministry of Defence is not in a position to give purchase guarantee for products to be manufactured. However, the planned acquisition programme for such equipment and overall requirements would be made available to the extent possible. (*ix*) The capacity norms for production will be provided in the licence based on the application as well as the recommendations of the Ministry of Defence, which will look into existing capacities of similar and allied products. (*x*) Import of equipment for pre-production activity including development of prototype by the applicant company would be permitted. (*xi*) Adequate safety and security procedures would need to be put in place by the licensee once the licence is granted and production commences. These would be subject to verification by authorized Government agencies. (*xii*) The standards and testing procedures for equipment to be produced under licence from foreign collaborators or from indigenous R & D will have to be provided by the licensee to the Government nominated quality assurance agency under appropriate confidentiality clause. The nominated quality assurance agency would inspect the finished product and would conduct surveillance and audit of the Quality Assurance Procedures of the licensee. Self-certification would be permitted by the Ministry of Defence on case to case basis, which may involve either individual items, or group of items manufactured by the licensee. Such permission would be for a fixed period and subject to renewals. (*xiii*) Purchase preference and price preference may be given to the Public Sector organizations as per guidelines of the Department of Public Enterprises.		

Sl.No.	Sector/Activity	% of FDI Cap/Equity	Entry Route
	(*xiv*) Arms and ammunition produced by the private manufacturers will be primarily sold to the Ministry of Defence. These items may also be sold to other Government entities under the control of the Ministry of Home Affairs and State Governments with the prior approval of the Ministry of Defence. No such item should be sold within the country to any other person or entity. The export of manufactured items would be subject to policy and guidelines as applicable to Ordnance Factories and Defence Public Sector Undertakings. Non-lethal items would be permitted for sale to persons/entities other than the Central of State Governments with the prior approval of the Ministry of Defence. Licensee would also need to institute a verifiable system of removal of all goods out of their factories. Violation of these provisions may lead to cancellation of the licence. (*xv*) Government decision on applications to FIPB for FDI in defence industry sector will be normally communicated within a time frame of 10 weeks from the date of acknowledgement.		
SERVICES SECTOR			
INFORMATION SERVICES			
6.2.7	**Broadcasting**		
6.2.7.1	**Terrestrial Broadcasting FM (FM Radio) subject to** such terms and conditions as specified from time to time by Ministry of Information and Broadcasting for grant of permission for setting up of FM Radio Stations	26% (FDI, NRI & PIO investments and portfolio investment)	Government
6.2.7.2	**Cable Network, subject to** Cable Television Network Rules, 1994 and other conditions as specified from time to time by Ministry of Information and Broadcasting	49% (FDI, NRI & PIO investments and portfolio investment)	Government
6.2.7.3	**Direct–to-Home subject to** such guidelines/terms and conditions as specified from time to time by Ministry of Information and Broadcasting	49% (FDI, NRI & PIO investments and portfolio investment)	Government

Sl.No.	Sector/Activity	% of FDI Cap/Equity	Entry Route
		Within this limit, FDI component not to exceed 20%	
6.2.7.4	**Headend-In-The-Sky (HITS) Broadcasting Service** refers to the multichannel downlinking and distribution of television programme in C- Band or Ku Band wherein all the pay channels are downlinked at a central facility (Hub/teleport) and again uplinked to a satellite after encryption of channel. At the cable headend these encrypted pay channels are downlinked using a single satellite antenna, transmodulated and sent to the subscribers by using a land based transmission system comprising of infrastructure of cable/optical fibres network.		
6.2.7.4.1	**FDI limit in (HITS) Broadcasting Service is subject to** such guidelines/terms and conditions as specified from time to time by Ministry of Information and Broadcasting.	74% (total direct and indirect foreign investment including portfolio and FDI)	Automatic up to 49% Government route beyond 49% and up to 74%
6.2.7.5	**Setting up hardware facilities such as up-linking, HUB etc.**		
	(1) Setting up of Up-linking HUB/Teleports	49% (FDI & FII)	Government
	(2) Up-linking a Non-News & Current Affairs TV Channel	100%	Government
	(3) Up-linking a News & Current Affairs TV Channel **subject to** the condition that the portfolio investment from FII/NRI shall not be "persons acting in concert" with FDI investors, as defined in the SEBI (Substantial Acquisition of Shares and Takeovers) Regulations, 1997	26% (FDI & FII)	Government
6.2.7.5.1	***Other conditions:***		
	(*i*) All the activities at (1), (2) and (3) above will be further subject to the condition that the Company permitted to uplink the		

Sl.No.	Sector/Activity	% of FDI Cap/Equity	Entry Route
	channel shall certify the continued compliance of this requirement through the Company Secretary at the end of each financial year. (*ii*) FDI for Up-linking TV Channels will be subject to compliance with the Up-linking Policy notified by the Ministry of Information & Broadcasting from time to time.		
6.2.8	**Print Media**		
6.2.8.1	Publishing of Newspaper and periodicals dealing with news and current affairs	26% (FDI and investment by NRIs/PIOs/FII)	Government
6.2.8.2	Publication of Indian editions of foreign magazines dealing with news and current affairs	26% (FDI and investment by NRIs/PIOs/FII)	Government
6.2.8.2.1	***Other Conditions:***		
	(*i*) 'Magazine', for the purpose of these guidelines, will be defined as a periodical publication, brought out on non-daily basis, containing public news or comments on public news. (*ii*) Foreign investment would also be subject to the Guidelines for Publication of Indian editions of foreign magazines dealing with news and current affairs issued by the Ministry of Information & Broadcasting on 4.12.2008.		
6.2.8.3	Publishing/printing of Scientific and Technical Magazines/ specialty journals/periodicals, **subject to** compliance with the legal framework as applicable and guidelines issued in this regard from time to time by Ministry of Information and Broadcasting.	100%	Government
6.2.8.4	Publication of facsimile edition of foreign newspapers	100%	Government
6.2.8.4.1	***Other Conditions:***		
	(*i*) FDI should be made by the owner of the original foreign newspapers whose facsimile edition is proposed to be brought out in India. (*ii*) Publication of facsimile edition of foreign newspapers can be undertaken only by an entity incorporated or registered in India under the provisions of the Companies Act, 1956.		

Sl.No.	Sector/Activity	% of FDI Cap/Equity	Entry Route
	(*iii*) Publication of facsimile edition of foreign newspaper would also be subject to the Guidelines for publication of newspapers and periodicals dealing with news and current affairs and publication of facsimile edition of foreign newspapers issued by Ministry of Information & Broadcasting on 31.3.2006, as amended from time to time.		
6.2.9	**Civil Aviation**		
6.2.9.1	The Civil Aviation sector includes Airports, Scheduled and Non-Scheduled domestic passenger airlines, Helicopter services/Seaplane services, Ground Handling Services, Maintenance and Repair organizations; Flying training institutes; and Technical training institutions. For the purposes of the Civil Aviation sector: (*i*) "Airport" means a landing and taking off area for aircrafts, usually with runways and aircraft maintenance and passenger facilities and includes aerodrome as defined in clause (2) of section 2 of the Aircraft Act, 1934; (*ii*) "Aerodrome" means any definite or limited ground or water area intended to be used, either wholly or in part, for the landing or departure of aircraft, and includes all buildings, sheds, vessels, piers and other structures thereon or pertaining thereto; (*iii*) "Air transport service" means a service for the transport by air of persons, mails or any other thing, animate or inanimate, for any kind of remuneration whatsoever, whether such service consists of a single flight or series of flights; (*iv*) "Air Transport Undertaking" means an undertaking whose business includes the carriage by air of passengers or cargo for hire or reward; (*v*) "Aircraft component" means any part, the soundness and correct functioning of which, when fitted to an aircraft, is essential to the continued airworthiness or safety of the aircraft and includes any item of equipment; (*vi*) "Helicopter" means a heavier-than -air aircraft supported in flight by the reactions of the air on one or more power driven rotors on substantially vertical axis; (*vii*) "Scheduled air transport service" means an air transport service undertaken between the same two or more places and operated according to a published time table or with flights so regular or frequent that they constitute a recognizably systematic series, each flight being open to use by members of the public;		

Sl.No.	Sector/Activity	% of FDI Cap/Equity	Entry Route
	(*viii*) "Non-Scheduled Air Transport service" means any service which is not a scheduled air transport service and will include Cargo airlines; (*ix*) "Cargo airlines" would mean such airlines which meet the conditions as given in the Civil Aviation Requirements issued by the Ministry of Civil Aviation; (*x*) "Seaplane" means an aeroplane capable normally of taking off from and alighting solely on water; (*xi*) "Ground Handling" means (i) ramp handling, (ii) traffic handling both of which shall include the activities as specified by the Ministry of Civil Aviation through the Aeronautical Information Circulars from time to time, and (iii) any other activity specified by the Central Government to be a part of either ramp handling or traffic handling.		
6.2.9.2	**Airports**		
	(*a*) Greenfield projects	100%	Automatic
	(*b*) Existing projects	100%	Automatic up to 74% Government route beyond 74%
6.2.9.3	**Air Transport Services**		
	(*a*) Air Transport Services would include Domestic Scheduled Passenger Airlines; Non-Scheduled Air Transport Services, helicopter and seaplane services. (*b*) No foreign airlines would be allowed to participate directly or indirectly in the equity of an Air Transport Undertaking engaged in operating Scheduled and Non-Scheduled Air Transport Services except Cargo airlines. (*c*) Foreign airlines are allowed to participate in the equity of companies operating Cargo airlines, helicopter and seaplane services.		
	(1) Scheduled Air Transport Service/Domestic Scheduled Passenger Airline	49% FDI (100% for NRIs)	Automatic
	(2) Non-Scheduled Air Transport Service	74% FDI (100% for NRIs)	Automatic up to 49% Government route beyond 49% and up to 74%

Sl.No.	Sector/Activity	% of FDI Cap/Equity	Entry Route
	(3) Helicopter services/seaplane services requiring DGCA approval	100%	Automatic
6.2.9.4	**Other services under Civil Aviation sector**		
	(1) Ground Handling Services **subject to** sectoral regulations and security clearance	74% FDI (100% for NRIs)	Automatic up to 49% Government route beyond 49% and up to 74%
	(2) Maintenance and Repair organizations; flying training institutes; and technical training institutions	100%	Automatic
6.2.10	**Courier services for carrying packages, parcels and other items which do not come within the ambit of the Indian Post Office Act, 1898 and excluding the activity relating to the distribution of letters.**	100%	Government
6.2.11	**Construction Development: Townships, Housing, Built-up infrastructure**		
6.2.11.1	Townships, housing, built-up infrastructure and construction-development projects (which would include, but not be restricted to, housing, commercial premises, hotels, resorts, hospitals, educational institutions, recreational facilities, city and regional level infrastructure)	100%	Automatic
6.2.11.2	Investment will be subject to the following conditions: (1) Minimum area to be developed under each project would be as under: (*i*) In case of development of serviced housing plots, a minimum land area of 10 hectares (*ii*) In case of construction-development projects, a minimum built-up area of 50,000 sq.mts		

Sl.No.	Sector/Activity	% of FDI Cap/Equity	Entry Route
	(*iii*) In case of a combination project, any one of the above two conditions would suffice (2) Minimum capitalization of US$10 million for wholly owned subsidiaries and US$ 5 million for joint ventures with Indian partners. The funds would have to be brought in within six months of commencement of business of the Company. (3) Original investment cannot be repatriated before a period of three years from completion of minimum capitalization. Original investment means the entire amount brought in as FDI. The lock-in period of three years will be applied from the date of receipt of each installment/tranche of FDI or from the date of completion of minimum capitalization, whichever is later. However, the investor may be permitted to exit earlier with prior approval of the Government through the FIPB. (4) At least 50% of each such project must be developed within a period of five years from the date of obtaining all statutory clearances. The investor/investee company would not be permitted to sell undeveloped plots. For the purpose of these guidelines, "undeveloped plots" will mean where roads, water supply, street lighting, drainage, sewerage, and other conveniences, as applicable under prescribed regulations, have not been made available. It will be necessary that the investor provides this infrastructure and obtains the completion certificate from the concerned local body/service agency before he would be allowed to dispose of serviced housing plots. (5) The project shall conform to the norms and standards, including land use requirements and provision of community amenities and common facilities, as laid down in the applicable building control regulations, bye-laws, rules, and other regulations of the State Government/Municipal/Local Body concerned. (6) The investor/investee company shall be responsible for obtaining all necessary approvals, including those of the building/layout plans, developing internal and peripheral areas and other infrastructure facilities, payment of development, external development and other charges and complying with all other requirements as prescribed under applicable rules/bye-laws/regulations of the State Government/Municipal/Local Body concerned. (7) The State Government/Municipal/Local Body concerned, which approves the building/development plans, would monitor compliance of the above conditions by the developer.		

Sl.No.	Sector/Activity	% of FDI Cap/Equity	Entry Route
	Note: (*i*) The conditions at (1) to (4) above would not apply to Hotels & Tourism, Hospitals, Special Economic Zones (SEZs), Education Sector, Old age Homes and investment by NRIs. (*ii*) FDI is not allowed in Real Estate Business.		
6.2.12	**Industrial Parks – new and existing**	**100%**	**Automatic**
6.2.12.1	(*i*) "Industrial Park" is a project in which quality infrastructure in the form of plots of developed land or built up space or a combination with common facilities, is developed and made available to all the allottee units for the purposes of industrial activity. (*ii*) "Infrastructure" refers to facilities required for functioning of units located in the Industrial Park and includes roads (including approach roads), water supply and sewerage, common effluent treatment facility, telecom network, generation and distribution of power, air conditioning. (*iii*) "Common Facilities" refer to the facilities available for all the units located in the industrial park, and include facilities of power, roads (including approach roads), water supply and sewerage, common effluent treatment, common testing, telecom services, air conditioning, common facility buildings, industrial canteens, convention/conference halls, parking, travel desks, security service, first aid center, ambulance and other safety services, training facilities and such other facilities meant for common use of the units located in the Industrial Park. (*iv*) "Allocable area" in the Industrial Park means— (*a*) in the case of plots of developed land- the net site area available for allocation to the units, excluding the area for common facilities. (*b*) in the case of built up space- the floor area and built up space utilized for providing common facilities. (*c*) in the case of a combination of developed land and built-up space- the net site and floor area available for allocation to the units excluding the site area and built up space utilized for providing common facilities. (*v*) "Industrial Activity" means manufacturing; electricity; gas and water supply; post and telecommunications; software publishing, consultancy and supply; data processing, database activities and distribution of electronic content; other computer related activities; basic and applied R&D on bio-technology, pharmaceutical sciences/life sciences, natural sciences and		

Sl.No.	Sector/Activity	% of FDI Cap/Equity	Entry Route
	engineering; business and management consultancy activities; and architectural, engineering and other technical activities.		
6.2.12.2	FDI in Industrial Parks would not be subject to the conditionalities applicable for construction development projects etc. spelt out in para 6.2.11 above, provided the Industrial Parks meet with the under-mentioned conditions: (*i*) it would comprise of a minimum of 10 units and no single unit shall occupy more than 50% of the allocable area; (*ii*) the minimum percentage of the area to be allocated for industrial activity shall not be less than 66% of the total allocable area.		
6.2.13	**Satellites – Establishment and operation**		
6.2.13.1	Satellites – Establishment and operation, subject to the sectoral guidelines of Department of Space/ISRO	74%	Government
6.2.14	**Private Security Agencies**	49%	Government
6.2.15	**Telecom Services** Investment caps and other conditions for specified services are given below. However, licensing and security requirements notified by the Department of Telecommunications will need to be complied with for all services.		
6.2.15.1	(*i*) **Telecom services**	74%	Automatic up to 49% Government route beyond 49% and up to 74%
6.2.15.1.1	***Other conditions:***		
	(1) ***General Conditions:*** (*i*) This is applicable in case of Basic, Cellular, Unified Access Services, National/International Long Distance, V-Sat, Public Mobile Radio Trunked Services (PMRTS), Global Mobile Personal Communications Services (GMPCS) and other value added Services. (*ii*) Both direct and indirect foreign investment in the licensee company shall be counted for the purpose of FDI ceiling. Foreign Investment shall include investment by Foreign Institutional Investors (FIIs), Non- resident Indians (NRIs), Foreign Currency Convertible Bonds (FCCBs), American		

Sl.No.	Sector/Activity	% of FDI Cap/Equity	Entry Route
	Depository Receipts (ADRs), Global Depository Receipts (GDRs) and convertible preference shares held by foreign entity. In any case, the `Indian' shareholding will not be less than 26 percent. (*iii*) FDI in the licensee company/Indian promoters/investment companies including their holding companies shall require approval of the Foreign Investment Promotion Board (FIPB) if it has a bearing on the overall ceiling of 74 percent. While approving the investment proposals, FIPB shall take note that investment is not coming from countries of concern and/or unfriendly entities. (*iv*) The investment approval by FIPB shall envisage the conditionality that Company would adhere to licence Agreement. (*v*) FDI shall be subject to laws of India and not the laws of the foreign country/countries. (2) ***Security Conditions:*** (*i*) The Chief Officer In-charge of technical network operations and the Chief Security Officer should be a resident Indian citizen. (*ii*) Details of infrastructure/network diagram (technical details of the network) could be provided on a need basis only to telecom equipment suppliers/manufacturers and the affiliate/parents of the licensee company. Clearance from the licensor (Department of Telecommunications) would be required if such information is to be provided to anybody else. (*iii*) For security reasons, domestic traffic of such entities as may be identified/specified by the licensor shall not be hauled/routed to any place outside India. (*iv*) The licensee company shall take adequate and timely measures to ensure that the information transacted through a network by the subscribers is secure and protected. (*v*) The officers/officials of the licensee companies dealing with the lawful interception of messages will be resident Indian citizens. (*vi*) The majority Directors on the Board of the company shall be Indian citizens. (*vii*) The positions of the Chairman, Managing Director, Chief Executive Officer (CEO) and/or Chief Financial Officer (CFO), if held by foreign nationals, would require to be security vetted by Ministry of Home Affairs (MHA). Security vetting shall be required periodically on yearly basis. In case something adverse is found during the security vetting, the direction of MHA shall be binding on the licensee.		

Sl.No.	Sector/Activity	% of FDI Cap/Equity	Entry Route
	(*viii*) The Company shall not transfer the following to any person/ place outside India:— (*a*) Any accounting information relating to subscriber (except for international roaming/billing) (Note: it does not restrict a statutorily required disclosure of financial nature) ; and (*b*) User information (except pertaining to foreign subscribers using Indian Operator's network while roaming). (*ix*) The Company must provide traceable identity of their subscribers. However, in case of providing service to roaming subscriber of foreign Companies, the Indian Company shall endeavour to obtain traceable identity of roaming subscribers from the foreign company as a part of its roaming agreement. (*x*) On request of the licensor or any other agency authorised by the licensor, the telecom service provider should be able to provide the geographical location of any subscriber (BTS location) at a given point of time. (*xi*) The Remote Access (RA) to Network would be provided only to approved location(s) abroad through approved location(s) in India. The approval for location(s) would be given by the Licensor (DOT) in consultation with the Ministry of Home Affairs. (*xii*) Under no circumstances, should any RA to the suppliers/ manufacturers and affiliate(s) be enabled to access Lawful Interception System(LIS), Lawful Interception Monitoring (LIM), Call contents of the traffic and any such sensitive sector/ data, which the licensor may notify from time to time. (*xiii*) The licensee company is not allowed to use remote access facility for monitoring of content. (*xiv*) Suitable technical device should be made available at Indian end to the designated security agency/licensor in which a mirror image of the remote access information is available on line for monitoring purposes. (*xv*) Complete audit trail of the remote access activities pertaining to the network operated in India should be maintained for a period of six months and provided on request to the licensor or any other agency authorised by the licensor. (*xvi*) The telecom service providers should ensure that necessary provision (hardware/software) is available in their equipment for doing the Lawful interception and monitoring from a centralized location. (*xvii*) The telecom service providers should familiarize/train Vigilance Technical Monitoring (VTM)/security agency		

Sl.No.	Sector/Activity	% of FDI Cap/Equity	Entry Route
	officers/officials in respect of relevant operations/features of their systems. (*xviii*) It shall be open to the licensor to restrict the Licensee Company from operating in any sensitive area from the National Security angle. (*xix*) In order to maintain the privacy of voice and data, monitoring shall only be upon authorisation by the Union Home Secretary or Home Secretaries of the States/Union Territories. (*xx*) For monitoring traffic, the licensee company shall provide access of their network and other facilities as well as to books of accounts to the security agencies. (*xxi*) The aforesaid Security Conditions shall be applicable to all the licensee companies operating telecom services covered under this circular irrespective of the level of FDI. (*xxii*) Other Service Providers (OSPs), providing services like Call Centres, Business Process Outsourcing (BPO), tele-marketing, tele-education, etc, and are registered with DoT as OSP. Such OSPs operate the service using the telecom infrastructure provided by licensed telecom service providers and 100% FDI is permitted for OSPs. As the security conditions are applicable to all licensed telecom service providers, the security conditions mentioned above shall not be separately enforced on OSPs. (3) The above General Conditions and Security Conditions shall also be applicable to the companies operating telecom service(s) with the FDI cap of 49%. (4) All the telecom service providers shall submit a compliance report on the aforesaid conditions to the licensor on 1st day of July and January on six monthly basis.		
6.2.15.2	(a) ISP with gateways (*b*) ISP's not providing gateways *i.e.* without gate-ways (both for satellite and marine cables) ***Note:*** The new guidelines of August 24, 2007 Department of Telecommunications provide for new ISP licenses with FDI up to 74%. (*c*) Radio paging (*d*) End-to-End bandwidth	74%	Automatic up to 49% Government route beyond 49% and up to 74%

Sl.No.	Sector/Activity	% of FDI Cap/Equity	Entry Route
6.2.15.3	(*a*) Infrastructure provider providing dark fibre, right of way, duct space, tower (IP Category I) (*b*) Electronic Mail (*c*) Voice Mail ***Note:*** Investment in all the above activities is subject to the conditions that such companies will divest 26% of their equity in favour of Indian public in 5 years, if these companies are listed in other parts of the world.	100%	Automatic up to 49% Government route beyond 49%
6.2.16	**Trading**		
6.2.16.1	(*i*) **Cash & Carry Wholesale Trading/Wholesale Trading (including sourcing from MSEs)**	100%	Automatic
6.2.16.1.1	***Definition:*** Cash & Carry Wholesale trading/Wholesale trading, would mean sale of goods/merchandise to retailers, industrial, commercial, institutional or other professional business users or to other wholesalers and related subordinated service providers. Wholesale trading would, accordingly, be sales for the purpose of trade, business and profession, as opposed to sales for the purpose of personal consumption. The yardstick to determine whether the sale is wholesale or not would be the type of customers to whom the sale is made and not the size and volume of sales. Wholesale trading would include resale, processing and thereafter sale, bulk imports with ex-port/ex-bonded warehouse business sales and B2B e-Commerce.		
6.2.16.1.2	**Guidelines for Cash & Carry Wholesale Trading/Wholesale Trading (WT):** (*a*) For undertaking WT, requisite licenses/registration/permits, as specified under the relevant Acts/Regulations/Rules/Orders of the State Government/Government Body/Government Authority/Local Self-Government Body under that State Government should be obtained. (*b*) Except in case of sales to Government, sales made by the wholesaler would be considered as 'cash & carry wholesale trading/wholesale trading' with valid business customers, only when WT are made to the following entities:		

Sl.No.	Sector/Activity	% of FDI Cap/Equity	Entry Route
	(I) Entities holding sales tax/VAT registration/service tax/excise duty registration; or (II) Entities holding trade licenses *i.e.* a license/registration certificate/membership certificate/registration under Shops and Establishment Act, issued by a Government Authority/Government Body/Local Self-Government Authority, reflecting that the entity/person holding the license/registration certificate/membership certificate, as the case may be, is itself/himself/herself engaged in a business involving commercial activity; or (III) Entities holding permits/license etc. for undertaking retail trade (like tehbazari and similar license for hawkers) from Government Authorities/Local Self Government Bodies; or (IV) Institutions having certificate of incorporation or registration as a society or registration as public trust for their self consumption. *Note:* **An Entity, to whom WT is made, may fulfill any one of the 4 conditions.** (*c*) Full records indicating all the details of such sales like name of entity, kind of entity, registration/license/permit etc. number, amount of sale etc. should be maintained on a day to day basis. (*d*) WT of goods would be permitted among companies of the same group. However, such WT to group companies taken together should not exceed 25% of the total turnover of the wholesale venture (*e*) WT can be undertaken as per normal business practice, including extending credit facilities subject to applicable regulations. (*f*) A Wholesale/Cash & carry trader cannot open retail shops to sell to the consumer directly.		
6.2.16.2	**E-commerce activities**	100%	Automatic
6.2.16.2.1	E-commerce activities refer to the activity of buying and selling by a company through the e-commerce platform. Such companies would engage only in Business to Business (B2B) e-commerce and not in retail trading, inter-alia implying that existing restrictions on FDI in domestic trading would be applicable to e-commerce as well.		
6.2.16.3	**Test marketing** of such items for which a company has approval for manufacture, provided such test marketing facility will be for a period of two years, and investment in	100%	Government

Sl.No.	Sector/Activity	% of FDI Cap/Equity	Entry Route
	setting up manufacturing facility commences simultaneously with test marketing.		
6.2.16.4	**Single Brand product retail trading**	100%	Government
	(1) Foreign Investment in Single Brand product retail trading is aimed at attracting investments in production and marketing, improving the availability of such goods for the consumer, encouraging increased sourcing of goods from India, and enhancing competitiveness of Indian enterprises through access to global designs, technologies and management practices. (2) FDI in Single Brand product retail trading would be subject to the following conditions: (*a*) Products to be sold should be of a 'Single Brand' only. (*b*) Products should be sold under the same brand internationally *i.e.* products should be sold under the same brand in one or more countries other than India. (*c*) 'Single Brand' product-retail trading would cover only products which are branded during manufacturing. (*d*) The foreign investor should be the owner of the brand. (*e*) In respect of proposals involving FDI beyond 51%, mandatory sourcing of at least 30% of the value of products sold would have to be done from Indian 'small industries/village and cottage industries, artisans and craftsmen'. 'Small industries' would be defined as industries which have a total investment in plant & machinery not exceeding US $ 1.00 million. This valuation refers to the value at the time of installation, without providing for depreciation. Further, if at any point in time, this valuation is exceeded, the industry shall not qualify as a 'small industry' for this purpose. The compliance of this condition will be ensured through self-certification by the company, to be subsequently checked, by statutory auditors, from the duly certified accounts, which the company will be required to maintain. (3) Application seeking permission of the Government for FDI in retail trade of 'Single Brand' products would be made to the Secretariat for Industrial Assistance (SIA) in the Department of Industrial Policy & Promotion. The application would specifically indicate the product/product categories which are proposed to be sold under a 'Single Brand'. Any addition to the product/product categories to be sold under 'Single Brand' would require a fresh approval of the Government.		

Sl.No.	Sector/Activity	% of FDI Cap/Equity	Entry Route
	(4) Applications would be processed in the Department of Industrial Policy & Promotion, to determine whether the products proposed to be sold satisfy the notified guidelines, before being considered by the FIPB for Government approval.		
	Financial Services Foreign investment in other financial services , other than those indicated below, would require prior approval of the Government:		
6.2.17	**Asset Reconstruction Companies**		
6.2.17.1	'Asset Reconstruction Company' (ARC) means a company registered with the Reserve Bank of India under Section 3 of the Securitisation and Reconstruction of Financial Assets and Enforcement of Security Interest Act, 2002 (SARFAESI Act).	49% of paid-up capital of ARC	Government
6.2.17.2	***Other conditions:***		
	(*i*) Persons resident outside India, other than Foreign Institutional Investors (FIIs), can invest in the capital of Asset Reconstruction Companies (ARCs) registered with Reserve Bank only under the Government Route. Such investments have to be strictly in the nature of FDI. Investments by FIIs are not permitted in the equity capital of ARCs. (*ii*) However, FIIs registered with SEBI can invest in the Security Receipts (SRs) issued by ARCs registered with Reserve Bank. FIIs can invest up to 49 per cent of each tranche of scheme of SRs, subject to the condition that investment by a single FII in each tranche of SRs shall not exceed 10 per cent of the issue. (*iii*) Any individual investment of more than 10% would be subject to provisions of section 3(3) (f) of Securitization and Reconstruction of Financial Assets and Enforcement of Security Interest Act, 2002.		
6.2.18	**Banking –Private sector**		
6.2.18.1	Banking –Private sector	74% including investment by FIIs	Automatic up to 49% Government route beyond 49% and up to 74%

Sl.No.	Sector/Activity	% of FDI Cap/Equity	Entry Route
6.2.18.2	*Other conditions:*		
	(1) This 74% limit will include investment under the Portfolio Investment Scheme (PIS) by FIIs, NRIs and shares acquired prior to September 16, 2003 by erstwhile OCBs, and continue to include IPOs, Private placements, GDR/ADRs and acquisition of shares from existing shareholders. (2) The aggregate foreign investment in a private bank from all sources will be allowed up to a maximum of 74 per cent of the paid up capital of the Bank. At all times, at least 26 per cent of the paid up capital will have to be held by residents, except in regard to a wholly-owned subsidiary of a foreign bank. (3) The stipulations as above will be applicable to all investments in existing private sector banks also. (4) The permissible limits under portfolio investment schemes through stock exchanges for FIIs and NRIs will be as follows: (*i*) In the case of FIIs, as hitherto, individual FII holding is restricted to 10 per cent of the total paid-up capital, aggregate limit for all FIIs cannot exceed 24 per cent of the total paid-up capital, which can be raised to 49 per cent of the total paid-up capital by the bank concerned through a resolution by its Board of Directors followed by a special resolution to that effect by its General Body. (*a*) Thus, the FII investment limit will continue to be within 49 per cent of the total paid-up capital. (*b*) In the case of NRIs, as hitherto, individual holding is restricted to 5 per cent of the total paid-up capital both on repatriation and non-repatriation basis and aggregate limit cannot exceed 10 per cent of the total paid-up capital both on repatriation and non-repatriation basis. However, NRI holding can be allowed up to 24 per cent of the total paid-up capital both on repatriation and non-repatriation basis provided the banking company passes a special resolution to that effect in the General Body. (*c*) Applications for foreign direct investment in private banks having joint venture/subsidiary in insurance sector may be addressed to the Reserve Bank of India (RBI) for consideration in consultation with the Insurance Regulatory and Development Authority (IRDA) in order to ensure that the 26 per cent limit of foreign shareholding applicable for the insurance sector is not being breached.		

Sl.No.	Sector/Activity	% of FDI Cap/Equity	Entry Route
	(*d*) Transfer of shares under FDI from residents to non-residents will continue to require approval of RBI and Government as per para 3.6.2 above as applicable. (*e*) The policies and procedures prescribed from time to time by RBI and other institutions such as SEBI, D/o Company Affairs and IRDA on these matters will continue to apply. (*f*) RBI guidelines relating to acquisition by purchase or otherwise of shares of a private bank, if such acquisition results in any person owning or controlling 5 per cent or more of the paid up capital of the private bank will apply to non-resident investors as well. (*ii*) Setting up of a subsidiary by foreign banks (*a*) Foreign banks will be permitted to either have branches or subsidiaries but not both. (*b*) Foreign banks regulated by banking supervisory authority in the home country and meeting Reserve Bank's licensing criteria will be allowed to hold 100 per cent paid up capital to enable them to set up a wholly-owned subsidiary in India. (*c*) A foreign bank may operate in India through only one of the three channels viz., (*i*) branches (*ii*) a wholly-owned subsidiary and (*iii*) a subsidiary with aggregate foreign investment up to a maximum of 74 per cent in a private bank. (*d*) A foreign bank will be permitted to establish a wholly-owned subsidiary either through conversion of existing branches into a subsidiary or through a fresh banking license. A foreign bank will be permitted to establish a subsidiary through acquisition of shares of an existing private sector bank provided at least 26 per cent of the paid capital of the private sector bank is held by residents at all times consistent with para (*i*) (*b*) above. (*e*) A subsidiary of a foreign bank will be subject to the licensing requirements and conditions broadly consistent with those for new private sector banks. (*f*) Guidelines for setting up a wholly-owned subsidiary of a foreign bank will be issued separately by RBI (*g*) All applications by a foreign bank for setting up a subsidiary or for conversion of their existing branches to subsidiary in India will have to be made to the RBI. (*iii*) At present there is a limit of ten per cent on voting rights in respect of banking companies, and this should be noted by potential investor. Any change in the ceiling can be brought		

Sl.No.	Sector/Activity	% of FDI Cap/Equity	Entry Route
	about only after final policy decisions and appropriate Parliamentary approvals.		
6.2.19	**Banking- Public Sector**		
6.2.19.1	Banking- Public Sector **subject to** Banking Companies (Acquisition & Transfer of Undertakings) Acts 1970/80. This ceiling (20%) is also applicable to the State Bank of India and its associate Banks.	20% (FDI and Portfolio Investment)	Government
6.2.20	**Commodity Exchanges**		
6.2.20.1	1 Futures trading in commodities are regulated under the Forward Contracts (Regulation) Act, 1952. Commodity Exchanges, like Stock Exchanges, are infrastructure companies in the commodity futures market. With a view to infuse globally acceptable best practices, modern management skills and latest technology, it was decided to allow foreign investment in Commodity Exchanges. 2 For the purposes of this chapter, (*i*) "Commodity Exchange" is a recognized association under the provisions of the Forward Contracts (Regulation) Act, 1952, as amended from time to time, to provide exchange platform for trading in forward contracts in commodities. (*ii*) "recognized association" means an association to which recognition for the time being has been granted by the Central Government under Section 6 of the Forward Contracts (Regulation) Act, 1952 (*iii*) "Association" means any body of individuals, whether incorporated or not, constituted for the purposes of regulating and controlling the business of the sale or purchase of any goods and commodity derivative. (*iv*) "Forward contract" means a contract for the delivery of goods and which is not a ready delivery contract. (*v*) "Commodity derivative" means- • a contract for delivery of goods, which is not a ready delivery contract; or • a contract for differences which derives its value from prices or indices of prices of such underlying goods or activities, services, rights, interests and events, as may be notified in consultation with the Forward Markets Commission by the Central Government, but does not include securities.		

Sl.No.	Sector/Activity	% of FDI Cap/Equity	Entry Route
6.2.20.2	**Policy for FDI in Commodity Exchange**	49% (FDI & FII) [Investment by Registered FII under Portfolio Investment Scheme (PIS) will be limited to 23% and Investment under FDI Scheme limited to 26%]	Government (For FDI)
6.2.20.3	***Other conditions:***		
	(*i*) FII purchases shall be restricted to secondary market only and (*ii*) No non-resident investor/entity, including persons acting in concert, will hold more than 5% of the equity in these companies.		
6.2.21	**Credit Information Companies (CIC)**		
6.2.21.1	Credit Information Companies	49% (FDI & FII)	Government
6.2.21.2	***Other Conditions:***		
	(1) Foreign investment in Credit Information Companies is subject to the Credit Information Companies (Regulation) Act, 2005. (2) Foreign investment is permitted under the Government route, subject to regulatory clearance from RBI. (3) Investment by a registered FII under the Portfolio Investment Scheme would be permitted up to 24% only in the CICs listed at the Stock Exchanges, within the overall limit of 49% for foreign investment. (4) Such FII investment would be permitted subject to the conditions that: (*a*) No single entity should directly or indirectly hold more than 10% equity. (*b*) Any acquisition in excess of 1% will have to be reported to RBI as a mandatory requirement; and (*c*) FIIs investing in CICs shall not seek a representation on the Board of Directors based upon their shareholding.		
6.2.22	**Infrastructure Company in the Securities Market**		
6.2.22.1	Infrastructure companies in Securities Markets, namely,	49% (FDI & FII) [FDI limit	Government

Sl.No.	Sector/Activity	% of FDI Cap/Equity	Entry Route
	stock exchanges, depositories and clearing corporations, in compliance with SEBI Regulations	of 26 per cent and an FII limit of 23 per cent of the paid-up capital]	(For FDI)
6.2.22.2	***Other Conditions:***		
6.2.22.2.1	FII can invest only through purchases in the secondary market		
6.2.23	**Insurance**		
6.2.23.1	Insurance	26%	Automatic
6.2.23.2	Other Conditions:		
	(1) FDI in the Insurance sector, as prescribed in the Insurance Act, 1938, is allowed under the automatic route. (2) This will be subject to the condition that Companies bringing in FDI shall obtain necessary license from the Insurance Regulatory & Development Authority for undertaking insurance activities.		
6.2.24	**Non-Banking Finance Companies (NBFC)**		
6.2.24.1	Foreign investment in NBFC is allowed under the automatic route in only the following activities: (*i*) Merchant Banking (*ii*) Under Writing (*iii*) Portfolio Management Services (*iv*) Investment Advisory Services (*v*) Financial Consultancy (*vi*) Stock Broking (*vii*) Asset Management (*viii*) Venture Capital (*ix*) Custodian Services (*x*) Factoring (*xi*) Credit Rating Agencies (*xii*) Leasing & Finance (*xiii*) Housing Finance (*xiv*) Forex Broking (*xv*) Credit Card Business (*xvi*) Money Changing Business (*xvii*) Micro Credit (*xviii*) Rural Credit	100%	Automatic

Sl.No.	Sector/Activity	% of FDI Cap/Equity	Entry Route
6.2.24.2	*Other Conditions:*		
	(1) Investment would be subject to the following minimum capitalisation norms: (*i*) US $0.5 million for foreign capital up to 51% to be brought upfront (*ii*) US $ 5 million for foreign capital more than 51% and up to 75% to be brought upfront (*iii*) US $ 50 million for foreign capital more than 75% out of which US$ 7.5 million to be brought upfront and the balance in 24 months. (*iv*) 100% foreign owned NBFCs with a minimum capitalisation of US$ 50 million can set up step down subsidiaries for specific NBFC activities, without any restriction on the number of operating subsidiaries and without bringing in additional capital. **The minimum capitalization condition as mandated by para 3.10.4.1, therefore, shall not apply to downstream subsidiaries.** (*v*) Joint Venture operating NBFCs that have 75% or less than 75% foreign investment can also set up subsidiaries for undertaking other NBFC activities, subject to the subsidiaries also complying with the applicable minimum capitalisation norm mentioned in (i), (ii) and (iii) above and (vi) below. (*vi*) Non-Fund based activities: US $0.5 million to be brought upfront for all permitted non-fund based NBFCs irrespective of the level of foreign investment subject to the following condition: It would not be permissible for such a company to set up any subsidiary for any other activity, nor it can participate in any equity of an NBFC holding/operating company. *Note:* The following activities would be classified as Non-Fund Based activities: (*a*) Investment Advisory Services (*b*) Financial Consultancy (*c*) Forex Broking (*d*) Money Changing Business (*e*) Credit Rating Agencies (*vii*) This will be subject to compliance with the guidelines of RBI. *Note:* (*i*) Credit Card business includes issuance, sales, marketing & design of various payment products such as credit cards, charge cards, debit cards, stored value cards, smart card, value added cards etc. (*ii*) Leasing & Finance covers only financial leases and not operating leases.		

Sl.No.	Sector/Activity	% of FDI Cap/Equity	Entry Route
	(2) The NBFC will have to comply with the guidelines of the relevant regulator/s, as applicable		
6.2.25	**Pharmaceuticals**		
6.2.25.1	Greenfield	100%	Automatic
6.2.25.2	Existing Companies	100%	Government

Chapter 7

Remittance, Reporting and Violation

7.1 Remittance and Repatriation

7.1.1 Remittance of sale proceeds/Remittance on winding up/Liquidation of Companies

(*i*) Sale proceeds of shares and securities and their remittance is 'remittance of asset' governed by The Foreign Exchange Management (Remittance of Assets) Regulations 2000 under FEMA.

(*ii*) AD Category-I bank can allow the remittance of sale proceeds of a security (net of applicable taxes) to the seller of shares resident outside India, provided the security has been held on repatriation basis, the sale of security has been made in accordance with the prescribed guidelines and NOC/tax clearance certificate from the Income Tax Department has been produced.

(*iii*) *Remittance on winding up/liquidation of Companies:* AD Category-I banks have been allowed to remit winding up proceeds of companies in India, which are under liquidation, subject to payment of applicable taxes. Liquidation may be subject to any order issued by the court winding up the company or the official liquidator in case of voluntary winding up under the provisions of the Companies Act, 1956. AD Category-I banks shall allow the remittance provided the applicant submits:

(*a*) No objection or Tax clearance certificate from Income Tax Department for the remittance.

(*b*) Auditor's certificate confirming that all liabilities in India have been either fully paid or adequately provided for.

(*c*) Auditor's certificate to the effect that the winding up is in accordance with the provisions of the Companies Act, 1956.

(*d*) In case of winding up otherwise than by a court, an auditor's certificate to the effect that there are no legal proceedings pending in any court in India against the applicant or the company under liquidation and there is no legal impediment in permitting the remittance.

7.1.2 Repatriation of Dividend

Dividends are freely repatriable without any restrictions (net after Tax deduction at source or Dividend Distribution Tax, if any, as the case may be). The repatriation is governed by the provisions of the Foreign Exchange Management (Current Account Transactions) Rules, 2000, as amended from time to time.

7.1.3 Repatriation of Interest

Interest on fully, mandatorily & compulsorily convertible debentures is also freely repatriable without any restrictions (net of applicable taxes). The repatriation is governed by the provisions of the Foreign Exchange Management (Current Account Transactions) Rules, 2000, as amended from time to time.

7.2. Reporting of FDI

7.2.1 Reporting of Inflow

(*i*) An Indian company receiving investment from outside India for issuing shares/convertible debentures/preference shares under the FDI Scheme, should report the details of the amount of consideration to the Regional Office concerned of the Reserve Bank not later than 30 days from the date of receipt in the Advance Reporting Form enclosed as **Annex-5**.

(*ii*) Indian companies are required to report the details of the receipt of the amount of consideration for issue of shares/convertible debentures, through an AD Category-I bank, together with a copy/ies of the FIRC/s evidencing the receipt of the remittance along with the KYC report (enclosed as **Annex-6**) on the non-resident investor from the overseas bank remitting the amount. The report would be acknowledged by the Regional Office concerned, which will allot a Unique Identification Number (UIN) for the amount reported.

7.2.2 Reporting of issue of shares

(*i*) After issue of shares (including bonus and shares issued on rights basis and shares issued under ESOP)/fully, mandatorily & compulsorily convertible debentures/fully, mandatorily & compulsorily convertible preference shares, the Indian company has to file Form FC-GPR, enclosed in **Annex-1**, not later than 30 days from the date of issue of shares.

(*ii*) Form FC-GPR has to be duly filled up and signed by Managing Director/ Director/Secretary of the Company and submitted to the Authorized Dealer of the company, who will forward it to the Reserve Bank. The following documents have to be submitted along with the form:

(*a*) A certificate from the Company Secretary of the company certifying that:

(A) all the requirements of the Companies Act, 1956 have been complied with;

(B) terms and conditions of the Government's approval, if any, have been complied with;

(C) the company is eligible to issue shares under these Regulations; and

(D) the company has all original certificates issued by authorized dealers in India evidencing receipt of amount of consideration.

Note: For companies with paid up capital with less than ₹5 crore, the above mentioned certificate can be given by a practicing company secretary.

(*b*) A certificate from Statutory Auditor or Chartered Accountant indicating the manner of arriving at the price of the shares issued to the persons resident outside India.

(*c*) The report of receipt of consideration as well as Form FC-GPR have to be submitted by the AD Category-I bank to the Regional Office concerned of the Reserve Bank under whose jurisdiction the registered office of the company is situated.

(*d*) Annual return on Foreign Liabilities and Assets **(Annex 7)** should be filed on an annual basis by the Indian company, directly with the Reserve Bank. This is an annual return to be submitted by 31st of July every year, pertaining to all investments by way of direct/portfolio investments/reinvested earnings/other capital in the Indian company made during the previous years (*i.e.* the information submitted by 31st July will pertain to all the investments made in the previous years up to March 31). The details of the investments to be reported would include all foreign investments made into the company which is outstanding as on the balance sheet date. The details of overseas investments in the company both under direct/portfolio investment may be separately indicated.

(*e*) Issue of bonus/rights shares or stock options to persons resident outside India directly or on amalgamation/merger/demerger with an existing Indian company, as well as issue of shares on conversion of ECB/royalty/lumpsum technical know-how fee/import of capital goods by units in SEZs, has to be reported in Form FC-GPR.

7.2.3 Reporting of transfer of shares

Reporting of transfer of shares between residents and non-residents and vice-versa is to be done in Form FC-TRS (**Annex 8**). The Form FC-TRS should be submitted to the AD Category-I bank, within 60 days from the date of receipt of the amount of consideration. The onus of submission of the Form FC-TRS within the given timeframe would be on the transferor/transferee, resident in India. The AD Category-I bank, would forward the same to its link office. The link office would consolidate the Form FC-TRS and submit a monthly report to the Reserve Bank.

7.2.4 Reporting of Non-Cash

Details of issue of shares against conversion of ECB have to be reported to the Regional Office concerned of the RBI, as indicated below:

(*i*) In case of **full conversion** of ECB into equity, the company shall report the conversion in Form FC-GPR to the Regional Office concerned of the Reserve Bank as well as in Form ECB-2 to the Department of Statistics and Information Management (DSIM), Reserve Bank of India, Bandra-Kurla Complex, Mumbai – 400 051, within seven working days from the close of month to which it relates. The words "ECB wholly converted to equity" shall be clearly indicated on top of the Form ECB-2. Once reported, filing of Form ECB-2 in the subsequent months is not necessary.

(*ii*) In case of **partial conversion** of ECB, the company shall report the converted portion in Form FC-GPR to the Regional Office concerned as well as in Form ECB-2 clearly differentiating the converted portion from the non-converted portion. The words "ECB partially converted to equity" shall be indicated on top of the Form ECB-2. In the subsequent months, the outstanding balance of ECB shall be reported in Form ECB-2 to DSIM.

7.2.5 Reporting of FCCB/ADR/GDR Issues

The Indian company issuing ADRs/GDRs has to furnish to the Reserve Bank, full details of such issue in the Form enclosed as **Annex 9**, within 30 days from the date of closing of the issue. The company should also furnish a quarterly return in the Form enclosed as **Annex 10**, to the Reserve Bank within 15 days of the close of the calendar quarter. The quarterly return has to be submitted till the entire amount raised through ADR/GDR mechanism is either repatriated to India or utilized abroad as per the extant Reserve Bank guidelines.

7.3 Adherence to Guidelines/Orders and Consequences of Violation

FDI is a capital account transaction and thus any violation of FDI regulations are covered by the penal provisions of the FEMA. Reserve Bank of India administers the FEMA and Directorate of Enforcement under the Ministry of Finance is the authority for the enforcement of FEMA. The Directorate takes up investigation in any contravention of FEMA.

7.3.1 Penalties

(*i*) If a person violates/contravenes any FDI Regulations, by way of breach/non- adherence/non-compliance/contravention of any rule, regulation, notification, press note, press release, circular, direction or order issued in exercise of the powers under FEMA or contravenes any conditions subject to which an authorization is issued by the Government of India/FIPB/Reserve Bank of India, he shall, upon adjudication, be liable to a penalty up to thrice the sum involved in such contraventions where such amount is quantifiable, or up to two lakh Rupees where the amount is not quantifiable, and where such contraventions is a continuing one, further penalty which may extend to five thousand Rupees for every day after the first day during which the contraventions continues.

(*ii*) Where a person committing a contravention of any provisions of this Act or of any rule, direction or order made there under is a company

(company means any body corporate and includes a firm or other association of individuals as defined in the Companies Act), every person who, at the time the contravention was committed, was in charge of, and was responsible to, the company for the conduct of the business of the company as well as the company, shall be deemed to be guilty of the contravention and shall be liable to be proceeded against and punished accordingly.

(*iii*) Any Adjudicating Authority adjudging any contraventions under 6.3.1(i), may, if he thinks fit in addition to any penalty which he may impose for such contravention direct that any currency, security or any other money or property in respect of which the contravention has taken place shall be confiscated to the Central Government.

7.3.2 Adjudication and Appeals

(*i*) For the purpose of adjudication of any contravention of FEMA, the Ministry of Finance as per the provisions contained in the Foreign Exchange Management (Adjudication Proceedings and Appeal) Rules, 2000 appoints officers of the Central Government as the Adjudicating Authorities for holding an enquiry in the manner prescribed. A reasonable opportunity has to be given to the person alleged to have committed contraventions against whom a complaint has been made for being heard before imposing any penalty.

(*ii*) The Central Government may appoint as per the provisions contained in the Foreign Exchange Management (Adjudication Proceedings and Appeal) Rules, 2000, an Appellate Authority/Appellate Tribunal to hear appeals against the orders of the adjudicating authority.

7.3.3 Compounding Proceedings

Under the Foreign Exchange (Compounding Proceedings) Rules 2000, the Central Government may appoint 'Compounding Authority' an officer either from Enforcement Directorate or Reserve Bank of India for any person contravening any provisions of the FEMA. The Compounding Authorities are authorized to compound the amount involved in the contravention to the Act made by the person. No contravention shall be compounded unless the amount involved in such contravention is quantifiable. Any second or subsequent contravention committed after the expiry of a period of three years from the date on which the contravention was previously compounded shall be deemed to be a first contravention. The Compounding Authority may call for any information, record or any other documents relevant to the compounding proceedings. The Compounding Authority shall pass an order of compounding after affording an opportunity of being heard to all the concerns as expeditiously and not later than 180 days from the date of application made to the Compounding Authority. Compounding Authority shall issue order specifying the provisions of the Act or of the rules, directions, requisitions or orders made there under in respect of which contravention has taken place along with details of the alleged contraventions.

Annexure 1

FC-GPR

(*To be filed by the company through its Authorised Dealer Category-I bank with the Regional Office of the RBI under whose jurisdiction the Registered Office of the company making the declaration is situated as and when shares/convertible debentures are issued to the foreign investor, along with the documents mentioned in item No. 4 of the undertaking enclosed to this Form*)

Permanent Account Number (PAN) of the investee company given by the Income Tax Department	☐☐☐☐☐☐☐☐☐☐☐☐☐☐
Date of issue of shares/ convertible debentures	☐☐☐☐☐☐☐☐

No.	Particulars	(In Block Letters)
1.	Name	
	Address of the Registered Office	
	State	
	Registration No. given by Registrar of Companies	
	Whether existing company or new company (strike off whichever is not applicable)	Existing company/ New company
	If existing company, give registration number allotted by RBI for FDI, if any	
	Telephone	
	Fax	
	e-mail	
2.	Description of the main business activity NIC Code	
	Location of the project and NIC code for the district where the project is located	
	Percentage of FDI allowed as per FDI policy	
	State whether FDI is allowed under Automatic Route or Approval Route (strike out whichever is not applicable)	Automatic Route/Approval Route

3	**Details of the foreign investor/collaborator***	
	Name Address Country Constitution/Nature of the investing Entity [Specify whether 1. Individual 2. Company 3. FII 4. FVCI 5. Foreign Trust 6. Private Equity Fund 7. Pension/Provident Fund 8. Sovereign Wealth Fund (SWF)[1] 9. Partnership/Proprietorship Firm 10. Financial Institution 11. NRIs/PIO 12. Others (please specify)] Date of incorporation * If there is more than one foreign investor/collaborator, separate Annex may be included for items 3 and 4 of the Form.	
4	**Particulars of Shares/Convertible Debentures Issued**	
(*a*)	**Nature and date of issue**	

	Nature of issue	*Date of issue*	*Number of shares/ convertible debentures*
01	IPO/FPO		
02	Preferential allotment/ private placement		
03	Rights		
04	Bonus		
05	Conversion of ECB		
06	Conversion of royalty (including lump sum payments)		

1 SWF means a Government investment vehicle which is funded by foreign exchange assets, and which manages those assets separately from the official reserves of the monetary authorities.

07	Conversion against import of capital goods by units in SEZ		
08	ESOPs		
09	Share Swap		
10	Others (please specify)		
	Total		

(*b*) Type of security issued

No.	Nature of security	Number	Maturity	Face value	Premium	Issue Price per share	Amount of inflow*
01	Equity						
02	Compulsorily Convertible Debentures						
03	Compulsorily Convertible Preference shares						
04	Others (please specify)						
	Total						

(*i*) In case the issue price is greater than the face value please give break up of the premium received.

(*ii*) * In case the issue is against conversion of ECB or royalty or against import of capital goods by units in SEZ, a Chartered Accountant's Certificate certifying the amount outstanding on the date of conversion

(*c*)	**Break up of premium**	**Amount**
	Control Premium	
	Non competition fee	
	Others@	
	Total	

@ ***please specify the nature***

(*d*)	**Total inflow** (in Rupees) on account of issue of shares/convertible debentures to non-residents (including premium, if any) vide (*i*) Remittance through AD: (*ii*) Debit to NRE/FCNR A/c with Bank_________ (*iii*) Others (please specify) Date of reporting of (i) and (ii) above to RBI under Para 9 (1) A of Schedule I to Notification No. FEMA 20/2000-RB, dated 3-5-2000, as amended from time to time.	
(*e*)	**Disclosure of fair value of shares issued****	
	We are a listed company and the market value of a share as on date of the issue is*	
	We are an un-listed company and the fair value of a share is*	

** *before issue of shares* * (***Please indicate as applicable***)

5. Post issue pattern of shareholding								
			Equity			***Compulsorily convertible Preference Shares/Debentures***		
Investor category			No. of shares	Amount (Face Value) ₹	%	No. of shares	Amount (Face Value) ₹	%
(*a*)	Non-Resident							
	01	Individuals						
	02	Companies						
	03	FIIs						
	04	FVCIs						
	05	Foreign Trusts						
	06	Private Equity Funds						
	07	Pension/Provident Funds						
	08	Sovereign Wealth Funds						
	09	Partnership/ Proprietorship Firms						
	10	Financial Institutions						
	11	NRIs/PIO						
	12	Others (please specify)						
	Sub Total							
(*b*)	Resident							
Total								

Declaration to be Filed by the Authorised Representative of the Indian Company: (*Delete whichever is not applicable and authenticate*)

We hereby declare that:

1. We comply with the procedure for issue of shares/convertible debentures as laid down under the FDI scheme as indicated in Notification No. FEMA 20/2000-RB, dated 3-5-2000, as amended from time to time.

2. The investment is within the sectoral cap/statutory ceiling permissible under the Automatic Route of RBI and we fulfill all the conditions laid down for investments under the Automatic Route namely (strike off whichever is not applicable).

~~(*a*) Foreign entity/entities (other than individuals), to whom we have issued shares have existing joint venture or technology transfer or trade mark agreement in India in the same field and Conditions stipulated at Para 4.2 of Consolidated FDI policy Circular of Government of India have been complied with.~~

OR

Foreign entity/entities—(other than individuals), to whom we have issued shares do not have any existing joint venture or technology transfer or trade mark agreement in India in the same field. For the purpose of the 'same' field, 4 digit NIC 1987 code would be relevant.

(*b*) We are not an Industrial Undertaking manufacturing items reserved for small sector.

OR

We are an Industrial Undertaking manufacturing items reserved for small sector and the investment limit of 24% of paid-up capital has been observed/requisite approvals have been obtained.

(*c*) Shares issued on rights basis to non-residents are in conformity with Regulation 6 of the RBI Notification No FEMA 20/2000-RB, dated 3-5-2000, as amended from time to time.

OR

Shares issued are bonus.

OR

Shares have been issued under a scheme of merger and amalgamation of two or more Indian companies or reconstruction by way of de-merger or otherwise of an Indian company, duly approved by a court in India.

OR

Shares are issued under ESOP and the conditions regarding this issue have been satisfied.

3. Shares have been issued in terms of SIA/FIPB approval No._ dated

4. We enclose the following documents in compliance with Paragraph 9 (1) (B) of Schedule 1 to Notification No. FEMA 20/2000-RB, dated 3-5-2000:

(*i*) A certificate from our Company Secretary certifying that

(*a*) all the requirements of the Companies Act, 1956 have been complied with;

(*b*) terms and conditions of the Government approval, if any, have been complied with;

(*c*) the company is eligible to issue shares under these Regulations; and

(*d*) the company has all original certificates issued by authorised dealers in India evidencing receipt of amount of consideration in accordance with paragraph 8 of Schedule 1 to Notification No. FEMA 20/2000-RB, dated 3-5-2000.

(*ii*) A certificate from Statutory Auditors/SEBI registered Category I Merchant Banker/Chartered Accountant indicating the manner of arriving at the price of the shares issued to the persons resident outside India.

5. Unique Identification Numbers given for all the remittances received as consideration for issue of shares/convertible debentures (details as above), by Reserve Bank.

R														

(Signature of the Applicant)*:______________________

(Name in Block Letters):______________________

(Designation of the signatory):______________________

Place:

Date:

(* To be signed by Managing Director/Director/Secretary of the Company)

Certificate to be Filed by the Company secretary[1] of the Indian Company Accepting the Investment

(*As per Para 9 (1) (B) (i) of Schedule 1 to Notification No. FEMA 20/2000-RB, dated 3-5-2000*)

In respect of the abovementioned details, we certify the following:

1. All the requirements of the Companies Act, 1956 have been complied with.

---

1 If the company doesn't have a full time Company Secretary, a certificate from a practicing Company Secretary may be submitted.

2. Terms and conditions of the Government approval, if any, have been complied with.

3. The company is eligible to issue shares/convertible debentures under these Regulations.

4. The company has all original certificates issued by AD Category-I banks in India, evidencing receipt of amount of consideration in accordance with paragraph 8 of Schedule 1 to Notification No. FEMA 20/2000-RB, dated 3-5-2000.

(Name and Signature of the Company Secretary) (Seal)

For Use of the Reserve Bank Only

Registration Number for the FC-GPR:

R													

Unique Identification Number allotted to the Company at the time of reporting receipt of remittance

R													

Annexure 2

Terms and conditions for Transfer of Shares/Convertible Debentures, by way of Sale, from a Person Resident in India to a Person Resident Outside India and from a Person Resident Outside India to a Person Resident in India

1.1 In order to address the concerns relating to pricing, documentation, payment/receipt and remittance in respect of the shares/convertible debentures of an Indian company, in all sectors, transferred by way of sale, the parties involved in the transaction shall comply with the guidelines set out below.

1.2 Parties involved in the transaction are (a) seller (resident/non-resident), (b) buyer (resident/non-resident), (c) duly authorized agent/s of the seller and/or buyer, (d) Authorised Dealer bank (AD) branch and (e) Indian company, for recording the transfer of ownership in its books.

2. Pricing Guidelines

2.1 The undernoted pricing guidelines are applicable to the following types of transactions:

(*i*) Transfer of shares, by way of sale under private arrangement by a person resident in India to a person resident outside India.

(*ii*) Transfer of shares, by way of sale under private arrangement by a person resident outside India to a person resident in India.

2.2 Transfer by Resident to Non-resident (*i.e.* to incorporated non-resident entity other than erstwhile OCB, foreign national, NRI, FII)

Price of shares transferred by way of sale by resident to a non-resident where the shares of an Indian company are:

(*a*) listed on a recognized stock exchange in India, shall not be less than the price at which the preferential allotment of shares can be made under the SEBI guidelines, as applicable, provided the same is determined for such duration as specified therein, preceding the relevant date, which shall be the date of purchase or sale of shares,

(*b*) not listed on a recognized stock exchange in India, shall not be less than the fair value to be determined by a SEBI registered Category I Merchant Banker or a Chartered Accountant as per the discounted free cash flow method.

The price per share arrived at should be certified by a SEBI registered Category I Merchant Banker or a Chartered Accountant.

2.3 Transfer by Non-resident (*i.e.* by incorporated non-resident entity, erstwhile OCB, foreign national, NRI, FII) **to Resident**

Sale of shares by a non-resident to resident shall be in accordance with Regulation 10B(2) of Notification No. FEMA 20/2000-RB, dated 3-5-2000 which shall not be more than the minimum price at which the transfer of shares can be made from a resident to a non-resident as given at para 2.2 above.

3. Responsibilities/Obligations of the parties

All the parties involved in the transaction would have the responsibility to ensure that the relevant regulations under FEMA are complied with and consequent on transfer of shares, the relevant individual limit/sectoral caps/foreign equity participation ceilings as fixed by Government are not breached. Settlement of transactions will be subject to payment of applicable taxes, if any.

4. Method of payment and remittance/credit of sale proceeds

4.1 The sale consideration in respect of the shares purchased by a person resident outside India shall be remitted to India through normal banking channels. In case the buyer is a Foreign Institutional Investor (FII), payment should be made by debit to its Special Non-Resident Rupee Account. In case the buyer is a NRI, the payment may be made by way of debit to his NRE/FCNR (B) accounts. However, if the shares are acquired on non-repatriation basis by NRI, the consideration shall be remitted to India through normal banking channel or paid out of funds held in NRE/FCNR (B)/NRO accounts.

4.2. The sale proceeds of shares (net of taxes) sold by a person resident outside India may be remitted outside India. In case of FII, the sale proceeds may be credited to its special Non-Resident Rupee Account. In case of NRI, if the shares sold were held on repatriation basis, the sale proceeds (net of taxes) may be credited to his NRE/FCNR(B) accounts and if the shares sold were held on non repatriation basis, the sale proceeds may be credited to his NRO account subject to payment of taxes.

4.3 The sale proceeds of shares (net of taxes) sold by an OCB may be remitted outside India directly if the shares were held on repatriation basis and if the shares sold were held on non-repatriation basis, the sale proceeds may be credited to its NRO (Current) Account subject to payment of taxes, except in the case of OCBs whose accounts have been blocked by Reserve Bank.

5. Documentation

Besides obtaining a declaration in the enclosed Form FC-TRS (in quadruplicate), the AD branch should arrange to obtain and keep on record the following documents:

5.1 For sale of shares by a person resident in India

(*i*) Consent Letter duly signed by the seller and buyer or their duly appointed agent indicating the details of transfer *i.e.* number of shares to be transferred, the name of the investee company whose shares are being transferred and the price at which shares are being transferred. In case there is no formal Sale Agreement, letters exchanged to this effect may be kept on record.

(*ii*) Where Consent Letter has been signed by their duly appointed agent, the Power of Attorney Document executed by the seller/buyer authorizing the agent to purchase/sell shares.

(*iii*) The shareholding pattern of the investee company after the acquisition of shares by a person resident outside India showing equity participation of residents and non-residents category-wise (*i.e.* NRIs/OCBs/foreign nationals/incorporated non-resident entities/FIIs) and its percentage of paid up capital obtained by the seller/buyer or their duly appointed agent from the company, where the sectoral cap/limits have been prescribed.

(*iv*) Certificate indicating fair value of shares from a Chartered Accountant.

(*v*) Copy of Broker's note if sale is made on Stock Exchange

(*vi*) Undertaking from the buyer to the effect that he is eligible to acquire shares/convertible debentures under FDI policy and the existing sectoral limits and Pricing Guidelines have been complied with.

(*vii*) Undertaking from the FII/sub account to the effect that the individual FII/Sub account ceiling as prescribed by SEBI has not been breached.

5.2. For sale of shares by a person resident outside India

(*i*) Consent Letter duly signed by the seller and buyer or their duly appointed agent indicating the details of transfer *i.e.* number of shares to be transferred, the name of the investee company whose shares are being transferred and the price at which shares are being transferred.

(*ii*) Where the Consent Letter has been signed by their duly appointed agent the Power of Attorney Document authorizing the agent to purchase/sell shares by the seller/buyer. In case there is no formal Sale Agreement, letters exchanged to this effect may be kept on record.

(*iii*) If the sellers are NRIs/OCBs, the copies of RBI approvals evidencing the shares held by them on repatriation/non-repatriation basis. The sale proceeds shall be credited NRE/NRO account, as applicable.

(*iv*) Certificate indicating fair value of shares from a Chartered Accountant.

(*v*) No Objection/Tax Clearance Certificate from Income Tax authority/ Chartered Account.

(*vi*) Undertaking from the buyer to the effect that the Pricing Guidelines have been adhered to.

6. Reporting requirements

6.1 Reporting of transfer of shares between residents and non-residents and vice versa is to be done in Form FC-TRS. The Form FC-TRS should be submitted to the AD Category-I bank, within 60 days from the date of receipt of the amount of consideration. The onus of submission of the Form FC-TRS within the given timeframe would be on the transferor/transferee, resident in India. The AD Category-I bank, would forward the same to its link office. The link office would consolidate the Forms and submit a monthly report to the Reserve Bank[1].

For the purpose the Authorized Dealers may designate branches to specifically handle such transactions. These branches could be staffed with adequately trained staff for this purpose to ensure that the transactions are put through smoothly. The ADs may also designate a nodal office to coordinate the work at these branches and also ensure the reporting of these transactions to the Reserve Bank.

6.2 When the transfer is on private arrangement basis, on settlement of the transactions, the transferee/his duly appointed agent should approach the investee company to record the transfer in their books along with the certificate in the Form FC-TRS from the AD branch that the remittances have been received by the transferor/payment has been made by the transferee. On receipt of the certificate from the AD, the company may record the transfer in its books.

6.3 The actual inflows and outflows on account of such transfer of shares shall be reported by the AD branch in the R-returns in the normal course.

6.4 In addition the AD branch should submit two copies of the Form FC-TRS received from their constituents/customers together with the statement of inflows/outflows on account of remittances received/made in connection with

1 To the Chief General Manager-in-Charge, Reserve Bank of India, Foreign Exchange Department, Foreign Investment Division, Central Office, Mumbai

transfer of shares, by way of sale, to IBD/FED/or the nodal office designated for the purpose by the bank in the enclosed proforma (which is to be prepared in MS-Excel format). The IBD/FED or the nodal office of the bank will in turn submit a consolidated monthly statement in respect of all the transactions reported by their branches together with copies of the FC-TRS Forms received from their branches to Foreign Exchange Department, Reserve Bank, Foreign Investment Division, Central Office, Mumbai in soft copy (in MS- Excel) by e-mail to fdidata@rbi.org.in

6.5 Shares purchased/sold by FIIs under private arrangement will be by debit/credit to their Special Non Resident Rupee Account. Therefore, the transaction should **also** be reported in Form LEC (FII) by the designated bank of the FII concerned.

6.6 Shares/convertible debentures of Indian companies purchased under Portfolio Investment Scheme by NRIs, OCBs cannot be transferred, by way of sale under private arrangement.

6.7 On receipt of statements from the AD, the Reserve Bank may call for such additional details or give such directions as required from the transferor/transferee or their agents, if need be.

Annexure 3

Documents to be submitted by a person resident in India for transfer of shares to a person resident outside India by way of gift

(*i*) Name and address of the transferor (donor) and the transferee (donee).

(*ii*) Relationship between the transferor and the transferee.

(*iii*) Reasons for making the gift.

(*iv*) In case of Government dated securities and treasury bills and bonds, a certificate issued by a Chartered Accountant on the market value of such security.

(*v*) In case of units of domestic mutual funds and units of Money Market Mutual Funds, a certificate from the issuer on the Net Asset Value of such security.

(*vi*) In case of shares and convertible debentures, a certificate from a Chartered Accountant on the value of such securities according to the guidelines issued by Securities and Exchange Board of India or DCF method for listed companies and unlisted companies, respectively.

(*vii*) Certificate from the concerned Indian company certifying that the proposed transfer of shares/convertible debentures by way of gift from resident to the non-resident shall not breach the applicable sectoral cap/FDI limit in the company and that the proposed number of shares/ convertible debentures to be held by the non-resident transferee shall not exceed 5 per cent of the paid up capital of the company.

(*viii*) An undertaking from the resident transferor that the value of security to be transferred together with any security already transferred by the transferor, as gift, to any person residing outside India does not exceed the rupee equivalent of USD 50,000 **during a calendar year.***

* RBI's AP (DIR Series) Circular No. 14, dated 15-9-2011.

Annexure 4

Definition of "relative" as given in section 6 of Companies Act, 1956

A person shall be deemed to be a relative of another, if, and only if:

(*a*) they are members of a Hindu undivided family; or

(*b*) they are husband and wife; or

(*c*) the one is related to the other in the manner indicated in Schedule IA (as under):

1. Father.
2. Mother (including step-mother).
3. Son (including stepson).
4. Son's wife.
5. Daughter (including step-daughter).
6. Father's father.
7. Father's mother.
8. Mother's mother.
9. Mother's father.
10. Son's son.
11. Son's son's wife.
12. Son's daughter.
13. Son's daughter's husband.
14. Daughter's husband.
15. Daughter's son.
16. Daughter's son's wife.
17. Daughter's daughter.
18. Daughter's daughter's husband.
19. Brother (including step-brother).
20. Brother's wife.
21. Sister (including step-sister).
22. Sister's husband.

Annexure 5

Report by the Indian company receiving amount of consideration for issue of shares/Convertible debentures under the FDI Scheme

(*To be filed by the company through its Authorised Dealer Category-I bank, with the Regional Office of the Reserve Bank under whose jurisdiction the Registered Office of the company making the declaration is situated, not later than 30 days from the date of receipt of the amount of consideration, as specified in para 9 (I) (A) of Schedule I to Notification No. FEMA 20/2000- RB, dated 3-5-2000*)

Permanent Account Number (PAN) of the investee company given by the IT Department	

No.	Particulars	(In Block Letters)	
1.	Name of the Indian company Address of the Registered Office		
	Fax		
	Telephone		
	e-mail		
2	**Details of the foreign investor/collaborator**		
	Name Address Country		
3.	Date of receipt of funds		
4.	Amount	In foreign currency	In Indian Rupees
5.	Whether investment is under Automatic Route or Approval Route If Approval Route, give details (ref. no. of approval and date)	Automatic Route/Approval Route	
6.	Name of the AD through whom the remittance is received		
7.	Address of the AD		

A Copy of the FIRC evidencing the receipt of consideration for issue of shares/convertible debentures as above is enclosed.

(Authorised signatory of the investee company) (Stamp)	(Authorised signatory of the AD) (Stamp)

For Use of the Reserve Bank Only

Unique Identification Number for the remittance received: | | | | | | | | | | | | | |

Annexure 6

Know Your Customer (KYC) Form in respect of the non-resident investor

Registered Name of the Remitter/Investor (Name, if the investor is an Individual)	
Registration Number (Unique Identification Number* in case remitter is an Individual)	
Registered Address (Permanent Address if remitter Individual)	
Name of the Remitter's Bank	
Remitter's Bank Account No.	
Period of banking relationship with the remitter	

* Passport No., Social Security No, or any Unique No. certifying the *bona fides* of the remitter as prevalent in the remitter's country

We confirm that all the information furnished above is true and accurate as provided by the overseas remitting bank of the non-resident investor.

(Signature of the Authorised Official of the AD bank receiving the remittance)

Date: Stamp:

Place:

Annexure 7

Annual Return on Foreign Liabilities and Assets

(*Return to be filled under AP* (*DIR Series*) *Circular No. 45, dated 15-3-2011 to the Department of Statistics and Information Management, RBI, Mumbai*)

Please read the guidelines/definitions carefully before filling-in the Return

Section I

Identification Particulars

For RBI's use

1. **Name and Address of the Indian Company** | **COMPANY CODE**

____

____

____

City: Pin:

State:_______________________

2. Income-Tax allotted PAN Number of Company:

3. Registration No given by the Registrar of Companies:

4. Name of the Contact Person: _______________ Designation: _______

Tel. No. (with STD code):_______________ Fax:_______________

e-mail:_______________

5. Account closing date: (dd/mm/yy) Web-site (if any):_______________

6. In case of change in Company Name and/or activity, specify the old and new Company Name and activity:

Old Company Name _______________ New Company Name _______

Effective Date_______________

Old Activity: _______________ New Activity_______________

7. Nature of Business: Please tick (✓) the appropriate group of activity to which your principal line of business pertains and also mention, if possible the NIC code in the bracket.

Industry	Revenue (%)	Industry	Revenue (%)	Industry	Revenue (%)	Industry	Revenue (%)
1. Power ( )		2.Electrical and Electronics ( )		3. Non - financial services ( )		4. Financia Services ( )	
5.Telecom ( )		6. Hotels and Tourism ( )		7. Metallurgical Industry and Mining ( )		8. Food Processing Industry ( )	
9. Transpor-ttion ( )		10. Petroleum and Natural Gas ( )		11. Chemicals (other than fertilizers) ( )		12. Construction ( )	
13. Software and ITES/ BPO ( )		14. Pharma-ceutical ( )		15. Other ( )			

For RBI's use (Industry Code)

8. Whether your company is listed in India [please tick (✓)]?

Yes		No	

9. Whether your company has any Foreign Collaboration? If yes, please indicate whether it is (please tick the appropriate one)

Yes		No	

(*a*) Technical collaboration		(*b*) Financial collaboration (foreign equity participation)		(*c*) Both	

Block 1A: Total Paid up Capital of Indian Company

Item	**End-March of previous FY**		**End-March current FY**	
	Number of Shares	**Amount in ₹ lakh**	**Number of Shares**	**Amount in ₹ lakh**
1.0 Total Paid-up Capital [(i)+(ii)]				
(*i*) Ordinary/Equity Share				
(*ii*) Preference Share [(*a*)+(*b*)]				
(*a*) Participating				
(*b*) Non-participating				

Item	**End-March of previous FY**		**End-March current FY**	
	Number of Shares	**Amount in ₹ lakh**	**Number of Shares**	**Amount in ₹ lakh**
2.0 Non-resident Equity Holdings				
1 Individuals				
2 Companies				
3 FIIs				
4 FVCIs				
5 Foreign Trusts				
6 Private Equity Funds				
7 Pension/Provident Funds				
8 Sovereign Wealth Fund (SWF)§				
9 Partnership/ Proprietorship firms				
10 Financial Institutions				
11 NRIs/PIO				
12 Others (please specify)				

Note: FY: Financial Year

Block 1B : Free Reserves and Surplus and Retained Profit

Item	**Amount in ₹ lakh as at the end – March of**	
	Previous FY	**Current FY**
3.1 Free Reserves and Surplus as at the end of		
	Amount in ₹ lakh	
	During Previous FY	**During Current FY**
3.2 Profit (+)/Loss (-) after tax		
3.3 Dividend Declared (excluding tax on dividend)		
3.4 Retained Profit/loss (3.4 = 3.2 - 3.3)		

Section II

Foreign Liabilities

2. Investments made under Foreign Direct Investment (FDI) scheme in India:

In case of listed companies, equity should be valued using share price on closing date of reference period, while in case of unlisted companies, Own Fund of Book Value (OFBV) Method should be used (*see the attached guidelines for details*)

Block 2A: Foreign Direct Investment in India (10% or more Equity Participation)

[Please furnish here the outstanding investments *made under the FDI Scheme in India* by Non-resident Direct investors, who were individually holding **10 per cent or more** ordinary/equity shares of your company on the reporting date]

If this block is ***Non-NIL****, then please give the Name and Addresses of your subsidiary in India, if any,* in BLOCK 9.

Name of the non-resident Company/Individual	Type of Capital	Country of non-resident investor	Equity holding (%)	Amount in ₹ lakh as at the end of		
				March Previous FY	December Current FY	March Current FY
	1.0 Equity Capital (1.0 = 1.2-1.1)					
	1.1 Claims on Direct Investor					
	1.2 Liabilities to Direct Investor					
	2.0 Other Capital (2.0 = 2.2-2.1)					
	2.1 Claims on Direct Investor					
	2.2 Liabilities to Direct Investor					
	3.0 Disinvestments in India during the year					

Note:

(*i*) if investor is a company, then country is the country of incorporation;

(*ii*) Please use different sheet using same format to report different non-resident company/individual.

Block 2B: Foreign Direct Investment in India (Less than 10% Equity Holding)

[Please furnish here the outstanding investments *made under the FDI Scheme in India* by Non-resident Direct investors, who were individually holding **less than 10 per cent** ordinary7equity shares of your company on the reporting date]

Name of the non-resident Company/Individual	Type of Capital	Country of non-resident investor	Equity holding (%)	Amount in ₹ lakh as at the end of		
				March Previous FY	December Current FY	March Current FY
	1.0 Equity Capital (1.0 = 1.2-1.1)					
	1.1 Claims on Direct Investor					
	1.2 Liabilities to Direct Investor					
	2.0 Other Capital (2.0 = 2.2-2.1)					
	2.1 Claims on Direct Investor					
	2.2 Liabilities to Direct Investor					
	3.0 Disinvestments in India during the year					

Note:

(*i*) if investor is a company, then country is the country of incorporation;

(*ii*) Please use different sheet using same format to report different non-resident company/individual.

3. Portfolio and Other Liabilities to Non-residents (*i.e.* position with unrelated parties)

Block 3A: Portfolio Investment

Please furnish here the outstanding investments by non-resident investors made under the **Portfolio Investment Scheme in India**. In case of listed companies, equity should be valued using share price on closing date of reference period, while in case of unlisted companies, Own Fund of Book Value (OFBV) Method should be used. (*see the attached guidelines for details*)

Portfolio Investment	Country of non-resident investor	Amount in ₹ lakh as at the end of	
		March Previous FY	March Current FY
1.0 Equity Securities			
2.0 Debt Securities (2.0 = 2.1+2.2)			
2.1 Bonds and Notes (original maturity more than 1year)			
2.2 Money Market Instruments (original maturity upto1year)			
3.0 Disinvestments in India during the year			

Note: **Data pertaining to each type of investment are to be reported consolidating the information country-wise. If more countries are involved to report the data for the particular type(s) of investment, it should be reported in the same format using additional sheets separately for each country.**

Block 3B: Financial Derivatives (with non-resident entities only)

Please furnish here the outstanding foreign liabilities on account of financial derivatives contract **entered into with non-residents.**

Financial Derivatives	Country of non-resident investor	Amount in ₹ lakh as at the end of	
		March Previous FY	March Current FY
(*i*) Notional Value			
(*ii*) Mark to market value			

Note: **If more countries are involved to report the data for the particular type(s) of investment, it should be reported in the same format using additional sheets separately for each country.**

Block 3C: Other Investments

This is a residual category that includes all financial outstanding not considered as direct investment or portfolio investment (**outstanding liabilities with Unrelated Parties**)

Other Investment	Country of non-resident lender	Amount in ₹ lakh as at the end of	
		March Previous FY	March Current FY
4.0 Trade Credit (4.0 = 4.1+4.2)			
4.1 Short Term (4.1 = 4.1.1+ 4.1.2)			
4.1.1 Up to 6 Months			
4.1.2 6 Months to 1 Year			
4.2 Long Term			
5.0 Loans (5.0 = 5.1+5.2)			
5.1 Short Term			
5.2 Long Term			
6.0 Other Liabilities (6.0= 6.1+6.2)			
6.1 Short Term (up to 1yr.)			
6.2 Long Term			

Note:

(*i*) Data pertaining to each type of investment are to be reported consolidating the information country wise. If more countries are involved to report the data for the particular type(s) of investment, it should be reported in the same format using additional sheets separately for each country.

(*ii*) At item 5.0, loan should include the ECB loan other than those taken from non-resident parent company. ECB loan taken from parent company abroad should be shown under Other Capital of Block 2A.

Section III

Foreign Assets

1. Please use the **exchange rate as at end-March/end-December** (as applicable) of reporting year while reporting the **foreign assets in ₹ lakh**.

2. In case, the overseas company is listed, equity should be valued using share price on closing date of reference period, while in case of unlisted company, use Own Fund of Book Value (OFBV) method for valuation of equity (*see the attached guidelines for details*)

Block 4: Direct Investment Abroad under Overseas Direct Investment Scheme

Block 4A: Direct Investment Abroad (10% or more Equity holding)

[Please furnish here your outstanding investments in Non-resident enterprises [Direct Investment Enterprises (DIE)], **made under the Overseas Direct Investment Scheme**, in each of which **your company** hold **10 per cent or more** Equity shares on the reporting date]. *If this block is* ***Non-NIL****, then please furnish the information* in BLOCK 6.

Name of the non-resident Direct Investment Enterprise (DIE)	Type of Capital	Country of non-resident DIE	Equity holding (%)	Amount in ₹ lakh as at the end of		
				March Previous FY	December Current FY	March Current FY
	1.0 Equity Capital (1.0 = 1.1-1.2)					
	1.1 Claims on Direct Investment Enterprise					
	1.2 Liabilities to Direct Investment Enterprise					
	2.0 Other Capital (2.0 = 2.1-2.2)					
	2.1 Claims on Direct Investment Enterprise					
	2.2 Liabilities to Direct Investment Enterprise					
	3.0 Disinvestments made abroad during the year					

Note: **Please use separate sheets in the above format to report for separate DIEs**

Block 4B: Foreign Direct Investment Abroad (Less than 10% Equity holding)

[Please furnish here your outstanding investments in non-resident enterprises (Direct Investment Enterprises DIE), **made under the Overseas Direct Investment Scheme**, in each of which **your company holds less than 10 per cent** Equity shares on the reporting date].

Name of the non-resident enterprises	Type of Capital	Country of non-resident enterprises	Amount in ₹ lakh as at the end of		
			March Previous FY	December Current FY	March Current FY
	1.0 Equity Capital (1.0 = 1.1-1.2)				
	1.1 Claims on non-resident Enterprise abroad				
	1.2 Liabilities to non-resident Enterprise abroad				
	2.0 Other Capital (2.0 = 2.1-2.2)				
	2.1 Claims on non-resident Enterprise abroad				
	2.2 Liabilities to non-resident Enterprise abroad				
	3.0 Disinvestments made abroad during the year				

***Note:* Please use separate sheets in the above format to report different non-resident fellow enterprises.**

Portfolio and Other Assets Abroad (*i.e.*, position with unrelated parties)

Block 5A: Portfolio Investment Abroad

1. Please furnish here the outstanding investments in non-resident enterprises, **other than those made under Overseas Direct Investment Scheme** in India (*i.e.*, other than those reported in Block 4A and 4B).

2. In case overseas companies are listed, equity should be valued using share price on closing date of reference period, while in case of unlisted companies, use Own Fund of Book Value Method (OFBV) (*see the attached guidelines for details*)

Portfolio Investment	Country of non-resident enterprise	Amount in ₹ lakh as at the end of		
		March Previous FY	December Current FY	March Current FY
1.0 Equity Securities				
2.0 Debt Securities (2.0=2.1+2.2)				
2.1 Bonds and Notes (original maturity more than 1year)				
2.2 Money Market Instruments (original maturity up to 1year)				
3.0 Disinvestments Abroad during the year				

***Note:* Data pertaining to each type of investment are to be reported consolidating the information country-wise. If particular type(s) of investment spreads over more than one country, it should be reported in the above format using separate additional sheet for each country.**

Block 5B: Financial Derivatives (with non-resident entities only)

Please furnish here the outstanding claims on non-residents on account of financial derivatives contract **entered into with Non-residents.**

Financial Derivatives	**Country of non-resident enterprise**	**Amount in ₹ lakh as at the end of**	
		March Previous FY	**March Current FY**
(*i*) Notional Value			
(*ii*) Mark to market value			

Note: **If particular type(s) of investment spreads over more than one country, it should be reported in the above format using separate additional sheet for each country.**

Block 5C: Other Investment (Outstanding claims on Unrelated Parties):

This is a residual category that includes all financial outstanding claims not considered as direct investment or portfolio investment.

Other Investment	**Country of non-resident enterprise**	**Amount in ₹ lakh as at the end of**	
		March Previous FY	**March Current FY**
4.0 Trade Credit (4.0=4.1+4.2)			
4.1 Short Term (4.1=4.1.1+4.1.2)			
4.1.1. Up to 6 Months			
4.1.2. 6 Months to 1 Year			
4.2 Long Term			
5.0 Loans (5.0=5.1+5.2)			
5.1 Short Term (Up to 1 year)			
5.2 Long Term			
6.0 Other Assets (6.0=6.1+6.2)			
6.1 Currency and Deposits			
6.2 Others			

***Note*:**

(*i*) **Data pertaining to each type of investment are to be reported consolidating the information country wise. If particular type(s) of investment spreads over more than one country, it should be reported in the above format using separate additional sheet for each country.**

Block 6: Equity Capital, Free Reserves and Surplus of Direct Investment Enterprise Abroad

[Please report here the total equity, the **equity held by your company** and the total free reserves and surplus of those non- resident enterprises in each of which **your company held 10 per cent or more** shares on the reporting date].

If this block **is** *Non-NIL then please make sure that you have provided the relevant information* in BLOCK 4A.

Name of the DIE	Item	Currency	Amount in Foreign Currency as at the end of (in actual)	
			March Previous FY	March Current FY
(1)	(2)	(3)	(4)	(5)
	1. Total Equity of DIE			
	2. Equity of DIE held by you			
	3. Free Reserves and Surplus of DIE			
	4. Dividend Received by you **during the year**			
	5. Amount of your Profit retained by DIE **during the year**			

Note: **If your company is a Direct Investor in more than one DIE, the data should be provided in the same format in respect of each such DIE using additional sheets.**

Block 7: Contingent Foreign Liabilities

[Please report here the relevant details about the contingent foreign liabilities of **your company**]

Description of Contingent Liability	Country	Currency#	Amount in Foreign Currency as at the end of (in actual)	
			March Previous FY	March Current FY
(1)	(2)	(3)	(4)	(5)

Note: # Currency of denomination of the contingent foreign liability should be mentioned in Col. 3. Refer to the details on Contingent liabilities given in Annex.

Block 8: Employee Information of reporting Indian company

	As at the end-March of	
	Previous FY	Current FY
No. of Employees on Payroll		

Block 9: Name(s) and Address(es) of your subsidiary in India

Sr. Nos.	Name of Subsidiary in India*	Your Equity holding in subsidiary %	Address	Retained profit/loss of your subsidiary in India during the current FY (Amount in ₹ lakh)

Certificate

We hereby certify that all the facts and figures furnished in this schedule reflect the accurate position of the company and reported after understanding all the items of all the blocks of the schedule.

Place:

Signature and Name of the Authorised person

Date:

Concepts and Definitions to be used while filling-in the Annual Return on Foreign Liabilities and Assets

Residence of Enterprises

An enterprise is said to have a center of economic interest and to be a resident unit of a country (economic territory) when the enterprise is engaged in a significant amount of production of goods and/or services there or when it owns land or buildings located there. The enterprise must maintain at least one production establishment in the country and must plan to operate the establishment indefinitely or over a long period of time.

Free Reserves and Surplus (Block 1B, Item 3.1)

Free Reserves and Surplus should **include** all unencumbered reserves such as

(*i*) General Reserve net of losses, if any

(*ii*) Capital Reserve

(*iii*) Development Rebate Reserve

(*iv*) Premium on shares

(*v*) Dividend Equalization Reserve

(*vi*) Investment Allowance **(utilized)** Reserve.

Free Reserves and Surplus should **exclude** Tax provisions and other items such as

(*i*) provision for deferred taxation

(*ii*) Tax Equalization Reserve

(*iii*) Investment Allowance **(unutilized)** and

(*iv*) Revaluation Reserve

Retained Profit (Block 1B, Item 3.4)

Retained profit = Profit after tax – Dividend declared (excluding tax on dividend) (*i.e.* Item 3.4 = Item3.2 minus Item 3.3, of Block 1B)

A. Direct Investment

Direct investment is a category of international investment in which a resident entity in one economy (direct investor (DI) acquires a lasting interest in an enterprise resident in another economy (Direct Investment Enterprise (DIE). It consists of two components, viz., Equity capital and Other Capital.

(*i*) **Equity Capital under Direct Investment**

It covers (1) Equity in branches and all shares (except non-participating preferred shares) in subsidiaries and associates; (2) Contributions such as the provision of machinery, land and building(s) by a direct investor to a DIE by equity participation; (3) Acquisition by a DIE of shares in its direct investor, termed as Reserve investment (*i.e.* claims on DI).

(*a*) **Foreign Direct Investment in India** (Block 2A, 2B)

If the Indian company has issued the shares to non-resident entities under the FDI scheme in India, then it should be reported under the Foreign Direct Investment in India (Liabilities), Section II of the return. If the non-resident entity **holds the 10 per cent or more** equity/ordinary shares in the reporting Indian company, then it should reported under **Block 2A** (item 1.2, liabilities to direct investment). However, if the non-resident entity holds **less than 10 per cent** of the equity capital of reporting Indian company, then it should be reported under **Block 2B** (item 1.2, liabilities to direct investment). In both the cases, the investing non-resident entity is called as the Direct Investor (DI) while the reporting Indian company is called as Direct Investment Enterprise (DIE).

If the **reporting Indian company** also holds the **equity shares in its DI** company abroad and if its share is **less than 10 per cent** of equity capital of DI company, then it is called as **reverse investment** and same should be **reported under item 1.1** (claim on direct investor) of the respective block *i.e.* **Block 2A or 2B**.

(*b*) **Foreign Direct Investment abroad by Indian companies** (Block 4A and 4B)

If the reporting Indian company invest in equity shares of non-resident company, under the Overseas Direct Investment scheme in India, *i.e.* investment in Joint venture or Wholly owned subsidiaries abroad, then it should be reported under the Foreign Direct Investment abroad, Section III. If the equity holding of Indian company in non-resident company is **10 per cent or more**, then it should be reported under **Block 4A** (item 1.1 claim on DIE), **otherwise**, it should be reported under **Block 4B** (item 1.1, claim on DIE). In both the cases, Indian company is called as the Direct Investor (DI) while the non-resident company is called as Direct Investment Enterprise (DIE).

If the **non-resident DIE** also holds the **equity shares in Indian reporting company** (DI) and if its share is **less than 10 per cent** of equity capital of reporting company, then it is called as **reverse investment** and same should be reported **under item 1.2** (liabilities to DIE) of the respective block *i.e.* **Block 4A or 4B.**

(*ii*) **Other Capital under Direct Investment** (Block 2A, 2B, 4A and 4B)

The **other capital** (inter-company debt transactions) component of direct investment covers the outstanding liabilities or claims arising due **borrowing and lending of funds, investment in debt securities including non-participating preference shares, trade credits, financial leasing, share application money, between direct investors and DIEs and between two DIEs that share the same Direct Investor**. Non-participating preferred shares owned by the direct investor are treated as debt securities and should be included in Other Capital.

B. Portfolio Investment

(*i*) **Portfolio Investment** (Block 3A and 5A)

It covers **external claims by or liabilities to reporting Indian company** in equity and debt securities **other than those included in direct investment** (Block 2A, 2B and 4A, 4B). Debt securities include long-term bonds and notes, short-term money market instruments.

Any investment is made **by the non-resident entities in Indian company** under the **Portfolio Scheme in India** should be should be reported under **Block 3A** (Portfolio liabilities).

Any investment made **by the Indian company** in foreign shares and/or debt securities, **apart from the investment made under the Overseas Direct Investment Scheme**, should be reported under **Block 5A** (Portfolio assets).

(*ii*) **Equity Securities** (Block 3A and 5A, Item 1.0)

Equity securities are instruments acknowledging the holders' claim to the residual income of the issuing enterprise after the claims of all creditors have been met. These include ordinary shares, stocks, participating preference shares, depository receipts (ADRs/GDRs) denoting ownership of equity securities issued to non-residents, shares/units in mutual funds and investment trusts, equity securities that are sold under repurchase agreement, equity securities that are sold under securities lending arrangement.

(*iii*) **Debt Securities** (Block 3A and 5A, Item 2.0)

These include bonds and notes, money market instruments.

(*iv*) **Bonds and Notes** (Block 3A and 5A, Item 2.1)

This category includes debt securities with original contractual maturities of more than one year (long-term). It includes the long-term securities such as Debentures, Non-participating preference shares, Convertible bonds, Negotiable certificates of deposit, Perpetual bonds, Collateralized mortgage obligations, Dual currency, Zero coupon and other Deep discounted bonds, Floating rate bonds and Index-linked bonds.

(*v*) **Money Market Instruments** (Block 3A and 5A, Item 2.2)

These short-term instruments include treasury bills, commercial paper, banker's acceptances, short-term negotiable certificates of deposit and short-term notes issued under note issuance facilities. It may be noted that the instruments that share the characteristics of money market instruments but are issued with maturities of more than one year are classified as Bonds and Notes.

C. Financial Derivatives (Block 3B and 5B)

Financial derivatives are linked to a specific financial instrument, indicator, or commodity and through which specific financial risks can be traded in the financial markets in their own right. Derivative instruments include futures, interest and cross-currency swaps, forward rate agreements, forward foreign exchange contracts, credit derivatives and various types of options.

D. Other Investments: (Block 3C and 5C)

This is a residual category that **includes** all financial outstanding **not considered as direct investment or portfolio investment** such as:

(*i*) **Trade Credits** (Block 3C and 5C, Item 4.0)

Trade credits are assets and liabilities that arise from the **direct extension of credit** from a **supplier to a buyer** for transactions in **goods and services** and **advance payments** by buyers for transactions in goods and services and for work in progress. **Trade credit assets** are **advance payments** made by **importer (you)** for (your) imports or **credit extended by exporter (you)** directly to (your) importer. **Trade credit liabilities** are **advance payment received** by the exporter (you) for (your) exports or **credit received by importer (you)** directly from (your) exporter. It may be noted here that **funding provided by an enterprise other than the supplier** for the purpose of purchasing goods or services is treated **as a loan** and not as trade credit.

(*ii*) **Loans** (Block 3C and 5C, Item 5.0)

Loans are direct lending of funds by a creditor to a debtor through arrangements. These include, loans to finance trade (*i.e.* Buyers' credit in which a bank or a financial institution or an export credit agency in the exporting country extends a loan directly to a foreign buyer or to a bank in the importing country to pay for the purchase of goods and services), mortgages and other loans and advances. Financial leases and repurchase agreements are also considered loans.

Note that **loan received from the non-resident direct investor** should be reported under **Other Capital of Block 2A or 2B** while **loan extended** to your **subsidiaries/associates abroad** should be reported under **Other Capital of block 4A or 4B**. These outstanding loans should be reported under the loan item of Block 3C or 5C.

(*iii*) **Other Liabilities and Assets** (Block 3C and 5C, Item 6.0)

These are the residual items that include all external financial liabilities and assets not recorded elsewhere in the liabilities/assets. These are miscellaneous accounts receivable and payable such as accounts relating to interest payments in arrears, loan payments in arrears, wages and salaries outstanding, prepayments of insurance premiums, taxes outstanding and the like.

(*iv*) **Long-term and Short-term Investment** (Block 3C and 5C)

Long-term investment is defined as investment with an original contractual maturity of more than one year. Short-term investment includes currency, investment payable on demand or with an original contractual maturity of one year or less.

E. Disinvestments in India and Abroad (Item 3.0 in Block 2A, 2B, 3A, 4A, 4B and 5A)

Any disinvestments made by non-resident direct investor of the reporting Indian company during the year should be reported in Block 2A and Block 2B and portfolio disinvestments in Block 3A. Likewise, any disinvestment made by the reporting Indian company in its DIE abroad during the year should be reported in Block 4A and 4B and portfolio disinvestments by reporting company should be reported in Block 5A.

F. Contingent Liabilities (Block 7)

Contingent liabilities are obligations that **arise from a particular discrete event(s), which may or may not occur**. Contingent liabilities are (i) **explicit - arise from a legal or contractual arrangement** (Loan and other payment guarantees, credit guarantees, Contingent credit availability guarantees, exchange rate guarantees, etc) and (ii) **implicit - do not arise from a legal or contractual source, but recognized after a condition or event is realized.**

If the Indian company has extended a guarantee to a loan taken by non-resident entity (may be its subsidiary abroad), such guarantees are part of contingent foreign liabilities. In this case, under column1 of block 7, "Loan Guarantee" needs to be mentioned.

Country should relate to the country of location of the non-resident creditor involved in the transaction. To illustrate, as mentioned above, if the contingent foreign liability is in connection with guarantees on loans, the country of location of the non-resident creditor to whom such guarantees are given, needs to be reported in column 2.

Seal

Annexure 8

Form FC-TRS

<table>
<tr><td colspan="3">Declaration regarding transfer of shares/compulsorily and mandatorily convertible preference shares (CMCPS)/debentures by way of sale from resident to non resident/non-resident to resident</td></tr>
<tr><td></td><td colspan="2">(to be submitted to the designated AD branch in quadruplicate within 60 days from the date of receipt of funds)</td></tr>
<tr><td></td><td colspan="2">The following documents are enclosed
For sale of shares/compulsorily and mandatorily convertible preference shares/debentures by a person resident in India
(i) Consent Letter duly signed by the seller and buyer or their duly appointed agent and in the latter case the Power of Attorney Document.
(ii) The shareholding pattern of the investee company after the acquisition of shares by a person resident outside India.
(iii) Certificate indicating fair value of shares from a Chartered Accountant.
(iv) Copy of Broker's note if sale is made on Stock Exchange.
(v) Declaration from the buyer to the effect that he is eligible to acquire shares/compulsorily and mandatorily convertible preference shares/debentures under FDI policy and the existing sectoral limits and Pricing Guidelines have been complied with.
(vi) Declaration from the FII/sub account to the effect that the individual FII/Sub account ceiling as prescribed has not been breached.
Additional documents in respect of sale of shares/compulsorily and mandatorily convertible preference shares/debentures by a person resident outside India
(vii) If the sellers are NRIs/OCBs, the copies of RBI approvals, if applicable, evidencing the shares held by them on repatriation/non-repatriation basis.
(viii) No Objection/Tax Clearance Certificate from Income Tax Authority/Chartered Account.</td></tr>
<tr><td>1</td><td>Name of the company</td><td></td></tr>
<tr><td></td><td>Address (including e-mail, telephone Number, Fax no)</td><td></td></tr>
<tr><td></td><td>Activity</td><td></td></tr>
<tr><td></td><td>NIC Code No.</td><td></td></tr>
<tr><td>2</td><td>Whether FDI is allowed under Automatic route</td><td></td></tr>
<tr><td></td><td>Sectoral Cap under FDI Policy</td><td></td></tr>
</table>

3	**Nature of transaction** (*Strike out whichever is not applicable*)	Transfer from resident to non resident/Transfer from non resident to resident
4	**Name of the buyer**	
	Constitution/Nature of the investing Entity Specify whether 1. Individual 2. Company 3. FII 4. FVCI 5. Foreign Trust 6. Private Equity Fund 7. Pension/Provident Fund 8. Sovereign Wealth Fund (SWFπ) 9. Partnership/Proprietorship firm 10. Financial Institution 11. NRIs/PIOs 12. Others	
	Date and Place of Incorporation	
	Address of the buyer (*including e-mail, telephone number. Fax no.*)	
5	**Name of the seller**	
	Constitution/Nature of the disinvesting entity Specify whether 1. Individual 2. Company 3. FII 4. FVCI 5. Foreign Trust 6. Private Equity Fund 7. Pension/Provident Fund 8. Sovereign Wealth Fund (SWF∏) 9. Partnership/Proprietorship firm 10. Financial Institution 11. NRIs/PIOs 12. others	
	Date and Place of Incorporation	
	Address of the seller (*including e-mail, telephone Number Fax no*)	
6	**Particulars of earlier Reserve Bank/FIPB approvals**	

7	**Details regarding shares/compulsorily and mandatorily convertible preference shares (CMCPS)/debentures to be transferred**				
	Date of the transaction	***Number of shares CMCPS/ debentures***	***Face value in ₹***	***Negotiated Price for the transfer**in ₹***	***Amount of consideration in ₹***
8	**Foreign Investments in the company**		*No. of shares*		*Percentage*
		Before the transfer			
		After the transfer			
9	**Where the shares/CMCPS/debentures are listed on Stock Exchange**				
	Name of the Stock exchange				
	Price Quoted on the Stock exchange				
	Where the shares/ CMCPS/debentures are Unlisted				
	*Price as per Valuation guidelines**				
	*Price as per Chartered Accountants */** Valuation report (CA Certificate to be attached)*				

Declaration by the transferor/transferee

I/We hereby declare that:

(*i*) The particulars given above are true and correct to the best of my/our knowledge and belief.

(*ii*) I/We, was/were holding the shares compulsorily and mandatorily convertible preference shares/debentures as per FDI Policy under FERA/FEMA Regulations on repatriation/non repatriation basis.

(*iii*) I/We, am/are eligible to acquire the shares compulsorily and mandatorily convertible preference shares/debentures of the company in terms of the FDI Policy. It is not a transfer relating to shares compulsorily and mandatorily convertible preference shares/debentures of a company engaged in financial services sector or a sector where general permission is not available.

(*iv*) The Sectoral limit under the FDI Policy and the pricing guidelines have been adhered to.

Signature of the Declarant or his duly authorised agent

Date:

Note:

In respect of the transfer of shares/compulsorily and mandatorily convertible preference shares/compulsorily and mandatorily convertible debentures from resident to non resident the declaration has to be signed by the non resident buyer, and in respect of the transfer of shares/compulsorily and mandatorily convertible preference shares/compulsorily and mandatorily convertible debentures from non-resident to resident the declaration has to be signed by the non- resident seller.

Certificate by the AD Branch

It is certified that the application is complete in all respects.

The receipt/payment for the transaction are in accordance with FEMA Regulations/Reserve Bank guidelines.

Signature

Name and Designation of the Officer

Date: Name of the AD Branch

AD Branch Code

π SWF means a Government investment vehicle which is funded by foreign exchange assets, and which manages those assets separately from the official reserves of the monetary authorities.

∏ SWF means a Government investment vehicle which is funded by foreign exchange assets, and which manages those assets separately from the official reserves of the monetary authorities.

Annexure 9

Form DR

[Refer to paragraph 4(2) of Schedule 1]

Return to be filed by an Indian Company who has arranged issue of GDR/ADR

Instructions

The Form should be completed and submitted to the Reserve Bank of India, Foreign Investment Division, Central Office, Mumbai.

1. Name of the Company
2. Address of Registered Office
3. Address for Correspondence
4. Existing Business (please give the NIC Code of the activity in which the company is predominantly engaged)
5. Details of the purpose for which GDRs/ADRs have been raised. If funds are deployed for overseas investment, details thereof

6. Name and address of the Depository abroad
7. Name and address of the Lead Manager/Investment/Merchant Banker
8. Name and address of the Sub-Managers to the issue
9. Name and address of the Indian Custodians
10. Details of FIPB approval (please quote the relevant NIC Code if the GDRs/ADRs are being issued under the Automatic Route)
11. Whether any overall sectoral cap for foreign investment is applicable. If yes, please give details

12. Details of the Equity Capital	Before Issue	After Issue
(*a*) Authorised Capital		
(*b*) Issued and Paid-up Capital		
(i) Held by persons Resident in India		
(*ii*) Held by foreign investors other than FIIs/NRIs/PIOs/OCBs (a list of After Issue foreign investors holding more than 10 percent of the paid-up capital and number of shares held by each of them should be furnished)		
(*iii*) Held by NRIs/PIOs/OCBs		
(*iv*) Held by FIIs		
Total Equity held by non-residents		
(*c*) Percentage of equity held by non-residents to total paid-up capital		

13. Whether issue was on private placement basis. If yes, please give details of the investors and GDRs/ADRs issued to each of them
14. Number of GDRs/ADRs issued
15. Ratio of GDRs/ADRs to underlying shares
16. Issue Related Expenses
    (*a*) Fee paid/payable to Merchant Bankers/ Lead Manager
        (*i*) Amount (in US$)
        (*ii*) Amount as percentage to the total issue
    (*b*) Other expenses
17. Whether funds are kept abroad. If yes, name and address of the bank
18. Details of the listing arrangement

Name of Stock Exchange

Date of commencement of trading

19. The date on which GDRs/ADRs issue was launched
20. Amount raised (in US $)
21. Amount repatriated (in US $)

Certified that all the conditions laid down by Government of India and Reserve Bank of India have been complied with.

Sd	Sd
Chartered Accountant	Authorised Signatory of the Company

Annexure 10

Form DR - Quarterly

[Refer to paragraph 4(3) of Schedule 1]

Quarterly Return

(to be submitted to the Reserve Bank of India, Foreign Investment Division, Central Office, Mumbai)

1. Name of the Company
2. Address
3. GDR/ADR issue launched on
4. Total No. of GDRs/ADRs issued
5. Total amount raised
6. Total interest earned till end of quarter
7. Issue expenses and commission etc.
8. Amount repatriated
9. Balance kept abroad - Details
   (*i*) Banks Deposits
   (*ii*) Treasury Bills
   (*iii*) Others (please specify)
10. No. of GDRs/ADRs still outstanding
11. Company's share price at the end of the quarter
12. GDRs/ADRs price quoted on overseas stock exchange as at the end of the quarter

Certified that the funds raised through GDRs/ADRs have not been invested in stock market or real estate.

Sd	Sd
Chartered Accountant	Authorised Signatory of the Company

THE END

Personal Notes

Personal Notes